THE MATTER OF ART

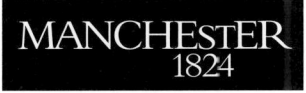

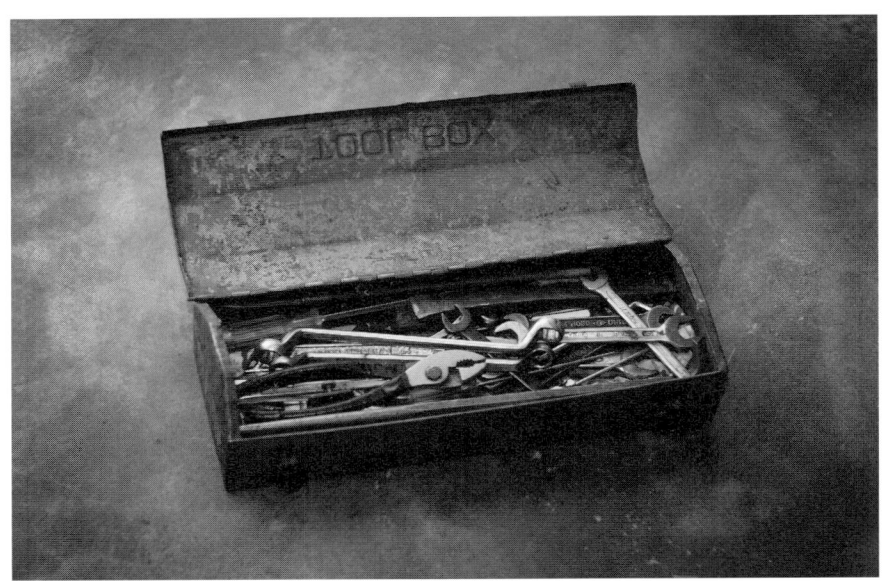

Yasser Chalid, *Toolbox*, 2011

The matter of art

MATERIALS, PRACTICES,
CULTURAL LOGICS, c. 1250–1750

*Edited by Christy Anderson,
Anne Dunlop and Pamela H. Smith*

Manchester University Press

Copyright © Manchester University Press 2015

While copyright in the volume as a whole is vested in Manchester University Press, copyright in individual chapters belongs to their respective authors, and no chapter may be reproduced wholly or in part without the express permission in writing of both author and publisher.

Published by Manchester University Press
Altrincham Street, Manchester M1 7JA, UK
www.manchesteruniversitypress.co.uk

British Library Cataloguing-in-Publication Data
A catalogue record for this book is available from the British Library

Library of Congress Cataloging-in-Publication Data applied for

ISBN   978 07190 9060 8   hardback

First published 2015

The publisher has no responsibility for the persistence or accuracy of URLs for any external or third-party internet websites referred to in this book, and does not guarantee that any content on such websites is, or will remain, accurate or appropriate.

Typeset by
Graphicraft Limited, Hong Kong
Printed in Great Britain by TJ International Ltd, Padstow

Contents

List of figures   *page* vii

List of contributors   xiii

Introduction   1

Part I   Matter

1. The matter of the medium: some tools for an art-theoretical interpretation of materials   21
   Ann-Sophie Lehmann
2. The matter of ideas in the working of metals in early modern Europe   42
   Pamela H. Smith
3. On the origins of European painting materials, real and imagined   68
   Anne Dunlop
4. Gold coins and gold leaf in early Italian paintings   97
   Irma Passeri

Part II   Practices

5. The 'Genealogy of Jean le Blanc': accounting for the materiality of the medieval Eucharist   119
   Aden Kumler
6. Lead white's mysteries   141
   Spike Bucklow
7. Material distinctions: plaster, terracotta, and wax in the Renaissance artist's workshop   160
   Eckart Marchand

8 Rocks and reverence: Inka and Spanish perceptions of
   stonework in the early modern Andes   180
   Carolyn Dean

Part III Cultural logics

9 Precious stones, mineral beings: performative materiality
   in fifteenth-century northern art   205
   Brigitte Buettner
10 Carving life: the meaning of wood in early modern
   European sculpture   223
   Christina Neilson
11 *Arti povere*, 1300–1650   240
   Michael Cole
12 Polish stone, Venetian glass, and red Hungarian marble:
   the materials of a Renaissance chapel in Jagiellonian
   Poland   263
   Katie Jakobiec
13 Reveal or conceal: chopines and the display of material
   wealth in early modern Valencia and Venice   283
   Elizabeth Semmelhack
14 Entanglements of body, text, and stone: the crafting and
   connoisseurship of inkstones in eighteenth-century China 309
   Dorothy Ko

Index   334

Figures

Frontispiece: Yasser Chalid, *Toolbox*, 2011 (Photo: Yasser Chalid – Indonesia)

2.1. Native silver, Freiberg District, Erzgebirge, Saxony, Germany, Houston Museum of Natural Science (Photo: Image in the public domain: http://commons.wikimedia.org/wiki/File:WLA_hmns_Silver.jpg) *page* 46

2.2. Hans Leinberger (1480–after 1530), *Mass for victims of a mining accident*, c. 1510–20, limewood relief, 33.5 × 33.5 cm, Inv. 463, Berlin, Skulpturensammlung und Museum für Byzantinische Kunst, Staatliche Museen (Photo: Joerg P. Anders. Art Resource, NY) 47

3.1. Gentile da Fabriano, *Madonna and Child*, c. 1421, tempera on panel, 60 × 45 cm, Museo Nazionale di San Matteo, Pisa (Photo: Scala/Art Resource, NY) 69

3.2. Gentile da Fabriano, detail of Mary's robes and halo (Zenodot Verlagsgesellschaft mbH) (Photo: Yorick Project, image in the public domain, licensed by GNU Free Documentation) 70

3.3. Gentile da Fabriano, fictive inlays and precious stones (reverse of Figure 3.1) (Photo: Scala/Art Resource, NY) 70

3.4. Pietro Lorenzetti, *Diptych with the Madonna and Child and the Man of Sorrows*, c. 1330, tempera on panel, 35.3 × 26 cm, Lindenau-Museum, Altenburg, inv. 47 (Photo: Lindenau-Museum, by permission) 71–2

3.5. Pietro Lorenzetti, fictive inlays (reverse of *Man of Sorrows* panel in Figure 3.4) (Photo: Lindenau-Museum, by permission) 73

3.6. Languedoc, *Detti di filosofia in versi provenzali*, c. 1380? Biblioteca nazionale centrale, ms. Palatino 586. Florence (Photo: Biblioteca nazionale centrale, by permission) 85

4.1.	Master of Rosano, painted crucifix, twelfth century, Monastery of Santa Maria, Rosano, Florence (Ministero per i Beni e le Attività Culturali – Opificio delle Pietre Dure di Firenze, Archivio Fotografico)	98
4.2.	Master Guglielmo, painted crucifix, 1138, Cathedral of Sarzana, La Spezia (Ministero per i Beni e le Attività Culturali – Opificio delle Pietre Dure di Firenze, Archivio Fotografico)	99
5.1.	*La genealogie de Jean le Blanc*, c. 1570–1624, engraving; British Museum, 1880,0710.838 (Photo: © Trustees of the British Museum)	119
5.2.	Host press, late medieval (?), once belonging to the parish church of Saint-Pierre, Peyrelevade (Corrèze, France) (Photo: Aden Kumler)	126
5.3.	Inner surface of incised paten of a late medieval (?) host press, collection of the Musée du Hiéron, Paray le Monial (Photo: Aden Kumler)	127
5.4.	Attributed to Diego de la Cruz, *The Mass of Saint Gregory* (detail), c. 1490, oil and gold on panel, Philadelphia Museum of Art, EW1993-127-1	129
5.5.	Ulm Workshop, *Host Mill retable*, c. 1470, oil on panel, Ulmer Museum, Inv. AV 2150 (Photo: Schmidt-Glassner, © Ulmer Museum)	133
6.1.	A coiled sheet of urine-sprinkled lead metal after exposure to vinegar fumes under horse-dung for a month (Photo: Spike Bucklow)	143
6.2.	A leaf as painter's palette (FM MS 1-2005 fol. 44r), (Photo: by permission of the Syndics of the Fitzwilliam Museum, University of Cambridge)	151
6.3.	A cripple (painted in lead white) consulting a wolf-doctor, who inspects a flask of urine (FM MS 1-2005 fol. 98r) (Photo: by permission of the Syndics of the Fitzwilliam Museum, University of Cambridge)	152
6.4.	A multiple-headed marginal figure (FM MS 1-2005 fol. 64r) (Photo: by permission of the Syndics of the Fitzwilliam Museum, University of Cambridge)	153
6.5.	A contemplative figure (FM MS 1-2005 fol. 190r) (Photo: by permission of the Syndics of the Fitzwilliam Museum, University of Cambridge)	154
7.1.	Michelangelo, *Slave*, 1516–19, wax model for one of the unfinished statues for the Tomb of Pope Julius II, Victoria and Albert Museum, London (Photo: © Victoria and Albert Museum, London)	162

List of figures

7.2.	Giambologna, *Head*, c. 1578, clay, Victoria and Albert Museum, London (Photo: © Victoria and Albert Museum, London)	163
7.3.	Baccio Bandinelli, *Giants*, before 1520, lime-based plaster, Gardens of the Villa Madama, Rome (Photo: Jill Sinclair)	165
7.4.	*Ex voto* portrait figure surrounded by cast wax *ex voti*, seventeenth century, Santa Maria delle Grazie, near Mantua (re-cast and re-arranged in the eighteenth century)	169
7.5.	Antonio del Pollaiuolo, *Young Man in Pageant Armour*, c. 1450, terracotta, Museo Nazionale del Bargello, Florence (Photo: © Alinari)	171
8.1.	Inka, megalithic walls, Saqsaywaman, early sixteenth century (Photo: Carolyn Dean)	183
8.2.	Inka, high-prestige coursed stonemasonry, 1450–1530 (Photo: Carolyn Dean)	185
8.3.	Inka, high-prestige uncoursed, polygonal stonemasonry, 1450–1530 (Photo: Carolyn Dean)	186
8.4.	Colonial Inka, portal, 1550–1750, Cuzco (Photo: Carolyn Dean)	194
8.5.	Pre-Hispanic Inka and Spanish Colonial, Qurikancha-Santo Domingo exterior, 1450–1824, Cuzco (Photo: Carolyn Dean)	195
9.1.	Jean Fouquet, *Virgin and Child*, Melun Diptych, right wing, c. 1452–55, Antwerp, Koninklijk Museum voor Schone Kunsten (Photo: Scala/Art Resource, NY)	206
9.2.	Pearl shell, Matthaeus Platearius, *Le livre des simples médecines*, Burgundy, 1470s, Paris, Bibliothèque nationale de France, Ms. Fr. 9137, fol. 204 (Photo: BnF)	208
9.3.	Crown of Margaret of York, 1460s, silver-gilt, enamels, precious stones, h. 13.2 cm, d. 12.5 cm, Aachen, Cathedral Treasury (Photo: Foto Marburg/Art Resource, NY)	211
9.4.	Watercolour of the *Three Brothers' Brooch*, before 1504, 21 × 18 cm, Basel, Historisches Museum, Inv. 1916.475 (Photo: Historisches Museum Basel)	214
9.5.	Hubert and Jan van Eyck, *Ghent Altarpiece*, open position, completed 1432, Ghent, Cathedral of St Bavo (Photo: Erich Lessing/Art Resource, NY)	217
10.1.	Lando di Pietro, *Head of Christ*, fragment from a crucifix, 1338, Basilica dell'Osservanza, Siena (Photo: 'Foto LENSINI Siena', Basilica dell'Osservanza, Siena, and Ministero per i Beni e le Attività Culturali,	

	Soprintendenza per i beni storici artistici ed ednoantropologici per le province di Siena e Grosseto, Siena)	227
10.2.	Desiderio da Settignano, completed by Giovanni d'Andrea, *Mary Magdalen*, begun 1458, Santa Trinita, Florence (Photo: Gabinetto Fotografico, Soprintendenza Speciale per il Polo Museale della città di Firenze)	229
10.3.	Nero Alberti, *Saint Roch*, 1528, Comune de Pergola, Marche (Photo: Sante Castignani)	230
10.4.	Giuliano or Benedetto da Maiano, *Crucifix*, c. 1474, Museo d'Arte Sacra, San Gimignano (Photo: 'Foto LENSINI Siena' and Museo d'Arte Sacra di San Gimignano)	232
11.1.	Tintoretto, *Baptism of Christ*, 1579–81, oil on canvas, Sala Superiore, Scuola Grande di San Rocco, Venice (Photo: Art Resource)	241
11.2.	Giotto, *Miracle of the Crucifix*, fresco, Upper Church, San Francesco, Assisi (Photo: Art Resource)	244
11.3.	Giotto, *Christ Preaching before Honorius III*, Upper Church, San Francesco, Assisi (Photo: Art Resource)	245
11.4.	*Allegory of Poverty*, c. 1330, Lower Church, San Francesco, Assisi (Photo: Art Resource)	246
11.5.	Michele Giambono, *Man of Sorrows*, c. 1430, tempera and gold on panel, Metropolitan Museum of Art, New York (Photo: Art Resource)	248
11.6.	Gentile da Fabriano, *Coronation of the Virgin*, c. 1420, tempera and gold on panel, J. Paul Getty Museum (Photo: Getty Museum)	249
11.7.	Antonio del Pollaiuolo, *Tomb of Sixtus IV*, 1484–93, bronze, St Peter's, Vatican (Photo: Art Resource)	251
11.8.	Tintoretto, *Annunciation*, 1583–87, oil on canvas, Sala Inferiore, Scuola Grande di San Rocco, Venice (Photo: Art Resource)	254
11.9.	Salvator Rosa, *The Genius of Salvator Rosa*, c. 1662, engraving (Photo: Michael Cole)	257
11.10.	Giovanni Benedetto Castiglione, *The Genius of Castiglione*, c. 1645–47, engraving (Photo: Michael Cole)	258
11.11.	Michelangelo Merisi, called 'Caravaggio', *The Fortune Teller*, 1595, oil on canvas, Louvre, Paris (Photo: Art Resource)	259
12.1.	Bartolommeo Berrecci, Sigismund Chapel (interior), 1519–33, Krakow (Photo: Katie Jakobiec)	263

12.2.	Bartolommeo Berrecci, Sigismund Chapel (exterior), 1519–33, Krakow (Photo: Katie Jakobiec)	264
12.3.	Bartolommeo Berrecci, Sigismund Chapel (detail), 1519–33, Krakow (Photo: Katie Jakobiec)	265
12.4.	Bartolommeo Berrecci, Sigismund Chapel (detail), 1519–33, Krakow (Photo: Katie Jakobiec)	269
12.5.	Benedikt Ried, Vladislav Hall, c. 1500, Prague (Photo: Katie Jakobiec)	274
12.6.	Benedikt Ried, Riders' Staircase, Prague (Photo: Katie Jakobiec)	275
12.7.	Hans Spiess, Vladislav Oratory, St Vitus Cathedral, 1490–93, Prague (Photo: Katie Jakobiec)	276
12.8.	Hans Spiess, Vladislav Oratory (detail), St Vitus Cathedral, 1490–93, Prague (Photo: Katie Jakobiec)	277
12.9.	St Anne's Church, c. 1501, Vilnius (Photo: Katie Jakobiec)	278
12.10.	St Anne's Church (detail of brick), c. 1501, Vilnius (Photo: Katie Jakobiec)	279
13.1.	Small terracotta statue of Aphrodite, Greek, first century BCE, Louvre, Paris (Photo: © Réunion des Musées Nationaux-Grand Palais/Art Resource, NY)	285
13.2.	Watercolour of Spanish ladies, c. 1540, Museo Stibbert (Photo: Image © Museo Stibbert)	289
13.3.	Spanish chopines, probably Valencian, sixteenth century, Museu Diocesà i Comarcal de Solsona, Spain (Photo: © Museu Diocesà i Comarcal de Solsona)	291
13.4.	Spanish chopines, probably Valencian, before 1540, Kunsthistorisches Museum Wien, Sammlung Schloss Ambras (Photo: © Kunsthistorisches Museum Wien, Sammlung Schloss Ambras)	293
13.5.	Venetian chopines, late sixteenth century, Museo Stefano Bardini (Photo: © Fototeca dei Musei Civici Fiorentini)	297
13.6.	Engraving of Venetian bride with her dancemaster by Giacomo Franco, c. 1591–1609, The Metropolitan Museum of Art, Harris Brisbane Dick Fund 1938 38.38.7 (Photo: © The Metropolitan Museum of Art)	302
13.7.	Venetian engraving of *Courtesan and Blind Cupid*, publisher Pietro Bertelli, c. 1563, Metropolitan Museum of Art 55.503.30. (Photo: © The Metropolitan Museum of Art. Art Resource, NY)	303

13.8.	Venetian engraving of *Courtesan and Blind Cupid*, publisher Pietro Bertelli, c. 1563, Metropolitan Museum of Art 55.503.30 (Photo: © The Metropolitan Museum of Art. Art Resource, NY)	304
14.1.	Carving an inkstone, Huanggang village, Zhaoqing, Guangdong province, China (Photo: Dorothy Ko)	309
14.2.	A scholar sitting on an outdoor mat, holding a writing brush and a blank scroll; his butler grinding ink on an inkstone. Detail from Zhang Lu 張路 (1464–1538), Handscroll of the Lord of Huainan Seeking Immortality, Collection of the Tianjin Museum, Tianjin, China (Photo: Dorothy Ko)	311
14.3.	Fetishized imperfections (*shipin* 石品) on the surface of Duan stone. Duan Inkstone Factory, Zhaoqing, Guangdong province, China (Photo: Dorothy Ko)	315
14.4.	Rubbing of 'Twin swallows' inkstone bearing Gu Erniang's mark, Qing dynasty (1644–1911), Collection of Tianjin Museum, Tianjin, China (Rubbing courtesy of Cai Hongru)	323
14.5.	Rubbing of 'Ink drops' inkstone showing Huang Ren's portrait, Qing dynasty (1644–1911), Collection of Tianjin Museum, Tianjin, China (Rubbing courtesy of Cai Hongru)	329

Contributors

Christy Anderson is an architectural historian and has published on English architecture, architectural photography, and Renaissance literature. Her introduction to the history of European architecture of the fifteenth and sixteenth centuries appeared as one volume of the Oxford History of Art (*Renaissance Architecture*, 2013); and her new study of building materials in early modern architecture is forthcoming with the title *Fusible Stones and Solidified Juices: The Matter of Renaissance Buildings*.

Spike Bucklow trained as a chemist, undertook research into cockroach sex pheromones and then made special effects for the TV and movie industries. He retrained as a painting conservator and obtained a PhD in the history of art, supervised by John Gage at Cambridge. He now teaches painting conservation at the Hamilton Kerr Institute, Cambridge. His research interests include artists' materials and methods.

Brigitte Buettner is Louise I. Doyle 1934 Professor in the Art Department at Smith College. A specialist of medieval art, she has published on Boccaccio, late medieval manuscripts, and rituals of gift-giving, and is currently finishing a book on the cultural meanings and uses of precious stones in the Middle Ages.

Michael Cole is Professor of Art History and Archaeology at Columbia University. His most recent book is *Ambitious Form: Giambologna, Ammanati, and Danti in Florence* (2011). His recent essays on the materials of art include 'Francesco Mochi: Size, Scale and Stone' (in *Critical Perspectives on Roman Baroque Sculpture*, ed. Anthony Colantuono and Steven Ostrow, 2013), 'The Cult of Materials' (in *Renouveau et invention: La Sculpture à travers ses histoires matérielles*, ed. Martina Droth and Sébastien Clerbois, 2011), 'Bronze' (in *The Classical Tradition*, ed. Anthony Grafton, Glenn Most, and Salvatore Settis, 2011), and 'Bernini Struts' (in *Projecting Identities: The Power of Material Culture*, ed. Joanna Sofaer Derevenski, 2007).

Carolyn Dean, Professor of Pre-Hispanic and Colonial Latin American Visual Culture at the University of California, Santa Cruz, researches Inka visual and performance culture before and after Spanish colonization. Her recent book, *A Culture of Stone: Inka Perspectives on Rock* (2010), considers various aspects of Inka rock work.

Anne Dunlop is Associate Professor of Art History at Tulane University. She works on the art and culture of medieval and early modern Europe, and her interest in the cross-cultural meanings of materials comes out of a larger research project on 'Eurasian Exchange and Artistic Change in Italy, c. 1250–1450'. She has been a fellow at CASVA, Villa I Tatti, the Getty Research Center, and the British School at Rome. Her publications include 'Drawing Blood', RES (Fall 2013); 'Carrying the Weight of Empire', in *Matters of Weight*, ed. David Young Kim (2013); *Painted Palaces: The Rise of Secular Art in Early Renaissance Italy* (2009), and *Art and the Augustinian Order in Early Renaissance Italy*.

Katie Jakobiec received her PhD from the University of Toronto in 2014. Her dissertation, 'Grain, Stone, Red Velvet: The Material Assemblages of a City on the Vistula River in Poland, c. 1555–1655' examined a merchant community in Kazimierz Dolny, Poland.

Dorothy Ko is a cultural historian whose current research focuses on the history of things in pre-industrial China, especially the epistemology of female artisans – weavers, embroiderers, potters, and inkstone carvers, for example, who learned their craft by non-textual means. The author of *Cinderella's Sisters: A Revisionist History of Footbinding* (2005) and other monographs, she is Professor of History at Barnard College, Columbia University.

Aden Kumler is Associate Professor in the Department of Art History at the University of Chicago. She received her PhD in the History of Art & Architecture from Harvard University in 2007, and the LMS from the Pontifical Institute of Mediaeval Studies in 2012. The author of *Translating Truth: Ambitious Images and Religious Knowledge in Late Medieval France and England* (2011), she is currently working on a study of economies of form, substance, and accidents organized in relationship to the medieval multiples of coin, host, and seal.

Ann-Sophie Lehmann is Associate Professor at the Department of Media and Culture Studies, Utrecht University. Her research develops historical and theoretical perspectives on the production of artefacts in old and new media environments and proposes a process-based approach to visual culture. Recent publications include *New Perspectives in Iconology: Visual Studies and Anthropology* (2012), edited with Barbara Baert and Jenke van den Akkerveken, and 'Showing Making: On Visual Documentation and Creative Practice', *Journal of Modern Craft* 1/5 (2012): 9–24. In 2013, Lehmann was a Scholar at the Getty Research Center in Los Angeles, with a project titled 'Coloring Life, Crafting Images'.

Eckart Marchand is Academic Assistant at the Warburg Institute Archive, University of London. He was Lecturer in the History of Italian Renaissance Art at Reading University from 2003 to 2007. His publications include *Gebärden in der Florentiner Malerei* (2004), an edition of journals and sketchbooks by John Flaxman from his journey to Italy in 1787–94 (2010), and *Plaster Casts: Making, Collecting and Displaying from Classical Antiquity to the Present* (co-edited with Rune Frederiksen, 2010). He is presently working on the use of plaster casts in artists' studios from the Renaissance to the eighteenth century.

Christina Neilson is Assistant Professor of Renaissance and Baroque Art History at Oberlin College. She is the author of 'Rediscovered photographs of two terracotta modelli by Verrocchio', *The Burlington Magazine* vol. 154 (November, 2012) and *Parmigianino's* Antea: *A Beautiful Artifice* (2008), an exhibition she curated at The Frick Collection. A recent recipient of fellowships from the NEH and Villa I Tatti, the Harvard Center for Italian Renaissance Studies in Florence, she is currently completing a book on Andrea del Verrocchio's unusual techniques of manufacture.

Irma Passeri is Associate Conservator of Paintings at the Yale University Art Gallery. She received a degree in the Conservation of Easel Paintings in 1998 at the conservation school of the Opificio delle Pietre Dure in Florence, Italy. In 2010 she received a degree from the University of Tuscia, Viterbo, in the Conservation of Cultural Heritage, with a course of study in 'Tecnologie della Conservazione e il Restauro dei Beni Culturali'. After working in the laboratory of the Opificio delle Pietre Dure for a few years, Irma was invited by the Yale University Art Gallery in 2001 to restore the large dossal depicting the *Virgin and Child with Saints Leonard and Peter* by the Master of the Magdalene. From 2002 to 2004 she restored the *Portrait of Alessandro de Medici* by Pontormo at the Philadelphia Art Museum, and in 2005 she returned to the Opificio to collaborate on the restoration of the *Polyptych of the Intercession* by Gentile da Fabriano from the church of San Niccolò Oltrarno in Florence. At the Yale University Art Gallery her treatments focus on the Early

Italian painting collection. She has published on Italian approaches to the treatment of loss compensation, and on materials and techniques of Italian paintings, including a co-authored essay, 'Technique and Pontormo's Portrait of Alessandro de' Medici,' with Mark Tucker, Ken Sutherland, and Beth Price, for the 2004 catalogue *Pontormo and Bronzino, the Medici, and the Transformation of the Renaissance Portrait*.

Elizabeth Semmelhack has been the Senior Curator of the Bata Shoe Museum since 2000 and her work focuses on the construction of gender in relation to dress, with a particular interest in the history of elevating footwear. She has curated numerous exhibitions that explore this history and has written extensively on the subject. Related publications include: 'Above the rest: Chopines as trans-mediterranean fashion (*Spanish Journal of Cultural Studies*, 2013); *On a Pedestal: Renaissance Chopines and Baroque Heels* (2009); *Heights of Fashion: A History of the Elevated Shoe* (2008) and 'A Delicate Balance: Women, Power and the High Heel', in *Shoes: A History from Sandals to Sneakers* (2006). She is currently working on her upcoming book *Shoe* for Reaktion Press.

Pamela H. Smith is Seth Low Professor of History at Columbia University, where she teaches courses in early modern European history and history of science. Her books include *The Business of Alchemy: Science and Culture in the Holy Roman Empire* (1994); *Merchants and Marvels: Commerce, Science and Art in Early Modern Europe*, co-edited with Paula Findlen (2002); *The Body of the Artisan: Art and Experience in the Scientific Revolution* (2004), and *Making Knowledge in Early Modern Europe: Practices, Objects, and Texts, 1400–1800*, co-edited with Benjamin Schmidt (2008). She has published numerous articles on early modern European artisanal knowledge and culture, and, in current research, she is attempting to reconstruct the vernacular knowledge of early modern European metalworkers from a variety of disciplinary perspectives.

Introduction

Christy Anderson, Anne Dunlop, Pamela H. Smith

> (E)very property is a condensed story. To describe the properties of materials is to tell the stories of what happens to them as they flow, mix and mutate.
>
> (Tim Ingold, 'Materials against materiality')[1]

THINGS, objects, materials, and materiality have infiltrated almost every aspect of scholarship in recent years. There is nothing new about this, of course, as a concern with objects and the human experience of the external world has been a central philosophical concern since at least the early twentieth century with the advent of phenomenology, itself tracing a genealogy back to Marx's critique of Hegel's philosophy of history in *The German Ideology* (1845–46):

> In direct contrast to German philosophy which descends from heaven to earth, here we ascend from earth to heaven. That is to say, we do not set out from what men say, imagine, conceive, nor from men as narrated, thought of, imagined, conceived, in order to arrive at men in the flesh. We set out from real, active men, and on the basis of their real life-process we demonstrate the development of the ideological reflexes and echoes of this life-process. The phantoms formed in the human brain are also, necessarily, sublimates of their material life-process, which is empirically verifiable and bound to material premises. Morality, religion, metaphysics, all the rest of ideology and their corresponding forms of consciousness, thus no longer retain the semblance of independence. They have no history, no development; but men, developing their material production and their material intercourse, alter, along with this their real existence, their thinking and the products of their thinking. Life is not determined by consciousness, but consciousness by life.[2]

It is thus by now an obvious point that even the most abstract ideas may also exist as things in the world. Take the metre, created in the wake of the French Revolution to be a rational unit of measurement. Since 1983 it has been defined as the distance travelled by light in a vacuum in 1/299,792,458th of a second. But that distance was chosen so it would correspond to a physical thing, a metal bar, that sits in the French National Archives in Paris. This 'metre of the Archives' is the second metre of record: the first was made of a platinum alloy that proved unstable over time, and so, by 1889, the metre no longer measured a metre and had to be remade. The bar in turn was supposed to correspond to 1/10,000,000th of the distance from the North Pole to the Equator on a median passing through Paris. But the metre is suspiciously close to a unit of measurement that had been in common use in Paris from at least the Middle Ages – the thing existed long before any abstract definition.[3] As things in the world, derived from things in the world and from the everyday practices of real people, even abstract ideas carry the material traces of the accidents, presuppositions, and processes that produced them.

It is our goal in this book to place matter and its manipulation back into the definition of the early modern artwork. We wish to explore the physical and lived reality of the things that were defined as art, a much broader category in the early modern period than today, and to use the criteria of this pivotal moment to interrogate and evaluate its own production. The period between about 1250 and 1750 was marked by intense interest in and examination of the stuff of the world. This was the age that shaped our modern ideas of art and artistry, and, by attending to the material nature of early modern objects, we also aim to question our own categories of art and visual culture. Such a project demands an opening up of the usual disciplinary boundaries; it also cuts across traditional categories of period or school. The three editors of this volume are an architectural historian, an art historian, and a historian of science. The chapters that follow draw on trends in literary studies, sociology, architecture, anthropology, and conservation studies, just to name a few. Some chapters are case studies of particular objects, makers, or commissions. Others look instead at the broader understandings and implications of particular materials. But they are linked by their drive to focus on materials in order to think differently about the relations of people and objects throughout the early modern world.

The study of materials in art and architecture, early modern or otherwise, intersects with several other threads in recent scholarship. While the connection between intellectual and material life is a long enduring object of study, much of the present exploration is phrased in terms of 'material culture'. Materials can be foregrounded in material culture studies, or just one more bit of evidence in the history of an object.[4] The trajectory of material culture studies should be seen as a parallel study to the history of materials, sharing the close attention to the object and its constitution. And material culture's attention to a wide range of object types, from high style to the vernacular, artist-designed as well as collaborative projects, offers a model of method that embraces cultural history. While there are many shared interests between studies of materials and material culture, the essential difference is one of focus on the ways in which materials themselves bring with them to the object their own histories of origins and associations. Much of the critique of new historicist studies has been the loss of the object, the description of a deeply worked context that was difficult to connect back to the artwork itself. One of the most compelling aspects of the chapters in this collection, and the broader interest in materials in current scholarship, is the way this more materialist approach allows us to connect the object with its context in a distinctly tangible way. That focus on materials forms a path into the study of the artist and craftsperson, their practices and knowledge, the desires of the patron, and the cultural significance of the object itself.

Anthropologists argue for the entanglement of humans and the material world: in the foundational work of Alfred Gell, that entanglement is both real, a form of decoration on objects, and the mental state created in viewers and users. Gell linked this entanglement to the agency of objects, their ability to act in the world, and he suggested that the inability to imagine the conditions of production of an object, to understand the relations of cause and effect, might be one way to define artworks as a subsection of artificial objects.[5] Tim Ingold, in his drive to break down the binary oppositions of subject and object, and nature and culture, speaks of flows of matter and materials, rather than bounded, discrete things. He is therefore sceptical of the concepts of 'materiality' and 'material culture', as they foster a view of things in which form is imposed on inert matter from without, rather than things being 'generated and dissolved within the fluxes of materials across the interface between substances and the medium that surrounds them'.[6]

Because Ingold views things as actively caught up in and contributing to flows – rather than exercising agency of a more conventional sort – and thereby contributing to the shaping of the lifeworld, he takes issue with another extremely influential scholar, Bruno Latour, whose work argues that 'mute' living and non-living objects exercise agency in the constitution of scientific facts and theories. Latour has exerted a powerful force in many disciplines, especially the sociology of knowledge and the history of science. In *We Have Never Been Modern* and further writings on actor–network theory, Latour and others have sought to lay out a method by which historians and anthropologists can provide accounts of the agency of material objects and nonhuman entities (what he names quasi-objects). In explicating quasi-objects, Latour argues that the objects of science (objects like the metre) do not exist apart from human culture, but are instead entirely embedded within and constituted by that culture, including its material components. Latour contends that the conventional mode of viewing the objects of science as pure nature, rather than as the 'nature–culture hybrids' that they are, removes science and its objects from the sphere of questioning and political dispute, thus distorting decision-making in science policy. Historians of science in particular have employed this recent work to consider how objects of science – intellectual and material, often both – emerge out of material, intellectual, and cultural fields (or, as one might phrase it, out of lifeworlds), to go on to shape these fields in further ways.[7]

To study materials means to return to objects, yet not objects in isolation. It is not a reactionary turn against studying art as a cultural artefact, but rather comes from the understanding that artworks, like other objects, are always tempered by the conditions of production, their physical creation out of the materials of the earth.[8] Materials are always understood in the conditions and events of their time; they are imbued with political meaning and shaped by the beliefs of their creators and audiences. For the ancient writer Lucretius, in his *De rerum natura*, the vitality of materials was inherent in the world's elemental structures, and inevitably produced the collisions and accidents that affected history and social conditions. As Manuel De Landa has written, 'we live in a world populated by structures – a complex mixture of geological, biological, social, and linguistic constructions that are nothing but accumulations of materials shaped and hardened by history.'[9] Matter is the substratum of the social, and it is no coincidence that those interested in breaking down the barriers between high culture and the wider lived experience of the past have so often focused on things as agents and vehicles.[10]

If De Landa is interested in vast territories of time and the interactions of materials with social structures, others have sought to understand how materials engage with the spaces of the psyche, of the imaginary. Here materials as historical artefacts exist in a middle zone between tangible substance and poetic creation, and the historian must take both these aspects into account in the study of how materials were used and understood. Gaston Bachelard's study of the four elemental materials in the Western tradition in his books on water, fire, air, and water propose what he calls a theory of reverie to describe this intermediate place between rational consciousness and the unconscious, provoked by our interactions with the material world.[11] Not quite daydreaming, and not solely located in the unconscious, Bachelard's philosophical approach takes into account what could be called the creative impulse or art-making: 'the explanation by the useful must give way to the explanation by the agreeable, the rational explanation must give way to the psychoanalytical explanation.'[12] Adrian Stokes's 1934 book *Stones of Rimini* might be taken as a precursor of Bachelard's call; it started with a rumination on the birth of modern limestone in ancient waters, and traced a distinction in fifteenth-century sculpture between carving and modelling that is ultimately medium- as much as process-based.[13] For Stokes, modelling was using stone as a 'suitable' medium, and valued the plastic form created. But carving was an act of bringing stone to life through figurative and emotional engagement with it, a kind of coaxing into being of the fluid and changeable qualities of the stone itself.

Until very recently, Stokes remained an idiosyncrasy in art history, which formed as an academic discipline around disembodied images – slides and scans – often with a privileging of the visual over the tactile or practical qualities of a work. Stokes wrote as the field was engaging strongly with iconology, a project based in the finding of meaning in figuration and textual sources rather than in making and craftsmanship. As a practice constructed around the close examination of things, however, art and architectural history has had a long tradition of physical and technical examination of objects: what they were made of, and how they might be repaired, restored, or preserved. Both museum and field work require an engagement with the physical condition of the artefact or building, and these issues are at the centre of conservation and conservation studies, which have their own highly specialized literature: it is possible to determine the purity of the gold used on an icon painting, what proteins are present in pigments, or the refraction index of the glass used in seventeenth-century houses. But in the field at large such information has mostly been used to locate objects in time and space, and to determine forgeries; art history has traditionally been concerned with ascribing authorial names to objects, and materials have been mined for information about where things were produced and by whom, as much as for their subsequent history. There has been limited interest in materials or production as bearers of meaning – as social and historical agents – in their own right, let alone a willingness to take them as entries into the socially and historically contingent spaces of the imaginary, of 'reverie', that Bachelard so beautifully described.

Of course there have always been exceptions, and they come up again and again as reference points in the chapters that follow here. Significantly, they have often come from the most important thinkers in the field. Julius von Schlosser wrote on the uses and meanings of wax, and Michael Baxandall's *Limewood Sculptors of Renaissance Germany* began from the cell structure of linden trees and ended with the social and political world of the sculptors who responded to these properties.[14] Romanticism and especially the Arts and Crafts movement of the nineteenth century created an interest in pre-industrial techniques of building and fabrication: Mary Merrifield collected and edited treatises on early painting techniques, and Ruskin chose the title *The Stones of Venice*, with an opening chapter called 'The Quarry', for what is essentially a social history of the city. Art historians interested in artistic production as a social field sometimes studied workshop practice.[15] The project of the social history of art in the 1970s and 1980s brought a new focus to this work, and a concern with both objects and makers as agents of social and historical change. Growing fundamentally from Marx's insistence on the material conditions of society (although the term 'dialectical materialism' was not itself used by Marx), the social historians of art often worked in dialogue with cultural historians and cultural studies. They insisted on the work of the artist as a class-based labour with its own dynamic and customs, and stressed the role of objects, high and low, in the creation of class, taste, and historical change.[16] Objects were examined as evidence but also as agents of otherwise unrecorded or under-recorded lived historical experience – the lives of the poor, or women, for instance.[17] Historical research on materials and material culture increased exponentially, as did studies of consumption, commerce and of production, including the production of ideology or power through conspicuous consumption.[18]

The current engagement with matter in art and cultural history is however more far-reaching and fundamental. It is not simply a late version of the high-modernist credo of truth to materials. It has come about in part through dissatisfaction with the oddly disembodied sign or image of recent art history, but it is also linked to a much larger cultural interest in things, which may in turn be spurred partly by the increasingly disembodied nature of information and images in a digital age.[19] Against globalized networks of data, a focus on the importance of the handmade and the specific object can seem like an act of resistance, even a form of grace.[20] It may be too much to say that media studies has reverse-engineered an interest in media as physical things, but certainly contemporary artists and architects interested in materials have encouraged an interest for historians in the use and understanding of materials in the past.[21]

At the same time, the drive to write a more global history has focused, among other issues, on 'commodity chains' and networks of exchange, and artworks and other objects of commerce have been used to write different accounts of the early modern past. It has become clear that the associations of materials, while culturally specific, might also cut across both distance and time.[22] Throughout the medieval and early modern world, the trade in luxury goods was predicated on the value given to precious materials such lapis lazuli from Afghanistan or Armenia, rock crystal from the Middle East, South American feather objects, or textiles from China and Central Asia.[23] This is not news to historians of non-Western art and vernacular traditions,[24] but it is another reason why, in assembling the chapters of this volume, we have sought out contributors from so many different formations and fields. Materials and technologies may start out very local, but they often have a fluidity of circulation that overturns older art-historical ideas of discrete cultures, nations, or schools.

The chapters themselves have been grouped in three large categories – 'Matter', 'Practices', and 'Cultural Logics' – which are intended to move roughly from the most concrete to the most abstract aspects of objects. The specific issues of each section are outlined here below. In practice, however, these three aspects – material, making, and meaning – are as entangled as the human–object relations that Tim Ingold lays out, and, like the condensed stories of matter in our epigraph, issues flow together across chapters, mixing and mutating throughout the sections of the book.

Matter

The early modern artwork was above all a particular kind of physical object and presence. Through the skilful manipulation of materials – from wood, marble, paint, and plaster to brick, gold, and gems – artisans and artists from Peru to China sought to move the viewer, to create new and unexpected experiences, and to make objects communicate with rapidly evolving and ever more exacting audiences. When artisans began to work, their first concern was the material they would use. What was the best material for the purpose at hand? Where could they find it; what skills, tools, and time would it require; what effects would it allow; and how much would it cost? What associations did it bring in its wake? As the artisan explored the properties of the materials, he or she might find that the qualities of materials allowed certain techniques, thus fostering particular skills. The materials themselves could 'train' the makers, and impose form on the work of art.[25] As craft and artistic techniques of working particular materials were institutionalized, social groupings and communities, as well as rituals and hierarchies, formed, and codified bodies of knowledge and intellectual frameworks about the behaviour of natural materials emerged.

Ann-Sophie Lehmann, a historian of art and of media whose chapter begins the section, holds that the recent 'material turn' in art history possesses no coherent theory of materials. Her goal therefore is to sketch out both a theory of materials and a methodology for how such a theory might be elaborated, including the re-making and authentic reconstruction of works of art. After surveying a variety of de-materializations and re-materializations of art history and theory, she discusses the relationship of Gottfried Semper's *Kunstwerden* and Alois Riegl's *Kunstwollen*, and lays out a 'theoretical toolbox' for interpreting materials. Lehmann employs this tool kit, and its underlying principle that materials make meaning, by examining the use of oil as a medium in fifteenth-century Netherlandish panel painting. As she stresses, oil has been the ultimate medium without meaning in art history, recognized only as a carrier of colour and form enabling representation, and relegated in the interpretation of artworks to a kind of 'pure material', devoid of meaning. In Lehmann's exploration of oil as an active creator of meaning, she begins with its properties or 'affordances' (a term she borrows from Gibson) that make meanings possible, including the meaning of representation itself. Oil paint's property of vanishing entirely affords the artist the capacity to make viewers believe that it is real hair or bark or skin before them on the surface of a painting.

Like Lehmann's examination of oil, research on Renaissance bronzes has given rise to fruitful new approaches in recent art history.[26] Bronze is an alloy, an artificial metal invented by humans, and as such it brings to a head the question of the relationship between art of the human hand and natural materials, as well as of the behaviour of matter. Such questions were laid out in the 1540 *De la Pirotechnia* by the metalworker and author Vannoccio Biringuccio.[27] The chapter from historian of science Pamela Smith emerges from a desire to attend to materials in the ways expressed by Biringuccio, in order to explore the lifeworld of the artist and craftsperson and the entanglement of the human body and natural materials within it. She finds Biringuccio articulating principles of metallic generation and transformation, and these are also more methodically developed by the teacher of Greek, city physician, and mine shareholder Georgius Agricola, in his many learned books. Smith's chapter shows that Agricola's ideas and knowledge about mining and metalworking coalesced not only through his reading of ancient and medieval texts, but also by his close association with miners, and his attempts to translate and codify their language and their experience into theory and text. A study of his work reveals the process by which a theoretical corpus of knowledge emerges out of the experience of working matter, or, we might say, how matter gives rise to ideas.

Art historian Anne Dunlop's chapter moves to the materials of European painters in the fourteenth and fifteenth centuries. She begins from a small panel done in Florence by Gentile da Fabriano in the early 1420s, a study in itself of materials and their representation. She notes that the early development of such painting came in the wake of the thirteenth-century Mongol conquests, which brought new trade, images, and exchange. Dunlop argues that this affected early Italian painting in at least two ways. The quality and quantity of imported materials increased, and this had an immediate impact on production. Beyond this, however, such materials were linked to the same exotic places and spaces as the holy figures that painters worked to represent, and the transformation of matter into Mary or Jesus by painters could be seen to mirror God's own creation in miniature. By tracing the routes that pigments travelled to reach Florence, and the methods by which they were produced, Dunlop shows the important associations of place and meaning they both maintained and acquired over distance and culture.

The first section concludes with a close examination of a material of great resonance in the early modern period – gold. Regarded as ripening beneath the hot sun of Africa, gold was used both for coinage and, in the form of gold leaf, for paintings. As paintings conservator Irma Passeri shows in her chapter, most Mediterranean gold derived from Africa, and, by following the movement of gold from Africa to Europe in the medieval and Renaissance period, she suggests that the increased availability of gold in Italy in the thirteenth and fourteenth century, and the capacity to mould and shape it, translated directly into the expressive ambitions of a painting. In addition, of course, the value of gold, both as an item of coinage (with economic and social functions) and as a marker within a social system heightened its significance in works of art.

Taken together, the chapters in the first section provide a variety of different approaches to materials, but all point to the overarching thrust of this volume, expressed above in the epigraph from Tim Ingold's work: matter can only be studied through its properties, and this necessitates investigation into the mutual interaction of people and materials – of the ways in which humans shaped materials into things, and the ways in which those things in turn shaped human culture and society.

Practices

In the second section, the focus is on the spaces and skills of production – the workshops, quarries, ovens, and kilns where matter was transformed, and the bodies, knowledge, and lore that allowed one thing to be shaped into another. If matter was believed to be pregnant with meaning, this was because it reflected an attitude about the vitality of the world and its substances. All materials came from natural sources, but some remained close to their first states, while others were transformed radically through mechanical, chemical, or other means. Throughout all these manipulations, however, materials were thought to retain the potency of the earth, the first divine creation. As God created the earth and all it contained, so too artisans and artists could extend sacred creation through their own labour.

The increasing virtuosity of early modern artisans was met with an equal desire to distinguish the artist from the artisan, intellectual labor from manual work. In seeking to establish a hierarchy of the arts and of artistic production, one strategy was to value an abstracted ideal of artistic conception over the material execution of any given object – to de-materialize the activity of making. The debate over social status in the arts was often framed around materials: around who had the knowledge and access to transform the stuff of nature. Specialized texts such as treatises or manuals emphasized the importance of materials, and viewers as well as artisans had an understanding of materials, their preciousness, the difficulty of their manipulation, and their suitability for different types of objects. Yet the detailed information of how matter might be manipulated was often a closely guarded trade secret, linked to disciplines like alchemy as a knowledge for the initiated. Moreover, processes of making and the patterns of practice were often shown and learned through the senses and never intended to be described in words. This is a major theme in this section and for *The Matter of Art* as a whole: the struggle to describe matter and its transformation into materials, and then to communicate these ideas to others.

The chapters in this section move from the most ephemeral and malleable materials to the most enduring and recalcitrant, from bread to stone through earth, wax, plaster and pigment. They cluster around the problem of transformation, both how this might be accomplished and what transformation might imply – what did it mean to make one thing out of another? The first chapter, by Aden Kumler, takes on the most profound transformation of all: how something made by human hands can stand in for, or even become, the divine. In 'The "Genealogy of Jean le Blanc"'[1], Kumler explores the European Eucharist, that small mixture of water and grain that, according to Catholic theology, became the real flesh of Christ through the rite of the Mass. There was enormous anxiety to produce the purest hosts from the finest flour; the rituals around the making and baking of hosts overlapped with the liturgy in which they were used, and they tended to erase, as much as possible, the man-made status of the wafers. Kumler highlights the paradox at the heart of these practices and debates: if the host became the body of God, then its prior purity was a moot point; if it did not, then it was only flour and water, the most ordinary and banal substances, and no amount of special treatment could make it anything but a base thing falsely presented as something sacred.

In Spike Bucklow's contribution, a study of lead white, one of the oldest and most basic pigments of the painter's palette, becomes a way to think through the problem of transformation in the widest sense. Lead white, basic lead carbonate, can be found in use by painters from at least 3000 BCE, and it is still used to create an intense bright colour. Its fabrication was well known and involved some of the humblest materials: in one recipe, metal was exposed to vinegar and left to ferment in horse dung. It also occurred naturally. Yet, as Bucklow shows, this common substance held a series of mysteries within itself. Its exact production relied on the knowledge of makers and apprentices, and it could go badly wrong. Lead is extremely poisonous, both in immediate exposure and in contact over time. More fundamentally, in the polarities that structured the premodern European cosmos, the creation of this simple pigment transformed black into white, hot and dry into cold and wet; Bucklow writes that it ultimately suggested that 'opposite states lay latent within each other', and that appearances 'rode upon a substrate that was in a constant state of flux'.

Eckart Marchand looks at plaster, clay, and wax, widely used in Renaissance sculptors' workshops and widely ignored in most art-historical writing. In a system where the real and symbolic worth of sculpture was linked to difficulty – the innate difficulty of carving stone or the practical difficulty of casting molten bronze – these three malleable materials were relatively little valued. All three, as Marchand shows, were used in early but formative stages of creating work, though their different properties lent them to distinctive uses. Clay and plaster were seldom used in their 'naked' state, without gilding or colour; they seem to have been valued for their ability to reference other materials. Conversely, wax had been associated with memory since antiquity, and its imagined origins – as the unadulterated nectar of flowers – led it to be compared to the virgin birth. Marchand suggests that these associations, joined with wax's property of flesh-like translucency, encouraged its use in votive settings, and lent it to the recording of the sculptural process itself.

The idea that the process of production is always integral to the meaning of the thing produced lies at the heart of the final chapter in this section, 'Rocks and reverence', by Carolyn Dean. Dean is focused on stone in Andean building and culture, where Inka builders worked with giant blocks to create the most important ritual and civic structures. When the Spanish claimed this territory, they also laid claim to these buildings and a modified version of this architectural tradition. In both cultures, stone was the greatest and most significant building material, and Dean traces the very physical and technical work that such architecture required. She argues that two fundamentally different understandings of stone shaped Inka and Spanish interactions. For the Inka, building was a process of domesticating living partners in their environment. Stones were worked by being 'nibbled', allowing themselves and their essence to be incorporated into the Inka social order. They might bleed or refuse to be moved if they were not willing to find a place there. For the Spaniards, stone was instead a symbol, linked to permanence and to the taming of nature in culture; the model was adversarial, not complementary.

These brief summaries also make clear the ways in which practices and theory cannot be separated. From the making of bread wafers or white paint to the laying of masonry, making was embedded in systems of belief about acting in and on the world in the largest sense. This is the central theme of the third section of the volume, 'Cultural logics'.

Cultural logics

Studies of materials begin with a close attention to the qualities of the matter out of which they are created, and they move outward to offer an understanding of how that material was understood at a particular moment and in a precise place. Materials have scientific properties that are measurable. Yet how those properties are employed and how they are understood are a product of culture, those adaptive patterns of behaviour that evolve over time and tie practices to a particular place.[28] Stone, for example, may have distinct physical qualities, but how its qualities are understood and then employed is the product of the interaction of matter, circumstance, and beliefs.

Materials are enmeshed with the physical as well as the societal structures of any age, and constantly in motion. Materials have a history that may be charted over the short and long term. The story of materials begins with the history of matter, and matter is a product of the earth with its geological time frame. One way to think about the cultural logics of materials, therefore, is to see them is as part of historical epochs and central to the social structures with which they engage. This dynamic approach links human institutions such as cities, trade networks, and linguistic systems with a slowly evolving material world.

For the patrons of architecture, the cost of materials was the first concern. If labour was relatively inexpensive, the purchase and transportation of stone constituted the majority of the budget. Other materials were more local, such as terracotta and brick made from nearby clay reserves. No observer of high-style buildings would have failed to notice that the materials out of which they were made were precious and a display of great monetary resources. So too in painting, where the use of exotic and imported materials such as lapis lazuli imbued a work with a preciousness that permeated all aspects of the object and its subject. Brigitte Buettner's chapter explores the interaction of ingenuity and value in the paintings of Jean Fouquet. That artist's exquisite rendering of materials, the gems and silks that envelop saints and patrons, was not only an opportunity to showcase his artistic skill; it emerged from the very real interaction of artisans with their materials. Buettner refers to the geological energy of the precious stones depicted, following a medieval tradition of ascribing meaning to specific gemstones. By the early modern period, however, the relationships between material identification and significance had shifted, opening up new avenues and demands for artists to capture the potency of materials in what they painted.

When artists chose not to employ these materials and to paint in a 'poor manner' they brought into question the artistic practices Buettner describes. A mode of painting that appeared materially deficient shifted the attention to other issues of painting's purpose, at times aligning it with ancient practices or the identity of the commissioning patron. Looking broadly at art from the fifteenth through to the seventeenth centuries, Michael Cole identifies a growing emphasis on impoverishment in art-making, which includes attention to personal poverty or humility, a bare or stripped-down style, and an impoverished use or representation of the materials of painting and sculpture. One example is the experimentation by artists with Pliny's injunction to employ only a four-colour palette. As Michael Baxandall pointed out many years ago, if artists intentionally eschewed the use of rich materials, value could shift to the abilities of the artist who was able to do so much with so little. Yet the monetary worth of art, and the prestige of artists, required a delicate balance between a visual vocabulary that embraced a changing aesthetic and the traditional value of art as an object of preciousness.

The study of materials highlights networks of alliances that go against the usual groupings of art object or typology. Artisans with an expertise and knowledge of a specific material might make devotional works as well as utilitarian objects. Against that technical skill, however, materials did take on nuanced meanings based on their use. Christina Neilson examines the varieties of wood used for religious sculpture, suggesting that the type of wood aligned with the particular figure depicted and with intended use. This alliance between form and material emerged from the early modern understanding of wood (and the trees from which it was taken) as having a similarity to flesh and the human body.

In Ming and Qing China, inkstones made from the hard Duan riverstones came to be associated with the body of the male scholar, taking on the attributes of the connoisseur and collector. Yet the smooth surface, lovingly caressed by its owner, was also the product of the labour of the miner whose tacit knowledge of local geology was essential in releasing the stone from the earth. Equally subsumed was the skill of the artisan who carved the stone. As Dorothy Ko shows in her chapter, the cultural authority given to writing in seventeenth-century China had the effect of diminishing the value of the labourer and artisans whose knowledge was not recorded in texts (as was the experience of the connoisseur). Ko traces a geography of skills associated with the production of inkstones, and the projection of the desires of the patrons on to the material objects he owned.

Wood, stone, wax, silk, pigments: these materials accumulated new and heightened meanings as their use intersected with new social conditions. It is often in a moment of change or contestation that a material received a heightened charge: a new ruler requests his architect to use a type of marble used by his political rival, as Katie Jakobiec's chapter describes in her contribution on the materials used by eastern European architects in Poland and Lithuania. By approaching the architecture of the Jagiellonian court by attending first to its materials, rather than simply its style, Jakobiec presents a view of the building world as a site of court politics, where allegiances were played out in material choices.

Luxury goods are usually made from exotic stuff, and their power was predicated on the ability to interact with the physicality of the materials put to more mundane uses.[29] The transformation of shoes, for example, into objects of status and luxury was predicated on the introduction of exotic materials into their production. In her chapter on the chopine, Elizabeth Semmelhack describes how in Valencia and Venice the simple substructure of cork and wood that made up the structure of the shoe was covered with luxury stuffs, shifting attention to the surface of the shoe. The shoe, as just one aspect of an elaborately controlled dress, achieved a new status on account of its surface transformation.

Writing on the occasion of the construction of a man-made lake in Dallas, the philosopher and priest Ivan Illich traced the meanings of water as an object of myth and practical purpose. Illich called for a historicity of matter, of what he called 'stuff', from the Bible through to modern urban planning: 'For not only does the way an epoch treats water and space have a history: the very substances that are shaped by the imagination – and thereby given explicit meanings – are themselves social creations to some degree'.[30] In returning to the fluid meanings of matter in an age as obsessed with its manipulation and definition as our own, this volume provides multiple approaches to the study of materials, none of them necessarily definitive, but all arguing for taking things and stuff as primary points of embarkation in understanding the material and intellectual culture of the past.

Notes

1 Tim Ingold, 'Materials against materiality', *Archaeological Dialogues*, 14 (2007), pp. 1–16, p. 14.
2 Karl Marx and Friedrich Engels, *The German Ideology* (1845–6), in *The Marx and Engels Reader*, ed. Robert C. Tucker, 2nd ed. (New York: W.W. Norton, 1978), pp. 154–5.

3   Steven Shapin, 'Plus or minus one ear', *London Review of Books* (30 August, 2012), pp. 8–10.
4   For example, see Sara Pennell, '"For a crack or flaw despis'd": Thinking about ceramic durability and the "everyday" in late seventeenth- and early-eighteenth-century England', in Tara Hamling and Catherine Richardson (eds), *Everyday Objects: Medieval and Early Modern Material Culture and Its Meanings* (Farnham and Burlington, VT: Ashgate, 2010), pp. 27–40.
5   Alfred Gell, *Art and Agency: Towards an Anthropological Theory* (Oxford: Oxford University Press, 1998). See also Liana Chua and Mark Elliott (eds), *Distributed Objects: Meaning and Mattering after Alfred Gell* (New York and Oxford: Berghahn Books, 2013); Daniel Miller (ed.), *Materiality* (Durham, NC and London: Duke University Press, 2005); and Ian Hodder, *Entangled: An Archaeology of the Relationships between Humans and Things* (Chichester: Wiley-Blackwell, 2012).
6   Tim Ingold, *The Perception of the Environment: Essays in Livelihood, Dwelling and Skill* (London and New York: Routledge, 2000), and 'Materials against materiality', p. 1.
7   For example, Ursula Klein and E.C. Spary, *Materials and Expertise in Early Modern Europe: Between Market and Laboratory* (Chicago: University of Chicago Press, 2010); Lorraine Daston (ed.), *Things that Talk: Object Lessons from Art and Science* (New York: Zone Books, 2004); Lorraine Daston and Peter Galison, *Objectivity* (New York: Zone Books, 2007); and Bruno Latour, *On the Modern Cult of the Factish Gods* (Durham, NC and London: Duke Unviersity Press, 2010).
8   Michael Cole, 'The cult of materials', in Sébastien Clerbois and Martina Droth (eds), *Revival and Invention: Sculpture through Its Material Histories* (Oxford: Peter Lang, 2011), pp. 1–15; and the fundamental book by Thomas Raff, *Die Sprache der Materialien: Anleitung zu einer Ikonologie der Werkstoffe* (Berlin: Deutscher Kunstverlag, 1994).
9   Manuel De Landa, *A Thousand Years of Nonlinear History* (New York: Zone Books, 2000), p. 25. Also see, from very different perspectives, John Brinckerhoff Jackson, 'Stone and its substitutes', in his *Discovering the Vernacular Landscape* (New Haven, CT and London: Yale University Press, 1984), pp. 103–12; Sonia Macrì, *Pietre viventi: I minerali nell'immaginario del mondo antico* (Turin: UTET 2009); and Jane Bennett, *Vibrant Matter: A Political Ecology of Things* (Durham, NC and London: Duke University Press, 2010).
10 The reorganization of the British and European galleries at the Victoria and Albert Museum is a good example. Rather than displaying artworks as discrete objects, the curators chose to suggest (fictive) environments built around the works of the collections. For related studies, see Marta Ajmar and Flora Dennis (eds), *At Home in Renaissance Italy* (New Haven, CT and London: Yale University Press, 2006); Michelle O'Malley and Evelyn Welch (eds), *The Material Renaissance* (Manchester: Manchester University Press, 2007). For the premises of such studies, see Michel De Certeau, *The Practice of Everyday Life*, trans. Stephen Rendall (Berkeley and London: University of California Press, 1984).
11 Gaston Bachelard, *La Psychanalyse du feu* (Paris: Gallimard, 1938); *L'Eau et les rêves: Essai sur l'imagination de la matière* (Paris: J. Corti, 1942); *L'Air et les songes: Essai sur l'imagination du mouvement* (Paris: J. Corti, 1943); *La Terre et les rêveries du repos* (Paris: J. Corti, 1948).
12 Gaston Bachelard, *The Psychoanalysis of Fire* (Boston, MA: Beacon Press, 1964), p. 33. Also see Mary McAllester Jones, *Gaston Bachelard: Subversive Humanist* (Madison: University of Wisconsin Press, 1991).
13 Adrian Stokes, *Stones of Rimini* (New York: Schocken, 1985); see also Stephen Bann (ed.), *The Coral Mind: Adrian Stokes's Engagement with Architecture, Art History, Criticism, and Psychoanalysis* (University Park: Pennsylvania State University Press, 2007).
14 Julius von Schlosser, *Geschichte der Porträtbildnerei in Wachs* (Vienna: Tempsky, 1911); English edition and translation in Roberta Panzanelli (ed.), *Ephemeral Bodies: Wax Sculpture and the Human Figure* (Los Angeles, CA: Getty Research Institute, 2008); and

Michael Baxandall, *The Limewood Sculptors of Renaissance Germany* (New Haven, CT and London: Yale University Press, 1982).

15 One example: Martin Wackernagel, *The World of the Florentine Renaissance Artist: Projects and Patrons, Artists and Art Markets*, trans. Alison Luch, 2nd ed. (Toronto, ON: University of Toronto Press, 2011), first published in Leipzig by E.A. Seemann in 1938.

16 On the relations to nineteenth-century theories of *Kulturgeschichte*, and to Marx, see Peter N. Miller, 'Introduction: The culture of the hand', in Peter N. Miller (ed.), *Cultural Histories of the Material World* (Ann Arbor: The University of Michigan Press, 2013), pp. 2–6. In Britain in particular this work was in dialogue with cultural historians such as Stuart Hall and the Birmingham School.

17 See for instance Jules David Prown, 'Mind in matter: An introduction to Material Culture Theory and Method', *Winterthur Portfolio* 17 (1982), pp. 1–19. Two recent cultural historians who use objects to shed light on the lives of women are Raffaella Sarti, *Europe at Home: Family and Material Culture, 1500–1800* (New Haven, CT: Yale University Press, 2004), and Laurel Thatcher Ulrich, *The Age of Homespun: Objects and Stories in the Creation of an American Myth* (New York: Vintage Books, 2002).

18 Examples, among many others: Suzanne B. Butters, *The Triumph of Vulcan: Sculptors' Tools, Porphyry, and the Prince in Ducal Florence*, 2 vols (Florence: Leo S. Olschki, 1996); Ulinka Rublack, 'Matter in the material Renaissance', *Past and Present*, 219 (May 2013), pp. 41–85; Paula Findlen (ed.), *Early Modern Things: Objects and their Histories* (New York: Routledge, 2012), especially the useful introduction; Georges Didi-Huberman, 'Viscosities and survivals: Art history put to the test by the material', in Panzanelli (ed.), *Ephemeral Bodies*; Peta Motture and Michelle O'Malley (eds), *Re-Thinking Renaissance Objects: Design, Function and Meaning* (Oxford: Wiley-Blackwell, 2011).

19 An accessible account is Daniel Miller, *Stuff* (Cambridge and Malden, MA: Polity Press, 2010), which also offers a good overview of Miller's important work on the cultural meanings of things.

20 For instance, Matthew B. Crawford, *Shop Class as Soulcraft: An Inquiry into the Value of Work* (New York: Penguin Press, 2009).

21 Kate Lloyd Thomas (ed.), *Material Matters: Architecture and Material Practice* (London and New York: Routledge, 2007).

22 Two examples among many: Mark Kurlansky, *Salt: A World History* (New York: Penguin Books, 2002); Kris Lane, *The Colour of Paradise: The Emerald in the Age of Gunpowder Empires* (New Haven, CT and London: Yale University Press, 2010). See more generally: Arjun Appadurai (ed.), *The Social Life of Things: Commodities in Cultural Perspective* (Cambridge and New York: Cambridge University Press, 1986).

23 It can only be mentioned in passing here that the early modern interest in things was not only a European phenomenon. This is one reason why the 2008 conference of the Comité international d'histoire d'art, on the theme of cross-cultural exchange, had a multi-day session dedicated to the theme 'Materiality across Cultures': Jaynie Anderson (ed.), *Crossing Cultures: Conflict, Migration, and Convergence* (Melbourne: Miegunyah Press, University of Melbourne, 2009), pp. 466–519. Thus, for instance, the historian of China Craig Clunas has demonstrated the Ming and Qing culture of valuation and connoisseurship: *Superfluous Things: Material Culture and Social Status in Early Modern China* (Honolulu: University of Hawaii Press, 2004). The work of Carolyn Dean, a contributor to this volume, shows that both Inka and Spanish cultures had a fascination with stone in post-conquest Peru, though their interest took very different forms: *A Culture of Stone: Inka Perspectives on Rock* (Durham, NC: Duke University Press, 2010). See also the essays by Anna Contadini and Lisa Monnas, in Lieselotte E. Saurma-Jeltsch and Anja Eisenbeiss (eds), *The Power of Things and the Flow of Cultural Transformations: Art and Culture between Europe and Asia* (Berlin and Munich: Deutscher Kunstverlag, 2010).

Introduction

24 See, for example, Dora P. Crouch and June G. Johnson, *Traditions in Architecture: Africa, America, Asia, and Oceania* (Oxford and New York: Oxford University Press, 2001).

25 Ann-Sophie Lehmann, 'Wedging, throwing, dipping and dragging: How motions, tools and materials make art', in Barbara Baert and Trees de Mits (eds), *Folded Stones* (Ghent: Institute for Practice-Based Research in the Arts, 2009), pp. 41–60.

26 Much work was driven by the Renaissance bronze project begun by the Getty Museum in the 1990s, but there have been many recent exhibits on bronze and on individual artists or national traditions, including of course, *Bronze!* at the Royal Academy of Art in London. For recent studies, see Volker Krahn (ed.), *Von allen Seiten schön: Bronzen der Renaissance und des Barock* (Berlin and Heidelberg: Edition Braus, 1995); Edgar Lein, *Ars Aeraria: Die Kunst des Bronzegießens und die Bedeutung von Bronze in der florentinischen Renaissance* (Mainz: Philipp von Zabern, 2004); Victoria Avery, *Vulcan's Forge in Venus' City: The Story of Bronze in Venice, 1350–1650* (Oxford: Oxford University Press, 2012), and the essay by Pamela H. Smith in this volume.

27 Vannoccio Biringuccio, *Pirotechnia* (1540), trans. Cyril Stanley Smith and Martha Teach Gnudi (Cambridge, MA: Harvard University Press, 1966), pp. 215–16.

28 See for example the discussion in Tim Ingold, 'Stories against classification: Transport, wayfaring and the integration of knowledge', in his *Being Alive. Essays on Movement, Knowledge and Description* (London and New York: Routledge, 2011), pp. 156–64.

29 Peter Noever (ed.), *Global Lab: Kunst als Botschaft, Asien und Europa, 1500–1700* (Ostfildern: Hadje Cantz Verlag, 2009), p. 29.

30 Ivan Illich, *H_2O and the Waters of Forgetfulness: Reflections on the Historicity of Stuff* (Berkeley, CA: Heyday Books, 1985), p. 4.

Part I ✧ Matter

1 ✧ The matter of the medium: some tools for an art-theoretical interpretation of materials

Ann-Sophie Lehmann

MATERIALS, in spite of their decisive role in determining the meanings and effects of visual artefacts, have long been overlooked in art-theoretical discussions. Following an analysis of possible reasons for art theory's marginal interest in the subject, this chapter argues that the recent 'material turn' in art history and adjacent fields is still in need of a coherent theoretical framework in order to analyse how concrete materials and techniques make and achieve meaning. By bringing together elements from actor–network theory (ANT) with approaches to materiality in art history, media studies, anthropology, philosophy, and psychology, a preliminary theory for the interpretation of materials is outlined. The resulting 'theoretical toolbox' and the various tools it contains are fleshed out with regard to one specific example, the oil medium in fifteenth-century Netherlandish panel painting.

Kunstwerden *and* Kunstwollen: *de- and re-materializations in art history*

'Papers and signs are incredibly weak and fragile', writes Bruno Latour in his essay 'Visualization and Cognition: Drawing Things Together', and exactly because they are made of more flexible and frail materials than the things they describe, they are able to dominate those things.[1] Latour's primary example is the map, a mere drawing on paper that, in the hands of a colonial power, can help to occupy and subjugate entire countries. Therefore, he writes, if we want to understand how visual artefacts acquire significance and power, we must investigate the 'imaging craftsmanship' of their makers and the materials that go into the crafting.[2] Latour suggests this approach for scientific drawings, yet based on two simple premises, it also applies to the making of all sorts of visual artefacts made from all kinds of materials: fragile or durable, liquid or solid. The premises are that (a) materials are a meaningful component of visual artefacts, and that (b) materials cannot be separated from representation.

As obvious as they may seem, these assumptions are in stark contrast with dominant art-theoretical tradition, which generally favours a separation between meaning and material. That tradition assumes that the meaningful conception of art occurs prior to its respective materializations into concrete works of art. This dualist concept is rooted in the so-called hylomorphic model or paradigm, an Aristotelian concept of formation in which an ideal image of a form precedes the material appearance of that form in the physical world.[3] Positioning mind over matter, this model is intrinsically hierarchical and is echoed by many other dualist constellations (e.g. culture–nature, male–female, theory–practice, line–colour). Accordingly, art works were and are still most often understood as material manifestations of an immaterial idea. 'Idea' has been defined differently throughout history, for instance, in terms of divine inspiration in the Renaissance, as creative intuition and ingenious fantasy in the eighteenth and nineteenth centuries, or as knowledgeable design and intellectual concept in modernity. Notwithstanding the diversity of these definitions, material figures unvaryingly as the stuff needed to translate the immaterial into tangible things, yet is given little part in the original conception – and therefore is merely a carrier of meaning, but not meaningful in itself.

Although materials in twentieth-century art certainly emancipated themselves into meaningful substances,[4] the dualistic model and materials' implicit subordination prevailed in art-theoretical discourse. The notion of the immaterial image, for instance, tied in well with the equation of image and text that took place in the wake of the linguistic turn in the 1960s.[5] William J.T. Mitchell, whose writings inspired the 'pictorial turn' in the early 1990s, described images as visual metaphors that freeze the temporality of speech into spatially arranged patterns.[6] Fundamental to such a definition is the primacy and hegemony of language. The problem with the 'reading' of images as texts, as has frequently been pointed out, is the loss of historical and context-bound information that images carry through their material presence.[7] But even in the refashioning of art history as visual studies and *Bildwissenschaft* that followed the 'pictorial turn', the notion that an immaterial idea prefigures material execution remained intact, for instance in Mitchell's clear differentiation between image (the transportable form) and picture (its various material manifestations) or in Hans Belting's *Bild-Anthropologie* which presents the human body as the medium that transforms mental into material images.[8] Gottfried Boehm recently criticized the persistent division of idea and matter in contemporary art theory, yet without offering clear alternatives.[9]

The dominance of the hylomorphic paradigm in art theory is paired with an institutional neglect of material. A discipline that incorporates a highly sophisticated knowledge of materials, art history has paradoxically defined itself through a series of de-materializations by perpetually moving the visual arts out of the domain of material praxis and into the supposedly higher realm of theory.[10] Thus did the visual arts become one of the free arts, when, around 1500, they were emancipated from the craft trades. In the process, the artist's practical knowledge that Pamela Smith has aptly dubbed 'artisanal epistemology'[11] is marginalized, or rather subdued, in emerging art-theoretical writings in the following centuries, culminating in a dominant Hegelian aesthetics which celebrated the greatest work of art as one that overcame its materiality.[12] Around 1900, this paradigm was reinforced once more when in the effort to establish art history as an academic discipline in the university, the subject was stripped of its materiality, and the latter was associated with non-academic spaces and activities (e.g. making, collecting and preserving art in the studio and the museum).

Paradigmatic for the opposition between the material and the ideal is Alois Riegl's criticism of the work of Gottfried Semper. To understand the influence of this conflict on the development of art theory throughout the twentieth century, it is worth going into some detail. A practising architect and artist, Semper had been aggravated by the marginalization of material's role in contemporary theoretical discourse.[13] With his *Style in the Technical and Tectonic Arts* (Berlin, 1860–63), Semper presented a thorough framework for the study of the role materials and techniques played in the evolution of artistic style.[14] Semper's so-called 'practical aesthetics' focused on the applied arts (architecture, ceramics, and textiles), and until around 1900 his ideas enjoyed wide popularity, even in the wider context of emerging materialist philosophy on the continent and Great Britain.[15] Riegl knew and appreciated Semper's writings. However, in the preface to his first *magnum opus*, the 'Problems of Style', which he wrote during his employment as curator of textiles at the Österreichische Museum für Kunst und Industrie (Museum of Applied Arts), he severely criticized the over-eager 'post-Semperists' for their reductionist view of Semper, according to which art was exclusively shaped by tools and materials, just as humans, according to post-Darwinist theories of evolution, were exclusively shaped by nature.[16] To counter their ideas, he introduced the famous term *Kunstwollen* ('will to art/will of art') that foregrounded the creative capacity and intellectual inspiration of humans to make, perceive, and enjoy art.[17] Riegl's criticism had been directed at his immediate surroundings, where the director of the Museum für Kunst und Industrie had introduced a strictly technology- and material-based approach to the collection, leaving, in Riegl's view, no room for the creative dimension of the applied arts, thereby threatening to reduce their history to a mere mechanical affair.[18] His initial target remained ignorant of the critical stance, but after Riegl's appointment at the University of Vienna, his *Kunstwollen*, which essentially related a period's style to an overarching *Zeitgeist*, caught on as an influential concept and put Hegelian idealism, and with it a teleological model of development, right back at the centre of art-theoretical discussion, where the concept is debated still today.[19] Semper's 'practical aesthetics', on the other hand, inspired by a criticism of those very ideas that fuelled Riegl's concept, were not pursued much further.

It is interesting that these two exponents of the conflict between materialism and idealism had in fact been striving for a model that incorporated both perspectives. That their theories paralleled rather than opposed each other is illustrated by the hitherto unnoticed fact that Riegl's *Kunstwollen* was not so much a new invention, but, rather, a witty modification of Semper's term *Kunstwerden* ('becoming of art').[20] Semper had coined this expression in the preface to *Style in the Technical and Tectonic Arts* to characterize the key aim of his undertaking – namely, to understand 'the work of art . . . as a result of *all* the factors involved in its creation' (italics added). This could be achieved by studying individual cases in order 'to explore . . . the regularity and order that become apparent in artistic phenomena during the creative process of becoming' and consequently deduce 'the general principles, the fundamentals of an empirical theory of art'.[21]

The phrasing 'all the factors involved' in the creative process of becoming (*Kunstwerden*) is crucial, because these factors, according to Semper, include the element of human creativity and intellect, which Riegl felt had been lost in post-Semperist interpretations.[22] Rather than opposing *Kunstwerden*, in which materials and human intervention were equally incorporated, Riegl's *Kunstwollen* must have been intended as a shift in focus in order to correct the misreading of Semper. To change the neutral *werden* (becoming) into the purposeful *wollen* (wanting), it can be argued, was a means to emphasize the role of human intention within the process of art-making. When, in the twentieth century, Riegl's writings became far more influential than Semper's, what had been intended to balance Semperism came to stand for the primacy of idea alone, and the initial connection between *Kunstwerden* and *Kunstwollen* was severed, leaving Riegl to appear as sole inventor of the latter.[23] Today, *Kunstwollen* is still familiar to most students of art history while its predecessor is virtually unknown. The clash between Semper and Riegl, therefore, is a historiographical construct, the result of the interpretation of their ideas rather than their initial intentions.

A final example of an influential suppression of materials in art history is Erwin Panofsky's conceptualization of iconology as a pictorial language.[24] The abstraction inherent to iconology constituted an extremely useful and sophisticated method to study the meaning of motifs, but it also had institutional and political motives.[25] Not only did iconology entrench the discipline of art history deeply in the intellectual tradition of humanism, therefore making it more of a theoretical profession; by turning material works of art into signs it also provided a rescue (if only symbolic) from the propagandist abuse of art's material qualities under the National Socialist regime that Panofsky had fled, where the expressive lines of Dürer's woodcuts were deemed Aryan, and Rembrandt's earthy hues Germanic.[26]

These dematerializations (sketched out only briefly here and in need of a more thorough historiographical study) have resulted in the fact that art history today can make use of numerous theories and methods to study style, form, aesthetics, perception, reception, iconography, iconology, and so forth, but has no coherent theory of materials that one could pick from a library shelf or assign to students to read. The extremely vast knowledge of materials that art history has always had at its disposal is accordingly treated as practical wisdom, or is isolated in highly specialized subdisciplines such as museum sciences and technical art history, which have established their own research platforms, conferences, and professional journals, yet only infrequently act as envoys to the realm of art theory.[27]

Since the early 1990s, however, a movement has emerged that can be described as a re-materialization of art history and of art theory. At the beginning of the 1990s, individual publications as well as larger research projects made the decisive first step in this direction.[28] A growing body of studies of individual artistic materials, of materials in crafts, and of the history and historicity of materials in the history of science, confirm the relevance of this research subject.[29]

Currently, design studies, craft studies, and material culture studies programs are being established in academia, yet art history and visual studies have been slow to follow their lead. One of the reasons may indeed be the lack of a coherent theory of materials. To push further the re-materialization of art history, therefore, a theoretical framework for analysing the significance and impact of materials is needed. James Elkins has recently questioned whether material can be theorized at all. Theory, he states rhetorically, may at most occupy itself with the materiality of art, but not with its material.[30] Indeed, recent theoretical discussions focus on the materiality of things and objects. This abstraction from the actual, however, is often characterized by a certain vagueness (the 'stoniness' of the stone, the 'digitality' of the digital), and thereby rather constitutes a further distancing from actual materials, preventing their serious inclusion in theoretical analysis.[31]

Likewise, a theory of materials cannot be obtained by simply focusing on material instead of the immaterial, thereby flipping the hierarchy of the hylomorphic paradigm on its head. For in so doing, the dualism would still be maintained.[32] Ideally, a theory of materials ignores the dichotomy and moves on to advance a contemporary version of Semper's *Kunstwerden* that enables a careful analysis of how art is made by equally considering all elements employed in art's becoming.

A 'theory of materials' as toolbox

Actor–network theory (ANT), chiefly developed by Bruno Latour and John Law, shows some interesting parallels to Semper's ideas, not only because it envisages an empirical study of processes, but chiefly because of its fundamental sensitivity to things, materials, and processes. This sensitivity is expressed through the agnostic treatment of human and non-human objects as possible actors and possessors of agency.[33] To think of materials as active agents in processes of art-making helps to free them from their subjection within art-theoretical discourses, and to approach all elements involved in these processes (material, tools, creators, and their ideas and actions) unbiased with regard to their possible influence on the outcome.[34] The idea that material possesses agency is, however, still quite unspecific and needs to be refined by joining this general notion with other theories – some stemming from within art history, others from psychology, sociology, and anthropology – that have presented material as a meaningful element of artistic creation. In the following, I bring together some of Latour's ideas with those of other writers in order to put forward a preliminary 'theory of materials'. This theory is conceived as a metaphorical toolbox, which contains various implements, and which can be added to at any time. The purpose of this admittedly eclectic procedure is threefold. First, it signifies openness, because it does not force an overarching theory upon all materials, but rather, allows for the particular material to inquire after tools that are suitable to interpret it. Secondly, it wants to emphasize that theoretical elements can vary, change, and be expanded upon, and are, in fact, themselves materials and therefore never superior to the materials they aim to describe. Lastly, it shows that any theory of materials must be interdisciplinary.

The name of the toolbox has been supplied by media scholar Rudolf Arnheim. In the personal note preceding a selection of writings published as *Film as Art* (1957), Arnheim writes that he had begun in the mid-1920s to prepare detailed records of a 'theory of materials' (he uses the German term *Materialtheorie*): 'It was a theory meant to show that artistic and scientific descriptions of reality are cast in moulds that derive not so much from the subject matter itself as from the properties of the medium

– or *material* – employed.'³⁵ Arnheim does not mention his *Materialtheorie* again in this book or in other published writings. However, the fundamental assumption that materials make meaning clearly underlies his unique and well-informed scrutiny of the formal and technical elements of film and other media. It is also paramount to the book's central hypothesis, that the creative use of film's material limitations (the initial absence of sound and colour) constitutes the very source of its artistic character. When *Film as Art* was published, this notion had already been outdated by technological innovations and represented a somewhat conservative and antiquated film aesthetic. Apart from the general lack of interest in materials in art and media studies, this may explain why Arnheim's rigorous material perspective on media and his *Materialtheorie* were not further developed in subsequent research, and why his brief definition is all we have.

Arnheim's idea that the materials used in forming 'descriptions of reality' shape these as much or even more than the things they describe harks back to Semper's emphasis on the study of *Kunstwerden*, and prefigures Latour's notion that materials hold power over images. The presumption that materials shape meaning, therefore, forms the outer casing of the 'theory of materials' toolbox. In order to fill this box with specific tools, the following paragraphs engage with a substance, which is especially illustrative of the relation between material and meaning.

Oil as intermediary and mediator

Ever since its use as a chief medium in early Netherlandish painting, beginning around 1420, oil has had such an influence on the development of Western painting that, to this day, oil painting is considered the equivalent of 'High Art'. Additionally, the countless images we encounter in contemporary visual culture do in fact still submit to the standards set by oil painting. Whether on an iPad, on Facebook, in magazines, or pinned to a wall, these images are almost always quadrangular, multicoloured, with a glossy surface, and they are transportable, as were the paintings by Jan van Eyck and his contemporaries.

Lasting colour, gloss, and robustness are but a few of the characteristics initially made possible by oil as a binding medium. Interestingly enough, this inconspicuous substance's enormous influence has only recently emerged as a subject of independent study.³⁶ Whereas colour pigments and their exotic, animalistic, or mysterious origins have aroused lively research interest and material iconography has focused on substances clearly pregnant with meaning, such as gold, felt, plastic, or porphyry, oil is barely recognized as a material as such. This situation may be due to its colourlessness, for although it owes much of its success to transparency, an invisible material will also be quickly overlooked, a fact which renders oil a particularly interesting substance to develop a theory of materials.

Until very recently, research into oil has been asymmetrically distributed in art history. Where the field is understood as an interpretive discipline, oil is accepted as an element of the so-called *ars nova*,[37] and as a component of the historiography within Vasari's founding myth of oil painting – but it does not constitute an explicit topic of research. However, where art history appears as natural science, oil is the focus of attention, and is a constant topic of investigation.

The imbalance may be explained by a conception of oil as a substance that enables, but does not cause, the realistic representation of images. It is, to speak with Latour, treated as an 'intermediary': 'An *intermediary* . . . is what transports meaning or force without transformation: defining its inputs is enough to define its output. For all practical purposes, an intermediary can be taken as a black box.'[38] Latour opposes 'intermediaries' to 'mediators', whose input leads to changes in context. Mediators 'transform, translate, distort, and modify the meaning or the elements they are supposed to carry', and their specificity must always be taken into account.[39] Latour explains this difference between intermediary and mediator by means of two materials, nylon and silk. Seen as pure carriers of meaning – silk connotes highbrow culture, nylon the lowbrow – they are intermediaries. If, however, we make explicit the direct relationship between materials and social strata, and demonstrate how differences in the materials' chemical composition, manufacturing, and durability lend symbolic charge to each, they become mediators.[40]

As a rule, leading interpretations of early Netherlandish painting, from Max Friedländer and Erwin Panofsky up through the present, treat oil paint as a prerequisite for the new visual realism. The source and significance of this realism, however, are attributed to religious, cultural, or social conditions (theological documents, Burgundian court culture, the rise of the bourgeoisie in Flanders, the existence of optical lenses and scientific treatises etc.),[41] and are seldom linked with the particular material and the attendant technique that it produced. The perception of oil as medium, as a substance that *carries* meaning, but has none of its own, conforms to the description of the intermediary.

In technical art history, on the other hand, oil and its interaction with pigments form a chemical mystery that must be deciphered. Ever since Vasari posited Jan van Eyck as the founder of oil painting over five hundred years ago, painters, historiographers, and theoreticians have speculated about the nature of this mystery.[42] Experiments were already being carried out in the eighteenth century to reclaim the status of founder for other painters and countries, or for earlier periods.[43] Van

Eyck's primacy finally declined when Lessing discovered, in the Wolfenbüttel library, recipes for oil paint contained in the treatise *De diversis artibus* (c. 1120) by the German monk Theophilus.[44] Thereafter, it was assumed that the secret was no longer contained within the invention itself of the paint, but within a particular ingredient or means of preparing the oil. During a detailed analysis in the 1950s of the Ghent Altarpiece, which included material testing of several panels, the formula 'oil + x' was noted, and the unknown factor was assumed to be a resinous ingredient. When a study of the tests was taken up again at the beginning of the 1980s, 'x' was asserted to be a proteinaceous substance, and van Eyck's secret declared to be an emulsion.[45] Throughout the 1990s, chemists Ashok Roy and Raymond White of the National Gallery in London tested the collection's numerous early Netherlandish paintings, publishing the results in appendices of the *National Gallery Technical Bulletin*. In a synthesizing publication, they contested the theory of the additive, arguing that van Eyck's secret lay in the exclusive use of oil: 'there is no substance that x can be substituted for, there is only oil: Van Eyck was simply a fabulous painter, who exploited the possibilities of the medium to its fullest extent.'[46] In more recent research, however, proteins have reappeared – possibly as migrants to the upper layers of paint from the priming – and other, older theories are again studied – for instance, the suspicion that van Eyck added essential oils to the linseed oil.[47] And so the search for the secret continues, posing the same question with the assistance of ever-newer technologies. If one were to undertake anthropological research[48] in the laboratories of the London National Gallery, the Dörner Institute in Munich, the KIK/IRPA (The Royal Institute for Cultural Heritage) in Brussels, or of the Getty Conservation Institute in Los Angeles, it could well lead to the realization that oil, via many different scientific methods and instruments, is again and again reconstructed as a mysterious object. It is located, isolated, and analysed within the constellation of a paint sample, and the understanding of chemical alterations in pigment-oil and oil-protein compounds ever increases. However, as long as this knowledge is not brought to bear on the meaning of images, oil, in technical art history as well as art theory, remains an intermediary; a black box whose contents are scrutinized without taking into consideration its transformative effect on the thing it describes.

In order to mobilize technical art history's valuable findings for the study of the relationship between material and depiction, oil must be promoted from its intermediary position into that of 'full-blown mediator'.[49] Since the beginning of this century, technical art history and art history have indeed moved closer in the effort to achieve a better understanding of this relation. Oil, for instance, is investigated within the *Malsystem* ('system of painting'), a term denoting the material structure and specific process employed to achieve a certain element of depiction.[50] The relationship between material, process, and representation becomes especially apparent when it is studied with regard to particular motifs (e.g. how water, shadows, reflections, skin, or gold brocade are painted). Such an iconographical perspective requires the interweaving of art theory, scientific analyses, and historical research of textual sources such as recipes, contracts, and guild charters.[51] It is within this integrative approach that the material is made visible as a mediator. In other words, its mediating potential can only become apparent if the complex network of the elements in which it exists is brought to light. To do this is the work of the researcher and the first tool to go into the theoretical toolbox.

Oil as enchanted technology
In her short historiography of the study of materials in the history of science, Ursula Klein recently stated that 'the "history of technology", taken literally, is not the history of machines and other artefacts, but the history of the *study* of the arts'.[52] This observation shows how intimately linked art and technology suddenly become when we begin to think from the perspective of material. Twenty years earlier, astonished at the neglect of technology in art-theoretical discussions, anthropologist Alfred Gell made a related argument in his article titled 'The Technology of Enchantment and the Enchantment of Technology'.[53] With the objective to free art objects from their static position as emanating beauty or profound meaning, he placed their material production centre-stage. Much like Latour had claimed in 'Drawing Things Together' a few years before, Gell writes, 'the power of art objects stems from the technical processes they objectively embody... The enchantment of technology is the power that technical processes have of casting a spell over us so that we see the real world in an enchanted form.'[54]

Two phenomena, apparently opposed – technology and enchantment – are, then, identified as mutually implicated in an art object's power (or 'agency', as Gell later calls it).[55] Works of art are the result of technical processes, hence of the manipulation of material, and are therefore in the position to enchant the viewer – that is, to change his or her perception of the world. The concept of enchanted technology bridges the discrepancy outlined in the previous paragraph between the relative absence of materials in art-historical discourses (where illusionism, meaning, or aesthetics are discussed) and their isolated presence in scientific discourse (where technology is discussed).

More specifically, it enables us to understand painting with oil as an exceptionally enchanting technology. For although Gell at first defends his thesis by reference to the Trobriand Islanders' (Papua New Guinea) ornamentation on prow-boards, whose colourful carvings have a magical effect upon the enemy, he demonstrates the universal relation between enchantment and technology using an example from Western art, the famous *trompe l'oeil* by John Frederik Peto *Old Time Letter Rack* (Museum of Fine Arts, Boston, 1894):

> The painting's power to fascinate stems entirely from the fact that people have great difficulties in working out how coloured pigments (substances with which everybody is broadly familiar) can be applied to a surface so as to become an apparently different set of substances, namely, the ones which enter into the composition of letters, ribbons, drawing-pins, stamps, bits of string, and so on. The magic exerted over the beholder by this picture is a reflection of the magic which is exerted inside the picture, the technical miracle which achieves the transubstantiation of oily pigments into cloth, metal, paper, and feather.[56]

Gell's description is easily applied to any arbitrarily chosen early Netherlandish painting, whose fascination for laypeople seeing it with the naked eye, as well as for experts whose technological exploration is equipped with Optivisor and macro lenses, resides in the desire to understand how the mimetic relationship is achieved between the image's material (oil, pigments, layers, and application of paint) and the material of the object being portrayed (e.g. stone, bronze, skin, hair, water). What Gell describes as the transubstantiation of oily pigments into represented materials allows us to approach technology and magic, and hence material and representation, as a unity, constituting the second theoretical tool for a theory of materials. The religious metaphor that Gell uses, however, should not suggest that the process of transformation evades analysis. Scrutinizing it merely calls for more precise instruments to add to the toolbox.

Oil and its affordances

The theory of affordances, developed during the 1970–80s by the psychologist James J. Gibson, can provide such instruments.[57] The concept of affordances signifies that the properties of a thing, a substance or material encourage the performance of particular actions with them. Hence, the earth offers us the possibility to walk upon it (Gibson's example); a chair affords us the possibility to sit in it (designers were the first outside of the field of psychology to embrace Gibson's theory, as it offered an excellent framework to understand the shaping of things towards their affordances;[58] software design has also recently made use of it);[59] stones afford not only the ability to build houses, but the destruction of shelter as well. This final example is important, for the affordances of a particular thing or substance should by no means be confused with the demand for a 'truth to materials' voiced by the Arts and Crafts movement and the German *Werkbund* around 1900, both of which were highly charged with idealistic notions about 'right' and 'wrong' applications of materials.[60]

To perceive the environment through the concept of affordances leads to a reversal of the anthropocentric notion of causality, in which idea, action, and material result neatly follow from one another. Instead, the theory of affordances generates an alternative chain in which material provides the starting point for an idea and draws out certain actions. This reversal makes manifest the agency of things, and hence Gibson's immense significance for ANT, which is built on the premise that not only humans but also 'things . . . might authorize, allow, afford, encourage, permit, suggest, influence, block, render possible, forbid, and so on'.[61]

Applied to the material oil, the theory of affordances helps us to discover how the technology of enchantment is worked. Gibson divides physical matter into three categories: media (e.g. air, light), substances (all materials) and surfaces (where media and substances meet). Substances are understood with regard to their material specificity: viscosity, cohesion, and composition.[62] As a substance, oil is a fluid. Due to their extremely polymorphous shape, Gibson links fluids to the production of forms and, therefore, to depiction: 'fluid substances . . . can be poured, spilled, splashed, and they can be smeared, painted, and dabbled in. The human infant explores these possibilities with great zest; the adult artisan has learned to perceive and take advantage of them.'[63] Along with its general affordance of depiction due to its fluidity, certain oils, like linseed and walnut oil, have more specific properties that support not only the extreme refinement, but also the preservation, of depiction. The multitude of oil's affordances may explain why it took artisans a comparatively long time 'to perceive and take advantage of them', and why, once they had mastered the possibilities, the splendid realism typical of early Netherlandish painting was achieved so quickly.

There is, first, oil's viscosity, which facilitates the mixing of pigments and results in paint's extreme degree of manipulability, so that it may be blended on the palette and even on the panel or canvas. Due to the relatively high viscosity (which may be lessened with thinners or increased through drying it), oil has a certain degree of plasticity, and can be flattened out or assume a spatial texture. Oil's transparency, probably its most celebrated property, enables the production of glazes, and produces a refraction of light within layers of paint, resulting in sheen and a high saturation of colour.[64] Because it is slow-drying, oil paint can, moreover, be reworked over long periods, allowing for improvement and smooth transitions between different colour zones. In drying, linseed oil's chemical composition changes irreversibly; it polymerizes and is, therefore, stable and lasting.

Generally, it is this complex conglomeration of properties that enabled realistic depiction. When Panofsky (whose few observations about material are very astute) wrote that 'the paint that renders skin, or fur, or even the stubble on an imperfectly shaved face seems to assume the very character of what it depicts',[65] he was only partially correct, for oil paint not only appears to assume the character of what it represents; it actually possesses some of the properties of the materials that it emulates. Thus, paint's plasticity affords the possibility of creating structures through manipulation by brushes, combs, or textiles that convey the texture of hair, fur, or coarse fabric. Its transparency makes possible the mimetic rendition of water, along with semi-translucent substances such as marble, smoke, and human skin. Furthermore, oil forms an actual skin when it dries, a fact that heightens even more the mimetic relationship between the material of paint and the material depicted.[66] Its very transparency, though, veils its own material presence, making the viewer forget the substance that has achieved the depiction, thereby encouraging the illusion of the immediate presence of what is represented. In addition, the permanence of oil paint, once dried, has not only allowed for the preservation of images over centuries, but also has the affordance of transportability: the technology's triumphal procession comes about, thanks not to copies in other media, or written reports about these images, but, rather, to the actual export of oil paintings to Italy, Spain, Portugal, Germany, Poland, and other European countries.[67]

The medium's agency then, emerges from these affordances, which together engage in a mimetic appropriation of the world. Agency, as defined by Latour, 'lies in the blind spot in which society and matter exchange their properties', meaning that we generally do not tend to notice the ways in which everyday objects shape the actions we are accustomed to carrying out with them.[68] This definition can be expanded to depiction because oil, the invisible mediator, is quite literally such a blind spot. Within a painting, oil paint literally enacts the exchange of properties between 'matter and society' as it is transformed into skin, hair, portrait, landscape, architecture, and so on, and in this process disappears behind the things it is employed to depict. Hence, oil's most powerful affordance is, perhaps, this suggestion of not being there, of veiling its material presence, which time and again coaxes the viewer into forgetting the matter of the medium.

Incidentally, from this material affordance of seeming immaterial, a relationship can be established between materials as disparate as oil, wax, glass, plastic, and even computer graphics. All of these materials are to a greater or lesser extent viscose, (semi-)transparent and polymorphous, and afford a high degree of visual realism when used to fabricate two- or three-dimensional representations of the world.[69]

The theory of affordances therefore allows for an acute and detailed interpretation of what materials do and achieve; it opens up new perspectives on the relation between materials and brings to light the active nature of material properties. In keeping with the metaphor of the toolbox, it may be likened to a set of wrenches used to wriggle free the various bolts, nuts, and pipes that hold together the enchantment of technology. Taking things apart and neatly analysing the different affordances and restrictions of a material is extremely useful, yet also leads to a static enumeration of properties. In processes of production, however, materials are hardly ever static. They interact with tools, makers, and each other.[70] To analyse the role of materials within the dynamics of *Kunstwerden* is, perhaps, the most difficult task of a theory of materials.

Oil in motion, or Latour's paintbrush
In his introduction to ANT, *Reassembling the Social*, Bruno Latour records a fictitious conversation between a professor and a PhD student who discuss how ANT can, or rather, cannot, be applied to a research question.[71] To begin with, the professor regrets the dominance of the term 'network'. A network suggests a static arrangement that can be captured in a diagram, or by drawing a map of agents and their various actions and connections, but 'really we should say "worknet" instead of "network." It's the work, and the movement, and the flow, and the changes that should be stressed.' Understandably, the student is confused by the professor's debunking of his own theory: 'Do you mean to say that once I have shown that my actors are related in the shape of a network, I have not yet done an ANT study?' The professor answers, 'That's exactly what I mean: ANT is more like the name of a pencil or a brush than the name of a specific shape to be drawn or painted.'[72] That is not to say, the professor hastens to add, that ANT is a neutral tool for tracing the connections in a network; for coal produces quite different lines from a pencil or a brush.

With these metaphors deriving from artistic techniques, Latour makes explicit that ANT as a theory is itself a mediator. It sets things in motion and alters what it means to show. The metaphor works so well because this is indeed exactly what materials do in processes of artistic creation. To describe this mechanism, we need a tool that does not freeze material's movement, but, rather, makes its dynamism available to experience. Keeping Latour's metaphor in mind, we may imagine this instrument as a bristly, multi-purpose paintbrush. But how can it be put to use?

The question of how to describe the complex interaction between materials and the maker of artefacts returns us to the hylomorphic model and its inherent opposition between ideas and materials. If we are to leave this model behind, as I have suggested earlier, we need to know to what degree material really is active, compared with the tool in the hand and the ideas in the head of the artist. For paintings are certainly not produced by oil and pigments alone. Is it, then, ideas after all that set the process of creation in motion, even if they are most certainly influenced by an understanding of the materials employed? And even if we assume human and non-human agents as having equal chances for exhibiting agency, they remain separate entities and we have to ask how agency is distributed between them. In the book *Material Agency*, which grapples with this question, archaeologist Lambros Malafouris describes how a potter throws clay on the wheel, and states that agency is established in the space *between* all the elements involved: 'while agency and intentionality may not be properties of things, they are not properties of humans either; they are the properties of *material engagement*, that is, of the grey zone where brain, body and culture conflate'.[73]

Just like Semper's theories prefigure the notion of material agency, this 'grey zone' of interaction had been recognized by earlier writers as a place rich in action. John Dewey, in his 1934 book *Art as Experience*, not only presented the artworks' material production as an intellectual performance, but also offered a model for studying this performance.[74] First, Dewey cleverly circumvents the dominant dualism of idea and material by a simple yet effective relabelling: everything that is usually ascribed to the mind and therefore deemed immaterial – thoughts, observations, memories, fantasies, feelings – he describes as 'inner material'.[75] Everything the artist encounters on the exterior of his or her body is 'outer material'. The artistic process of production is consequently a dynamic interaction between inner and outer materials: 'the physical process develops imagination, while imagination is conceived in terms of concrete material'.[76] This early definition of what Malafouris succinctly describes as material engagement does not, however, provide the researcher of material with a straightforward methodology. On the one hand, the joining of inner and outer materials makes a claim of universality (for in which creative process would they *not* come together?), but at the same time only allows itself to be observed in action, in living contexts, in which, for instance, the investigator looks over a painter's shoulder.

While attending a summer school where historical reconstructions of early Netherlandish oil paintings from the collection of the Amsterdam Rijksmuseum were being prepared, I witnessed an explicit reflection on the exchange of inner and outer materials.[77] One of the participants was visibly struggling to represent the long hair of the female saint depicted in the painting. She had no prior experience with oil paint and explained to me, 'I just wanted to paint the hair quickly, but it didn't look good, and then I realized that I had to think about how the paint felt against the panel, and what shape it made when I moved the brush, and then I understood how I needed to guide the brush to paint the hair so that it looked like hair.' Observing inexperienced and experienced painters systematically over a longer period of time will certainly yield valuable descriptions of material engagement. But can there also be a historical study of material engagement? Though we cannot bring back to life their precise actions, the analysis of written sources, of visual documentations of making and the re-enactment of processes certainly allows for the reconstruction of the material engagement of past artists.[78] If we condense these approaches into a tool for the theoretical toolbox, its Latourian affordance to affect the very thing it aims to analyse should not be forgotten.

With these sketchy outlines for a 'theory of materials', I hope to have shown that materials can be theorized, that such a theorization helps to establish materials as a subject of academic research, and, finally, that assuming the perspective of materials yields a rich historiography of theoretical approaches, which may facilitate the further re-materialization of a discipline that knows so much about materials.

Notes

This chapter is a revised version of my article 'Das Medium als Mediator: Eine Materialtheorie für (Öl-)Bilder', *Zeitschrift für Ästhetik und Allgemeine Kunstwissenschaften*, 57:1 (2012), pp. 69–88. I thank Katy Scrogin for the translation and Sybille Lammes for the generous financial support. I also thank Marianne van den Boomen, Anne Dunlop, and Paul van den Akker for their invaluable comments.

1 Bruno Latour, 'Visualization and cognition: Drawing things together', *Culture Technique* 14 (1985), pp. 1–32, here at p. 29.

2 Latour, 'Visualization', p. 3.

3 Erwin Panofsky presented the first in-depth discussion of the concept with his *Idea: A Concept in Art Theory* (Columbia: South Carolina Press, 1968). See also Georges Didi-Huberman, 'Die Ordnung des Materials: Plastizität, Unbehagen, Nachleben', in Wolfgang Kemp et al. (eds), *Vorträge aus dem Warburg Haus*, vol. 3 (Berlin: Akademie Verlag, 1999), pp. 1–30; and recently Tim Ingold, 'The textility of making', *Cambridge Journal of Economics* 34 (2008), pp. 91–102; and Tim Ingold, *Making: Anthropology, Archaeology, Art and Architecture* (London: Routledge, 2013).

4 Didi-Huberman, 'Ordnung'; Lucy Lippard (ed.), *Six Years: The Dematerialization of the Art Object from 1966–1972* (New York: Praeger, 1973); Amanda du Preez, '(Im)materiality: On the matter of art', *Image & Text* 14 (2008), pp. 30–41.

5 Roland Barthes, 'Is painting a language?', *The Responsibility of Forms: Critical Essays on Music, Art and Representation*, trans. Richard Howard (New York: Hill & Wang, 1985), pp. 149–52.

6 W.J.T. Mitchell, 'Ekphrasis and the other', *South Atlantic Quarterly* 91 (1992), p. 697.

7 Robert Morris, 'Looking at saying in W.J.T. Mitchell', *Culture, Theory and Critique* 50 (2009), p. 236.

8 W.J.T. Mitchell, 'Four fundamental concepts of image science', in James Elkins (ed.), *Visual Literacy* (New York: Routledge, 2008), especially pp. 16–17; Hans Belting, 'Image-medium-body: A new approach to Iconology', *Critical Inquiry* 31 (2005), pp. 302–19.

9 Gottfried Boehm, 'Glossar. Grundbegriffe des Bildes: Ikonische Differenz', *Rheinsprung 11, Zeitschrift für Bildkritik* 1 (2011), pp. 170–6, here at p. 175. http://rheinsprung11.unibas.ch/archiv/ausgabe-01/glossar/ikonische-differenz/6.html (accessed on 28 January 2014).

10 Didi-Huberman, 'Ordnung', p. 4.

11 Pamela H. Smith, *The Body of the Artisan: Art and Experience in the Scientific Revolution* (Chicago: University of Chicago Press, 2004).

12 Monika Wagner, *Das Material der Kunst: Eine andere Geschichte der Moderne* (Munich: C.H. Beck, 2001).

13 Harry Francis Mallgrave, *Gottfried Semper: Architect of the Nineteenth Century* (New Haven, CT: Yale University Press, 1996), esp. p. 366. For an excellent discussion with regard specifically to wood, see Monika Wagner, 'Wood: Primitive material for the creation of German sculpture', in Christian Weikop (ed.), *New Perspectives on Brücke Expressionism: Bridging History* (Farnham: Ashgate, 2011), pp. 71–89.

14 Gottfried Semper, *Style in the Technical and Tectonic Arts* (Berlin, 1860–3), intro. and trans. Harry Francis Mallgrave and Michael Robinson (Los Angeles: Getty Publication Programs, 2004).

15 Mallgrave, *Semper*, pp. 356–81.

16 Alois Riegl, *Stilfragen: Grundlegungen zu einer Geschichte der Ornamentik* (Berlin: Verlag van Georg Siemens, 1893), pp. vi–vii. Translated as *Problems of Style: Foundations for a History of Ornament*, trans. Evelyn Kain (Princeton: Princeton University Press, 1992).

17 The translations of *Kunstwollen* vary considerably. Panofsky's article about the concept 'Der Begriff des Kunstwollens' was translated as 'The concept of artistic volition', trans. Kenneth J. Northcott and Joel Snyder, *Critical Inquiry* 8:1, pp. 17–33. Margaret Olin wisely refrains from a direct translation; see *Forms of Representation in Alois Riegl's Theory of Art* (University Park: Pennsylvania State University Press, 1992), esp. pp. 148–53. Benjamin Binstock suggests 'will of art' (see Alois Riegl, *Historical Grammar of the Visual Arts*, trans. Jacqueline E. Jung, foreword by Benjamin Binstock (New York: Zone Books 2004), p. 14).

18 Diana Reynolds, 'Semperianismus und *Stilfragen*: Riegls Kunstwollen und die "Wiener Mitte"', in Rainald Franz and Andreas Nierhaus (eds), *Gottfried Semper und Wien* (Vienna: Böhlau Verlag, 2007), pp. 85–96.

19 For the influence of *Kunstwollen* on twentieth-century art and art theory, see Margaret Iversen, *Alois Riegl: Art History and Theory* (Cambridge, MA: MIT Press, 1993); Mike Gubser, *Time's Visible Surface: Alois Riegl and the Discourse on History and Temporality in Fin-de-siècle Vienna* (Detroit: Wayne State University Press, 2006), esp. chapter 9, where all relevant literature is discussed; Peter Noever, Artur Rosenauer, and Georg Vasold (eds), *Alois Riegl Revisited: Contributions to the Opus and its Reception* (Vienna: Austrian Academy of Sciences 2010); and Reinhold Heller, 'Some reconsiderations of Brücke's "New German Style": Shape, components and ramifications', in Weikop (ed.), *New Perspectives*, pp. 57–70.

20 Though Riegl does not explicitly refer to Semper's concept, his intimate knowledge of Semper's writings, as well as the syntactical and conceptual resemblance of the two terms, can leave little doubt as to his intention. To understand *Kunstwollen* as an answer to *Kunstwerden* also grounds the term in Riegl's immediate intellectual environment, thereby lending focus to prior interpretations which have related it to a wide array of thinkers, ranging from Schiller and Hegel to Schopenhauer, Nietzsche, Freud, and many others. See Andrea Reichberger, *Riegls 'Kunstwollen': Versuch einer Neubetrachtung* (Sankt Augustin: Academia Verlag, 2003), esp. pp. 24–8.

21 Semper, *Style*, pp. 71–2; see also Mallgrave, *Semper*, pp. 273–4.

22 Semper himself writes that material was ultimately subservient to ideas, criticizing the 'materialists' of his era, much like Riegl would do later. Semper, *Style*, p. 77. Riegl acknowledges Semper's opinion repeatedly in *Stilfragen*, pp. vii, 6.

23 In 1920, Panofsky hailed him as the 'creator' of the concept of *Kunstwollen*; see Panofsky, *Artistic Volition*, p. 28.

24 Erwin Panofsky, *Studies in Iconology: Humanistic Themes in the Art of the Renaissance* (New York: Oxford University Press, 1939).

25 For an early criticism of iconology's inherent abstraction from material and creative process, see Pierre Bourdieu, *Outline of a Theory of Practice* (Cambridge: Cambridge University Press, 1977).

26 Ulrike Wendland, *Biographisches Handbuch deutschsprachiger Kunsthistoriker im Exil: Leben und Werk der unter dem Nationalsozialismus verfolgten und vertriebenen Wissenschaftler*, 2nd ed. (Munich: K.G. Saur, 1999), pp. 484–97; and Erwin Panofsky, *Korrespondenz 1910 bis 1968: Eine kommentierte Auswahl in fünf Bänden*, ed. Dieter Wuttke (Wiesbaden: Harrassowitz, 2001).

27 Erma Hermens gives an excellent overview of the history of the field and pleads for a better integration with traditional art historical approaches in 'Technical art history: The synergy of art, conservation and science', in Matthew Rampley et al. (eds), *Art History and Visual Studies in Europe: Transnational Discourses and National Frameworks* (Leiden: Brill, 2012), pp. 151–65. See also Maryan W. Ainsworth, 'From connoisseurship to technical art history: The evolution of the interdisciplinary study of art', *Getty Conservation Institute News Letter* 20 (2005). www.getty.edu/conservation/publications_resources/newsletters/20_1/feature.html (accessed on 28 January 2014).

28 For instance the *Rembrandt Research Project* or the *Material Ikonographie* research project at the University of Hamburg. Among the relevant publications are Ernst van de Wetering, *Rembrandt: The Painter at Work* (Amsterdam: Amsterdam University Press, 1997); Monika Wagner, *Material in Kunst und Alltag* (Berlin: Akademie Verlag, 2002); Dietmar Rübel, Monika Wagner, and Vera Wolff (eds), *Materialästhetik: Quellentexte zu Kunst, Design und Architektur* (Berlin: Reimer, 2005); Monika Wagner, Dietmar Rübel and Sebastian Hackenschmidt (eds), *Lexikon des künstlerischen Materials: Werkstoffe der modernen Kunst von Abfall bis Zinn*, 2nd ed. (Munich: C.H. Beck, 2010); Barbara Naumann, Thomas Strässle, and Caroline Torra-Mattenklott (eds), *Stoffe: Zur Geschichte der Materialität in Künsten und Wissenschaft* (Zurich: vdf Hochschulverlag AG, 2006); Thomas Raff, *Die Sprache der Materialien: Anleitung zu einer Ikonologie der Werkstoffe* (Munich: Wanmann Verlag, 2008).

29 For example: Melanie Gifford, 'Fine painting and eloquent imprecision: Gabriel Metsu's painting technique', in Adriaan E. Waiboer (ed.), *Gabriel Metsu* (New Haven, CT: Yale University Press, 2010), pp. 154–79; Glenn Adamson, *Thinking Through Craft* (London: Berg, 2007); Ursula Klein and E.C. Spary (eds), *Materials and Expertise in Early Modern Europe: Between Market and Laboratory* (Chicago: University of Chicago Press, 2010).

30 James Elkins, 'On some limits of materiality in art history', in Stefan Neuner and Julia Gelshorn (eds), *31: Das Magazin des Instituts für Theorie* 12, special issue *Taktilität: Sinneserfahrung als Grenzerfahrung* (2008), pp. 25–30.

31 Recently, scholars in material-culture studies have started to criticize the vague definition of materiality in their field. See Tim Ingold in 'Materials against materiality', *Archeological Dialogues* 14 (2007), pp. 1–16; Tim Ingold, 'Toward an ecology of materials', *Annual Review of Anthropology* 41 (2012), pp. 427–42; and Birgit Mayer and Dick Houtman (eds), *Things, Religion and the Question of Materiality* (New York: Fordham University Press 2012).

32 In the process of discussing objects as non-human actors, Latour warns against wanting to resolve or overcome dichotomies, and suggests that we ignore them instead. Bruno

Latour, *Reassembling the Social: An Introduction to Actor-Network-Theory* (Oxford: Oxford University Press, 2005), p. 76.

33 John Law and John Hassard (eds), *Actor Network Theory and After* (Oxford: Blackwell: 1999).

34 Carl Knappet and Lambros Malafouris (eds), *Material Agency: Towards a Non-Anthropocentric Approach* (New York: Springer, 2008).

35 Rudolf Arnheim, *Film as Art* (Berkeley: University of California Press, 1957), p. 2.

36 Jeroen Stumpel, *The Impact of Oil: A History of Oil Painting in the Low Countries and its Consequences for the Visual Arts 1350–1550*, Project Description (Utrecht, 2008). www.uu.nl/faculty/humanities/EN/research/research-institutes/ogk/research/arthistory/research/Pages/theimpactofoil.aspx (accessed on 20 February 2014).

37 Panofsky appropriated this term from musicology to describe the impact of oil painting: see Ann-Sophie Lehmann, 'Ars nova in een flesje', *Kunstschrift* 5 (2010), pp. 28–39.

38 Latour, *Reassembling the Social*, p. 39.

39 Latour, *Reassembling the Social*, p. 39.

40 Latour, *Reassembling the Social*, p. 40.

41 See, for instance, Hans Belting, *Spiegel der Welt: Die Erfindung des Gemäldes in den Niederlanden* (Munich: C.H. Beck, 2010).

42 For the historiography, see Pim Brinkman, *Het geheim van Van Eyck* (Zwolle: Waanders, 1993).

43 Jilleen Nadolny, 'A problem of methodology: Merrifield, Eastlake and the use of oil-based media by medieval English painters', in *ICOM 14th Triennial Meeting The Hague Reprints*, vol. 2 (London: Maney Publishing, 2005), pp. 1028–33.

44 Erhard Brepohl, *Theophilus Presbyter und das mittelalterliche Kunsthandwerk: Gesamtausgabe der Schrift De Diversis Artibus*, Vol. 2 (Cologne: Böhlau, 1999).

45 Elise Effmann, 'Theories about the Eyckian painting medium from the late-eighteenth to the mid-twentieth centuries', *Reviews in Conservation* (2006), pp. 17–26; Leslie Carlyle and Maartje Witlox, 'Historically accurate reconstructions of artists' oil painting materials', in Mark Clarke, Joyce H. Townsend, and Ad Stijnman (eds), *Art of the Past: Sources and Reconstructions* (London: JG Publishing, 2005), pp. 53–9.

46 Raymond White, 'Van Eyck's technique: The myth and the reality II', in Susan Foister et al., *Investigating Jan van Eyck* (Turnhout: Brepols, 2000), p. 104.

47 Nienke Woltman, 'De toevoeging van vluchtige oliën aan het olieverfmedium in de zestiende-eeuwse schilderpraktijk van de Nederlanden' (Masters thesis, University of Amsterdam, 2010).

48 Bruno Latour and Steve Woolgar, *Laboratory Life: The Social Construction of Scientific Facts* (Beverly Hills: Sage Publications, 1979).

49 Latour, *Reassembling the Social*, p. 173.

50 Christoph Schölzel, 'Jan van Eycks Bindemittel: Ein Geheimnis?', in *Das Geheimnis des Jan van Eyck: Die frühen niederländischen Zeichnungen und Gemälde in Dresden* (exhibition catalogue Gemäldegalerie Dresden; Munich: Deutscher Kunstverlag, 2005), p. 35.

51 Hermens, *Technical Art History*, pp. 164–5; and Marjolijn Bol and Ann-Sophie Lehmann, 'Painting skin and water: Towards a material iconography of translucent motifs in early Netherlandish painting', in Lorne Campbell et al. (eds), *Rogier van der Weyden in Context: Underdrawing and Technology in Painting* (Walpole: Leuven/Paris, 2012).

52 Ursula Klein and E.C. Spary, 'Introduction: Why materials?' in Klein and Spary (eds), *Materials and Expertise*, pp. 1–23, here at p. 17.

53 Alfred Gell, 'The technology of enchantment and the enchantment of technology', in Alfred Gell, *The Art of Anthropology: Essays and Diagrams*, ed. Eric Hirsch (London and New Brunswick: The Athlone Press, 1999), pp. 159–86.

54 Gell, *Enchantment*, p. 162.

55 Alfred Gell, *Art and Agency: An Anthropological Theory* (Oxford: Clarendon Press, 1998).

56 Gell, *Enchantment*, p. 170.

57 James Jerome Gibson, *The Ecological Approach to Visual Perception* (Boston, MA: Houghton Mifflin, 1979); James Jerome Gibson, 'The theory of affordances', in Robert Shaw and John Bransford (eds), *Perceiving, Acting and Knowing: Toward an Ecological Psychology* (New York: Halsted Press, 1977), pp. 67–82. On the history and application of the theory in media studies, see Nicole Zillen, 'Die (Wieder-)Entdeckung der Medien: Das Affordanzkonzept in der Mediensoziologie', *Sociologica Internationalis: Internationale Zeitschrift für Soziologie, Kommunkations- und Kulturforschung* 46:2 (2009), pp. 161–81. See also Henry S. Jenkins, 'Gibson's "affordances": evolution of a pivotal concept', *Journal of Scientific Psychology* (December, 2008), pp. 34–45.

58 Donald A. Norman, *The Design of Everyday Things* (New York: Basic Books, 1988).

59 Zillen, 'Affordanzkonzept', especially part III, 'Das Affordanzkonzept in der neueren Medienforschung', and Mirko Tobias Schäfer, *Bastard Culture: How User Participation Transforms Cultural Production* (Amsterdam: Amsterdam University Press, 2011).

60 Glenn Adamson, 'Introduction to section 3: Modern craft: idealism and reform', *The Craft Reader* (Oxford and New York: Berg Publishers 2010), pp. 135–8.

61 Latour, *Reassembling the Social*, p. 72.

62 Gibson, 'Medium, substances, surfaces', in *The Ecological Approach*, pp. 16–32.

63 Gibson, *The Ecological Approach*, pp. 24–5.

64 See Marjolijn Bol, 'Oil and the translucent: Varnishing and glazing in practice, recipes and historiography, 1100–1600' (PhD dissertation, Utrecht University, 2012).

65 Erwin Panofsky, *Early Netherlandish Painting, Its Origins and Character* (Cambridge, MA: Harvard University Press, 1953), p. 181.

66 Ann-Sophie Lehmann, 'Fleshing out the body: The "colours of the naked" in Dutch art theory and workshop practice 1400–1600', in Ann-Sophie Lehmann and Herman Roodenburg (eds), *Body and Embodiment in Netherlandish Art*, Nederlands Kunsthistorisch Jaarboek 58 (Zwolle: Waanders, 2008), pp. 108–31.

67 See Paula Nuttall, *From Flanders to Florence: The Impact of Netherlandish Painting 1400–1500* (New Haven, CT and London: Yale University Press, 2004).

68 Bruno Latour, *Pandora's Hope: Essays on the Reality of Science Studies* (Cambridge, MA: Harvard University Press, 1999), p. 190.

69 Ann-Sophie Lehmann, 'Taking the lid off the Utah teapot: Towards a material analysis of computer graphics', *Zeitschrift für Medien- und Kulturforschung* 1 (2012), pp. 157–72.

70 Tim Ingold writes that the only way to understand the constant flux of materials is to follow their movement. See Ingold, *Making*, 'The materials of life'.

71 Latour, *Reassembling the Social*, pp. 141–56.

72 Latour, *Reassembling the Social*, p. 143.

73 Lambros Malafouris, 'At the potter's wheel: An argument for material agency', in Knappet and Malafouris, *Material Agency*, p. 22.

74 John Dewey, *Art as Experience* (New York: Capricorn Books, 1934), p. 73.

75 Dewey, *Art as Experience*, p. 74.

76 Dewey, *Art as Experience*, p. 75.

77 Amsterdam-Maastricht Summerschool, *The Impact of Oil* (Universiteit van Amsterdam/Rijksmuseum, 26 August–2 September 2011). www.amsu.edu/en/course/3401/the-impact-of-oil-historical-painting-techniques-in-early-netherlandish-painting (accessed on 28 January 2014).

78 Ann-Sophie Lehmann, 'Showing making: On visual documentation and creative practice', *Journal of Modern Craft* 5:1 (2012), pp. 9–24. For a successful example of the re-enactment of material engagement, see Pamela H. Smith and Tony Beentjes, 'Nature and art, making and knowing: Reconstructing sixteenth-century life casting techniques', *Renaissance Quarterly* 63 (2010), pp. 128–79.

2 ✧ The matter of ideas in the working of metals in early modern Europe

Pamela H. Smith

[O]ne should gather experience in these mineral diseases and learn in those places where these diseases are and live: for the physician becomes learned through this exercise and experience. For even if I would report and describe everything, still no one would be able to understand it without the experience. Thus if he wants to have the experience, let him acquire it where it is, that is among the mineral diseases. For who could be taught the knowledge of experience from paper, since paper has the property to produce lazy and sleepy people, who are haughty and learn to persuade themselves and to fly without wings, all of which things are repugnant to the physician. Therefore the most fundamental thing is to hasten to experience.

(Theophrastus von Hohenheim, called Paracelsus)[1]

The artifact, in short, is the crystallization of activity within a relational field.

(Tim Ingold)[2]

Matter

HISTORIANS OFTEN talk about science and its theories as existing within a realm of ideas, with written texts the carriers of these ideas across time and space. The protagonists of this type of history are thinkers engaging with texts and influencing the textual corpus through their writing. This chapter posits a different realm for the emergence of ideas and theories, one in which ideas emerge from the interaction of the human hand with the material world. In the production of works of art, and, more generally, in all human acts of making, we can view matter as undergoing a series of transformations – first into the 'raw materials' of human use, then into objects through work of the human hand, and, finally, given meaning and significance in human culture and society. All matter thus possesses particular properties which enable the manufacture of certain kinds of materials and objects by means of specialized practices and technologies. Humans assign meanings to these practices and objects, and these meanings are both embedded within and help to extend systems of belief (or, 'theories') about the matter, practices, and things they incorporate. We should not view this as a linear, or uncomplicated, process, as various cultural frameworks constrain the ideas or theories that emerge from the human activity of transforming matter. For example, social hierarchies consign some labourers in matter to untouchables; religious practices give distinct meanings to some objects or materials and not to others; analogies with coexisting areas of the lifeworld, such as organic growth or sexual reproduction, provide explanatory systems; and pre-existing bodies or systems of knowledge – often in the form of written texts – help shape attitudes to, and ideas about, matter. This chapter's exploration of pre-industrial mining and ideas about the genesis of metals in the matrix of the earth seeks to locate in a historically specific example the reciprocal dynamic by which matter gives rise to practices and objects, which themselves produce systems of belief that, in their turn, further inform ideas about the treatment of materials and practices.

Matter and the human body

In this reciprocal process between materials, hand, cognition, and intellect, the environment and the human body mingle. Indeed, tool use and the acquisition of skills can ultimately be viewed as biological processes of interaction of the human body with the environment.[3] We are accustomed today to starting from a distinction between human and environment, and nature and culture, but both evolutionary theory and everyday experience belie these distinctions.[4] Take, for example, the ancient human activity of wood cultivation and management, in which the matter of made things is *grown* by practices like pollarding every year for narrow poles, by coppicing every five to seven years, or for larger poles every twenty years, and fostering the decades-long, sometimes century-long, growth of individual tall trees for ships' masts, and house frames. Joiners and carpenters employed the properties of living wood in their practices also, for example, in splitting wood along its growth rays, or in making a join strong by forming holes in green wood and joining them by pins of dry wood; as the green wood dries, it grips the pin ever tighter.[5] The still-living wood is part of the process of making. Where in these practices of wood cultivation does growing stop and human making begin?

The human body is an integral part of this continuum of growing and making. Consider its uses in the early modern workshop: it functioned as a tool in myriad ways – for warming, blowing, handling, manipulating, sensing, tasting, and providing force and dexterity, just to name a few of its functions. The human body was also a source of substances employed in manufacture – including urine, excrement, blood, ear wax, and saliva; and the body was a model for natural processes – for the fermentation, digestion, concoction, purging, and excretion of the human body provided a conceptual framework for the transformation of materials in nature. Moreover, the quotidian stuff that sustained growth in the human body – including bread, butter, eggs, milk, honey, figs, and garlic – was also employed on a daily basis in workshop practices. And it was by means of the body and its learned gestures and techniques that the embodied and collaborative knowledge of craft was produced and reproduced, passed on from one generation to the next.[6]

The workshop functioned as an extension of the capacities and products of the human body. But the body was more than a tool in production – it was also implicated in the work: the bodies of metalworkers and the very matter upon which they laboured interpenetrated each other: bad breath could prevent the adhesion of metal gilding, and, conversely, metal fumes were known to shorten the lives of metalworkers, and records of their practice give evidence that they ate bread and butter before starting work because bread was viewed as a perfectly tempered food that filled the stomach and prevented the subtle metal vapours from being drawn into the body. At the same time, the hot, wet qualities of butter counteracted the miasmic exhalations of the minerals and metals rising up from the ground or billowing out from the smelting furnace. In eating butter, these artisans operated within the Greco-Roman-Arabic health worldview based on an Aristotelian framework of the four elements and qualities; that is, all things were composed of mixtures of the four elements – earth, water, air, and fire – and exhibited varying characteristics according to their qualities – wet, cold, dry, and hot. In this scheme, butter was hot; metal vapours were cold.[7] This was also the framework for the explanation from mine manager, engineer and author of *De la Pirotechnia* (1540) Vannoccio Biringuccio for what happened when bronze was poured into a cold mould – the cold, moist mould overcame the nature of bronze and turned it back to its primordial earthy-watery state.[8]

The human body and natural materials shared many properties. To take one example from metalworking: the idea of *temper* was crucial in the mental world of early modern Europeans. 'Temper' meant to balance by mixing, and a person's temperament was determined by a balance of the four qualities – hot, wet, dry, cold – and their instantiation in the humours: black bile, phlegm, blood, and yellow bile. Each individual's unique combination of the four qualities and humours could be tempered by diet, exercise, purging, and so on. This process of tempering was crucial to human health. Metals too partook in this system and their balance of qualities could be rectified by tempering, as steel was tempered (sometimes using the urine of pre-pubescent boys), and copper was given temper and tone by tin in making the alloy, bronze. Minerals and humans alike received their temper from the movements of the heavens, for the sun was a source of growth for all living things – gold grew better along riverbanks warmed by the sun and in south-facing veins, and, in the common understanding of health and identity in early modern Europe, the celestial spheres and bodies determined the temperament of human beings at their conception and birth, just as they did for metals. This was a theological vision as well as a cosmological one, and gave rise to all manner of practices, such as baptizing mines and invoking God and the saints before a bronze pour.[9]

Metalworkers viewed the matter they worked as capable of growth. They daily employed processes in the production of goods that we conceptualize as typical of organic growth, such as in a pigment recipe for a gold colour that calls for mixing mercury with a fresh hen's egg and then putting it back under the hen to heat slowly,[10] or the use of constant slow heat produced by thermophilic bacteria in putrefying horse manure for a slow heat in numerous metalworking procedures.[11] Formations brought out of the *veins* in the body of the earth, such as the pure strands of native silver (Figure 2.1), were self-evident proof for the growth and ripening of metals in the earth. Artisanal manuals and recipe collections mixed procedures for grafting and growing plants, fermenting liquids, and healing humans and animals with instructions for producing objects from ingredients we would now call inorganic because they were viewed as operating according to the same principles. Blood and metal were related as well. We know from the work of Michael Cole and Francesca Bewer that blood and bronze were often brought into a symbolic and/or material relationship,[12] and blood appears among the ingredients and operations of numerous metalworking recipes: the blood of goats, oxen, foxes, rams, of a menstruating woman and of the dragon tree – a red resin.[13] The colour red appears to have been seen as possessing many of the attributes of blood, and it too is mentioned frequently in both medicinal and metalworking recipes.[14]

Mining

This entanglement of the human body with matter is especially clear in the labour of mining and metalworking, in which the bodies of miners and smelters are penetrated by the very matter upon which they labour. Their bodily striving brings the materials to the earth's surface and then draws out the metals from the matrix of their ores, but in this process, the spirits and humours of the metals and minerals mix with those of the metalworkers, and they affect and shape each other in distinctive ways.

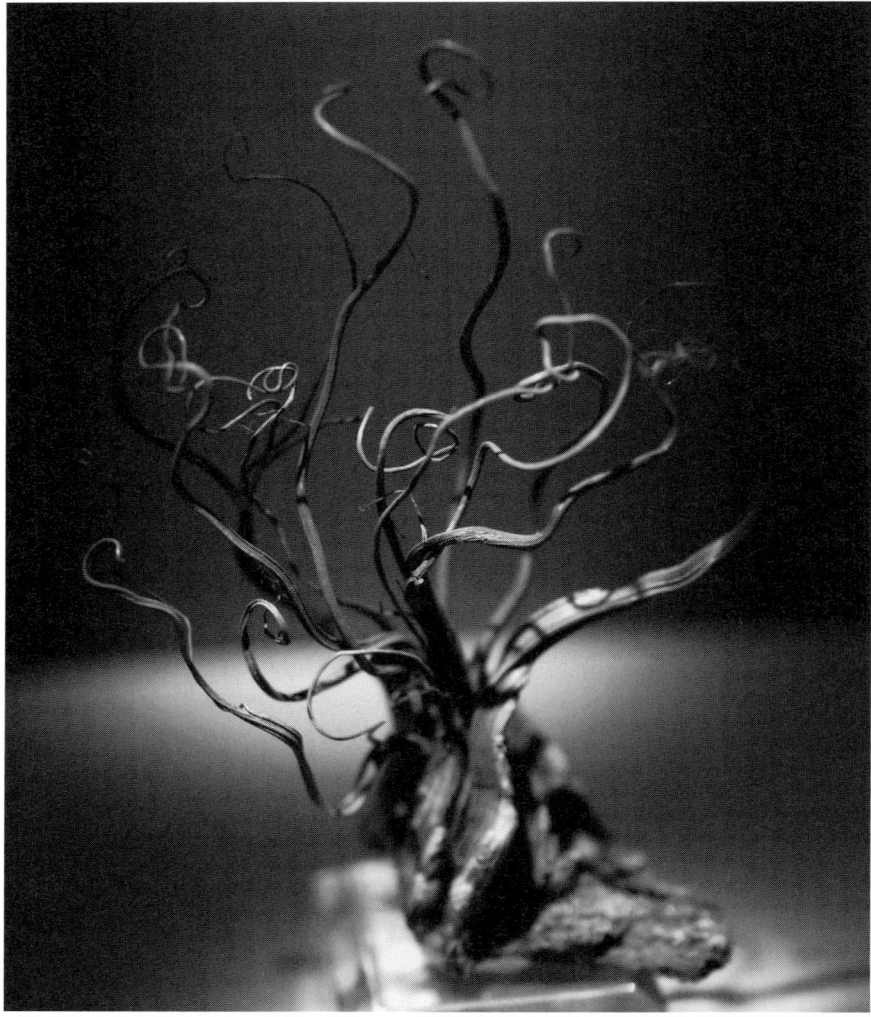

2.1. Native silver, Freiberg District, Erzgebirge, Saxony, Germany, Houston Museum of Natural Science

Grounding his account on German physician Daniel Sennert's work, Joannes Jonston wrote in his 1657 *A History of the Wonderful Things of Nature*: 'Truly the Flux of Veins hath somthing proportionable to vegetable nature; and the relation of a Physitian of Friberg, that, in the Lungs of such as use to dig in Mines, their bodies being opened when they are dead, you shall find the same Mettals grown hard, wherein they laboured being alive (*Sennertus lib de consensu et diss. Chymicorum et Galenicorum*) seems to intimate as much.'[15] A vivid emblematic evocation of the co-penetration of human body and the material of the earth can

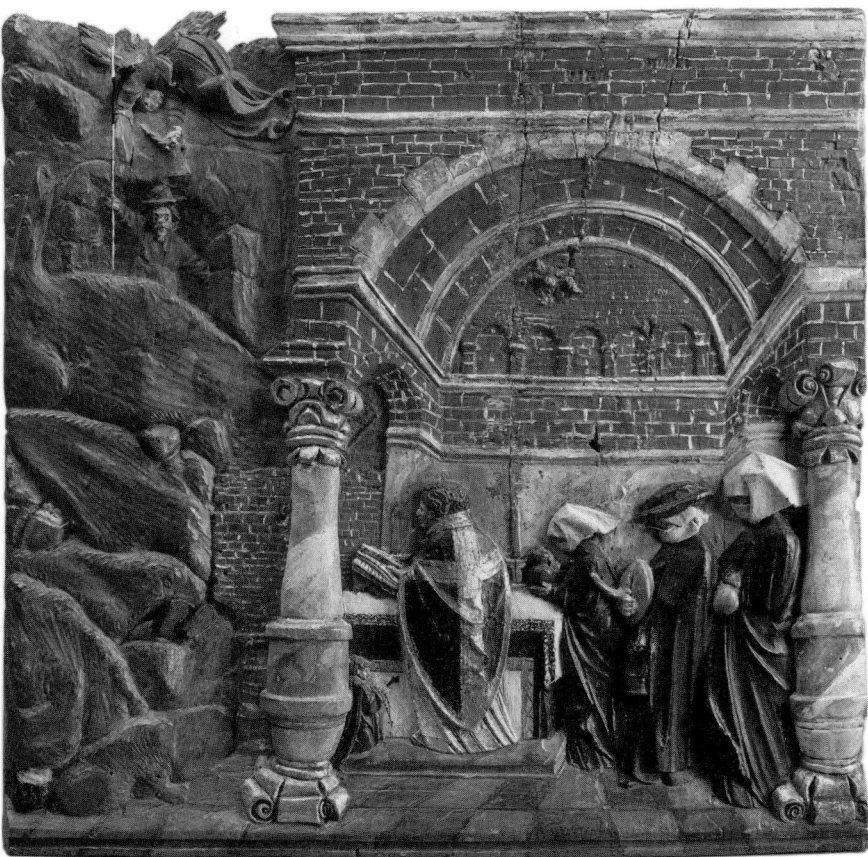

2.2. Hans Leinberger (1480–after 1530), *Mass for victims of a mining accident*, c. 1510–20, limewood relief, 33.5 × 33.5 cm., Inv. 463, Berlin, Skulpturensammlung und Museum für Byzantinische Kunst, Staatliche Museen

be seen in an early sixteenth-century relief altarpiece commemorating a mine accident that shows the limbs and a head of dead miners protruding from the mass of rock and earth of the collapsed shaft (Figure 2.2). This representation shows the endpoint of the struggle with matter that shaped the bodies of miners. Like other craftspeople, their specific bodily labour formed their musculature and posture, and the matter they worked marked their bodies by distinctive diseases. In his remarkable treatment of the diseases of miners, the sixteenth-century religious, medical and intellectual reformer Paracelsus forcefully conveyed this view of the permeability and porosity of the human body. In the 1530s, he described human beings as affected by the four elements because all resemble foetuses lying in the matrix:

> For all of us, although we are grown up, still lie in the mother and the uterus surrounds us all and whatever lies in the uterus must be the same as that which the uterus is and bears. Thus all the elements and everything that has been generated are around us. And we walk and wander among them. Therefore we are as loose and soft as a chick in its shell; for all the rays of the planets and of the limbus, which is the seed, enter into us and produce an essential action, for heaven and earth are the uterus and both are one thing. And man is the least thing and yet everything.[16]

Paracelus' evocative statement of the formation of humans in the matrix of the material world is echoed by a goldsmith two generations later in his discussion of the shaping of stones by the climate and influences of the heavenly bodies:

> The precious stones are eyther Gems, or Marble, Gems [are] grown for the most parte in the east Countries, because the temperature of the Clymatt is there fitt to generate them, and also in Persia, phrigia, Thracia, Media, Cappadocia, Arabia, Scythia, Cyprus & in Germanys alsoe. Those which growe in the Indies are for the most parte more precious & harder then they which are found elswhere. Sometyme they grow amontest the Rockes, Sometyme in the Mynes: the Thynne matter being seperated from the impurest; and the influence of the heavens by continewance of tyme makes it a most pure stone; They are bred of other Stones, as pearles are of Sea oysters, They have goodly vertues and properties whereby we may with pleasure observe their consent and agreement with the heavens for if they be like the heavens in brightnes, clerenes and no waye stayned in purities, wee may eselie coniecture that the caelestiall bodies are prodigall in transfusing & bestowing their vertues upon them.[17]

Mining and ancient texts

The interaction of the human body with matter itself occurred especially in the extraordinarily intense sensory engagement – looking, touching, tasting, smelling, and even hearing – of the work of prospecting, the beginning of all mining, smelting, and metalworking. Minerals and ores are found in a great variety of combinations in very different locations; indeed, the particularity of geological phenomena, or 'fossils' (i.e. things dug up) led ancient authors to lament the impossibility of a scientific nature of the study of stones, earths, and minerals because the variety of these materials made them incapable of being marshalled into systematic generalized knowledge. Indeed, this attitude to mining and metalworking on the part of the ancients allows us to trace the trajectory from matter to ideas with particular clarity. Because no significant corpus of ancient texts on metals and minerals, and mining and smelting, existed, we can observe the emergence of a theory of the origin and genesis of metals from the handwork of mining. When mining expanded in Central Europe in the fifteenth and sixteenth centuries, several attempts were made to articulate and codify mining knowledge in writing in a way that had not occurred previously in European history. This attempt at codification occurred in conjunction with a greater exchange between labourers and elites (artisans and scholars), and in an economic context in which new forms of exploiting the diggings forced nobles, merchants, and scholarly elites to work together and gave more power to miners and prospecting entrepreneurs.[18] Because no ancient texts existed which dealt with the labour of mining (only Pliny made brief allusions to mining), scholar-physicians, mining officials, and others authored texts that were informed by miners and metalworkers about the processes by which materials were transformed in the mines and smelting huts. They took up mine labourers' beliefs and their experience of matter, sometimes assimilating these beliefs and experience within already existing textual corpuses, drawing frameworks from biblical and alchemical texts, as well as what little ancient writing existed on stones, earths, and metals, and often making their understanding of vernacular experiences the basis for new theories and worldviews.

The first example of this codification was written before the central European mining boom, but serves as an introduction to the problem of mining, metalworking, and ancient authority. In the thirteenth century, the cleric, teacher, and church administrator Albertus Magnus (1193?–1280) could not believe that he would not someday locate an ancient corpus of writing on metals, but, after searching for some years for what he believed must be a lost book of Aristotle on the formation of metals and stones, he finally gave up and decided to write a work that would fill in for Aristotle's lost book:

> Our method in this work will be to follow the sequence of Aristotle's thought, and to say in explanation and demonstration of it whatever may seem necessary; but without any quotation of the text. And also we shall put in digressions, so as to clarify difficulties as they arise or to add whatever may make the Philosopher's thought clearer to anyone . . . And we shall make additions wherever books are incomplete, and wherever they have gaps in them, or are missing entirely – whether they were left unwritten by Aristotle or, if he did write them, they have not come down to us.[19]

Albertus travelled widely as an administrator of the Dominican Order, noting that he made 'long journeys to mining districts, so that I could learn by observation the nature of metals. And for the same reason I have inquired into the transmutations of metals in alchemy, so as to learn from this, too, something of their nature and accidental properties.'[20]

Everywhere he went he observed craftspeople – stonemasons, miners, smelters, alchemists, and metalworkers – and recorded his conversations with them. He observed that when miners 'go into the mines they cover their mouths and noses with two or three layers of cloth so that their breathing may not be too much injured by the vapour – for this is where the greatest damage is done, as we have said.'[21] In discussing the cause of different hardness in stones, Albertus cites the experience of builders and stonemasons who know that if an unctuous material is heated, it will cohere, while if it is watery, it will evaporate, like chalk.[22] He records the experience of stonemasons who know which stones will break into thin slabs,[23] while he looks to the practices of founders to explain the cause of conglomerated stones: he theorizes that these stones are produced by nature in the same way that crucibles are made for casting metals – that is, old pottery is crushed and calcined (or heated) then again mixed with moist clay from which crucibles are formed, which themselves are then solidified by firing. He notes a continuum between natural processes and human art: 'Nor is there any reason, either, why it should be said that bricks are made only artificially and not naturally. For if tenacious clay is mixed in the earth and afterwards baked by the heat enclosed there, a better brick is made in the earth, naturally, than is made artificially.' This happens best along shores of seas and banks of rivers, because those places are mixed with moisture and warmed by rays of the sun.[24] In the case of metallic transmutation, Albertus cites the evidence of his own eyes when, down in a mine, he saw a vein flowing from a single source that was in one area pure gold, and in another area silver with a stony calk mixed with it. Miners and smeltermen told him that this very frequently happens, 'and therefore they are sorry when they have found gold, for the gold is near the source, and then the vein fails'.[25]

Out of his observations, his conversations with craftsmen, and his reading of Aristotle and the newly translated Arabic alchemical texts, including Avicenna, Albertus formulated a theory of the genesis of minerals and metals in the earth recorded in his work *De mineralibus*, probably finished in the 1260s and first published in Italy in the 1490s. He came to see the formation of metals in the earth as like the processes that took place in the crucibles and distillation flasks of 'alchemical' (by which he meant what we would call 'chemical') vessels. The earth formed natural vessels in which stone, minerals, and metals were generated.[26] In keeping with Aristotelian causal explanation, Albertus named the *efficient* cause of metals as the heat that mixed earth and water;[27] the specific form of the metal (when it melts and solidifies) – its *formal* cause – as imposed by 'the formative power in nature, poured into the stars of heaven'; and its *essential* cause the power of the planets.[28] By the time he travelled to Venice, Albertus had formulated a theory and could give an expert answer to queries about stone: when in Venice, he saw marble being cut with saws to decorate the walls of a church. When the two slabs were placed side by side, there was a most beautiful picture of a king's head with a crown and a long beard, which had a single fault: the middle of the forehead seemed too high. He was asked why the forehead was disproportioned, to which he answered that the stone had been hardened from a vapour, and, in the middle, the vapour had risen up too far because the heat was greater there, as also happens in clouds. When these vapours were subjected to the influence of a place and a mineralizing power, they fashioned many figures in stones.[29]

Like Albertus, sixteenth-century scholars living and working in the mining boom towns of Central Europe – including the surveyor of St Annaberg, Freiberg *Stadtphysicus* and eventual *Bürgermeister* Ulrich Rülein von Calw (*c.* 1465–1523), and the St Joachimsthal *Stadtphysicus* and mining shareholder Georgius Agricola (1493–1555) – often had to abandon the works of the authors they read in their university years to make first-hand observations, asking questions as they went of the workers. St Annaberg, Freiberg, and St Joachimsthal sat at the centre of a tremendous mining boom in Central Europe. From 1460 until the 1550s (when New World silver brought down the value of precious metals), the princes and merchants of central Europe enjoyed a tremendous surge in prosperity fuelled by innovations in mining. Silver production increased five-fold in this period. Although silver had been mined in central Europe since ancient times, a turning point came in the 1450s when the technique of separating silver from copper ores by means of lead was introduced into central Europe (apparently from China where it had been discovered in the eleventh century). This made profitable the greater capital investment in the large and complex machines needed for digging deep shafts to follow rich veins and the new methods of drainage and ventilation that made possible these shafts. Simultaneously, the rediscovery of the blast furnace meant more effective cast-iron tools for digging and breaking up the ore could be produced at a lower cost. In the wake of large-scale capital investment, independent partnerships of miners and smelters gave way to managers operating mines on behalf of absentee shareholders, including nobles, large merchants, and even monasteries and universities.

In this boom, towns grew from small hamlets to tens of thousands of inhabitants in a matter of years. In their medical duties and in the material conditions of their lives in these boom towns, von Calw and Agricola were thus confronted with a world far different from that for which their training in ancient languages and classical medical authors had prepared them. As city physicians both these men dealt with the illnesses of miners, and as municipal officials and mine shareholders they were naturally interested in the discovery of rich ores as the basis of both civic and personal wealth. The discovery of ores necessitated an understanding of where metals 'grew' in the earth. In theorizing about the origin and genesis of metals, these two physicians could draw upon Aristotle's very brief discussion in *Meteorologica* that rocks and metals were formed by the exhalation of hot vapours which then congealed in the cold of the earth. They also drew upon Theophrastus on earths and stones, Pliny's brief mentions of mining, medieval gem books, Albertus' *De mineralibus*, medical authorities, and alchemical authors who posited the 'principles' of sulphur and mercury as the underlying substratum of all metals. Apart from Albertus, none of these works, however, treated mining or had very much to say about the genesis of metals in the earth.

Both von Calw's single *Bergbuchlein* (published anonymously *c.* 1500) and Agricola's very numerous texts on mining and metals (published from 1530 to 1556) are marked – as was Albertus' *De mineralibus* – by their exchange with miners. The *Bergbuchlein* is written as a dialogue between Daniel, a *Bergverständiger* (a 'knower' of mining), and his apprentice.[30] Agricola modelled his first work on mining, *Bermannus, sive de re metallica dialogus* (1530), directly on the *Bergbuchlein*, writing it as a dialogue between a 'learned miner, *Bermannus*', and two traditionally trained physicians, one expert in Latin and one in Arabic and Greek. The miner teaches about mining terms and concepts which gives rise to conversation among the scholars about the relationship of these new terms to ancient texts, practices, and medicines. At several points, Agricola warns his reader through the miner Bermannus that mining must be discussed with new terms because either the ancient texts have not come down to us or these subjects were unknown in antiquity.[31]

As well as relying upon textual authorities and local mining informants, von Calw and Agricola also used analogies from other observations they had made in related areas: for example, Agricola used the mechanics of distillation to explain the formation of minerals and stones, and he used the analogy of the human body in which various liquids were produced and excreted as the basis of his theory that mixtures of water and earth form different 'juices' of the earth that ultimately lead to the formation of all stones, earths, minerals, ores, and metals.[32] In addition, von Calw and Agricola also took over the *method* by which miners themselves made knowledge.

Prospecting

Miners were in the business of identifying rich veins of ore, but this was always very locally specific knowledge because the formation of mineral outcroppings is always extremely variable. *Prospecting* was the method by which miners produced theories about the formation of stones, ores, metals, or *fossils* (literally, 'things dug up', as Agricola called his treatise on subterranean phenomena)[33] that allowed them to decide to begin to dig and tunnel in particular locations. Thus, *place* – the landscape – became a crucial part of miners' theories about how ores and minerals formed in the earth, and where they might best be discovered.[34] Prospecting consisted in *recognizing signs* based on prior experience of fruitful ore strikes. Although the miners needed specific knowledge of the characteristics of place, they also needed to formulate some more general principles, such as the favourable strike and dip of veins, veinlets, and other feeders, 'which are supposed to be responsible for ores, so that miners follow such indications in their prospecting and have developed certain theories on the subject', as the St Annaberg native Lazarus Ercker, superintendent of mines and comptroller of the Holy Roman Empire under Rudolf II, wrote in his 1574 *Treatise on Ores and Assaying*.[35]

Both the method and the theorizing of prospecting involved the use of all five senses to sample and sound out the earth that lay on the surface or in exploratory diggings. Miners seeking out the hidden riches below the ground had to scour the surface of the earth for clues to what lay below.[36] The earliest written vernacular evidence of miners' practices and ideas occurs in a mining ballad, 'Märe vom Feldbauer', written down between 1330 and 1350. This ballad contained miners' vernacular terms recorded for the first time referencing the orientation and formation of the veins. These terms were those collected from miners by von Calw and Agricola and, indeed, continued to be employed by scholars through the eighteenth century and beyond.[37]

The five senses

Looking carefully and observing the loose rocks as well as outcroppings where veins came to the surface obviously formed a primary tool of prospecting. Miners made a close study of rocks and the ground, looking carefully at the *Geschüb*, or 'alluvial fragments' – a flood of rocks washed out of a vein which miners followed into the earth and the vein of ore. In addition, they looked for the effects of underground vapours, such as fog lying low over the ground, discoloured leaves and plants, stunted growth and twisted roots. The author of *De la Pirotechnia*, Vannoccio Biringuccio, visualized minerals growing under the earth like the branches of a tree, striving continually skyward and drawing up the adjacent material, until they 'arrive at the summit of the mountain and emerge with clear sign, sending forth, in place of leaves and blossoms, blue or green fumosities, marcasites with small veins of heavy mineral, or other composition of tinctures.'[38] With this model in mind, Biringuccio's *Pirotechnia* described the visible signs of each of the six true metals and numerous semi-minerals, which he believed to be the beginnings of minerals, often distinguishing between what 'natural philosophers say' and what 'practical men' observe.[39] Silver, for example, is found either near or mixed together with marcasites of a yellow colour like gold. Those that are most promising to the prospector 'approach white as nearly as possible and be of minute grain and in small quantities . . . The closer together and finer they are the better the minerals that they point out.'[40] Copper ore is recognized by the shiny specks, like talc, of a greenish cast, with a metallic taste in stones on the surface of the earth. Often these stones lie on a bed of 'viscous and green putrefaction'.[41] What Biringuccio called the 'semi-metal' mercury (and other writers considered one of the seven true metals) is engendered in places of 'abundant water and trees, and the grasses are very green, because it has a moist coolness in it and does not give off dry vapours as sulphur, vitriol, salt, and similar minerals do.' However, the trees do not produce blossoms or come to fruit, and in April and May the places where mercury is found produce thick and dense vapours which do not rise very high due to their heaviness.

Tasting was central to understanding the stones and soils discovered while prospecting, and was carried out either by placing the soil or crushed rock directly on the tongue or by putting it in a vessel full of rain water (rain water was pure, containing no components leached from the ground), working it with the hands, then sipping the water. Biringuccio recommends tasting to know the properties of soils and earths: for example, in the making of saltpetre, one must taste the 'mercurial soil' 'with the tongue to find if it is biting, and how much so'.[42] In *De natura fossilium* (1546), Agricola gives ample evidence of these practices, detailing the eight varieties of taste and their corresponding minerals: sweet (melitites), oily (marl), bitter (nitrum), salty (halite), acrid (lime), astringent (red ochre), acidulous, and mixed (astringent and acrid).[43] He notes that each metal has a distinctive taste which can be ascertained by placing water in a vessel made from the metal and allowing it to stand: copper is bitter and unpleasant, iron less so, and tin has the weakest taste.[44] The taste of sulphur is 'oily and unpleasant'.[45] Agricola makes taste an attribute of things themselves, theorizing that it comes into being when the elements mix. The elements themselves do not have any taste or smell, but the mixture of elements in the matrix of the earth gives rise to these properties.[46]

Odour could also be useful in identifying the presence of useful *fossiles*, for, as Agricola noted, certain minerals have an odour when struck with an iron or stone: for example, Hildesheim marble gave off the odour of burning horn. The odour of sulphur was like 'that of thunder and lightning and is similar to the odour that comes from certain ores when they are roasted. When sulphur is burned it is very irritating to the nose.'[47] Like Agricola's *De natura fossilium*, Alvaro Alonso Barba's *El Arte de los Metales* began by briefly mentioning the many colours by which we know the earths, minerals, stones, and salts, and then recounted at length the tastes and smells by which they may be more certainly known. Barba begins, for example, with 'Common Earth', or ordinary soil, which 'smells strongly, after the heat of the East Winds, when it receives the touch of the first Rains'.[48] He notes that in the Entremoz in Portugal and in the Natá of Panama some muds exhale a strong smell when it rains, and he takes over from Agricola the story of a sweet smelling silver ore. As Agricola had written in 1545, 'Recently a silver vein has been discovered in a prospect named St Fabius and St Sebastian near Marienburg and the ore from this vein, when broken in the mine or after it is carried outside, gives off an odour which is pleasing to everyone. Prince Henry [of Saxony], who was present at the time the vein was discovered, was so pleased that he exclaimed, "This is Calcutta, India." Aromatic gums come to us from that city.'[49] Barba records the exclamation as referring to 'Civet, that land of India so famous for its Perfumes'.[50] Agricola goes on to note that, when heated, gold has a sweet odour detected with difficulty; silver a fetid odour; copper and iron a fetid odour; lead, bismuth, and zinc a dull odour. Odour was given off by some minerals when crushed in a mortar: realgar gives off the odour of sulphur, for example. Many minerals smell of bitumen, some of garlic, and geodes from Misena and others have an odour of violets, but Agricola notes, not in this case from the stone, but from the moss.[51] Agricola attributes odour, too, to the mixing of primal elements, for, as experience shows, when water and earth mix, an odour rises from them, as Barba had observed in examples from the Old and New Worlds.[52]

Minerals could also be differentiated by touch, as Agricola noted, because they contain warmth and coolness, as well as moisture and dryness. Some veins do not feel hot to the miners, but when the ore is brought to the surface and a person buries his hands in it, it burns the hands.[53] Hearing, too, played a part, for metals and earths could be recognized by the sounds they caused: tin, for example, when bent or squeezed between the teeth, made cracking sounds, 'like that which water makes when it is frozen by cold'. Conversely, tin also affected the 'sweetness' of other metals, hardening them and making them sonorous, 'just as if it puts the spirit there and vitalizes the substances'.[54] Good iron was indicated by the presence of bole and another red, soft, fat earth that did not make any crackling noise when squeezed by the teeth.[55]

Knowledge from the senses

The prospector's mingling of his five senses with the matter of the earth involved cognition. Use of the five senses was the beginning of knowledge, but the sensory observations were then made into knowledge by repeated *experience*. As Biringuccio envisaged this process of knowledge making:

> All things created by God have some particular gift or power. If we humans cannot see it, it is because of our defective vision, in our little knowledge, and in our lack of careful thought concerning the necessity of seeking hidden things. Certainly those things that have such inner powers, like herbs, fruits, roots, animals, precious stones, metals, or other stones, can be understood only through oft-repeated experience. Others do not need so much knowledge, and belief for their powers are obvious and shown to us at all times by their effects. They reveal themselves to us through the sense of sight by their splendour and variety of colours, through the sense of smell by their odours, through the sense of hearing by the melody of the harmonious or unpleasantly discordant repercussions of the air. They likewise manifest themselves by their softness or harshness. As you see, all those things, according to their limits, are conveyed by the ordinary senses to the mind, by whose distinctions all their species, both harmful and beneficial, are discerned. Then they are reviewed by the judgment in all their degrees of perfection and imperfection, so that whoever seeks them with careful study or with experience often finds them.[56]

In other words, all the particular sensory data collected in repeated investigations by the prospecting miner was generalized into a collection of theoretical frameworks by which the miner could make predictions about where it would be most profitable to begin digging. While scholars such as Agricola codified these theories by writing them down in books, miners codified their embodied knowledge in the dowsing rod. As historian Warren Dym has shown, the dowsing rod was employed since ancient times to locate water and minerals, and was seen in early modern European mining as a self-evident component of the knowledge and expertise of the miner. A man (never a woman) who attained this expertise was known as a *Bergverständiger* – he could speak the lingo, the *Bergsprache*, and possessed 'mountain science': *Bergwissenschaft*. Dowsing involved mind and body, and dowsers were asked to focus their 'impressions and thoughts',[57] indicating both the sensory and cognitive aspects of their activities. As Dym recounts, dowsing continued to form the basis of the 'mining science' taught at the Freiberg Academy into the eighteenth century. To modern ears, dowsing might sound ludicrous; however, dowsers were generally experienced miners who possessed a reservoir of knowledge and observational skills that allowed them to attend to and integrate many particulars of the landscape – plant growth, rock outcroppings, gravel wash and silt found in streams, the taste and smell of water running through the land, direction of mineral veins, and so on. Perhaps the dowsing rod helped focus their attention into a state of subsidiary awareness of all these particular observations which made them able to discern more likely locations of ore. And, significantly, as a recognizable symbol of social and epistemic authority, the dowsing rod then enabled them to declare this knowledge more authoritatively because, in its visible dipping movement, it provided an external demonstration to observers. As the culmination of vernacular knowledge-making in prospecting, the dowsing rod codified miners' theories about ores and metals.

Practice into theory

We can see how the method of prospecting and the knowledge derived from it contributed directly to theories about the genesis and composition of minerals and metals in the work of Georgius Agricola. In addition to the examples provided above, we find the observations of miners repeatedly used to give credence to a theory. For example, both miners and theorists believed that mineral fumes gave clues to the earth's contents underground and provided support to a theory that minerals were generated by these mineral exhalations. In Germany, these fumes were known by miners as underground 'weathers' or *Witterungen*, often referred to as *Dünste*, *Broden*, *Dämpfe*, and *exhalationes*, and were believed to be given off as the minerals grew in the earth, and stirred up into a wind by the air that moved through the earth.[58] In *On the Cosmos* (pseudo-)Aristotle wrote that 'the wind... lashes about enveloped in the earth with tumultuous force. The blasts of wind that enter the earth are recondensed also by the moisture that is hidden in the earth.'[59] Agricola and Paracelsus took over this theory in part, but they also incorporated the miners' stories about sprites and spirits that inhabited the diggings as the cause of exhalations. Agricola classified the spirits into evil and simply mischievous, recounting an example from the Rosenkranz mine in which an evil spirit killed twelve miners through its miasmic breath. The other, milder *Geister*, which were known by the Germans as *Kobolden*, imitated humans, giggled 'as if from joy' and amused themselves with harmless deceptions. Some called them

Bergmännlein, because they were dwarf-like, and, while they looked like old men and were dressed like miners, they occupied themselves with hurrying around in the mines, appearing to do work, but actually doing nothing. Although they occasionally annoyed the workers by throwing gravel, they hardly ever did any harm, unless ridiculed by the miners. In this, Agricola writes, they were similar to the spirits who appeared seldom to humans but every day do a part of the work and take care of the animals. Germans call them 'Guttell' and others 'Trulle' (trolls). These latter are of both male or female sex and live among other peoples, such as the Swedes, whom they serve. The *Berggeister* work mainly in mines that had proven themselves or about which investors were hopeful; thus the miners are not afraid of them, but take it as a good sign and 'are of good spirit and work all the harder'.[60]

Paracelsus, too, wrote that underground 'weather' could be caused by the spirits and sprites of the subterranean world. Paracelsus noted that in mines all over Germany 'Bergmännlein' made their homes. These spirits also appeared in woodlands, around springs, but were especially prevalent in the mines. While the presence of gnomes was a sign of the productivity of the mines, humans had to show respect for these guardians of the earth's treasure. Any harm done to the spirits could cause them to transmute noble metals into worthless dirt. This was especially true of 'Kobolden' who produced a corrosive ore, called by the miners 'Kobolderz', which corrupted valuable metal ores. Paracelsus took up this terminology for what today is known as a cobalt-containing ore, and, by means of his writings, this terminology flowed seamlessly from miners' beliefs to chemistry textbooks, and today Paracelsus is viewed in the history of chemistry as the discoverer of cobalt.[61] The vernacular practices of mining and making here gave rise directly to theory.[62]

Another area in which miners' reports and the writings of the ancients combined to support and develop theories about the origin of minerals was the presence of water in the mines: prospecting led to theories about the importance of water in the genesis of minerals, indeed, all writers who maintain this view of the watery generation of metals appealed to the experience of miners. Thus, Biringuccio recalls a mine in Austria, very rich in copper and silver, a huge enterprise, in which much water fell continuously from various openings, like a heavy rain, but this 'did not surprise me since I had always understood that water was the primary and peculiar companion of minerals, indeed that it was perhaps the very reason for the generation of their substance'. Biringuccio continued, 'All mountains from which abundant waters spring also abound in minerals.'[63]

Agricola formulated a theory that the water running through the earth, carrying with it all kinds of juices and settling in enclosed spaces generated, as if in a vessel or a matrix, the minerals and metals. Water breaks off bits of rock and soil as it flows into and through the earth, and as it settles and is filtered, it ends up on the bottom of the 'vessels' of the earth, turns to slime and then hardens into a type of 'earth'.[64] Agricola's theories about the genesis of rocks, minerals, and metals are viewed as the basis of 'scientific' geology.[65]

Fat and lean

A final example of the emergence of theory from matter and practice can be found in a recurrent paradigm employed in mines, metalworking shops, and the books of scholars: the framework of fat and lean. Miners spoke of *Guhr* or *Steinmark*,[66] and generalizing theorists such as Agricola wrote of the 'marrow of stones'.[67] This was analogous to the fatty substance of bone marrow, and was seen to be responsible for the generation of mineral ores. The paradigm of lean and fat appears in myriad writings in the sixteenth century, in the records of both craftspeople and scholars. For example a late sixteenth-century collection of recipes and techniques includes many references to 'greasy' and 'fatty' lead, and 'greasy sands'.[68]

Agricola discusses fat and lean extensively, calling on the authority of Pliny, who he said had given an excellent description of the role of fat earth in increasing the productivity of soils: 'It is a sort of soft fat of earth and, like the glandular organs in the body, there thickens itself with a nucleus of richness. There are many varieties, the best being found in characteristic veins.'[69] In *De natura fossilium*, Agricola classified earths and minerals by their dry or lean qualities, with many grades of dryness and unctuousness: those that burned, such as sulphur, jet, bitumen and amber, were the most unctuous.[70] Bitumen and sulphur caught fire easily because of their fatness.[71] Fire drives the marrow out of the earth, where it extrudes from rock outcroppings.[72] The leanest earths included sandstone, salt, and ochre. In order to test the leanness of an earth, it should be softened with water, thoroughly worked with the hands, then a small ball formed and thrown on the ground. If it cracks, it is 'meagre'; if not, it is unctuous. Some earths are so unctuous they melt like butter on the tongue.[73] Agricola appears to have studied the practices of farmers, detailing the soils cultivated by farmers and those used by potters, fullers, painters, carpenters, and other artisans. Farmers, he wrote, select unctuous sandy soil for growing sesame; indeed, he noted that farmers classify soils first according to fertility, sterility or intermediate qualities, then according to denseness and porosity, and finally according to taste.[74] Agricola speaks of twenty-one species of earths of interest to farmer, nine species of rich earths and six each of poor and intermediate:

> Rich or unctuous earths are the best since in these, especially in the sweet varieties, there exists a juice which nourishes the grain. Rich porous earths are the best of all since they yield the finest produce. Porous earths require the least work and afford the greatest yield. . . . Poor soils are improved by manure and marl (*marga*, lime) . . . Marl is nothing other than a very rich, compact earth . . . When dried it changes into sand, *tofus*, or a harder rock and when moistened, into some sort of juice that is known by the same name, *marga*.[75]

The rock is crushed and sprinkled over fields. This 'tempering' earth could also be useful in medicines, for when the white juice 'Steinomarga' is drunk it can stop profuse bleeding, and in general has the same medicinal properties as Samian earth.[76]

The concept of a generative 'fat' thus seems to have emerged out of agriculture, in which rich, unctuous soils produced bountiful crops, and from scholars who called upon the writings of Theophrastus on soils in agriculture (generalizations which themselves must have arisen from the experience of farmers) as the basis of their theorizing. In *De causis plantarum*, Theophrastus mentioned 'fat soil' as a 'better producer of grain, leaner soil of trees'. As evidence, he noted that 'vegetables and cereals thrive in fat soils, and all these plants are by their nature spare; for the naturally spare requires fatter food'.[77] Theophrastus gives further proof of this paradigm by comparing it to medical ideas about the beneficial character of rich food for starving humans – 'they not only take the greatest delight in this fat food but gain in colour and strength; for their spare bodies require plenty of fat food, and they get no benefit from dry and spare food because they cannot assimilate it, being apt instead to contract various diseases, especially those of the digestive tract. The case is the same (they say) for trees as well, except that the tree continues as before, whereas when the human body has recuperated it passes to an austere and fatless diet.'[78]

The paradigm of fat and lean also appears to have formed a common currency in metalworkers' shops. From Agricola, we hear that smelters in the Saxon mines draw off the fatty sulphur and bitumen by floating it on water: 'Beneath the plate are placed pots containing water, into which the sulphurous or bituminous vapour descends, and in the water the fat accumulates and floats on the top. If it is sulphur, it is generally of a yellow colour; if bitumen, it is black like pitch. If these were not drawn out they would do much harm to the metal when the ore is being smelted. When they have thus been separated they prove of some service to man, especially the sulphurous kind.'[79] In *De la Pirotechnia*, Biringuccio explained the strength and durability of crucibles by reference to fat and lean: use of lean clay or crushed stone clay that 'seems to be arid and resistant' will make the crucible more able to resist the fire. In this case, the natural fatness of clay must be mixed with talc, finely ground and sifted iron scale or young ram's-horn ashes.[80] Biringuccio extensively discusses fat and lean in relation to alloying metals and in the making of silver coins (actually an alloy of copper and silver), where silver is cast in hot iron plates greased with fat to make the metal run more fluidly into the mould.[81] In mixing an alloy of copper and tin, Biringuccio advises that after adding 'the quantity of tin that you think will corrupt it best', when it appears entirely liquid and clear, and flashes like the sun, and when the flames which still issue from the metal are almost white and without smoke, skim it with a skimmer of dry wood, then throw in some lard or other animal fat mixed with tartar or saltpetre, or add ram's horn and heat it well.[82]

Most significantly, Biringuccio notes that in casting bronze the channels through which the metals flow into the mould are greased with pig fat or tallow in order to make the metals more fluid.[83] In addition, if a box mould is formed from lean sand, it receives the fatness of a metal particularly well, resulting in a well-formed cast with a very good surface impression.[84] He explains the need, when casting bronze cannons, to have a quantity of bronze at the mouth of the mould so that it presses down and makes the other parts 'fat'. He advises adding tin to the furnace or putting it in the channels down which the bronze flows so that the feeding head becomes 'fat with tin, where it will press down and give fatness to the muzzle', thus producing a cast that is 'close, dense, and safe, and pleasing to the sight in its beauty'.[85] Without this, the metal would remain 'lean and brittle'. Again, in casting guns, tin must be added right at the end of the pour to add 'unctuousness', so that the metal mass is solid and without small holes, which would result from a lean mixture.[86] Today, we would term this process 'inverse segregation', in which the addition of tin compensates for the fact that in the last parts of the alloy to solidify, tin content is lower and thus the metal does not flow and often is more brittle at that point.[87] For Biringuccio, animal fats, tallow, tin, fluxes such as borax and crushed glass, all kinds of gum, Grecian pitch, common oil, soft soap, ram's-horn scrapings, and the smoke of pine resin or turpentine were all unctuous and fatty, and thus the cause both of the metals running more fluidly and producing a denser cast.[88] Leanness resulted in brittleness that could nevertheless withstand heat, while unctuous fatness led to greater liquidity and greater strength through malleability.

The polarity of fat and lean informed Agricola's theory of the genesis of minerals in the earth. In *De ortu*, Agricola asks what causes the heat that miners encounter as they dig down into the earth. He notes that there are many theories about this put forward by learned authors, and they include heating by the sun; wind penetrating into the earth and heating up by its constant motion; water becoming hot by falling on the rocks; but miners, Agricola says, can testify every working day that none of these happen.[89] Rather, Agricola says that by carefully observing the veins, one can conclude that water flows along the veins and deposits its generative component in to receptacles (the *matrix*) in which the veins then grow and burst out on to the surface in outcrops. Agricola saw veins as generative and formative receptacles (like wombs or matrices) in which the ores form. Miners knew that every vein had a floor and a ceiling, it had clefts (at which cruciform intersection the vein could be especially rich), and outcroppings where it burst on to the surface. As the water runs through the earth and settles into vessels, it takes on certain characteristics: for example, if it runs through soft rock, such as Kalkstein, it produces fat earths such as chalk, clay, marl, and *Steinsalz*, and when it runs through sandstone, lean earths are created. Once deposited in the veins, it is cooked by a fire kept burning by a fat substance, such as bitumen or sulphur.[90] This fire sometimes burns so hot that it can drive out the stone marrow from the earth, such as when one finds sulphur protruding out of the earth in volcanic regions.[91] For Agricola, fat earths resulted from slow fermentation in a medium heat of the air's humidity. If the earth's heat became too fierce, the substances would turn out lean.[92] Interestingly, in articulating this idea of the generation of fat earths, Agricola might have been following the 'secrets' of metalworkers, as recorded by Benvenuto Cellini (1500–71), who made a particularly unctuous clay (resembling a medicinal 'salve') for small moulds by mixing clay and wool with water until it resembled bread dough, beating it with an iron rod, then fermenting it for some time in the warmer months. Because it fermented, it was believed to hold together better.[93] Thus, the paradigm of fat and lean (and the generative nature of putrefaction) appears to have arisen not only in observation by and of farmers, but also from the practices of foundrymen in which it played a central part in the making of moulds and crucibles, and in the alloying of metals.

Fat earths were central in mine prospecting, as miners sought out *Steinmark* or *Steinomarga*, 'stone marrow', in mines. They played an important role in smelting ores, the most striking example being the use of what is known today as fluorite – a mineral that appears to have been formed by flowing and congealing liquid. In *Bermannus*, Agricola discusses the qualities of stone marrow, which he states is not so fat and tough as clay.[94] He notes that what the miners call *Flußspate* and scholars call *Fluores* for its appearance as a solidified flow is added by metalworkers to ores and metals on melting in order to enhance their fluidity. It continued to be used for centuries as a flux in iron smelting to make iron flow and its slag congeal, which allowed their easier separation.[95] In the seventeenth and eighteenth centuries, chemical philosophers such as Johan Rudolf Glauber and Herman Boerhaave identified stone marrow, which they called by the miners' term *Guhr*, with the generative substance of metals,[96] and it remained an object of investigation into the nineteenth century.[97] Once more, we see how the theory of the generation of metals, codified by scholars in the sixteenth and seventeenth centuries, emerged out of a combination of textual authority and the labour of metalworkers and miners.

Conclusion

This chapter sought, first, to suggest the entanglement of the human body with matter, and, second, to show how theories about the origin and genesis of metals emerged out of that entanglement, specifically, out of the experience of working matter by mining and metalworking. The itinerary from matter through the action of the human body into ideas is easier to trace in mining and metalworking because by the sixteenth century the embodied knowledge and artisanal experience in mining had not yet been codified in an extensive textual tradition. In other spheres of human experience and natural enquiry – such as medicine and agriculture – the formation of theoretical frameworks out of the embodied experience of matter and their codification in writing had occurred centuries or millennia earlier. Thus the practices (and sources recording such practices) of vernacular theorizing are less visible to historians because they are obscured by deep layers of an authoritative textual corpus. In mining, however, the miners' experience of nature and matter can still be glimpsed in the theories of metallic genesis that came to be codified in the texts of sixteenth-century scholars.

Notes

1. Theophrastus von Hohenheim, called Paracelsus, 'On the miners' sickness and other miners' diseases', trans. George Rosen, in Henry E. Sigerist (ed.), *Four Treatises of Theophrastus von Hohenheim called Paracelsus* (Baltimore, MD: The Johns Hopkins University Press, 1941), p. 91.
2. Tim Ingold, *The Perception of the Environment: Essays in Livelihood, Dwelling and Skill* (London and New York: Routledge, 2000), p. 345.
3. See Raymond Tallis, *The Hand: A Philosophical Inquiry into Human Being* (Edinburgh: Edinburgh University Press, 2004), and especially Ingold, *Perception of the Environment*.
4. Among other disciplines, anthropology and sociology of knowledge (especially that inspired by actor–network theory) have produced much work contesting this dichotomous view.
5. Robert Tarule, *The Artisan of Ipswich: Craftsmanship and Community in Colonial New England* (Baltimore, MD: The Johns Hopkins University Press, 2004), chapter 1.
6. For a discussion of craft practices such as these, see Pamela H. Smith, *The Body of the Artisan* (Chicago: University of Chicago Press, 2004).

7 For a fuller statement of and references to the foregoing discussion, see Pamela H. Smith 'Making as knowing: craft as natural philosophy', in Pamela H. Smith, Amy R. W. Meyers, and Harold J. Cook (eds), *Ways of Making and Knowing: The Material Culture of Empirical Knowledge* (Ann Arbor: University of Michigan Press, 2014).

8 Vannoccio Biringuccio, *The Pirotechnia*, trans. Cyril Stanley Smith and Martha Teach Gnudi (New York: Basic Books, 1943), p. 250.

9 For these practices, see my discussion in Smith, 'Making as knowing'.

10 Anon., *Kunstbüchlein* (Augsburg: Michael Manger, 1538), fol. 19v.

11 The warmth of dung, approximately equal to a hen brooding an egg, was classified as the first degree of heat by the medical and chemical systematizer Herman Boerhaave (1669–1738). See John C. Powers, 'Measuring fire: Herman Boerhaave and the introduction of thermometry into chemistry', in Seymour Mauskopf, Bill Newman, and Matthew Eddy (eds), *Chemical Knowledge in the Early Modern World*, Osiris 29 (forthcoming, 2014).

12 Francesca G. Bewer, 'The sculpture of Adriaen de Vries: A technical study', in Debra Pincus (ed.), *Small Bronzes in the Renaissance* (Washington, DC: Center for Advanced Study in the Visual Arts, 2001), pp. 159–93. Michael W. Cole, 'Cellini's blood', *The Art Bulletin* 81:2 (1999), pp. 215–35; Michael W. Cole, *Cellini and the Principles of Sculpture* (Cambridge: Cambridge University Press, 2002); and Michael W. Cole, 'The Medici *Mercury* and the breath of bronze', in Peta Motture (ed.), *Large Bronzes in the Renaissance* (New Haven, CT: Yale University Press, 2003), pp. 129–53.

13 On different sorts of blood, see for example the recipes in the collection written down in the Monastery of Tegernsee in the fourteenth and fifteenth centuries: Anna Bartl, Christoph Krekel, Manfred Lautenschalger, and Doris Oltrogge, *Der 'Liber illuministarum' aus Kloster Tegernsee* (Stuttgart: Franz Steiner Verlag, 2005), and especially the discussion by Christoph Krekel and Manfred Lautenschlager, 'Bearbeitung von Glas, Edestein, Bein und Horn', p. 675.

14 I treat this in Pamela H. Smith, 'Vermilion, mercury, blood, and lizards: Matter and meaning in metalworking', in Ursula Klein and Emma Spary (eds), *Materials and Expertise in Early Modern Europe: Between Market and Laboratory* (Chicago: University of Chicago Press, 2010), pp. 29–49.

15 Joannes Jonstonus, *A History of the Wonderful Things of Nature* (London: John Streater, 1657), p. 92. My thanks to Dániel Margócsy for this reference.

16 Paracelsus, 'On the miners' sickness', p. 112.

17 H.G., 'The goldsmith's storehouse', 1604, Folger Library, V.a. 179, fol. 59r.

18 See the useful Jon U. Nef, 'Mining and metallurgy in medieval civilisation', in M.M. Postan and Edward Miller (eds), asst. Cynthia Postan, *The Cambridge Economic History of Europe*, vol. 2: *Trade and Industry in the Middle Ages*, 2nd ed. (Cambridge: Cambridge University Press, 1987).

19 Quoted in Albertus, *Book of Minerals*, trans. Dorothy Wyckoff (Oxford: Clarendon Press, 1967), p. xxviii.

20 Albertus, *Book of Minerals*, p. 153.

21 Albertus, *Book of Minerals*, p. 153.

22 Albertus, *Book of Minerals*, chapter 4, pp. 46–7.

23 Albertus, *Book of Minerals*, pp. 48–9.

24 Albertus, *Book of Minerals*, p. 51.

25 Albertus, *Book of Minerals*, p. 200.

26 Albertus, *Book of Minerals*, p. 200.

27 Albertus, *Book of Minerals*, pp. 165–6.

28 Albertus, *Book of Minerals*, pp. 169–70. For Aristotle, any explanation consisted of explicating the four causes – the material, formal, efficient and final: i.e. the material of which a thing consists, the form of the thing, the cause by which it is brought into being, and its use or function.
29 Albertus, *Book of Minerals*, p. 128.
30 Wilhelm Pieper, *Ulrich Rülein von Calw und sein Bergbüchlein, Freiberger Forschungshefte* (East Berlin: Akademie Verlag, 1955). Facsimile reprint of the first edition (1505) of the *Bergbüchlein*, Bibliothèque Nationale, Paris. See also Anneliese Grünhaldt Sisco and Cyril Stanley Smith (eds), *Bergwerk – und Probierbüchlein: a translation from the German of the Bergbüchlein, a sixteenth-century book on mining geology, by Anneliese Grünhaldt Sisco; and of the Probierbüchlein, a sixteenth-century work on assaying* (New York: American Institute of Mining and Metallurgical Engineers, 1949).
31 Georgius Agricola, *Bermannus, sive de re metallica* (Basel: Froben, 1530), trans Helmut Wilsdorf (Berlin: VEB Deutscher Verlag der Wissenschaften, 1955), p. 126.
32 Georgius Agricola, *De ortu et causis subterraneorum libri V* (Froben, 1544; republished 1555), *Ausgewählte Werke*, trans. Georg Fraustadt and Hans Prescher (Berlin: VEB Deutscher Verlag der Wissenschaften, 1956), p. 9.
33 Georgius Agricola, *De natura fossilium*, ed. and trans. Mark Chance Bandy and Jean A. Bandy (New York: Geological Society of America, 1955).
34 This converged with the importance given to place by Albertus in his theory that minerals came into being through the influence of the planets as it rained down on particular locales.
35 Lazarus Ercker, *Treatise on Ores and Assaying* (1580), trans. Anneliese Grünhaldt Sisco and Cyril Stanley Smith (Chicago: University of Chicago Press, 1951), p. 12.
36 Warren Alexander Dym, 'Mineral fumes and mining spirits: Popular culture in the *Sarepta* of Johann Mathesius (1504–65)', *Renaissance and Reformation Review* 8 (2006), pp. 161–85, pp. 169ff.
37 Georg Schreiber, *Der Bergbau in Geschichte, Ethos und Sakralkultur*, Wissenschaftliche Abhundlungen der Arbeitsgemeinschaft für Forschung des Landes Nordrhein-Westfalen, 21 (Cologne and Opladen: Westdeutscher Verlag, 1962), p. 186. A discussion of Agricola's publication of vocabulary lists is in the 1955 edition of Agricola, *Bermannus*: the 1518 and 1527 editions of the *Wormser Bergbuch* included vocabulary lists (p. 175). Agricola published 76 vernacular miners' expressions with the first edition of his *Bermannus* and 127 with the next edition (p. 169).
38 Biringuccio, *Pirotechnia*, p. 13.
39 Biringuccio, *Pirotechnia*, p. 46.
40 Biringuccio, *Pirotechnia*, pp. 46–7.
41 Biringuccio, *Pirotechnia*, pp. 53–4.
42 Biringuccio, *Pirotechnia*, p. 405.
43 Agricola, *De natura fossilium*, p. 7.
44 Agricola, *De natura fossilium*, p. 8.
45 Agricola, *De natura fossilium*, p. 59.
46 Agricola, *De ortu*, pp. 100–2.
47 Agricola, *De natura fossilium*, pp. 8, 59.
48 Alvaro Alonzo Barba, *Arte de los Metales*, originally written as a report in 1637 and published in Madrid in 1640, trans. Ross E. Douglass and E.P. Mathewson (New York: John Wiley & Sons, 1923), p. 3.
49 Agricola, *De natura fossilium*, p. 7.
50 Barba, *Arte*, p. 3.

51 Agricola, *De natura fossilium*, p. 7.
52 Agricola, *De ortu*, p. 101.
53 Agricola, *De natura fossilium*, p. 8.
54 Biringuccio, *Pirotechnia*, pp. 60–1.
55 Biringuccio, *Pirotechnia*, p. 67.
56 Biringuccio, *Pirotechnia*, p. 114.
57 Warren Alexander Dym, *Divining Science: Treasure Hunting and Earth Science in Early Modern Germany* (Leiden: Brill, 2010).
58 For an overview, see Dym, 'Mineral fumes and mining spirits', pp. 170–2.
59 Pseudo-Aristotle, *On the Cosmos*, trans. E.S. Forster and D.J. Furley, Loeb Classical Library, vol. 3 (Cambridge, MA: Harvard University Press, 1955), pp. 375–7.
60 Georgius Agricola, *De animantibus subterraneis liber* (Froben, 1549, then revised 1556), *Ausgewählte Werke*, trans. Georg Fraustadt and Rolf Hertel (Berlin: VEB Deutscher Verlag der Wissenschaften, 1961), pp. 199–200.
61 Charles Webster, 'Paracelsus and demons: Science as a synthesis of popular belief', *Scienze credenze occulte livelli di cultura* (Florence: Leo S. Olschke, 1982), pp. 3–20, 18.
62 Other examples include Isaac Beeckman and Descartes, as recounted by Klaas van Berkel, *Isaac Beeckman (1588–1637) en de Mechanisering van het Wereldbeeld* (Amsterdam: Rodopi, 1983).
63 Biringuccio, *Pirotechnia*, pp. 20–1.
64 Agricola, *De ortu*, p. 131.
65 While Agricola's theories arose in a reciprocal dialogue with metalworkers and textual authorities, he did not agree with everything he heard from miners; for example, he does not agree with the miners who say that all fat substances adhering to stone in the mines are sulphur (*De ortu*, p. 167). Interestingly, on the basis of eyewitness observation, Bernard Palissy disputed that the so-called 'fat earths' are fatty. He argued that if they were fatty, cloth fullers would not use them to get the fat out of cloth. Palissy saw the generative component in these earths as salt (or the fifth element, as he called it), rather than fat. Bernard Palissy, *Admirable Discourses on the nature of waters and fountains, either natural or artificial, on metals, salts and salines, on rocks, earths, fire and enamels* (1580), trans. Aurele la Rocque (Urbana: University of Illinois Press, 1957), p. 221.
66 Dym, 'Mineral fumes and mining spirits', pp. 179–80. The first to use the term 'Guhr' in writing was the St Joachimsthal preacher, Johannes Mathesius. Anna Maria Alfonso-Goldfarb and Marcia H.M. Ferraz, '*Gur, Ghur, Guhr* or *Bur*? The quest for a metalliferous prime matter in early modern times', *The British Journal for the History of Science* 46 (2013): pp. 23–37, at pp. 24–5.
67 Agricola, *Bermanus*, p. 158.
68 Anonymous, Ms. Fr 640, probably late sixteenth century, Bibliothèque nationale, Paris, fols 159r–v and 90r. The framework of lean and fat is found in earlier texts such as the late-fourteenth-century Cennino D'Andrea Cennini, *Il libro dell'Arte (The Craftsman's Handbook)*, English trans. Daniel V. Thompson, Jr. (New York: Dover, 1960), with reference to pigments, such as pp. 26, 30.
69 Agricola, *De natura fossilium*, p. 24.
70 Agricola, *De natura fossilium*, p. 9.
71 Agricola, *De ortu*, p. 124.
72 Agricola, *De ortu*, p. 124.
73 Agricola, *De natura fossilium*, p. 22.
74 Agricola, *De natura fossilium*, p. 23.

75 Agricola, *De natura fossilium*, pp. 21–4.
76 Agricola, *De natura fossilium*, p. 24.
77 Theophrastus, *De causis plantarum*, trans. Benedict Einarson and George K.K. Link (Cambridge, MA: Harvard University Press, 1976), vol. 1, book II, 4.2, p. 225.
78 Theophrastus, *De causis plantarum*, vol. 1, book II, 4.5–4.6, pp. 227–8.
79 Georgius Agricola, *De re metallica* (1556), trans. Herbert Clark Hoover and Lou Henry Hoover (New York: Dover Publications, 1950), p. 276.
80 Biringuccio, *Pirotechnia*, p. 391.
81 Biringuccio, *Pirotechnia*, p. 361.
82 Biringuccio, *Pirotechnia*, p. 296.
83 Biringuccio, *Pirotechnia*, p. 257.
84 Biringuccio, *Pirotechnia*, p. 324.
85 Biringuccio, *Pirotechnia*, p. 260.
86 Biringuccio, *Pirotechnia*, p. 297.
87 Biringuccio, *Pirotechnia*, p. 260n.
88 Biringuccio, *Pirotechnia*, pp. 332 ff.
89 Agricola, *De ortu*, p. 95.
90 Agricola, *De ortu*, p. 98.
91 Agricola, *De ortu*, p. 140. In this theory (pp. 133ff.), Agricola was arguing against Albertus, *De mineralibus*, who wrote that the growth of different minerals is to be attributed to the power of the stars (*De ortu*, p. 180), and against Paracelsus' statement in 'On the miners' sickness' that 'the seeds of the metals and the minerals have been sowed in the earth' (p. 108).
92 Agricola, *De ortu*, p. 137.
93 Benvenuto Cellini, *Traktate über die Goldschmiedekunst und die Bildhauerei (I trattati dell' oreficeria e della scultura di Benvenuto Cellini)*, trans. Ruth and Max Fröhlich, with technical commentary by Erhard Brepohl (Cologne, Weimar, and Vienna: Böhlau Verlag, 2005), p. 169.
94 Agricola, *Bermannus*, p. 158.
95 Agricola, *Bermannus*, pp. 162–3.
96 On Glauber's equation of 'Gur' with sulphurous spirit of vitriol (sulphuric acid), see Anna Marie Roos, *The Salt of the Earth: Natural Philosophy, Medicine, and Chymistry in England, 1650–1750* (Leiden: Brill, 2007), pp. 41, 46. On Boerhaave's use of Guhr, see John Powers, 'Scrutinizing the alchemists: Herman Boerhaave and the testing of chymistry', in Lawrence M. Principe (ed.), *Chymists and Chymistry: Studies in the History of Alchemy and Early Modern Chemistry* (Sagamore Beach, MA: Science History Publications, 2007), pp. 227–38. For seventeenth-century alchemical/chemical theorizers, 'Fatty earth' would also come to be seen as a foundational and transformative element in many material processes, informing the concept of 'phlogiston' and then 'oxygen'.
97 Alfonso-Goldfarb and Ferraz, 'Gur, Ghur, Guhr or Bur?', pp. 26–8. Even Isaac Newton wrote of 'Gur': William R. Newman, 'Newton's theory of metallic generation in the previously neglected text "Humores minerals continuo decidunt"', in Principe (ed.), *Chymists and Chymistry*, pp. 89–99, at p. 91.

3 ✧ On the origins of European painting materials, real and imagined

Anne Dunlop

THE SMALL PANEL reproduced here (Figure 3.1), by the artist Gentile da Fabriano, was painted in Florence in the early 1420s, possibly for the Archbishop of Pisa.[1] At first glance it is a typical Madonna image. Mary sits on a golden brocade cushion, covered in a deep blue robe also edged in gold. An elaborate plum-coloured fabric hangs behind her, dotted with dark-centred gold rosettes; the ground is covered with another fabric, this one gold with green and red fan-shaped flowers. Christ lies on cloth-of-gold in Mary's lap. The two gaze intently at each other, her hands crossed on her breast in adoration. It is a gesture she often makes in images of the Annunciation, and the suggestion of that moment is picked up on Mary's robes. Along the border and pooling at her feet are parts of the 'Ave Maria' written in small gold letters.

Yet while these Latin words are not easy to read, her enormous halo has a very clear inscription, right at the centre of the composition, in Kufic lettering (Figure 3.2). The Arabic inscription has been read several ways, but it may be the beginning of the Shahada, or creed of belief of Islam, 'there is no God but God'.[2] Its inclusion tends to locate the luxurious fabrics around Mary more specifically: they are Islamic textiles, with the most luxurious, the cloth-of-gold under Christ, identifiable as the 'nasij' woven from gold thread in central Asia. The back of the panel is a further shock, a complete reversal of the lush texture and pattern of the front. Turning the panel in one's hands (Figure 3.3) reveals a stark painted grid of inlaid marbles and precious stones, as close to geometric abstraction as Western painting would come before Piet Mondrian. Fictive porphyry is shown on the two long sides, and the centre seems to be serpentine marble. The framing elements would be marble from Carrara, while the four corners have notional insets of gems – lapis lazuli, amethyst, onyx, and amber or possibly topaz. The pieces between are perhaps to be understood as spinel rubies, much valued in medieval and Renaissance Europe.

On the origins of European painting materials

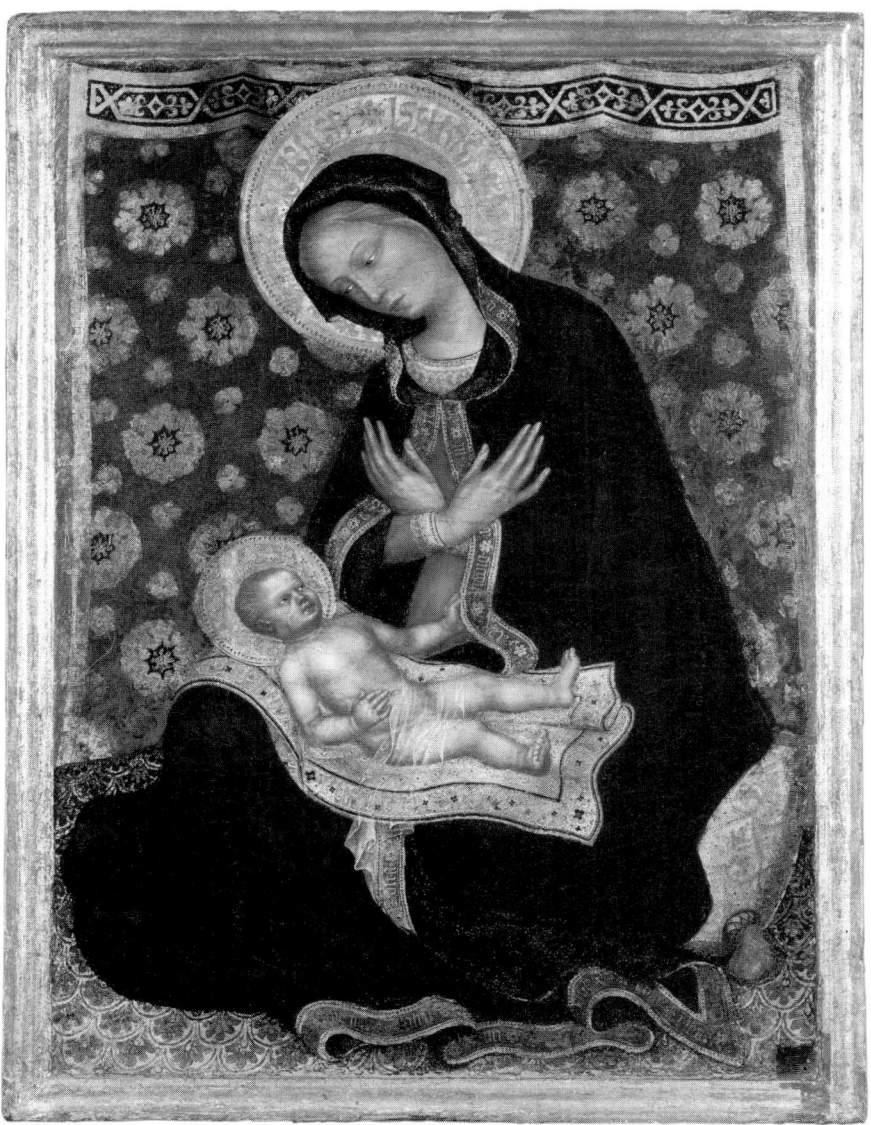

3.1. Gentile da Fabriano, *Madonna and Child*, c. 1421, tempera on panel, 60 × 45 cm, Museo Nazionale di San Matteo, Pisa

There are many other painted panels with 'stone' backs from the fourteenth and fifteenth centuries: a *Madonna and Child with Man of Sorrows* by Pietro Lorenzetti (Figure 3.4) has fictive metalwork and a splash of marble hardstone (Figure 3.5), while a *Madonna and Child* by Lippo Memmi offers painted marble and porphyry.[3] Such paintings are partial descendants of the portable hardstone altars created for elite

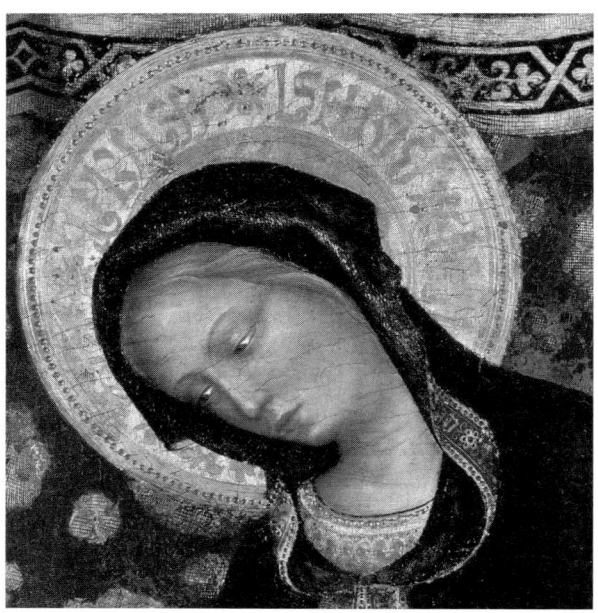

3.2. Gentile da Fabriano, detail of Mary's robes and halo (Zenodot Verlagsgesellschaft mbH)

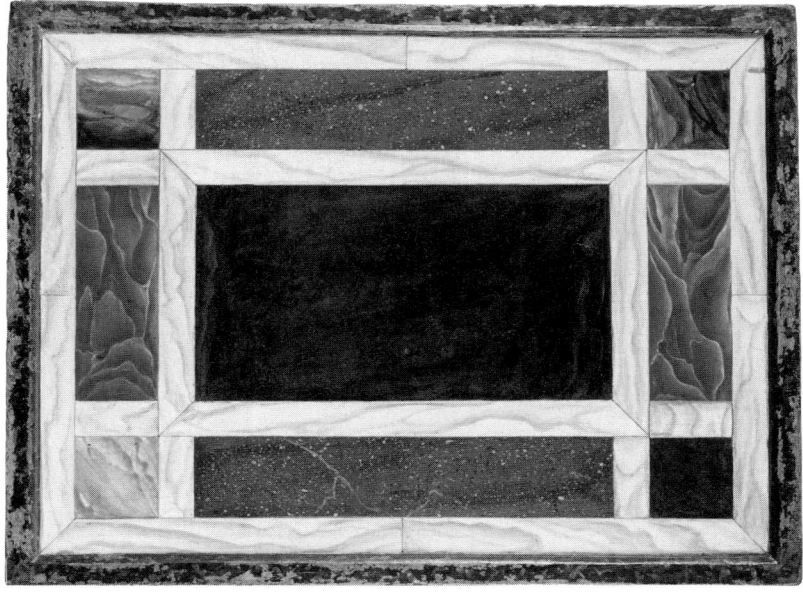

3.3. Gentile da Fabriano, fictive inlays and precious stones (reverse of Figure 3.1)

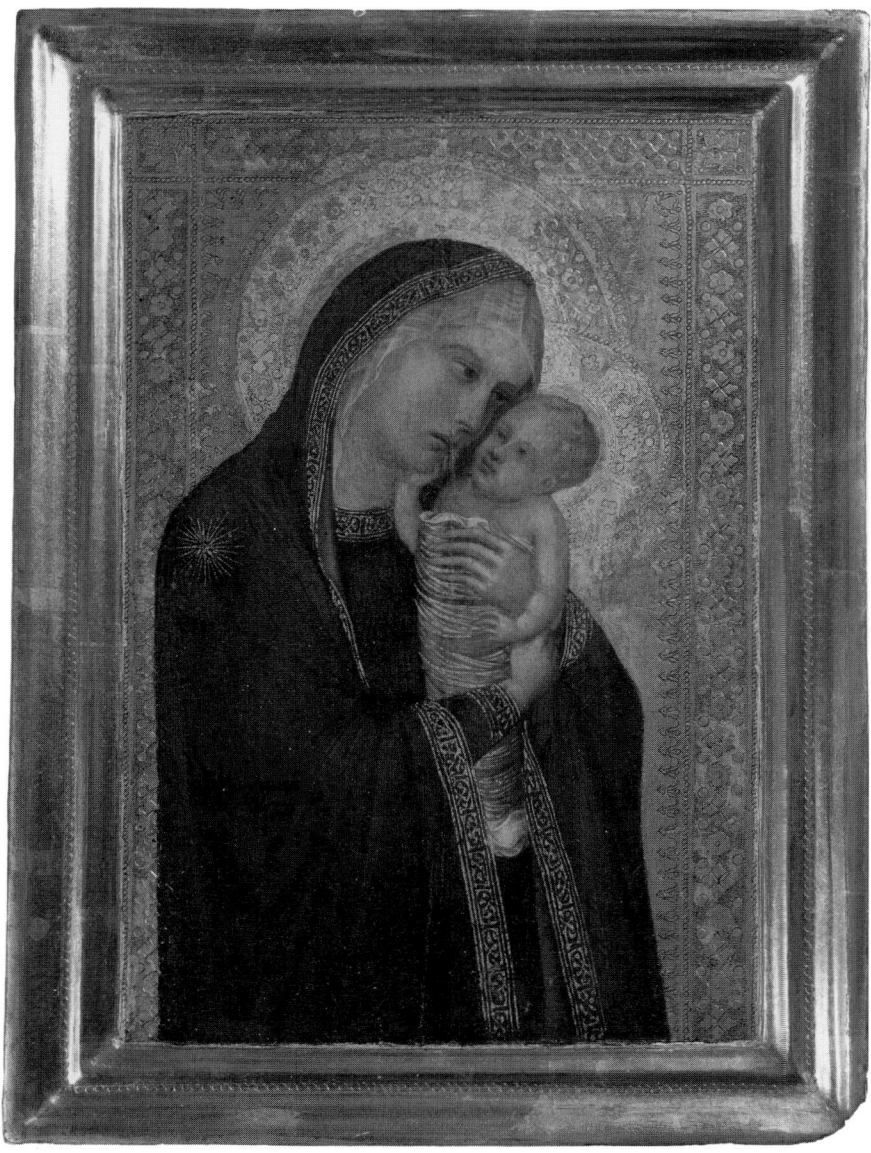

3.4. Pietro Lorenzetti, *Diptych with the Madonna and Child and the Man of Sorrows*, c. 1330, (left panel), tempera on panel, 35.3 × 26 cm, Lindenau-Museum, Altenburg, inv. 47

patrons throughout the Middle Ages.[4] Yet they also propose a conceptual link between the holy bodies they represent on their fronts and the fictive stones on the versos. In what follows, I will explore this link, and I will argue that it was intimately tied to ideas of origins, the spaces and forces that had shaped both saints and stones. This essay is intended

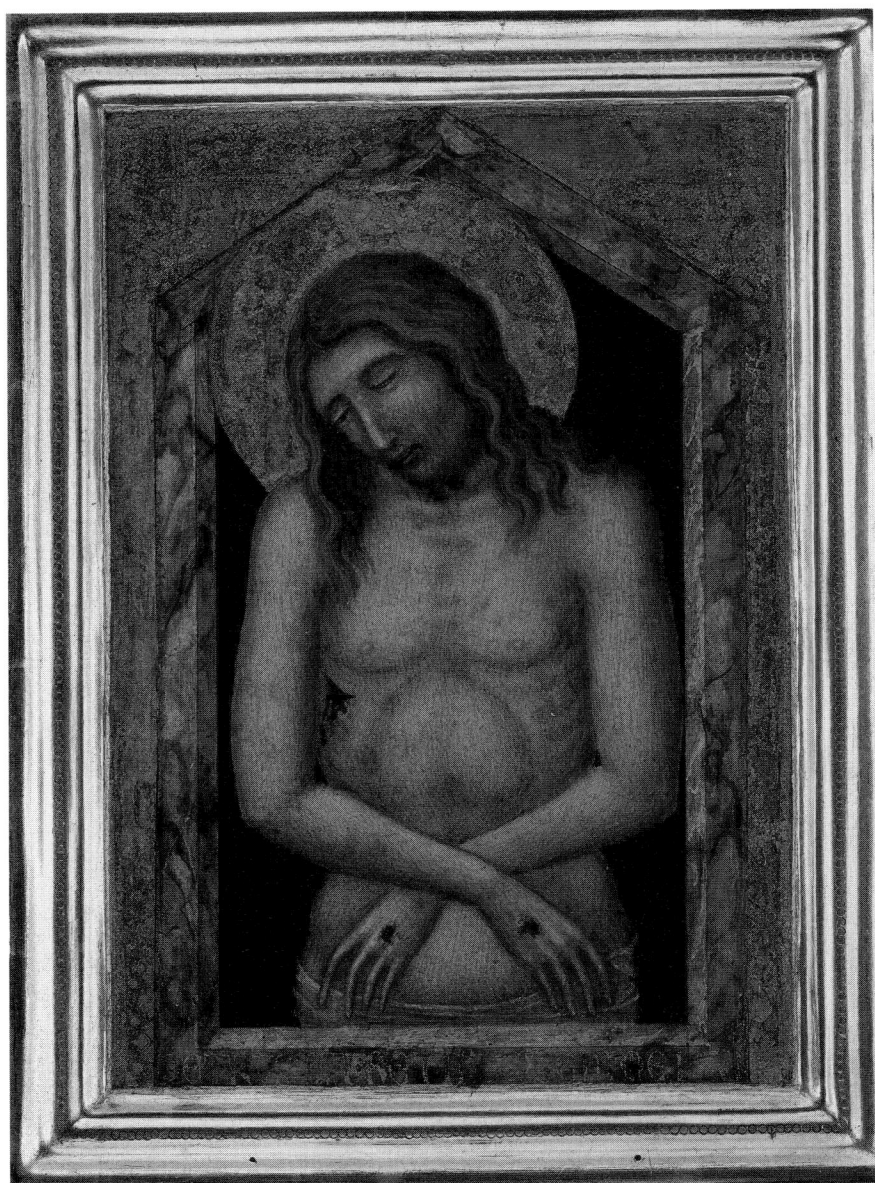

3.4. Pietro Lorenzetti, *Diptych with the Madonna and Child and the Man of Sorrows*, c. 1330, (right panel), tempera on panel, 35.3 × 26 cm, Lindenau-Museum, Altenburg, inv. 47

to complement the other essays on painting and pigments in this volume by providing a broad overview of tempera materials and techniques in the moment before the adoption of oil as pre-eminent medium. Beyond this, however, it is an argument for the semantic power of these materials.[5] A panel like Gentile's Madonna was made of pigments every bit as exotic

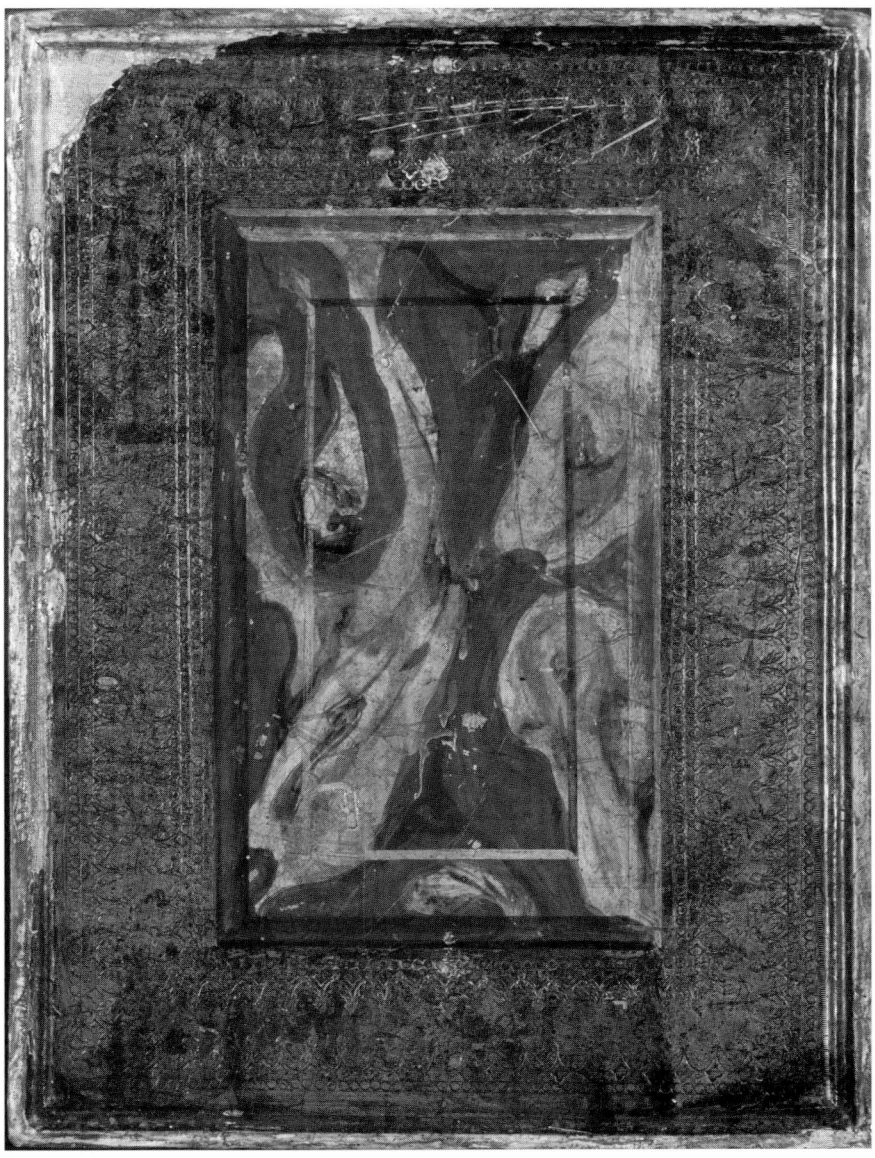

3.5. Pietro Lorenzetti, fictive inlays (reverse of Figure 3.4)

as Mary's nest of textiles or her kufic-inscribed halo – Asian stones and African gold, silver and tin from northern Europe and earths from local sources. At a moment when the idea of these spaces and places was shifting radically and rapidly, the geographies of materials, real and imagined, were at the heart of their associated meanings. In what follows I will take each of these points in turn.

Eggs and earths, stones and skins

Almost all our sources on early European painting are treatises on the properties and miseries of materials.[6] When Gentile and his contemporaries made a panel painting, they combined disparate materials with practical chemistry based on years of training, and things might go wrong at almost every step of production.[7] The panels themselves were most commonly made from local poplar, a fast-growing, lightweight, and soft wood found all over Italy, though walnut, oak, and other woods are also found. Poplar's major drawback is that it is quite sensitive to swings in temperature and humidity, and can bow and crack over time; it also is subject to dry rot as well as insect infestation.[8] Nails used to hold together the different elements were wrapped in tin to contain the inevitable rust. The wood was then coated with albumen-based glue size, derived from boiled-down fish scales, rabbit sinews, bits of parchment, animal skins, or other organic matter. This glue served to anchor multiple layers of linen and gypsum, or calcium sulphate dihydrate, a chalky substance found throughout the Mediterranean and easily ground to an opaque and porous white powder and paste. Ideally, coarser and then finer layers of gesso were brushed on, all bound to the panel with the same glue size. In the treatise on techniques written by the painter Cennino Cennini around 1400, he says that the first glue layers gave the wood an appetite for the gesso layers.[9] Once this relatively smooth and uniform surface for painting had been created, underdrawings, called *sinopie*, might be done in local charcoals or in sinoper, a red earth tone named for its origins near the Turkish city of Sinop. Areas to be gilded were often marked off by incised lines around the design, and received a ground of red clay called bole, its colour derived from the presence of iron oxides. Bole came from both local sources and modern Turkey and Armenia. Bole was ground with water and brushed on with either diluted glue size or egg white.

To make the actual image, any large areas of metal were applied first, soaked into the bole layer with correct amounts of water and ideally on damp days so that the bole would remain soft and humid. Given that silver will tarnish quickly, even when varnished, it is relatively uncommon, though occasionally found in small areas, usually glazed to provide some protection. Gold leaf on the other hand was widely used as a background, sometimes with decorative forms or important areas like haloes built up with gesso forms underneath them. The gold leaf was usually derived from beaten coinage, and there were specialists, the *battiloro*, who did this work. In Florence, the rate was set by guild statute: one florin coin was to yield a hundred gold leaves, giving some idea of the thinness and fragility of them.[10] If successfully applied, this gold could then be burnished, worked, punched, and tooled, either with patterned tools or freehand.[11]

At this point colouring could start, but here things got truly complicated. Tempera is a wet medium, closer in behaviour to watercolour than oil, with low refraction and high chroma, meaning that colours are pure, opaque, and intense. Paint was made of colouring agents drawn from organic, inorganic, and artificial materials, normally suspended in the yolk of chicken eggs. Cennino Cennini notes that eggs too contributed colour: city hens produced whiter yolks and country hens redder ones, meaning that city eggs were good for pale colours and country eggs for warmer ones.[12] Some oils, typically linseed or walnut, were also used, both with added colour to create tone, and, more generally, for glazing and varnishes.[13] Details might finally be picked out in gold dust stuck down with glue.

Early Italian painters were masters of the highly polished surface; tempera encourages hard outlines and hard reflection. But one of tempera's fundamental properties is that it does not blend easily. Layer can be built on layer, but the first must be dry enough not to gum up on contact, and yet not so dry that there is only temporary adherence. Further, not all pigments could be used together or were stable over time.[14] To build complex colours, layers of different types of colourant could be used. In central Italy, for instance, flesh tones were normally created by layering the opaque and highly reflective lead white – that is, lead carbonate – with vermilion, an intense red-orange that is chemically red mercuric sulphide, over terreverte. The first two were artificial compounds, although vermilion also occurs in nature; the last was an earth deriving a green tinge from the presence of the minerals glauconite or celadonite. Cennino often points to the limits or problems of materials, and his remarks are now supported by modern conservation science. He notes for instance that vermilion will turn black if used alone; a modern conservator blames the presence of alkali metal halides.[15] Another common red pigment, red lead, also turns if not protected by varnishes (it forms lead dioxide when exposed to air), and red from hematite, in addition to being difficult to grind, doesn't work on panel either.[16] Greens were not much better. Terreverte was found easily in central Italy, and was cheap and stable, but dull. What Cennino calls blue-green, the gemstone malachite ground into a powder, is pale and washed out and loses colour if ground too much; it was also, clearly, more expensive. *Verderame* or verdigris, created by exposing copper to vinegar, is quite stable, but Cennino felt it faded.[17] Cennino notes green can be created from various combinations of blue and yellow, including orpiment (arsenic trisulphide) and *indacho*. But *indacho* is indigo dye, imported and expensive and subject to fading, and Cennino condemns orpiment as it turns black in air and will make you sick if it gets in your mouth.

Most valued for blues was lapis lazuli, or ultramarine, the usual colour of the Virgin Mary's robe and still a semi-precious stone.[18] Chemically, it is the most complex of the mineral pigments, and its basic structure was not understood until the nineteenth century; diagrams of its molecules look something like three-dimensional and slightly melted snowflakes suspended within cubes which have octahedrons at the corners.[19] Its intense hue comes from a substance called lazurite; the colour is ultimately derived from the presence of sulphur.[20] The other components of the lattice are oxygen and sodium, silicon and aluminium. To make the mineral suitable for painting, the blue lazurite must be separated from the colourless calcite in which it occurs. It is a laborious process, as Cennino and others note, done by grinding dry pigment, combining the pulverized mixture into a mass with pine resin, gum mastic, and/or beeswax, and then kneading it and working it over two to four weeks. This mixture was then placed in a basin with an alkaline solution of potassium carbonate typically obtained from ash; the separated pigment was eventually collected by decanting. Lapis is intensely coloured and extremely stable once all this is done, particularly in tempera; the egg yolk binder seems to coat and protect the colour against atmospheric gases and the discoloration that can occur in other media, including in oil.[21] Unfortunately, as the name 'ultramarine' suggests, lapis was imported, and by far the most expensive material of the palette. In an account of 1347 the price hovered between about three and four lire an ounce, an amount that bought one hundred leaves of gold leaf, and by 1394 it was costed at six lire and fourteen soldi an ounce.[22]

For most painting, a different mineral, azurite, was used instead. It is a copper-based blue chemically related to malachite, and much less stable over time.[23] Azurite was cheaper than lapis, though not cheap, as it was also imported. Major sources came from northern Europe and as such it was called German blue, 'azzurro della Magna' or 'della Magnia'. Renaissance viewers saw this expense. In contracts, the cost of materials, and responsibility for them, is normally defined; in the few comments we have on art before Vasari, cost is often stressed.[24] Precious materials would attract the worshipper's gaze; they stressed the patron's or the owner's wealth, and also honoured the holy figures. This aspect of conspicuous consumption is often noted by modern scholars. Yet there is another side to these pigments which deserves attention, already suggested in their premodern names: ultramarine, blue of Germany, or 'indacho bacchadeo', combining the material's origin in far-off India and its normal trade route into Europe via Baghdad, the most powerful city of the Islamic world. The materials of early painting were tied to a wider world and all the marvels in it, and these real and imagined geographies were arguably inherent to the meanings of the panels created with them.

The expanding world

From the modern point of view, a defining feature of early painting is the use of gold grounds. Such works are still sometimes called 'gold backs', a designation that overlaps with the older term 'primitives'. But as discussed in this volume by Irma Passeri, the gold that backed European Madonnas around 1300 or 1400 had only recently become so profuse.[25] For much of the Middle Ages, sub-Saharan Africa was the major source of old-world gold. 'Ghana the land of gold' is first mentioned at the end of the eighth century by a geographer, Al-Faziri, in far-away Baghdad.[26] In the tenth century, the mines of the Bambouk region on the Senegal river in modern Mali were recorded by the geographer and poet al Hamdani (c. 893–945) in the south of the Arabian peninsula, who claimed the mines of the kingdom of 'Ghanah' were the most productive in the world.[27] The rise in the late twelfth century of the kingdom of Mali on the Niger river increased the volume of exchange, both because of the strength and stability of the state, and because new mines were opened at Boure.[28] From Mali, gold was ferried across the Sahara by camel caravans, running north via Awdaghost (modern Tegdaoust), or Taghaza to Sijilmasa (near modern Rissani, Morocco). This trans-Saharan trade exchanged gold for salt and other commodities, and it was encouraged by successive Islamic states in the Magrib.[29] By the thirteenth century, the northern terminus was in modern Tunisia, controlled by the Hafsid dynasty of Tunis. The Hafsids signed trade treaties with Pisa, Venice, Genoa, and Sicily in the 1230s, and by the end of the 1250s had risen to such power that the sharif of Mecca recognized the Tunisian ruler as Calif of Islam.[30] By the same era Italian merchant ships had increased in size, and no longer had to use Sicily as a stepping stone back to their own ports. Metal was shipped into Europe on Italian, especially Venetian, galleys.[31]

These changes in the gold trade coincided with a shift in European demand. For much of the medieval period, European states used silver for coinage.[32] In the thirteenth century, however, expanding and ever-wealthier Italian trade states shifted to gold currency, and weakening Islamic states in the Magrib were moving to silver. Unlike gold, silver was a northern European commodity. The main mines were in Central Europe: Silesia, Hungary, Bohemia, and Germany.[33] There were also sources in Dalmatia, and from the fourteenth century and especially in the fifteenth, silver was extensively mined, along with lead, copper, tin, and some gold, in Serbia and Bosnia. The trade from Dalmatia was controlled by merchants and owners from the Republic of Ragusa, which was subject directly to Venice until 1358; even after that, however, this metal flowed overwhelmingly into Venice, usually on Venetian ships, before making its way south across the Mediterranean.[34] A Venetian merchant's book known as the *Zibaldone da Canal* noted that the bankers of Venice bought silver from Germany and Hungary, which was impure, and refined it, and that the mint in Venice would pay merchants for gold but refused anything that was less than 23.5 carats in purity.[35] The first significant European gold mine was only opened in Serbia in 1252, the same year that both Genoa and Florence began minting gold coins as trade currency rather than as coins of record.[36] By the trecento all the major Italian trading powers were minting gold coins, and what happened next was predictable. From about 1240 to 1340, the cost of gold almost doubled in southern Europe, even as trade volumes increased, and it almost trebled in northern Europe, where demand in the south encouraged a flow out of local economies. The situation stabilized in the 1360s, but there was further inflation in the mid-quattrocento.[37]

Lapis lazuli, the other major precious pigment, was also newly profuse, and even more exotic. Though found in Georgia and Armenia, the major sources were in central Asia.[38] Its usual names still reflect this journey: 'lapis lazuli' is a linguistic hybrid, the Latin word for stone joined to a Latinized form of the Persian word for blue; ultramarine, meaning 'from over the sea' was first used as an adjective, to distinguish the blue from other forms. The most important mine was at Sar-el-Sang, 3,600 metres above sea level in the mountains in what is now northeastern Afghanistan. Because of weather the mines are still accessible for no more than five months a year; the path to them is rebuilt every spring after the winter snows and rains. Rocks will vary from a few kilograms to as much as 100 kilograms, though most are small. Lapis is found in veins of limestone or occasionally granite, and always contains calcite and pyrite. Traditionally, the mineral was extracted by heating the rock around it with small fires and then rinsing the stone with cold water. The sudden change in temperature would cause small splits, making the stone easier to cleave with pick-axes. Lapis was a minor if notable commodity in Asian trade into Europe. Given the relatively small volumes involved, stones may have been carried among merchants' personal effects, thereby subtracting them from customs records and import duties.[39]

What had opened these trade routes to bring these materials and others into Europe, and what drove the rise of gold-based currency of record in Italian states, was the rise of Chinggis Khan (d. 1227), who, after conquering all traditional Mongol territories, moved out to take over much of the known world.[40] His name means Oceanic Ruler (i.e. ruler without end), and from 1206 he led Mongol armies in ever-expanding campaigns. The Mongols practised a form of inheritance that divided goods and power among all surviving sons but made all younger brothers subject to the oldest. At Chinggis's death the Mongol territories were divided among his four sons. By the winter of 1240–41, the armies of his successor Ögödei (r. 1229–41) had advanced into central Europe, occupying Hungary and reaching into Austria. In 1258, under Möngke Khan (r. 1251–59), the Mongols conquered Baghdad, traditional capital of the Muslim world. Their westward expansion was only halted by their 1260 defeat at Ayn Jalut by the Mamluk state of Egypt and Palestine. In the east, Kubilai (r. 1260–94) conquering southern China, declared a new, Mongol dynasty, the Yuan, in 1271. It would endure for almost a hundred years. The four khanates of Chinggis's descendants were quickly shaped by pre-existing cultures, and the links among them weakened with constant disputes of precedence and inheritance.[41] Yet for more than a century it was possible to travel through central Europe to the coast of China with a single form of laissez-passer through a single geopolitical space; and the Persian Ilkhanate in particular occasionally sought Latin Christian alliances in its struggles against both the Mamluks and other khanates.[42]

Janet Lippman Abu-Lughod notes that by the thirteenth century Eurasian trade was organized in eight blocks, which overlapped in specific towns and regions.[43] Until the Mongol rise, the Italians had successfully monopolized trade into and out of the European zone, with Genoa controlling links to the land routes through Asia, and Venice the links to Alexandria. But they had little direct access to zones immediately beyond Europe, in Muslim territories controlled by Mamluk, Arab, and Persian traders. The Mongols opened these routes, sometimes by destroying existing local powers; they also encouraged trade through a whole series of measures, including paper currency and state-sponsored way-stations. It has been argued that the Italian Renaissance as a cultural and artistic movement was driven by the immense surplus wealth that Italians accrued as the European middlemen for all this commerce.[44] In any case it seems less surprising that in the first decades of the trecento an Italian merchant gave a quite casual account of how to reach China, with a total travelling time of 271 to 284 days by ox, horse, water, camel, and donkey. He noted what could be bought and traded en route, with silk and fabrics alongside artists' pigments like lapis, indigo, and vermilion.[45] Ambassadors, legates, and missionaries also wrote accounts of their travels, as European courts and the papacy sought to establish relations and also congregations in the Asian East. A Franciscan, John of Plano Carpinis, was sent as an emissary to the Great Khan at the capital in Karakorum by Pope Innocent IV in 1240; on his return to Europe in 1241 John wrote a full account of his travels. He would be followed by other clerics, William of Rubruck, Odoric of Pordenone, and many others.⁴⁶ The most famous travellers of European history, Marco Polo and the imaginative Sir John Mandeville, also emerged in this moment.⁴⁷ There seems to have been a thirst for new information about this expanded world, and again, not only in Europe. In Baghdad, the Persian grand vizier and writer Rashid al Din (1247–1318), a Jewish convert to Islam who served the Mongol rulers, wrote a long history of the world and the place of the Mongols within it, including separate sections on China, India, and the 'Franks'.

As people circulated, so did commodities, ideas, and technologies, including those involved in European painting. We can take lapis as an example. In Italy quantities of lapis lazuli waxed and waned in these geopolitical shifts. Lapis is strongly attested in mid- and later duecento Siena, for instance, but occurs more sparingly as the trecento progresses and the Mongol empires begin to crumble.⁴⁸ Significantly, Duccio's two-metre-tall and four-metre-wide *Maestà* uses only lapis for its blues, despite its enormous size.⁴⁹ Just as importantly, however, a new technology for the creation of lapis pigment emerged. Lapis used in the Middle Ages was simply ground up and made into a paste. The laborious method of purifying and decanting described above, which results in a much richer and purer blue, is first recorded in the *Liber claritas*, probably translated into Latin in the thirteenth century. It was based on the work of a writer called Abu Ibn Musa Jabir Hayyan (d. c. 815), known as Geber in European sources and active at the court of Harun al Rashid.⁵⁰ After the thirteenth century, this new and better method is offered by almost any writer on pigments, including Cennino Cennini, as we have seen.⁵¹ Yet while renewed contact changed supplies and uses of pigments, it did not supplant old ideas about the places that produced them. Having examined the geographies of major pigments according to modern understanding and reconstruction, we can now turn to trecento and quattrocento ideas about these sources.

The secret life of pigments

Medieval Europe had inherited a worldview based in conflicting pagan sources and clear religious symbolism. Jerusalem lay at the centre (the navel) of a world in three parts: Africa, Europe, and Asia. Eden and Paradise lay in the east, although it was not clear where, and the races of each continent were the descendants of Noah's three sons, dispersed after the Flood. This is the form embodied by the so-called T-O maps, with the Don, the Nile, and the Mediterranean separating the three continents. The concept was given its canonical form by the fifth-century Spanish priest Orosius, in his *Historiarum adversus paganos, libri septem*.⁵² It was further spread by Isidore of Seville, whose *Etymologiarum* became the encyclopedia of subsequent Christians. More than 660 copies were created of Isidore's work in the Middle Ages, often illustrated with T-O maps.[53] Alongside this Christian cosmos there was information inherited from pagan sources, above all Pliny's first-century *Natural History*, which for instance placed what we call China off the west coast of Gaul and described its inhabitants as above-average height, golden-haired, and blue-eyed.[54] Brunetto Latini's encyclopedic *Livre dou Tresor* of the later duecento repeated this account almost verbatim.[55] Pliny in turn had inherited accounts of freaks and marvels going back at least to Herodotus, the *Indica* of Ctesias (c. 401 BCE), and Skylax, sent in the sixth century BCE by Darius of Persia to create an account of the Indus valley.

What this looked like as a mental world map is suggested by the so-called Catalan Atlas, done by the Jewish mapmaker Abraham Cresques around 1375 almost certainly as a gift from the ruler of Aragon to King Charles V of France.[56] Here the world beyond Europe extends further and in more detail than ever before. It is still sketchy for Africa beyond the Sahara, but the profusion of gold and ivory is noted in the descriptions of places and the ruler Musa Melli, called 'lord of the negroes of Guinea' (Mansa Musa of Mali, r. c. 1312–27), is shown holding an enormous gold coin. The King of Nubia is described as the enemy of Prester John. In Asia, a caravan of merchants crosses the central plain; beyond them, however, the Three Wise Men ride out of the east toward Bethlehem. In the east Kebek Khan is pictured, and said to be the most powerful ruler in the world (he ruled the Chagadai Khanate 1309–10 and 1318–26). At the edge of the world, behind the walls of Gog and Magog erected by Alexander the Great and protected by a demon, the Antichrist waits to claim the earth at the end of time. In the meanwhile, sources of gold and spices, stones and pearls, are marked all along the coast of Asia, men obtain diamonds from mountains, and pearl-fishers breathe under the sea by using incantations.

Something conceptually similar emerges in Marco Polo's mentions of lapis, blue stones of intense colour. These occur in three places, each more fantastic than the last. Polo explained that lapis lazuli was mined as veins in the mountains of a Muslim kingdom called Balascam (Badakhshan, the modern region of Sar-el-Sang), ruled by the descendants of Alexander the Great and the daughter of Darius of Persia; two nearby mountains were of made of silver and gold, a detail which can be traced back at least to pagan tales of Chryse and Argyre, mountains of gold and silver on islands in the India Sea, sometimes guarded by dragons or griffins, relayed among others by Pomponius Mela and Isidore of Seville.[57] Further east, according to Polo, there was lapis in the kingdom of Tenduc, ruled by the descendants of the legendary Christian king Prester John, all of whom were called George. This Christian kingdom was a high medieval legend, and had found new life with the initial coming of the Mongols.[58] Polo added that this kingdom also produced cloth of gold called *nasji*. On this, as with many trade goods, he was carefully exact. *Nasij*, from the Arabic *nasaja*, to weave, was in fact the most significant luxury good of the Mongol period, the cloth of gold that became court dress at the Yuan court and that clothed, covered, sheltered, and rewarded the highest elites of the Mongol courts. It is the cloth that Gentile da Fabriano has represented under the infant Christ Child. The merchant Pegolotti called these clothes 'nachetti', and by the fourteenth century Italians would get rich producing passable imitations.[59] Finally, but most importantly, in the imperial city of Kubilai Khan himself, there was an artificial hill covered with the most beautiful trees in the world, topped by a blue-green palace.[60] In Marco Polo's accounts, as on the Catalan Atlas maps, new knowledge and old myths coexisted.

This was also true for artists and their materials. We rate stones by chemical structure, hardness, or crystalline patterns. Metals are defined by their atomic structure and subsequent place on the periodic table. And yet with all their listed properties they are still a bit uncanny. Some will glow when rubbed, and others after exposure to light, a phenomenon already known to Herodotus.[61] Magnetic stones will draw metals to themselves or push them away; one stone can appear to grow from another and colours shift as crystalline patterns change in relation to ambient temperature and incorporated mineral impurities. The most famous stones, like the Hope Diamond, are often cursed in popular imagination. This ambivalent status has long roots. From the beginning in the Christian West, gems and precious metals were associated with the other-worldly and the world elsewhere, as Brigitte Buettner discusses in this volume. In the second chapter of Genesis, the first of the four rivers of Paradise, the Phison, comes from the land 'where the gold groweth', and where bdellium and onyx are found. In Exodus 28:9–21, twelve different precious stones adorned the breastplate of the priest Aaron, one each for the twelve tribes of Israel. The last book of the Bible, Revelation, describes the Heavenly Jerusalem as adorned with these same stones.[62] Augustine of Hippo suggested that diamonds, magnetic stones, and even quicklime showed that no marvel was beyond God's power; it was their oddity that caused the human mind to look beyond them to seek divine purpose.[63]

Such writers were helpful for those, like the twelfth-century Abbot Suger of Saint-Denis, who sought to justify the use of precious materials for church and cult. Such passages associated gold and gems with the Holy Land, and the phenomenon of pilgrimage is a reminder that sacred power had specific locations; materials brought from Africa or Asia came from the lands where Christ and his ancestors had walked. Yet what

Suger said is revealing: the beauty of gold and stones allowed him to feel he dwelt in a world between the shit and sediment of the earth and the purity of Heaven.⁶⁴ Like their exotic origins, this in-between quality is a persistent theme in premodern sources on gems and metals.

For Europeans around 1400, stones were classified above all by colour, leading to confusion in terminology.⁶⁵ Like everything in the world, they were mixtures of the four elements, fire, air, water, and earth – in this case, earth and water. And they hovered between the animate and the inanimate. The basic idea was Aristotelian, and laid out in the *Metrologia* and the *De sensu*, but it came into the later medieval West supplemented by Avicenna's (unattributed) explanation that water allowed a kind of coagulation of the earth to occur, under the action of either heating or cooling.⁶⁶ Metals were generated from the mixture of mercury and sulphur, their different natures produced by the greater or lesser presence of impurities from the four elements. Stones were made from the mixture of earth and water, their colours and properties depending on the amount of incorporated moisture and the specific earths in which they were generated.⁶⁷ Thus Albertus Magnus, in the mid-thirteenth-century *De lapidibus*, argued that stones were produced by a 'virtus generativa' or generative power, most common in India and the East, that imparted form to the four elements of creation.⁶⁸ This virtue generated stones in the same way that male seed impressed form on female menstrual matter in the human act of conception.⁶⁹ The power that created stones and metals was the same divine action that created human beings, and – crucially – that allowed human beings to create objects that continued to be linked to the properties of the natural world that had produced them:

> The principle of this science is that all things whatsoever, whether made by nature or by art, receive their impulse in the first place from the powers of heaven. In nature there is no doubt of this. But even in art it is recognized, because some [impulse], at the right time and not before, incites the heart of a man to make [something]. And this [impulse] can only be the power of heaven as the above-mentioned wise men say . . . Therefore we must conclude that if a figure is impressed upon matter, either by nature or by art, [with due regard to] the configuration of heaven, some force of that configuration is poured into the work of nature or of art.⁷⁰

The generation of these materials also gave them specific powers. Thus for example Albertus noted the use of lapis as a pigment, but also that it was a remedy for black bile, fainting, fever, and sickness in the eyes.⁷¹ The most popular lapidary of the period, by Marbode, Bishop of Rennes, written before 1190, claimed that lapis strengthened the body, and protected against harm, fraud, and terror. It could aid escape from prison, locked doors, or bonds. When taken internally, it had the power to cool the sick and to prevent excessive perspiration. It also cured eye sores, headaches, and ulcers of the tongue. Ground into milk, it cured sores in general. More generally, it had the power to overcome envy, reconcile people to God, and lead them to prayer.[72] It was also universally agreed that gold, the perfect metal, prolonged human life and greatly aided health.

Stones and metals also slipped between the organic and the inorganic, between geology and biology. Pliny's *Historia naturalis* explained that dragon's blood, a pigment used for painting, came from the petrified blood shed in fights between elephants and lions; and both Pliny and Albertus described stones that were formed in the bodies of fish or animals, or in the nests of serpents.[73] Albertus Magnus wrote: 'the specific form of individual stones is mortal, just as men are; and if [stones] are kept for a long time, away from the place where they were produced, they are destroyed.'[74] He also noted that he had seen a human skull with gold dust growing in the sutures of the bones, as if the one had generated the other.[75] An odd herbal from the Languedoc (Figure 3.6) showed lapis being mined from a deep pit guarded by a dragon, though the text in this part is missing and so we have no further explanation of its properties. It also, however, noted that gold was a metal which 'comforted all the members of the body and preserved youth'.[76] Like many other premodern elites, Italians sought to benefit from this life-extending power: at a banquet held in 1368 at the court of Milan, almost everything served in the eighteen courses had an outer covering of gold leaf, magnificent but also beneficent.[77]

We may seem to be a long way from painting, but painters spread this lore as they shared their own practical arts. Knowledge of the properties of metals and stones was disseminated through three major sources: lapidaries like those by Albertus and Marbode, treatises on alchemy, and recipe books for pigments and dyes made by artists and craftsmen. Each of these had a different emphasis, but the boundaries between them were porous, and perhaps also their audiences.[78] Just as lapidaries, by association of ideas, often discussed painting, painters' recipes were shared by alchemists.[79] Painters were reminded of the far-off origins and the associated properties of their materials every time they bought pigments from the *speziali*: thus in the pigment manuscripts, mostly Italian, collated by Jean Le Begue, we find: 'To make fine azure – you must take the Indian or Persian azure stone which comes from beyond the sea, and which is kept by the apothecaries, who use it in some of their medicines. That which has white veins is better than that which

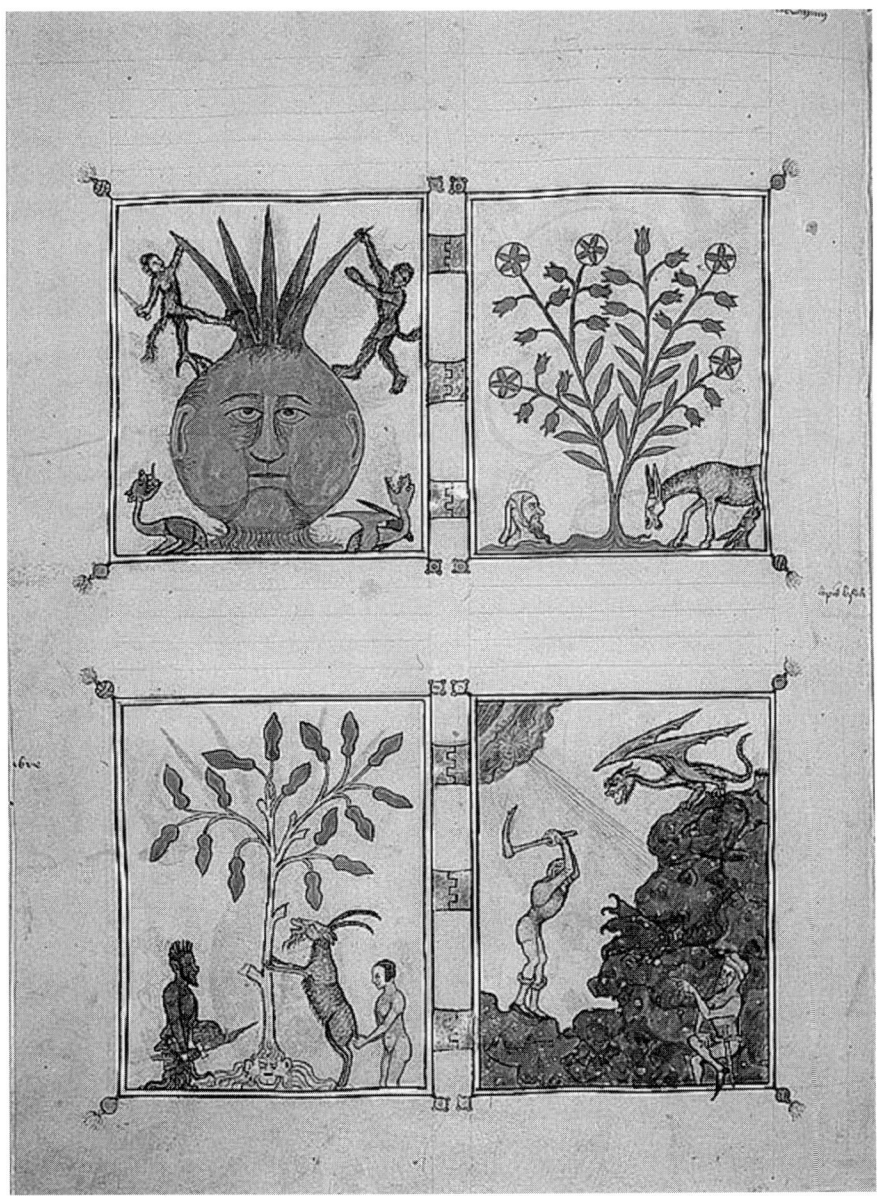

3.6. Languedoc, *Detti di filosofia in versi provenzali*, c. 1380? Biblioteca nazionale centrale, ms. Palatino 586. Florence

has gold veins.'[80] Like Albertus or Marbode, artists placed their materials on a scale ranging from the fully natural to the fully artificial, or at least they tried to do so: Cennino notes that he had heard *giallarino* (lead-tin yellow) came from volcanoes ('luogho di grande arsure di montagnie'), adding that it was therefore artificial, 'artificiato', but not alchemical, 'd'archimia'.[81] With more explicit intellectual ends, Alberti, in his 1435 *De pictura*, tied what he called the four basic colours – red, blue, green, and beige-grey – to the four elements of creation – fire, air, water, and earth. The remaining two colours, black and white, were light and darkness.[82] Painters were even associated with magic stones in broader culture. Boccaccio's tale of the artists Bruno and Buffalmacco tricking their fellow painter Calandrino with 'invisible stones' is only the most famous example.[83]

This play of visibility and invisibility moves us back to painting. When Cennino Cennini wrote his treatise on materials, he began by defining painting in just these terms, as the skills for 'revealing the unseen things hiding themselves within natural ones, and making the absent visible to the eye'.[84] It is a definition that points to surfaces, and to substances, and the most compelling evidence of artists' ideas about materials comes from the works themselves, like Gentile da Fabriano's little panel with its lavish front and stark and startling back (Figure 3.1). The *Madonna and Child* in Pisa was used for private prayer, and meant to be kept close to see how the materials of the work make up the image. At close hand there is a constant oscillation between surface and depth, substance and representation. The Madonna's collar and cuffs have been rendered by gold punched and scratched with the back of Gentile's brushes (Figure 3.2), as close to a gestural moment as tempera will allow. The fabric hanging behind the Virgin was created by laying an intense red lake pigment (now darkened) over the gold ground, and the florets scored freehand and stained with lapis at their centres.[85] The artist even stained the areas around the inscriptions on Mary's robe to make the letters stand out further against the metal ground. Mary herself is almost entirely a flat body of lapis. There is very little modulation to her form, beyond small lightened sweeps on her proper left side to suggest the folds made by the fabric collecting on the cushion. Elsewhere the painter created folds entirely by the sinuous line of the fabric edging and by clustering and spacing out small gold dots on the revealed green lining of her cloak, notably around Mary's face; at the bottom of her robe they trail like stippled stars.

All this is visible on the surface, and points to the process of making. It is harder to see how intimately Gentile knew his materials and how he experimented with the properties of his paints. Counter-intuitively, he often used colours with good opaque coverage in what seems to be oil binders to create glazes; conversely, he chose colours with greater transparency to cover ground.[86] Most complicated of all were his flesh-tones, which created a porcelain smoothness out of lead white probably mixed with some earth in an ochre tone; shadows were brushed on in a dark brown-green, and then the features were reinforced with a black-brown line. For lighter areas, a rosy colour was then laid on top, probably made from lead white with vermilion. Gentile used very little pigment to make flesh, and a lot of binder – which seems to have been both tempera and oil. From this mix of elements – earths and artificial compounds, dry egg and fatty oil – flesh was created.

The back of the panel is literally a different matter (Figure 3.3). Where the front surface is all surface effect and careful blending of intense colour, the dominant colour on the back is white, used here not only as a notional framework, but also to create almost all the surface effects, including transparency, ironically, while the only white used as white on the front is the cloth on Christ, almost transparent. Though the starkness of the white gridding is exacerbated in photos – the illusion of inlaid sections is much more convincing on the actual panel – it still seems as if two different modes of painting are in operation on the two sides of the work: the materials here are falser than the figures they serve to make. It is this distinction that suggests Gentile's thinking about the links of holy bodies and fictive stones that underpinned his own creation. In the years before his 1427 death, Gentile made a number of small devotional panels that were entirely painted over a gold ground, despite the cost and the reduced adhesion of tempera on metal. These had an extremely limited palette, using only dark outlines for features and lakes for colour.[87] The front of the Pisa panel is one of these panels. The holy figures float here entirely over gold, and Mary in particular is made almost entirely of lapis inflected by the same substance.

Mary and Christ were other-worldly creatures, and their images in a devotional image were not to be conflated with any existence in the viewer's world. The problem, once painters moved away from pure convention in their renderings, was how to create both presence and distance, how to make sure that the image pointed to a world beyond it. One way was to evoke distance in the most straightforward terms, and arguably this is one reason for the exotic textiles and for Mary's Arabic-inscribed halo that Gentile has pictured here. But these same far-off places had also created the strange properties of the stones and metals incarnating the holy figures by Gentile's hands. When Cennini spoke of revealing the hidden and absent within the natural, he might have been describing the back and front of this panel: when Gentile and his contemporaries painted the backs of their panels with fictive gems and metals, they were also evoking the hidden acts of creation that brought both art and matter into being, the power that once, in far-away Nazareth, had brought Christ into the world with the assent of his mother Mary.

Notes

I am grateful to my co-editor Pamela Smith for comments on this essay. Thanks also to Irma Passeri for discussions about goldbacks over the years.

1 Laura Laureati and Lorenza Mochi Onori (eds), *Gentile da Fabriano and the Other Renaissance* (Milan: Electa, 2066), cat. VI.1, 248–51. It has been suggested that the patron was Alemanno Adimari, Archbishop of Pisa (d. 1422), also resident with the papal *curia* in Florence in these years. Gentile painted a fresco, now lost, for Adimari's tomb in Santa Maria Nuova, Rome.

2 Vincenza Grassi, 'Le iscrizioni arabo-islamiche nell'opera di Gentile da Fabriano', in Andrea De Marchi (ed.), *Nuovi studi sulla pittura tardogotica: Intorno a Gentile da Fabriano* (Livorno: sillabe, 2008), pp. 33–44. The question of the inscription is surprisingly complicated. Martin Forstner, 'Zu Madonna mit der Schahada', *Zeitscrift der Deutschen Morgenländischen Gesellschaft* 122 (1972), pp. 102–7, sees the creed on both the halo and the border of the cloth-of-gold under the Child. Grassi reviews the earlier literature, but argues instead that the inscription is only pseudo-Kufic, and that the creed is on the border of the cloth-of-gold only. Conversely, Marco Bussagli, 'Misteri d'Oriente', *Art e dossier* 21 (May 2006), pp. 36–41, sees the creed on the halo alone.

3 Both are now in Altenburg. See Jochen Sander, 'Marien- und Christusbilder, depictions of the Virgin Mary and Christ', in *Kult Bild: Das Altar- und Andachtsbild von Duccio bis Perugino. Cult Image: Altarpiece and Devotional Painting from Duccio to Perugino* (Petersberg and Frankfurt am Main: Michael Imhof Verlag and Städelsches Kunstinstitut, 2006), pp. 177–211, at 178–84.

4 There is a beautiful example from Hildesheim with Purbeck marble, crystals, and ivories, now in the British Museum For this object: www.britishmuseum.org/explore/highlights/highlight_objects/pe_mla/p/portable_altar.aspx; www.britishmuseum.org/explore/highlights/article_index/c/conservation_hildesheim_altar.aspx (accessed on 5 February 2014).

5 I would cite Thomas Raff, *Die Sprache der Materialien: Anleitung zu einer Ikonologie der Werkstoffe* (Munich: Deutscher Kunstverlag, 1994) as the foundational study of materials as signifiers in premodern Western art.

6 For early treatises, see Mark Clarke, *The Art of All Colours: Mediaeval Recipe Books for Painters and Illuminators* (London: Archetype, 2001), with further bibliography; Sandro Baroni, 'I ricettari medievali per la preparazione dei colori e la loro trasmissione', in Paola Antonella Andreuccetti and Iacopo Lazzareschi Cervelli (eds), *Il colore nel Medioevo: Arte, simbolo, tecnica. Atti del Convegno di Studi, Lucca, 23–24 novembre 2007*, 3 vols (Lucca: Istituto Storico Lucchese, 2009), vol. 1, pp. 117–44; and Salvador Muñoz Viñas, 'Original written sources for the history of medieval painting techniques and materials: A list of published texts', *Studies in Conservation* 43 (1998), pp. 114–24. A number of early treatises are brought together in Mary P. Merrifield, *Original Treatises on the Arts of Painting*, 2 vols (New York: Dover, 1967), a re-edition of her 1849 publication.

7 For an overview of tempera practice, see David Bomford et al. (eds), *Art in the Making: Italian Painting before 1400* (London and New Haven, CT: National Gallery Company, distributed by Yale University Press, 1989); Jo Kirby, David Saunders, and John Cupitt, 'Colorants and colour change', in Tonnie Bakkenist et al. (eds), *Early Italian Paintings: Techniques and Analysis. Symposium, Maastrict, 9–10 October 1996* (Maastricht: Limburg Conservation Institute, 1997), pp. 65–71; Spike Bucklow, *The Alchemy of Paint: Art, Science, and Secrets from the Middle Ages* (London and New York: Marion Boyers, 2009); and Anne Dunlop, 'Materials, origins, and the nature of early Italian painting', in Jaynie Anderson (ed.), *Crossing Cultures: Conflict, Migration, and Convergence* (Melbourne: Miengunyah Press, 2009), pp. 472–6.

8 Bomford et al. (eds), *Art in the Making*, pp. 11–16, which notes that because of deforestation, Italian painters may have had little choice but to use poplar. In northern Europe,

the harder, denser, and more stable oak was preferred. See more generally: Kathleen Dardes and Andrea Rothe (eds), *The Structural Conservation of Panel Paintings: Proceedings of a Symposium at the J. Paul Getty Museum, April 1995* (Los Angeles: Getty Conservation Center, 1998); and Luca Uzielli and Marco Fioravanti, 'Il comportamento fisico-meccanico del legno nei dipinti su tavola', in Marco Ciatti et al. (eds), *Dipinti su tavola: La tecnica e la conservazione dei supporti* (Florence: Edifir, 1999), pp. 37–58.

9   Cennino Cennini, *Il libro dell'arte*, ed. Fabio Frezzato (Vicenza: Neri Pozza, 2003), p. 143: 'E ssai che ffa la prima cholla con acqua? Che viene a essere men forte e a punto, chome fussi digiuno e mangiassi una presa di confetto e beessi un bichiere di vino buono, ch'è uno invitarti a disinare; chosì è questa cholla, è un farsi acchostare il legniame a ppigliare le cholle e giessi.' Frezzato's edition is based on the two early manuscripts of the treatise, the Codex Mediceo Laurenziano P. 78.23 and Codex Riccardiano 2190, and includes (pp. 235–318) a useful technical appendix on pigments and methods. The standard English translation, based on the same manuscripts, is *The Craftsman's Handbook: The Italian 'Il Libro dell'arte'*, trans. Daniel V. Thompson, Jr. (New York: Dover Publications, 1933. 1960). For the book and its context: Wolf-Dietrich Löhr and Stefan Weppelmann (eds), *'Fantasie und Handwerk': Cennino Cennini und die Tradition der toskanischen Malerei von Giotto bis Lorenzo Monaco* (Berlin: Gemäldegalerie Staatliche Museen zu Berlin, 2008); and Andrea Bolland, 'Art and humanism in early Renaissance Padua: Cennini, Vergerio and Petrarch on imitation', *Renaissance Quarterly* 49 (1996), pp. 469–87.

10 Alessandro Guidotti, 'Battiloro e dpintori a Firenze fra Tre e Quattrocento: Bastiano di Giovanni e la sua clientela (dal Catasto del 1427)', in Cristina De Benedictis (ed.), *Scritti di storia dell'arte in onore di Roberto Salvini* (Florence: Sansoni, 1984), pp. 239–49; Robert Sabatino Lopez, 'Back to gold, 1252', *Economic History Review* 9 (1956), pp. 219–40. The Italian coins were twenty-four carat, weighing 3.53 grams in Florence, and 3.52 grams in Genoa.

11 These decorative punches were specific enough that they have sometimes been used as evidence for attributions. For an overview, see Erling Skaug, 'Painters, punchers, gilders or goldbeaters? A critical survey report of discussions in recent literature about early Italian painting', *Zeitschrift für Kunstgeschichte* 71 (2008), pp. 571–82.

12 Cennini, *Libro dell'arte*, pp. 170–1.

13 Yvonne Szafran and Narayan Khandekar, 'Varnish and early Italian paintings: Evidence and implications', in Bakkenist et al. (eds), *Early Italian Paintings*, pp. 108–19; Cennini, *Libro dell'arte*, pp. 129–32.

14 For early pigments and their properties, in addition to the sources above, see Anita Albus, 'Of lost colors', in *The Art of Arts: Rediscovering Painting*, trans. Michael Robertson (New York: Alfred A. Knopf, 2000), pp. 293–360; Philip Ball, *Bright Earth: Art and the Invention of Color* (Chicago: University of Chicago Press, 2001), especially pp. 24–102; and Robert L. Feller (ed.), *Artists' Pigments: A Handbook of their History and Characteristics*, 4 vols. (Washington, DC: National Gallery of Art, 1986–2007). There are a number of study institutes and collections for historical pigments, including at the Getty Conservation Institute, Los Angeles.

15 Vincent Daniels, 'The blackening of vermilion by light', in James Black (ed.), *Recent Advances in the Conservation and Analysis of Artifacts* (London: University of London Summer Schools Press, 1987), pp. 280–2. See also Rutherford J. Gettens et al., 'Vermilion and cinnabar', *Studies in Conservation* 17 (1972), pp. 45–69. Additional sources are given below.

16 Similar woes are traced in other painters' handbooks, including the Strasbourg manuscript of Master Henry of Lubeck, done in the later fifteenth century: *The Strasburg Manuscript: A Medieval Painters' Handbook translated from the Old German*, trans. Viola and Rosamund Borradaile (New York: Transatlantic Arts, 1966).

17 Rutherford J. Gettens and Elisabeth West Fitzhugh, 'Malachite and green verditer', *Studies in Conservation* 19 (1974), pp. 2–23.

18 There is a huge literature on lapis and ultramarine, following Michel Pastoureau, *Bleu: Histoire d'une couleur* (Paris: Le Seuil, 2000). For a first overview, see Bomford et al. (eds), *Art in the Making*, pp. 34–6; Claire da Cunha, *Le lapis lazuli: Son histoire, ses gisements, ses imitations* (Monaco: Editions Le Rocher, 1989); Spike Bucklow, 'A tale of two blues', in Stella Panayotova (ed.), *The Cambridge Illuminations: The Conference Papers* (London and Turnhout: Harvey Miller, 2007), pp. 205–13; and Spike Bucklow, 'Lapis lazuli: Moving stones at the heart of power', in Jaynie Anderson (ed.), *Crossing Cultures: Conflict, Migration and Convergence. The Proceedings of the 32nd International Congress in the History of Art* (Melbourne: Miegunyah Press, 2009), pp. 468–71.

19 Joyce Plesters, 'Ultramarine blue, natural and artificial', *Studies in Conservation* 11 (1966), pp. 62–91, here at p. 65. Plesters notes that the approximate chemical formula is $Na_{8-10}Al_6Si_6O_{24}S_{2-4}$.

20 D.D. Hogarth and W.L. Griffin, 'New data on lazurite', *Lithos* 9 (1976), pp. 39–54.

21 Kirby et al.; 'Colorants and colour change', pp. 65–71; and 'Researchers find why ultramarine blue fades', *ScienceDaily*, 10 October 2006, www.sciencedaily.com/releases/2006/10/061002214727.htm (accessed 6 July 2011).

22 Bomford et al. (eds), *Art in the Making*, pp. 201–2, and pp. 205–6 for tables of equivalence for weights and measures. There were twenty soldi in one libra. One ounce was approximately twenty-eight grams. See more generally: Jo Kirby, 'The price of quality: Factors influencing the cost of pigments during the Renaissance', in Gabriele Neher and Rupert Shepherd (eds), *Revaluing Renaissance Art* (Aldershot: Ashgate, 2000), pp. 19–42.

23 Rutherford J. Gettens and Elisabeth West Fitzhugh, 'Azurite and blue verditer', *Studies in Conservation* 11 (1966), pp. 54–61.

24 Michelle O'Malley, *The Business of Art: Contracts and the Commissioning Process in Renaissance Italy* (New Haven, CT and London: Yale University Press, 2005), pp. 101–48, Anabel Thomas, *The Painter's Practice in Renaissance Tuscany* (Cambridge: Cambridge University Press, 1995). O'Malley notes (p. 46) that blue and gold were the only colours consistently mentioned in contracts, and that even a medium-grade lapis was twelve times as costly as the most expensive azurite (p. 68). In the appraisal of Cosmè Tura's lost frescoes at Belriguardo five different blues were listed and appraised: 'azuro di biacha', indigo, 'azuro todescho grosso' and 'fino', and ultramarine (p. 66).

25 Irma Passeri, 'Gold coins and gold leaf', in this volume.

26 Nehemia Levtzion, *Ancient Ghana and Mali* (London: Methuen, 1973), pp. 124–52. See also Raymond Mauny, *Tableau géographique de l'Ouest Africain au Moyen Age d'après les sources écrites, la tradition et l'archéologie* (Amsterdam: Swets and Zeitlinger, 1967), p. 3.

27 Thomas Walker, 'The Italian gold revolution of 1252: Shifting currents in the pan-Mediterranean flow of gold', in J.F. Richards (ed.), *Precious Metals in the Later Medieval and Early Modern Worlds* (Durham, NC: Carolina Academic Press, 1983), pp. 29–52, here at p. 33.

28 Andrew M. Watson, 'Back to gold – and silver', *Economic History Review* 20 (1967), pp. 1–34, here at p. 28.

29 Levtzion, *Ancient Ghana and Mali*, pp. 124–52; Mauny, *Tableau géographique de l'Ouest Africain*, pp. 354–441.

30 Walker, 'The Italian gold revolution', pp. 37, 50.

31 Philip D. Curtin, 'Africa and the wider monetary world, 1250–1850', in Richards (ed.), *Precious Metals in the Later Medieval and Early Modern Worlds*, pp. 231–68, here at pp. 233–41.

32 Watson, 'Back to gold – and silver', p. 1.

33 Balint Homan, 'La circolazione delle monete d'oro in Ungheria dal X al XIV secolo e la crisi europea dell'oro nel secolo XIV', *Rivista italiana di numismatica e scienze affini* 35 (1922), pp. 109–56.

34 Desanka Kovacevic, 'Dans la Serbie et la Bosnie mediévales: Les mines d'or et d'argent', *Annales ESC* 15/2 (1960), pp. 248–58.

35 Beinecke Library, Yale University, ms. 327, unpaginated. There is a published edition: *Merchant Culture in Fourteenth Century Venice: The Zibaldone da Canal*, ed. and trans. John E. Dotson (Binghamton, NY: Medieval and Renaissance Texts and Studies, 1994), p. 32. The manuscript seems to have been compiled in the later trecento from early trecento materials; a later owner, one Niccolò da Bartolomeo da Canal, gave it its usual name. Later in the book (p. 83 in the edition), under the date 20 August 1311, there is information about the gold trade of Tunis, 'which is the capital of the kingdom of all Barbary'.

36 Walker, 'The Italian gold revolution of 1252', p. 43. Information on the extent of European gold production is contradictory. Louise Robbert, 'Monetary flows: Venice 1150 to 1400', in Richards (ed.), *Precious Metals in the Later Medieval and Early Modern Worlds*, pp. 53–77, at pp. 66–9, argues that Hungarian sources were important after 1337, when export of gold was made legal.

37 Watson, 'Back to gold – and silver', pp. 25–6; Nevtzion, *Ancient Ghana and Mali*, pp. 133–5. Homan, 'La circolazione delle monete d'oro', suggests that the shifts in the relative value of gold and silver were also driven by papal bans on trade with Muslim Egypt and by periodic Hungarian bans on the export of silver.

38 For mines and distribution: Lissie von Rosen, *Lapis Lazuli in Geological Contexts and in Ancient Written Sources* (Partille: Paul Åströms, 1988), pp. 8–20.

39 Louisa C. Matthews, '"Vendecolori a Venezia": The reconstruction of a profession', *Burlington Magazine* 144 (2002), pp. 680–6, at 682. Similarly, indigo is widely seen as a pigment in the thirteenth century, but unusual in the fourteenth.

40 For an overview see Christopher Dawson, *Mission to Asia* (Toronto, ON: University of Toronto Press, 1980), pp. vii–xxxviii; and Peter Jackson, *The Mongols and the West, 1221–1420* (Harlow: Pearson Longman, 2005). For an introduction to the art and culture of these states, see Stefano Carboni and Linda Komaroff (eds), *The Legacy of Genghis Khan: Courtly Art and Culture in Western Asia, 1256–1353* (New York: Metropolitan Museum, 2002); and James C.Y. Watt (ed.), *The World of Khubilai Khan: Chinese Art in the Yuan Dynasty* (New York: Metropolitan Musuem, 2010).

41 The Persian Ilkhanate fell in 1353. The Khanate of the Golden Horde in Russia and the steppes splintered into small states, as did the central Asian Chaghadai Khanate. In 1368 the Mongol Yuan dynasty of China was overthrown and then succeeded by the Han Chinese Ming dynasty.

42 Jackson, *The Mongols and the West*, pp. 165–95, gives an overview.

43 Janet Lippman Abu-Lughod, *The World System in the Thirteenth Century: Dead-End or Precursor?* (Washington, DC: American Historical Association, c. 1993), pp. 4–11; and more broadly Janet L. Abu-Lughod, *Before European Hegemony: The World System A.D. 1250–1350* (New York and Oxford: Oxford University Press, 1989). Through Italian ports like Genoa and Venice, trade between southern and northern Europe intersected with trade within the Mediterranean and Black Sea. At Alexandria it met the trade of the Red Sea region, and in Palestine, partially occupied by crusaders, it intersected with the trading zone centred on Baghdad and the Persian Gulf. These Middle Eastern zones were in turn linked to the enormously rich trade worlds of the Indian Ocean. A first trading region circled the Arabian Sea, while a second moved around India into the seas of Indonesia, south-east Asia, and the Bay of Bengal. The final and most important trade zone centred on China, where a

sea trade ran from the Bay of Bengal and Indonesia up the South China and East China Sea. Land routes, the so-called Silk Roads, moved from northern China through the oasis routes of Central Asia into the Caspian and Black Seas.

44 Richard A. Goldthwaite, *Wealth and the Demand for Art in Italy 1300–1600* (Baltimore, MD and London: The Johns Hopkins University Press, 1993), especially pp. 12–40.

45 Francesco Balducci Pegolotti, *La practica della mercatura*, ed. Allan Evans (Cambridge, MA: Medieval Academy of America, 1936), pp. 21–3; English trans. Robert S. Lopez and Irving W. Raymond, *Medieval Trade in the Mediterranean World: Illustrative Documents Translated with Introductions and Notes* (New York: Columbia University Press, 1955 and 1990), pp. 108–14 and pp. 353–8. The manuscript is in Florence, Riccardiana, ms. 2441, transcribed by Filippo Frescobaldi and dated 19 March 1472. It was probably compiled between about 1310 and the 1340s; Pegolotti was posted to Cyprus in the 1320s, which may be when much of the information was gathered. See in general Luciano Petech, 'Les marchands italiens dans l'empire mongol', *Journal Asiatique* 250 (1962), pp. 549–74.

46 In addition to Dawson, *Mission to Asia*, see Michèle Guéret-Laferté, *Sur les routes de l'Empire Mongol: Ordre et rhétorique des relations de voyage aux XIIIe et XIVe siècles* (Paris: Honoré Champion, 1994); and Gregory G. Guzman, 'European clerical envoys to the Mongols: Reports of Western merchants in Eastern Europe and Central Asia, 1231–1255', *Journal of Medieval History* 22 (1996), pp. 53–67. For Italian colonies in the far East: Robert Sabatino Lopez, 'Nuove luci sugli italiani in Estremo Oriente prima di Colombo', in Paolo Revelli and Giuseppe Rosso (eds), *Studi Colombiani: Atti del Convegno Internazionale di Studi Colombiani*, 3 vols (Genoa: Arti Grafiche ed Affini, 1952), vol. 3, pp. 337–98.

47 And not only Europeans: perhaps the greatest premodern traveller of all time, Ibn Battuta (1304–68/9), also travelled in this period and wrote about his experiences, as did Kubilai's emissary to Europe and the papacy, Rabban Bar Sauma, in the years 1287–88. See *The Travels of Ibn Battuta AD 1325–1354*, 4 vols, trans. H.A.R. Gibb and C.F. Beckingham (London: Hakluyt Society, 1994); David Waines, *The Odyssey of Ibn Battuta: Uncommon Tales of a Medieval Adventurer* (London and New York: I.B. Tauris, 2010); and *Storia di Mar Yahballaha e di Rabban Sauma. Un orientale in Occidente ai tempi di Marco Polo* (Turin: Silvio Zamorani, 2000), pp. 75–95.

48 Cathleen Hoeniger, 'The identification of blue pigments in early Sienese paintings by color infrared photography', *Journal of the American Institute for Conservation* 30 (1991), pp. 115–24. But cf. the exchange of letters by Hoeniger and Dan Kushel in the same journal, issue 31 (1992), pp. 141–3.

49 The limited palette of the *Maestà* (seven pigments and gold) was established in a 1952–58 restoration by Cesare Brandi. See Alessandro Bagnoli et al. (eds), *Duccio: Alle origini della pittura senese* (Cinisello Balsamo, MI: Silvana Editoriale, 2003), cat. pp. 2, 208–33.

50 Lucretia Kargère, 'The use of lapis lazuli as a pigment in medieval Europe', *Met Objectives* 4 (Spring 2003), pp. 5–7; Bucklow, *The Alchemy of Paint*, p. 44.

51 The most striking example is the anonymous mid-quattrocento writer of the north Italian *Segreti per colori*, who begins his manuscript with a whole section called 'De multis et diversis azurris naturalibus fiendis', and repeats the method later in the treatise that is reproduced in Merrifield, *Original Treatises*, vol. 2, pp. 340–83 and pp. 500–1. The second and third chapters are on making artificial blues and on making blues from plant sources. Merrifield (pp. 112–13) notes that ultramarine blue seems to have been unknown to Petrus of S. Audemar (Pierre de Saint-Omer), who compiled recipes before the end of the thirteenth century.

52 Orosius, *Le storie contro i pagani*, 4 vols, ed. Adolf Lippold, trans. Aldo Bartalucci (Rome: Fondazione Lorenzo Valla and Milan: Arnoldo Mondadori, 1976), 1, p. 16. For an overview, see: Alessandro Scafi, *Mapping Paradise: A History of Heaven on Earth* (Chicago: University of Chicago Press, 2006), pp. 160–90 and plates; J.B. Harley and David Woodward, *The*

On the origins of European painting materials

History of Cartography, Vol. 1: Cartography in the Prehistoric, Ancient, and Medieval Europe and the Mediterranean (Chicago: University of Chicago Press, 1987); and George H.T. Kimble, Geography in the Middle Ages (London: Methuen, 1938).

53 David Woodward, 'Medieval mappaemundi', in Harley and Woodward, The History of Cartography, Vol. 1, pp. 286–370, here p. 301.

54 Pliny, Historia naturalis X: Books 36 and 37, trans. D.E. Eichholz. Loeb Classical Library 419 (Cambridge, MA: Harvard University Press, 1962), book VI, p. 54: 'primi sunt hominum qui vocantur Seres, lanicio silvarum nobiles, perfusam aqua depectentes frondium canitiem ... Seres mites quidem, sed et ipsi feris similes coetum reliquorum mortalium fugiunt, commercia exspectant', p. 378 (VI, 88: 'ipsos [i.e. "Seras"] vero excedere hominum magnitudinem, rutilis comis, caeruleis oculis, oris sono truci, nullo commercio linguae. Cetera eadem quae nostri negotiatores: fluminis ulteriore ripa merces positas iuxta venalia tolli ab iis si placeat permutatio ...' p. 404.

55 Brunetto Latini, Li Livres dou Tresor, ed. Spurgeon Baldwin and Paul Barrette (Tempe: Arizona Center for Medieval and Renaissance Studies, 2003), p. 94. This edition is taken from ms. Escorial L-II-3, written for Alfonso X el Sabio of Castille. The passage reads: 'Aprés cellui outre toute habitasion des homes trouvons nos homes qui sont apellé Seir, que de foillies & d'ecorgies d'arbres, por force d'eiue, font une laine dont il se vestent lor cors. & sont humbles & passibles entr'iaus, & refusent compagnie d'autre jent: mes li nostre mercheant passent un leur fluves, & trovent sous la riviere toute mainiere de mercheandisse, que la puet estre trovés. & sans nul parlement, il s'esgardent as oils le pris de caschune; & quant il l'ont veu, il portent ce que il veulent & laissent la vaillance ou leu meimes.'

56 The map is in the Bibliothèque nationale, Paris, ms espagnol 30, as six parchment sheets (65 × 25 cm) mounted on wood and with leather bindings. For good online images, see: http://expositions.bnf.fr/ciel/index2.htm (accessed on 5 February 2014). There is a large bibliography on this work, but the best introduction is Hans-Christian Freiesleben, Der Katalanische Weltatlas vom Jahre 1375 (Stuttgart: Brockhaus Komm. Gesch., 1977). For a verbal equivalent, written, I suspect, by someone looking at a similar map, see Marcos Jiménez de la Espada (ed.), Book of the Knowledge of All the Kingdoms, Lands, and Lordships that are in the World, and the Arms and Devices of each Land and Lordship, or of the Kings and Lords who possess them. Written by a Spanish Franciscan in the Middle of the XIV Century, trans. Sir Clements Markham (London: Hakluyt Society, 1912).

57 Thomas Suárez (ed.), Early Mapping of Southeast Asia (Berkeley, CA: Periplus Editions, 1999), p. 72.

58 C.F. Beckingham, 'The achievements of Prester John' and 'The quest for Prester John', both in Between Islam and Christendom: Travellers, Facts and Legends in the Middle Ages and Renaissance (London: Variorum Reprints, 1983), pp. 4–24 and pp. 291–310.

59 Thomas T. Allsen, Commodity and Exchange in the Mongol Empire: A Cultural History of Islamic Textiles (Cambridge: Cambridge University Press, 1997), especially pp. 1–4 and pp. 60–70. See also Linda Komaroff, 'The transmission and dissemination of a new visual language', in Carboni and Komaroff (eds), Legacy of Genghis Khan, pp. 169–95; and James C.Y. Watt and Anne E. Wardwell, When Silk was Gold: Central Asian and Chinese Textiles (New York: Metropolitan Museum in cooperation with the Cleveland Museum of Art, 1997), especially the essay by Morris Rossabi, 'The silk trade in China and Central Asia', pp. 7–19.

60 Marco Polo, Il Milione, ed. Daniele Ponchiroli (Turin: Einaudi, 2005), pp. 37–8, 66–8, 82. This edition includes a modern Italian translation, 227–429; for English, see: Marco Polo, The Travels, trans. Ronald Latham (London: Penguin, 1958), pp. 76–7, 105–6, 127. See more generally Franco Brunello, Marco Polo e le merci dell'Oriente (Vicenza: Neri Pozza, 1986). In the case of the Khan's garden palace, both the English and the modern Italian translation use the word lapis explicitly, but Polo may in fact have meant azurite, as he speaks of 'terra dello azzuro, ch'è tutta verde'.

61 Sidney H. Ball, 'Luminous gems, mythical and real', *Scientific Monthly* 47 (1938), pp. 496–505, here at 499.

62 Revelation 21:18–21: 'And the building of the wall thereof was of jasper stone: but the city itself pure gold, like to clear glass. And the foundations of the wall of the city were adorned with all manner of precious stones. The first foundation was jasper: the second sapphire: the third, a chalcedony: the fourth, an emerald: The fifth, sardonyx: the sixth, sardius: the seventh, chrysolite: the eighth, beryl: the ninth, a topaz: the tenth, a chrysoprasus: the eleventh, a jacinth: the twelfth, an amethyst. And the twelve gates are twelve pearls, one to each: and every several gate was of one several pearl. And the street of the city was pure gold, as it were transparent glass.'

63 Augustine, *The City of God*, trans. Marcus Dods (New York: Modern Library, 2000), pp. 766–71. There are hundreds of similar passages in the medieval period. For compilations of allegorical links to colours and stones, see for example: Christel Meier, *Gemma spiritalis: Methode und Gebrauch der Edelsteinallegorese vom frühen Christentum bis ins 18. Jahrhundert* (Munich: W. Fink, 1977); Rudolf Suntrup '"Color coelestis": Himmel, Ewigkeit und ewiges Leben in der allegorischen Farbendeutung des Mittelalters', in *Cieli e terre nei secoli XI–XII: Orizzonti, percezioni, rapporti. Atti della tredicesima Settimana internazionale di studio Mendola, 22–26 agosto 1995* (Milan: Vita e Pensiero, 1998), pp. 235–60; and more generally John Gage, *Colour and Culture: Practice and Meaning from Antiquity to Abstraction* (London: Thames & Hudson, 1993). There is also now a CD publication with handbook, *Lexikon der Farbenbedeutungen im Mittelalter*, directed by Christel Meier-Staubach and Rudolf Suntrup, but I have not seen it.

64 *Abbot Suger on the Abbey Church of St.-Denis and its Art Treasures*, ed. and trans. Erwin Panofsky and Gerda Panofsky-Soergel, 2nd ed. (Princeton, NJ: Princeton University Press, 1979), pp. 63–5, Latin text 62–4: 'videor videre me quasi sub aliqua extranea orbis terrarum plaga, quae nec tota sit in terrarum faece nec tota in coeli puritate, demorari, ab hac etiam inferiori ad illam superiorem anagogico more Deo donante posse transferri.' Suger had just cited Ezekiel 28, 13: 'Thou wast in the pleasures of the paradise of God: every precious stone was thy covering: the sardius, the topaz, and the jasper, the chrysolite, and the onyx, and the beryl, the sapphire, and the carbuncle, and the emerald: gold the work of thy beauty: and thy pipes were prepared in the day that thou wast created.'

65 Hans Lüschen, *Die Namen der Steine: Das Mineralreich in Spiegel der Sprache* (Thun: Ott, 1979). There is an enormous bibliography on lapidaries and the powers of stones. For an introduction, see: Camillo Leonardi, *Les pierres talismaniques: Speculum lapidum, livre III*, ed. and trans. Claude Lecouteux and Anne Monfort (Paris: Presses de l'Université de Paris-Sorbonne, 2002), pp. 7–41; Joan Evans, *Magical Jewels of the Middle Ages and the Renaissance Particularly in England* (Oxford: Clarendon, 1932); Léon Baisier, *The Lapidaire Chrétien, Its Composition, Its Influence, Its Sources* (Washington, DC: The Catholic University of America, 1936); and the essay of Brigitte Buettner in this volume.

66 Robert Halleux and Anne-Françoise Cannella, 'Entre technologie et alchimie: De la teinture du verre à la fabrication des fausses pierres précieuses', in Andreuccetti and Cervelli (eds), *Il colore nel Medioevo*, vol. 2, pp. 41–58, at p. 46.

67 Albertus Magnus, *Book of Minerals*, trans. Dorothy Wyckoff (Oxford: Clarendon Press, 1967), p. 13.

68 Albertus, *Book of Minerals*, pp. 138–9: 'And the reason why stones of this sort come rather from India and Egypt than from any other region is that the power of the planets is most effective in those places, because they lie either under the equator, or between the equator and the tropic, or in the fourth clime.'

69 Albertus, *Book of Minerals*, p. 22.

70 Albertus, *Book of Minerals*, pp. 134–6.

71 Albertus, *Book of Minerals*, p. 125.

72 Marbode of Rennes' (1035–1123) *De Lapidibus considered as a Medical Treatise with Text, Commentary and C.W. King's Translation together with Text and Translation of Marbode's Minor Works on Stones*, ed. John M. Riddle (Wiesbaden: Franz Steiner Verlag, 1977).

73 For examples in Pliny, *Historia naturalis*, p. 37, lines 142–205. In Sonia Macri's excellent book, *Pietre viventi: Le minerali nell'immaginario del mondo antico* (Turin: UTET, 2009), she notes that stories about stones in antique sources moved them rhetorically from invisibility into visibility. The Island of Topazes, for instance, was constantly shrouded in mist and fog, and its stones could not be seen in daylight. She speculates that stones underwent a 'demineralizing' shift or journey, which in turn rendered them supernatural. This might be effected for instance by the flight of eagles, carrying the stones from the hidden valleys where they lurked (a scene shown occurring in Asia on the Catalan Atlas, for instance), a movement which also carried them from the depths to the skies, from earth to light. It makes sense, therefore, that there were stones created by lightning or rain, which dropped to earth out of the heavens themselves. Above all, this explains the supernatural luminosity of stones, which allied them to the eyes of their viewers. For this reason, eyes might be healed by stones, and stones might have the same diseases as eyes. Pliny uses the word 'scabritia' for both impurities of stones and diseases of the eyelids; and Artemidoros interpreted a dream in which rings with stones were lost as an augur of blindness. See Macri, *Pietre viventi*, pp. 87–92 for these examples.

74 Albertus, *Book of Minerals*, p. 66.

75 Albertus, *Book of Minerals*, p. 232.

76 'Aurum es metalli caut e sec ses & plus temprat que negun autre. Et es vena de terra e conforta totz los membres del cors e conserva Iuventut et c.' The manuscript, 'Detti di filosofia in versi provenzali', is in the Biblioteca Nazionale Centrale in Florence, ms. Palatino 586. It has been digitized: www.bncf.firenze.sbn.it/Bib_digitale/Manoscritti/Palat586/main.htm (accessed on 5 February 2014). It is unfinished, and sixty-three folios. The text ends on fol. 29v, and on 30r it was taken up and illuminated by a different hand in two steps. The plants were drawn in outline (these continue to the end of the book) and then coloured with bas-de-page marginalia often added on either side of the horizon line. The lapis scene is unusual, however, in making a narrative within the scene itself. There is another mining scene traced out on p. 84 in the modern pagination. Matteo Milani, 'Aloes es caut e sec . . . : edizione di un erbario occitano (Firenze, Biblioteca nazionale centrale, Palatino 586)', *La Parola del Testo* 8/2 (2004), pp. 369–91; and Minta Collins, *Medieval Herbals: The Illustrative Tradition* (London and Toronto, ON: The British Library and University of Toronto Press, 2000), pp. 265–8, notes.

77 Jacqueline Proust, 'L'aurum potabile au temps de la Renaissance en France et en Angleterre', in M.T. Jones-Davies (ed.), *L'or au temps de la Renaissance: du mythe à l'économie* (Paris: Université Paris-Sorbonne, 1978), pp. 15–26. In a similar vein, the treatise on diet by the most famous doctor of quattrocento Italy, Michele Savonarola, dedicated to Borso d'Este of Ferrara around 1450, concludes with a medicine intended to extend life and cure everything from paralysis to leprosy; gold is the first and major ingredient. See Michele Savonarola, *Libreto de tutte le cosse che se magnano: un'opera di dietica del sec. XV*, ed. Jane Nystedt (Stockholm: Almqvist & Wiksell International, 1988), p. 193. The menu of the banquet, for the wedding of Violante Visconti and Lionel, Duke of Clarence, is given by John Larner, *Italy in the Age of Dante and Petrarch, 1216–1380* (London and New York: Longman, 1980), pp. 211–13.

78 Halleux and Cannella, 'Entre technologie et alchimie', pp. 42–5.

79 A. Wallert, 'Alchemy and medieval art technology', in Z.R.W.M. von Martels (ed.), *Alchemy Revisited: Proceedings of the International Conference on the History of Alchemy at the University of Groningen, 17–19 April 1989* (Leiden: Brill, 1990), pp. 154–61. The third book of the *Speculum lapidum* by Camillo Leonardo (c. 1500) begins with a discussion of the best

sculptors and painters of his age (whom he identifies as Mantegna, Perugino, Giovanni Bellini, Piero della Francesca, and Melozzo da Forlì): *Les pierres talismaniques*, pp. 48–50.

80 'Manuscripts of Jehan Le Begue', in Merrifield, *Original Treatises*, vol. 1, pp. 1–321, at pp. 316–17: 'Pour faire fin azur – Vous devez prendre la pierre de lazur qui est Inde ou Pers, et vient des parties doultremer, et se treuve sur les appothicuaries qui en font aucunes medicines; et celle qui a vaines blanches vault mieulx que celle que les a dor . . .' The manuscript was compiled and transcribed in 1431, but much of the material is Italian from the later fourteenth century.

81 Cennini, *Libro dell'arte*, p. 96.

82 Leon Battista Alberti, *On Painting and On Sculpture: The Latin Texts of* De Pictura *and* De Statua, ed. and trans. Cecil Grayson (London: Phaidon, 1972), p. 47: 'there is fire-colour, which they call red, and the colour of air which is said to be blue or blue-gray, and the green of water, and the earth is ash-coloured. We see that all other colours, like jasper and porphyry stone, are made from a mixture.' Latin text, p. 46: 'Namque est ignesus, ut ita loquar, color quem rubeum vocant, tum et aeris qui celestis seu caesius dicitur, aquaeque color viridis; terra vero cinereum colorem habet. Ceteros omnes colores veluti diaspri et porphyrii lapidis ex permixitione factos videmus.'

83 Boccaccio, *Decamerone*, Day 8, third story. A man called Maso decides to trick Calandrino. Finding Calandrino admiring the paintings and decoration of San Giovanni, he begins to discuss magic stones. Calandrino is drawn into the conversation, and told that there are two kinds available nearby: the sandstones of Settignano and the millstones of Montisci, which come from an area near an emerald mountain that shines at night. And then there are heliotropes, which make bearers invisible, and are blackish stones found in the Mugnone valley. Calandrino rushes to tell his friends Bruno and Buffalmacco, who realize the game afoot and agree to accompany him the following Sunday. Calandrino loads his body with stones and the others pretend they cannot see him, stoning him all the way home. When his wife sees him and asks what he has been thinking, Calandrino flies into a rage, believing that, as a woman, she has stripped the stones of their power. Calandrino is left angry and with a house filled with rocks.

84 Cennini, *Libro dell'arte*, p. 62; 'quest'è un'arte che ssi chiama dipignere, che conviene avere fantasia e hoperazione di mano, di trovare cose non vedute chacciandosi sotto ombra di naturali e fermarle con la mano, dando a dimostrare quello che nonne sia.'

85 Andrea De Marchi, *Gentile da Fabriano: Un viaggio nella pittura italiana alla fine del gotico* (Milan: Federico Motta Editore, 2006), p. 202.

86 Roberto Bellucci and Cecilia Frosinini, 'Tecnica e stile: Appunti su Gentile da Fabriano', in Andrea De Marchi et al. (eds), *Gentile da Fabriano: Studi e ricerche* (Milan: Electa, 2006), pp. 54–65, here at p. 57.

87 Bellucci and Frosinini, 'Tecnica e stile', pp. 61–2. Gentile da Fabriano may have used leftovers from goldsmithing, much less pure than gold from florins, but already altered by human hands.

4 ✧ Gold coins and gold leaf in early Italian paintings

Irma Passeri

A FULL UNDERSTANDING of the techniques encountered in works of art requires knowledge of artists' materials, their cultural and historical significance, and their physical and chemical characteristics. To go beyond the painted image can elucidate not only the moment of artistic creation and its final product, but also the complex and varied social structures and economic realities that shaped a painter's workshop, or *bottega*. Therefore the understanding of a work of art must encompass the contributions of the anonymous craftsmen who cooperated directly or indirectly in its creation (for example the carpenters, goldbeaters, gilders, and the apothecaries or pharmacists who supplied pigments); it also requires study of the artists' materials, including their origins, trade, and chemical, physical, and mechanical properties.

This essay focuses on gold leaf production in order to examine one of the most important materials used in medieval and early Renaissance works of art. The varying quality of gold leaf in paintings from the twelfth to the fifteenth centuries is examined and contextualized in relation to the gold trade between Europe and Africa; and it is suggested that the analysis of gold in earlier works provides greatly needed information, given a dearth of early documentary sources. The gold of artworks is linked to gold as a shifting trade commodity, and requires discussion of the types of gold traded in the Mediterranean basin during this period. This permits a contextualization, through identification of the materials of works of art as visual expressions of the economic, political, and cultural status of a city, county, monastery, or church, and the patronage that supported them. The essay therefore discusses coins and the circulation of gold in the Mediterranean basin; it then examines the control of the guilds in the production of gold leaf; and finally, it offers examples of gold leaf analysis in two key early works.

The development of the medieval economy and gold trade is reflected in the history of coin production, and offers insight into the sources of gold used for minting coins. After the introduction, in 1252, of 23.75 to 24 carat gold coins in Florence, Genoa, and Venice, coins became the source for gold leaf in paintings; and while it is impossible to determine, because of a dearth of documents, that twelfth-century gold leaf was obtained by beating gold coins, analysis of works will suggest this may also have been so. Therefore, to understand the use of low-carat gold leaf,[1] like that found in the crucifix by an anonymous master for the monastery of an order of nuns in Rosano dated circa 1130, and the crucifix by Master Guglielmo for the church of Sarzana dated 1138 (Figures 4.1 and 4.2), it is necessary to know the history of early medieval coinage. Valuable information on the provenance, quality, and quantity of the gold and silver in circulation in Italy and across Europe

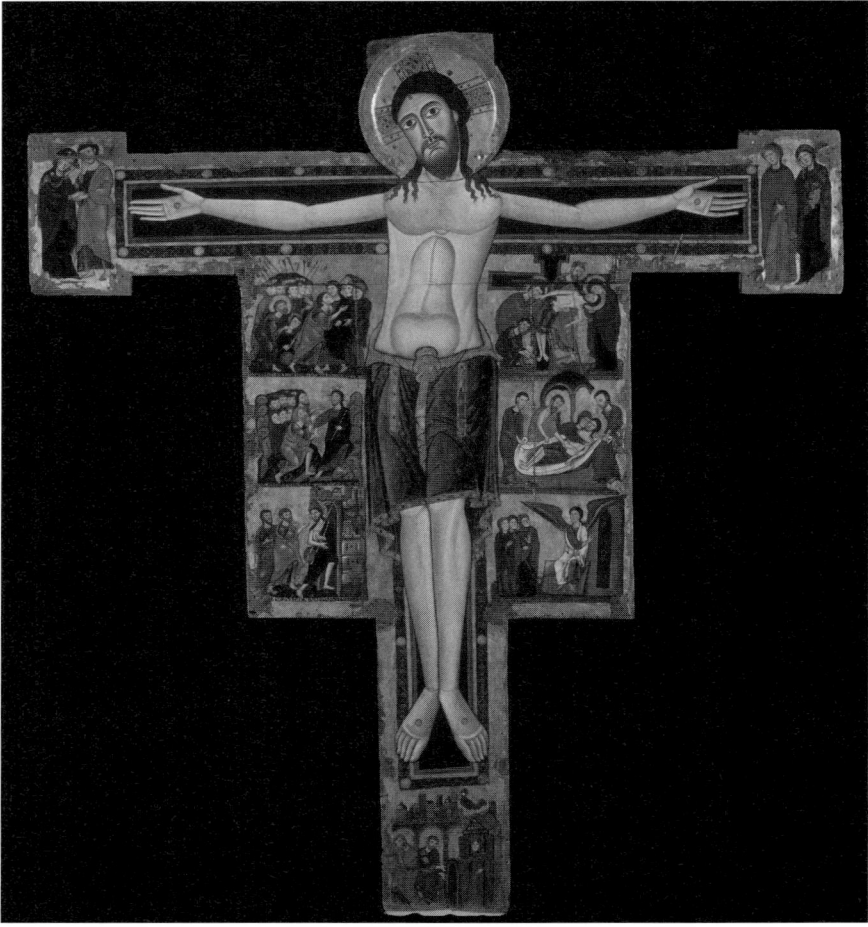

4.1. Master of Rosano, painted crucifix, twelfth century, Monastery of Santa Maria, Rosano, Florence

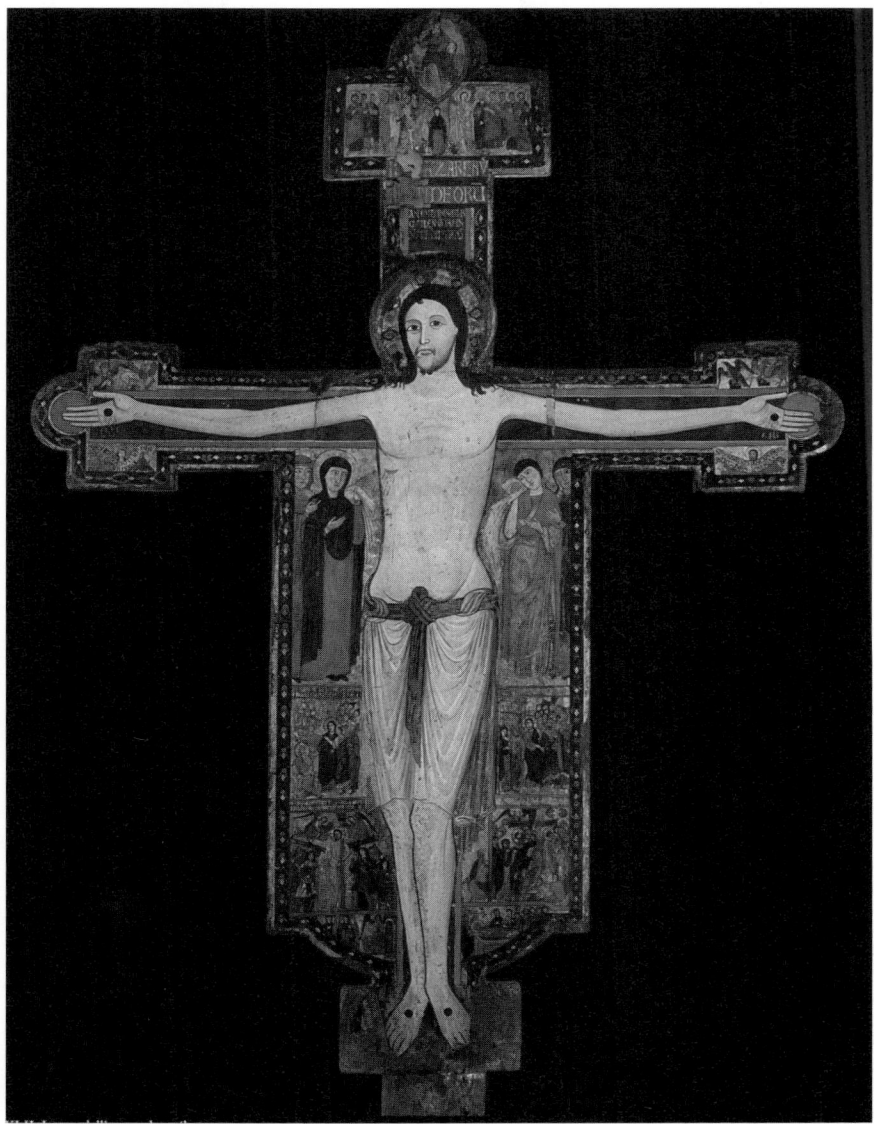

4.2. Master Guglielmo, painted crucifix, 1138, Cathedral of Sarzana, La Spezia

can thus be obtained. Significant material is also traceable in medieval treatises like the third book of the twelfth-century treatise *Schedula diversarum artium* by Theophilus, where the author dedicates four chapters to different types of gold of diverse geographical origins: 'Gold from the land of Havilah', described in the Genesis being surrounded by the river Phison, which is one of the rivers that runs out of the Garden of Eden; 'Arabic gold', which is described as very precious and red in colour;

'Spanish gold', 'which is compounded from red copper, basilisk powder, human blood, and vinegar'; and 'Sand gold', from the banks of the Rhine.[2] The hearsay qualities of these chapters reflects the strong allure that the writer and many others before or after him had towards gold and silver, their desire to own, possess and understand the physical and chemical properties of precious metals. Furthermore they allude to the availability of different gold alloys to the artist.

From the eighth to the mid-thirteenth century a limited amount of gold circulated in the Mediterranean basin.[3] In the eleventh and twelfth centuries, in a few areas of the Italian peninsula, gold started to circulate more widely, brought in from Africa to the south of Italy, Sicily, Genoa, and Pisa. In Southern Italy, from the eleventh century onward, we see a flow of gold powder from western Africa (now Senegal). Some of this gold arrived as a duty from African rulers to Christian kings; some of it was involved in intensive commercial activities. In the 1180s, Genoese merchants, following a three-step route, exported European goods to Tunis. Imported African gold was unloaded in Sicily, where the vessels were loaded with Sicilian goods, which were then transported to Genoa. The role of coordinators and intermediaries in trade allowed the Genoese access to gold.[4]

In the south of Italy, during the Norman and Swabian Hohenstaufen dynasties, gold was employed to coin the tari, a coin that was composed of 16.3 parts of gold with the remaining 7.6 being silver and copper. Its weight varied from 0.23 to 2.62 grams. Silver formed the basis of the main coinage system; gold circulated in the form of bars or dust, and foreign gold coins were also available. Along the Mediterranean coast from Spain to Syria, Muslim dinars and Castilian anfusi also circulated. These coins were high in gold content. In 1231 in Sicily and in the south of Italy, there was a sufficient amount of gold to allow the Holy Roman Emperor Frederick II to coin in the mints of Brindisi and Messina the 'double gold dinar' known as the augustales. The augustales weighed about 5.3 grams and was 20.5 carat gold. Analyses done on a few augustales confirmed the gold content of the alloy.[5]

In the twelfth century, gold metal still reached the Italian peninsula in the form of tribute from African rulers or as a result of commercial activity with Africa. Senegalese gold reached the northern Italian merchants and the Genoese in particular; here notarial documents of the decade from 1180 to 1190 show payments in tari and African gold bullion, recorded under the term 'paiola' or 'pagliola', though commercial trades with Africa, in which gold might have been included, are recorded since 1162.[6] Documents, in which the word 'paiola' is cited, become more frequent in the thirteenth century. The gold of the pagliola, whose origins the Genoese eagerly sought, came from the sands of Senegalese rivers in a region called Palola or Palolus, from which the terms 'paiola' and 'pagliola' derive.⁷ Analysis of the Senegalese gold, carried out in the 1800s, showed that it was relatively pure: gold 869.7 millesimal (less than 21 carats) and silver 105.3 millesimal (a little more than 2.5 carats)⁸. In Genoese documents of the first half of the thirteenth century, the same purity is recorded, oscillating between 20, 21, and 21.5 carats. Notarial registers also record that the gold of pagliola was sold in *virgis* or bars stamped officially by the city. African alluvial gold, used for the coinage of Sicilian coins (and the gold content in pagliola gold and augustales are the same), was also found in Pisa in powdered or bar form, and Sienese merchants were aware of the existence and high quality of the African gold.⁹

It is important to remember the relation that Genoese merchants had with Genoese Franciscan friars in Morocco during the early decades of the thirteenth century (they also were interested in the extraction of gold); and the desire that the Genoese Pope Innocent IV had to convert Moroccan rulers to Christianity, in order to garner territorial concessions for their Christian compatriots. This allowed the establishment of commercial bases along the Atlantic coast and facilitated the gold trade. The Genoese would later find, in the city of Safi (Morocco), a landing stage closer to the gold-bearing African region of Palolus.¹⁰

For about five hundred years, from the eighth to the thirteenth centuries, there was not nearly as much gold in the West as there had been in antiquity. Gold had not disappeared, but rather its supply and availability was greatly reduced due to social, economic, and political circumstances in Europe, and its commercial and political relationships with North Africa. Gold coins were always minted, even in the Dark Ages. Two regions close to the Arabic and Byzantine world, Spain and the south of Italy, remained fairly loyal to the use of gold coins. Historians have argued that the return of gold to Europe in the twelfth and thirteenth centuries was related to a renewed capacity of the West to export goods and import gold from Africa.¹¹ The gold was put into wider circulation in the form of coins; an increase in the availability and supply of gold, and the cost of gold compared to silver are also factors to be considered. If the return of gold coinage is linked to an evolution of the European economy, the decrease in value or price of gold as compared to silver – which goes down, in 1252, to 8.5 to 1 – must have played an important role as well. In Europe between the mid-thirteenth and the fourteenth centuries the value of gold increases again.¹²

By contrast, until Venice established close relations with the northwest regions of Africa in the later thirteenth century, the Venetian gold supply was not large enough to allow for the coinage of gold money. In the second half of the thirteenth century, however, large quantities of gold from southern Italy, Sicily, central Europe, and Africa started to arrive in Venice. Gold was refined near Rialto, and in 1269 the Venetian government decreed that gold sold in the city had to be of a fixed fineness of 23.25 carat. In 1284 the fabrication of gold bars was largely substituted by the coinage of the ducat, which weighed 3.56 grams and was 23.75 carat; the Venetian government specified that the ducat needed to be '. . . tan bona et fina per aurum vel melior ut est florenus' ('as good and pure gold as the florin, or better').[13]

The so-called return to gold in Italy's monetary system in the twelfth and thirteenth centuries is reflected in works of art by an extensive and increasing use of gold leaf, and is perhaps related to an increase in the availability of gold. This is not to suggest a direct link between the gold metal used in coinage and in art. It only suggests that the economic, political, and social circumstances of this period caused an increase in the circulation of gold. The passage from a Europe relatively poor in gold to an area very rich in the precious metal was a gradual process that must have had an impact on artistic production, in particular on the choice of materials used.

For medieval and Renaissance artists, the creative moment was converted into an image through the careful knowledge and use of materials. The choice of one material over another and the capacity to mould or shape it were important expressive tools. Ancient and medieval treatises focus on the transformation and manipulation of substances, knowledge that was conveyed through the formulae of recipes.[14] The quality of an artistic product reflects the deep knowledge of the craftsman or artist, derived from a long and rigorous apprenticeship in the *bottega*.[15] Likewise, the quality of a work of art exemplifies the economic, political, and social status of the city, church, or family for which it was produced. In the late Middle Ages and early Renaissance, all professions were organized into guilds; these were associations which regulated the production, materials, work, ethics, and the life of their members within a given city's jurisdiction. Thus, for instance, the rigorous rules of Florentine guilds are the result of a complex organizational system put in place by a society that wanted to control and supervise the products of its artists, which were seen as a visual manifestation of the city's economic status and cultural refinement.[16] The enrolment in the guilds also protected the artisans from outside competition and ensured a quality control of the members. This control becomes clear when reading the regulations imposed by the guild in the use or substitution of painters' materials; of particular interest are the rules, discussed below, related to the production of metal leaf, specifically gold leaf, employed to make a flat gold background or to be used as a decorative element with mordant gold and shell gold in panel paintings.

Noteworthy examples of the desire to introduce high standards, directly linked to the production of gold leaf for works of art, are the regulations that governed the introduction, production, and circulation of the gold florin of Florence, a coin that was well regarded in Europe for its stable value: it had a weight and alloy composition that fluctuated only slightly from 1252, when it was introduced, throughout the centuries.[17] In 1252, a sufficient quantity of gold was passing through Genoa and Florence to allow the minting of gold coins. The genovino and the florin, minted just a few months apart, are almost identical in mass: the first weighed 3.53 grams, the second 3.54 grams. The gold employed was of a high quality: 23.75 to 24 carat. These new currencies attest that Genoa and Florence had attained considerable political and economic importance in the panorama of the Italian peninsula. Initially the genovino and florin were employed for internal use (within the city domain), but soon after they became important international currencies.[18]

The reappearance of gold coins in Europe both illustrated the economic development of those cities that introduced them into their monetary systems, and served as an affirmation of their political prestige.[19] The quality and the widespread circulation of the gold coins exemplified the wealth of the city or realm that used them. The burden of representing a government's economic stability and affluence required strict controls on coinage production. The monitoring of the alloy's purity and the weight and aspect of the coin was delegated to an authority such as a mint. Control was exerted during the circulation as well as the production of the coins; for example, a specific professional figure called *saggiatore* (tester) was in charge of verifying the weight of the florin with a *saggiolo* and a scale. All coins that did not conform to the mint's set standards were marked and pulled from circulation.[20]

Surviving painters' contracts and accounts, and Cennino Cennini's late fourteenth-century treatise *Il libro dell'arte*, record that gold leaf was manufactured by beating gold coins, and indicated the number of leaves produced (100 to 145 per coin).[21] This is not mentioned by the Guild of the Doctors and Apothecaries statutes in which the goldbeaters were enrolled. A reference to the use of gold coinage can be found in the statutes of the goldsmiths' guild, the Arte di Por Santa Maria, of 1335, chapter XXI, 'De deaurandis rebus infrascripto modo', where the use of gold exclusively from Florentine coinage is required for artworks.[22] For the goldbeaters, Florentine gold coins were a reliable source that offered them, the artist, and the patron assurance that their leaves would be made of the highest quality gold available.

Cennino Cennini's close attention to gilding does not extend to discussing the size or production of gold leaf. But this information can be found in earlier sources such as *Schedula diversarum artium*, the twelfth-century treatise by Theophilus, where the technique described is surprisingly similar to the one still used today. In chapter XXIII, 'Gold leaf', Theophilus's description of gold leaf production comprises several phases: first the gold metal was beaten on a flat surface with a hammer to obtain a thin metal foil, then the gold foil was cut into squares two fingers wide and stacked between squares of red-pigmented linen paper or parchment four fingers wide. The pile of gold and parchment was inserted into a parchment pouch, which was then beaten on a flat surface with a hammer to obtain thin leaves of gold. When the margins of the gold square bulged over the margin of the parchment squares, the goldbeater cut the extra gold and continued the beating process until he was satisfied with the thickness of the leaves, which could be 'thin or moderately thick'. The process was repeated as many times as needed. Nevertheless, the thickness was still sufficient to cut the gold leaves with scissors and into the size needed to decorate the background space.[23]

Although Theophilus's chapter can be found in the painting section of his treatise, presumably because of the association between gold leaf and its use in paintings and manuscript illumination, it must have been evident to the writer that the production of gold leaf required a technical skill specific to goldbeaters or goldsmiths. Also the tools described are those that can be found in a goldbeater's or goldsmith's *bottega* and not in that of a painter. Cennino's *Il libro dell'arte* was written for a society with a different structure, and though it describes gilding techniques, as well as the quality, thickness, and sources for gold leaf, Cennino deliberately avoids mentioning the process of making leaf, and thus makes a clear distinction between goldbeaters and painters.

In 1315, for the first time, metal beaters were enrolled in the Florentine Guild of the Doctors and Apothecaries as new members, and they are described as those who sell and beat gold, silver, and tin into thin sheets, 'vendunt et operantur aurum et argentum et stangnum battutum'.[24] Thereafter their activity was strictly regulated by the guild.[25] The 1403 reform of the painters' guild statutes first mentions the size of the gold, silver, and *oro di metà* leaves. *Oro di metà* is a laminated leaf made of two sheets – one of silver and one of gold – which are beaten together.[26] They are described at the end of the Codex C of the Statutes: 'ogni pezzo d'oro puro o vero d'oro fine debba essere e sia di misura e a misura, la quale è pe' consoli della dett'arte ordinata. La qual misura è più nona parte e meno octava parte d'un braccio alla misura di Firenze, e ogni pezzo d'oro di metà e d'ariento debba essere e sia di misura e a misura l'altra maggiore pe' detti consoli ordinata, maggior cioè l'octava parte e minore (i) la settima parte del braccio sopra detto' ('That each piece of pure gold or better fine [gold] must be, and is, of the measure ordered by the consuls of the guild. The measure is more than a ninth part and less than an eighth part of one braccio to the Florence measure, and each piece of half gold and silver [leaf] must be, and is, of measure and of higher measure ordered from the said consuls, greater that is eight part and minor the seventh part of the above mentioned *braccio*'). The dimensions of each gold leaf were fixed, one-ninth to one-eigth of a *braccio fiorentino*, which is about 6.5 to 7.3 centimetres per side; although this regulation was instituted only in 1403, it probably codified a practice already in use. The size of gold leaf is confirmed by treatises, both ancient and modern: Pliny talks about a large leaf 'quattro dita in ambo i lati' – four fingers wide on each side – that is, around 7.5 to 8 centimetres; and Theophilus talks about a red-pigmented linen paper leaf four fingers wide that was used as a size reference during the beating of the gold leaf.[27] The silver and *oro di metà* leaves were fixed at one-eighth to one-seventh of a *braccio fiorentino* (circa 7.3–8.3 centimetres); the larger dimension of these metal leaves is related to the cost of the metal, which was relatively inferior in respect to gold.

The thickness of the gold leaf is not discussed in the guild's statutes, although it appears from the painters' contracts and accounts and from Cennino Cennini's treatise that the thickness was necessarily determined by the number of leaves per coin. Knowing the weight of the florin, the number of leaves per coin, and the dimension and the density of the gold, conservators and scientists at the National Gallery of London have calculated that medieval gold leaf had a thickness of around 2.69 microns. This has been confirmed by analysis of original medieval and Renaissance metal leaves.[28]

Cennino Cennini dedicates a chapter to the topic, 'What gold is good for burnishing and for mordant gilding, and what thickness'. In it he writes, 'Let me tell you that for the gold which is laid on flats they ought not to get more than a hundred leaves out of a ducat, whereas they do get a hundred and forty five; because the gold for the flat wants to be rather dull . . . On mouldings or foliage ornaments you will make out better with thinner gold; but for the delicate ornaments of the embellishment with mordants it ought to be very thin gold, and cobweb-like.'[29] He advises using the thicker leaf for flat backgrounds, as it is most suitable for burnishing, and would create the effect of a solid metal surface. Thinner leaves are more appropriate for mordant gilding and frame mouldings, adapting more readily to the complicated profile of the exterior frame elements.

The Guild of the Doctors and Apothecaries regulated and controlled the production of the goldbeaters in order to prevent fraud. Goldbeaters who violated the guild's regulations were punished. To control the production of metal leaf in Florence the guild introduced professional figures called *cercatori*,[30] or searchers, who ensured that the goldbeater was supplying the artist with leaves that adhered to the guild's standards. Similar regulation also extended to painters, who were forbidden to substitute *oro di metà* or tinted silver for gold, tin for silver, or the blue pigment azurite for the semi-precious ultramarine.[31] Similar prohibitions can also be read in the statutes of the guilds of Siena and Perugia.[32]

Although it is not common to have the gilded backgrounds of panel paintings analysed to confirm the gold content of the metal leaves, a few tests have been performed and published by the Opificio delle Pietre Dure in Florence. Works that have been tested include: the *Annunciation* by Lorenzo Monaco from the church of Santa Trinita, Florence (1423); the predella with the story of *Saint Julian Killing His Parents*, from the museum of Ingres of Montauban (1425); the *Saint Julian* from the museum Diocesano of Florence (1424–25); the *Saint Paul* by Masaccio from the museum Nazionale of Pisa (1426); and the *Linaioli Altarpiece* by Beato Angelico, from the museum of San Marco, Florence (1433). X-ray fluorescence spectroscopic (XRF) analysis of these paintings confirms a high gold content in the metal leaf, and the absence of silver or copper impurities.[33] An interesting counterexample is offered by three works of the painter Gentile da Fabriano, the *Polyptych of Valle Romita* (1410–12), *Crucifixion* (1400–10) from the Pinacoteca di Brera, and the *Polyptych of the Intercession* from the church of San Niccolò Oltrarno in Florence (1420s). XRF analysis of gilded backgrounds and decorations on all three of Gentile's panels has detected silver and copper impurities in the gold leaf, suggesting that the metal leaves were obtained not from gold coins but perhaps by melting down gold objects made by previous goldsmiths' art.[34]

While we are almost certain that panel paintings executed after the mid-thirteenth century have gold backgrounds made with the highest quality gold available – that is, the gold derived from coins – this is not the case for paintings created before this date. Therefore, when conservators at the Opificio delle Pietre Dure in Florence treated two twelfth-century paintings, the crucifix by an anonymous master for the monastery of an enclosed order of nuns in Rosano dated circa 1130, and the crucifix by Master Guglielmo from the Cathedral of Sarzana dated 1138 (Figures 4.1 and 4.2), careful attention was given to the gold backgrounds.[35] While low-carat gold in the regions of Tuscany and Liguria is documented during the period when the two crucifixes were produced, only a handful of documents and contracts can still be connected to early works of the twelfth century, and medieval treatises such as Theophilus's *Schedula diversarum artium* do not offer information on the source of gold for metal-leaf production. Thus analysis of the gold leaf can be useful in the identification of the materials employed.

The chemical alloy composition of the gold leaf used in both crucifixes is very similar and allows for a comparison with the type of gold that was circulating in the twelfth century in Italy. In both crucifixes, preliminary XRF analysis performed in the gilded areas revealed the use of a low-carat gold leaf. The alloy composition contained relatively high amounts of silver, on the order of 5 per cent to 15 per cent for the crucifix by Master Guglielmo and 7 per cent to 15 per cent for the crucifix of Rosano, and little to no copper; placing the gold leaf at 22.8 to 20.4 carat.[36] Both crucifixes are characterized by gold leaf of a pale colour, which is partially due to the poor state of preservation of the gilded background and the absence of an orange-red bole layer underneath the metal leaf that would have imparted a warm quality to the metal.[37] But it should not be overlooked that the tonality of the gold is also influenced by the presence of different elements in the alloy: for example, copper and silver. A low-carat gold leaf, rich in silver content, will appear whiter in tone compare to one that has high content of gold such as a 23.75 or 24 carat leaf. This is because 'silver displays high reflectivity over most of the visible range of the electromagnetic spectrum, while gold and copper give high reflectivity only at longer wavelengths. These differences in reflectivity, account for the perceived colour of gold and copper in contrast to the whiteness of silver in leaf alloys.'[38] Furthermore, when gold leaf is thinly beaten it becomes almost transparent and the transmitted light appears of greenish-blue tonality and reflects the yellow and red bands of the visible spectrum.

Although it is impossible to confirm that the gold leaf employed in both crucifixes was partially if not completely manufactured with pagliola gold (which is 20 to 21.5 carat), it appears that we can infer a relationship between the gold circulating in raw and in coin forms, and that employed by the artists for these paintings. Also the development of gold geology, mining techniques and the process of refining the metal determined the physical properties and chemical qualities of the gold employed in the metal leaf production.

It is interesting that in both crucifixes the bole layer underneath the metal leaf is missing. Though it is impossible to affix a precise date for the use of a bole-based preparatory layer for gilding, it is reasonable to say that from the mid-thirteenth century, red-orange bole layers become commonly used by gilders. Gilders used different coloured grounds for gold and silver leaf in order to obtain specific visual effects. In fact it is not uncommon to find no red-orange preparatory layer for gilding in a number of early medieval paintings dated from the twelfth to the mid-thirteenth century.[39] The gold leaf was instead laid directly on to a meticulously smoothed and polished gesso ground; the leaf was then adhered to the surface with an aqueous adhesive, like a glair or animal glue; when the surface had dried the gold leaf was burnished. The smooth white gesso ground enhanced the surface texture and chromatic hues of the metal leaf. In Byzantine paintings the use of a highly polished white gesso layer as a preparatory layer for gold leaf is often seen.[40] Theophilus describes the application of metal leaf directly on to a gesso ground in the chapter 'Gold leaf':

> In laying on [the gold] take glair, which is beating out of the white of an egg without water, and with it lightly cover with a brush the place where the gold is to be laid. Wet the point of the handle of the brush in your mouth, touch a corner of the leaf that you have cut, and so lift it up and apply it with the greatest speed. Then smooth it with the brush. At this moment you should guard against drafts and hold your breath because, if you breathe, you will lose the leaf and find it again only with difficulty. When this piece has been laid on and has dried, lay another piece over it in the same way, if you wish, and also a third, if necessary, so that you can polish it all the more brightly with a tooth or a stone. If you wish, you can also lay this leaf in the same way on a wall or a ceiling panel.[41]

A counterexample of this practice is also described by Theophilus in 'How gold and silver are applied in books'; here he advises the use of a red coloured preparation ground for gilding with a powered gold mixed to glue:

> Next, take pure minium, add a third part of cinnabar to it, and grind it on a stone with water. When it is carefully ground, beat the glair out of the white of an egg (in summer with water, in winter without water). When this is pure, put the minium into a horn and pour the glair over it. Put in a stick and stir it a little. Then, using a brush, cover with it all those places on which you want to apply gold.[42]

Cennino Cennini offers as an alternative to the use of bole a layer of green earth or terre verte: 'You may do also as our forefathers used to . . . and then gild with terre-verte.'[43] Green earth is a natural earth pigment with a limited covering power. Because terre verte cannot be finely ground it creates a granular surface that is subsequently imparted to the thin metal leaf, which will reflect the light in a more diffused way. Furthermore, terre verte does not burnish with the same lustre as bole and provides a cool tonality to the gold leaf.[44]

Because analysis of the chemical alloy composition of the gold leaf in early Italian painting has not been extensively performed, it is difficult to know whether the crucifixes of Rosano and Sarzana are unique or reflect a broader aspect of gold-leaf production. A better understanding of the gilding materials used in early medieval Italian paintings will require more analysis of gold backgrounds: this might show a progressive change in the quality of the gold employed in the manufacture of metal leaves from the twelfth to fifteenth centuries. Such progression in quality would prompt a closer look at the areas of extraction and refinement of the metal, a consideration of the type of gold alloys circulating, and the economic and commercial status of those geographical regions of Italy where gold was being traded and used. It might then be possible to see an increase in quality from the twelfth to the mid-to-late thirteenth century, when we know that gold leaf was generated by using gold coins of the highest purity.

Notes

1. For high-carat gold leaf in early Italian paintings we mean a metal leaf made of a gold of a fineness of 23.75 to 24 carat, where minimal or non-quantities of silver and or copper are present in the alloy; for a low-carat gold leaf, a metal that averages between 18 and 22 carat gold.
2. Theophilus, *On Divers Arts: The Foremost Medieval Treatise on Painting, Glassmaking and Metalwork*, trans. J.H. Hawthorne and C.S. Smith (Chicago: University of Chicago Press, 1963), pp. 118–20.
3. C.H.V. Sutherland, *L'oro* (Milan: Mondadori Editore, 1961), pp. 17–168; P. Spufford, *Money and Its Use in Medieval Europe* (New York: Cambridge University Press, 1988); R.S. Lopez, *Settecento anni fa: Il ritorno all'oro nell'occidente duecentesco*, Rivista Storica Italiana, LXV – Fascicolo I (Naples: Edizioni Scientifiche Italiane, 1953).
4. Spufford, *Money and Its Use*, pp. 163–86; and R.S. Lopez, 'I Genovesi lungo le coste dell'Atlantico: Secoli XII e XIII', in *Studi sull'economia genovese nel Medio Evo* (Turin: S. Lattes, 1936), pp. 40–5.
5. Lopez, *Settecento anni fa*, pp. 24–5 and 31–2; Spufford, *Money and Its Use*, p. 169; the augustales had a gold fineness of 0.854, p. 406.
6. Lopez, 'I Genovesi lungo', and 'Dai Vivaldi ai Malocello: Progressi tecnici e cambiamento di obbiettivi nella navigazione', also in *Studi sull'economia genovese*, pp. 45–9.
7. The terms 'paiola' or 'pagliola' may be derived from an island generated by the Bambuk's rivers, which is now identified with Wangara, and that the medieval cartographers called Palola or Palolus, see R. Lopez, 'Il retroterra sudanese. L'oro di Pagliola: la produzione e i metodi di scambio', in *Studi sull'economia genovese*, pp. 34–40.
8. Lopez, *Settecento anni fa*, p. 31 and note 2. Carat purity is measured as twenty-four times the purity by mass. A 24 carat gold is the finest type of gold (99.9 per cent Au), a lower-carat gold such as a 21 carat gold is composed of twenty-one parts gold and three parts of another metal (silver or and copper); the millesimal fineness system can be additionally used to describe the purity of precious metals, which is defined by parts per thousand of pure metal in the alloy.
9. Lopez, *Settecento anni fa*, pp. 30–1; Spufford, *Money and Its Use*, p. 176.
10. Lopez, 'I Genovesi lungo', pp. 42–3, and 'L'elemento religioso', in *Studi sull'economia genovese*, pp. 8–11.
11. Spufford, *Money and Its Use*, pp. 163–86.
12. The gradual increase of the price of gold in the thirteenth century is related to the fact that from 1252 it was being employed for monetary purposes: see, on the subject, C. Desimoni, 'La moneta e il rapporto dell'oro all'argento dai secoli XII al XV', in *Reale*

Accademia dei Lincei (Rome: Tipografia della R. Accademia dei Lincei, 1895); and Anne Dunlop's chapter in this volume. If Italy and Europe were fairly rich in silver, Africa was rich in gold and scarce in silver, making the silver valued more than gold in the African world. African rulers traded large quantities of white metal with gold, which starts flowing into northern and southern Italy and Spain in the twelfth and thirteenth century; see Spufford, *Money and Its Use*.

13 Spufford, *Money and Its Use*, p. 178; the Florentine and Genoese examples were soon imitated in France and in England.

14 Teofrasto di Ereso, *Liber de lapidibus graece et latine cum brevis annotationibus*, fourth century; Marcus Vitruvius Pollio, *De architectura libri decem*, 27 CE; Gaius Plinius Secundus, *Naturalis historia, libri triginta septem*, first century BCE; Dioscoride Pedanio, *De materia medica*, first to second century, BCE; Anonymous, *Manoscritto lucchese n. 490 (Compositiones ad tingenda musiva)*, eighth century BCE; Heraclius, *De coloribus et artibus romanorum*, tenth to thirteenth century; Anonymous Bernese, *De clarea*, eleventh century; Teophilus Presbyter, *Schedula diversarium atrium*, eleventh to twelfth century; Anonymous, *Mappae clavicula*, twelfth century; Pietro di San'Audemar, *Liber magistri petri de sancto audemaro de coloribus faciendis*, thirteenth to fourteenth century; Anonymous, *De arte illuminandi*, second half of the fourteenth century; Cennino Cennini, *Il libro dell'arte*, end of the fourteenth century. Recipes related to the preparation of art materials or the making of works of art were collected in manuscripts, which often had a heterogeneous and encyclopedic character. Medieval treatises started focusing more attention on one or more areas of art production. Most of the surviving treatises have a miscellaneous character, in which prescriptions of artists' materials and techniques are mixed with pharmaceutical, medicinal, botanical, culinary, and cosmetic instructions. These literary sources transmitted technological knowledge, and they offer important insights into the cultural and artistic scene of the time period. Although it is unclear for whom these manuscripts were written and collected, their production and circulation can be identified in the scriptoria of the monasteries, in the court artists' studios, and later in the medieval botteghe. P. Castelli, 'I segreti delle botteghe: I ricettari', in *Lorenzo Ghiberti: materiali e ragionamenti* (Florence: Centro Di, 1978); S. Bordini, *Materia e immagine: Fonti sulle tecniche della pittura* (Rome: Leonardo – De Luca Editori, 1991), pp. 7–31; C. Strehlke and C. Frosinini, *The Panel Paintings of Masolino and Masaccio*, The Role of Technique 5 (Milan: Continents Edition, 2002); Wolf-Dietrich Lohr and S. Weppelmann (eds), *Fantasie und Handwerk: Cennino Cennini und die Tradition der toskanischen Malerei von Giotto bis Lorenzo Monaco* (Berlin: Hirmer Verlag, 2008).

15 Cennino Cennini's chapter 'The system by which you should prepare to acquire the skill to work on panel' describes the different steps of an artist's apprenticeship, which should last for a total of twelve years: *The Craftsman's Handbook: 'Il Libro dell'Arte' Cennino d'Andrea Cennini*, trans. Daniel V. Thompson (New York: Dover, 1960), pp. 64–5. Cennino's description contradicts the regulations of the Guild of the Doctors and Apothecaries, which suggests a much shorter apprenticeship of at least three years: R. Ciasca, *Gli statuti dell'arte dei medici e speziali* (Florence: Tipografia del Secolo, 1922), note 1, statute of 1349, no. LXII, p. 181; also R. Ciasca, *L'arte dei medici e speziali nella storia e nel commercio fiorentino* (Florence: Leo S. Olschki, 1927), pp. 177–89. A. Guidotti, 'Il mestiere di dipintore nell'Italia del due-trecento', in E. Castelnuova (ed.), *La pittura in Italia: Il Duecento e il Trecento* (Milan: Electa, 1986). R. Bellucci and C. Frosinini proposed a revision of the role and function of Cennino's treatises, suggesting that the rigid adherence to old rules and practice recorded by the late thirteenth-century artist and writer doesn't reflect the artistic scene and practical work organization in Florence at the end of the fourteenth century. Cennino's treatise should be seen more as a reference book for the guild than a manual, reflecting the conservative approach of the guild towards its old and new members. R. Bellucci and C. Frosinini, 'Working together: Technique and innovation in Masolino's and Masaccio's panel paintings', in Strehlke and Frosinini, *The Panel Paintings*, pp. 29–31.

16 To practise a given craft you needed to enrol in a guild and pay a membership fee. In 1315 in Florence, painters were included in the guild of the Arte dei Medici e Speziali (Doctors and Apothecaries); among their members were the *speziali* or apothecaries, described in the 1297 statues guild as those 'who buy sell and work ... colours'. Different, although related, trades might be enrolled in the same guild, as they were dealing with analogous materials; thus we find in the Medici and Speziali highly specialized professions such as *battilori* (goldbeaters), *orpellai* (decorators of non-precious materials), *legnaioli* (carpenters), *forzerinai* (casket-makers), *cofanai* (makers of chests or cassoni), *miniatori* (illuminators), *naibi* (painters of playing cards), or *imbiancatori* (house painters) alongside painters and apothecaries. The painters' statutes of Florence, Siena, and Perugia still survive, and though guild regulations vary from city to city, common aspects in the way they controlled the life and work of the members can be found. For example in 1315–16 the Florentine statutes admonish the selling of German azurite as ultramarine, or saffron from Catalonia mixed with saffron from Tuscany; the same sort of materials admonishment can be found in the guild statutes of Siena of 1355, where it is forbidden to substitute gilded silver for pure gold, or tin for silver. The work and materials employed by an artist were also controlled by written contracts that were drawn up between the artist and the patron prior to the making of the work of art. See Ciasca, *Gli statuti dell'arte*; Ciasca, *L'arte dei medici e speziali*; Guidotti, 'Il mestiere di dipintore'; L. Indrio, 'Firenze nel Quattrocento: Divisione ed organizzazione del lavoro nelle botteghe', *Ricerche di Storia dell'Arte* 38 (1988–89); Ugo Procacci, *Studio sul catasto fiorentino* (Florence: Leo S. Olschki, 1996); D. Bomford, J. Dunkerton, D. Gordon, and A. Roy (eds), *Art in the Making: Italian Painting before 1400* (London: National Gallery Publications, 1989), pp. 6–7; Bellucci and Frosinini, 'Working together'.

17 The florin, issued from 1252 to 1533, did not change much in weight and remains stable in gold content: its weight varied from 3.33 grams to 3.55 grams. Spufford, *Money and Its Use*, p. 406; Bomford et al., *Art in the Making*, p. 22.

18 Spufford, *Money and Its Use*, p. 177.

19 Lopez, *Settecento anni fa*.

20 M. Bernocchi, *Le monete della Repubblica fiorentina*, vol. 3: *Documentazione* (Florence: Leo S. Olschki, 1976), pp. 1–14.

21 Cennini, *The Craftsman's Handbook*, 'What gold is good for burnish and for mordant gilding, and what thickness', chapter 139, pp. 84–5. Surviving contracts and expense accounts informs us of the use of coins for the production of gold leaf and the number of leaves obtained by gold coins: the contract dated 17 April 1320 for Pietro Lorenzetti's polyptych for Santa Maria della Pieve, Arezzo, reads: 'Laborando in campis et spatiis ipsarum figurarum de optimo auro de C [cento] folis pro floreno' ('excellent gold of a hundred sheets per florin'); C. Merzenich, 'Dorature policromie delle parti architettoniche nelle tavole a'altare toscane fra trecento e quattrocento', *Kermes* 9/26 (May–August 1996), pp. 56–7. It appears that one hundred leaves per coin was commonly used, and this is true for the accounts related to the polyptych for the high altar of San Pier Maggiore, Florence, painted by Jacopo di Cione, where three different payments are related to gold leaf of the quality of one hundred leaves per coin, 'per cento pezzi d'oro per li fregi ... a 2 dì settembre [1371], fior. 1 d'oro'. Bomford et al., *Art in the Making*, p. 22; for the specific payments see Appendix III, pp. 197–200; Merzenich, *Dorature policromie*, p. 57. In the fifteenth century a payment for a lot of 1,000 gold leaves for the important high altarpiece of San Egidio painted by Lorenzo Monaco, 'E a dì 31 d'ottobre 1420, fiorini 8 lire 1 per pezzi M [=mille] d'oro da Pietro di Francesco battiloro' testifies that goldbeaters were also producing a lower-quality leaf of 125 per coin, which reflects a desire to save money: Merzenich, *Dorature policromie*, p. 58.

22 U. Dorini, *Statuti dell'arte di Por Santa Maria del tempo della Repubblica* (Florence: Leo S. Olschki, 1934).

23 'Take some Byzantine parchment, which is made from flax fibre, and rub it on both sides with the red pigment that is made by burning very finely ground and dried ochre. Then polish it very carefully with the tooth of a beaver, a bear, or a boar, until it becomes bright and the pigment sticks fast as a result of the friction. Then cut this parchment with scissors into square pieces, four fingers wide and equally long. After this make a sort of pouch of the same size out of calf vellum and sew it together firmly. Make it large enough to be able to put a lot of pieces of the reddened parchment into it. After doing this take pure gold and thin it out with a hammer on a smooth anvil, very carefully, so as not to let any break occur in it. Then cut into square pieces, two fingers in size. Then put a piece of the reddened parchment into the pouch and in the middle on top of it a piece of gold, then another piece of parchment and again a piece of gold, and continue doing so until the pouch is filled and there is always a piece of gold interleaved in the centre. Then you should have a hammer cast from brass, narrow near the handle and broad at the face. Hammer the pouch with it on a large flat smooth stone, lightly, not heavily. After frequent inspections you will decide whether you want to make the gold completely thin or moderately thick. If the gold spreads too much as it is thinned and projects out of the pouch, cut it off with small light scissors made for this purpose alone. This is the recipe for making gold leaf. And when you have thinned it out according to your liking, with the scissors cut as many pieces of it as you want, and with them ornament the halos around the heads of figures, stoles, hems of robes, etc., as you like.' Theophilus, *On Divers Arts*, pp. 29–31; Bomford et al., *Art in the Making*, pp. 21–4. Ancient and medieval techniques on beating gold in thin sheets can be found in G. Plinio Secondo, *Storia naturale*; Dioscorides, *De materia medica*, first century BCE, 'Pedanii dioscoridis anazarbei de materia medica libri quinque', ed. C.G. Kuhn (Lipsia, 1829); the sections related to gold leaf are published by Merzenich *Dorature policromie*, p. 54; Anonymous, *Manoscritto lucchese n. 490 (Compositiones ad tingenda musiva)*, eighth century, BCE; H. Hedfors, *Compositiones ad tingenda musiva* (Uppsala, 1932).

24 Ciasca, *Gli statuti dell'arte*, p. 77.

25 In the fourteenth century, and most probably before that, goldbeaters were mainly involved in two areas of art production: one was that of painted objects, which was under the control of the Guild of the Doctors and Apothecaries; the second one was related to textiles woven with gold threads, which was under the jurisdiction of the guild of Por Santa Maria. In this last corporation we also find cited, from 1375, goldbeaters related to goldsmiths, who were also members of the guild of Por Santa Maria. These specific work associations (goldbeater–painter, goldbeater–weaver, goldbeater–goldsmith) are strictly related to the type of material produced and its specific use. We also find goldbeaters as members of the Compagnia di San Luca, where numerous painters were enrolled. Ciasca, *Gli statuti dell'arte*; Dorini, *Statuti dell'arte di Por Santa Maria*; A. Guidotti, 'Battiloro e dipintori a Firenze fra tre e Quattrocento: Bastiano di Giovanni e la sua clientela (dal Catasto del 1427)', in *Scritti di Storia dell'Arte in onore di Roberto Salvini* (Florence: Sansoni, 1984), pp. 239–49; J. Nadolny, 'Some observations on northern European metalbeaters and metal leaf in the late Middle Ages', in R.A. Rushfield and M.W. Ballard (eds), *The Materials, Technology, and Art of Conservation: Studies in Honor of Lawrence J. Mejewski on the Occasion of his 80th Birthday* (New York: Conservation Centre of the Institute of Fine Arts, New York University, 1999); Bellucci and Frosinini, *Working Together*, pp. 56–7, and note 3.

26 The *oro di metà* leaf has been found in a limited number of paintings and can be confused with a silver leaf when the upper gold sheet becomes abraded. Cennino warns on the use of *oro di metà* because it tarnishes; on the subject of *oro di metà* see Cennino Cennini, *The Craftsman's Handbook*, p. 60; E. Skaug, 'Cennino Cennini's "oro di metà"', in C. Manganelli del Fa, M. Matteini, B. Santi, and E. Skaug, *Cennino Cennini's 'Oro di metà': A Possible Interpretation* (this manuscript, dated April 1983, was never published and a copy was left to the library of the scientific department of the Opificio delle Pietre Dure, Florence);

E.S. Skaug, 'Cenniniana: Notes on Cennino Cennini and His Treatise', *Arte Crist* 31/754, pp. 15–22; E. Skaug, *Punch Marks from Giotto to Fra Angelico: Attribution, Chronology, and Workshop Relationships in Tuscan Panel Painting c.1330–1430* (Oslo: IIC Nordic Group, 1993); M. Ciatti and C. Frosinini (eds), *La Madonna di San Giorgio alla Costa di Giotto* (Florence: Edifir, 1995), pp. 70-3 (on p. 73 it is cited that *oro di metà* has been also found in the Madonna del Popolo, Brancacci chapel, church of Carmine, Florence, and in the Giottesque crucifix of Santa Felice, Florence). The production of a double leaf, gold and silver, for threads, is described by Theophilus, 'Soldering gold and silver together', in *On Divers Arts*, p. 156.

27 Ciasca, *Gli statuti dell'arte*. 'Reform of 1403 Rubrica IIII', *Misura dell'oro e dell'argento battuto*, p. 371; the size of the gold and silver leaf is drawn at the end of the codex, see p. 377. The writer has measured the size of the gold leaf in several paintings that were in the conservation laboratories of the Opificio delle Pietre Dure in Florence in 1998–99 and they average between 6.5 and 8.5 centimetres: Coppo di Marcovaldo, *Madonna and Child* from Santa Maria Maggiore, Florence; Giotto, *Crucifix* from Santa Maria Maggiore, Florence; Lorenzo Monaco, *Coronation of the Virgin* from the Uffizi; and Lorenzo Monaco *Annunciation* from Santa Trinita, Florence. The gilded areas in the crucifix of Sarzana show that small and irregular gold leaf was used; this may be related to the fact that the gilded area was limited in size and did not require the use of large leaf.

28 Bomford et al., *Art in the Making*, p. 22. The scientific laboratory of the Opificio delle Pietre Dure in Florence confirmed that the gold leaf analysed has a thickness of around two to two and a half microns. Medieval gold leaf was much thicker and easier to handle, compared to modern leaf; in fact, Cennino writes in the chapter 'How to Gild on Panel', 'take your fine gold, and pick up the leaf carefully with a pair of tweezers or small pincers'. Cennini, *The Craftsman's Handbook*, chapter 134, p. 80; similarly, Teophilus advises cutting the gold leaf to the size needed with scissors: Teophilus, 'Gold leaf', in *On Divers Art*, chapter 23, p. 31. I. Passeri, *Techniche di lavorazione delle foglie metalliche nei dipinti su tavola e organizzazione del mestiere tra XIII e XV secolo: Proposte circa i metodi di pulitura* (unpublished thesis, Opificio delle Pietre Dure e Laboratori di Restauro, 1998).

29 Cennini, *The Craftsman's Handbook*, chapter 138, pp. 84–5. Cennino writes about a ducat and not a florin coin as a source for gold; this is perhaps related to the fact that he lived for a period of time in Padua. Bellucci and Frosinini, *Working Together*, p. 29.

30 'Et che e consoli le dette misure per loro ordinate continuamente debbino apresso a loro o presso al notaio della dett'arte tenere marchiata del loro marchio, et le dette misure così marchiate dare a cercatori che ànno a cercare delle cose divietate tra gli artefici della dett'arte, e per essi cercatori far cercare colla detta misura e investigare se le predette cose s'oservano; e trovati colpevoli, punire e condempnare secondo la forma del presente ordinamento.' The size of the leaf is reported at the end of the codex, Ciasca, *Gli statuti dell'arte*, pp. 371, 377.

31 In the statute of 1315, Rubrica XII: 'Item, quod nullus de dieta arte possit, audeat, vel presummat committere aliquam fraudem in arte predicta, in mittendo vel ponendo argentum prò auro, aurum di meta prò auro fini, et azzurum de Alamania prò ultramarino, nec similia, unde opus aliquod dapnum recipiat, sub pena soldorum quadraginta f. p., et quotiens, et ad restituendum dapnum quod recipuretur ex malitia supradicti, seu sequeretur exinde.' Ciasca, *Gli statuti dell'arte*, p. 82.

32 In the guild of Siena 'Breve dell'Arte dei Pittori Senesi' of 1355, the following is required: 'Di non mettere uno oro per uno altro, o uno colore per altro'; chapter 14, 'Ancho ordiniamo, che nullo de' l arte de' dipentori ardisca over presuma di mettare ne' lavorii che facesse altro oro o ariento o colori che avesse promesso, sì come oro di metà, per oro fino, e stagno per ariento, azzurro de la Magna per azurro oltramarino, biadetto overo indico per azzurro, terra rossa o minio per cinabro; e chi contrafacesse per le predette cose

sia punito et condannato per ogni volta in x libr.'; G. Milanesi, 'Breve dell'arte de' pittori senesi', in *Documenti per la storia dell'arte senese* (Siena: O. Porri, 1854), p. 7; furthermore, in the painters' guild of Perugia's *Odinamenta hominus artis pictorum civitatis Perusi'*, Chapter 3, we read: 'Item dicimus et ordinamus quod quiquicunque de dicta arte promittet dare alicui aurum finum in aliquo opere et dabit argentum superauratum, nomine pene. C. sold. den. solvere teneatur'; and in Chapter 4: 'Item dicimus et ordinamus quod quicunque promictet alicui dare argentum finum et dabit stangnum pro argento, nomine pene. XL. sold. den. solvere teneatur', L. Manzoni, *Statuti e matricole dei pittori delle città di Firenze, Perugia e Siena nei testi originali del secolo XIV* (Perugia: Perugia Unione Tipografica Coop., 1904) p. 159.

33 XRF analysis allows the identification of the chemical elements present in the gold leaf and makes it possible to calculate the percentage of impurities present in the alloy.

34 P. Maioli and C. Seccaroni, 'Analisi XRF su tre opere di Gentile da Fabriano', in M. Ciatti and C. Frosinini, with the collaboration of R. Bellucci, *Il Gentile risolto: Il politico dell'Intercessione di Gentile da Fabriano* (Florence: Edizioni Edifir, 2006), pp. 199–211.

35 M. Ciatti and C. Frosinini, with the collaboration of R. Bellucci, *Pinxit Guillielmus: Il restauro della Croce di Sarzana* (Florence: Edifir Edizioni, 2001); M. Ciatti, C. Frosinini, and R. Bellucci, *La Croce dipinta dell'Abazia di Rosano, Visibile ed Invisibile, studio e restauro per comprensione* (Florence: Edifir Edizioni, 2007).

36 Bellucci, 'La Croce di Sarzana tra materia e immagine', in *Pinxit Guillielmus*, pp. 41–54; P. Moioli and C. Seccaroni, 'Caratterizzazione non distruttiva mediante analisi di fluorescenza X dei pigmenti', in *Pinxit Guillielmus*, pp. 83–8. Ciatti, Frosinini, and Bellucci, *La Croce dipinta dell'Abazia di Rosano*, p. 117 and P. Moioli, C. Seccaroni, *Caratterizzazione non distruttiva dei pigmenti della Croce di Rosano mediante spettrometria XRF* in Ciatti, Frosinini, and Bellucci, *La Croce dipinta*, pp. 175–7; Passeri, *Techniche di lavorazione*; also, Unn Plahter, 'The crucifix from Hemse: Analyses of the painting technique', *Restauro* 1 (January 1884), pp. 35–44; the gold decoration in the Crucifix from Hemse was analysed and resulted to be 22 carat gold. It is also important to note that any calculation of the alloy composition should take in consideration the thickness of the metal leaf.

37 Bellucci, *La Croce di Sarzana*, p. 46; R. Bellucci, 'Materia ed ipotesi: La tecnica artistica della Croce di Rosano', in Ciatti, Frosinini, and Bellucci, *La Croce dipinta*, p. 117. J. Nadolny, 'All that's burnished isn't bole. Reflections on medieval water gilding part 1: Early medieval to 1300', in J. Nadolny, K. Kollandsrud, M.L. Sauerberg, and T. Frøysaker (eds), *Medieval Painting in Northern Europe: Techniques, Analysis, Art History* (London: Archetype Publications, 2006).

38 Andrew Lins, 'Basic properties of gold', in D. Bigelow, E. Cornu, G.J. Landrey, and C. van Horne (eds), *Gilded Wood: Conservation and History* (Madison, CT: Sound View Press, 1991), pp. 17–23.

39 Bole or 'Armenian' bole is an aluminum silicate or clay rich in iron oxide that confers to the material a red-orange tonality. The easy-to-grind clay, as well as the soft greasy texture allows the bole to produce a cushioning smooth layer on which the gold leaf can be laid, burnished, punched, and tooled. Cennino suggested grinding and mixing the bole with a dilute egg white and applying it in several coats in the areas to be gilded. Cennino Cennini, 'How to lay bole on panel, and how to temper it', Chapter 131, and 'Another way to temper bole on panel, for gilding', Chapter 132, in *The Craftsman's Handbook*, pp. 79–80. Nadolny, 'All that's burnished isn't bole'.

40 M. Matteini and A. Moles, 'Tecniche della pittura antica: Le preparazioni del supporto', *Kermes* 4 (January–April 1989), pp. 49–62.

41 Theophilus, *On Divers Arts*, pp. 29–31.

42 Theophilus, *On Divers Arts*, pp. 36–7.

43 Cennino Cennini, 'How you may gild on panel with terre-verte', *The Craftsman's Handbook*, Chapter 133, p. 80.

44 Two paintings by Giotto show the use of terre verte: a small panel with the Pentecost, dated around 1310–18, at the National Gallery in London and the Saint Stephan, dated around 1330–35, at the Horne Museum in Florence. Bomford et al., *Art in the Making*, p. 69.

Part II ✧ Practices

5 ✧ The 'Genealogy of Jean le Blanc': accounting for the materiality of the medieval Eucharist

Aden Kumler

IN A PROTESTANT print from circa 1570–1624, the tattered sails of windmills and the exposed lath and crumbling plaster of a granary shed subtly index the ruinous state of Catholic claims to the *corpus Christi* (Figure 5.1).[1] Within an impossible landscape, we are offered a clear view of ecclesiastical industry. The print meticulously plots the fabrication of communion wafers or hosts from the sowing of a wheat field, through the reaping, threshing, winnowing, and milling of the grain, to the cooking and impressing of wheaten paste in a host press

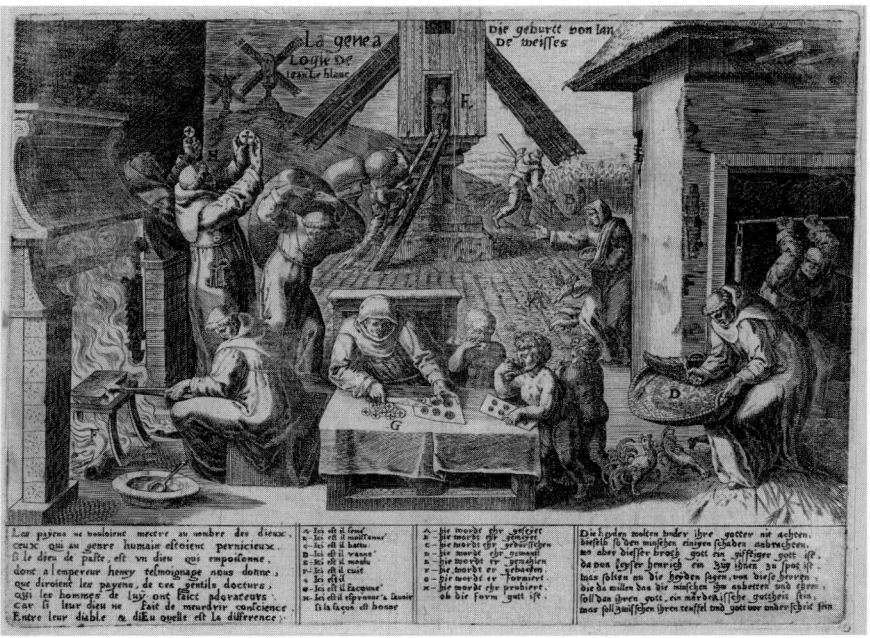

5.1. *La genealogie de Jean le Blanc*, c. 1570–1624, engraving, British Museum, 1880,0710.838

set in the fire, the excision of round wafers from cooked unleavened sheets, and, finally, the examination of each cross-stamped wafer, a visual inspection intent on discovering and rejecting flawed hosts.

Each stage in the production process detailed in the image is keyed by a roman capital to verses below. And so we learn: 'Here he is sown,/ here he is harvested,/ here he is beaten,/ here he is winnowed,/ here he is milled,/ here he is cooked,/ here he is,/ here he is tested to see if the workmanship is good.'[2] The 'he' in question is the bilingual shaped print's eponymous 'Jean le Blanc' / 'Jan de Weisses' and it is his 'genealogie' or 'geburtt' that the print carefully traces. The French and German poems set in the lower corners of the sheet castigate this Catholic 'dieu de paste / broth gott'. Denying that even the pagans would have admitted such a poisonous deity into their pantheon, the short poems ascribe to the Catholics' deified material thing the power of murdering consciences.[3]

La genealogie de Jean le Blanc's insistence on the inanity of an edible divinity, its claims to lay bare the wheaten device at the heart of a dangerous, if absurd, system of cultic deception, resound throughout reform accounts of the Catholic sacrament.[4] In England, the prolix reformer Thomas Becon (1512/13–67) denounced the Catholic 'new-baken little great god' in strikingly similar terms:

> A wonderful god it is that ye set forth to the people to be worshipped. Not many days past it was corn in the ploughman's barn; afterward the miller ground it to meal; then the baker, mingling a little water with it, made dough of it, and with a pair of hot printing-irons baked it. Now at the last come you, blustering and blowing, and with a few words spoken over it, ye charm the bread on such sort that either it trudgeth straightways away beyond the moon, and a fair young child above fifteen hundred years old, come in the place of the bread; or else, as the most part of you papists teach, of the little thin cake ye make the very same body of Christ was born of Mary the virgin, and died for us upon the altar of the cross, the bread being turned into the natural flesh of Christ, and the accidents of the bread only remaining, according to the doctrine of pope Nicholas and pope Innocent.[5]

For Becon, as for many reformers, the consecrated wafer was a point of obvious vulnerability precisely because the host, after the consecration, seemed so manifestly and empirically *not* what its devotees proposed it to be. Jean le Blanc, the reformers insisted, was an impossible, risible fabrication: a 'Jack-in-the-Box' whose whiteness was no more or less than the appearance of fine wheat flour and whose presence on the altar owed more to the mill and the miller than any miracle or divine dispensation.[6] Over and over again, reformers urged their audiences to take a long, hard look at the host. There was, they insisted, no incarnate but divine body to be found on the altar or in monstrances. Instead, they argued, the wheaten wafer was as it always had been, in material or substantial terms: a made thing whose genealogy could be traced back from clerical hands to the host press, the millstone, and the wheat field.

Confronting the Catholic Eucharist, the incredulity of reformist conviction and polemic was two-fold. On the one hand, reformers rejected traditional claims for Christ's invisible but substantial presence lurking behind, or under, the persistent appearance, or 'accidents', of the transubstantiated wafer and wine. At the same time, they also refused to believe that Christian men and women, presented with an honest account of the Eucharist's materiality, could continue to adore this 'bread god'. Meticulously delineating each stage in the fabrication of the host, *La genealogie de Jean le Blanc* adduces the very existence of that process as irrefutable evidence for the inescapable artefactual character of the host. 'Surely you can recognize a material thing, made by artifice, when you see it?' the print seems to ask its beholder. The premise of the print's relatively understated visual polemic is clear: to document Jean le Blanc's material origins and genealogy is to render apparent, even self-evident, the insurmountable difference between a piece of bread and the deity, between the material and the divine.

In the remainder of this chapter I will take the Protestant print as an invitation to look closely at the host made by the Middle Ages and rejected by reformers. *La genealogie de Jean le Blanc*'s confidence that a clear, close-hand view of the material production of the Eucharistic wafer would undo its claims upon divine presence is, I will suggest, stranger than we have recognized. For the host's roots in sod, its origins in seed, its refinement and formation under the pressure of the mill stone and the hot iron surface of the host press were hardly well-kept secrets in the Middle Ages. Indeed, the medieval Eucharistic situation is marked by a sustained, if often polyvalent engagement with materials and material processes. Attending to the material facture of the sacramental elements of wafer and wine and their visible, tactile and metaphorical properties, medieval people fabricated not only the offerings destined for the altar, but also a complex, vital economy of materials, making, meaning and metamorphosis.[7]

In material terms, the Western medieval sacrament of the altar required three things: flour, water, and wine. By the ninth century in the West, unleavened bread (*azyma* or *panis infermentatus*) came to be preferred for use in the Mass; with the eruption of the Azymite Controversy in the eleventh century it became a subject of ritual divergence and intense debate.[8] Decrying the Byzantine ritual use of leavened bread, Western ecclesiastics mounted a series of interconnecting arguments for their ritual practice. Christ, they claimed, would have offered his disciples unleavened bread at the Last Supper in conformity with Jewish law.[9]

There was also Paul's testimony in First Corinthians to be reckoned with: 'know you not that a little leaven corrupteth the whole lump? Purge out the old leaven, that you may be a new paste, as you are unleavened ... Therefore let us feast, not with the old leaven, nor with the leaven of malice and wickedness; but with the unleavened bread of sincerity and truth.'[10]

This Pauline association of leavening with pollution, sin, and malice, intensified by the Azymite controversy, was powerful and long-lived in the medieval West. Not only did it authorize the unleavened host as the correct type of altar bread, it also laid the foundation for a powerful tradition of tropological thought and practice, organized in relation to Eucharistic materiality.[11]

Throughout the Middle Ages ecclesiastics attempted to authorize their ritual practice with reference to Christ's example, prophecy (typologically construed), and the metaphors and tropes that permeate both the Old and the New Testaments. Thus, in accordance with the account in John 19:34 of the water and blood that flowed from the lance wound Christ received on the cross, priests added a small amount of water to the sacramental wine in the Mass. Likewise, Christ's parabolic self-identification with a grain of wheat (John 12:24–5) and as the 'true vine' (John 15:1) and medieval Christological interpretations of Isaiah 63:2–3 ('Why then is thy apparel red, and thy garments like theirs that tread in the winepress? I have trodden the winepress alone') and Genesis 49:11 ('He shall wash his robe in wine, and his garment in the blood of the grape') ensured that the material elements of wheaten wafer and communion wine were invested with sacral, Christological connotations long before they were ritually consecrated on the altar.[12]

Non-scriptural criteria were also brought to bear on the sacramental species of wheaten wafer and wine, criteria that manifest a sophisticated and sustained engagement with the substantial qualities and empirical properties of things seen, touched, tasted, and smelled. As we shall see, medieval theory and practice cultivated an acute sensitivity to the specific character of materials and material things in the economy of the sacred. The stakes of this analytic and creative engagement with material forms of meaning were nowhere higher than in the making of the material species that came to be the body of Christ in the Mass.

As we might expect, questions of purity and pollution loomed large. Writing in 798, Alcuin admonished his brethren in Lyon: 'the bread, which is consecrated into the Body of Christ, ought to be of the cleanest, without the leavening of any other infection, and the water [ought to be] the purest, without any filth, and the wine should be most purified and free from the admixture of any other liquid.'[13] The necessity of pure sacramental species is a constant refrain in early medieval capitularies and in high and late medieval synodal and provincial statutes.[14] Yet this policing of the boundary between the pure and impure hardly exhausted medieval thinking about the wafer and wine destined for the altar. As we shall see, the sacramental elements were both produced by and generative of a medieval tradition of materialist hermeneutics, an intense mode of apperception that found and made meaning with raw materials and manufactured objects alike.

The wheat used in the making of Eucharistic hosts is a case in point. Already in the early Middle Ages Western ritual tradition prescribed that the Eucharistic host be made with the finest, most expensive grade of wheat flour (*triticum* or *farina triticea*).[15] The ubiquity of this specification extended even to secular law codes such as Alfonso X's *Las siete partidas* (1256–65), which echoed ecclesiastical authorities when it insisted that the host 'must be made of wheat flour (*farina de trigo*) mixed up with water alone, without yeast or any other substance whatever; and the priest must make it very cleanly'.[16]

A repetitious corpus of texts prescribing the use of fine wheat flour in making hosts was accompanied in the period by imaginative forms of exegesis that took up the specific qualities of various types of grain. Even scholastic *magristi* were sensitive to the differentiated potential of grains, each variety of cereal acting as a touchstone in a complex web of moralizing associations. Taking up the question 'is wheaten bread required for the matter of this sacrament?' in his *Summa theologiae*, Thomas Aquinas ruminated:

> It seems that the matter of this sacrament does not require that the bread should be wheaten bread (*panis triticeus*). This sacrament is a memorial of our Lord's passion. Yet barley bread seems more in keeping with the passion of our Lord than wheaten bread; in the first place, it is rougher . . . Again, in natural things the shape (*figura*) is the sign of the specific nature (*speciei*). But some cereals have the same shape (*figuram*) as wheat (*grano tritici*), thus *far* and *spelta*, from which in certain regions altar bread is made . . . Furthermore, if you mix a thing with something else you no longer have one specific nature. But it is scarcely possible to have pure wheaten flour (*farina triticea*) without some admixture of some other cereal, unless one most carefully selects the grains.[17]

Scriptural citations feature very little in Thomas's analysis. Instead, it is the material form, colour, and natural properties of specific cereals that attract his exegetical attention. The theological, even soteriological valence of specific materials is cast into even higher relief as Thomas explains why barley, despite its apparent analogic attractiveness, is not an appropriate material for the host:

> Barley bread serves to signify the hardness of the Old Law. First, because of its harshness. Then again, because as Augustine says, 'the pith of the barley grain which has a shell most difficult to remove, signifies either the Law itself, which was so given that in it the vital nourishment of the soul was covered over by corporeal signs; or the people itself, which had not yet been freed from fleshly desire, which like a shell stuck close to its heart.' But this sacrament pertains to the *easy yoke* of Christ and to the truth which is already made manifest and to a spiritual people. Hence barley bread would not be suitable matter for this sacrament.[18]

With Augustine's help, Aquinas articulates a relational *distinctio* of fine wheat from obdurate barley. As Aquinas explains earlier in his response, *panis triticeus* is the paradigmatic bread; all other breads seem to be only substitutes for this fine wheat bread that *confortat hominem* (strengthens/comforts mankind).[19] It comes as no surprise, then, that he concludes: *propria materia hujus sacramenti est panis triticeus* (the proper material of this sacrament is bread made of fine wheat flour).[20] Thomas's exegesis is at once a tropological and typological account of different grains as specific materials.[21] Underlying this mode of thought and interpretation we can detect a conception of the material in which substance and semantics coincide. In the case of many medieval discussions of the sacramental elements, this interpretation of materials works from the altar to the field and back again in a complex and relational material poetics.

The wine employed in the Mass never garnered the intense attention that medieval thinkers lavished on wheat; it was, nonetheless, a matter for deliberation. Although there is evidence for some variation in practice, particularly in the early Middle Ages – witness an eleventh-century English statute expressly forbidding the use of beer in the Mass – a consistent consensus deemed wine, with the admixture of a modicum of water, to be the preferred sacramental liquid.[22] Ecclesiastical authorities agreed that either red or white wine could be employed in the Mass, but the formal qualities of red wine – its resemblance to blood – made it particularly suited to the sacred signifying work of a sacrament.[23] As John de Burgh put it in his influential manual for priests: 'although red wine ought to be preferred because of its more overt resemblance to blood, it is not a necessity for the sacrament.'[24]

What was a necessity, everyone agreed, was that the liquid that would be substantially transformed into Christ's blood be wine, not vinegar or water. For some authorities, the possible confusion of white wine with water sufficed to recommend the exclusive use of red wine.[25] Other authors insisted that the admixture of too much water in wine of any colour would have the effect of absorbing the substance of wine in the substance of water, resulting in a liquid ontologically more water than wine and so materially diverted from its proper sacramental state. Statutes issued in 1350 for the diocese of Sodor and Man instructed clergy to take:

> the utmost care that the wine in which [the sacrament] is celebrated should not be corrupt or changed into vinegar and that it should rather be red than white. Nevertheless, the holy [sacrament] is truly confected with white [wine], but not with vinegar, since in vinegar all the substantial powers [of wine] are changed, and wine loses its potency. And let water be added in a moderate quantity, so that the wine is not absorbed by the water, but rather the water by the wine.[26]

As in Aquinas's consideration of the sacramental aptitude of different grains, the statute emphasizes the material specificity of wine and its particular substantial powers (*substantiales vires*). The loss of these potent properties renders the liquid that remains unfit for the altar, precisely because it no longer possesses wine's quiddity. It is this principle that also governs medieval concern about the ratio of water to wine: too much water drowns the substantial presence of wine, resulting in liquid that cannot accomplish the sacramental – that is sacredly signifying – labour for which it was appointed.

The confusion of liquids and liquid proportions at the altar, like the offering of a wine corrupted into vinegar or the consecration of an impure host, were dire scenarios. Canons attributed to Egbert, the eighth-century Archbishop of York, went so far as to propose penalizing the use of impure material elements in the Mass as if it were a kind of villainous re-crucifixion of Christ: 'priests of God should always diligently take care that the bread and wine and water, without which masses are celebrated pointlessly, should be pure and clean; for if it is celebrated otherwise, unless true penitence comes to the rescue, they shall be punished with those who offered vinegar mixed with gall to the Lord.'[27]

The introduction of compromised, confused, or corrupted materials into the ritual frame – even before the moment of consecration – had serious consequences. Precisely because of their insistent materiality, and the privileging of that specific materiality, the sacramental species required special handling.

Medieval scrutiny of materials and materials practices seem to have intensified further when it came to the actual making of hosts. The Carolingian Bishop Theodulf of Orléans (760–821) stipulated that priests in his jurisdiction should fabricate altar breads themselves, or, at the very least, should closely supervise their production:

The breads that you offer to God in the sacrifice should be made resplendently and diligently, either by you yourselves or by your boys [i.e. servants] in your presence; and you should diligently note that the bread, the wine, and the water, without which masses cannot be celebrated, should be handled most cleanly and carefully, and let nothing filthy or unapproved be found in these things, in accordance with what Scripture says: *Let the fear of the Lord be with you, and do all things with diligence!* (2 Par. 19:7).[28]

This designation of host-making as a sacerdotal undertaking, animated by a God-fearing diligence, is a recurring refrain in the centuries following. Theodulf's injunction was reiterated and expanded upon in an Anglo-Saxon text circulating in the eleventh century, and synodal statutes and manuals for priests throughout the late Middle Ages maintain both the letter and the spirit of these prescriptions.[29]

From the beginning of the medieval period, concerns for material purity and sacerdotal diligence set altar bread apart from other, more ordinary forms of bread. By the eleventh century, if not earlier, however, the Western host was further distinguished – even from other unleavened breads consumed in Europe – by its facture and form.[30] The distinctness of the communion wafer was a specific material and formal effect, obtained by the use of a special implement, the host press (Figure 5.2).[31] The host press was an ironwork tool consisting of a flat paten end, incised on one interior surface with decorated roundels, each corresponding to a wafer, and long scissor-like handles (Figure 5.3). When hosts were made, the inner surface of one paten would be covered with a paste composed exclusively of fine wheat flour and water, and the tool's terminal plates would be closed. Set over a fire, the paste would heat and harden into a thin, white sheet impressed with a number of disks, each stamped in low relief with various motifs and sacred abbreviations.

In the early and high Middle Ages, host production was supposed to be an ecclesiastic monopoly. Indeed, just as capitularies and synodal statutes throughout the period insisted that each parish priest should be responsible for making the wafers he consecrated in the Mass, so too

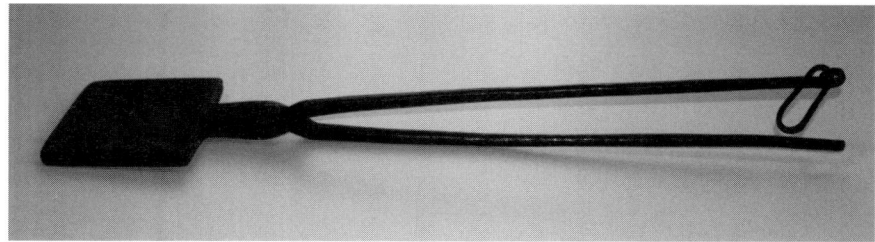

5.2. Host press, late medieval (?), once belonging to the parish church of Saint-Pierre, Peyrelevade (Corrèze, France)

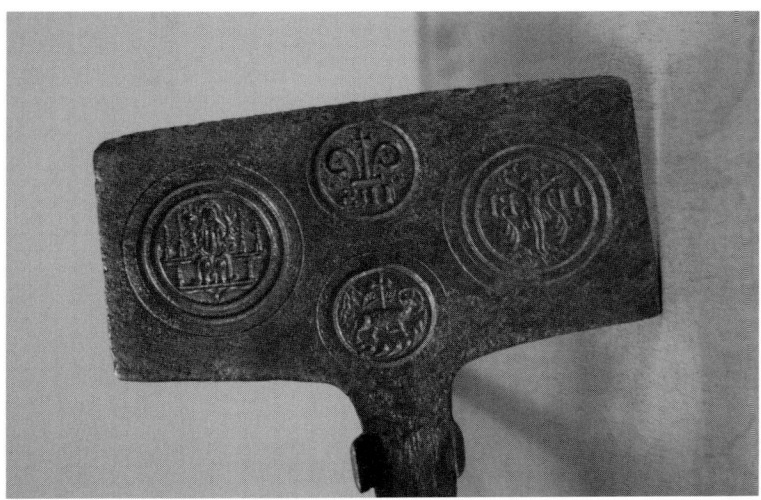

5.3. Inner surface of incised paten of a late medieval (?) host press, collection of the Musée du Hiéron, Paray le Monial

the regulations that governed monastic life laid down precise directions for how hosts should be made and by whom. From Lanfranc's Constitutions for the Benedictine community at Christ Church, Canterbury (c. 1077),[32] to Uldaric's Customary for the Benedictine Abbey of Cluny[33] and the Constitutions composed for the Cluniac Abbey of Hirsau by its reforming Abbot William (d. 1091),[34] monks were enjoined to take every care in the fabrication of hosts.

Monastic customaries elaborated a regime of exacting, regimented host production usually supervised by the sacristan, but involving multiple members of the monastic community and their servants. Instructions given to the brethren at the Benedictine Abbey of Eynsham (Oxfordshire) in the thirteenth century are characteristic of this tradition of rigorous, scrupulous fabrication.[35] The subsacristan was charged with ensuring that the hosts made by the brethren would be superlatively clean and respectable (*mundissime et honestissime*). Accordingly, the wheat to be used was chosen grain by grain (*granatim*) and entrusted to a servant of good repute (*famulo bonae opinionis*) who would take the grain to the mill in a clean cloth sack, specifically designated for the purpose. Before the milling of the flour destined to become wafers could commence, the mill stones had to be purged of any impurities: at Eynsham this involved a preliminary grinding of other wheat intended to flush out any dirt that might have clung to the surface of the stones.

Once the milling of the flour for wafers was completed, it was brought back to the Abbey and boulted within a curtained space prepared by the sacristan for that purpose.³⁶ Not only were the brethren and abbey servants required to wash their faces and hands before undertaking the labour that followed, but the customary further specifies that they were to be dressed in albs with their heads veiled by amices (*albis induantur, capita amictibus velent*), vestments closely associated with the liturgy of the Mass. Undoubtedly, these sartorial stipulations witness to the desire to keep hair from falling into and polluting the species, but they also reveal the quasi-liturgical aura that surrounded the production of wafers, at least in monastic milieus. Vested, with a fire supplied with specially prepared firewood (*ligna valde sicca . . . ante multos dies de industria per-parata*), monastic host-makers would sprinkle the specially prepared flour with water, working this mixture into a paste on a pristine surface (*tabula mundissime*). As this paste cooked in host presses set over the fire, the monks were directed to recite the psalms of the hour in which they worked, but otherwise to keep silent.³⁷

The imposition of silence during the making of hosts at Eynsham was almost certainly motivated by the desire to keep the brethren's breath or saliva from the species, a preoccupation expressed in a customary from the Benedictine Abbey of Cluny: 'with the greatest diligence let them take care that in no way should their saliva, nor even their breath, come in contact with the hosts.'³⁸ Throughout the production process, as described in monastic regulations, measures were taken not simply to prevent a confusion or pollution of materials, but also to control and regularize the material substance and facture of the finished wheaten wafers. From the veiling of the monks' heads and the retention of their breath and spittle, to the use of the host press, the process was itself designed to ensure a serial production of uniform wafers and to eliminate any trace of the human hand.

The hosts made at Eynsham, like those made throughout Europe in the medieval period, were emphatically material objects. They were, at the same time, objects whose specific formal and material features bore no apparent signs of manufacture, if we take that term in its most literal sense of 'handmadeness'. The surfaces of wafers did not register the hands that had threshed the wheat, operated the mill, and held the host press. In this respect, the instructions for making wafers that survive in multiple versions from the Middle Ages can be read as directions for the material production of an object in which the suppression of all indices of the human or the contingent allowed for a significant privileging of form, surface, and opaque material substance (Figure 5.4).

The specificity of the host, its constitution through specific, repeated characteristics – wheatness, roundness, thinness, whiteness, purity – was no accident of ritual practice or taboo. The medieval host's specific materiality, form, and facture were deliberately cultivated, both by the

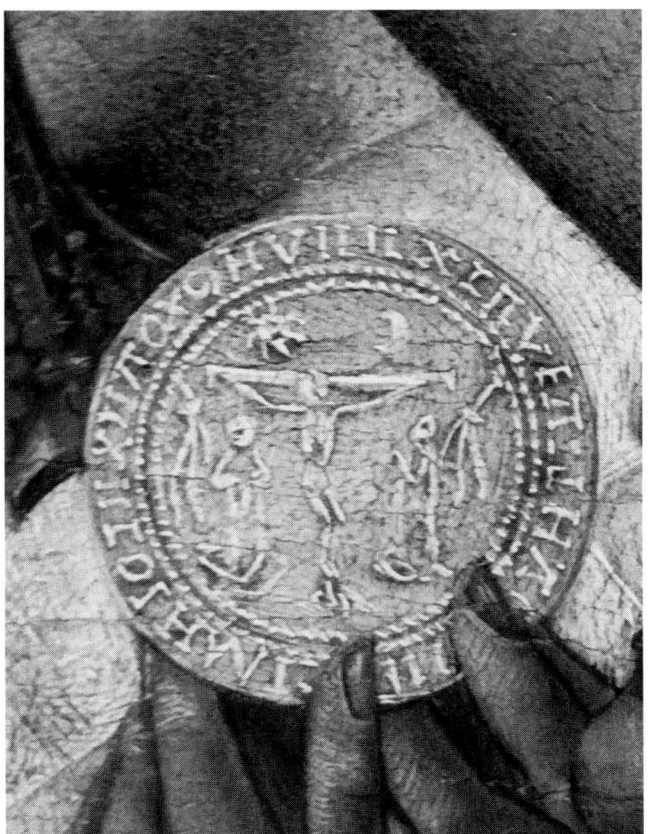

5.4. Attributed to Diego de la Cruz, *The Mass of Saint Gregory* (detail), c. 1490, oil and gold on panel, Philadelphia Museum of Art, EW1993-127-1

fabrication process and by discourses that surrounded the wafer as object. The Sodor and Man statutes of 1350 articulate a terse account of how the host ought to be constituted and why: 'The wheaten host should be round and whole and without blemish, like the lamb without a blemish who has not had a bone removed from it. Hence the verse: Christ's host should be clean, wheaten, thin, not large, round, unleavened. It is inscribed, not cooked in water but baked in fire.'[39] Similarly, the host's material and formal properties were tropologically appropriated by Robert Mannying of Brunne's early fourteenth-century treatise, *Handlyng Synne*:

> You know well that the host is but a little thing to see. So should we be little in will, little and meek without ill will . . . The host is made of wheat, the most admirable grain that men eat. So should we be meek and kind . . . The paste for the host should not be made of any kind of sour dough, for the sour dough makes the sweetness that comes from the flour all sour. By

> this sour dough is signified that envy is a wicked thing... There is also a power in the wheat that is very contrary to slothfulness, for grains of wheat will not prick, as do oats and barley. Nor should we have any prickle [or sting] of too much idleness... The paste of the host, as said before, shall not be of mixed grain, but all only of wheat. The mixture of grain men should leave aside. And this signifies that in no way should we mix ourselves with covetousness... Also, you see that the host is thin, and there is no dark flour in it. And that will truly signify in opposition to the sin of gluttony... And you see that the host is white, and so we should have no delight in any kind of carnal offense of lechery, that makes us black.[40]

Through an elaborate, systematic tropological inventory not only of the host's properties, but also of a range of grains, the text exhorts its audience to morally and spiritual conform to the host; a form of *imitatio* not of Christ, but of the white wheaten object designed for the Mass. Through tropological ekphrases of various grains, as well as the wafer and wine fabricated for the Mass, medieval thinkers elaborated a materialist hermeneutics that was both deductive and constructive. Offered exemplars for their own moral and spiritual formation and reformation in the form of wheat, communion wafer, and sacramental wine, medieval men and women were urged to undertake an *imitatio rerum* emphatically grounded in the material world.[41]

In the midst of these tropological ekphrases and prescriptive pragmatic accounts of the host and wine, surely there lurks a massive contradiction. Certainly, late medieval dissidents and early modern reformers argued there was a problem at the heart of the Catholic sacrament, a problem that, quite literally, could not be overlooked. It was that persistent, opaque, material problem that prints like *La genealogie de Jean le Blanc* attempted to lay bare.

Either all the fuss about the making of the medieval host, all the engineering of its ontology and appearance, was the meticulous fabrication of a sham god – a bit of bread that only ever remained a bit of bread – and so the Mass was nothing better than a spectacle designed to frame a very underwhelming idol. Or if some substantial change did take place in the Mass in which wheaten and viniferous substances yielded to the invisible but real hypostatic presence of Christ, surely all the elaborate measures taken to produce, refine, control, and shape the materiality of the Eucharistic species were profoundly irrelevant. In yet blunter terms: either the medieval account of the materiality of the Eucharist was a fraud tending toward idolatry, or it was a nonsensical labouring of materials that culminated only in an evacuation of substance, an emptiness where there used to be a specific object.

In subtle ways, this dichotomous view of the materiality of the Eucharistic species as either fraud or irrelevance continues to condition our obliviousness to crucial aspects of the medieval sacrament and the real interest of medieval accounts of its materiality. Indeed, scholarly enthusiasm for medieval texts and works of art that propose epiphanic modes of 'seeing through' or 'seeing beyond' the consecrated species has privileged the miraculous over the manufactured in ways that ultimately fail to adequately account for the materiality of the sacrament. By way of a conclusion, I want to suggest that if our accounts of the Eucharist only ever begin with the apotheosis of wafer and wine and the advent of the ineffable *corpus Christi*, we risk a kind of blindness to the persistent significance of materiality and material processes in the medieval Eucharistic situation.

Whether favouring the term transubstantiation, or preferring several other variant terms and phenomenal accounts for the change that took place on the altar with the pronunciation of the consecration form, theologians in the later Middle Ages generally agreed that a real change took place in the Mass whereby the substance of the wafer and wine ceased to exist as they had existed and the *corpus Christi* came to be present on the altar.[42] At the same time, however, theologians, monastics, parish priests, and lay devotees all knew from first-hand experience that the appearance of the sacramental species *did not change*. When celebrants and communicants looked, smelled, and tasted, they perceived the wheaten wafer that had been brought to the altar by the deacon and they observed the same wine within the gleaming interior of the chalice.

The apparent absence of change in the sacramental species was no secret or suppressed phenomenon in the period: it was constantly remarked upon, promoted, and attended to. When James Ryman saluted the Eucharist in song as 'God in fourme of brede' he emphatically acknowledged that 'it semeth white, yet it is rede, and it is quik and semeth dede'.[43] *Handlyng Synne* offers its audience a yet more extended meditation on the post-consecration state of things:

> If you see it [Christ's presence] not with bodily sight, Your soul within shall believe it right. And if you taste no flavour, but truly wine and bread of flour, that is the wisdom of God's arrangement . . . by sight it seems bread and it truly has the flavour of bread, Neither your sight nor your touch, has there any certain thing. What then shall best save you, if not the steadfast belief you shall have? Steadfast belief in every part shall then truly save you.[44]

Circulated widely among both the clergy and the laity in late medieval England, *Handlyng Synne* urged devotees to concentrate their attention upon the seeming empirical persistence of the species after the consecration. Neither sight nor taste, it muses, can discern the change worked by the consecration. This sacramental situation – the persistence of the accidents, despite the substantial non-presence of the material elements – was to be desired, *Handlyng Synne* suggests. It was precisely in confronting and contemplating the *unchanged* accidents that the devotee could 'beleue . . . ryght'.

The persistence of the accidents of wafer and wine involved medieval devotees in a difficult discipline of attention. Attending Mass, witnessing the elevation of the host in the priest's hands, watching the celebrant communicate from paten and chalice, and perhaps even gazing at the host reserved in a monstrance, medieval Christians were confronted with a visible, tactile paradox: the empirical presence of a substantial absence. What is more, they were explicitly exhorted to linger in that paradoxical situation; to keep looking, not so much through or beyond the species, but rather *at* their persistent, opaque forms. And if we attend to the persistence of the specific objects of wafer and wine within the Mass, we can recognize that much of the 'ocular piety' that we have come to associate with Eucharistic devotion was precisely a practice of attending to those things that the authors of monastic customaries, the designers of host presses, and the workers in the vineyard had fabricated: works of a technical, labour-intensive *ars*, if not art, that demanded and rewarded close attention both before and after they were consecrated.

The obduracy of the accidents is a crucial aspect of late medieval conceptions of what transpired in the Mass, and it is a phenomenal account of the Eucharist that our current accounts of the sacrament as spectacle or epiphany have largely ignored, despite the compelling testimony of countless medieval texts and works of art. It is, I think, one of the chief preoccupations of the central *Hostienmühle* panel of an altarpiece painted in Ulm in around 1470, today preserved in the Ulmer Museum (Figure 5.5).[45]

At the apex of the panel's cruciform composition, the four zoocephalic Evangelists and the Virgin Mary empty sacks of grain into a hopper, supervised from above by the Holy Spirit. Just below, in a kind of manufacturing miracle worked by the apostles, we see perfect white hosts tumbling out from between two small millstones. This cascade of hosts is depicted in mid-descent against the upper curve of the mill wheel, separated by the smallest of intervals from the diminutive haloed head of the Christ Child, naked within a golden chalice held by the four 'Latin' doctors of the Church: Jerome, Ambrose, Gregory the Great, and Augustine.

As many interpreters have recognized, the panel invites its beholders to a complex meditation on the change worked in the Mass; a substantial change of species to body, here rendered in terms that are quite literal in their mimetic details and allegorical in their collective effects.[46] The altarpiece's exploration of the before and after of Christ's substantial presence in the sacrament is in part a meditation on ecclesial unity: the

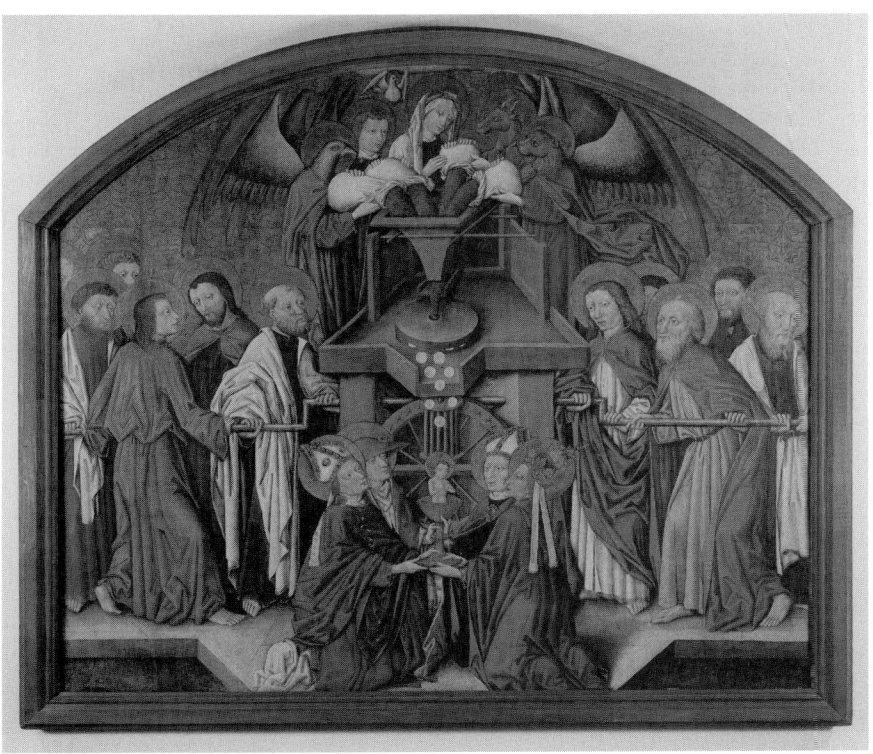

5.5. Ulm Workshop, *Host Mill retable*, c. 1470, oil on panel, Ulmer Museum, Inv. AV 2150

corpus mysticum of the communion of the faithful realized, sacramentally, in relation to the *corpus Christi*.[47] There may also be a subtle play within the panel's figural composition on traditional typological inflections of this iconographic type: an allegory of the supersession of laws and of divine favour in which the tough raw material of the Mosaic law is refined, tempered, and ultimately transformed by the teleological progress of Christian salvation history and its heroes: Mary, the Evangelists, the Apostles, the Fathers.

Yet within the dense allusive economy of the panel, amidst a dazzling array of vivid surface effects, we confront, once again, the tactile and visible forms of the material wafer. As the panel's horizontal axis of apostolic exertion intersects with its vertical axis of salvific transformation, it is the painter's rendering of these discrete, white, bright material objects that holds the eye. Like the accidents of wafer and wine that lingered in the devotee's vision after the Christic presence was announced by the elevation, so too the white hosts tumbling from the mill stones remain: passages of pigment and oil made to account for the persistent, opaque effects of the materiality of the medieval Eucharist.

Notes

1 Bilingually entitled *La genealogie de Jean le Blanc* and *Die Geburtt von Ian de Weisses*, the print (190 × 253 mm) survives in at least five impressions: in addition to the sheet in the British Museum reproduced here, the Rijksmuseum (Amsterdam), Hessische Landes- und Hochschulbibliothek (Darmstadt), SvS (Rotterdam), Bibliothèque nationale de France (Paris) and the Herzog August Bibliothek (Wolfenbüttel) preserve copies. For a brief notice with further references, see: Wolfgang Harms et al. (eds.), *Die Sammlung der Herzog August Bibliothek in Wolfenbüttel: Kommentierte Ausgabe*, 3 vols, Deutsche illustrierte Flugblätter des 16 und 17 Jahrhunderts (Munich: Kraus International Publications, 1980), 2, pp. 98–9 (No. 50).

2 'A – Ici est il semé/ hie wordt ehr geseyet; B – Ici est il moissonné/ hie wordt ehr gemeyet; C – Ici est il battu/ hie wordt ehr gedorsschen; D – Ici est il vanné/ hie wordt ehr gewantt; E – Ici est il moulu/ hie wordt er gemahlen; F – Ici est il cuit/ hie wordt er gebacten; [orphaned incomplete line in French]; G – Ici est il façouné/ hie wordt er formiert; H – Ici est il esprouué a sauoir si la façon est bonne/ hie wordt ehr probiert, ob die form gutt ist.' Translations are mine, unless otherwise noted.

3 'Les payens ne vouloient mectre au nombre des dieux/ ceux qui au genre humain estoient pernicieux/ si le dieu de paste, est vn dieu qui empoisonne/ dont a lempereur henry tesmoignage nous donne/ que diroient les payens, de ce gentils docturs/ qui les hommes de luy on faict adorateurs/ car si leur dieu ne fait de meurdrir conscience/ Entre leur diable & dieu quelle est la difference'; 'Die heyden wolten under ihre gotter nit achten/ dieselb so den minschen einigen schaden anbrachten/ wo aber diesser broth gott ein gifftiger gott ist/ da von keyser henrich ein zu(e)g ihnen zu spot ist/ was solten nu die heyden sagen, von diese herren/ die da willen das die minschen ihm anbetten und ehren/ soll dan ihren gott, ein morderissche gottheit sein/ was soll zwisschen ihren teuffel und gott vor underschiet sein'; I'm grateful to Christopher Wild for his comments on the German and I thank Gwendolyn Collaço and Alexandra Marraccini for their helpful suggestions.

4 From a large and growing literature on early modern Eucharistic polemic, both Catholic and Protestant, as well as the sacramental theologies articulated by reformers, I found the following studies particularly illuminating: Frank Lestringant, *Une sainte horreur, ou, Le voyage en Eucharistie: XVIe–XVIIIe siècle*, Histoires (Paris: Presses universitaires de France, 1996); Stephen Greenblatt, 'Remnants of the sacred in early modern England', in Margreta De Grazia, Maureen Quilligan, and Peter Stallybrass (eds), *Subject and Object in Renaissance Culture* (Cambridge: Cambridge University Press, 1996); Christopher Elwood, *The Body Broken: The Calvinist Doctrine of the Eucharist and the Symbolization of Power in Sixteenth-century France*, Oxford Studies in Historical Theology (New York: Oxford University Press, 1999); Jeff Persels, '"The Mass and the fart are sisters": Scatology and Calvinist rhetoric against the Mass 1560–63', in Jeff Persels and Russell Ganim (eds), *Fecal Matters in Early Modern Literature and Art: Studies in Scatology*, Studies in European Cultural Transition, vol. 21 (Aldershot and Burlington, VT: Ashgate, 2004); George Hoffmann, 'Anatomy of the Mass: Montaigne's "cannibals"', *PMLA* 117:2 (2002); Pierre Deyon, 'Sur certaines formes de la propagande religieuse au XVIe siècle', *Annales Histoire Sciences Sociales* 36:1 (1981); Luc Racaut, *Hatred in Print: Catholic Propaganda and Protestant Identity during the French Wars of Religion*, St Andrews Studies in Reformation History (Aldershot and Burlington, VT: Ashgate, 2002); Stephen Greenblatt, 'La souris mangeuse d'hostie: Les miettes du repas eucharistiques', *Traverses* 5 (1993); Philip Benedict, 'Of marmites and martyrs: Images and polemics in the wars of religion', in *The French Renaissance in Prints from the Bibliothèque nationale de France* (Los Angeles: Grunwald Center for the Graphic Arts, University of California, Los Angeles, 1994), pp. 120–1.

5 Thomas Becon, 'The displaying of the Popish Mass', in John Ayre (ed.), *Prayers and Other Pieces of Thomas Becon* (Cambridge: Cambridge University Press, 1844), p. 261.

6 On the derisive appellation 'Jean le Blanc', see Francis Clark, *Eucharistic Sacrifice and the Reformation* (Westminster, MD: Newman Press, 1960), p. 178; Lestringant, *Une sainte horreur*, pp. 76–9. For further examples of reformist satire on the theme of Jean le Blanc or the Dieu de paste, see *La Legende veritable de Jean le Blanc* and *Le Passe-Temps de Jean le blanc*, reprinted in Anatole de Montaiglon (ed.), *Recueil de poésies françoises des XVe et XVIe siècles, morales, facétieuses, historiques*, 13 vols (Paris: P. Jannet, 1858), 8, pp. 105–25, 126–38. See also the further variants on this theme published in Henri Léonard Bordier (ed.), *Le chansonnier huguenot du XVIe siècle* (Geneva: Slatkine Reprints, 1969), pp. 149–54, 158–61.

7 Caroline Bynum has recently proposed a powerful account of the role materiality played in late medieval Christian materiality: Caroline Walker Bynum, *Christian Materiality: An Essay on Religion in Late Medieval Europe* (New York: Zone Books and Cambridge, MA: The MIT Press, 2011). While Bynum emphasizes the transforming and transformative character of 'holy matter' in the Middle Ages, here I want to suggest that we should also take seriously the powerful part played by more mundane, ordinary and non-miraculous materials and conceptions of matter (or materiality) in medieval religious and visual-material culture.

8 On the historical antecedents and theological–political contours of the Azymite Controversy, see Georgij Avvakumov, *Die Entstehung des Uniongedankens: Die lateinische Theologie des Hochmittelalters in der Auseinandersetzung mit dem Ritus der Ostkirche*, Veröffentlichungen des Grabmann-Institutes zur Erforschung der Mittelalterlichen Theologie und Philosophie Bd 47 (Berlin: Akademie Verlag, 2002), pp. 29–159. The Byzantine position, represented by Patriarch Michael Cerularius, is examined in Mahlon H. Smith, *And Taking Bread . . . : Cerularius and the Azyme Controversy of 1054*, Théologie historique 47 (Paris: Beauchesne, 1978).

9 Whereas the Latin church relied upon the chronology advanced by the synoptic Gospels in which the Last Supper took place after all leavening and leavened food stuffs had been purged from Jewish households in preparation for the Passover meal, the Byzantine church favoured the chronology proposed by John's Gospel in which the Last Supper took place before preparations for Passover had begun: Smith, *And Taking Bread*, p. 32.

10 'Nescitis quia modicum fermentum totam massam corrumpit? Expurgate vetus fermentum, ut sitis nova conspersio, sicut estis azymi . . . Itaque epulemur: non in fermento veteri, neque in fermento malitiæ et nequitiæ: sed in azymis sinceritatis et veritatis.' 1 Corinthians 5:6–8. All biblical texts are quoted in the Vulgate translation: Robert Weber and Bonifatius Fischer (eds), *Biblia Sacra iuxta vulgatam versionem*, quartam emendatam. ed. (Stuttgart: Deutsche Bibelgesellschaft, 1994). English translations quoted from *The Holy Bible Douay Rheims Version*, trans. Bishop Richard Challoner, revised ed. (Rockford, IL: Tan Books and Publishers, 2000).

11 The western church's commitment to an unleavened host and the association of leavening with malice did not weaken in the later Middle Ages; from among a host of examples, see the assertion 'Debet panis consecrandus esse azimus id est sine fermento malicie' (The bread to be consecrated must be unleavened, that is without the leaven of malice) in the late fourteenth-century *Pupilla oculi*, a widely circulating manual for the clergy: Johannes de Burgo, *Pupilla oculi omnibus sacerdotibus tam curatis, q[uam] non curatis, summe necessaria* (Paris: Jahanne [sic] Paruo, 1527), part 4, c. 3 (n.p.).

12 See, for example, the catena of these scriptural touchstones in Guillaume Durand, *Rationale Divinorum Officiorum: I–IV*, Anselmus Davril and T.M. Thibodeau (eds), *Corpus Christianorum: Continuatio Mediaevalis* 140 (Turnhout: Brepols, 1995), pp. 442–3 (4, 41, 6).

13 '. . . panis, qui in corpus Christi consecratur, absque fermento ullius alterius infectionis, debet esse mundissimus; et aqua absque omni sorde purissima, et vinum absque omni commistione alterius liquoris [nisi aquae] purgatissimum . . . Ex aqua et farina panis fit qui consecratur in corpus Christi: aqua et vinum in sanguinem consecrabitur Christi.'

Epistola 90 in Alcuin, *Epistolae*, ed. J.P. Migne, PLL 100 (Paris: Migne, 1844–65), cols. 289A–B.

14 Concern for the sacrament's material purity and integrity is further discussed in Miri Rubin, *Corpus Christi: The Eucharist in Late Medieval Culture* (Cambridge: Cambridge University Press, 1991), pp. 38–49.

15 Medieval Latin terminology for grains is complex and often involves no little ambiguity; for further clarification and discussion, see Georges Comet, *Le paysan et son outil: Essai d'histoire technique des céréales: France, VIIIe–XVe siècle*, Collection de l'École française de Rome 165 (Rome: École française de Rome, 1992), pp. 199–292; Georges Comet, 'Dur ou tendre? Propos sur blé médiéval', *Médiévales* 16–17 (1989). For a magisterial review of ecclesiastical teaching, tradition, and a range of practices concerning the choice of materials used in the western Eucharist, with consideration of contemporary pastoral questions, see Roger Gaise N'ganzi, *Les signes sacramentels de l'Eucharistie dans l'Église latine: Études théologiques et historiques*, Studia Friburgensia n. F. 89 (Fribourg: Éditions Universitaires, 2001).

16 'E este pan, a que llaman Hostia, deue ser fecho de farina de trigo, amasada tan solamente con agua, sin leuadura, e sin otro mezclamiento ninguno: e deuelo fazer el Clerigo muy limpiamente.' Gregorio López de Tovar (ed.), *Las Siete Partidas del Sabio Rey Don Alonso el Nono glosadas por el licenciado Gregorio López*, 4 vols (Madrid: la Oficina de Benito Cano, 1789), 1, pp. 59–60 (1.4.52). English translation modified slightly from Robert Ignatius Burns (ed.), *Las Siete partidas*, trans. S.P. Scott, Middle Ages series (Philadelphia: University of Pennsylvania Press, 2001), vol. 1, p. 39. On medieval Iberian taxonomies of wheat and wheaten breads with particular attention to Eucharistic tropes, see Terry Mount, 'Levels of meaning: Grains, bread, and bread making as informative images in Berceo', *Hispania* 76:1 (1993).

17 Latin and English translation (slightly modified) in: Thomas Aquinas, *Summa theologiae: The Eucharistic Presence (3a. 73–8)*, ed. and trans. William Barden (Cambridge: Blackfriars and New York: McGraw-Hill, 1965), 58, pp. 30–3 (3a, 74, 3)

18 Aquinas, *Summa theologiae*, ed. Barden, pp. 32–3 (3a, 74, 3, ad. 1).

19 Aquinas, *Summa theologiae*, ed. Barden, pp. 32–3 (3a, 74, 3, resp.).

20 Aquinas, *Summa theologiae*, ed. Barden, p. 32 (3a, 74, 3 resp.).

21 For further discussion of Thomas's treatment of *triticum*, see also Comet, *Le paysan et son outil*, pp. 210–11.

22 'Quod sacrificium de cervisia, vel sola aqua non fiat, sed solummodo de vino aqua mixto.' From the *capitula* of a legatine council held at Winchester in April 1070 CE: M. Brett et al. (eds), *Councils & synods, I: A. D. 871–1204. Part II, 1066–1204* (Oxford: Clarendon Press, 1981), p. 575 [6]. Wilkins had previously designated this canon as belonging to the 1076 council convened at Winchester: David Wilkins, *Concilia Magnae Britanniae et Hiberniae*, 4 vols (Londini: Sumptibus R. Gosling, 1737), vol. 1, p. 365 [6}.

23 Quoting Augustine, Peter Lombard provides a concise preliminary definition of a sacrament in his influential *Sententiae*: 'Augustinus in libro X De civitate Dei: "Sacramentum est sacrae rei signum" . . . Item, sacramentum est invisibilis gratiae visibilis forma.' Peter Lombard, *Sententiae in IV Libris Distinctis*, vol. II, *Spicilegium Bonaventurianum*; 5, 3rd ed. (Grottaferrata: Editiones Collegii S. Bonaventurae ad Claras Aquas, 1981), p. 232 (L. 4, D. 1, c. 2).

24 '. . . quamvis vinum rubeum sit preeligendum propter expressiorem similitudinem sanguinis nec est de necessitate sacramenti': Burgo, *Pupilla oculi omnibus sacerdotibus tam curatis, q[uam] non curatis, summe necessaria*, part 4, c. iii (n.p.).

25 Josef A. Jungmann, *Missarum sollemnia: Explication génétique de la messe romaine*, 3 vols (Paris: Aubier, 1952), 2, p. 311. For further discussion, see Pierre-Marie Gy, 'Le vin rouge

est-il préférable pour l'Eucharistie?', in Martin Klöckener and Arnaud Join-Lambert (eds), *Liturgia et unitas: Liturgiewissenschaftliche und ökumenische Studien zur Eucharistie und zum gottesdienstlichen Leben in der Schweiz; Études liturgiques et oecuméniques sur l'Eucharistie et la vie liturgique en Suisse: in honorem Bruno Bürki* (Freiburg: Universitätsverlag and Geneva: Labor et Fides, 2001); Ferdinando Dell'Oro, 'Il vino nella liturgia latina del Medioevo', in Gabriele Archetti (ed.), *La civiltà del vino: Fonti, temi e produzioni vitivinicole dal Medioevo al Novecento. Atti del convegno, Monticelli Brusati, Antica Fratta, 5–6 ottobre 2001, Atti delle Biennali di Franciacorta 7* (Brescia: Centro culturale artistico di Franciacorta e del Sebino, 2004).

26 'Summopere praecauentes ne vinum cum quo celebratur sit corruptam, vel in acetum commutatum, et quod potius sit rubrum, quam album. In albo tamen bene conficitur sacrum, et non de aceto, cum in aceto mutantur omnes substantiales vires, et vinum vim amisit. Et aqua in tam modica quantitate apponatur ut non vinum ab aqua, sed aqua a vino absorbeatur': David Wilkins, *Concilia Magnae Britanniae et Hiberniae*, 4 vols. (Londini: Sumptibus R. Gosling, 1737), vol. 3, p. 11 [2].

27 'Sacerdotes Dei diligenter semper procurent, ut panis et vinum, et aqua, sine quibus nequaquam missae celebrantur, pura et munda fiant; quia si aliter agatur, cum his qui acetum cum felle mixtum Domino optulerunt, nisi vera poenitentia subvenerit, punientur': Benjamin Thorpe (ed.), *Ancient Laws and Institutes of England*, 2 vols. (London: Printed by G.E. Eyre and A. Spottiswoode, 1840), vol. 2, p. 111 [100]. Dating from the eleventh century, these were attributed to the eighth-century Anglo-Saxon Archbishop's aegis.

28 'Panes, quos Deo in sacrificium offertis, aut a uobis ipsis, aut a uestris pueris coram uobis, nitide ac studiose fiant; et diligenter obseruetis, ut panis, et uinum et aqua, sine quibus missae nequeunt celebrari, mundissimae atque studiose tractentur, et nichil in his uile, nihil inprobatum inueniatur, iuxta illud, quod ait scriptura: "Sit timor Domini uobiscum, et cum diligentia cuncta facite!"' Hans Sauer (ed.), *Theodulfi Capitula in England: Die altenglischen Übersetzungen, zusammen mit dem lateinischen Text*, Münchener Universitäts-Schriften: Institut für Englische Philogie: Texte und Untersuchungen zur englischen Philologie (Munich: Wilhelm Fink Verlag, 1978), p. 310 [5].

29 In the Anglo-Saxon translation and expansion of Theodulf of Orléans's first Capitulary, *ibid.*, p. 311 [5]. An antiquated modern English translation is available in Thorpe (ed.), *Ancient Laws and Institutes of England*, pp. 405, 407. I am grateful to Damian Fleming for his generous elucidation of philological aspects of the Anglo-Saxon text, which I hope to examine more fully elsewhere.

30 For further discussion of the range of breads produced in the Middle Ages, with consideration of non-sacramental unleavened breads, see A.M. Bautier, 'Pain et pâtisserie dans les textes médiévaux aux latins antérieurs au XIIIè siècle', in Denis Menjot (ed.), *Manger et boire au Moyen Age: Actes du Colloque de Nice (15–17 octobre 1982)*, Publications de la Faculté des lettres et sciences humaines de Nice, 1st series, no. 27–28 (bis) (Paris: Belles Lettres, 1984); Françoise Desportes, *Le pain au Moyen Âge* (Paris: O. Orban, 1987); Carole Lambert, 'Rites eucharistiques dans les us et coutumes alimentaires au bas Moyen Âge', *Religiologiques* 17 (1998); Kirk Ambrose, 'A medieval food list from the monastery of Cluny', *Gastronomica* 6:1 (2006); Max Währen, 'Brot und Gebäck im Mittelalter und als Primärquellen im Abendmahlsbild', in Hermann Eiselen (ed.), *Gesammelte Aufsätze und Studien zur Brot- und Gebäckkunde und -geschichte: 1940–1999* (Ulm: Deutsches Brotmuseum, 2000).

31 For several recent discussion of host presses, with references to the older, largely antiquarian literature, see Lluïsa Amenós, 'Hostier i neulers medievals del Museu Episcopal de Vic', *Quaderns del Museu* 1 (2005); M. Sunyol i Busquets, 'Estudi d'un hostier medieval del 1339', *Acta historica et archaeologica mediaevalia* 9 (1988); Patricia Sela del Pozo Coll, 'Imágenes en las hostias eucarísticas: Origen y significación de motivos iconográficos

presentes en un medio secunadrio', in Inés Monteira Arias, Belén Muñoz Martínez, and Fernando Villaseñor Sebatián (eds), *Relegados al margen: Marginalidad y espacios marginales en la cultura medieval* (Madrid: Consejo Superior de Investigaciones Científicas, 2009); Aden Kumler, 'The multiplication of the species: Eucharistic morphology in the Middle Ages', *RES: Anthropology and Aesthetics* 59–60 (2011). See also the essays collected in Oliver Seifert (ed.), *Panis angelorum – Das Brot der Engel: Kulturgeschichte der Hostie* (Ostfildern: J. Thorbecke, 2004).

32 David Knowles and Christopher Nugent Lawrence Brooke (eds), *The Monastic Constitutions of Lanfranc*, Oxford Medieval Texts, revised ed. (Oxford: Clarendon Press, 2002), pp. 124–5.

33 Udalricus Cluniacensis, *Antiquiores consuetudines Cluniacensis monasterii*, ed. J.P. Migne, PL 149 (Paris: Migne, 1853), cols 757A–758A (L. 3, c. 13). For further discussion of these very influential directions, see Dominique Iogna-Prat, *Order and Exclusion: Cluny and Christendom Face Heresy, Judaism, and Islam, 1000–1150*, Conjunctions of Religion & Power in the Medieval Past (Ithaca, NY: Cornell University Press, 2002), pp. 200–1.

34 Wilhelmus Hirsaugiensis, *Constitutiones Hirsaugienses*, ed. J.P. Migne, PLL 150 (Paris: Migne, 1844–65), cols 1086C–1087D (L. 2, c. 32).

35 For these instructions see Antonia Gransden (ed.), *The Customary of the Benedictine Abbey of Eynsham in Oxfordshire*, Corpus consuetudinum monasticarum (Siegburg: F. Schmitt, 1963), pp. 178, ll. 7–26.

36 'Reportata farina secretarius vas et locum quo farina bulitari debet in circuitu cortina paret.' Gransden (ed.), *The Customary of the Benedictine Abbey of Eynsham*, p. 178. The Latin phrasing is ambiguous: it may refer simply to a temporary curtained space within the monastery or, more specifically, to a curtained-off part of the cloister walk (*curcuitu*).

37 'Cura eciam faciendi hostias super subsacristam est, quae ut mundissime et honestissime fiant summopere studere debet. In primis frumentum cum magno studio granatim eligatur, electum in sacculo mundo et de bono panno facto et ad hoc opus tantum parato ponatur et a famulo bonae opinionis ad molendinum deferatur. Quo delato famulus aliud frumentum in ipso molendino moli prius faciat, ut illud unde hostiae fieri debent sine aliqua sorde moli postea valeat. Reportata farina secretarius vas et locum quo farina bulitari debet in circuitu cortina paret. Ipsemet vero indutus alba et velato amictu capite hoc opus agat. Eo autem die quo hostiae fieri debent secretarius et fratres qui eum adiuvare debent, anequam incipiant manus et facies lavent, albis induantur, capita amictibus velent. Qui ferrum tenebit et focum faciet, famuli erunt monachorum. Unus de revestis super tabulam mundissimam ipsam farinam aqua consergat et manibus fortiter conpingat et maceret. Qui ferra in quibus hostiae coquuntur tenet, manus cirotecis involutos habeat. Interim, dum ipsae hostiae fiunt et coquuntur, dicant ibidem fratres psalmos familiares horarum et horas canonicas. Silencium nisi cum necesse fuerit teneant. Ligna valde sicca esse debent et ante multos dies de industria praeparat. Subsacrista eciam cum ispas hostias parat alba induetur et capud amicto velatum habebit': Gransden (ed.), *The Customary of the Benedictine Abbey of Eynsham*, p. 178 (ll. 7–26). The Eynsham customary was composed some time between c. 1228/29 and c. 1300.

38 'summopere cavent ut nonmodo saliva, sed nec flatus eorum aliquo modo ad hostias pertingere possit': Marquard Herrgott (ed.), *Vetus disciplina monastica; seu, Collectio auctorum Ordinis S. Benedicti maximam partem ineditorum* (Parisiis: Typis C. Osmont, 1726), p. 249.

39 'Hostia de frumento fit rotunda et integra, et sine macula, quia agnus extitit sine macula, et os non fuit communutum ex eo. Unde versus: candida, triticea, tenuis, non magna, rotunda expers fermenti non mista, sit hostia Christi. Inscribatur aqua, non cocta sed igne sit assa.' Wilkins, *Concilia* vol. 3, p. 11 [2]. English translation from Rubin, *Corpus Christi*, p. 39.

40 'Þou wost weyl þat þe vbble/ Ys but a lytyl þyng to se./ So shul we be lytyl yn wyl,/ Lytyl & meke wyþ outen yl . . . / Þe vbble ys made of whete,/ Þe loueliest corne þat men ete./

So shuld we be meke & louely . . . / Þe past of þe vbble nat ne ogh/ Be made of any maner of soure dogh,/ For þe sour dogh makþ al soure/ Þe suetnes þat cumþ of þe floure./ By þys sour dogh ys tokenyng/ Þat enuye ys a wykked þyng, . . . / A vertu also yn þe whete ys/ Þat ys moche aʒens sloghnes,/ For whete cornes wyl nat prykke/ As otes doun or barlykke./ Ne we shuld nat haue any prykyl/ Of ydelnes ouer mykyl . . . / Þe paste to þe vbble seyd byforn/ Shal nat be of medled corn/ But al only of whete,/ Þe mastlyoun shul men lete./ Þat yche meneþ: wyþ no wyse/ we shul vs medel wyþ coueytyse . . . / Also þou seest þe vbble ys þynne/ And gret dunhede ys noun þer ynne./ And þat wyl weyl sygnyfye/ Aʒens þe synne of glotonye./ For þere ne wyl þe sacrament reste/ Þere glotonye wyl hym out keste . . . / And þou seest þe vbble ys whyte,/ And we shul haue noun delyte,/ Of no maner of flesshely lak,/ Of lecherye þat makþ vs blak.' Robert Mannyng, *Handlyng synne*, ed. Idelle Sullens, Medieval & Renaissance Texts & Studies 14 (Binghamton, NY: Medieval & Renaissance Texts & Studies, 1983), pp. 251-3 (ll. 10091-146).

41 Although considerable attention has focused on how medieval people understood sacramental communication as a form of *imitatio* in which the devotee was incorporated in Christ's mystical body and assimilated, in some fashion, to the Christic body *per se*, the conformation of devotee to sacramental *materials* (even before their consecration in the Mass) that I emphasize here has yet to receive the attention it warrants. On medieval communion as a Christomimetic act involving eating and being eaten, see Caroline Walker Bynum, *Holy Feast and Holy Fast: The Religious Significance of Food to Medieval Women* (Berkeley: University of California Press, 1987), esp. pp. 48-67; Caroline Walker Bynum, 'Women mystics and Eucharistic devotion in the thirteenth century', in *Fragmentation and Redemption: Essays on Gender and the Human Body in Medieval Religion* (New York Zone Books and Cambridge, MA: The MIT Press, 1991).

42 For further discussion of the range of models and terms for how Christ's real presence was realized in the Eucharist among theologians of the high and later Middle Ages, see Gary Macy, *The Theologies of the Eucharist in the Early Scholastic Period: A Study of the Salvific Function of the Sacrament According to the Theologians, c. 1080-c. 1220* (Oxford: Clarendon Press, 1984); Gary Macy, 'The "dogma of transubstantiation" in the Middle Ages', in *Treasures From the Storeroom: Medieval Religion and the Eucharist* (Collegeville, MN: Liturgical Press, 1999); Caroline Walker Bynum, *Wonderful Blood: Theology and Practice in Late Medieval Northern Germany and Beyond*, The Middle Ages Series (Philadelphia: University of Pennsylvania Press, 2007); Rubin, *Corpus Christi*, esp. pp. 12-163. On the introduction of 'transubstantiation' into the theological lexicon, see Joseph Goering, 'The invention of transubstantiation', *Traditio* 46 (1991).

43 Cambridge, University Library, MS Ee.I.12, fol. 49v; transcribed in Richard Leighton Greene (ed.), *The Early English Carols* (Oxford: Clarendon Press, 1935), p. 219 (no. 318).

44 'Ʒyf þou se hyt nat wyþ bodyly syght,/ Þy soule wyþ ynne shal beleue hyt ryght./ And ʒyf þou fele no sauour,/ But ryghtly wyne & brede of flour,/ Þat ys þe wysdom of goddes ordynaunce,/ For to saue vs alle fro þys chaunce./ . . . Hyt semeþ brede as be syght,/ And as brede sauer haþ ryght./ Noþer þy syghte no þy felyng/ Hast þou on no certeyn þyng./ What shal þan þe most saue/ But stedfast beleue þat þou shalt haue?/ Stedfast beleue of euerydeyl,/ Þat shal þan, saue þe weyl.' Mannyng, *Handlyng synne*, p. 249 (ll. 9983-10002).

45 The Ulm panel (137 × 156 cm) has most recently been discussed in Seifert (ed.), *Panis angelorum – Das Brot der Engel: Kulturgeschichte der Hostie*, pp. 122-3. For further consideration of the iconography of the so-called *Hostienmühle* or *Sakramentsmühle* (including discussion of the Ulm altarpiece), see Heinrich Schulz, 'Die mittelalterliche Sakramentsmühle', *Zeitschrift für bildende Kunst* 63; Alois Thomas, 'Die mystische Mühle', *Die Christliche Kunst: Monatsschrift für alle Gebiete der christlichen Kunst und Kunstwissenschaft* 31 (1934/35); H. Rye-Clausen, *Die Hostienmühlenbilder im Lichte mittelalterlicher Frömmigkeit* (Stein am Rhein: Christiana-Verlag, 1981); P. Remigius Boving, 'Zur Theologie eines Altarbildes aus der ehemaligen Franziskanerkirche in Göttingen', *Franziskanische Studien* 5 (1918); Heinrich

Herzberg, *Die Mühle zwischen Religion und Aberglauben* (Berlin: Verlag für Bauwesen, 1994), pp. 13–21. The *Hostienmühle* is often related to the earlier iconographic formula of the so-called 'Mystic Mill', best known from a nave capital from Vézelay; see, with further bibliography, Kirk Ambrose, 'The "Mystic Mill" capital at Vézelay', in Steven A. Walton (ed.), *Wind & Water in the Middle Ages: Fluid Technologies from Antiquity to the Renaissance*, Penn State Medieval Studies, 2 (Tempe, AZ: ACMRS, 2006). In the Middle Ages sacramental wine and its production were also given an allegorizing iconographic treatment in the so-called *Christus in der Kelter* or Christ in the Wine Press schema, which cannot be explored here; for further discussion see Alois Thomas, *Die Darstellung Christi in der Kelter: Eine theologische und kulturhistorische Studie, zugleich ein Beitrag zur Geschichte und Volkskunde des Weinbaus*, ed. Matthias Zender and Franz Josef Heyen, Quellen und Abhandlungen zur mittelrheinischen Kirchengeschichte 37, 2nd ed. (Düsseldorf: Schwann, 1981); Alois Thomas et al., *Der Keltertreter: Über das neuerworbene Triptychon des Mittelrhein-Museums Koblenz aus der Zeit um 1500*, Mittelrheinische Helfte 5 (Koblenz: Görres-Verlag, 1980); Danièle Alexandre-Bidon (ed.) *Le pressoir mystique: Actes du Colloque de Recloses (27 mai 1989)* (Paris: Éditions du Cerf, 1990); Gerald Maier, '"Hostienmühle" und "Christus in der Kelter": Zur Allegorie des Altarsakraments an Beispielen von Malmsheim, Deufringen, Gärtringen und Herrenberg', *Leben mit Vergagenheit: Jahrbuch des Heimatgeschichtsvereins für Schönbuch und Gäu e.V.* 5 (2007); James H. Marrow, *Passion Iconography in Northern European Art of the Late Middle Ages and Early Renaissance: A Study of the Transformation of Sacred Metaphor into Descriptive Narrative*, Ars neerlandica 1 (Kortrijk: Van Ghemmert, 1979), pp. 83–94.

46 Several interpreters have insisted that the *Hostienmühle* iconography cannot be a 'depiction' or 'illustration' of transubstantiation, *strictu senso*, because of its emphasis on the active labour of the Evangelists, Mary, and the Apostles. In this view, the iconography is instead either primarily typological in orientation, or else concerned with an incarnational theology of the word made flesh. See, for example, Thomas's remark: 'Die mystische Mühle ist also mehr als ein einfaches Symbol der Transsubstantiation, nämlich eine allegorische hochdramatische Erzählung vom Escheinen Christi, des wahren Himmelsbrotes, das von Maria den Menschen geschenckt wurde, als Brot des Glaubens helles Licht verbreitend und als heiliges Brot der Eucharistie das ewige Leben gewährleistend.' Thomas, 'Die mystische Mühle', p. 139.

47 The best account of the idealizing ecclesiological import of medieval conceptions of the *corpus Christi* remains Henri de Lubac (ed.), *Corpus mysticum: L'eucharistie et l'église au moyen âge*, revised and augmented 2nd ed. (Paris: Aubier, 1949).

6 ✧ Lead white's mysteries

Spike Bucklow

LEAD WHITE is ubiquitous in the European painting tradition – found in the oldest surviving works, right up to those executed in the mid-twentieth century. Today, relatively little mystery surrounds the material. It is a white crystalline solid that can be described chemically as basic lead carbonate ($2PbCO_3.Pb(OH)_2$). Like most heavy metal compounds, it has a relatively high refractive index.[1] This optical property helps account for its popularity amongst painters, since its refractive index is significantly greater than that of linseed, poppy, or walnut oil, which are the standard media for European oil painting. The difference between the refractive indices of the pigment and media results in a high degree of light scattering within the mixture, so thin layers of lead white dispersed in oil produce very opaque paint films. Other whites available to artists before the early twentieth century, like chalk, had refractive indices closer to those of oils, so they generally made more transparent paint films. The pigment's popularity with painters was reinforced by the way it interacted chemically with oils to produce very robust and intensely white paint films.

Artists' manuals recommended the use of lead white in flesh paint (usually tinted with vermilion on panels or earths on walls).[2] According to just one manual, other uses included tinting paper, lightening blues, painting brocades, panel painting and gilding in general, and even fixing broken glass and fine dishes.[3] It follows that wherever a good strong, bright white was required, lead white was recommended. The chemical analysis of microscopic samples taken from paintings confirms that lead white was the main white pigment until the beginning of the twentieth century. It was, for example, in England's most prestigious thirteenth-century painting,[4] and also on the palette of England's most prodigious nineteenth-century painter.[5] Lead white had other uses – including cosmetic and medical[6] – but this chapter focuses on its role in painting.

Lead white's widespread use as an artists' material – as attested by the results of several decades of scientific analysis of paintings – is also suggested by its wide variety of names. In English alone, lead white has also been known as Apulian white, Flake white, French white, Cremnitz white, Krems white, Vienna white, Berlin white, silver white, slate white, white lead, and ceruse or cerussa. Painters also employed lead white mixed with chalk, a mixture known as both ceruse and Spanish white. From the seventeenth century onwards, several variants of basic lead carbonate were also used as white pigments, including lead acetate, known as sugar of lead, and lead sulphate, known as Flemish white.[7] Chemically, lead white is identical to a natural mineral that is now called hydrocerussite. The Roman architect Vitruvius recorded that this relatively rare mineral was once been mined in Rhodes but that, in his lifetime, the artists' material was manufactured artificially.[8] This chapter considers that manufacturing process and its cultural significance in medieval and early modern Europe.[9]

The manufacture of artificial or synthetic pigments might initially be considered an early modern or modern phenomenon. However, Vitruvius was not the first to mention the manufacture of lead white as a synthetic pigment. Theophrastus described its manufacture centuries earlier,[10] and another description occurs in clay tablets of about 1700 BCE, retrieved from the library of Assurbanipal.[11] These records of a synthetic chemical process are significantly pre-dated by the practice itself, as lead white was amongst artists' materials found in the ruins of Ur, dated to around 3000 BCE.[12]

In his early twelfth-century artists' treatise, the Benedictine monk and practising craftsman Theophilus described lead white's manufacture. He said that sheets of lead metal should be sprinkled with urine and vinegar and placed in an oak box under a pile of horse-dung for a month, after which they could be retrieved and a white powder could be scraped off.[13] The present author followed Theophilus' instructions (Figure 6.1). The principle that underlies Theophilus' recipe is the corrosion of lead with acidic fumes provided by the vinegar or horse-dung. Many recipes survive which describe numerous variations on the same theme.[14] Chemically, the vinegar (or acetic acid) is warmed by the fermenting dung and its fumes react with the lead to produce lead acetate (or sugar of lead). Upon exposure to the carbon dioxide released by the fermenting dung, the lead acetate is converted into basic lead carbonate.[15] The chemical process is as follows:

$$2Pb + 2CH_3COOH + O_2 \rightarrow Pb(CH_3COO)_2 \cdot Pb(OH)_2$$

followed by

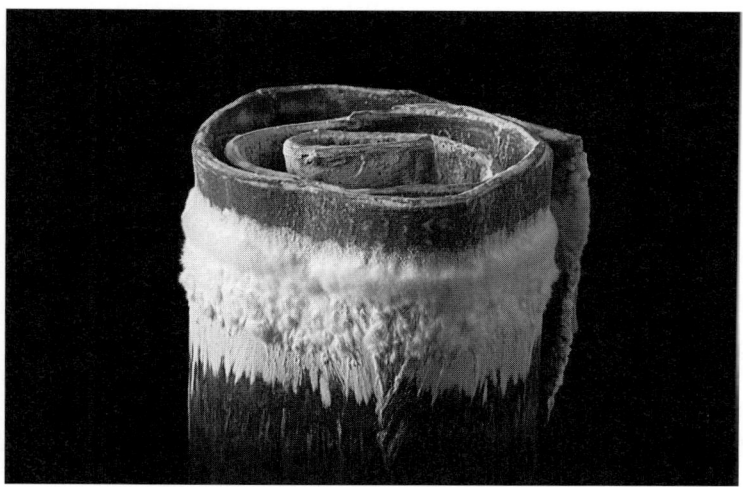

6.1. A coiled sheet of urine-sprinkled lead metal after exposure to vinegar fumes under horse-dung for a month

$$Pb(CH_3COO)_2.Pb(OH)_2 + 2CO_2 \rightarrow$$
$$3Pb(CH_3COO)_2 + H_2O + PbCO_3.Pb(OH)_2$$

Theophilus' procedure is essentially the same as that described briefly by Theophrastus and Vitruvius and in more detail by early modern authors. In 1678, for example, the manufacture of lead white was described in the *Philosophical Transactions* of the Royal Society. Lead was cast into thin strips one yard long and six inches wide, then rolled into loose coils. Pots were partly filled with vinegar and the lead coils were suspended over the vinegar within the pots, which were then closed with a lead lid. A wide area of ground was prepared with horse-dung and four hundred such lead-and-vinegar pots were arranged on the horse-dung. Four layers of pots were stacked and covered with more horse-dung. After a period of several weeks, the lead coils were retrieved and the white encrustation was knocked off.[16]

Alternative methods of making lead white were introduced in the eighteenth and nineteenth centuries, and in fact alternative methods may also have been available earlier. In the mid-thirteenth century, for example, Albertus Magnus mentioned the alchemists' *lac virginis*, or Virgin's milk, which may have been a precipitate of lead carbonate caused by mixing solutions of sugar of lead (lead acetate) and lye (potassium carbonate).[17] However, the method described above, called the stack, vinegar or Dutch method, was exclusively mentioned by artists and was still being used for the commercial production of lead white pigment through the nineteenth century, and by the Glasgow Lead and Colour Works in 1901.[18]

Theophilus' recipe, like the numerous variations that preceded and followed it, was eminently practical, and it involved cheap, readily available materials. The process also required little effort. In fact, artists knew that under the right conditions the white pigment could even make itself with no human intervention. For example, lead white was known to form slowly where the underside of lead roofing was exposed to oak beams. (Oak is a particularly acidic wood and the fumes it emits will, over an extended period, corrode lead metal.) One late seventeenth-century artists' treatise even recommended that the attics of old buildings should be inspected as a potential source of the material for painters who ran out of the white pigment.[19]

What mystery?

It might therefore appear that the manufacture of lead white held little or no mystery in the medieval and early modern worlds since the ingredients were common and the process was well documented, easy to carry out, and could even occur spontaneously.

However, the ingredients, the process, and the product were not without risk and the outcome was not always predictable. The Fellows of the Royal Society were concerned about the erratic results achieved by the industrial-scale process and they were also concerned about the well-being of workers who could suffer abdominal pains and shortness of breath, both symptoms of chronic lead poisoning, as well as blindness and paralysis, which are symptoms of acute lead poisoning.[20] (The health risks associated with lead white and its manufacture were well known to earlier practitioners and are well documented.)[21]

Together, human risks and variable outcomes are indications that there might be more to the process of making lead white than is at first apparent. And while Theophilus described lead white's manufacture, he invariably omitted many practical details that could be crucial to a successful outcome. For example, if the container that held the vinegar and lead was air-tight, then carbon dioxide would not be available to convert the acetate into a carbonate. Such undocumented details doubtless accounted for the erratic yields noted by Vernatti and the Fellows of the Royal Society. (The issue of safety depended upon whether or not the lead white could be ingested during the process of removing the powder from the metal.)

In his artists' treatise of around 1400, Cennini acknowledged that lead white's production held some mystery. He did not describe the process, as did Theophilus, but merely said that lead white was 'made alchemically'.[22] Cennini implied that he bought the pigment rather than made it himself, since there are other materials, such as glue, that he recommended getting at the 'druggist'.[23] And, like the manufacturing process, a certain level of skill was required when buying materials from druggists. For example, when buying 'alchemical' vermilion from the druggist, Cennini recommended buying unbroken crystals, since the powdered form could have been adulterated with red lead or brick dust.[24] Similarly, when buying lead white, the 'choicest sort' was to be found on the top of the 'little cakes like goblets or drinking glasses' and was 'shaped like a cup'.[25] This statement is very specific but is also very difficult to interpret with much confidence. No reason is given why one part of a lump of lead white might be better than another part of the same lump, and we can only conjecture that the alchemists' or druggists' method of making lead white involved a partial separation of material in the final stages. It is possible that the differences between the top and the bottom of the lump – a dense aggregate of microscopic crystals – involved some physical property, such as crystal size. Alternatively, the differences may be chemical, with more or less water-soluble lead acetate present in the top or bottom of the lump of lead carbonate. The reasons for the difference are unknown.

Such conjecture or speculation about the meaning of artists' manuals shows that even the existence of a very detailed recipe does not preclude a mystery. And mysteries were openly acknowledged within recipes, such as one from the *Mappae clavicula* that referred to a process described 'as a sacred thing' to be kept secret so that 'you will not as a prophet have given it away'.[26] There are several dictionary definitions of 'secret', a word that derives from the Latin, to separate or set apart. These definitions include: (1) things to be kept private, not to be made known or exposed to view, or to be known only by a limited number of people; (2) a true but not generally understood method of attaining some goal such as health or happiness; (3) a mystery or thing for which explanation is sought in vain. Lead white was one of the cheapest materials used by painters. The first kind of secret is therefore unlikely to be the most important one associated with the pigment. The second kind of secret has already been alluded to in questions about the variability of yield and quality in the product of a single process. Thus it remains to consider the manufacture of lead white as a secret of the third kind.

In the Middle Ages, crafts were known as 'mysteries' and the artist's or craftsperson's manipulation of materials was widely recognized as a type of secret. The inherently mysterious nature of the crafts was alluded to in the public domain. For example, the popular *Romance of the Rose* asked: 'Have we not seen how those that are expert in glass-making can, through a simple process of purification, use ferns to produce both ash and glass? Yet glass is not fern, nor fern glass.'[27] And Chaucer's *Canterbury Tales* also commented upon the mysterious commonplace: 'others said how strange it was to learn/ That glass is made out of the ash of fern,/ Though bearing no resemblances to glass;/ But being used to this, they let it pass.'[28] Theophilus described the glass-making process, but he used the ash of beech-wood logs rather than ferns.[29]

Cennini did not mention the process of glass-making but would probably have agreed with Albertus Magnus, who described the manufacture of glass as 'alchemical',[30] like his own description of lead white's manufacture. Parallels between the two processes were reinforced because lead white is the product of a metal, and glass was considered to be related to metals (the molten material is still referred to as 'metal'). Glass-making and making metallic products like lead white were both eminently practical activities but, in medieval technology, practicality did not preclude mystery. Robert Kilwardby, a thirteenth-century Archbishop of Canterbury, said 'the speculative sciences are practical and the practical sciences speculative'.[31] The first half of Kilwardby's statement is a worldly justification for theology and the second half suggests that technical treatises could be approached in the same manner as any other medieval 'mirror', like the bestiaries, herbals, and lapidaries that contained animal, vegetable, and mineral lore yet also reflected different aspects of cosmology and of God. Medieval and early modern cosmology have been addressed in great detail elsewhere and this is not the place to review the literature. However, the operative relationship between such cosmological theories and the technological practices of making art has not been approached in any detail.[32] A very brief overview of the cosmology relevant to the manufacture of lead white is therefore in order.

Operative cosmologies

Just as the recipe for making lead white was effectively unchanged for millennia, so too certain fundamentals of the cosmology within which the activity took place also remained stable.[33] The medieval or early modern artists', alchemists', druggists', and informed patrons' understanding of the specialist process and pigment would have drawn upon their everyday understanding of metals. Metals owed their properties to a combination of the 'power of Earth' (dryness, coldness, and heaviness) and the power of the planets 'which send out light and nobility',[34] hence metals were to be understood in terms of elements and planets.

People's understanding of such technical matters was reinforced by their understanding of their own bodies, since the elements and planets were also thought to influence physiological and psychological temperaments. The elements – fire, air, water, and earth – were related to the humours – choleric, sanguine, phlegmatic, and melancholic – through their paired fundamental qualities – dry–hot, hot–wet, wet–cold, and cold–dry – respectively. The human physical and mental constitution was also related to the planets, as suggested by the adjectives – lunatic, mercurial, venereal, sunny, martial, jovial, and saturnine – corresponding to the Moon, Mercury, Venus, the Sun, Mars, Jupiter, and Saturn – respectively.[35]

In his mid-thirteenth-century treatise *The Book of Minerals*, Albertus Magnus was simply rephrasing a commonplace when he wrote 'as in animal bodies, there must be . . . a blending of humours in the metal'.[36] In this cosmology, planets and metals were connected. The Moon was connected to silver, Mercury to mercury, Venus to copper, the Sun to gold, Mars to iron, Jupiter to tin, and Saturn to lead.[37] These planetary correspondences were common knowledge, as was lead's connection to the melancholic humour.[38]

In the *Book of Minerals*, Albertus Magnus summarized and synthesized traditional metal-lore. In his scientific view, all metals were a combination of heavenly and earthly powers that corresponded to the alchemical principles sulphur and quicksilver, and the Aristotelian principles fire and water, respectively.[39] The malleability of metals – their ability to liquefy and solidify, to be worked and to bend – was seen as the inevitable consequence of their inherent 'moisture', which was contrasted with the 'dryness' in stones that caused them to be brittle, friable, or crumbly and to shatter.[40] All seven metals of his system were related, and Albertus Magnus said that 'the production of metals is cyclical, from each other, just as the production of the elements is cyclical'.[41]

In lead metal, the Earthly power dominated the heavenly power, which accounted for its 'dark-coloured, heavy, cold' qualities.[42] Consequently, lead was an 'imperfect' metal.[43] The domination of Earth, or Water, accounted for its 'dull' taste.[44] The Earth, Water, or Quicksilver in lead was 'not of good quality' but was 'cold and constricting'. The interaction of these qualities with male humours gave lead metal its 'special power over sexual lust and nocturnal emissions', for example, and men were advised to strap lead plates at night to their thighs to control these.[45]

Albertus Magnus's rationalization of the process of converting lead metal into lead white was framed in terms of Earth, Water, or Quicksilver,[46] and, since the watery part of lead 'evaporates in the fire',[47] the remaining white stuff, lead's 'rust', is 'nothing but burnt earthiness'.[48] The fire that evaporates the watery part of lead is provided by the vinegar since although 'vinegar is dull on account of its coldness, it is nevertheless sharp in its action, because it is the remains of a sort of Fire that has arisen from it, just as ash is the remains of Fire in wood'.[49] The residues of 'Fire' in vinegar – acids produced by fermentation – and in ash – alkalis produced by physical fire – were both capable of burning. One burnt lead to make lead white, the other burnt sand to make glass, and both could burn flesh.

A mystery

Albertus Magnus' commentary on the craft processes might seem at first sight to be an attempt at demystification, yet his endeavour to understand materials was undertaken within a neo-Platonic framework in which God was the mysterious First Mover of all things.[50] From the medieval point of view, the lead white pigment with which artists painted was a burnt, earthy, and rust-like material that was dry and friable, an 'infusible' powder that would not melt when heated. Yet it was derived from a metal that was by definition 'fusible' or malleable and which melted when heated.[51] In other words, the artists' secret involved taking a material that belonged in one category and transforming it into a material that belonged to the opposite category.

The theoretical significance of this transformation would have been apparent to artists like Cennini, Theophilus, or the unknown author of the *Mappae clavicula*. Of course, it is impossible to make definitive statements about the level of knowledge possessed by individual artists who did not write treatises. However, technical details of glass production were casually alluded to in popular poetry, so some craft mysteries were evidently appreciated beyond the confines of guilds in which they were practised.

Poets felt it worth noting that 'glass is not fern, nor fern glass' and their fictional characters found the material transformation of one into the other to be 'strange', but nonetheless 'let it pass'. Artists making lead white could similarly have noted that 'fusible is not infusible, nor infusible fusible' and the strangeness of their material transformation would have been reinforced by the colour change. Classically, lead was known as *plumbum nigrum*, or black lead, to distinguish it from *plumbum album*, or tin,[52] so the artists' initial ingredient was black,[53] but the final result was white and 'black is not white, nor white black'.

While 'glass is not fern, nor fern glass', people 'let it pass' because the glass-making processes was widely rationalized as enabling the manifestation of something that was naturally latent in the cinders of ferns, and indeed, in ferns themselves. For example, in the fourteenth century, Richardus Anglicus said the art of glassmaking was 'nothing but an aid to nature' since, if the essence of glass was 'not hidden in the cinders, art would by no means be able to make glass from it'.[54] It should be said that such an argument would not have appealed greatly to Albertus Magnus, who, in the context of metals, refuted the related beliefs of Hermes, Anaxagoras and others. According to him, these authorities were mistaken in claiming that 'all things contain all things' and that forms could be latent, with one manifest and another occult or with one revealed and another concealed, so that 'lead is gold inside and lead outside'.[55] Nonetheless, Albertus' refutations were only necessary because such beliefs were extremely widely held. Albertus wrote for theologians and philosophers, but painters and patrons were more likely to adhere to the widespread views with which Albertus took issue.[56]

Applying that same (popular) explanation to the making of lead white from black lead would have profound implications for the nature of matter because – unlike fern ash and glass, which are both material composites – fusible and infusible, and black and white, are conceptual categories that are, moreover, defining polar opposites.

In the Middle Ages, a lay person who was interested in transformations might turn to Ovid's *Metamorphoses*, and there he or she would find that to turn 'black to white and white to black' was a 'trick' performed by Autolycus, which was worthy of 'his crafty father', Hermes.[57] The artists' material – a black that was turned into a white – therefore embodied half a Hermetic trick, which is consistent with Cennini's statement that it was 'made alchemically' since Hermes was the father of alchemy. And Cennini also knew that, under the right circumstances, the artists' material could, of its own volition, complete the trick. He said that one should avoid using this particular white pigment on walls because there, 'in the course of time, it turns black'.[58] One of the secrets that artists openly shared with their readers was that their most important white came from black and could go back to black.[59]

On a wall, lead white is turned black by exposure to air pollution, but while the colours black and white have obvious cultural associations, the spontaneous reversion of white to black was not necessarily interpreted as the corruption of purity. This is evident because another of the artists' staple materials engaged in an analogous behaviour that might seem to signal the purification of corruption. In another pigment recipe, Cennini recommended the second joints and wings of a capon, 'just as you find them under the dining-table' as an ingredient for an artists' material.[60] These white bones could be charred to make a black pigment. And, when used as a black pigment in oil, bone black can spontaneously turn white over time.[61] Cennini does not mention this, but his recipe does acknowledge that bone can be burned more thoroughly to make a pure white ash. So artists also knew of a white that makes a black that degradation or further processing could make white again.

Artists converted white bones into a black pigment and black metal into a white pigment, and both pigments could return to something that resembled their original state. In pre-Newtonian colour theory, black and white were the two extreme colours, the poles that defined the scale within which all the other colours lay.[62] However, artists knew that these two definitively different colours were very closely connected, not circuitously via all the colours or via intermediate shades of grey but directly through the behaviour of materials on their palette. The relationship between the artists' blacks and whites was more profound than the relationship between the glaziers' ferns and glass. The artists' blacks and whites could suggest that opposite states lay latent within each other, thereby undermining any and all definitive categorical understanding of the world, the logical conclusions of which were explored by Nicholas of Cusa.[63] Lead white (and bone black) hinted that appearances were fleeting and rode upon the back of a substrate that was in a constant state of flux.

Prime matter

One can assume that practising artists were primarily interested in the world of appearances. Otherwise they would have pursued a different vocation. Yet, in attempting to imitate the appearance of nature, artists needed some working knowledge of the operations of nature in order to transform their materials in a repeatable fashion. Artists were connected with the vocation that grappled most deeply with a practical understanding of the operation of nature – medicine – through their patron saint, St Luke,[64] and through the suppliers of equipment and pre-made pigments, the apothecaries.[65] Through such contacts, they could have interpreted the 'alchemical' transformation of a black fusible metal into a white infusible powder in terms of 'elemental matter',[66] the single matter that God separated when creating the world.[67]

Elemental, or prime, matter is not mentioned by Theophilus or Cennini. Yet it is not in the nature of commonplaces to be documented explicitly – as the poet said, 'being used to this, they let it pass'.[68] And even Albertus Magnus, who objected to the idea that the 'form of all metals is one and the same',[69] acknowledged the cycling of metals and elements as different forms of (the same) matter.[70] So, from the craft point of view, it would have appeared that in order to transform a black metal into white powder, artists assisted nature in the movement of one matter through some of its mineral forms. Unless the unknown patron dabbled in alchemy, they might not have appreciated the mystery of helping prime matter transform in the mineral realm. But they would almost certainly have appreciated the mystery of helping prime matter transform in the vegetable realm and would have recognized the same idea being played out in a different arena: anyone in the position to commission a richly illuminated manuscript would be able to afford a garden in which the craft of tree-grafting could be practised.

A text written in 1305 said that it was 'a great beauty and pleasure to have in one's garden trees variously and marvellously grafted, and many different fruits growing on a single tree'.[71] Elaborate and fanciful grafting was far from a merely utilitarian activity – it alluded to the

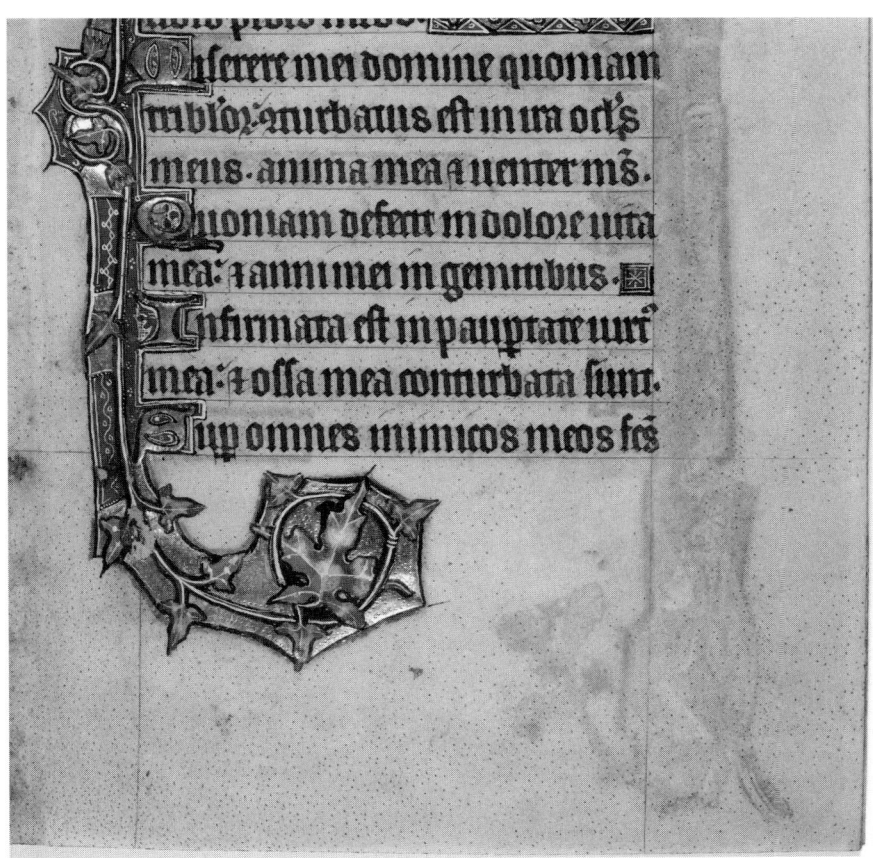

6.2. A leaf as painter's palette (FM MS 1-2005 fol. 44r)

multiple branches of the Tree of Knowledge in the Garden of Eden – and it continued up to the seventeenth century.[72] Like gardening in general, it was an activity that had moral overtones as an ordering of the world according to a perceived divine plane, with the craft serving to domesticate both nature and man.[73] From a cosmological point of view, the ability to graft different viable fruit-bearing branches on to a single root-stock could be interpreted as supporting the idea of a single matter that was capable of manifesting itself in many forms (Figure 5.2).

The single tree bearing many different fruit may be a vegetable analogue of the mineral that can appear black and white (and black again), and if it also had an analogue in the animal kingdom it might be a beast with one body sprouting many heads. A plethora of such creatures populate the margins of the Macclesfield Psalter of ca. 1330, a very high-quality illuminated manuscript with which this chapter is illustrated. The visual programme of this manuscript was executed by two unknown

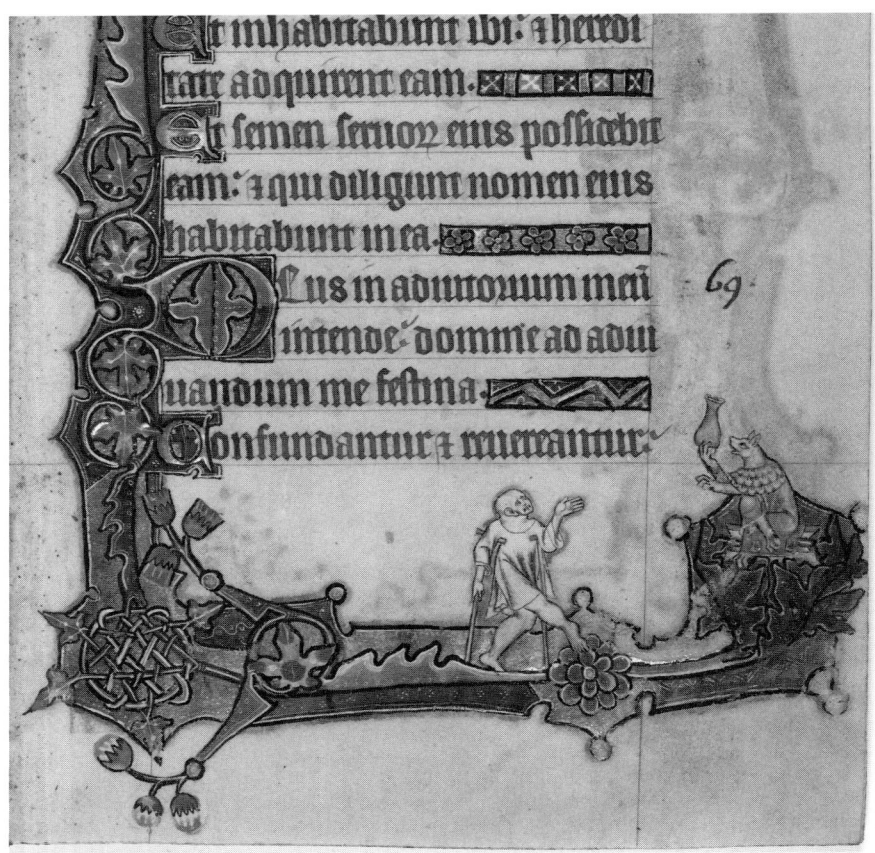

6.3. A cripple (painted in lead white) consulting a wolf-doctor, who inspects a flask of urine (FM MS 1-2005 fol. 98r)

painters in East Anglia, guided by a Dominican advisor.[74] The pattern of pigment use in this manuscript suggests that the artists had an interest in their materials (Figure 6.3) and the bizarre marginalia suggest an awareness of several cosmological principles that lead white exemplified as a synthetic – multivalent – material. From a cosmological point of view, these monstrous hybrids could suggest (amongst other things) the many faces or appearances of which a single matter is capable (Figure 6.4). A patron's recreational grafting of fruit trees and an artist's ability to change colours are both examples of persuading matter to show one or another of its innumerable possible faces.

Placing lead metal under horse-dung for a month made an artists' material and involved an artists' secret, the apparent transformation of a material from one category (or 'species'), 'fusible', into its opposite, 'infusible', which, in the process, turned black into white. As a part of

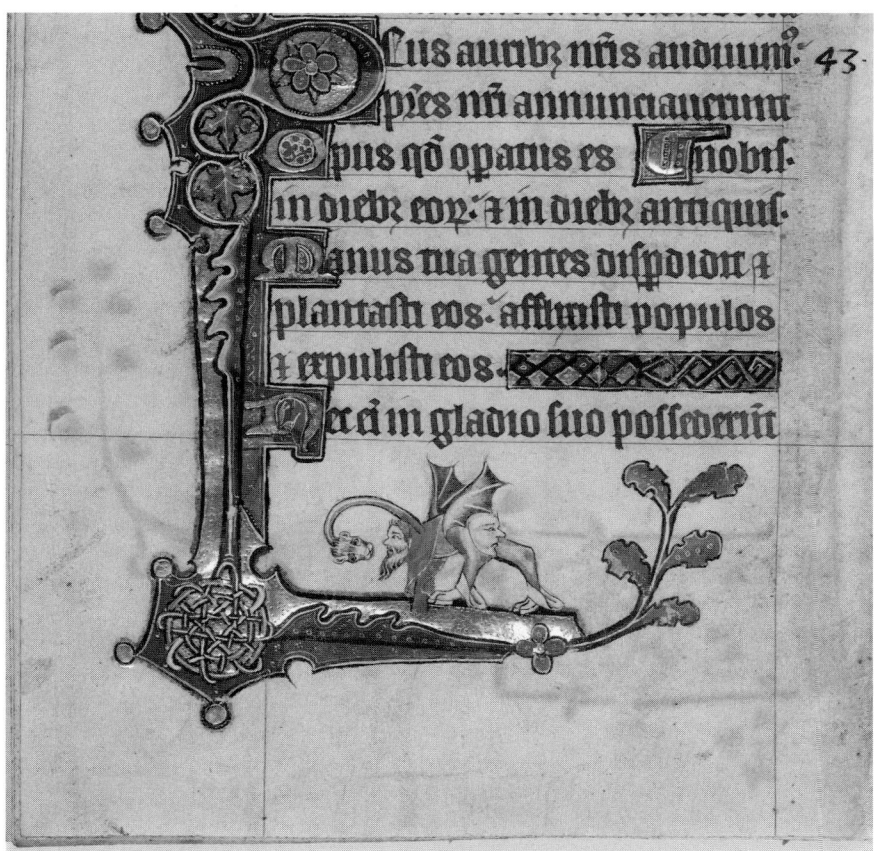

6.4. A multiple-headed marginal figure (FM MS 1-2005 fol. 64r)

a craft mystery, it tacitly touched upon a question about the nature of reality that the more didactic *Romance of the Rose* openly commented upon:

> Whatever may be true of species, individuals at least, when subjected to the operations of the intellect, can be changed into so many different forms, and their complexions so altered by various transformations, that this change can rob them of their original species and put them into a different one. . . . And thus species are transformed, or rather their individuals are alienated from them in substance and appearance, by Art . . . and by Nature.[75]

These two statements immediately precede and follow the observation that ferns could be transformed into glass. They come from a chapter on *Nature and Genius*, which is part of a text 'in which the whole art of love is contained'.[76] Although in this chapter these extracts have been interpreted in terms of the chemistry of artists' materials, they primarily

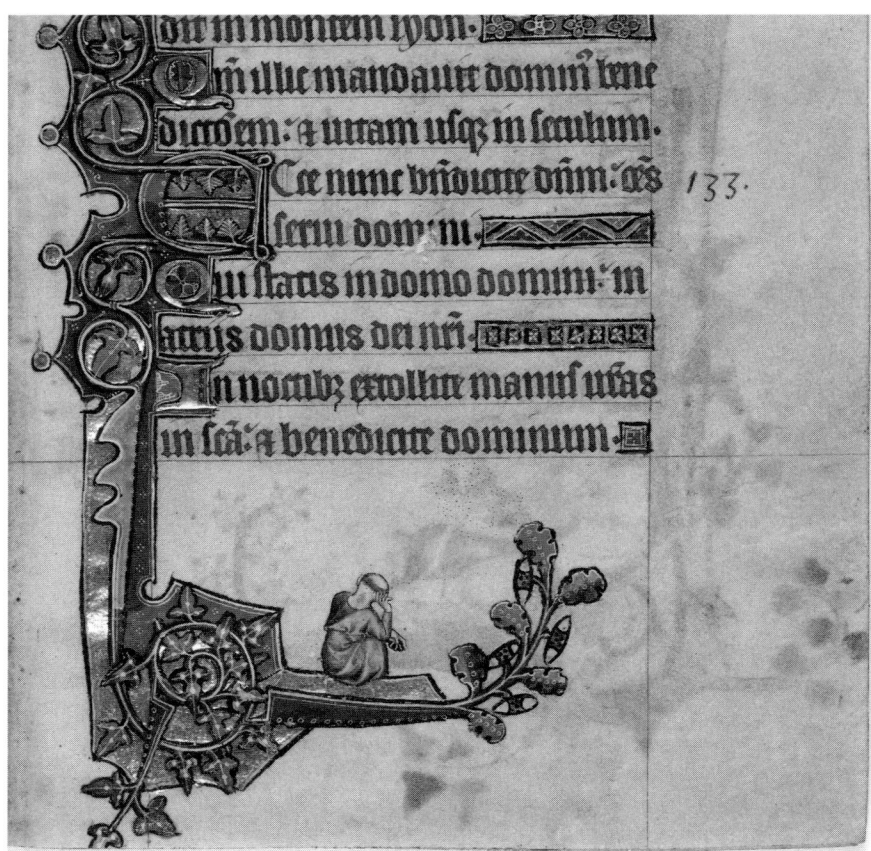

6.5. A contemplative figure (FM MS 1-2005 fol. 190r)

allude to the transformation of affections that can take place in the 'chemistry' that exists between lovers. And, in a psalter, the same transformation might appropriately be interpreted in terms of repentance, literally re-thinking (Figure 6.5). The possibility that individuals might change the course of true love or alter their spiritual destiny could be encouraged by one of the artists' most common pigments, which proved that a person who knew the secrets of nature could change black into white.

Conclusion

One of lead white's mysteries is the mystery of transformation. Mysteries are not resolved; they are acknowledged. Or, to be more accurate, paradigmatic examples are acknowledged in order that other instances may be recognized more easily.[77] Lead white is a paradigmatic example of change and the process may be interpreted as demonstrating the inherent mutability of matter, a tangible reflection of intangible prime matter. But material change was of interest to poets like Chaucer or de Lorris as well as to scientist-philosophers like Albertus Magnus or Anaxagoras. The essentially conservative painter (and his patron) may have been more interested in poetry than in philosophy, and his interest in a white powder that apparently lay latent in a black metal may have reinforced an idea that survives today in an English proverb – 'every cloud has a silver lining'.[78] And it should be acknowledged that the pre-modern connection between proverbs and technology was strengthened by the institution of apprenticeships which were as much extended periods of enculturation as inductions into craft practice, as the anthropologist David Killick has pointed out: 'the worldview and social persona of the apprentice are shaped by the apprenticeship, just as clay is shaped by the potter.'[79]

However, lead white, like all medieval materials, was multivalent. Its production was at once prosaic and alchemical, it was both medicinal and poisonous and, as an artists' pigment, it was reliable on panels but capricious on walls. This chapter does not therefore seek to imply that the material had an exclusive meaning. For different people, at different times, in different works of art, some of the material's cosmologically grounded associations may be more or less relevant.[80] So, when used to illuminate a manuscript with many-headed beasts, contemplative monks and self-referential allusions to the painting process, the material's mysterious transformation from black to white and fusible to infusible – evoking material change and prime matter – might seem more apt than evocations of Saturn, melancholy, lady's cosmetics or a cure for men's nocturnal emissions.

One of the purposes of marginal images in devotional manuscripts was to provoke different ways of thinking. They provided commentaries on the text that were sometimes so radically unexpected that their very obscurity challenged the reader to return to the text again and again in order to reconcile word and image.[81] And to contemporary readers, visual images were also appreciated as physical ensembles of materials with colour, texture, and numerous other attributes – ultramarine and gold being obvious luxury materials and lead white being a more modest one.

Chaucer's late-thirteenth-century physician knew 'the cause of every malady' as 'planets' and 'humours', 'whether dry, cold, moist or hot'.[82] The Italian painter Lomazzo wrote a treatise that was translated by a late-sixteenth-century English physician in which it was stated that: 'colours have different qualities, therefore they cause diverse effects in the beholders, which arise from an inwarde contrariety of their causes (as Aristotle teacheth).'[83]

In contemporary theory, people shared causes and qualities with, and were affected by, materials in paintings. In this chapter, the meanings associated with lead white in medieval and early modern painting illuminate one of the differences between the valences of materials then and now. Our own cosmology defines materials as inherently meaningless – unless ingested, the artists' pigment now has no significance other than its property of reflecting white light.[84] However, it is as well to recall that when artists' materials embodied humours and astrological forces and had commonplace uses outside the workshop, they possessed manifold meanings for the painters who used them and the patrons who appreciated them.

Notes

Details of the Macclesfield Psalter (FM MS 1-2005) are reproduced with the permission of the Syndics of the Fitzwilliam Museum, University of Cambridge. The author gratefully acknowledges the support of the Monument Trust.

1. The refractive index is the speed at which light travels through a material relative to the speed it travels through a vacuum.
2. Cennino Cennini, *The Craftsman's Handbook* (CXLVII), trans. D.V. Thompson (New York: Dover, 1960), p. 94.
3. Cennini, *The Craftsman's Handbook* (XVI, XVIII, XXXII), pp. 9, 11-2, 18; (LXI), p. 36; (CVII), p. 66; (CXLI), p. 87; (CXLV–CLII), pp. 91–7.
4. P. Binski and A. Massing (eds), *The Westminster Retable* (London: Harvey Miller, 2009), pp. 243, 438–9.
5. S. Bucklow and S. Woodcock (eds), *Sir John Gilbert* (London: Lund Humphries, 2011), pp. 240–3.
6. *Liber diversarum arcium* (I, xv, 3), in M. Clarke, *Medieval Painters' Materials and Methods* (London: Archetype, 2011), pp. 181–2 following Dioscorides, *De materia medica* (Book V, chapter lxxxviii, line 6), trans. L.Y. Beck (Hildesheim: Georg Olms Verlag, 2005), p. 372.
7. R.D. Harley, *Artists' Pigments, c. 1600–1835* (London: Butterworths, 1982), pp. 166–72, and R.J. Gettens, H. Kuhn, and W.T. Chase, 'Lead white', in A. Roy (ed.), *Artists' Pigments* (Oxford: Oxford University Press, 1997), vol. 2, pp. 67–70.
8. Vitruvius, *On Architecture* (VII, xii, 1 & 2), trans. F. Granger (London: Heinemann, 1962), vol. 2, p. 125.
9. It should be acknowledged that the manufacture of lead white was widespread. For example, it was practised in China from around 300 BCE. See J. Needham, *Science and Civilisation in China* (Cambridge: Cambridge University Press, 1976), vol. 5, 3, pp. 15–17.
10. E.R. Caley, 'Ancient Greek Pigments', *Journal of Chemical Education* 23 (1946), pp. 314–16, and E. Caley and J.F.C. Richards, *Theophrastus on Stones* (Columbus: Ohio State University, 1956), pp. 187–9.
11. R.C. Thompson, *The Chemistry of the Ancient Assyrians* (London: Luzac, 1925), vol. 9, p. 106; R.C. Thompson, *A Dictionary of Assyrian Chemistry and Geology* (Oxford: Oxford University Press, 1936), pp. 135–40.
12. J.R. Partington, *Origins and Development of Applied Chemistry* (London: Longmans, 1935), pp. 292–3.

13 Theophilus, *On divers arts* (I, 37), trans. J.G. Hawthorne and C.S. Smith (New York: Dover, 1979), pp. 41–2.
14 Including British Museum MS Sloane 122, fol. 92v. cited in Hartley, *Artists' Pigments*, p. 166.
15 D.V. Thompson, *The Materials and Techniques of Medieval Painting* (New York: Dover, 1956), pp. 92–3.
16 P. Vernatti, 'A relation of the making of ceruse', *Philosophical Transactions* 12 (1678), p. 935.
17 Albertus Magnus, *Book of Minerals* (II, iii, 2), trans. D. Wyckoff (Oxford: Clarendon, 1967), p. 132.
18 J. Sinclair, *General Report of the Agricultural State and Political Circumstances of Scotland* (Edinburgh, 1814), App. 2, p. 309, cited in A and N.L. Clow, *The Chemical Revolution* (London: Batchworth, 1952), p. 383.
19 John Smith (1687) cited in I. Bristow, *Interior House Painting Colours and Technology 1615–1840* (New Haven, CT: Yale University Press and the Paul Mellon Centre for Studies in British Art, 1996), p. 10.
20 Vernatti, 'A relation of the making of ceruse', p. 936.
21 Pliny the Elder, *Natural History* (XXXIV, 50, 167), trans. H. Rackham, vol. 9 (London: Heinemann, 1968), p. 249.
22 Cennini, *The Craftsman's Handbook* (LIX), p. 34.
23 Cennini, *The Craftsman's Handbook* (XXV), p. 14.
24 Cennini, *The Craftsman's Handbook* (XL), p. 24.
25 Cennini, *The Craftsman's Handbook* (LIX), p. 34.
26 *Mappa claviculae*, p. 14, in C.S. Smith and J.G. Hawthorne, 'Mappae clavicula', *Transactions of the American Philosophical Society*, 64:4 (1974), p. 32.
27 G. De Lorris and J. De Meun, *The Romance of the Rose* (approx. 1653–83), trans. F. Horgan (Oxford: Oxford University Press, 2008), p. 249.
28 Chaucer, 'The Squire's Tale' (Part I), *The Canterbury Tales*, trans. N. Coghill (Harmondsworth: Penguin, 1975), p. 414.
29 Theophilus, *On divers arts* (Book II, Chapter 4), pp. 52–3. Both beech and fern make 'forest' glass that is rich in potassium and is to be distinguished from glasses rich in sodium that are made from mineral rather than vegetable matter.
30 Albertus Magnus, *Book of Minerals* (I, i, 3), p. 15.
31 Robert Kilwardby, *De ortu scientiarum*, 40.393, cited in E. Whitney, 'Paradise restored: The mechanical arts from antiquity through the thirteenth century', *Transaction of the American Philosophical Society*, 80:1 (1990), p. 120.
32 An exception is M. Cole, 'Cellini's blood', *The Art Bulletin*, 81:2 (1999), pp. 215–35.
33 E. Grant, 'Aristotelianism and the longevity of the medieval world view', *History of Science* 16 (1978), pp. 93–106.
34 Albertus Magnus, *Book of Minerals* (III, i, 6), p. 168.
35 S. Bucklow, *The Alchemy of Paint* (London: Marion Boyars, 2009), pp. 43–74 and 109–40.
36 Albertus Magnus, *Book of Minerals* (III, i, 1), p. 155.
37 Chaucer, 'The Canon's Yeoman's Tale' (I), *The Canterbury Tales*, p. 475.
38 R. Wittkower, *Born under Saturn* (New York: Random House), 1963.
39 It should be noted that the principles, Earth, Water and Fire are not the same as the elements, earth, water and fire, although, as can be seen, the principles and elements share certain qualities.

40 Albertus Magnus, *Book of Minerals* (III, i, 3; III, ii, 1 & 2), pp. 159, 186–90.
41 Albertus Magnus, *Book of Minerals* (III, ii, 6), p. 200.
42 Albertus Magnus, *Book of Minerals* (III, i, 6), p. 168.
43 Albertus Magnus, *Book of Minerals* (III, i, 3), p. 161
44 Albertus Magnus, *Book of Minerals* (III, ii, 4), p. 195.
45 Albertus Magnus, *Book of Minerals* (IV, i, 3), p. 210, following Pliny, *Natural History* 9 (XXXIV, 69, 166), p. 247.
46 Albertus Magnus, *Book of Minerals* (IV, i, 3), pp. 210–11.
47 Albertus Magnus, *Book of Minerals* (III, ii, 5), p. 199.
48 Albertus Magnus, *Book of Minerals* (IV, i, 4), p. 216.
49 Albertus Magnus, *Book of Minerals* (IV, i, 3), p. 211.
50 Albertus Magnus, *Book of Minerals* (II, i, 1 & 4), pp. 55–8, 64–7.
51 Albertus Magnus, *Book of Minerals* (III, i, 3), pp. 159–60.
52 Pliny, *Natural History* 9 (XXXIV, 47, 156), p. 241.
53 'Some observations concerning the substance commonly called, black-lead, by the late Dr. Rob. Plot, F.R.S.', *Philosophical Transactions* 20 (1683–1775), p. 183.
54 Richardus Anglicus, *Correctio fatuorum*, cited in W.R. Newman, 'Alchemical and Baconian views on the art/nature division', in A.G. Debus and M.T. Walton (eds), *Reading the Book of Nature* (Kirksville, MO: Sixteenth Century Journal, 1998), p. 90.
55 Albertus Magnus, *Book of Minerals* (III, i, 8), pp. 174–5.
56 Other learned authors also felt the need to combat popular beliefs. Agricola, *De re metallica* (1556), I, trans. H.C. and L.H. Hoover (New York: Dover, 1950), pp. 1–24 is a sustained attempt to refute widespread beliefs about metals and mining, for example. Painters' treatises, however, were generally very conservative in tone.
57 Ovid, *Metamorphoses* 2 (XI, 313), trans. F.J. Miller (London: Heinemann, 1984), p. 143.
58 Cennini, *The Craftsman's Handbook* (LVIII), p. 34.
59 According to modern science, the two blacks are not the same – the first is metallic and the last is a sulphide – but, when used on walls, the material can appear to return to its original state.
60 Cennini, *The Craftsman's Handbook* (VII), p. 5.
61 A. van Loon and J. Boon, 'The whitening of oil paint films containing bone black', in J. Bridgland (ed.), *ICOM-CC 14th Triennial Meeting Conference Preprints* (London: James and James, 2005) pp. 515–18.
62 J. Gage, *Colour and Culture* (London: Thames and Hudson, 1993), p. 229.
63 Nicholas of Cusa, *Of Learned Ignorance*, trans. G. Heron (London: Routledge and Kegan Paul, 1954).
64 C. King, 'National Gallery 3902 and the theme of Luke the Evangelist as artist and physician', *Zeitschrift für Kunstgeschichte*, 48:2 (1985), pp. 249–55.
65 Cennini, *The Craftsman's Handbook* (XXV, XL, and LXII), pp. 14, 24, and 37.
66 De Lorris and De Meun, *The Romance of the Rose* (IX, c. 16040), p. 248.
67 Genesis 1:6.
68 Chaucer, 'The Squire's Tale' (I), *The Canterbury Tales*, p. 414.
69 Albertus Magnus, *Book of Minerals* (III, i, 7), pp. 172–3.
70 Albertus Magnus, *Book of Minerals* (III, ii, 6), p. 200.
71 Petrus de Crescentiis, *Liber ruralium commodorum*, cited in C. Thacker, *The History of Gardens* (Berkeley: University of California Press 1979), p. 85.

72 Thacker, *The History of Gardens*, p. 131.
73 S. Lerer, 'Artifice and artistry in Sir Orfeo', *Speculum* 60:1 (1987), pp. 95–6.
74 S. Panayotova, *The Macclesfield Psalter* (London: Thames & Hudson, 2008), p. 44.
75 De Lorris and De Meun, *The Romance of the Rose* (IX, c.16053–83), p. 249.
76 De Lorris and De Meun, *The Romance of the Rose* (I, c. 35), p. 3.
77 Aristotle, *Prior Analytics* (69 a 13–5) trans. H. Tredennick (London: Heinemann. 1962), p. 517.
78 See S. Shapin, 'Proverbial economies', *Social Studies in Science* 31:5 (2001), pp. 731–69.
79 D. Killick, 'Social constructivist approaches to the study of technology', *World Archaeology*, 36:4 (2004) p. 573. See also M. David and C. Kramer, *Ethnoarchaeology in Action* (Cambridge: Cambridge University Press, 2001), pp. 303–59.
80 In other words, the proliferation of meanings that is prized in art was supported by a science that – unlike modern science – was not averse to the proliferation of meaning. See F. Bastide, 'The iconography of scientific texts: Principles of analysis', trans. G Myers, in M. Lynch and S. Woolgar (eds), *Representation in Scientific Practice* (Cambridge, MA: The MIT Press, 1990), pp. 187–230.
81 M. Carruthers, *The Craft of Thought* (Cambridge: Cambridge University Press, 1998).
82 Chaucer, 'Prologue', *The Canterbury Tales*, p. 30.
83 Giovanni Paolo Lomazzo, *A Tracte Containing the Artes of Curious Paintinge Carvinge and Building*, trans. R. Haydocke (III, 11) (Farnborough: Gregg International, 1970), p. 112.
84 In fact, it can have meaning for the conservation scientist and economic historian since not all lead is the same. However, the differences – trace elements and isotope ratios – are not evident to the viewer and were not evident to the painter, so have retrospective forensic significance only. See, for example, D. Fabian and G. Fortunato, 'Tracing lead', in J. Kirby, S. Nash, and J. Cannon (eds), *Trade in Artists' Materials* (London: Archetype, 2010), pp. 426–46.

7 ✧ Material distinctions: plaster, terracotta, and wax in the Renaissance artist's workshop

Eckart Marchand

In a letter written in Venice, possibly on 15 July 1535, the poet Pietro Aretino thanked Giorgio Vasari for sending him a model of a head by Michelangelo, praising the expressiveness of the life-like work while exclaiming: 'Et è pur creta scolpita con le dita de la pratica in pochi tratti' (And it is only clay, sculpted with practised fingers in a few strokes).[1]

Aretino's statement reflects a common hierarchy of sculptors' materials, in which clay, together with plaster and wax, were considered base, while bronze and marble featured at the upper end of the scale. The historical reasons for this hierarchy of materials are well known: bronze and marble were associated with durability and the achievements of ancient Greece and Rome. Both materials were also expensive and difficult to obtain or produce. As a result of the ubiquitous *paragone* debate, in which painters scorned sculptors for the hard physical labour they had to perform, sculpture came to be defined by its *difficoltà*, something that working in clay, plaster, and wax lacked.[2]

While implying the low material value and status of clay, Aretino nevertheless invests the object of his contemplation with other values, reading it as an imprint of the forming fingers of the divine Michelangelo; thus it has become a relic of the artistic process, carrying the memory of the work of him who touched and formed it. This artistic value of the work stands in stark contrast to its material value.[3] Given the predominance of the *paragone* debate, comments that reflect the perception of plaster, wax, and clay during the period are relatively rare and by nature to be found outside the main art critical discourses. In this chapter I want to assess the uses of the three materials in the field of sculpture and relate these uses to their physical characteristics, availability, and price. Throughout this examination of the associations of these materials beyond the sculptor's workshop, I shall try to establish wider values and associations that may have attached to works made in these materials. In the nature of the argument, some of these connotations have to remain speculative.

The head Aretino was discussing was a model. Vasari, when addressing sculpture in the introduction to his *Lives*, mentions clay, wax, and *gesso* (plaster) as materials for three-dimensional models in the sculptor's design process, but he goes on to discuss only wax and clay.[4] Similarly, Cellini mentions clay and wax when referring to the initial models in which the artist develops the three-dimensional design.[5] The starting point was usually a wax model while clay was used for larger, secondary models, and plaster only for the full-scale model that featured late in the process. This seems to have been a fairly common sequence after the introduction of full-scale models in the early sixteenth century. Presentation models, to be shown to the patron, were made either of wax or terracotta.[6]

This discrimination in the use of the three materials at the different stages of the design process relates to their physical qualities. Wax, when mixed with turpentine, sawdust and/or other materials, could be worked at any time, as warming it with the hands would soften it (Figure 7.1). 'La cera sempre aspetta' is the beautiful line put into Ridolfo Sirigatti's mouth in Raffaello Borghini's dialogue *Il Riposo* of 1584.[7] Always ready for use, wax does not confront the modelling sculptor with any time limits. It also lends itself particularly well to copy modelling in front of existing works of art, a practice ascribed by Filippo Baldinucci to Giambologna, who, according to Baldinucci, went all over Rome to make models of what he saw. Baldinucci does not specify the material but clay would have been impractical and messy in this context.[8] Where the commission was for a bronze, the final model, eventually lost in the casting process, was made of wax, modelled around a core of clay, plaster, and other materials. If the softness and long-lasting malleability of wax meant that it was rarely used for large-scale models, another physical characteristic, that it turns liquid at relatively low temperatures, explains its use for lost wax casting, where the wax was melted out by heating the mould before pouring in the metal.[9]

Vasari describes modelling in wax and clay in some detail.[10] Working in wax, the sculptor would warm the material with his hands, add and remove material as he saw fit and provide the developing work with an internal armature of wire or wood. Clay, too, could be easily formed, but it had to be kept wet with soaked cloths and would eventually dry out and lose its manipulability.[11] Once turned into *terrasecca*, clay would gain some structural strength, but also a vulnerable, somewhat rough and porous surface. *Terrasecca* cannot be easily modified, and to revive it, one has to break up the material, pulverize it and mix it with water. Generally speaking, it is also unsuitable to record forms over a longer period, as it can easily be damaged and disintegrate. A few unfired clay

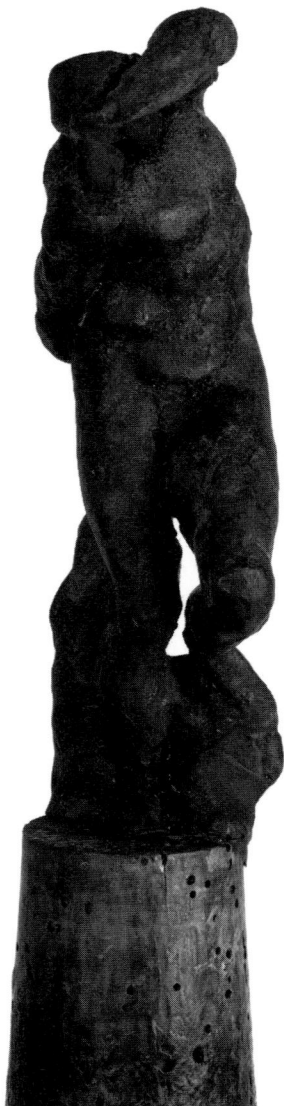

7.1. Michelangelo, *Slave*, 1516–19, wax model for one of the unfinished statues for the Tomb of Pope Julius II, Victoria and Albert Museum, London

models from the Renaissance have survived, such as Giambologna's full-scale clay model for the *Rape of the Sabine Women* in the Accademia in Florence (coated with plaster), and a clay mask by the same master in the Victoria and Albert Museum (Figure 7.2),[12] but ultimately, to make this material last, it had to be fired – a process that involved shrinkage and could easily result in the loss of the work.[13]

Material distinctions
163

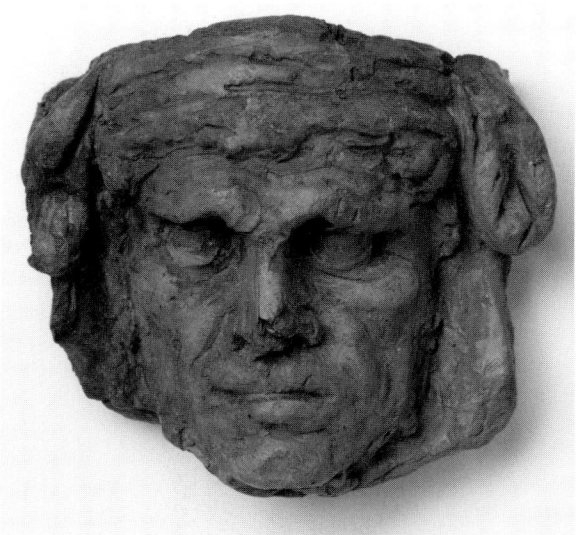

7.2. Giambologna, *Head*, c. 1578, clay, Victoria and Albert Museum, London

Plaster was well known in painters' and sculptors' workshops. The English term subsumes two different types of material: *gesso*, plaster made of gypsum, used for example by painters as a ground for tempera and oil paint on wood, stone or cloth; and *calcina*, lime-based plaster made of quick lime and sand (or pulverized stone) that was used for mortar, wall plaster and in the sixteenth century increasingly for architectural decorations.[14] It was therefore an important material for the building industry, as discussed by Richard Goldthwaite.[15] In sculptural practice both materials could be used for casting and modelling and while they have different material qualities (lime-plaster being harder and water resistant), in the finished product they are not easily distinguishable, particularly as they were often used in mixture with other materials.[16] Gypsum was locally available in several Italian regions, occurring in the hills near Bologna, Volterra, Siena, and elsewhere;[17] it was extracted from pits, baked at a low temperature and pulverized. Lime on the other hand was made from limestone that required a considerably higher baking temperature.[18] Where limestone was naturally abundant, as for example in Tuscany, it was quarried locally on the grounds surrounding a kiln, where the clay for the production of bricks was also dug up. Local authorities had an interest in ensuring the constant supply of building materials for their towns, which meant that, although not cheap in comparison to bricks,[19] lime was generally available.[20] The same may not have been the case for the considerably more expensive gypsum, a material that was less in demand, being used first of all by painters, goldsmiths, and sculptors.[21] As gypsum deposits were also rarer than the ubiquitous limestone, its availability would have depended on a workshop's geographical position. Thus, the Paduan Francesco Squarcione famously received from his pupil Marco Zoppo gypsum in lieu of payment for training, as Padua, unlike Zoppo's hometown, Bologna, did not have local deposits of this material.[22] A puzzling statement by Cellini about the supposed shortcomings of the gypsum available in Florence, as opposed to Mantuan or Paduan varieties, demonstrates not only the artist's ignorance in this matter (as Mantua and Padua did not have their own occurrences), it also reflects that, where possible, the material was sourced locally, allowing ill-informed speculation about the qualities of geographical varieties.[23]

In the fifteenth century, sculptors and painters used plaster (mostly gypsum-based) for reproductive purposes, making casts of human limbs and works by others that functioned as models for study in the workshop. The material was also chosen for final works of a devotional nature, such as the vast number of Virgin and Child reliefs and, less frequently, busts of saints, especially where established types of these were reproduced in series. If, as discussed above, Renaissance artists, especially in Tuscany, did not use plaster during the early stages of the design process, this may have related first of all to the time pressure set by the material itself. Once the pulverized plaster is mixed with water, this sets in motion chemical processes during which the material warms up and sets irreversibly.[24] It is also a grainy material and not as cohesive and flexible as wax or clay, and hence less compelling for modelling purposes. Once plaster has dried fully, it can still be manipulated with files, rasps, and saws, and one can easily add to it. In this state its physical qualities differ considerably from *terrasecca*: it has a hard and, if cast and/or filed down, potentially very smooth surface, and it is structurally sounder than clay. Even gypsum-based plaster is relatively resistant to water and physical impact when compared with clay. Large-scale works in plaster (like those in *terrasecca*) would have had wooden armatures inside. For final, full-scale models structural soundness was important both to sustain the models' own weight and to withstand wear and tear in the workshop.[25]

Regarding plaster and clay, an extension of these material choices can be found in the field of ephemeral or occasional sculpture. The use of painted cloth, wood, clay, and plaster decorations for festive entries in the sixteenth century, when entire cities were transformed to look like the New Rome, was largely dictated by time pressure, financial restraints, and/or the intended removal of the decorations after the relevant events.[26] Architectural decorations such as reliefs, figures in niches, and free-standing figures on top of triumphal arches were regularly made of lime-based plaster.[27] But colossal free-standing ephemeral sculptures,

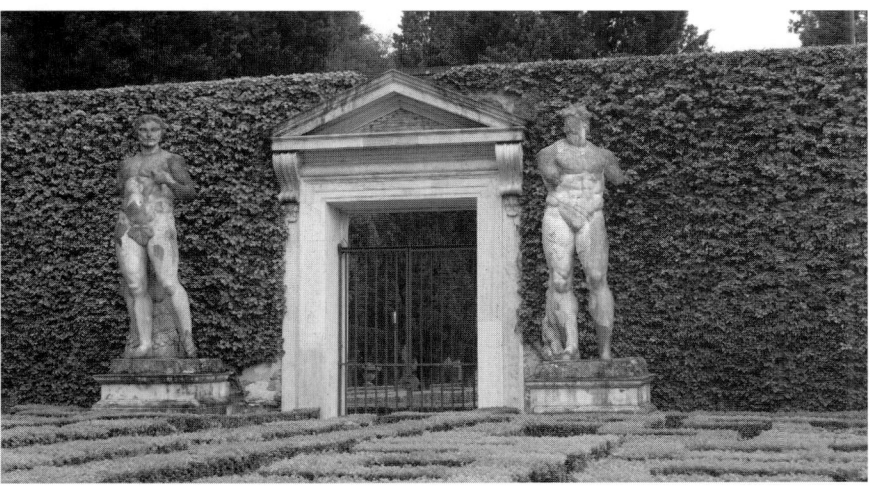

7.3. Baccio Bandinelli, *Giants*, before 1520, lime-based plaster, Gardens of the Villa Madama, Rome

such as Bandinelli's *Hercules* in the Florentine Loggia dei Lanzi, erected for the entry of Pope Leo X in 1515, were commonly made of clay.[28] The reason for these choices may lie with the above mentioned modelling qualities of clay and with the material's low price and local availability, both addressed below. In addition, clay was particularly suitable for the application of gilding.[29] I have argued elsewhere that the modern view of plaster as the ephemeral material *par excellence* may not have been shared by fifteenth- and sixteenth-century artists and patrons. In the sixteenth century, the use of (lime-based) plaster appears in fact increasingly in the realm of garden sculpture, as in the case of Baccio Bandinelli's colossal sculptures for the gardens of the Villa Madama near Rome (before 1520) (Figure 7.3). Issues of expense, time, and decorum may have made the white and relatively weather-resistant lime-based plaster an appropriate medium for garden, villa, and theatre decorations.[30]

For the modern spectator, plaster sculptures are primarily associated with whiteness. In the fifteenth century this would not have been the case, as most of these works were covered in polychromy. The above-mentioned devotional reliefs and busts of saints were painted to represent their subjects as life-like.[31] A decisively smaller group of works, including secular reliefs and heads of Famous Men, sported patinas to resemble bronze or gold.[32] Thus, while the owners of these works, and arguably also some of the beholders, may have been aware of the material of the objects they were looking at, they would not have associated plaster sculpture with any particular phenomenological characteristics. Painters and sculptors in the fifteenth century were of course familiar with the appearance of unpainted plaster surfaces – not only of incomplete works, but also of the above-mentioned workshop models. The latter, it seems, remained unpainted as their white and somewhat dull surface was ideal for drawing exercises, studying the rendering of volume through light and shade. It is tempting to speculate that it was in fact in the workshops of painters and sculptors such as Squarcione, Bellini, and Verrocchio that white plaster casts were invested for the first time with classical associations.[33] After all, casts of limbs or details of sculptures would often have had a fragmentary appearance not dissimilar to that of the fragments of ancient marble statuary that humanistically inspired patrons began to collect in this period.[34]

Instances where plaster was presented outside the workshop as a white material, without polychromy, bronze patina, or extensive gilding, mostly date from the sixteenth century and they appear in classicizing contexts. It is arguable that those who made or commissioned these works may have associated the use of plaster in these circumstances with classical practices, as mentioned by Pliny and experienced in the Domus Aurea.[35] Still, here too the material refers beyond its own materiality, standing in, as it does, for marble. Pomponio Gaurico in his 1504 treatise *On Sculpture* likens the whiteness of gypsum to that of marble, and Vasari, in his discussion of the sixteenth-century custom of *all'antica* stucco decorations, speaks of their permanence that, he claimed, made them similar to marble.[36] It appears that plaster, even when it was not covered in polychromy, was still read as referencing other, worthier materials, rather than attracting attention to itself. Thus, the major feature of plaster seems to have been its indexicality.

Though extremely variable in its appearance, wax is phenomenologically a much more distinct medium than plaster, and frequently recognizable by its translucent surface. It is also more complex in terms of its production, geographical origins, physical qualities, trade, historical associations, and uses. As a result, it was also by far the most expensive of the three materials studied in this essay.

Since classical antiquity, wax had been associated with memory. Famously, it was Aristotle who used the imprint of a seal in wax as a metaphor for human memory. Drawing especially on wax as a living medium that, depending on the temperature, could change its physical properties, the ancient philosopher compared the excitable minds of young children and old men that are unable to hold memories to the fluidity of warm wax.[37] Extensive myths had been woven since antiquity about the nature of wax and of the animals that produced it. It was believed to be a pure floral liquid, carefully chosen and collected by the bees, but not modified.[38] This belief also penetrated the semantics of wax in the context of the Christian church, where beeswax candles played a prominent role. Several early Christian versions of the *Exultet*, the Easter Song of Praise that early on Easter morning was sung in the Christian church as the new Easter candle was lit, dwell on the virginity of the bee and liken it to the whiteness of the (bleached) candle wax.[39] In fact, apart from artistic and the odd medical uses, wax had since late antiquity predominantly been consumed by the church. Demand in Europe far outweighed production. In Italy, beeswax was imported from Poland, Russia, Romania, Spain, Africa, and Corsica, with Venice acting both as an important centre for trade as well as for the production of bleached wax.[40] Throughout Europe, wax of different origins was on sale, with wax markets heavily regulated, and quality monitored and certified according to provenance, physical qualities, and purity.[41] In Florence, trading in wax fell under the remit of the *Arte dei Medici e Speziali*.[42] Accordingly it was *speziali*, such as the humanist Matteo Palmieri, with whom the Opera del Duomo dealt when selling wax that had been donated to the church on the feast days of Santa Reparata or San Zenobio, or when buying for its own donations to the nearby church of San Giovanni on the Florentine patron's feast day.[43] In the 1420s the per-pound price obtained by the Opera for the resale of its wax surplus amounted roughly to the daily wages of an unskilled worker, while the prices it paid to acquire wax were even higher.[44] Data like this have to be treated with caution[45] and do not reflect the wide range of different waxes available, but this illustrates sufficiently that, for large parts of the population, wax was not easily affordable. In fact, for illumination purposes, private households and even courts in the Renaissance used mainly tallow lamps that burned animal fat.[46]

Relatively expensive, supported by myths regarding its nature, imported from exotic places, and offered in different qualities according to its origin and treatment, wax featured prominently in civic and religious rites, which strongly affected its reception. Large quantities of wax, mainly in the form of candles, were given as tributes by subject territories and civic bodies to local churches on the annual feast days of civic patron saints. A fifteenth-century source records that at the Florentine feast of St John the Baptist, candles carried in procession weighed between one and one hundred pounds, and in 1336 the overall weight of wax donated during this annual festival was recorded as amounting to 3,657 pounds.[47]

Inside the churches, wax candles had of course important liturgical functions, notably as altar candles, without which no Mass could be celebrated, and including candles on the altars of individual saints. The most important candle, however, was the Easter Candle, which stood for the Resurrected Christ as the Light of the World and from which early in the Easter morning all other lights in the church were lit.[48] Consumption varied, depending on social and liturgical factors, but some churches used vast quantities of beeswax candles regularly throughout the year, and/or on important events and feast days. The Schloßkirche in sixteenth-century Wittenberg (Saxony) legendarily burned 35,570 pounds of wax in a year,[49] while, in Rome, the papal Master of Ceremonies, Johannes Burchard, recorded in his diary the use of two tons of wax for the nine-day-long funeral rites of Cardinal La Balue in 1491.[50]

Finally, wax featured in churches also in the form of votive gifts to saints and/or miraculous images, which, arguably, brings us back to the realm of sculpture. The most famous examples, mentioned also by Vasari, are the full-scale portrait *ex voti* of SS Annunziata in Florence and Santa Maria delle Grazie near Mantua (Figure 7.4), where wax used for hands and faces of the sitters appeared together with a variety of other materials, such as cloth.

Vasari discusses the work of the sculptors and *ceraiuoli* who made these full-size portraits. Wax can assimilate the appearance of human flesh, hair, and fingernails, without being painted, still maintaining its own translucent material surface. Vasari explains how Verrocchio and Orsino Benintendi achieved life-like appearances by colouring wax using various pigments.[51] While Vasari focuses on the technical and aesthetic dimension of these works and their fame beyond Florence for the artists and for the visitors of Santissima Annunziata, the wax used for the visible body parts of these life-size portraits would have emphasized the link of these sculptures to other, much more common votive wax offerings. In addition to the ubiquitous candles, there were various forms of wax donation that had a representational link to the limb or person that was prayed for, including blocks of wax of identical weight and candles of identical height.[52] The largest group by a long way, far outweighing the comparatively small number of full-scale portraits at Santissima Annunziata, were small-scale casts in the shape of human limbs or bodies. As a pure material with its above-mentioned religious associations, stable monetary value, and potential for strong representational qualities, particularly in relation to the human body, wax ideally fulfilled the votive functions.

To those whose arguments were not restricted by the *paragone* debate, artists' wax models may well have evoked the material's connection with memory. To them, wax could have appeared as the fitting matrix to record the sculptor's process. Equally it is conceivable that for the sixteenth-century beholder the perception of works in wax may have been informed by associations of the material to the sacred, both through its legendary origins as well as through its ecclesiastic uses.[53]

Clay, the starting point of this chapter, was definitely the cheapest of the three materials. In most cases it was sourced locally, even when the sculptor himself was not local.[54] Gian Carlo Gentilini suggests that

Material distinctions 169

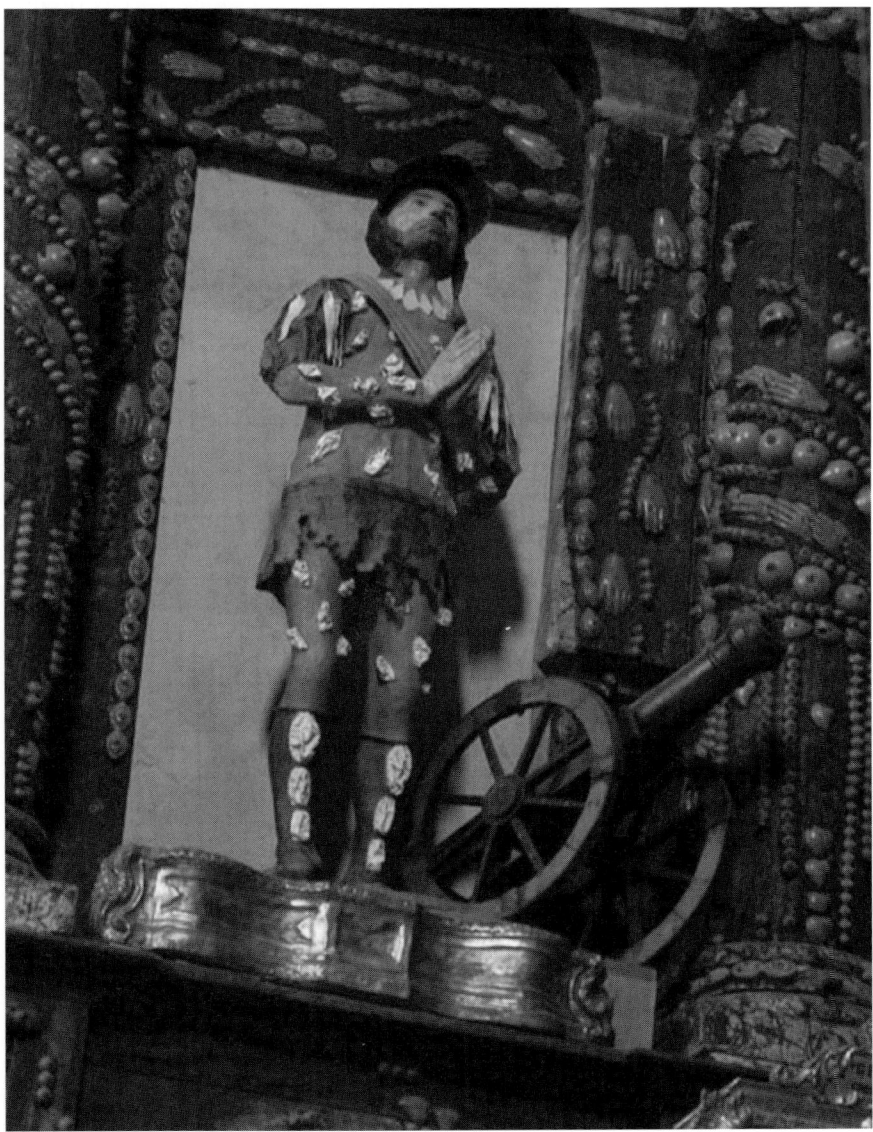

7.4. *Ex voto* portrait figure surrounded by cast wax *ex voti*, seventeenth century, Santa Maria delle Grazie, near Mantua (re-cast and re-arranged in the eighteenth century)

at least itinerant sculptors would have been able to make distinctions between the most important varieties of clay.[55] Once selected and sourced, clay also needed to be purified and manipulated. The skills involved, like those required for firing, were predominantly the domain of brick-makers and potters – that is, of craftsmen rather than practitioners of the liberal arts.[56] In fact, the most extensive and informative textual mention of working in clay comes from a potter, Cipriano Piccolpasso. His work *Li tre libri dell'arte del vasaio* is a practice-oriented text.[57] The opening passages immediately focus on the material of his craft and demonstrate a clear understanding of the varieties of clay, locally and in various other parts of Italy. But where Aretino in his letter to Vasari used the technical term *creta* (clay), dismissing the material value of his work, Piccolpasso speaks of *terra* (earth), a term with a huge semantic potential.[58] In the opening sentences the patriotic connotations of this term are immediately brought to the fore, as he discusses the use of clay in his adopted hometown, Urbino, mentioning its nearby river, geographical position and weather: 'The men of the potter's art in the city of Urbino use the clay [*terra*] which collects in the bed of the Metauro, and this they get in the summer more than at other times; ... When the rains fall in the Apennines at the roots of which the said river rises, its waters swell'. Turning to the techniques practised in his birthplace, Castel Durante, he uses the term in a different, closely related, meaning: 'The same method obtains in the land [*terra*] of Durante, my fatherland, which is washed on three sides by the said Metauro'.[59] In Renaissance Italy local crafts were of huge civic importance and the object of great pride. Civic pride and patriotism are clearly expressed as Piccolpasso refers to the raw material of his work.

When it comes to modelling in clay, positive comment can be found in Pomponio Gaurico's treatise of 1504, which stands firmly in the tradition of classical authors. Following ancient precedent, Gaurico describes modelling in clay as the oldest form of sculpture-making; as a Christian author he deviates from his classical sources as he mentions God as the first modeller who created the world and everything in it from clay.[60]

Firing, too, was a laborious and expensive act that required skill, equipment, and resources. Bruce Boucher reminds us that the technique evolved in the fifteenth century in a variety of non-classical contexts, drawing also on long-standing medieval traditions and skills of brickmakers and potters.[61] Thus there is a good argument that, in most cases, working in terracotta may have been seen as impressive modern craftsmanship rather than a revival of classical techniques or a process that supported more elevated connotations as argued by Gentilini and others.[62] Finally, one ought to consider that, like works in plaster, terracotta objects were frequently covered with polychromy that would have obviated any material-specific associations.

Nonetheless, as the product of a process that involves earth and fire, water and air, sculpture in terracotta might have supported elementary or alchemical associations.[63] Taking forward the image of God as the first sculptor, one might also expect a comparison of the process of firing with the breath of life that God gave to Adam. It is again in the classical context of Gaurico's treatise that clay, fire, and life are mentioned together, albeit in a passage that does not mention terracotta. In an unusual metaphorical reading of Prometheus' audacious theft of fire, Gaurico states that the ancient hero was such an excellent sculptor that *it was said* he stole from heaven a torch of life and implanted it into the clay (*vitalem igniculum limo imisisse*).[64]

The flame of life and a torch-wielding hero *all'antica* also feature in a flamboyant display of artistic invention on the breastplate of Antonio del Pollaiuolo's terracotta *Bust of a Young Man in Pageant Armour*, made a few decades earlier in Florence (Figure 7.5). Here the connection to

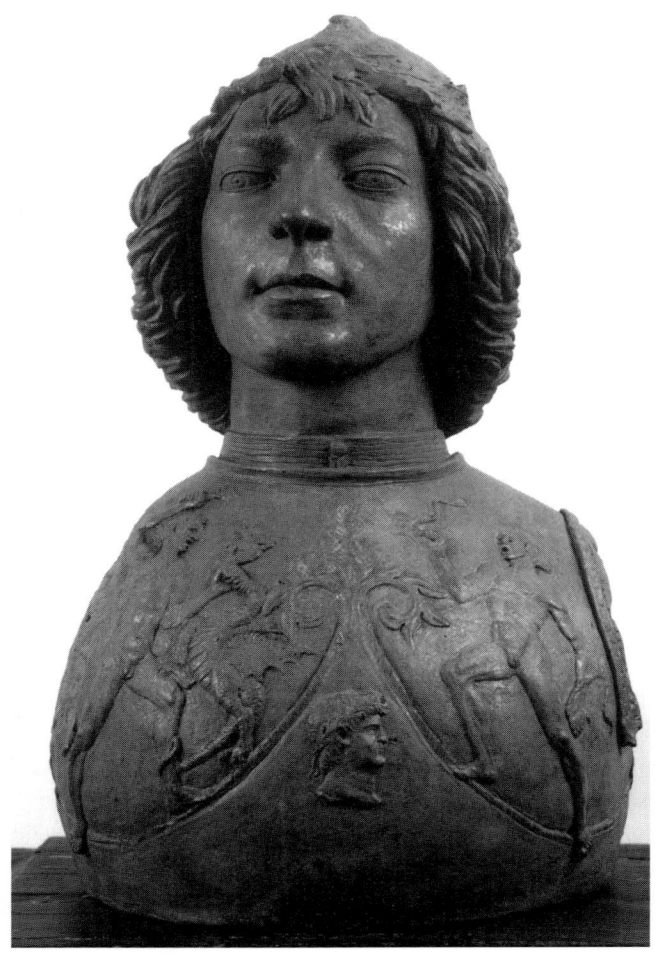

7.5. Antonio del Pollaiuolo, *Young Man in Pageant Armour*, c. 1450, terracotta, Museo Nazionale del Bargello, Florence

fired earth was obvious: originally only lightly tinted and gilded, the bust was always recognizable as a terracotta. A highly rhetorical representation of a Florentine youth with idealized features and fanciful *all'antica* armour, the bust is unlike other, more common, terracotta busts. These represent worthy Florentine patricians, occasionally using a deathmask. As objects in terracotta they hark back to Roman ancestral busts and are humble relatives of the Florentine honorary marble bust. Pollaiuolo's bust, instead, as argued by Alison Wright, is a terracotta in its own right, made to celebrate the chivalric achievements of a young member of an elite family. The young man was wearing a dragon-crowned fancy helmet, now partially broken off, and on his cuirass a central vase of fire is flanked by two heroes, one of whom wields a burning torch as he strangles a fiery dragon.[65] With Gaurico's reading of Prometheus in mind it is compelling to follow Wright's interpretation of the repeated representation of fire as an allusion to the sculptor's role as a god-like creator who fires the sculpture with life.[66]

Conclusion

Sidelined in the art-critical literature of the time, the three materials under discussion had a wide range of uses in the artist's workshop and beyond. Each material, due to distinct physical qualities, lent itself to specific tasks within the sculptor's practice. Beyond this there were other factors that would have conditioned the use and perception of these materials both inside the artist's workshop and beyond it. Financially, the hierarchy is obvious: clay, lime-based plaster, gypsum, wax, the latter being by far the most expensive. While this monetary scale might partly explain why wax was seldom used for large-scale models and why, in the realm of large-scale ephemeral monuments, clay was preferred over plaster, the choice of material for a work and its consequent reception may have been conditioned by the visibility of the material in the final work, its phenomenological distinctness, as well as by a wide range of associations that related to each material's origins, production methods, and uses beyond artistic practice. Georges Didi-Huberman has referred to the viscosity of wax to account for its neglect as an artistic medium by modern art historians.[67] In the Renaissance and outside the established art-critical discourses, works in wax and wax-working may have supported other associations that were informed rather by the myths of its origins and its trade that brought it into the realm of spices, as well as by its extensive theological and ecclesiastic associations. A model in wax may have been invested by the beholder with Aristotelian concepts of memory, as a fitting object to record the artist's forming movements. Such a perception may also have been conditioned by the association of wax with the sacred and with the memorializing and substitutional functions of the omnipresent wax *ex voti*. For clay, associations of divine creativity were voiced in the Renaissance. Works in plaster, at least during the fifteenth century, were often painted in polychromy to appear life-like. In the sixteenth century they appear to have been increasingly painted to look like bronzes, or were left unpainted. In these cases they may have been associated with classical practices and compared to ancient works. However, the uncovered plaster seems to have stimulated associations of marble, rather than ones that related to itself. Inorganic, burned before the forming act, and unpleasant to handle, plaster rather than clay may in practice have been perceived as the lowliest in the hierarchy of materials.

Notes

An early version of this chapter was presented at the Renaissance Society of America annual meeting 2010 in Venice as part of the panel *Visible Values: Making Distinctions in Late Fifteenth- and Sixteenth-Century Italy*. I should like to thank Michelle O'Malley for organizing the panel and Elizabeth Currie for steering the event. I am also grateful to Pamela Smith, Christy Anderson, and Anne Dunlop for inviting me to contribute to the present volume and for their generous and helpful comments on my text.

1. The original letter does not survive. The earliest publication gives the date 15 July 1538 (reiterated in Paolo Procaccioli (ed.), *Pietro Aretino, Lettere*, 5 vols (Rome: Salerno, 1997–2001; 1998), vol. 2, pp. 68–9, at 68, no. 63). This date has been convincingly questioned by Karl Frey, *Der Literarische Nachlass Giorgio Vasaris*, 3 vols (Munich: Georg Müller, 1923–40), I:35 (no. XIII), p. 39 (for the discussion of the date of the letter). This has been followed in later editions and studies, e.g. Ettore Camesasca (ed.), *Lettere sull'arte di Pietro Aretino, commentate da Fidenzio Pertile*, 3 vols (Milan: Edizioni del Milione, 1957–60; 1957), vol. 1, p. 25; Rick Scorza, 'Vasari, Borghini and Michelangelo', in Francis Ames-Lewis and Paul Joannides (eds), *Reactions to the Master: Michelangelo's Effect on Art and Artists in the Sixteenth Century* (Aldershot: Ashgate, 2003), pp. 180–210, at 208, note 59.

2. On the *fortuna critica* of terracotta and especially its low status in the context of the *paragone* debate see, e.g., Adalgisa Lugli, *Guido Mazzoni e la rinascita della terracotta nel quattrocento* (Turin: U. Allemandi, 1990), pp. 11–30, esp. 13–17; on the reception of wax (with a particular focus on the nineteenth and twentieth centuries): Georges Didi-Huberman, 'Die Ordnung des Materials', *Vorträge aus dem Warburg-Haus* 3 (1999), pp. 1–29, at 16–29; see 'Viscocités et survivances: L'histoire de l'art à l'épreuve du matériau', *Critique* 54:611 (1998), pp. 138–62 (English translation: 'Viscosities and survivals: Art history put to the test by the material', in Roberta Panzanelli (ed.), *Ephemeral Bodies: Wax Sculpture and the Human Figure* (Los Angeles: Getty Research Institute, 2008), pp. 154–69.)

3. The complex relationship of material and intellectual values and their roles in the reception of art objects during the period is discussed in Luke Syson and Dora Thornton, *Objects of Virtue: Art in Renaissance Italy* (London: British Museum, 2001), pp. 89–91.

4. Giorgio Vasari, *Le vite de' più eccellenti pittori scultori ed architettori*, ed. Gaetano Milanesi, 10 vols (Florence: Sansoni, 1906; reprint 1981), vol. 1, pp. 152–5; Johannes Myssok, *Bildhauerische Konzeption und plastisches Model in der Renaissance* (Münster: Rhema, 1999), pp. 65–70.

5. Benvenuto Cellini, 'Disputa infra la scultura e la pittura', in Paola Barocchi (ed.), *Scritti d'arte del cinquecento*, 3 vols (Milan and Naples: R. Ricciardi, 1971–77; 1971), vol. 1,

p. 597; for an almost identical passage see also 'Discorso sopra l'arte del Disegno', in *Scritti d'arte del cinquecento* (1973), vol. 2, p. 1932. For recent discussions of Cellini's design practice as reflected in his writings and surviving works see Michael W. Cole, *Cellini and the Principles of Sculpture* (Cambridge: Cambridge University Press, 2002); and Myssok, *Bildhauerische Konzeption*, pp. 59–64, 297–303.

6 For a fifteenth-century presentation model in terracotta see, e.g., Verrocchio's Finiguerra Monument; in Bruce Boucher (ed.), *Earth and Fire: Italian Terracotta Sculpture from Donatello to Canova* (exhibition catalogue New Haven, CT and London: Yale University Press, 2001), pp. 126–9; on wax models see Charles Avery, '"La cera sempre aspetta": Wax sketch-models for sculpture', *Apollo* 119 (1984), pp. 166–76.

7 Raffaello Borghini, *Il riposo* (Florence: Giorgio Marescotti, 1584), p. 136 (recte: 150); Charles Avery employed this line in the title of his ground-breaking article on Renaissance wax models 'La cera sempre aspetta'.

8 Filippo Baldinucci, *Notizie dei professori del disegno da Cimabue in qua*, 5 vols (Florence: V. Batelli e compagni, 1844–47) (1846), vol. 2, p. 565; Avery, 'La cera sempre aspetta', p. 173; Michael W. Cole, 'The figura sforzata: Modelling, power and the Mannerist body', *Art History* 24:4 (2001), pp. 520–51, at p. 525.

9 On the lost wax method, see, e.g., Richard E. Stone, 'Antico and the development of bronze casting in Italy at the end of the Quattrocento', *The Metropolitan Museum Journal* 16 (1981), pp. 87–116.

10 Vasari, *Le vite de' più eccellenti pittori scultori ed architettori*, vol. 1, pp. 152–5.

11 A general discussion of modelling in clay is provided in Nicholas Penny, *The Materials of Sculpture* (New Haven, CT and London: Yale University Press, 1993), pp. 201–14; for period-specific, close technical discussions see Giancarlo Gentilini, 'La scultura fiorentina in terracotta del Rinascimento: Tecniche e tipologie', in Maria Grazia Vaccari (ed.), *La scultura in terracotta: Tecniche e conservazione* (Florence: Centro Di, 1996), pp. 64–103; Charlotte Hubbard and Peta Motture, 'The making of terracotta sculpture: Techniques and observations', in Boucher (ed.), *Earth and Fire*, pp. 83–95, at pp. 83–5.

12 Charles Avery, *Giambologna: The Complete Sculpture* (Oxford: Phaidon and Christie's, 1987), pp. 69, 198, no. 198, fig. 81 (for the model in the Accademia); pp. 237, 275, no. 182, pl. 277 (for the *terra secca* model for the Florentine Palazzo Vecchietti in the Victoria and Albert Museum in London).

13 Penny, *The Materials of Sculpture*, p. 201; Hubbard and Motture, 'The making of terracotta sculpture', pp. 83–95, at pp. 84–5, 91–3.

14 Richard Goldthwaite, *The Building of Florence: An Economic and Social History* (Baltimore, MD and London: Johns Hopkins University Press, 1980), pp. 171, 206–7.

15 Goldthwaite, *The Building of Renaissance Florence*, pp. 171–212.

16 Claire Gapper, 'What is stucco? English interpretations of an Italian term', *Architectural History, Journal of the Society of Architectural Historians of Great Britain* 42 (1999) pp. 333–44; cf. Eckart Marchand, 'Reproducing relief: The use and status of plaster casts in the Italian Renaissance', in Donal Cooper and Marika Leino (eds), *Depth of Field: Relief Sculpture in Renaissance Italy* (Bern and Oxford: Peter Lang, 2007), pp. 191–221, at pp. 194–6. Lime-based plaster was typically mixed with sand or pulverized stone.

17 Pomponio Gaurico, *De sculptura*, ed. and trans. Paolo Cutolo (Naples: Edizioni scientifiche italiane, 1999), pp. 232–5. A document in the Archivio Statale di Siena (ASS, Balia 419, fol. 171v, 3 December 1504) makes mention of a gesso mine belonging to Pandolfo Petrucci. I am grateful to Philippa Jackson for generously sharing this information with me.

18 Penny, *Materials of Sculpture*, pp. 194–5; on gypsum as material see Augusto Giuffredi, *Manuale delle tecniche di formatura e fonderia* (Florence: Alinea, 2006), pp. 12–13; Marchand, 'Reproducing relief', pp. 191–221, at 194.

Material distinctions 175

19 William E. Wallace, *Michelangelo at San Lorenzo: The Genius as Entrepreneur* (Cambridge and New York: Cambridge University Press, 1994) pp. 91 and 144. Wallace states that for the building of the Biblioteca Laurenziana 'more was spent on lime than on bricks, the mortar costing more than the walls it held together'. On the prices of lime and bricks, see Goldthwaite, *The Building of Renaissance Florence*, pp. 198–9.

20 Goldthwaite, *The Building of Renaissance Florence*, pp. 187–8 (for Venice ensuring continuous supply from local kilns).

21 I am not aware of extensive studies of the price of gypsum, so the following cases (mainly from the sixteenth century) only give a general indication. In Padua, Francesco Squarcione was ordered on 9 October 1455 to repay Marco Zoppo for gypsum he had received from the latter at a rate of 6 denari to the pound – that is, 40 pounds to 1 lira (see note 22 below). The Opera del Duomo in Florence paid for gypsum delivered to Baccio Bandinelli on 13 December 1544, one lira ten soldi for fifty pounds of gypsum; on 21 March 1547, one lira five soldi for the same amount and on 6 November 1557, for twenty-eight pounds eighteen soldi. While this data suggests a relatively stable price during the wider span of the period, the varying Florentine prices may have reflected different traders and/or qualities of gypsum; Louis A. Waldman, *Baccio Bandinelli and Art at the Medici Court* (Philadelphia, PA: American Philosophical Society, 2004), pp. 277–9, 338, 633. For thirty-six istaiora lime delivered to Bandinelli's father on 14 June 1525, the Opera paid six lire and fifteen soldi, one *istaiora* (*staia*) being 22.4 litres; Waldman, *Baccio Bandinelli and Art at the Medici Court*, p. 74. See also the prices of lime mentioned in Goldthwaite, *The Building of Renaissance Florence*, p. 198.

22 'Documenti relativi alla pittura padovana del secolo XV', in Vittorio Lazzarini and Andrea Moschetti (eds), *Archivio Veneto* n. s., 15 (1908), pp. 72–190, 249–321; 16 (1908), pp. 68–102, at pp. 43, 149 (document XXXVIII, 24 May 1455); in 1455 Zoppo and his teacher fell out with one another and sought arbitration. The arbitors ordered Squarcione to return all of the remaining gypsum and to repay what he had used at a rate of 6 denari to the pound. The total weight of gypsum to be returned or repayed was stated as 3,500 pounds; Lazzarini and Moschetti (eds), *Archivio Veneto*, p. 43, 154 (document XL, 9 October 1455).

23 Stone, 'Antico and the development of bronze casting', pp. 108–9; Benvenuto Cellini, 'Della Sculptura', in *Opere di Benvenuto Cellini*, ed. Giuseppe Guido Ferrero (Turin: Unione tipografico-editrice torinese, 1971), pp. 751–804, at pp. 774–5.

24 Penny, *Materials of Sculpture*, 194; Giuffredi, *Manuale delle tecniche di formatura e fonderia*, pp. 12, 16; Marchand, 'Reproducing relief', pp. 191–221, 194.

25 Myssok, *Bildhauerische Konzeption und plastisches Model in der Renaissance*, p. 28; the author refers to Michelangelo's large-scale model of a river god in the Casa Buonarroti that contains clay, tow, wood, wool, and metal. Vasari, in his discussion of Tribolo's ephemeral equestrian monument to Charles V, mentions the (unhappy) collaboration with a carpenter who provided the armature for socle and horse; Vasari, *Le vite de' più eccellenti pittori scultori ed architettori*, vol. 6, p. 68.

26 On the organization of ephemeral sculpture in general see, e.g., Vicenzo Cazzato, 'Vasari e Carlo V: L'ingresso trionfale a Firenze del 1536', in Gian Carlo Garfagnini (ed.), *Giorgio Vasari tra decorazione ambientale e storiografia artistica* (Florence: Leo S. Olschki, 1985), pp. 179–204; on the potentially pressing timetable of the events see Paolo Fabbri, *Gusto scenico a Mantova nel tardo rinascimento* (Padua: Liviana, 1974), p. 13; see also Vasari's description of the only partly completed equestrian monument to Charles V by Tribolo in Vasari, *Le vite de' più eccellenti pittori scultori ed architettori*, vol. 6, p. 68.

27 Plaster statues on top of triumphal arches are mentioned, e.g., in the context of the entries of Philip of Habsburg and of Henry III of France to Mantua in 1549 and 1547, respectively: Fabbri, *Gusto scenico a Mantova nel tardo rinascimento*, pp. 9–13.

28 On Bandinelli's sculpture see John Shearman, 'The Florentine entrata of Leo X, 1515', *Journal of the Warburg and Courtauld Institutes* 38 (1975) pp. 136–54, at pp. 149–50, and note 41; Eckart Marchand, 'Plaster and plaster casts in the Italian Renaissance', in Rune Frederiksen and Eckart Marchand (eds), *Plaster Casts: Making, Collecting and Display*, Transformationen der Antike 18 (Berlin: Walter de Gruyter, 2010), p. 69, note 81 (with further literature).

29 In panel painting, bole, a particular fine type of clay, was used as an underlayer for the application of gold leaf; this is described by Cennino Cennini in his treatise probably written in early fifteenth-century Padua: Cennino d'Andrea Cennini, *The Craftsman's Handbook 'Il libro dell'arte'*, trans. Daniel V. Thompson, Jr. (New York: Dover Publications, 1960; 1933), pp. 79–80; for modern literature see, e.g., Jill Dunkerton, Susan Foister, Dillian Gordon, and Nicholas Penny, *Giotto to Dürer: Early Renaissance Painting in The National Gallery* (New Haven, CT and London: National Gallery Company and Yale University Press, 1991), p. 174.

30 Marchand, 'Plaster and plaster casts', pp. 67–70.

31 For a discussion of the uses of plaster in the period, see Marchand, 'Plaster and plaster casts', pp. 49–79; the literature on devotional images of the Virgin and Child is vast, see the recent contribution by Sarah Blake McHam, 'Now and then: Recovering a sense of different values', in Cooper and Leino (eds), *Depth of Field*, pp. 305–50, at pp. 309–45; on (the much less frequent) busts of saints see, e.g., Marc Bormand in Marc Bormand, Beatrice Paolozzi Strozzi, Nicholas Penny, *Desiderio da Settignano, Sculptor of Renaissance Florence*, exhibition catalogue, Paris 2006, Washington 2007 (Paris: Musée du Louvre Editions, 2007), pp. 132–5.

32 In Padua in 1591 Francesco Segala made two 'figure di stucho e finte di bronze' for the choir of the Santo, Bruce Boucher, *The Sculpture of Jacopo Sansovino*, 2 vols (New Haven, CT and London: Yale University Press, 1991), vol. 2, p. 336; another example for bronze patinated plaster sculpture are the twenty-eight heads of Roman emperors in the library of the Santo, of which seventeen survive; a document records a discussion on 6 November 1585 concerning the painting in bronze of this group, Irene Favaretto, 'Teste "all'antica"', in Giovanni Lorenzoni and Enrico Maria dal Pozzolo (eds), *Basilica del Santo: Dipinti, sculture, tarsie, disegni e modelli* (Padua: Centro studi antoniani and Rome: De Lucca, 1995), pp. 229–32, esp. p. 229.

33 On plaster casts in artists' collections see Marchand, 'Reproducing relief', pp. 191–221, at p. 207 with notes 29, 30; Irene Favaretto, *Arte antica e cultura antiquaria nelle collezioni venete al tempo della Serenissima* (Rome: 'L'Erma' di Bretschneider, 1990), pp. 65–70.

34 On the fragment and its interpretation in the Renaissance, see Leonard Barkan, *Unearthing the Past: Archaeology and Aesthetics in the Making of Renaissance Culture* (New Haven, CT and London: Yale University Press, 1999), pp. 119–207.

35 Pliny, *Naturalis historia*, vol. 35, p. 153; Nicole Dacos, *La découverte de la Domus Aurea et la formation des grotesques à la renaissance* (London: The Warburg Institute, 1969).

36 Gaurico, *De sculptura*, p. 232; Vasari, *Le vite de' più eccellenti pittori scultori ed architettori*, vol. 1, p. 166.

37 Didi-Huberman, 'Die Ordnung des Materials', pp. 5–6.

38 On wax and its associations in antiquity, the Middle Ages and the Renaissance, see Reinhard Büll, *Das große Buch vom Wachs: Geschichte Kultur Technik*, 2 vols (Munich: Callwey, 1977), vol. 1, pp. 10–28; on ancient myths relating to bees and honey, see Francois Quiviger, 'Honey from heaven', in Ulrich Pfisterer and Max Seidel (eds), *Visuelle Topoi: Erfindung und tradiertes Wissen in den Künsten der italienischen Renaissance* (Munich and Berlin: Deutscher Kunstverlag, 2003), pp. 317–21, and Hilda. M. Ransome, *The Sacred Bee* (London: George Allen & Unwin, 1937); on the bee in Christian theology: Manfred Misch, *Apis est animal – apis est ecclesia: Ein Beitrag zum Verhältnis von Naturkunde und Theologie*

in spätantiker und mittelalterlicher Literatur (Bern: Herbert Lang and Frankfurt: Peter Lang, 1974); on Renaissance perceptions of bees in general see Jonathan Woolfson, 'The Renaissance of bees', *Renaissance Studies* 24 (2009), pp. 281–300.

39 Büll, *Das große Buch vom Wachs*, vol. 2, p. 996.

40 Büll, *Das große Buch vom Wachs*, vol. 1, p. 163.

41 Büll, *Das große Buch vom Wachs*, vol. 1, pp. 152–87.

42 Raffaele Ciasca, *L'Arte dei Medici e Speziali nella storia e nel commercio fiorentino dal secolo XII al XV* (Florence: Leo S. Olschki, 1927; reprint 1977), pp. 371 and 377. The records of the Archivio dell'Opera del Duomo for the period of the construction of the dome of S. Maria del Fiore are now published on the web: English version: www.operaduomo.firenze.it/cupola/home_eng.html; Italian version: www.operaduomo.firenze.it/cupola/home.html (both accessed 24 June 2011). Matteo Palmieri's name appears frequently in this context in the documents, e.g. AOSMF, II-1-73, fol. 14v, b Deliberazioni (14 June 1418).

43 Donated as candles, wax loaves, or votive images, wax formed an important source of income, as surplus wax could be sold on to the trader; Büll, *Das große Buch vom Wachs*, vol. 1, pp. 174–6. For Siena Cathedral, the important role of wax in its finances has been illuminated by Andrea Giorgi and Stefano Moscadelli, 'Quod omnes cerei ad Opus deveniant: Il finanziamento dell'Opera del Duomo di Siena nei secoli XIII e XIV', *Nuova rivista storica* 85 (2001), pp. 489–584, especially p. 536; I am grateful to Philippa Jackson for bringing this text to my attention. For Florence Cathedral the published archival material highlights the economic importance of wax donations; see note 43 above. For Orsanmichele in Florence this has been discussed by Diane Finiello Zervas (ed.), *Orsanmichele a Firenze / Orsanmichele Florence* (Modena: Franco Cosimo Panini, 1996), pp. 79–82, and Zervas, *Orsanmichele: Documents 1336–1452 / documenti 1336–1452* (Modena: Franco Cosimo Panini, 1996) esp. p. 51, note 47.

44 Candles acquired by the Opera for the procession of San Giovanni on 16 July 1421 cost ten soldi (AOSMF, II-1-79, fol. c. 67, h, stanziamenti), while the price obtained by the Opera for the resale of its wax surplus varied during the 1420s between six soldi six denari on 18 April 1420 (AOSMF, II-1-78, fol. 25, b, deliberazioni) and eight soldi two denari the pound on 17 October 1426 (AOSMF, II-2-1, fol. 42v, d, deliberazioni). Over the same period the daily wages of an unskilled worker dropped from eleven soldi, one denaro to a temporary low of eight soldi, while a skilled labourer earned seventeen soldi, eight denari in 1420, twenty soldi in 1424 and seventeen soldi in 1426, Goldthwaite, *The Building of Renaissance Florence*, pp. 436–7.

45 The interpretation of such prices is notoriously problematic, as they are likely to have been conditioned by factors such as a the identity of the seller and the quality of the wax; see, e.g., the contributions in Michelle O'Malley and Evelyn Welch (eds), *The Material Renaissance* (Manchester and New York: Manchester University Press, 2007), esp. Evelyn Welch, 'Making money: Pricing and payments in Renaissance Italy', pp. 71–84 and Guido Guerzoni, 'The social world of price formation: Prices and consumption in sixteenth-century Ferrara', pp. 85–105.

46 Ursula Pfistermeister, *Wachs Volkskunst und Brauch: Ein Buch für Sammler und Liebhaber alter Dinge*, 2 vols (Nuremberg: H. Carl, 1982–83; 1982) vol. 1, p. 29; Helene Finkenstaedt and Thomas Finkenstaedt, *Stanglsitzerheilige und große Kerzen* (Weißenhorn: A.H. Konrad, 1968), p. 30.

47 On the procession on the feast of St John the Baptist in Florence see Pietro Gori, *Le feste fiorentine attraverso i secoli: Le feste per San Giovanni* (Florence: R. Bemporad & figlio, 1926), pp. 59–86; Heidi L. Chretien, *The Festival of San Giovanni: Imagery and Political Power in Renaissance Florence* (New York: Peter Lang, 1994), pp. 38–40. For the donations in 1369, see Gori, *Le feste fiorentine attraverso i secoli*, p. 60; for the weight of candles carried in procession see the fifteenth-century source *Istoria di Firenze di Goro Dati dall'anno*

MCCCLXXX all'anno MCCCCV (Florence: Giuseppe Manni, 1735), pp. 86–7; similar processions took place in other Italian cities, as, e.g., in Vicenza: Walter Stefani and Antonio Stefani, *Vicenza e la rua* (Vicenza: N. Pozza, 1985), p. 25.

48 For the meaning of light and the history of the candle in the Christian church see Büll, *Das große Buch vom Wachs*, vol. 2, pp. 959–99; Wolfgang Mühlbauer, *Geschichte und Bedeutung der (Wachs-)lichter bei den kirchlichen Funktionen: Ein Beitrag zur Liturgik, sowie für Prediger, Catecheten und religiöse Kunstanstalten* (Augsburg: Verlag der Kranzfelder'schen Buchhandlung, 1874); D.R. Dendy, *The Use of Lights in Christian Worship*, Alcuin Club Collections 41 (London: SPCK, 1959), this text includes the discussion of Anglican rites.

49 Büll, *Das große Buch vom Wachs*, vol. 2, p. 646; Charlotte Angeletti, *Geformtes Wachs: Kerzen, Votive, Wachsfiguren* (Munich: Callwey, 1980); Pfistermeister, *Wachs Volkskunst und Brauch*, p. 29; Celine Lausberg, *Beiträge zur Geschichte des Kerzenmachergewerbes im Mittelalter* (Duisburg: Ohlwein, 1929), p. 6.

50 Similar amounts were consumed at the funerals of other cardinals and of Pope Sixtus IV in 1484; Louis Thuasne (ed.), *Johann Burchard, Diarium* (Paris, 1883); vol. 1, 428–9; cited after Dendy, *The Use of Lights in Christian Worship*, pp. 105–7; Büll, *Das große Buch vom Wachs*, vol. 2, p. 649.

51 Vasari, *Le vite de' più eccellenti pittori scultori ed architettori*, vol. 1, pp. 152–3.

52 On wax *ex votos* in general see Büll, *Das große Buch vom Wachs*, vol. 2, pp. 905–8; most recently discussed by Megan Holmes, 'Ex-votos: Materiality, memory, and cult', in Michael W. Cole and Rebecca Zorach (eds), *The Idol in the Age of Art: Objects, Devotion and Early Modern World* (Aldershot: Ashgate, 2009), pp. 159–92; see also Jan Gerchow, 'Körper der Erinnerung, Votiv-, Stifter- und Grabbilder im Spätmittelalter', in Gerchow (ed.), *Ebenbilder. Kopien von Körper: Modelle des Menschen* (exhibition catalogue, Essen, Ruhrlandmuseum; Ostfildern-Ruit: Hatje Cantz, 2002), pp. 55–63; Georges Didi-Huberman, 'Heuristik der Ähnlichkeit: Der Fall der Votivbilder', in Gerchow (ed.), *Ebenbilder: Kopien von Körper*, pp. 65–72; Christine Göttler, '"Seelen in Wachs": Material, Mimesis und Memoria in der religiösen Kunst um 1600', in Gerchow, *Ebenbilder: Kopien von Körper*, pp. 83–96.

On the representational link of *ex votos* through weight or identical size see Holmes, 'Ex-votos', pp. 159–92, at p. 163; Didi-Huberman, 'Heuristik der Ähnlichkeit', p. 69. See also the seminal article by Julius von Schlosser, 'Geschichte der Porträtbildnerei in Wachs', *Jahrbuch der kunsthistorischen Sammlungen des allerhöchsten Kaiserhauses* 29:3 (1910–11), pp. 171–258 (English translation in Panzanelli, *Ephemeral Bodies*, pp. 171–314, and see also, in the same volume, Roberta Panzanelli, 'Compelling presence: Wax effigies in Renaissance Florence', pp. 13–39.)

53 A positive perception of wax (and the other two materials) is also implied in a passage of Pliny's *Natural History*. Georges Didi-Huberman, 'L'image-matrice: Généalogie et vérité de la ressemblance selon Pline l'Ancien Histoire Naturelle, XXXV, 1–7', *L'inactuel, psychoanalyse & culture: mensonges, verities* 6 (1996), pp. 109–25, esp. 117–18, discusses in psychoanalytical terms Pliny's expressed preference for ancestral images in wax, clay, and plaster over the collection of marble images of unknown people. Didi-Huberman argues that the art critical discourse since Vasari has suppressed the propagation of such positive perceptions of the cheaper materials.

54 Gentilini, 'La scultura fiorentina in terracotta del Rinascimento', pp. 67–8.

55 The two main types are dry, sandy clay that was dug up from river beds, and so-called *argilla di cava* that was fat and heavy and easy to model, most frequently used for small-scale works, as it shrinks rather dramatically.

56 On the technique and status of clay and terracotta see Gentilini, 'La scultura fiorentina in terracotta del Rinascimento'; Gentilini, 'Nella rinascita delle antichità', in *La civiltà del cotto: Arte della terracotta nell'area fiorentina dal XV al XX secolo* (exhibition catalogue Impruneta, 1980; Florence: Coop. Officine Grafiche Firenze, 1980), pp. 67–88; Bruce Boucher, 'Italian

Renaissance terracotta: Artistic revival or technological innovation?', in Boucher (ed.), *Earth and Fire*, pp. 1–31; Lugli, *Guido Mazzoni e la rinascita della terracotta nel quattrocento*, pp. 11–30.

57 Cipriano Piccolpasso, *Li tre libri dell'arte del vasaio*, ed. Giovanni Conti (Florence: All'insegna del giglio, 1976).

58 See Salvatore Battaglia, *Grande dizionario della lingua italiana*, 21 vols (Turin: Unione tipografico-editrice torinese, 1961–2002), s.v. 'Terra', vol. 20 (2000), pp. 941–6, esp. 942–3.

59 'Usano gli huomeni de l'arte de' vasi, nella città di Urbino, la terra che si colghie per il letto del Metauro, e quella colgano piu' ne l'istate che per altri tempi. . . . Quando cascano le piogge nel'Apenino, alla radice del quale nascie detto fiume, . . . '. 'Il medesmo muodo si tiene nella Terra di Durante, patria mia, la qual da tre lati bagnia il detto Metauro, come si dirà nel suo ritratto.' Piccolpasso, *Li tre libri dell'arte del vasaio*, pp. 35–6 (English translation: Piccolpasso, *The Three Books of the Potter's Art*, ed. and trans. Bernard Rackham and Albert van de Put (London: Victoria and Albert Museum, 1934), p. 7.)

60 Gaurico, *De sculptura*, p. 247; the topos that modelling in clay was the oldest sculptural technique can already be found in Pliny, *Naturalis historia*, vol. 35, pp. 45, 156.

61 Boucher, 'Italian Renaissance terracotta', pp. 1–31, esp. 1–5.

62 Gentilini, 'Nella rinascità dell'antichità'; Alison Wright, *The Pollaiuolo Brothers: The Arts of Florence and Rome* (New Haven, CT and London: Yale University Press, 2005), p. 147, note 171 (for further literature).

63 Vannoccio Biringuccio compares the attempts of early men to invent suitable building materials such as bricks and mortar through firing of the relevant raw materials, with the efforts of the alchemists of his time. This implies a devaluation of the alchemists' undertaking; it is not an attempt to ennoble the making of bricks or mortar; Vannoccio Biringuccio, *Pirotechnia* (1540), trans. Cyril Stanley Smith and Martha Teach Gnudi (Cambridge, MA: Harvard University Press, 1966), pp. 396–8, esp. 397. I should like to thank Pamela Smith for pointing me towards this reference.

64 Gaurico, *De sculptura*, p. 246; see also 247, note 6. Gaurico may have referred to Fulgentius' (2:79) account according to which Prometheus made human figures in clay that he provided with souls once he had stolen the divine fire from heaven. Fulgentius' version of the myth is discussed in Ernst Kris and Otto Kurz, *Legend, Myth, and Magic in the Image of the Artist: A Historical Experiment* (New Haven, CT and London: Yale University Press 1979), pp. 85–6. I am indebted to Anne Dunlop for pointing me towards this reference.

65 The other is holding two cords that the youth holds in emulation of Hercules as if he were fighting snakes; Wright, *The Pollaiuolo Brothers*, p. 148.

66 Wright, *The Pollaiuolo Brothers*, pp. 143–9, especially p. 149.

67 Didi-Huberman, 'Die Ordnung des Materials', pp. 16–29; 'Viscités et survivances', pp. 138–62 (English: pp. 154–69).

8 ✧ Rocks and reverence: Inka and Spanish perceptions of stonework in the early modern Andes

Carolyn Dean

PRIOR TO Spanish colonization, the Inka of western South America regarded the stones of which their temples were made to be as sacred as what the invading Spaniards would later identify as the 'idols' cosseted within.[1] The Inka not only carved and built with stone, they also revered, fed, clothed, and conversed with certain rocks which they regarded as sentient and potentially animate. Stone, to the Inka, was capable of hosting living essences and also of taking the form of humans and animals. Moreover, they believed that rock could resist human manipulation. As a consequence, building in stone evinced successful negotiations with nature; in general, the more finely worked the rock, the more it indexed the Inka's ability to coax cooperation from nature and tame the difficult terrain of the high Andes. Although Spaniards, who invaded the Andes in the early sixteenth century, widely praised Inka stonework, they did not hold the same regard for rock. Stone, to Spaniards was a prestigious building material, requiring craft specialization and an investment in labour; it was, however, not a sentient medium. They used already worked Inka ashlars to build Spanish-style structures, dismantling indigenous walls to erect elite residences, administrative buildings, chapels, churches, and cathedrals. To Spaniards, this re-use of Inka stonework actualized colonization and the religious conversion of indigenous Andeans to Roman Catholicism. To many Inka, however, the rocks probably remained sentient, regardless of their architectural context. Such differing perceptions of rock as a building material led to contrasting – even contradictory – understandings of colonial edifices constructed of stone.

Rock to the pre-Hispanic Inka
The Inka claimed a special relationship with rock.[2] In Andean oral culture the Inka are often said to talk to and interact with sentient and animate stone. Both in stories and in reality, the pre-Hispanic Inka engaged with

the earth and its stony extrusions in ways that underscored commonality and interdependence. The Inka understood themselves not as human beings separate and distinct from what we might term natural resources, but as co-dependent entities with the earth and its various parts. Stories featuring wilful rocks recorded the Inka's ability to forge alliances with potent petrous beings. Perhaps stories about *puruawqa* are the best examples of this. Briefly, *puruawqa* refers to rocks who became warriors when the Inka were threatened by a powerful enemy. Once the enemy had been defeated and Cuzco, the Inka's capital, was secure, the *puruawqa* re-petrified. Located in various places in and around Cuzco, *puruawqa* stones were objects of worship, and at least some of them were addressed individually by name. They were not specially carved or visually distinct from other rocks in the landscape. Rather, *puruawqa* were identified through oral culture and reverential practices. The *puruawqa* promised to aid the Inka in times of war whenever they were needed and, furthermore, it is alleged that the fear of the *puruawqa* discouraged other Andean peoples from resisting Inka domination. The Jesuit chronicler Bernabé Cobo, writing in the seventeenth century, stresses that visitors to pre-Hispanic Cuzco were shown the petrified warriors and told the story, adding 'then the strangers would be persuaded to worship the stones' (*a los forasteros . . . persuadían las adorasen*).[3] Whether through persuasion or coercion, inducing visitors to Cuzco to honour *puruawqa* was compelling them to acknowledge not just the history of the Inka's military success, but also the promise that the land itself would rise up in defence of the Inka.[4] We are told that the number of offerings made to the petrified warriors was great, and that the *puruawqa* were acknowledged whenever the ruler went to or returned from war, during coronations of rulers, and at all major festivals.[5] The Inka ruler and his military leaders surrounded themselves with these indefatigable petrous warriors. Additionally, the *puruawqa*'s promise of protection and future transformational abilities were properties projected on to stone more broadly such that rock used in Inka construction projects was similarly sentient and capable of self-determination.

One set of stories, widely told in the Andes both in pre-Hispanic and colonial times, directs attention to the immensity of the task of transporting megaliths, some weighing many tons, for use in Inka building projects.[6] According to accounts recorded in the Andes between 1553 and 1653, a giant stone was quarried and then transported a great distance by the Inka for use in a building project; during the journey, the weary rock refused to move any further and began to shed tears of blood.[7] In nearly all of the tired stone stories recorded by the chroniclers (perhaps because many of them collected their stories in Cuzco), the stone is identified as having been intended for the building complex overlooking Cuzco called Saqsaywaman, whose megalithic walls still amaze visitors to the site (Figure 8.1).[8] The Saqsaywaman complex was built by labourers summoned from throughout the empire who worked periodically for the state as a form of tribute. Its magnificent walls manifested the extensive resources of a state that could mobilize the labour required to cut, dress, transport, and erect structures of these Herculean rocks. Accounts recording the difficulties of transporting stones, especially recalcitrant ones, induce awe and so reinforce the grandeur of the structure. Stories about reticent stones also draw attention to the labour of moving *all* stones; they underscore the work of those who, under Inka direction, quarried, pulled, shaped, hoisted, and ultimately fixed stones into the impeccable walls of Inka structures.

The Jesuit Cobo also tells the story of a tired stone that resisted Inka efforts to place it in the walls of Saqsaywaman.[9] After it had fallen three times, killing a number of workers, the Inka called on 'sorcerers' who were capable of speaking to the stone. They determined that, if the Inka continued their efforts to force the stone into the structure, 'all would have a bad end'. As with the tired stones who cried blood, the Inka desisted in their efforts to force the intransigent stone to do as they desired. Tales of resistant – even homicidal – rocks suggest that those stones that were parts of walls were there because they wanted to be. Such stories, then, actually stress the reciprocal nature of building, an effort that requires not just human labour, craft, and technical acumen, but also the cooperation of the material from which buildings are made – the rocks themselves. Like the *puruawqa*, the resistant stones of legend signified the Inka's special abilities to forge alliances with the earth and its least compliant components.

Although the Inka were not the only Andean peoples to practise stonemasonry, much of their stonework was distinctive.[10] The archaeologist Susan Niles identifies three basic styles of Inka masonry based on the quality of fit.[11] The finest she calls high-prestige masonry, while fieldstone masonry describes unworked or barely worked stacked stone; in between is intermediate masonry. Inka high-prestige masonry particularly signed the presence of the Inka state and conveyed its abilities with regard to the sentient material of which its architecture was built. While an ordinary stone wall was *pirqa* in Quechua, the Inka's language, a dictionary of 1586 defines a stone wall constructed without mortar as 'canic pirca' (*kanij pirqa*), meaning 'nibbled wall'.[12] 'Nibbling' describes the process of, and techniques for, creating high-prestige masonry that has been identified and recreated by Jean-Pierre Protzen.[13] Once a block was roughed out, hammer-stones, ever decreasing in size, were used to refine the shape.[14] While initial strokes took large bites from the stone, gobbling its excesses, final work persistently nibbled away at the block

Rocks and reverence

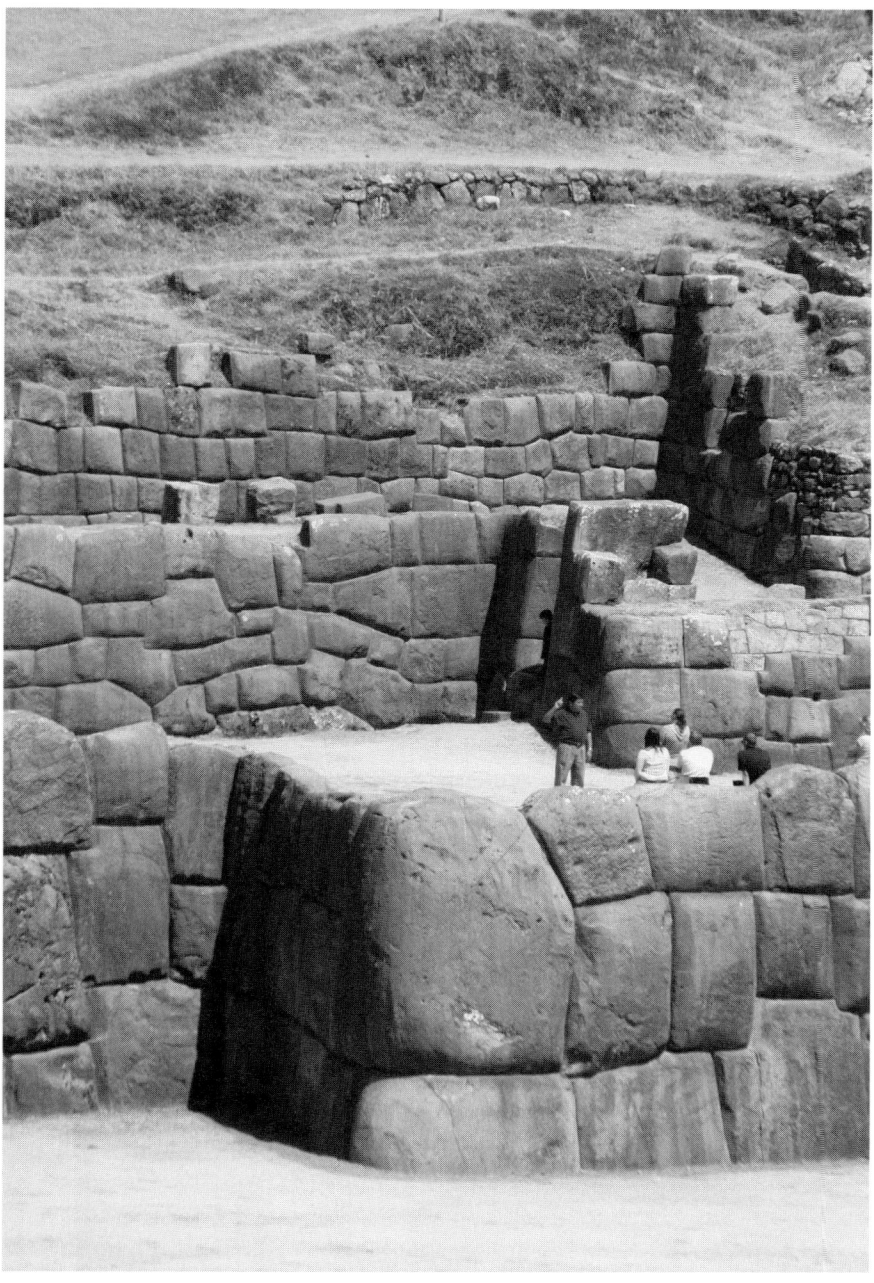

8.1. Inka, megalithic walls, Saqsaywaman, early sixteenth century

to achieve the desired result. Blocks were nibbled at the site of construction until they fitted precisely on top of, and next to, their nibbled peers. Walls where stone has been removed reveal the bedding joints achieved through the time-consuming, but not technically difficult, process of nibbling, fitting, nibbling, re-fitting, and so on.[15]

With regard to Andean textiles and metalwork, the archaeologist Heather Lechtman emphasizes the importance of the production history as recorded in the details of an object's structure; she concludes that meaning inhered in process, as well as product.[16] The same emphasis on process is true for Inka nibbled masonry.[17] Much of its significance derived from the evidence of the labour required to work the stones. Each finishing stroke of the hammer-stone left tell-tale bite marks that give the wall texture no matter how finely worked.[18] Even the very few examples of bas-relief decoration, such as serpents and pumas occasionally carved on isolated ashlars, do little to distract from the finely 'nibbled' stones making up high-prestige walls. Cobo, one of few Spaniards to show interest in Inka masonry practices, notes that the working of stone blocks was 'very hard and tedious' (*muy pesada y prolija*); he explains that, 'In order to fit the stones together, it was necessary to put them in place and remove them many times to check them.'[19] Cobo emphasizes the time involved in producing a wall of nibbled stone. The key to an Inka perspective, then, seems to be the concept of nibbling in which the *process*, the persistent working of individual blocks, not just the end *product*, the final wall or structure, is emphasized.

Because traces of the hammer-stone on the surface of a nibbled block constantly recall the work of production, the nibble marks are evidential, bearing witness to the working of the stone.[20] They cause the labour to be remembered and record the experience of the stone as it was transformed from the randomness of nature to Inka order. To build with stone or manipulate it in some way was to domesticate it; it was to render the chaos of nature conducive to human prosperity, and its pecked surface indexes the actions taken to tame it. The bites are the traces of the process through which a sentient and wilful substance was not just turned towards Inka purposes, but fully integrated into the Inka's cultural matrix. The dressed and fitted stone of which high-prestige walls are made might well be thought of as the most thoroughly tamed of all rock – and they bear the marks of their willing domestication.

Cut and fitted stonemasonry – what the Inka called nibbled masonry – has been studied extensively and numerous ways of categorizing its types or styles have been offered.[21] Most authors, following observations made by John Rowe in his 'Introduction to the archaeology of Cuzco' (1944), recognize two broad 'styles' of well-worked stone wall construction, both of which consist of nibbled blocks that are joined without

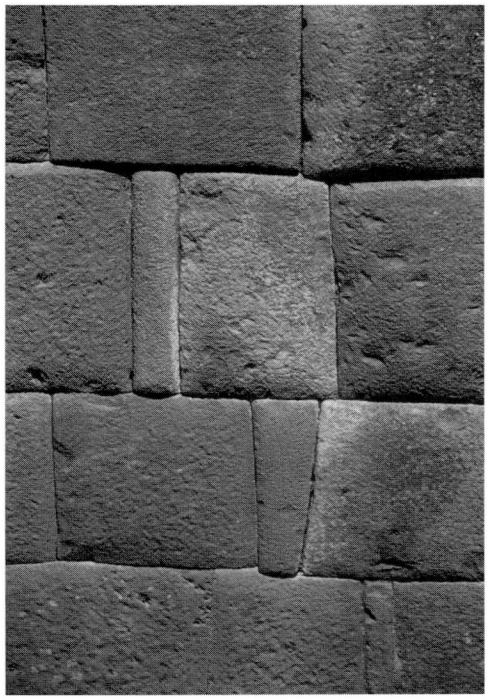

8.2. Inka, high-prestige coursed stonemasonry, 1450–1530

mortar.[22] In one style, the face of the wall is coursed, referring to rectangular-faced parallelepipeds (blocks with opposite sides parallel to one another), placed in relatively regular courses (Figure 8.2). In the second style, the face of the wall is uncoursed, composed of polygonal blocks of irregular, interlocking shapes (Figure 8.3). Rowe observes that whether the faces of stone blocks were rectangular or polygonal, both referred back to the humble built environment of Andean peasantry.[23] Rectangular-faced blocks are akin to square-cut blocks of sod, while polygonal masonry is a refinement of rustic fieldstone construction. Thus, high-prestige masonry gained meaning through comparison to architectural techniques used by Andean commoners. The labour of nibbling would have been clear, regardless of whether the blocks were coursed or not.

While the mostly regular parallelepipeds of coursed stonemasonry sometimes appear to be sized and shaped exactly alike, each is, in fact, distinct, and so worked to fit precisely where it is set. A nibbled wall, whether coursed or uncoursed, is unique in both its parts and its whole. All nibbled stone walls were prestigious; there is, however, distinct variation among them, from roughly nibbled to nearly smooth. Generally,

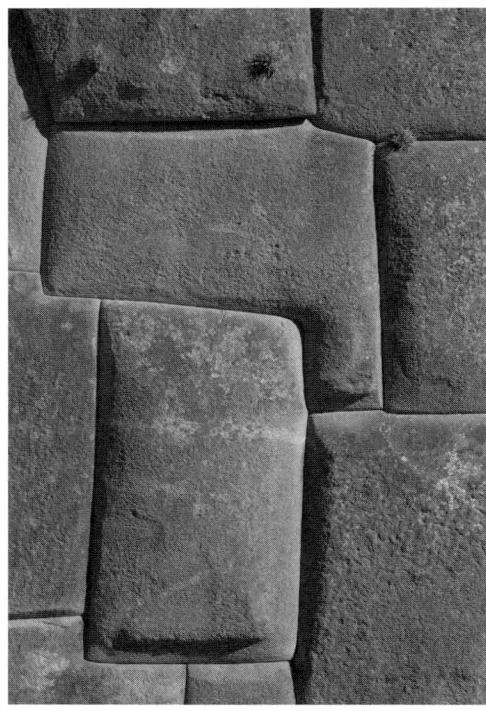

8.3. Inka, high-prestige uncoursed, polygonal stonemasonry, 1450–1530

the smaller the bite of the hammer-stone, the more time was spent refining the surface of the block. The marks of facture are thus not by-products of the process. Rather, they purposefully draw attention to the systematic series of actions that constitute the evidentiary value of nibbled rock. Once we understand the importance of process, of nibbling, to the Inka, we see that the dearth of adornment – so often puzzling to students of Inka masonry – makes perfect sense, for pervasive adornment of the stone's surface, whether through imagistic carving or decorative painting, would draw attention away from the joins and pecked surfaces. This emphasis on process also explains the infrequency with which paint or plaster was used on high-prestige walls.[24]

The nibbled wall might be seen as a metaphor for the Inka social order in which each individual 'fitted,' but not all fits were equal. If natural stone was an element of unordered nature, an unworked stone in a wall of stacked fieldstones suggests minimal ordering. A well-nibbled stone, with its minuscule peck marks embedded in a tightly bonded wall, represents a stone that has been brought into order through a time-consuming process. It was clearly prized for these qualities. Many parallels could be drawn between the nibbled walls and the Inka's social order. Suffice it to say that the finest integration and 'fit' were represented by the Inka and those commonly known as Inka-by-privilege (those few groups whom the Inka recognized as sharing many cultural traits, including their sense of order). Other groups who worked to better their 'fit' saw their value to the state increase and their prestige rise accordingly. The message of a wall of well-nibbled stones was that ordering processes leave traces discernible on the individual parts as well as in the whole. Within the Inka's well-established scopic regime in which rock was understood to be potentially animate and buildings were produced through negotiations with the medium of which they were made, a shaped stone was a sign of the state's civilizing presence.[25] Individuals were, in some sense, like stone blocks, some more thoroughly nibbled than others, but each bearing some trace of the fitting process. Populations dominated by the Inka clearly understood the political connotations of high-prestige masonry.[26]

Cobo indicates that stonemasons were one of only three or four types of craft specialists who worked exclusively for the Inka state;[27] surely he refers here to 'nibblers', since high-prestige masonry was linked directly to the state and its projects. A nibbled wall spoke not only to the state's control over these craft specialists, but also to characteristics the state deemed important: orderliness, organization, persistence, and the ability to deal with supernatural forces. Because stone was a potentially numinous material, the very working of it was significant. John Hemming and Edward Ranney suggest that working a stone 'could well have been a product of patriotic or pious devotion, a desire to build in the finest conceivable techniques for the most holy purposes'.[28] Nibbled masonry not only implied great technical expertise and political power, but had profound religious connotations as well.

For the Inka, sacredness was embedded in the material of the thing rather than in its form. Thus, the Inka identified sacred essence in a variety of hosts, and any particular essence was not necessarily reflected in its external appearance. Here some discussion of the Quechua notion of *kamay*, which is often translated as 'essence', is appropriate. The art historian Thomas Cummins explains how the sand used by the Inka to cover the central plaza of their capital city contained a sacred essence, a *kamay*, that was unique. Spanish authorities, finally recognizing that the sand of the plaza was held as holy by the indigenous residents of the city, ordered its removal and used it to make mortar for the construction of the cathedral.[29] Perhaps Spaniards reckoned that the sacred sand would reinforce the sanctity of their cathedral, but they did not understand that the natives of Cuzco might well distinguish the distinct building materials from the structure as a whole or the purpose for which the edifice was built. In other words, Spaniards could not separate the *kamay* from the sand. Essence was transubstantial, and so its significance was independent of form. Regardless of the shape it took, or how it was used, it was invested with its own sacred essence. Stone, like the sand of Cuzco's main plaza, possessed unique *kamay*. Its architectural contexts might vary, but its essence was stable. This regard for stone – as sentient, potentially animate, and invested with distinct *kamay* – informed Andean understandings of masonry structures.

Spanish regard for rock

In stark contrast to the Inka's perspective, Europeans historically have associated the veneration of sacred stones with primitive superstition. The ancient Greeks worshipped both *argoi lithoi*, which were unworked stones, as well as black meteoric stones called *baitulia* or *lithoi empsychoi* (animated stones).[30] From the earliest recorded times rocks such as these were anointed with precious oils and spoken to by devotees. Such practices were later derided as irrational superstitions by those who believed that anthropomorphic statuary was the proper focus of worship.[31] Spanish conquistadors and the colonizers who followed in their footsteps inherited aspects of this mindset, condemning reverence for natural rock.

While stone to the Spaniards might be viewed as incorporating life forces, it was not sentient and was not to be revered in and of itself, although it could be carved to represent sacred beings. It was, above all, a high-status building material. In Spanish tradition, and European tradition more generally, the finest buildings were made of worked stone. Masonry was an honoured profession and masons were respected craftsmen. Spaniards, who brought their notions about building materials with them to the Americas, constructed churches, state buildings, and elite residences of stone wherever possible. Although initially Spaniards were often compelled to erect structures of mud and straw, the intention was always to replace these relatively impermanent materials with stone or brick and to add tile roofs. Fire was the greatest threat to buildings in Europe, where the typical congested urban design featured flammable structures. Although in the high Andes, where oxygen is thin, great conflagrations are much less likely and earthquakes pose a much greater threat, the association of stone and permanence was so firmly fixed in the Spaniards' minds that they insisted on using stone. With regard to building in the Viceroyalty of Peru, art historian Valerie Fraser notes:

> Despite the earthquakes and despite the expense, during the second half of the sixteenth century many large stone or brick vaulted churches were begun on an ambitious scale. The tenacity of the ideas about architectural decorum was such that although the vaults of these churches came crashing

down with monotonous regularity, and with devastating effects on the church furnishings below – and indeed occasionally on the population too – lighter, more flexible roofing materials were scarcely even considered for generations.[32]

In Europe, walls and roofs of perishable materials signified low quality and poor engineering. Thus, despite the obvious advantages of lighter roofs in regions prone to earthquakes, Spaniards were a long time realizing them.

Spaniards understood architectural materials to reflect levels of civilization, and stone topped their building material hierarchy. Stone signalled permanence, not just of the structures Spanish colonizers built, but of their culture itself.[33] Hence, Spaniards disdained mud, reed, and even wood as impermanent building materials suited to poor people and unworthy cultures. They derided indigenous structures of perishable materials, commonly using the term *bohío* (hut), which they borrowed from the Carib and applied to all indigenous buildings made of straw or other non-permanent materials. Spaniards further imputed a lack of orderliness to communities with structures lacking stone components. In the Spanish mind, an important building simply could not be composed of mud or straw. Signs of civility and sociopolitical organization, what the Spaniards termed *policía*, included grid-planned towns with right angles, and buildings of stone with arches, columns, and architectural mouldings.[34] Having condemned various indigenous American built environments, Spaniards set about to build according to their own priorities. They believed proper edifices which were properly laid out would not only enact colonization, but facilitate enculturation. Fraser explains how settlement planning (the grid) and European-style architecture (arches, columns with bases and capitals) were to be 'so obviously superior and imposing that, almost despite themselves, the Indians [would] be awed into submission'.[35] Spaniards combined this approach with a strategy of substitution wherein places special or sacred to indigenous populations would be replaced with churches and shrines; at the very least a cross was to be erected on these spots.

While Spaniards dismissed most indigenous American building, Inka masonry was not subject to the same derision. Spaniards admired the ways the Inka brought order to their territories, something Inka imperial rhetoric also emphasized; formal road systems, bridges, storehouses, and building in stone were all signs of Inka *policía*. The Inka's stone structures were special marks of *policía*, being far more permanent and substantial than the *bohíos* the Spanish found elsewhere. Spaniards also repeatedly praised the tight joins exhibited in high-prestige Inka masonry, which required no mortar and into which a knife blade could not be inserted (as they frequently observed). Nevertheless, Spaniards had particular problems describing, with their customary architectural vocabulary, the uncoursed, polygonal style of Inka stonemasonry. The Inka's coursed style, with its rectangular-faced parallelepipeds, fitted Spanish conventions. The polygonal masonry, with its irregular shapes and lack of courses, violated Spanish expectations for high-quality stonework. Cobo, for example, uses the term *sillería* (ashlar masonry) to describe the Inka's coursed masonry, but *mampostería* for the uncoursed polygonal style.[36] *Mampostería*, meaning field-stone or rubble masonry, suggests little skill, causing Cobo to clarify that Inka 'mampostería' actually evinces considerable masonry expertise.[37]

Although Inka stonemasonry was widely lauded by Spaniards, the form of Inka structures and their building techniques were consistently derided. Cuzco's sixteenth-century Spanish magistrate Juan Polo de Ondegardo, after comparing Inka stonework favourably to that of ancient Rome, quickly adds that Inka buildings are 'without order or proportion, and low and even with little foundation' (*los edificios destos son sin horden ny proporcion y vajos e aun con poco cimyento*).[38] Similarly, the priest José de Acosta praises Inka masonry for its smoothness and precise joins, but observes that although Inka structures were often large they were 'badly arranged and utilized, and seemed no better than mosques or other barbarian buildings' (*estaban mal repartidos y aprovechados, propriamente como mezquitas o edificios de bárbaros*). He even identifies the lack of mortar as a deficit.[39] Spanish commentators repeatedly emphasize European technological superiority, wondering at what the Inka achieved *despite* their lack of tools, by which they meant iron tools. Cobo, for example, estimates that when the spectacular site of Saqsaywaman was under construction there were normally no fewer than thirty thousand labourers working on it; he goes on to say that such a high number of workers was 'not surprising since the lack of implements, apparatus, and ingenuity necessarily increased the amount of work'.[40] To put Cobo's argument more plainly: since the Inka did not possess iron tools and they were not very smart (they lacked ingenuity), they depended on considerable labour. Also frequently noted in Spanish commentary are the absence of arches and the lack of tile roofs, both of which were hallmarks of high-quality Spanish architecture. Any words of praise were thus mitigated by so-called Inka shortcomings.

Arches were a particular mark of European engineering supremacy. Arches enable high stone vaults spanning spacious interiors. In the Spanish mind, arches exemplified the art (*arte*) of architecture rather than the craft of building. Other signs of the art of architecture were columns with their bases and capitals. Cobo observes that nowhere in the Americas were found 'stones cut for arches, nor with the shape of bases, capitals, columns, nor other figures belonging to the art of architecture' (*piedras labradas para arquería, ni con forma de basas, capiteles, columnas, ni otras figuras que les suele dar el arte de arquitectura*).[41] From a Spanish perspective, while the Inka achieved great skill in stonemasonry, they never created the art of architecture because their structures did not include the particular features Europeans esteemed. Of these features the arch was singularly significant, marking both cultural superiority and religious triumph.[42] Fraser notes that in the sixteenth century throughout Spanish America churches had arched doorways while secular buildings had lintels; she concludes that arches particularly signalled the superiority of the monotheistic religion of the colonizers.[43]

Spaniards arrived in the Inka capital with a set of ideas about proper urban planning, and about what elite structures ought to look like. Cuzco's layout was generally well suited to Spanish purposes. It was organized according to a grid plan with a central plaza surrounded by stone edifices. The main plaza was overly large by European standards and so was diminished in size. Inka structures surrounding the plaza provided the foundations for many Spanish buildings. Gradually many walls were rebuilt or covered over, and the Inka's straw roofs were replaced with tiles. Whereas the Inka preferred rectangular structures without internal divisions, called *wasi*, which they made in many sizes to suit many different purposes, Spanish buildings typically had specialized interior spaces such as chapels, courtyards, and chambers to serve various functions.

Portals were a particular focus of renovation in order to fit hinged wooden doors with locks. Doorways were an important architectural focal point for Spaniards, who frequently commented disdainfully on the lack of proper portals in indigenous homes.[44] In colonial buildings the entrance is the primary formal feature, being the location through which all important visitors must pass. Sometimes the only architectural detail adorns the main portal, and even very plain edifices will often have elaborately ornamented entrances. The Inka, too, had focused attention on well-fashioned portals, but theirs did not feature hinged doors. Inka structures had open, trapezoidal portals which were wider at the bottom than at the top; sometimes doorways were covered by textiles or had wooden panels propped up to cover and guard the entrance. Door jambs from pre-Hispanic times had to be modified in order to accommodate the mandatory hinged doors swinging inward typical of Spanish structures.[45]

Like the doorway without a door to close, there were other features of Inka architecture that ran contrary to Spanish precepts about proper building. Inka openings with their customary trapezoidal outline violated the Spanish preference for right angles. What's more, the Inka employed wall batter, meaning that walls were thicker at the bottom than at the top and sloped inward. Although batter, like the use of trapezoidal openings, actually produced a more stable structure in zones subject to regular seismic activity, to Spaniards a leaning wall signalled structural instability. Arches, when built properly, are stable architectural features allowing for great wall height and for large expanses to be roofed; there are, however, many examples of European cities, with their cathedrals reaching ever increasing heights, whose citizens nervously watched as the stones of unstable walls slowly separated and began leaning despite the addition of flying buttresses and other architectural supports. To many a European, including many Spaniards, a leaning wall was an unstable thing that suggested a lack of technical expertise. Also contrary to Spanish sensibilities, and suggesting a lack of engineering acumen, was the Inka's typical thick stone wall. Europeans had worked for centuries to build higher and higher walls that were thin, but still stable. From the Romanesque period to the Gothic, walls decreased dramatically in thickness while growing in height. To Spaniards, then, the thick, battered Inka wall was not at all appealing. Cuzco, as the Inka had built it, was gradually refashioned into a Spanish city with vertical walls, rectangular doorways with carved ornamentation and hinged doors, rectangular windows, and churches with arches. Indigenous masons performed much of the labour of transformation. They reworked stone blocks to fit colonial structures, re-carved lintels, and applied mortar to parallelepipeds that once would have been nibbled to fit. If Fraser is correct, Spaniards understood the radical alteration of the indigenous built environment to actuate colonization and the enculturation of the Inka and other Andeans. But what did the Inka perceive? We do not have the documents to provide us with a thorough and nuanced indigenous perspective, but that does not mean we cannot speculate, informed by pre-Hispanic beliefs and practices.

Stone, form, and meaning in colonial Cuzco

Inka labourers under Spanish direction removed parallelepipeds from pre-Hispanic structures, transported them to edifices under construction, and fixed them with mortar into walls of colonial-period buildings. Cuzco's cathedral and many of its churches and elite residences evince this kind of repurposing of Inka stones. In the words of Garcilaso de la Vega, who lived in Cuzco as a child, 'The Spaniards . . . demolished the fortress [of Saqsaywaman] to build private houses in Cuzco. And to save themselves the expense, effort and delay with which the Indians worked the stone, they pulled down all the smooth masonry in the walls.'[46]

As Garcilaso notes, Saqsaywaman was a particularly well-scoured source of already worked stone. In 1571, the city's Spanish magistrate commented that Saqsaywaman could supply enough dressed stones to build four churches like those of Seville.[47] Other officials and chroniclers affirm extensive usage of stones from Saqsaywaman in the building of Spanish Cuzco.[48] Like Garcilaso, the Mercerdarian friar Martín de Murúa claimed that all Spanish structures built in Cuzco used stone from Saqsaywaman; he explained that the only reason any stones were left standing at the site was that the megaliths would have been too expensive to move and would have required the labour of too many natives.[49]

While most indigenous labour was unskilled, 'nibblers' also worked to build Spanish Cuzco. They produced bonded stonemasonry identical to the high-prestige masonry of pre-Hispanic times only without the wall batter of Inka structures. Windows and portals in colonial-period structures assume more rectangular shapes, and the doorways allow for hinged doors opening inward and are large enough to accommodate horses.[50] Sometimes the ashlars are worked with hammer-stones, as was the pre-Hispanic practice, but metal tools were introduced, producing tell-tale small, sharp, regularly spaced peck marks.[51] Stonemasonry in the labour-intensive Inka style is found only on façades and within vestibules; it is most frequently featured on portals, the parts of buildings Spaniards deemed most important and in which they would have invested the most skilled labour.[52] Some of the lintels found on secular buildings in Cuzco were no doubt repurposed from pre-Hispanic portals, but with their broader surfaces turned to face outward. To the broad face of the lintel figures and coats-of-arms were added, providing decoration that Spaniards found highly desirable, but that ran contrary to pre-Hispanic practices (Figure 8.4). Nevertheless, these doorways appear to have been constructed by indigenes using pre-Hispanic techniques. Sometimes the joins are mortarless and only the lack of the distinctive Inka trapezoid shape betrays a colonial-period date.

In part, Spaniards used native labour because it was available, but they also valued Inka stonework so long as the resultant buildings were without leaning walls, featured right angles, and had doors. Although we know from records that Inka labourers moved stone, and worked to erect many colonial-period structures, we see their colonial-period presence only rarely. Fraser argues that by erecting vertical walls with rectangular openings, indigenes were implicitly denying their own cultural values and replacing them with those of the colonizing Spaniards.[53] When we look at the Inka's most sacred temple, the Qurikancha, we see that the church of Santo Domingo, built in the sixteenth and seventeenth centuries, now dominates its indigenous foundations (Figure 8.5). The European-style church with its vertical walls, ashlars set in mortar, and repeated arches, surrounds and rises above a pre-Hispanic section of high-prestige masonry making up the curving wall at the base. It is

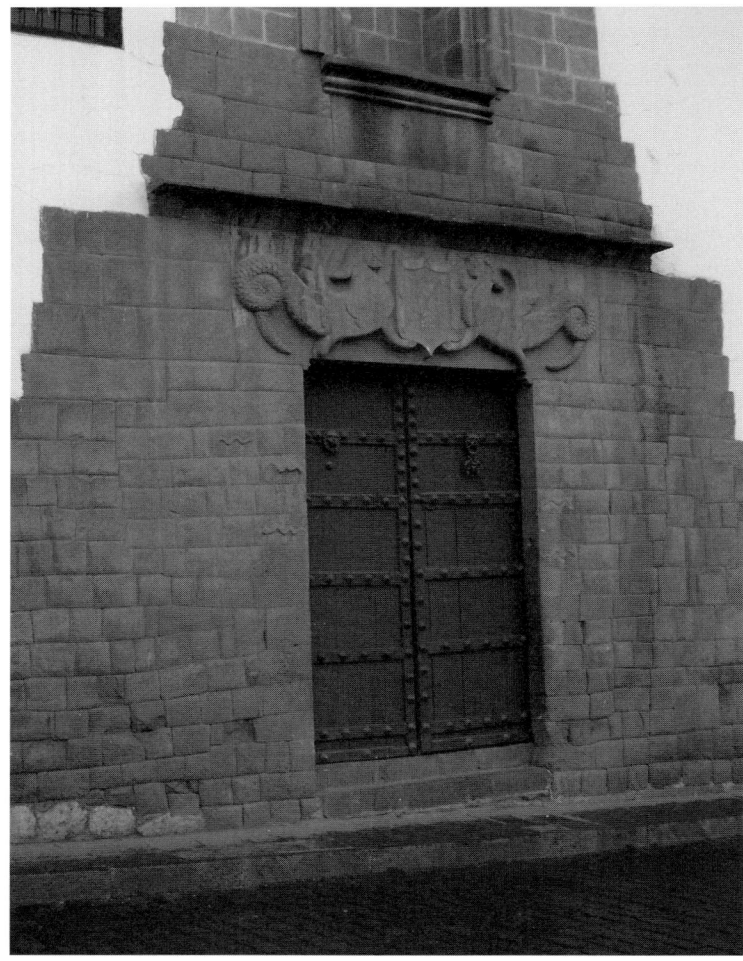

8.4. Colonial Inka, portal, 1550–1750, Cuzco

frequently said that, to the Spaniards, this culturally composite structure both illustrates and actuates colonization and religious conversion. The Spanish church replaces the Andean temple, and indigenous hands provided the labour for it to do so.

But were the Spaniards correct in thinking that recreating the European built environment would ensure that indigenes would adopt Roman Catholicism and Spanish ways of doing and thinking about things as quickly as they picked up metal tools and built using right angles? Did the Inka's sentient stones convert to Roman Catholicism as they were set in the walls of a church? At this point it might be useful to recall the Inka notion of essence (*kamay*) that could assume various forms. If the sand of Cuzco's plaza retained its *kamay* when used in the cathedral's

Rocks and reverence

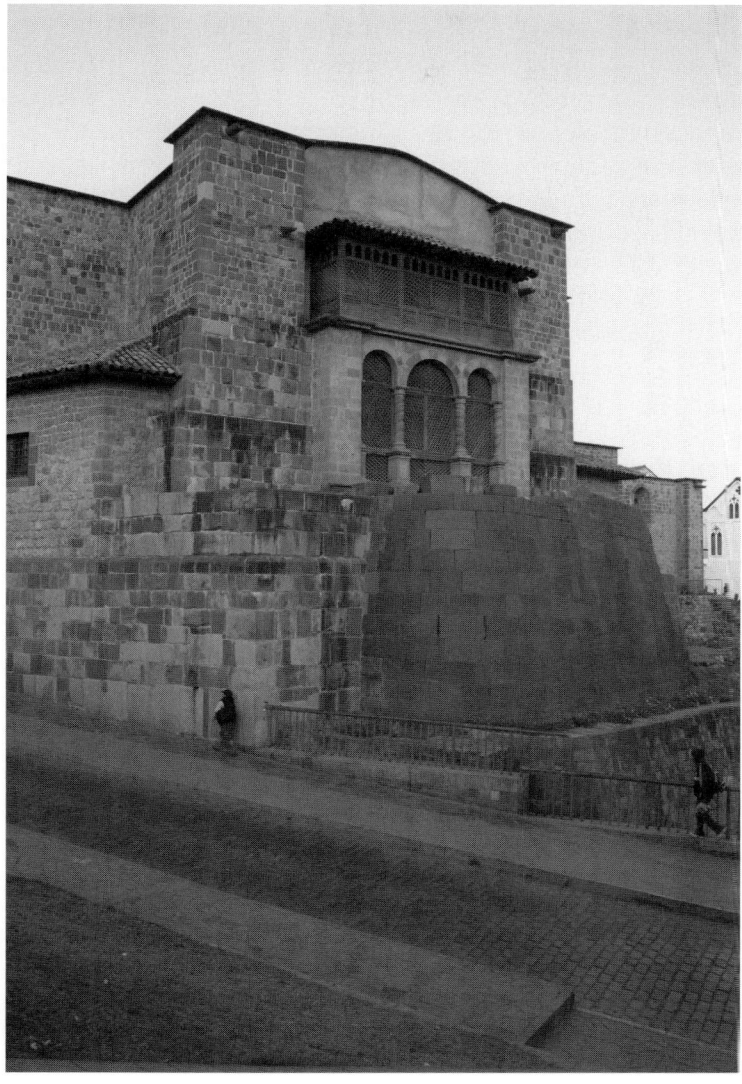

8.5. Pre-Hispanic Inka and Spanish Colonial, Qurikancha-Santo Domingo exterior, 1450–1824, Cuzco

mortar, then the stones of Inka temple walls were not likely to have lost their sanctity when re-contextualized. Unlike the exclusive beliefs of Christianity, which insist on adherence to a single set of beliefs, Andean religions were inclusive. While the Inka demanded that those groups they conquered revere the sun, their patron deity, they did not prohibit local and regional religious affiliations. Usually they incorporated local deities, generically called *waka*, into their pantheon. The Inka and other indigenes did not quickly comprehend that declaring allegiance to the Christian god meant abandoning their own. Indeed, many indigenous Andeans continued worshipping their *waka* while learning Catholic prayers and making the sign of the cross. Spaniards, for their part, were not prepared to recognize the ability of Andean rocks to host transubstantiated essences, nor did they comprehend the sentience of stone more generally. Thus Andean notions about rock were generally not targeted by tenacious extirpators of idolatry, who tended to focus on particular instantiations of reverence rather than the underlying belief systems.

Andeans understood the cosmos to be composed of necessary complements: day and night; up and down; right and left; male and female. The Spanish invasion added new sets of complements, such as Spaniard and Indian, and God and *waka*. Andean complementarity, in which each part is necessary (although usually not equal), differs from binary opposition, which is a feature of Western philosophy. In binary opposition, the members of pairs often struggle to eradicate their opposite. In Andean complementarity, both members of a pair are recognized as essential to each other's existence. While Spaniards, given their binary thinking, would have understood that Catholicism had triumphed over Andean *waka* (defeating them utterly), Andean complementarity recognized the essential value of both, each needing the other to define itself. We may surmise that even as churches rose from Inka stonemasonry foundations and Spaniards saw clear evidence of their own cultural and religious superiority, indigenous viewers recognized a necessary complementarity emerging between their culture and that of the Spaniards. Composite structures, such as the Qurikancha-Santo Domingo, at least for a time (until the exclusive nature of Christianity was made clear), may have actuated this *new* complementarity. Such buildings may have visualized – even demonstrated – ways that indigenous religious ideas could persist within Catholic structures. Discerning the hearts and minds of Andean residents of Cuzco and elsewhere is, of course, impossible, but the church buildings with their indigenous palimpsests were likely not always understood in the way Spaniards intended.

Stones – animate, sentient, and historical allies of the Inka – continued to give Cuzco an impressive form into the colonial period. Despite the founding of Lima as the Spanish capital, the Inka's capital was still the most sacred location in all of the Andes to the indigenous inhabitants of viceregal Peru. Surely the Inka continued to take pride in Cuzco and its grand stone edifices, even as they recognized formal differences between Inka and Spanish buildings. One key difference between Inka and Spanish approaches to building and the use of stone may not have been so much seen as discerned, and we glimpse it in the oral culture of the central Andes. In 1971, Alejandro Ortiz Rescaniere recorded a widely told Quechua story of indeterminate age. According to the story, the Creator had two sons: the Inka and Jesus Christ.[54] The Inka grew up, established a reciprocal relationship with Mother Earth and eventually married her. Together they produced children and they prospered. The Inka also learned to build in stone and so erected magnificent structures in Cuzco. Jesus Christ grew jealous of the Inka and, with the help of the moon, scared the Inka away by showing him a piece of paper with writing. Once the Inka was gone and 'unable to do anything, Jesus Christ attacked Mother Earth, cut off her head, then built churches on her'.[55] From an Andean perspective, as expressed in the story, Christian churches are only possible when the Inka is chased away by Jesus Christ, who also kills Mother Earth. Actions from the story underscore key features of the pre-Hispanic Inka built environment which are distinct from Spanish practices: settlement planning that acknowledged and even drew attention to local topography, thereby honouring the body of Mother Earth; the integration of rock outcrops into structures such that the outcrops marked the union of the Inka and Mother Earth; and the requisite negotiations with stone that allowed the Inka to produce civilization.[56] The story emphasizes that Inka interaction with the earth is procreative and characterized by reciprocity and negotiation; Inka and earth form a fruitful complementary pair. Buildings in stone and in Inka style are a mark of their union. 'Christian' building activity, on the other hand, is characterized as destructive to Mother Earth, who must die before churches can be built.[57] Although nearly two centuries have passed between the colonial period and the recording of this story, it nonetheless prompts us to wonder whether many indigenes ever set aside their beliefs about an animate earth and sentient stones. Rather, at its conclusion, the story hints that stones await the Inka's return when Mother Earth will be revived. Building, rather than being a triumphant gesture, will then once again be a negotiated process, a cooperative enterprise between medium and mason.

Notes

1 Juan de Betanzos, *Narrative of the Incas* (1557), ed. and trans. Roland Hamilton and Dana Buchanan (Austin: University of Texas Press, 1996), p. 48.

2 This section summarizes research more fully discussed in Carolyn Dean, *A Culture of Stone: Inka Perspectives on Rock* (Durham, NC: Duke University Press, 2010).

3 Cobo, *Inca Religion and Customs* (1653), ed. and trans. Roland Hamilton (Austin: University of Texas Press, 1990), p. 36; see also Cobo, *Obras del P. Bernabé Cobo*, ed. Francisco Mateos (Madrid: Real Academia Española, 1956), p. 162. Cobo writes, 'the fear inspired by the *pururaucas* was more effective than the fighting of the Inca's troops in all of their successful encounters because often the enemy would flee almost without putting up a fight'; see *Inca Religion*, p. 35.

4 Stories of stones animating in support of heroic or honoured individuals are a familiar theme in world folklore.

5 Cobo, *Inca Religion*, p. 36. Pedro de Cieza de León refers to a 'stone of war' (*la piedra de la guerra*) that was called upon for help when the Inka faced battle. He says that 'captains and leaders' (*capitanes y mandones*) were appointed beside the stone of war that was placed in the square of Cuzco; see Cieza de León, *Crónica del Perú, segunda parte*, ed. Francesca Cantù (Lima: Pontificia Universidad Católica del Perú, 1986), p. 182. Cieza's 'stone of war' may have been one of the *puruawqa*.

6 For a discussion of modes of transport, see Jean-Pierre Protzen, 'Inca stonemasonry', *Scientific American* 254:2 (1986), pp. 102–3.

7 Maarten Van de Guchte, 'El Ciclo Mítico de la Piedra Cansada', *Revista Andina* 4:2 (1984), pp. 539–56.

8 Betanzos, *Narrative of the Incas*, p. 157; Cieza, *Crónica del Perú*, pp. 148–9; 'El Inca' Garcilaso de la Vega, *Royal Commentaries of the Incas and General History of Peru* (1609–17), trans. Harold V. Livermore (Austin: University of Texas Press, 1966), p. 470; Martín de Murúa, *Historia general del Perú* (1613), ed. Manuel Ballesteros Gaibrois (Madrid: Historia 16, 1986), pp. 314–16; and Diego de Ocaña, *A través de la América del sur* (1580–1605), ed. Arturo Álvarez (Madrid: Historia 16, 1987), p. 225. According to the indigenous chronicler Felipe Guaman Poma de Ayala, the stone was quarried in Cuzco and was being taken to Guanuco; later, he reports, an attempt was made to take it to Quito in Ecuador. See Guaman Poma, *El primer nueva corónica y buen gobierno* (c. 1615), ed. John V. Murra and Rolena Adorno (Mexico: Siglo Veintiuno, 1988), p. 160 (162).

9 Cobo, *Inca Religion*, pp. 56–7.

10 Jean-Pierre Protzen and Stella Nair have shown that in form, style, and construction techniques, buildings at Tiwanaku are significantly different from those of the Inka; see Protzen and Nair, 'Who taught the Inca stonemasons their skills? A comparison of Tiahuanaco and Inca cut-stone masonry', *The Journal of the Society of Architectural Historians* 56:2 (1997), pp. 146–67.

11 Susan A. Niles, 'Niched walls in Inca design', *The Journal of the Society of Architectural Historians* 46:3 (1987), pp. 277–8.

12 Anonymous, *Vocabulario y phrasis en la lengua general de los Indios del Perú llamada Quichua y en la lengua Española* (1586), ed. Guillermo Escobar Risco (Lima: Instituto de Historia de la Facultad de Letras, 1951), p. 21.

13 Protzen, 'Inca stonemasonry' and 'Inca quarrying and stonecutting', *Ñawpa Pacha* 21 (1983), pp. 183–214.

14 According to Garcilaso de la Vega, a mestizo who grew up in sixteenth-century Cuzco, stonemasons worked their blocks with 'some black pebbles . . . with which they pounded rather than cut'; see Garcilaso, *Royal Commentaries*, p. 131. For a study of tools used by the Inka, see Robert B. Gordon, 'Laboratory evidence of the use of metal tools at Machu Picchu (Peru)', *Journal of Archaeological Science* 12 (1985), pp. 311–27.

15 While the load-bearing, horizontal joins of nibbled masonry usually fit perfectly throughout, vertical seams sometimes fit closely only to the depth of a few centimetres with mud or gravel used to fill the internal gaps that are not visible from the exterior of the wall.

16 Heather Lechtman, 'Cloth and metal: The culture of technology', in Elizabeth Hill Boone (ed.), *Andean Art at Dumbarton Oaks*, 2 vols (Washington, DC: Dumbarton Oaks Research Library and Collection, 1996), vol. 1, pp. 33–43. For the relationship of structure to meaning in Andean textile work see also William J. Conklin, 'Structure as meaning in ancient Andean textiles', in Boone (ed.), *Andean Art*, vol. 2, pp. 321–8. For additional observations on process and product in Andean metalwork, see Lechtman, 'Andean value systems and the development of prehistoric metallurgy', *Technology and Culture* 25:1 (1984),

pp. 1–36; 'Style in technology: Some early thoughts', in Heather Lechtman and Robert S. Merrill (eds), *Material Culture: Styles, Organization, and Dynamics of Technology* (St Paul, MN: West Publishing, 1977), pp. 3–20; and 'Technologies of power: The Andean case', in Patricia Netherly and John Henderson (eds), *Configurations of Power in Complex Society* (Ithaca, NY: Cornell University Press, 1993), pp. 244–80.

17 Stella Elise Nair, 'Of remembrance and forgetting: The architecture of Chinchero, Peru from Thupa, 'Inka to the Spanish Occupation' (PhD dissertation, University of California, Berkeley, 2003), p. 285.

18 Protzen and Nair, 'Who taught the Inca stonemasons their skills?', p. 156.

19 Cobo, *Inca Religion*, p. 228.

20 Nibbled rocks are 'deictic', a term Norman Bryson borrows from linguistics, to describe visual works that call attention to the means and manner of their own creation; see Bryson, *Vision and Painting: The Logic of the Gaze* (New Haven, CT: Yale University Press, 1983), p. 89.

21 See, for example, the following: Agurto Calvo, *Estudios acerca de la construcción, arquitectura, y planeamiento Incas* (Lima: Cámera Peruana de la Construcción, 1987); Valerie Fraser, *The Architecture of Conquest: Building in the Viceroyalty of Peru, 1435–1635* (Cambridge: Cambridge University Press, 1990); Graziano Gasparini and Luise Margolies, *Inca Architecture*, trans. Patricia J. Lyon (Bloomington: Indiana University Press, 1980); John Hyslop, *Inca Settlement Planning* (Austin: University of Texas Press, 1990); Ann Kendall, *Aspects of Inca Architecture: Description, Function, and Chronology* (Oxford: British Archaeological Reports, 1985); Kendall, 'Descripción e inventario de las formas arquitectónicas Inca: Patrones de distribución e inferencias cronológicas', *Revista del Museo Nacional* (Lima) 42 (1976), pp. 13–96; Vincent R. Lee, 'Design by numbers: Architectural order among the Inkas' (paper presented at the 36th Annual Meeting of the Institute of Andean Studies, Berkeley, Jan. 1996 (Wilson, WY: Lee, 1996)); Francesco Menotti, *The Inkas: Last Stage of Stone Masonry Development in the Andes* (Oxford: Archaeopress, 1998); Craig Morris and Adriana von Hagen, *The Cities of the Ancient Andes* (London: Thames & Hudson, 1998); Protzen, 'Inca stonemasonry'; and Protzen and Nair, 'Who taught the Inca stonemasons their skills?'

22 John Rowe, 'An introduction to the archaeology of Cuzco', *Papers of the Peabody Museum of American Archaeology and Ethnology* 27:2 (1944), pp. 3–59.

23 Rowe, 'Introduction to the archaeology of Cuzco', p. 24.

24 Some high-prestige masonry may have been covered over with paint or even plaster. It is likely that the layer of paint was not thick enough to mask the peck marks, yet, even in cases where the nibbling was not readily visible, people knew it was there and so its visibility may not have necessarily been paramount; see Lisa Senchyshyn Trever, 'Slithering serpents and the afterlives of stones: the role of ornament in Inka-style architecture of Cusco, Peru' (MA thesis, University of Maryland, College Park, 2005), p. 16; and Margaret Greenup MacLean, 'Sacred land, sacred water: Inca landscape planning in the Cuzco Area' (PhD dissertation, University of California, Berkeley, 1986), p. 49. For a discussion of the Inka use of paint and plaster in architectural decoration, see Protzen, 'Inca architecture', in Laura Laurencich Minelli (ed.), *The Inca World: The Development of Pre-Columbian Peru, A.D. 1000–1534* (Norman: University of Oklahoma Press, 1992), pp. 198–9.

25 Christian Metz introduced the term 'scopic regime' in relation to cinema to describe a hegemonic visuality; see Metz, *The Imaginary Signifier: Psychoanalysis and the Cinema* (Bloomington: Indiana University Press, 1982), p. 61.

26 Dennis Ogburn examines a number of ways the Inka enhanced the perception of an all-powerful state: the building of imperial temples and palaces, royal visits to the provinces, the maintenance of state infrastructure (roads, bridges, storehouses), the resettlement of sizable populations to far-flung parts of the empire, the transportation of luxury goods

from throughout the empire to Cuzco, and the transportation of large building stones from Cuzco to various parts of Tawantinsuyu; see Ogburn, 'Dynamic display, propaganda, and the reinforcement of provincial power in the Inca empire', *Archaeological Papers of the American Anthropological Association* 14 (2005), pp. 225–39.

27 Cobo, *Inca Religion*, p. 240.
28 John Hemming and Edward Ranney, *Monuments of the Incas* (Boston, MA: New York Graphic Society, 1982), p. 53.
29 Thomas Cummins, 'A tale of two cities: Cuzco, Lima, and the construction of colonial representation', in Diana Fane (ed.), *Converging Cultures: Art and Identity in Spanish America* (New York: The Brooklyn Museum, 1996), p. 161. Cummins follows Gerald Taylor and Frank Salomon, both of whom discuss the meaning of camay (kamay) in the early seventeenth-century Quechua Huarochirí manuscript; see Taylor, '*Camay, Camac* et *Camasca* dans le Manuscript Quechua de Huarochirí', *Journal de la Société des Américanistes* 63 (1974–76), pp. 231–44, and Salomon, 'Introductory essay: The Huarochirí Manuscript', in Frank Salomon and Jorge Urioste (eds and trans.), *The Huarochirí Manuscript: A Testament of Ancient and Colonial Andean Religion* (Austin: University of Texas Press, 1991), p. 16. For more on the Quechua root '*cama-*' see Marusz S. Ziólkowski, *La guerra de los wawqi: Los objetivos y los mecanismos de la rivalidad dentro de la elite Inka, siglos XV–XVI* (Quito: Abya-Yala, 1996), pp. 27–9.
30 David Freedberg identifies reverence for sacred rocks throughout the ancient Middle East, including the black stone kept in the Kaaba in Mecca, the primary Muslim shrine; see Freedberg, *The Power of Images: Studies in the History and Theory of Response* (Chicago: University of Chicago Press, 1989), p. 68. David Summers notes that 'the Greek term for an aniconic stone, *baetyl*, has been traced to the Hebrew *beth-el*, house of god'; he also discusses the use of aniconic stones in ancient Aegean cultures. See Summers, *Real Spaces: World Art History and the Rise of Western Modernism* (London: Phaidon, 2003), pp. 268–9.
31 Freedberg, *Power of Images*, p. 83.
32 Fraser, *Architecture of Conquest*, p. 110.
33 Fraser, *Architecture of Conquest*, p. 21.
34 For a full discussion of the notion of *policía*, see Fraser, *Architecture of Conquest*, pp. 24–5.
35 Fraser, *Architecture of Conquest*, p. 50.
36 Cobo, *Obras*, pp. 260–2.
37 Fraser, *Architecture of Conquest*, p. 32.
38 Polo de Ondegardo, 'Relación de los fundamentos acerca del notable daño que resulta de no guarder a los indios sus fueros (1571)', in Horacio H. Urteaga (ed.), *Informaciones acerca de la religión y gobierno de los Incas* (Lima: Imprenta y Librería Sanmartí, 1916), p. 107.
39 Acosta, *Historia natural y moral de las Indias* (1590), ed. Edmundo O'Gorman (Mexico: Fondo de Cultura Económica, 1940), p. 298; and Jane E. Mangan (ed.), *Natural and Moral History* (Durham, NC: Duke University Press, 2002), p. 351.
40 Cobo, *Inca Religion*, p. 229.
41 Cobo, *Obras*, p. 53.
42 Fraser, *Architecture of Conquest*, p. 166.
43 Fraser, 'Architecture and imperialism in sixteenth-century Spanish America', *Art History* 9:3 (1986), pp. 325–35.
44 Fraser, *Architecture of Conquest*, p. 47.
45 Fraser, *Architecture of Conquest*, p. 119; Emilio Harth-Terré, 'Contribución al estudio de la arquitectura del Cuzco: Los últimos canteros incaicos', *Actas del II Congreso Nacional de Historia* (Lima: Centro de Estudios Histórico-Militares del Perú, 1958), pp. 1–10.

46 Garcilaso, *Royal Commentaries*, p. 471.
47 Polo de Ondegardo, 'Relación de los fundamentos', p. 107.
48 See, for example, Pedro Sarmiento de Gamboa, *Historia de los Incas* (1572), ed. Angel Rosenblatt (Buenos Aires: Emecé Editorial, 1942), p. 137, and Francisco de Toledo, 'Carta al rey (1571)', in José Toribio Medina (ed.), *La imprenta en Lima (1584–1824)* (Santiago de Chile: Casa del Autor, 1904), p. 174.
49 Murúa, *Historia general del Perú*, p. 500.
50 Nair, personal communication, 28 April 2011.
51 Trever, 'Slithering serpents', p. 41.
52 Stella Nair is compiling an inventory and analysis of all indigenous stonemasonry dating to the Spanish colonial period and visible today in Cuzco (personal communication).
53 Fraser, *Architecture of Conquest*, p. 5.
54 The term 'Inka' is used in the story to refer to an indigenous culture hero associated with an ancient, idealized Andean past.
55 For the complete story, see Ortiz Rescaniere, 'El mito de la escuela', in Juan M. Ossio A. (ed.), *Ideología mesiánica del mundo andino* (Lima: Ignacio Prado Pastor, 1973), pp. 237–50. The quoted section reads in Quechua: 'Inka mañas imaruaytapis atis sañachu Sucristus magarun Allpa Mama Pachata, kunkanta kuchurun. Inglisiatas ruarachin.'
56 Carolyn Dean, 'The Inka married the Earth: Integrated outcrops and the making of place', *Art Bulletin* 89:3 (2007), pp. 502–18.
57 Western religious architecture, with some few exceptions, has a long history of dominating local topography which predates Christianity. Vincent Scully observes that the Greek temple stands in 'geometric contrast to the shapes of the earth' and also comments that the Temple of Hera at Paestum 'weighs heavily on the land'; see Scully, *The Earth, the Temple, and the Gods* (New York: Praeger, 1969), p. i.

Part III ✦ Cultural logics

9 ✧ Precious stones, mineral beings: performative materiality in fifteenth-century northern art

Brigitte Buettner

EVERYTHING in the painting is seductively lustrous (Figure 9.1). Our gaze glides over the ruby-red seraphim and sapphire-blue cherubim, then latches on to the marmoreal flesh of the child and mother. Other high-gloss, swelling forms demand our attention, like the satiny pearls dotting the textured crown and the gilded throne where they surround globular finials and sharply cut plaques. Of a luminous black, these are animated by white, red, and orangey veins, which re-direct our eyes toward the Virgin's pensive, slit-eyed head. The artist applied those lines with a restless brush, lodging a moment of pure paint into an otherwise congealed environment. That geological energy must have mattered to him because he duplicated it in the almost-but-not-quite identical sardonyx revetment with which he lined the perspectival room in the pendant panel, now several hundred miles away in Berlin.[1] There, the patron, presented by St Stephen, prays – across the frame and the vertiginous gap between the terrestrial and the celestial – to the object of his devotion. Étienne Chevalier was a high-ranking court official, trusted advisor of Charles VII, and, from 1452 to his death in 1474, Treasurer of France. While the exact circumstances of the commission are not documented, it is likely that Jean Fouquet created the gutsy diptych for public display above Chevalier's family tomb in the collegiate church of Notre-Dame in Melun.[2] Seizing the opportunity to memorialize himself, he demonstratively etched his name next to a penetrating self-portrait on a copper roundel, interpolated among other medallions and love-knots in the frame once draped in lush blue velvet strewn with pearls.

While playing up the contrasts – spatial, chromatic, material – between the two panels, Fouquet ensured that they remain dialectically linked. Hence the reciprocating gestures, the repetition of the sardonyx stone, or the reflected windows on the two visible finials, a conceit that allowed him to unsettle temporal and spatial incommensurability, to incorporate the contingent into the absolute. The painted windows may

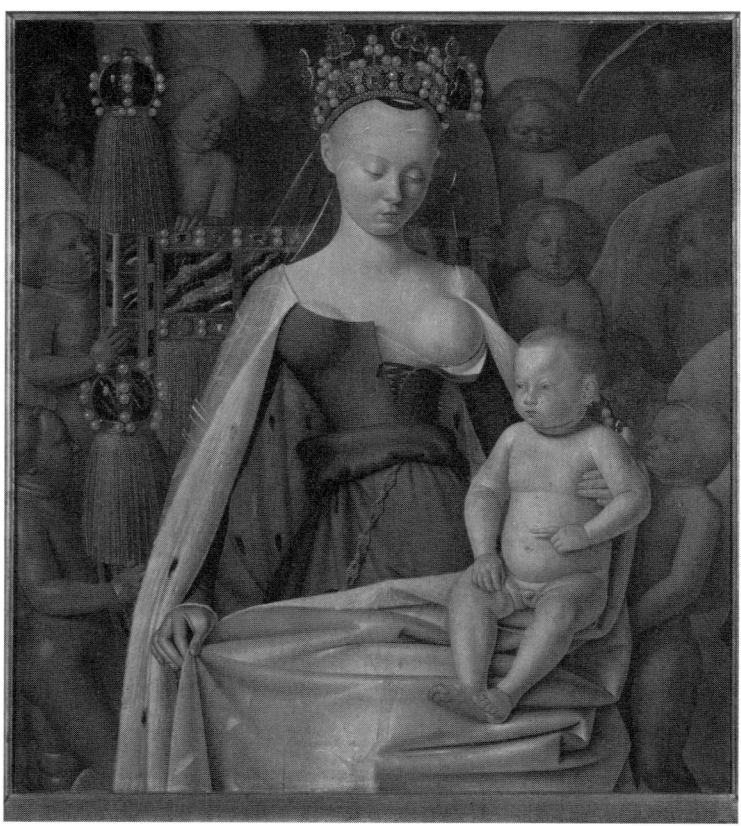

9.1. Jean Fouquet, *Virgin and Child*, Melun Diptych, right wing, c. 1452–55, Antwerp, Koninklijk Museum voor Schone Kunsten

have signalled meanings more specific – Chevalier's Parisian residence was famed for its generous fenestration. Certainly, their semantic reach was broader: cross-mullioned, they functioned as a time-worn metaphor for the Incarnation, the Virgin's undefiled body intact like glass hit, but not broken, by light. Contemporary viewers had ample opportunity to internalize such translated meanings from scriptural exegesis, hymns and Mariological poems, heard during sermons and read in devotional tracts. They also would have effortlessly joined the patron in savouring the Virgin's life-giving, spiritually regenerating milk. Maternal, maidenly, and sexual all at once, she is (un)dressed in a fashionable, tight-fitting blue gown framed by an ermine-lined mantle, its ghostly tint merging with her bleached flesh, its pyramidal shape extended by the virtually transparent veil. The bodice's contour-revealing cut is accentuated by the rolled-up fabric (which bulks up an impossibly thin waist), the delicate chemise and the laces that for centuries have been loosening in front of viewers' eyes to reveal that unforgettably spherical breast. The painting's measured stereometry is consonant with its restricted colour palette. The whites, reds, and blues are only relieved by splashes of gold and black, and punctuated by more discrete green pauses, the lace, a few emeralds, and, most puzzling, two leek-green stones prominently positioned on the crown's left fleuron. Are these a restorer's mistake? Or a clue about the twinned structure of the entire painting, Virgin and Child, seraphim and cherubim, human and divine, breasts, diptych? Most of the stones serve, however, to cement the painting's dominant chromatic range: balas rubies, polished into cabochons, and plump pearls affixed on to unobtrusive stems. One could have expected to see sapphires; yet the rectangular, table-cut stones are darker, of a shiny obscurity. Both that form and tint would indicate that these are diamonds, which by the middle of the fifteenth century had started their inexorable ascent toward the top of the hierarchy of gemmed value.

But in truth, these stones are illegible, hovering somewhere between sapphire and diamond. I like to think that this indeterminacy was purposeful, a means for Fouquet to invite multiple interpretations. Following long-standing allegorical explanations, the sapphire connoted the celestial and the regal, while the rare, most precious diamond of adamantine strength symbolized Christ himself. This surprising equivalence between god and mineral had been proposed as far back as the early Christian *Physiologus*, an influential Alexandrian compilation that inaugurated the tropological deciphering of things-of-nature. Systematically engineering links between the visible and the invisible, it hitched salient characteristics of animals and a handful of stones to divine beings, basic tenets of faith, moral truths, licit and illicit behaviour. And to the Virgin, signified by unblemished pearls.[3]

According to the *Physiologus* and the medieval and Renaissance bestiaries and lapidaries it inspired, pearl oysters dwell on the ocean floor. Except in the morning when they rise to the surface where, valves opened, they absorb drops of dew, a gossamer semen which eventually coagulates with their mucous core to form large single pearls or aggregates of smaller specimens (Figure 9.2). Should a sudden thunderstorm frighten the animals, it is a miscarriage, and pearly freaks the result.[4] But the pious *Physiologus* refuses to entertain that possibility: monstrosity is not part of its vocabulary insofar as the copulation of heaven and earth cannot but yield a flawless Incarnate.

Because things have a habit of dispersing in the quicksand of competing significations, such figurative readings were predestined for the multivalent. Red stones, whether sards, rubies, garnets, carnelians or the

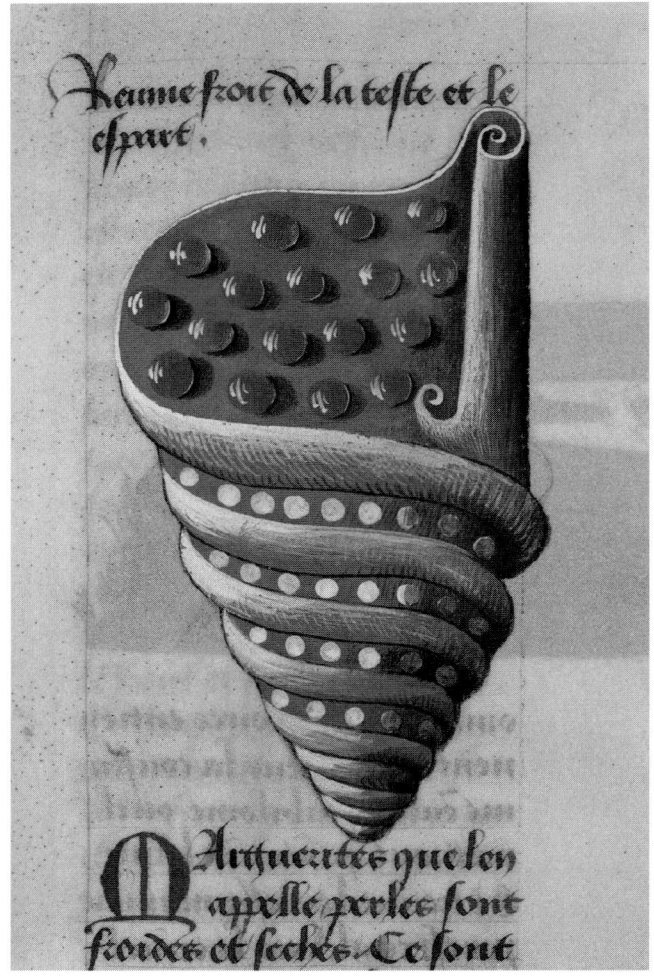

9.2. Pearl shell, Matthaeus Platearius, *Le livre des simples médecines*, Burgundy, 1470s, Paris, Bibliothèque nationale de France, Ms. Fr. 9137, fol. 204

much admired if entirely fictional carbuncle, could evoke the Passion and the sacrificial blood of martyrs; but also fire, though that could be unravelled as the spiritual love imparted by the Holy Ghost, the burning desire for charity, the scorching flames of Hell, and much more besides.[5] Such ready-made interpretative keys are attractive, especially when confronted with something as intractable to discourse as the mineral. I want to take a different route, however, and attend to what lies beyond textually based meanings. The aim is to restore stones' being, and, in the same move, mine their potential for variegated symbolic practices so as to show that mineral materiality was as loquacious as it was performative. From this vantage point, Fouquet's radically mineralized panel looks even less conventional; it's as if an alchemical operation had solidified ethereal flesh, and patches of utmost physical density had been summoned to embody non-human corporeality. This paradoxical communion of subjects and objects, here engendering rocky creatures, there procreating stones, is only conceivable against a background in which the absolute divide between the organic and the inorganic, the gelid boundaries between matter alive and dead were attenuated, perhaps altogether inoperative, certainly anachronistic. Foucault has taught us that these are modern certitudes. And to see the early modern 'prose of the world' instead as a system that ceaselessly wove strands across discontinuous orders of beings, powered by similitudes that encouraged animals to echo with stones, stones to rhyme with plants, and both to converse with humans. Similitudes, it bears stressing, are no more metaphors than analogies are allegories.[6] Stimulated by things' tangible fibres, they delved into the very thingliness of creatures: a pearly Virgin, imagined by an insightful painter who mused on the uncertain limits between metaphor (the Virgin as if a gem) and literalism (the Virgin is a gem).

Hyper-material and hyper-feminine, Fouquet's Madonna is a dual being through and through, especially if we accept the interpretation that she is a (not so) veiled portrait of an actual woman, Agnes Sorel, the first recorded official French royal mistress, and as much the stuff of legend as Joan of Arc, the other heroine who rescued Charles VII from gloom and doom.[7] Scholars have long debated the merits of this identification, first put forward by the antiquarian Denis Godefroy after his visit to the church of Melun in 1661. While it could be a romanticizing backformation, several copies of a sketch Fouquet drew of Sorel leave little doubt that he consented to his patron's wishes to fold the courtesan into the Virgin.[8] Virginal, Sorel was not. By the time of her death in 1450, caused by an overdose of mercury (either by accident or crime), she had given the king three daughters and was buried with a stillborn foetus.[9] Chevalier was one of the executors of her will, had been her close friend, and may have offered the Melun Diptych as a posthumous tribute. Nicknamed Dame de Beauté, a pun on both her beauty and the residence near Paris that she had received from the king, Sorel was unanimously extolled by her contemporaries for her physical charms. With regard to her character and social standing, opinions were considerably more divided. To some, she was a charitable saviour of the nation, rumoured to have pawned her jewels to pay for the king's soldiers; to others, she behaved like a Marie-Antoinette squanderer, depleting royal funds to finance her spendthrift habits. Georges Chastellain, the official Burgundian chronicler, subscribed to this latter view. Though he could be impartial when describing members of the opposite royalist camp, his pen-portrait of Sorel is vitriolic. A seductress of lowly birth, she had the presumption to keep a queenly estate, demanding the best in cuisine, furniture, linens, plate, and gems. It was her sartorial extravagance, however, that in Chastellain's view drove her off the map of acceptable norms. Showy and wasteful, her gowns were overly long, the headgear inordinately high, and, as Fouquet's portrait confirms, the cuts of her bodices, revealing her breasts down to the nipples, overtly provocative. But whereas the painter lifted his brush in fascinated attention, the writer took the path that maps legible surfaces on to a person's interiority, inevitably spiralling downward into an abysmal vision of moral turpitude, vanity, dissoluteness, promiscuity, all fuelling the general corruption that was pushing the French kingdom toward disaster.[10]

Chastellain and Fouquet agreed on one thing: the only treasure Sorel had to offer was her body. Unlike, that is, legitimate wives, who on top of producing one offspring after another brought copious dowries to replenish their husband's coffers with land, subjects, cash, and things. Precious things above all. To take just one example among many, when in 1389 the Milanese princess Valentina Visconti crossed the Alps to join her fiancé Louis of Orléans, her baggage contained crowns, belts, necklaces, brooches, rings, jewels, garments, books, and lots of money. From the meticulous inventories that were drawn upon receipt, we learn that the objects were loaded with some 125 rubies, 310 sapphires, 150 diamonds, 28 emeralds, and more than 7,000 pearls.[11] Two crowns are listed first, the larger of which must have been similar to the one rendered by Fouquet, and not very different from the one owned several decades later by Margaret of York (Figure 9.3).

This is one of the rare survivors of gem-encrusted luxury objects, produced in great quantity for wealthy consumers. Contemporaries categorized them as *joyaux*, a term that encompassed regalia, jewellery, and costly plate as well as fancy liturgical objects and relic containers. Far from registering as minor or decorative arts, such prestige objects had to satisfy sophisticated technical demands and aesthetic expectations. Yet crafted of metals, easy to melt, and bestrewn with gems, easy to detach, reuse or sell, they were vulnerable to destruction, and hardly any have survived the blows dispatched by later cash-strapped owners or by those who wanted something stylistically more *au courant*. If Margaret of York's crown escaped obliteration it is because it had become inalienable: the duchess had deposited it in the celestial bank vault by gifting it to a miracle-working image of Our Lady while on a pilgrimage to Aachen in 1474.[12] Whether the crown had been purpose-made for the sculpture (hence its small size) or refitted from the one Margaret wore at her wedding to Charles the Bold (hence the Cs and Ms tied by a love-knot and the quartered arms of Burgundy and England) remains

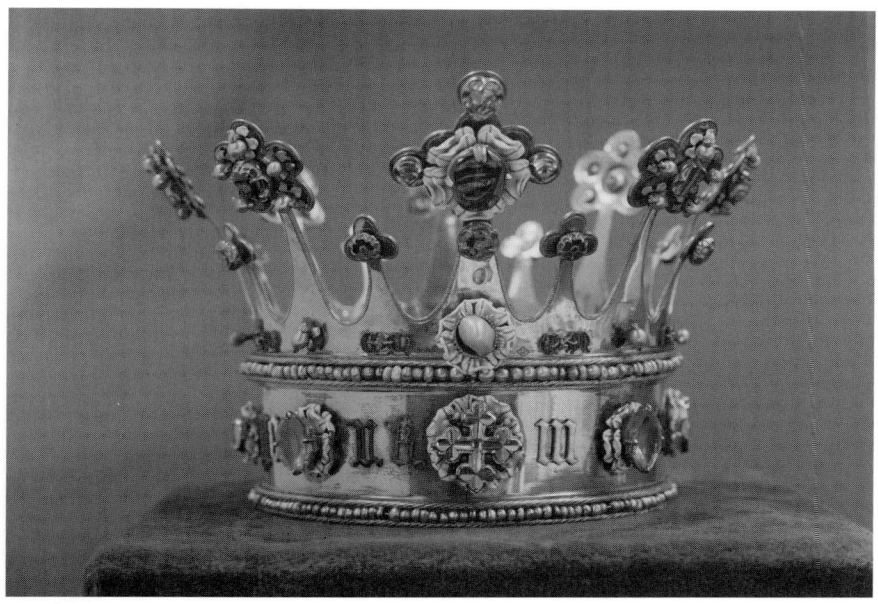

9.3. Crown of Margaret of York, 1460s, silver-gilt, enamels, precious stones, h. 13.2 cm, d. 12.5 cm, Aachen, Cathedral Treasury

a matter of debate. On the crown's body, white enamelled Yorkist roses harbour large sapphires and rubies; they alternate with the letters that spell out the owner's name, executed in opaque white, and translucent red and green enamel. The best stones, showing the most advanced cuts, each nestling within a double-petalled flower mark the frontal axis: a voluminous balas ruby hedged in by three multifaceted diamonds; a large natural pearl; and, on the circlet proper, an exquisitely wrought trefoiled diamond cross with a shield-shaped twinned diamond (macle) placed at the crossing of the arms.

It matters little for my purpose if this particular crown's first function was bridal or votive. Resplendent trappings were coterminous with any elite creature. Human or divine, Margaret or Mary had to abide by the same rule, and exude what Gaston Bachelard, who has written some of the best pages on the poetics of the mineral, nicely called 'droplets of concentrated ostentation'.[13] Failing to do so was tantamount to losing the most incontrovertible sign of distinction, meant being demoted to the level of those whose existence was, quite literally, lacklustre. The rapidly expanding market economy of the late medieval period did not fundamentally alter that class-specific logic; its terms simply shifted as new thresholds of prestige investment were devised, tested, enforced, transgressed. Though a persistent if inaccurate view has it that Sorel was the first to wear diamonds, she may have been the first commoner to do so openly. Middle-class buyers were asked to be content with cheaper jewels adorned with locally mined stones or glass imitations in lieu of the prised Oriental gems, so prominently foregrounded by Fouquet and which sumptuary laws endeavoured to earmark for the upper echelons.[14]

Not that there was no room for individual variation. Gemmophiles were free to embrace the dictates of jewelled existence, gemmophobes to distance themselves, and the majority that fell somewhere in between to modulate their materialism according to their means and preferences, provided that consumption and display remain commensurate with rank. No surprise, then, that fifteenth-century princely inventories list gem-set objects almost *ad nauseam*. And nowhere more so than in the vast material archive of the four Valois dukes of Burgundy, uncontested masters in the manipulation of courtly pomp, experts in overcoming friend and foe by the evidence of exalted materiality. When writing about Louis XI's official entry into Paris in the late summer of 1461, Chastellain cannot refrain from lingering on the unequalled opulence of the Burgundian delegation, its materials and colours so choreographed to throw Philip the Good into maximum relief:

> The duke of Burgundy wore a plume on his hat of inestimable price; it was garnished with nine large rubies, five large diamonds, three of the largest and clearest pearls on earth, and sixty-two other pearls of great value; and on the chamfer of his horse there were likewise nine large rubies interspersed with pearls without number. And on the sallet, carried behind him, was set a rich ruby of Flanders, the marvel [*outrepas*] of Christendom.[15]

Note the emphasis on the stones' large size. Most provocative seems the fact that a gem – simultaneously thing, commodity, and metonymy for the duke – could be hailed as *the* marvel of Christendom.

Whatever political motivation pushed him to accumulate more and more, Philip the Good was a passionate gemmophile. Permanently clad in black in memory of his murdered father, the third Burgundian duke interspersed the silks, damasks, and velvets he wore on ceremonial occasions with a sea of nacreous pearls, tender balas rubies, cerulean sapphires, verdant emeralds and, above all, sparkling diamonds. Of the seventy-two carts that transported his belongings from Dijon to Lille in 1435, five were requisitioned for his *joyaux*, equal to the number required by the kitchen.[16] Chastellain goes a step further, implying that the duke's passion bordered on lithomania: preferring to toy with his stones, 'of which he had more than anyone else', he refused to touch money because he considered it venal and vile.[17] The picture drawn by Leo of Rozmital, a Bohemian nobleman who in the 1460s travelled on a Grand

Tour to visit courts and shrines and beautiful women, is equally telling. When he and his companions stopped in Brussels, the protocol included a viewing of the host's jewels. While other courts reserved the same treat for distinguished guests, it is doubtful that Philip's peers were as fastidious in asking that a table be appointed upon which to exhibit a selection of 'clothes adorned with pearls and gems' as well as 'all the precious stones, arranged according to their various names'.[18]

The 'various names' may have designated classes of gemstones. Alternatively, they may have been given to discrete items since it was standard practice for princely collectors to salvage objects from worthless anonymity by subjectivizing them. The inventories of Jean de Berry list no fewer than twenty-five individually named stones, the majority of which are rubies and balas rubies – the Ruby of the Quail, the Ruby of the Mountain, the Balas of the Pope, and, as expected, the Ruby of Berry, labels clearly devised to particularize a shape, disclose a provenance, memorialize a donor.[19] When Berry's brother, Philip the Bold, the first duke of Burgundy, commissioned a pendant (later transformed into a brooch) from the fashionable goldsmith Hermann Ruissel, the inventories baptized it the Three Brothers, promptly anthropomorphizing the three 70-carat balas rubies that dominated its streamlined composition (Figure 9.4).[20]

Like most of its kin, it has been lost; more fortunate than others, its two-dimensional shadow survives in a handsome coloured drawing. It confirms that Ruissel used a discreet golden armature to foreground the stones, and that, in a studied contrast of colours, lustre, and volumes, he arrayed the table-cut rubies (simplified and darkened in this rendering) and four substantial pearls (one dangling) around a huge point-cut diamond octahedron, at that time the *ne plus ultra* of lapidary art and must-have things.[21]

Small size and mobility explain why gems were prone to vanish without a trace in the rubbish heap of history, except when their size, purity, or unusual mineralogical features marked them out for preservation. Thus equipped, they had a better chance to be singled out with a proper name, increasing the likelihood that they be viewed as memorials of affective bonds and dynastic heirlooms. Passing from hand to hand, generation to generation, gems and jewels not only accrued value but also crossed into the enchanted realm of things endowed with a 'cultural biography'.[22] Coated with this kind of transpersonal charisma, the Three Brothers' brooch weathered the Burgundian demise, and resumed its mineralizing work on Tudor bodies once Henry VIII bought it from the Fuggers in 1543. The Augsburg banking powerhouse had acquired it along with other prominent Burgundian *joyaux* some forty years earlier from the civic authorities of Basel, in whose hands they had landed as

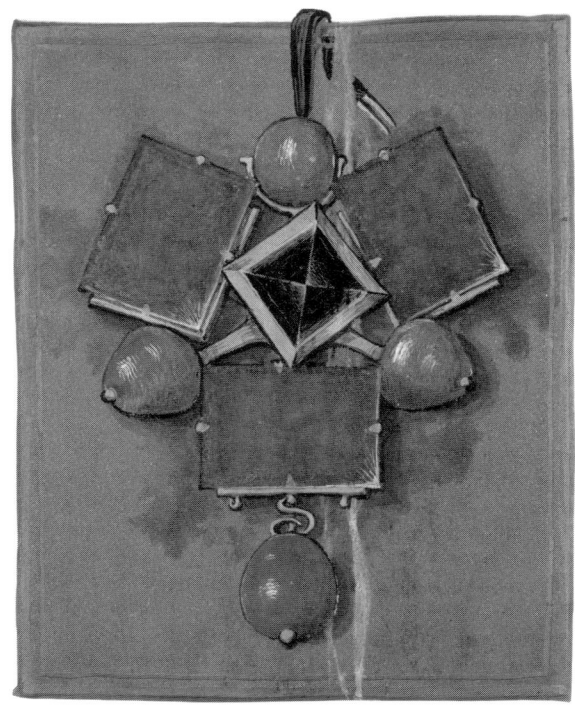

9.4. Watercolour of the *Three Brothers' Brooch*, before 1504, 21 × 18 cm, Basel, Historisches Museum, Inv. 1916.475

war spoils, retrieved after the crushing defeat of Charles the Bold at the battle of Grandson in 1476. Burgundian self-fashioning mandated that the duke enter the battlefield wielding a sword studded with gems, his body protected by a carapace of metal flashing with more.[23] Not content with these droplets of concentrated ostentation, he also brought along several loose stones, including his most eminent diamond, which in the words of Philippe de Commynes was 'perhaps the largest and finest jewel in Christendom'. Never mind the historian's hyperbole. The bauble failed to impress the Swiss ignoramus who drew it from its protective case, threw it back under the wagon mistaking it for glass, then thought better of it, and sold it to a priest for the risible sum of one florin.[24] That casual attitude short-changed (and unwittingly critiqued) the duke's attachment to the stone not only in an economic and social sense but also because it negated a quality that would have been paramount to its erstwhile owner: the diamond's talismanic role, its ability to render its owner invincible. Though it obviously failed to shield Charles from the realpolitik of iron-blows, common knowledge, reinforced by authoritative texts, the encyclopaedias and lapidaries with which his library was well stocked, had maintained it would – did not its very name, *adamas*, meaning invincible or indomitable, hold the promise to steel him down to his core?

In addition to preventing military defeat, lapidaries assured readers, stones could be deployed to blind enemies and split their lungs, detect spies, rout entire armies. Generally, however, their conduct was less bellicose, though it remained sufficiently vigorous to act on tissues and organs, influence minds, change the course of nature, interfere with the natural, meddle in the preternatural. Of immediate efficacy or predictive value, stones were capable of averting diseases or, if too late, of curing them; of making one clever and handsome; of multiplying crops and offering protection during trips; of scaring ghosts away and even of conjuring up the shadows of the dead. At Grandson, Charles the Bold also left behind a ring set with a *selenites* (not our moonstone), a gem reputed to bring relief to people afflicted with a wasting disease and to reconcile lovers, rekindling passion where it had dwindled. Such multitasking was typical, often facilitated by interconnected similitudes: given that the *selenites*, or at least a spot imprinted on it, seemed to wax and wane in synchrony with the phases of the moon, it made sense that its reach spread into disorders in which volume and intensity play a role. A striking illustration of a prose of the world premised on incessant exchanges between the astral, the earthly, and the human, the therapeutic energies of the *selenites* were far from metaphorical. Regulated by the underlying principles of sympathy and antipathy, they tapped into the forces that inhered in the entire cosmos, the same that emboldened red stones to operate as styptics and empowered wine-coloured stones, such as the amethyst, to prevent drunkenness. Of the virginal pearls, beautifully depicted in the Burgundian copy of the herbal known as the *Livre des simples médecines* (see Figure 9.2), one would have appreciated the cleansing properties, able to flush the body of excessive fluids as well as to bring solace to a heart heavy with sorrow.[25] Rippling from the animal to the human, coursing from the bodily to the mental, pearls additionally lessened bouts of melancholy and tamed bursts of anger – neither of which was foreign to Charles the Bold.

This is the crux of my story: the lapidary vulgate was concerned with what it called stones' virtues (*virtutes*). Accordingly, getting a grip on minerals' workings imposed itself as urgent a hermeneutic task as explicating their doctrinal significance. The ability to affect and effect was deemed so key that it was taken as the touchstone by which to determine whether a clump of earth was or not precious. Although it need not be the case, the aesthetic and the performative conveniently coincided in the most highly valued gemstones. Those, invariably, hailed from the East. There, far away, close to the sun, the earthly paradise within reach, nature bestowed her gifts with unmatched prodigality while the impoverished West was essentially bereft of her most accomplished masterpieces. Natural rarities hauled for a hefty price half way across the globe proved even more irresistible with this veneer of Edenic exoticism. Short of that, other mythologizing tales about minerals' origins kept gemmophiles both satiated and always craving for more, bigger, and better. Lapidaries tend to shy away from geographic information. Travel literature filled that gap, offering a respectable selection of stony Shangri-Las: Taprobane (Sri Lanka) awash in sapphires and rubies of dimensions that strain belief; mysterious Scythia, blessed with emerald-filled crags, cursed with fierce griffins to guard them; India and the Valley of Diamonds of Sinbad and Marco Polo fame; and the much searched-for though by definition always-elusive realm of Prester John watered by the gem-packed Idonus, a textual tributary of one of the four rivers of Paradise.

Genesis states that the Phison circles the land of Havilah 'where gold groweth' and that it carries in its waters 'bdellium and the onyx stone' (Genesis 2:11–12). Not only did that become shorthand for gems in general but it also provided the foundational proof that the mineral kingdom had been brought into being by God himself. In the Ghent Altarpiece (Figure 9.5), this river has been represented with thoughtful attention. Still a rivulet, channelled through a devilish spout, it trickles around the panelled marble basin of the Fountain of Life before emptying out, beyond the frame, on to the actual altar next to which we can imagine the kneeling patrons Jodocus Vijd and Elizabeth Borluut. Prayers and visual contemplation guided them toward the redemptive waters, following in the footsteps of the endless mass of adoring righteous – martyrs, prophets, judges, knights, hermits, pilgrims – that pour in from the sides. These are the 'living stones' (1 Peter 2:5) that constitute the Heavenly Jerusalem, the metaphoric twins of the twelve precious stones that provide its foundation (Revelation 21:19–20). Eight being the number of Resurrection, the octagonal fountain is at once primeval and apocalyptic, its vivifying contents both the river of the Garden of Eden and the 'water of life, clear as crystal' that proceeds from the divine throne (Revelation 22:1). Barely perceptible to the unaware eye, a dense scattering of sapphires and rubies, crystals and pearls lines the streambed. Far fewer than the specimens mentioned in the Bible, they correspond to the ones we have seen all along, and that here continue to blaze, now in full sight, from the jewel-laden celestial court in the upper register painted by Jan, the younger and more famous of the two van Eyck brothers.[26]

But let us first move sideways, to the panel on the right where the approaching hermits are about to tread upon other stones. As our eyes

Precious stones, mineral beings 217

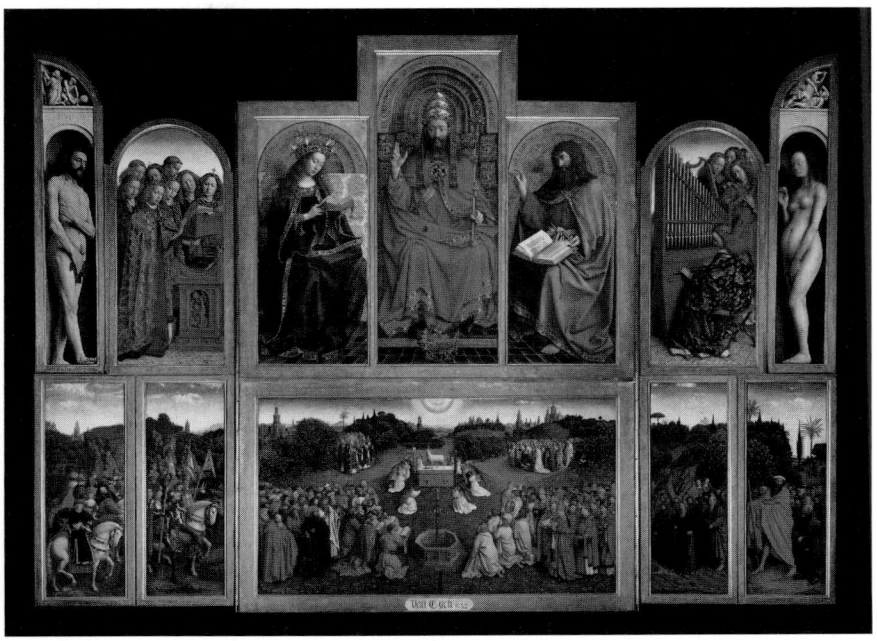

9.5. Hubert and Jan van Eyck, *Ghent Altarpiece*, open position, completed 1432, Ghent, Cathedral of St Bavo

crawl around the dried-out geological matrix, crystalline pebbles and a smattering of coral branches emerge while a burly pumice stone imposes itself toward the foreground where it hugs the tormented bedrock littered with wispy fossils.[27] Why crystal, coral, pumice? Keeping in mind that all were classified as minerals, and leaving aside whatever other significations (pictorial, allegorical, medicinal, magical) they may have conveyed,[28] I would suggest that van Eyck planted them there because he knew that all were brought into being through transmutation – ice frozen into crystal, underwater plant stiffened into coral, foam hardened into porous rock.[29] Rock crystal reappears in the compellingly illusionistic prayer beads fingered by St Anthony, which visually align with the hexagonal quartz underneath his left foot, one end chipped, as if damaged and yet capable of plenitude. Since it also provides the material for the most exalted object, the near-diaphanous, tubular sceptre held by the Almighty, one could say that the mineral universe of the Ghent Altarpiece has been calibrated so that the protracted transformation of the naturally rugged into the artfully contrived correlates with the long march from antediluvian creation to the ceasing of time.

In the Melun Diptych, Fouquet achieved something similar. He too resorted to geological transfiguration to lead us from the superbly rendered rough silex that features at the centre of the Berlin panel as St Stephen's lapidation stone to the room's manufactured marbles and – further up and away in time – to the gemmed celestial court in the Antwerp wing.[30] In Jan's handling, that place enjoys the same monopoly over brilliant *artificialia*, gems polished into rounded cabochons and chiselled into rectangles, lozenges, and pyramids; in short, perfection extracted from the evolving sublunar domain of *naturalia*. With unsurpassed phenomenological patience, he noted the patches of white on each of the hundreds, perhaps thousands of stones. And admitted the outside further by imprinting a stately Gothic window on to the bulging sapphire that anchors the cluster brooch worn by the first singing – and mediating – angel, a reflection in line with his better-known self-referential devices in other paintings. But, astute court artist that he was, he knew how to marry such peaks of visual gratification with the politics of representation. He therefore graduated his *joyaux*, saving the heftiest for the thoroughly mineralized King of Kings. On the clasp that fastens his ample vermilion cape, emeralds, sapphires, rubies, and pearls, in claw, box, and bowl settings, are massed around a sizeable point-cut diamond set in a slick box mount. Pared-down versions embellish the Virgin's glorious crown and the angels' circlets. All of these are viewed from an angle. Close scrutiny reveals that God's is not strictly frontal either: the painter rotated it ever so slightly and inclined the Holy Face ever so gently, thus allowing mineral apotheosis and beatific vision to jointly include the viewer's point of view.

Showing how things look and how we perceive them, how they obey or transcend physical constraints, was not enough for an artist of Jan's pictorial stamina. Though not alone in adapting his brushstrokes and pigments to the structure and texture of things, he did so more methodically, as if to imply that in yoking the optical to the tactile, he and his viewers could gain access to an object's essence, attain its inner truth, unlock the very soul of the matter.[31] His material imagination and medial sophistication are such that his signs turn into the hammer of the goldsmith, the needle of the seamstress, the weft of the weaver, the pipe of the glassblower, the quill of the scribe, and indeed the diamond point of the lapidary. Panofsky got it right when he said that the Flemish master 'builds his world out of his pigments as nature builds hers out of primary matter' and that his paintings can therefore claim 'to be both a real object – and a precious object at that – and a reconstruction rather than a mere representation of the visible world'.[32] Centuries earlier, Albrecht Dürer had expressed the same sentiment when writing that 'Jan's picture' struck him as *köstlich* (most precious) and *hoch verständig gemählt*, which can be translated as 'painted very knowledgeably'.[33]

We can press the implication of this intertwining of worth and ingenuity further. For if one wanted to reconstruct rather than merely mimic the real, then more had to be mobilized than shapes and outlines. Artists' fingers had to sink into stuff as they learned how to brew wood, chalk, oil, egg; how to grind, mix, and fire organic and mineral substances into representation; how to test materials' density and viscosity, creating with their demands and against their resistances; in sum, had to make materiality perform *in itself* before it could do so *for something else*. Take the way Jan fabricated his blues. Depending on their destination as sky, flower, cloth, or precious stone, he adjusted the proportions of lead white, azurite, and lapis lazuli. The intensely blue expanse of the Virgin's cloak, for example, consists of a fairly dense base layer of azurite into which some lapis has been injected, topped with a watery glaze of pure ultramarine. But gone is the azurite when we move to the sapphires: van Eyck let those sparkle as unadulterated lapis lazuli, combining in one and the same gesture material practice and mimetic theory. Analyses conducted during the 1951 restoration as well as later examinations have conclusively put to rest the guesswork about the Flemish master's painting technique. There is no wizardry about it; he did not use secret binding agents or a mysterious system of glazes. Its strength derived from the synthesis of unusually fine observational skills and a consummate knowledge of the medium; the virtuoso blending of visible paint particles suspended in invisible pine resin and linseed oil; the gradual shifting from translucent to transparent surfaces or light-absorbing to light-reflecting layers.[34] More than imitating everything under the sun, more than materializing things seen and unseen, pleasing patrons and viewers, the 'whole art of painting' must therefore appropriate nature's transformational energies, absorb its atoms to conjure up social subjects and desirable objects.[35] In its own way, this is an art of similitudes.

Notes

With my thanks to Michael Gorra, Craig Harbison, and Dana Leibsohn for their incisive comments. And to Nicola Courtright and Cynthia Hahn for having invited me to share an earlier version with their students.

1 Those plaques are sometimes identified as marbles, often as onyx. In lapidaries, the sardonyx is the only three-coloured stone with a black base. The most popular lapidary in the fifteenth century was Book 16 of Bartholomaeus Anglicus's *De proprietatibus rerum*, written in the mid-thirteenth century after earlier sources (such as Pliny, Isidore of Seville, the Venerable Bede, Marbode), and translated into several vernacular languages.

2 Most extensively examined by: C. Schaefer, 'Le Diptyque de Melun de Jean Fouquet conservé à Anvers et à Berlin', *Jaarboek van het Koninklijk Museum voor Schone Kunsten Antwerpen* (1975), pp. 7–100, shortened and revised in *Jean Fouquet an der Schwelle zur Renaissance* (Dresden: Verlag der Kunst, 1994), pp. 139–51; A. Châtelet, 'La *Reine Blanche* de Fouquet: Remarques sur le *Diptyque de Melun*', in A. Châtelet and N. Reynaud (eds), *Études d'art*

français offerts à Charles Sterling (Paris: Presses Universitaires de France, 1975), pp. 127–38; D. Thiébaut in F. Avril (ed.), *Jean Fouquet: Peintre et enlumineur du XVe siècle*, exhibition catalogue, Paris, Bibliothèque nationale de France (Paris: Hazan, 2003), pp. 121–37.

3   F. Carmody (ed.), 'Physiologus latinus versio Y', *University of California Publications in Classical Philology* 12 (1941), chapters 24 and 47 for the diamond, chapter 23 for the pearl. The online Aberdeen Bestiary Project (www.abdn.ac.uk/bestiary/intro.hti; accessed on 14 February 2014) offers convenient access to the English translation of an expanded version plus abundant documentation.

4   The template for subsequent descriptions is Pliny the Elder's *Natural History* 9.106–11, trans. H. Rackham (Cambridge, MA: Harvard University Press, 1983), pp. 234–9.

5   C. Meier, *Gemma spiritalis: Methode und Gebrauch der Edelsteinallegorese vom frühen Christentum bis ins 18. Jahrhundert* (Munich: W. Fink, 1977), pp. 147–52.

6   M. Foucault, *The Order of Things: An Archaeology of the Human Sciences* (New York: Pantheon, 1971), pp. 17–45. And, building on it, B. Latour, *We Have Never Been Modern*, trans. C. Porter (Cambridge, MA: Harvard University Press, 1993), pp. 51–69, for the argument that the Great Divide between sovereign subjects and supine objects is a foundational myth of modernity.

7   In the satirical poem *La Pucelle d'Orléans*, Voltaire was among the first to associate the two. It is evident that his fantasmatic description of Sorel's breast, inviting squeezing hands, voyeuristic gazes and kissing lips, was inspired by Fouquet's painting. For the ways in which the nineteenth century mythologized Sorel, see E. Schwartz, 'À propos du buste dit d'Agnès Sorel conservé à l'École des Beaux-arts: Les Fantaisies de la légende, de la politique et de l'histoire de l'art', *Bulletin archéologique du Comité des Travaux Historiques et Scientifiques* 29 (2002), pp. 81–103.

8   Avril (ed.), *Jean Fouquet*, pp. 149–53. X-ray analysis has shown that Fouquet copied the Antwerp Virgin through pouncing from a model over which he ended up painting, rather bafflingly, a portrait of Charles VII. See N. Reynaud, *Jean Fouquet*, Les Dossiers du Département de Peintures (Paris: Réunion des Musées Nationaux, 1981), pp. 12–22 and pp. 34–5; 'La Radiographie du *Portrait de Charles VII* par Fouquet', *Revue du Louvre* 33:2 (1983), pp. 97–9.

9   Her remains were exhumed in 2004. Extensive scientific analysis revealed high levels of mercury, which was used as a poison, a vermifuge, and to induce labour, all applicable to Sorel. Detailed by Pascal Dubrisay, *Agnès Sorel: Féminité et modernité* (Tours: Concept-Image, 2006).

10 Georges Chastellain, 'Chronique', in J. Kervyn de Lettenhove (ed.), *Oeuvres* (Brussels: Heussner, 1863–66), vol. 4, pp. 365–6, to which one can oppose the posthumous apology, perhaps inspired by the king, penned by Jean Chartier, *Chronique de Charles VII*, ed. Valet de Viriville (Paris, 1858), vol. 2, pp. 181–6. The most complete biography and reception history of Sorel remains Pierre Champion, *La Dame de Beauté: Agnès Sorel* (Paris: Honoré Champion, 1931), in particular pp. 37–41.

11 J. Camus, 'La Venue en France de Valentine Visconti, Duchesse d'Orléans, et l'inventaire de ses joyaux apportés de Lombardie', *Miscellanea di storia italiana*, series 3, 5 (1900), pp. 3–63.

12 P.W. Hammond, 'The coronet of Margaret of York', *The Ricardian* 6 (1984), pp. 362–5; E.G. Grimme, *Der Aachener Domschatz*, special issue of *Aachener Kunstblätter* 42 (1972), pp. 111–12; R. Marks and P. Williamson (eds), *Gothic: Art for England 1400–1547*, exhibition catalogue (London: Victoria & Albert Museum, 2003), pp. 154–5, no. 11; H. van der Velden, *The Donor's Image: Gerard Loyet and the Votive Portraits of Charles the Bold* (Turnhout: Brepols, 2000), pp. 215–17. And more generally on the typology of queenly crowns, P.E. Schramm et al., *Herrschaftszeichen und Staatssymbolik: Beiträge zu ihrer Geschichte vom dritten bis zum sechzehnten Jahrhundert* (Stuttgart: Hiersemann, 1954–78), vol. 3, pp. 991–1003.

13 G. Bachelard, *Earth and Reveries of Will: An Essay on the Imagination of Matter*, trans. K. Haltman (Dallas, TX: Institute of Humanities and Culture, 2002), p. 242.
14 R.W. Lightbown, *Mediaeval European Jewellery, with a Catalogue of the Collection in the Victoria & Albert Museum* (London: Victoria & Albert Museum, 1992), pp. 79–85.
15 Chastellain, 'Chronique', vol. 4, p. 77.
16 R. Vaughan, *Philip the Good: The Apogee of Burgundy* (New York: Barnes & Noble, 1970), p. 142.
17 Chastellain, 'Les Hauts Faits du duc de Bourgogne', in de Lettenhove (ed.), *Oeuvres*, vol. 7, p. 223.
18 M. Letts (ed.), *The Travels of Leo of Rozmital through Germany, Flanders, England, France, Spain, Portugal, and Italy, 1465–1467* (Cambridge: Cambridge University Press, 1957), p. 38.
19 J. Guiffrey, *Inventaires de Jean, Duc de Berry (1401–1416)* (Paris: E. Leroux, 1894–96), vol. 1, lxxxix–xcv; and more generally on the duke's passion for jewels, M. Camille, '"For our devotion and pleasure": The sexual objects of Jean, Duc de Berry', *Art History* 24:2 (2001), pp. 169–94.
20 E. Kovács, *L'Âge d'or de l'orfèvrerie parisienne au temps des princes de Valois* (Paris: Faton, 2004), pp. 152–79; F. Deuchler, *Die Burgunderbeute* (Bern: Stämpfli, 1963), pp. 123–4; S. Marti, T.H. Borchert, and G. Keck (eds), *Splendour of the Burgundian Court: Charles the Bold (1433–1477)*, exhibition catalogue (Brussels: Mercatorfonds, 2009), no. 97.
21 The best work on gem cutting and setting techniques during the fifteenth century is Fritz Falk, *Edelsteinschliff und Fassungsformen im späten Mittelalter und im 16. Jahrhundert. Studien zur Geschichte der Edelsteine und des Schmuckes* (Ulm: Kempter, 1975), of which a short English summary was published in *Princely Magnificence: Court Jewels of the Renaissance, 1500–1630* (London: Debrett's Peerage in association with the Victoria and Albert Museum, 1980), pp. 20–6.
22 I. Kopytoff, 'The cultural biography of things: Commodization as process', in A. Appadurai (ed.), *The Social Life of Things: Commodities in Cultural Perspective* (Cambridge: Cambridge University Press, 1986), pp. 64–91.
23 Deuchler, *Burgunderbeute*, p. 98; and for a broader discussion of the Burgundian 'language of splendour', M. Belozerskaya, *Rethinking the Renaissance: Burgundian Arts Across Europe* (Cambridge: Cambridge University Press, 2002).
24 Philippe de Commynes, *Mémoires* 5.2, ed. J. Blanchard (Geneva: Droz, 2007), vol. 1, p. 327, who concludes that the rich booty taught the Swiss one lesson: the value of money.
25 G. Malandin, F. Avril, and P. Lieutaghi, *Le Livre des simples médecines d'après le manuscrit français 12322 de la Bibliothèque Nationale de Paris* (Paris: Ozalid, 1986), p. 280, note 16; M. Platearius, *Le Livre des simples médecines*, ed. Paul Dorveaux (Paris: Société Française d'Histoire, 1913), p. 120, numbers 698–9: and, more generally, M. Collins, *Medieval Herbals: The Illustrative Traditions* (London: British Library, 2000).
26 Controversies about the respective contributions of Hubert and Jan are endemic in van Eyck studies, witness the exchange between H. van der Velden and V. Herzner published in *Simiolus* 35 (2011), pp. 5–39, 127–30, and 131–40.
27 K. Bé, 'Geological aspects of Jan van Eyck's "Saint Francis receiving the stigmata"', in *Jan van Eyck: Two Paintings of 'Saint Francis Receiving the Stigmata'* (Philadelphia, PA: Philadelphia Museum of Art, 1997), pp. 88–95.
28 For the medicinal dimension, see P.H. Jolly, 'Jan van Eyck's Italian pilgrimage: A miraculous Florentine Annunciation and the Ghent Altarpiece', *Zeitschrift für Kunstgeschichte* 61:3 (1998), pp. 369–94.
29 According to the definitions given by Isidore of Seville in his influential *Etymologies*, trans. S.A. Barney, W.J. Lewis, J.A. Beach, and O. Berghof (Cambridge: Cambridge University Press, 2006): crystal, 16.13.1 (p. 325), coral, 16.8.1 (p. 323), pumice 16.3.7 (p. 319).

30 On Fouquet's talent in portraying things as well as people, see Erik Inglis, *Jean Fouquet and the Invention of France: Art and Nation after the Hundred Years War* (New Haven, CT: Yale University Press, 2011); on temporal intimations, A. Acres, 'Small physical history: The trickling past of early Netherlandish painting', in C. Heck and K. Lippincott (eds), *Symbols of Time in the History of Art* (Turnhout: Brepols, 2002), pp. 7–25.

31 P. Schmidt, *The Adoration of the Lamb*, trans. L. Preedy (Leuven: Davidsfond, 2005), p. 9. And more broadly, L. Seidel, 'The value of verisimilitude in the art of Jan van Eyck', *Yale French Studies*, special issue: *Contexts: Style and Values in Medieval Art and Literature* (1991), pp. 25–43; 'Visual representation as instructional text: Jan van Eyck and *The Ghent Altarpiece*', in P.H. Smith and B. Schmidt (eds), *Making Knowledge in Early Modern Europe: Practices, Objects, and Texts, 1400–1800* (Chicago: Chicago University Press, 2007), pp. 45–67.

32 E. Panofsky, *Early Netherlandish Painting* (1953; New York: Harper & Row, reprint. 1971), p. 181; and W.R. Newman, *Promethean Ambitions: Alchemy and the Quest to Perfect Nature* (Chicago: Chicago University Press, 2004).

33 It is important to be literal here, as opposed to the painting 'full of thought' proposed by J.A. Goris and G. Marlier (eds), *Albrecht Dürer: Diary of His Journey to the Netherlands, 1520–1521*, trans. P. Troutman (Greenwich, CT: New York Graphic Society, 1971), p. 87; for the original see H. Rupprich, *Dürer: Schriftlicher Nachlass* (Berlin: Deutscher Verlag für Kunstgeschichte, 1956–69), vol. 1, p. 168.

34 P. Philippot, 'Vision et exécution eyckiennes', in P. Coremans (ed.), *L'Agneau mystique au laboratoire: Examen et traitement* (Antwerp: De Sikkel, 1953), pp. 94–7, and R. White, 'Van Eyck's technique: The myth and reality, II', in S. Foister, S. Jones, and D. Cool (eds), *Investigating Jan van Eyck* (Turnhout: Brepols, 2000), pp. 101–5.

35 This is inspired by the argument put forward by P.H. Smith in *The Body of the Artisan: Art and Experience in the Scientific Revolution* (Chicago: Chicago University Press, 2004), pp. 51–5. The 'whole art of painting' comes from the earliest recorded observation on the Ghent Altarpiece made in 1495 by the German humanist Hieronymous Münzer.

10 ✧ Carving life: the meaning of wood in early modern European sculpture

Christina Neilson

Wood was a favourite material for Renaissance sculpture. Because it was readily available across Europe, and because common species were not as expensive as other materials, many scholars have assumed that cost and availability were the reasons it was chosen. The surviving evidence, however, suggests that when wood was selected, often it was *not* because of cost or availability. Moreover, some subjects (such as the Penitent Magdalene) were made almost exclusively of wood in regions that otherwise preferred marble and bronze for sacred subjects. Why then was wood, and wood of particular species, chosen? This chapter examines wooden sculptures mainly of religious subjects from a range of regions, concentrating primarily on figural sculpture from the Italian peninsula. It explores how certain types of wood were chosen for their symbolic properties, properties that were believed to invest a sculpture with a spiritual force. It will be argued that wood was preferred for certain subjects because it was considered a living material that operated like a human body, with veins, humours, blood, and a complexion.[1]

The type of wood for sculpture was sometimes stipulated by guilds. In fourteenth-century Cologne, for example, only walnut was to be used for sacred objects, whereas in Lübeck it was oak.[2] At other times, commissioners demanded a specific wood. In 1389, for instance, the Lucchese artist Domenico di Fazino was ordered to use pearwood or wood from the tree known as 'gatto' (probably white poplar) for an Annunciate Virgin and Saint Michael Archangel.[3] On occasion, timber was provided by the patron. When Anton II Tucher, First Losunger (senior civic officer) of Nuremberg, commissioned Veit Stoss's *Annunciation of the Rosary* (1517–18, Saint Lorenzkirche, Nuremberg), he had a lime tree felled for the artist.[4] On 4 August 1408, Caterino di Corsino, from the *Operai del Duomo* in Siena, purchased wood for four figures to be carved by Francesco di Valdambrino.[5] Sometimes artists were responsible for selecting their own materials. Venetian woodcarvers Jacopo Moronzone and Lio Lupi supplied wood for several of their own commissions.[6] And it is implied in the case of Michel Erhart, who stored wood in a shed against the wall of the Dominican convent in Ulm.[7] The Venetian *intagliatore* Jacobello Foscolo may have been a dealer, as suggested by his acquisition of significant numbers of fir logs from a seller at Fonzaso in 1421.[8]

Why were certain species of wood chosen for sculptures? Theorists expounded on the best woods. According to a fourteenth-century English treatise on building, limewood and poplar were pleasant for carving.[9] Piero de' Crescenzi, author of an agricultural treatise (c. 1304–9), recommended poplar and limewood for sculpture;[10] but he noted that pearwood was used to make many beautiful things.[11] Leon Battista Alberti, following the ancients, recommended limewood (also jujube) above all others for wooden sculpture.[12] Giorgio Vasari concurred that limewood was the best, but he also praised boxwood and walnut.[13] Francesco di Giorgio Martini differed from these, stating that walnut and pear were most suitable for carving.[14]

Woods were probably chosen in large part because of their suitability for carving and their durability. Limewood's popularity was due to its homogeneity in all directions of growth, natural elasticity, and uniformly thin cells that make working with tools across the axial current easy.[15] Pearwood is fine and regular but it is hard and heavy to carve and so is best for details.[16] Poplar is easy to work, but it has a tendency to chip and split, and thus requires a gesso ground.[17] (And because it responds well to gesso, sculptors who intended to model with gesso chose poplar for this reason.)[18] Willow has a fine-to-medium texture, is easy to work with an attractive finish, and it does not split, but it does not allow for as good results in carving as pear or lime.[19] Figwood is coarse and its growth rings are irregular and walnut has a medium-to-fine texture with irregular fibres.[20]

Limewood grew in forests stretching from the Iberian Peninsula to the Caucasus.[21] Therefore it is no surprise that it tended to be the wood of choice for sculptures all over present-day Italy,[22] Germany, and Switzerland.[23] But it was not the cheapest wood, nor the most easily available (for instance, limewood was more expensive than poplar in Florence and cost more than beech and oak in Nuremberg).[24] And although southern Netherlandish sculptors tended to use oak for their carved altarpieces, which was available nearby, theirs was imported from the Baltic region, not the local variety.[25] In the Romanesque period, walnut was preferred for sculptures in Auvergne, France, but it was not obtainable in large, natural supply in that region.[26] And later, during the seventeenth century, Spanish confraternities chose cedar over other woods, ideally cedar 'de las Indias', which was especially costly as it had to be imported from the New World.[27]

Beyond qualities desirable for carving, types of wood may have been chosen for their symbolic significance. Wood was preferred for sculptures with moveable parts, a frequent feature of sacred performances.[23] These objects might have mobile limbs, or even eyes or tongues.[29] One crucifix from Reggio Emilia apparently stretched and moaned;[30] another, from Foligno, had eyes that opened and closed.[31] Other figures were used in sacred performances, such as Deposition and Epiphany plays;[32] or in processions, including those during outbreaks of plague.[33]

In all of these examples, wood enabled figures with jointed body parts that could move. Even more important though was the desire for lifelikeness, and wood was the perfect medium for this as it was considered to be a living material that operated like a body.[34] This attitude went back to the ancients. For Theophrastus, trees had parts that corresponded to veins, muscles, marrow, and flesh in animals. They depended on the humours (if they were not warm and moist, 'death and withering ensue[d]'),[35] and had a complexion (the heat of the lime tree explained why it blunted iron tools).[36] Hildegard of Bingen, who believed that because man was made from the earth, there remained present in the earth an analogy between the human body and all natural structures, wrote that the sap of fruit-bearing trees could be compared to a person's blood.[37] According to Albertus Magnus, wood resembled the human body in that it could suffer, rot or be blessed; and it could be infested with worms.[38] Piero de Crescenzi wrote that plants had veins and nerves, like animals,[39] and that during the autumn, the humours in plants became idle.[40] Leonardo da Vinci wrote that trees had humours, he compared the vessels of the human heart to the branches of a tree in a drawing, and his description of how a tree that has had some of its bark stripped off receives sap to that area resembles the process of scarring in human tissue.[41] And several writers compared the bark of trees to the flesh of men or animals.[42] It is no coincidence then that speaking statues were often of wood.[43] As a living material, wood played a powerful role in aiding the sense of animation of sculptures.[44]

But this attitude to wood as living was not only metaphorical; it shaped the creation of sculpture from the moment a tree was cut down. According to Alberti, the best time to fell wood was after the moon had set (to avoid unwanted influences on the humours).[45] Astrology too affected the creation of wooden sculpture. Alberti noted that 'material intended for movable objects ought to be cut and handled when the moon is in Libra or Cancer, but anything to be stable or immobile ought to be worked on while the moon is in Leo or Taurus, or the like'.[46] Contracts sometimes stipulated when to fell timber (for instance, the contract for a retable in Valladolid specified that 'all the wood for the said sculpture must be . . . cut in a good moon').[47]

When it came to making sculpture, the artist did not simply impose his or her will on to the medium. Instead, the sculptor worked with the wood to realize its inherent nature. Wooden figure sculptures tended to be made from hollowed out tree trunks, usually with the top of the body positioned as if the trunk were standing upright.[48] Each wood posed its own challenges, and sculptors had to work with these limitations.[49] As Michael Baxandall recognized decades ago, limewood sculptors had to cohere to or challenge the internal currents of that wood's 'starshake' (the radial patterns of splits caused by uneven shrinkage in drying). More ambitious German artists played with the starshake, creating expressive pieces that took advantage of limewood's internal mobility by carving radial, curving, and orbital sections.[50]

It is significant that almost all life-size crucifixes from the Italian peninsula were carved from wood as they represent Christ's human suffering upon the cross, a figure between life and death.[51] Wood, with its physical properties believed to resemble those of a human body, was fitting for these objects. Also, commentators made associations between timber and Christ's body, an attitude deriving from devotion to the wood of the cross, one of the most powerful relics.[52] The connection is evident in pictorial representations of Christ as the Man of Sorrows seated at the base of a tree, with which he is supposed to be confused,[53] and in the iconography of the Tree of Life, which appears occasionally in refectories, as at Santa Croce, Florence, where viewers were nourished.[54]

Sometimes the act of carving was spiritual. According to a medieval legend, Nicodemus carved a wooden crucifix, a mystical act shaped by his first-hand knowledge of Christ's body, which he removed from the cross after the Crucifixion (some believe this was the *Volto Santo*, later brought to Lucca).[55] Before making his statues, the Castilian Baroque sculptor Gregorio Fernández apparently prepared himself through rituals of prayer, fasting, and penitence, as well as taking the sacrament. He did this so that God would grant him a vision, which he recorded faithfully in wood.[56] And when the Sienese artist Lando di Pietro made his *Crucifix* (Figure 10.1), of which only the head survives, he inserted two notes on parchment into Christ's nostrils. In one, Lando expressed his desire for salvation through the act of carving, while the other referred to the dangers of conflating Christ and wood: '[I]t is he that one must adore and not this wood.'[57]

In Italy, crucifixes were usually carved from limewood[58] or poplar,[59] both of which had spiritual connotations. The associations of poplar, in particular, made it appropriate for crucifixes. According to Ovid, the poplar descended from the Heliades, sisters of Phaëton, who were transformed into trees marking the place by a river where they mourned their

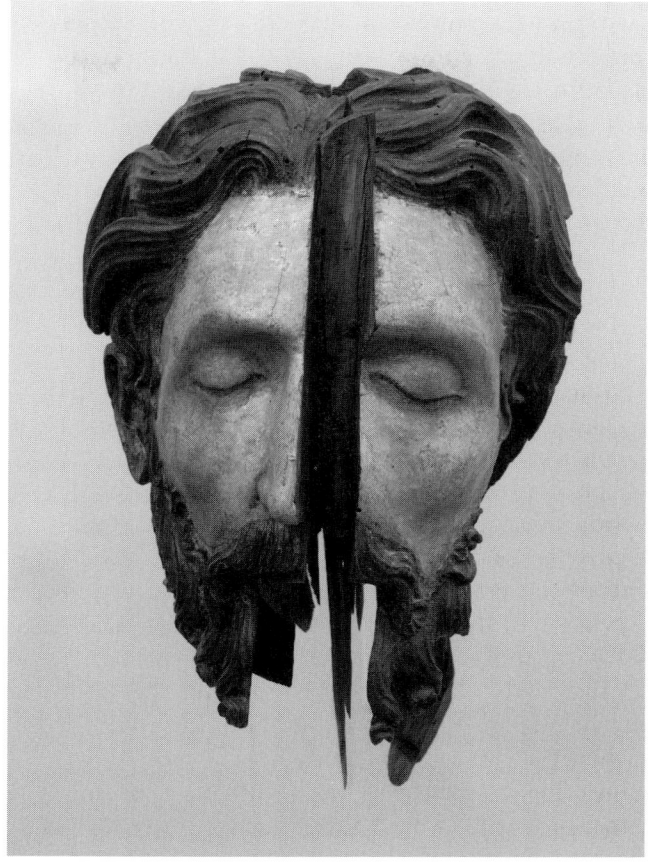

10.1. Lando di Pietro, *Head of Christ*, fragment from a crucifix, 1338, Basilica dell'Osservanza, Siena

brother's death after he was cast down by Zeus for mishandling the chariot of the Sun. As a result, poplars were associated with mourning, and in Christian iconography specifically, with the Passion and Resurrection of Christ.[60]

Sometimes walnut[61] or pearwood was used for crucifixes.[62] Each of these had spiritual associations, many well known to both learned and lay audiences.[63] Christ was compared to a nut in a medieval poem on the Nativity of Christ.[64] Richard of Saint Laurent compared Christ's flesh to a chestnut in a husk beset with thorns (little distinction was made between walnuts and chestnuts). Ambrose regarded the chestnut as a symbol for resurrection.[65] The three parts of the walnut symbolize the Trinity. Augustine considered the nut to be a symbol of Christ (the outer hull represents the flesh, the woody shell stands for the cross, and the kernel alludes to Christ's divine nature). Because it was enclosed in a husk covered with thorny spikes, it was associated with the torments of Christ. And sometimes the walnut was said to allude to the Resurrection because its tree can regenerate almost immediately after being cut down.[66] The pear tree was appropriate too because occasionally it was identified as the tree of knowledge, from which the cross was thought to have been made.[67]

As well as for crucifixes, wood was the preferred medium for statues of Mary Magdalen in Penitence. In fact, there are few known examples from Tuscany in any other medium, despite the fact that bronze and marble were favoured for sculptures, especially in Florence, and that terracotta was also a widely used material whose humbleness might seem appropriate for the subject.[68] Desiderio da Settignano's *Mary Magdalen* (Figure 10.2) was carved from willow, with intaglio additions in pearwood for some of the hair.[69] Willow had contradictory meanings suitable to the Magdalen. According to Berchorius, it symbolized the sinner, because the willow tree bends towards the water that it likes to grow near, indicating its weakness for worldly pleasures,[70] and, because it produces no seeds, the willow symbolized famine[71] and also chastity,[72] both of which applied to Mary Magdalen, who adopted an ascetic and pure existence after Christ's death. The willow symbolized grief, deriving from a reference in Psalm 137 to exiles hanging up their harps among the willows and weeping.[73] But it also symbolized the faithful (based on a reading of Isaiah 44:4 'And they shall spring up as . . . willows by the water courses').[74] All of these qualities were appropriate to Mary Magdalen. The intaglio additions in pear were suitable too as that tree was associated with Venus, because its leaves resemble a womb.[75] Thus Desiderio's sculpture expressed through its materials Mary Magdalen's sins and her later penance.

Wood was a popular material also for sculptures of Saint Roch, which tended to be carved from poplar,[76] and sometimes from fig- or limewood (Figure 10.3).[77] In this case, poplar may be read as an allusion to salvation, deriving from the ancient belief that its leaves cured snakebite.[78] Fig trees were particularly appropriate to Saint Roch because they offered consolation and food, according to Thomas the Cistercian, and protection from evil, qualities associated specifically with Saint Roch, who was a plague saint.[79] Roch was compared explicitly to a tree and his wounds to fruit in a late fifteenth-century breviary from Lübeck: 'The holy Rochus was as a tree that is planted in a watered place, when it is endowed with many good qualities', and 'he [Roch] offered himself as a servant to all with his abundant fruit'.[80]

Statues of Saint Roch were carried in processions, especially during outbreaks of plague,[81] and sometimes placed on altars in hospital

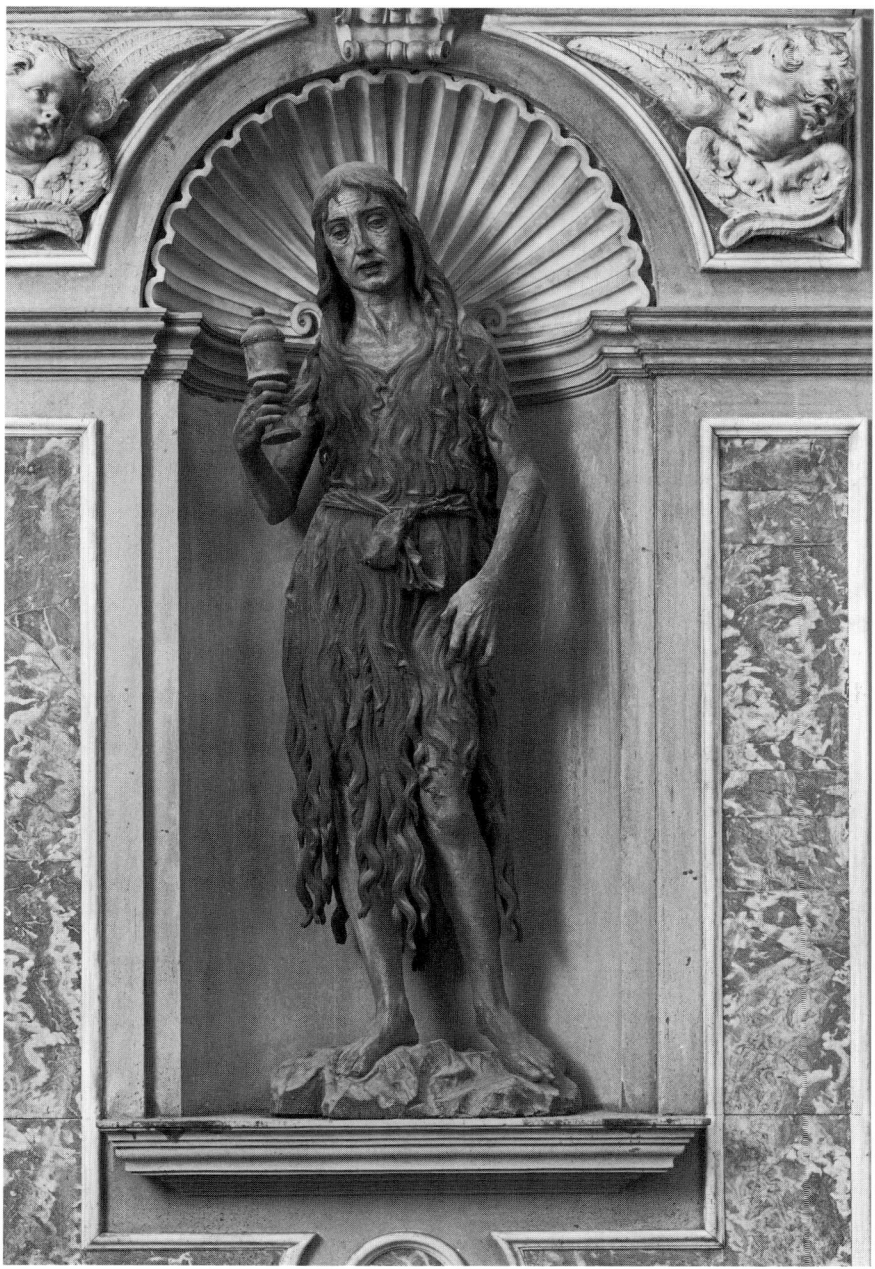

10.2. Desiderio da Settignano, completed by Giovanni d'Andrea, *Mary Magdalen*, begun 1458, Santa Trinita, Florence

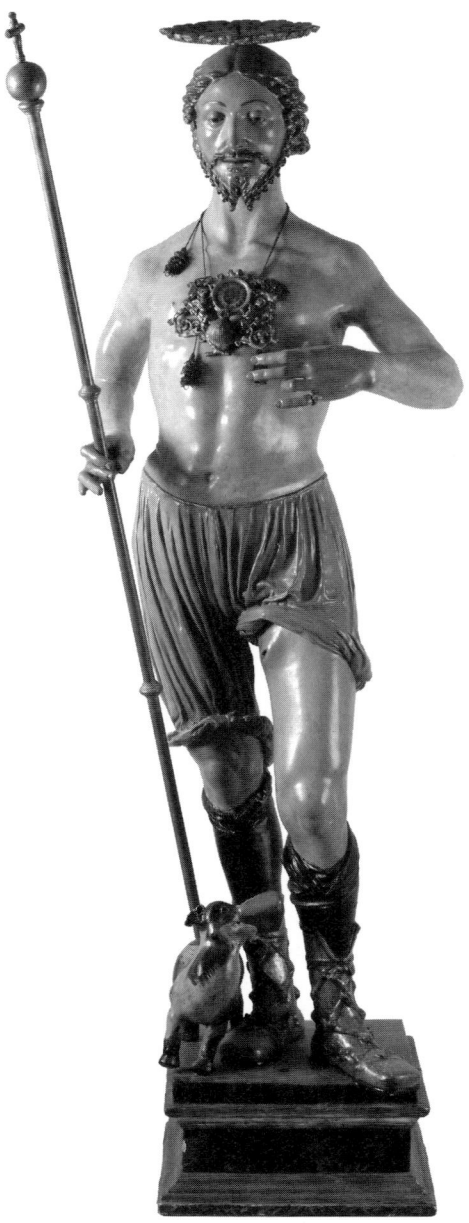

10.3. Nero Alberti, *Saint Roch*, 1528, Comune de Pergola, Marche

chapels.[82] According to popular belief, his body operated as a living 'lightning rod' (to adopt Leo Steinberg's phrase),[83] attracting the wrath of God in the form of a bubo to protect humanity.[84] It is significant for our purposes that Roch lived through his ordeal (which is what gave his followers hope). Thus the statues of him would have been regarded as living effigies and the properties of wood from which they were often made would have been fitting.

Occasionally statues were sculpted from sacred wood, such as the *Santo Bambino* in Santa Maria d'Aracoeli, Rome, made by a pious Minorite in Jerusalem from wood from the Mount of Olives,[85] and a colossal *San Cristoforo* (Duomo, Barga), said to have been carved from an ancient sacred tree.[86] In one remarkable crucifix, attributed to Giuliano or Benedetto da Maiano (Figure 10.4), the cross was carved in the form of a tree covered with leaves. This iconography recalls the thirteenth-century *Lignum vitae* by Saint Bonaventure, which describes the cross in arboreal form,[87] and the fourteenth-century French poem, the *Pèlerinage de l'âme* by Guillaume de Deguileville, which tells of how the dead Tree of Life could become green again only if the crucified Christ was grafted upon it, reviving it with his blood.[88]

It must be noted that sculptures were often painted. While this might be regarded as disguising the material from which the statue was made, an alternative reading is that it *extended* the already 'vital' quality of the material. This interpretation is supported by accounts of miraculous encounters between pious supplicants and painted statues in which the polychromy plays an important role. In one example, for example, from a thirteenth-century compilation, a sacristan was instructed by an animated statue of the Virgin to kiss her 'face colorée'.[89] And common in many tales of animate Madonnas is the emphasis placed on her seductive beauty and lifelikeness. (Ironically it was this that motivated many pledges of chastity by male devotees.)[90] As Andalusian painter Francisco Pacheco explained in a letter to sculptor Juan Martínez Montañés: 'The figure of marble and wood requires the painter's hand to come to life.'[91] It is no coincidence, therefore, to find instructions for making cosmetics and pigments side-by-side in recipe books,[92] and that painting flesh tones was known in Spain as *encarnación* ('making flesh').[93]

Wood was believed to resemble a human body and as such it was especially meaningful for mobile works of art. Carving crucifixes from wood aided in their verisimilitude as representations of Christ between life and death. In addition, the symbolic meanings of wood may explain the choice of timber for certain subjects, such as crucifixes, the Penitent Magdalen, and Saint Roch. Devotion to wood was also expressed through the use of sacred trees for sculptures. Rather than wood being used because it was cheap or easily available, the material itself had significance, which impacted on how wooden sculptures were experienced, both by their artists through making and by beholders through their devotion.

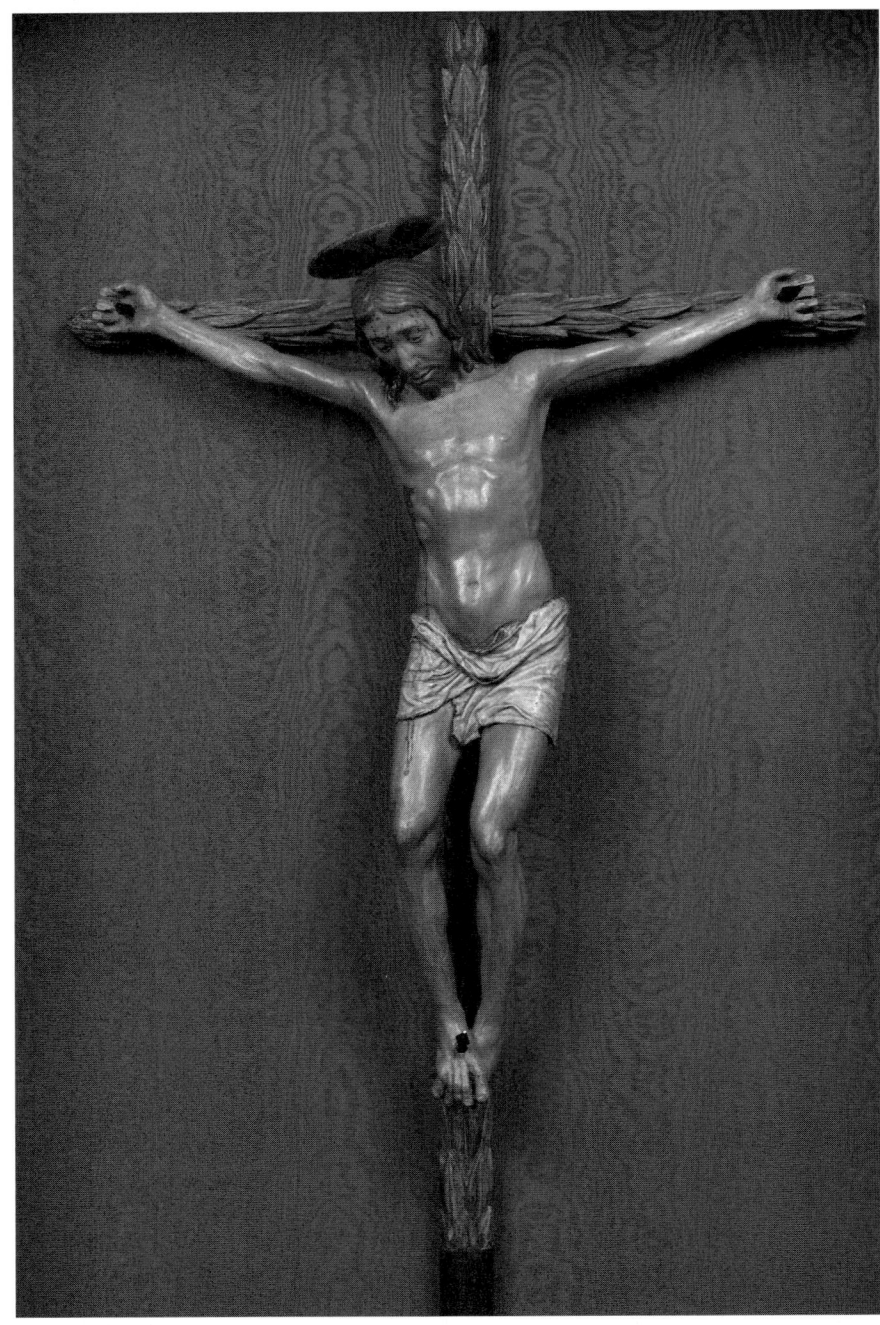

10.4. Giuliano or Benedetto da Maiano, *Crucifix*, c. 1474, Museo d'Arte Sacra, San Gimignano

Notes

1. Michel Pastoureau raised some similar issues in 'Introduction à la symbolique médiévale du bois', in *L'Arbre: Histoire naturelle et symbolique de l'arbre, du bois et du fruit au Moyen Age*. Les Cahiers du Léopard d'or 2 (Paris: Léopard d'or, 1993), pp. 25–40; and *Une histoire symbolique du Moyen Âge occidental* (Paris: Seuil, 2004).
2. Hans Huth, *Kunstler und Werkstatt der Spätgotik* (Darmstadt: Wissenschaftliche Buchges, 1925; repr. 1967), pp. 16, 55; and T. Brachert, 'Die Techniken der polychromierten Holzskulptur: Tl 1', *Maltechnik, Restauro* (1972), pp. 153–78, p. 156.
3. Archivio di Stato Lucca, *Notari* I, n. 228, c. 86 v., Ser Iacopo Turchi, published in Arnold Esch (ed.), *Arte e Pittura nel medioevo Lucchese* (Lucca: Elia Matteoni, 1994), pp. 314–16. 'Gatto' may relate to 'gattice' or 'gattero', terms for white poplar, especially in Tuscany. (Filippo Baldinucci, *Vocabolario toscano dell'arte del Disegno* (Florence: Studio per Edizioni Scelte, 1975), p. 65). Thanks to Giovan Battista Fidanza for this. A 1635 contract for a sculpture of Christ by Augustín Muñoz specified that 'the wood must be cypress', Susan Verdi Webster, *Art and Ritual in Golden-Age Spain: Sevillian Confraternities and the Processional Sculpture of Holy Week* (Princeton, NJ: Princeton University Press, 1998), p. 67. According to Giovan Battista Fidanza ('L'Archivio delle Identificazioni delle Specie Legnose dei Beni Storico-Artistici: per una migliore comprensione della vocazione formale del legno di statue, intaglio e tarsie', in Giovan Battista Fidanza and Nicola Macchioni (eds), *I legni dell'arte: L'Archivio delle Identificazione delle Specie Legnose dei Beni Storico-Artistici* (Fabriano: Fabriano Edizione, 2008), pp. 25–44, esp. 27, 29), wood might be mentioned in a contract if it was rare for the region.
4. Michael Baxandall, *The Limewood Sculptors of Renaissance Germany* (New Haven, CT, and London: Yale University Press, 1980), p. 271.
5. Siena, Op. Duomo, *Entrata e Uscita di Antonio di Jacopo di Dota* (1. maggio 1408–30 aprile, 1409), n. 8, c. 40 (n. 14 of *Memoriali e Bastardelli*), in Peleo Bacci, *Francesco di Valdambrino, emulo del Ghiberti e collaboratore di Jacopo della Quercia* (Siena: Istituto comunale d'arte e di storia, 1936), p. 161, doc. 4.
6. Anne Markham Schulz, *Woodcarving and Woodcarvers in Venice 1350–1550* (Florence: Centro Di, 2011), p. 30 and ns. 79–80.
7. Baxandall, *Limewood Sculptors*, p. 104.
8. Schulz, *Woodcarving*, pp. 30–1 and n. 85.
9. Bodleian Library, MS Auct. F. 5. 23, fol. 160a, quoted in Baxandall, *Limewood Sculptors*, p. 33.
10. Piero de' Crescenzi, *Trattato della agricoltura*, 3 vols (Milan: Dalla Società tipografica de' Classici italiani, 1805), vol. 1, p. 48.
11. Crescenzi, *Trattato della agricoltura*, vol. 2, p. 97.
12. Leon Battista Alberti, *On the Art of Building in Ten Books*, trans. J. Rykwert, N. Leach, and R. Tavernor (Cambridge, MA, and London: MIT Press, 1988), p. 45.
13. Giorgio Vasari, *On Technique, being the introduction to the three arts of design, architecture, sculpture and painting, prefixed to the Lives of the most excellent painters, sculptors and architects*, trans. Louisa S. Maclehouse, ed. G. Baldwin Brown (London: J.M. Dent, 1907), pp. 173–4.
14. Francesco di Giorgio Martini, *Trattati di architettura, ingegneria e arte militare*, ed. C. Maltese, transcription by L. Maltese Degrassi, 2 vols (Milan: Il Polifolo, 1967), vol. 2, p. 322.
15. Baxandall, *Limewood Sculptors*, p. 33; and Giovan Battista Fidanza, 'Caratteristiche tecnologie e formali delle specie legnose: una verifica su statue e intaglio di età moderna', in Giovan Battista Fidanza and Nicola Macchioni (eds), *Statue di Legno: Caratteristiche tecnologiche e formali delle specie legnose* (Rome: Istituto poligrafico e Zecca dello Stato, Libreria dello Stato, 2008), pp. 33–57, esp. 39–44.

16 Nicola Macchioni and Simona Lazzeri, 'L'identificazione delle specie legnose e la loro caratterizzazione tecnologia', in Fidanza and Macchioni (eds), *Statue di Legno*, pp. 9–31, esp. 25.

17 Fidanza, 'Caratteristiche tecnologie e formali delle specie legnose', pp. 36–7.

18 Thanks to Giovan Battista Fidanza for this point.

19 Fidanza, 'Caratteristiche tecnologie e formali delle specie legnose', pp. 44–5.

20 Macchioni, 'L'identificazione delle specie', p. 25. On the qualities of woods, see also the comments by the eighteenth-century French cabinetmaker M. Roubo in his treatise *L'Art du menuisier*, 6 vols (Paris: L.F. Delatour, 1769–75), vol. 1, pp. 23–7.

21 Marco Fioravanti, 'Specie legnose impiegate', in Giovanna Rasario (ed.), *Il Cavaliere da San Cassiano*, exh. cat., Museo Nazionale del Bargello, Florence, 31 March–30 June 1995 (Florence: SPES, 1995), pp. 86–90, esp. 87.

22 However, pine was preferred in the Alpine region. (Giuseppina Perusini, 'Tre sculture lignee molto venerate ma poco conosciute di Cortina d'Ampezzo', in Anna Maria Spiazza and Luca Majoli (eds), *La scultura lignea: Tecniche esecutive, conservazione e restauro*, Atti della giornata di studio, Belluno, 14 January 2005 (Cinisello Balsamo (Milan): Silvana, 2007), pp. 95–116, esp. 98.)

23 Baxandall, *Limewood Sculptures*.

24 See documents concerning wood purchasing by the Florentine *Operai del Duomo*: http://duomo.mpiwg-berlin.mpg.de (accessed on 14 February 2014). Baxandall, *Limewood Sculptors*, pp. 28–9.

25 Lynn F. Jacobs, *Early Netherlandish Carved Altarpieces, 1380–1550: Medieval Tastes and Mass Marketing* (Cambridge: Cambridge University Press, 1998), pp. 1, 175 and 243.

26 Ilene H. Forsyth, *Throne of Wisdom: Wood Sculptures of the Madonna in Romanesque France* (Princeton, NJ: Princeton University Press, 1972), p. 16.

27 Webster, *Art and Ritual*, p. 104.

28 Claudio Bernardi, 'Deposizioni e annunciazioni', in Francesca Flores d'Arcais (ed.), *Il teatro delle statue: Gruppi lignei di Depozione e Annunciazione tra XII e XIII secolo* (Milan: V&P, 2005), pp. 69–85, esp. 83. See E.C. Parker, *The Descent from the Cross: Its Relation to the Extra-Liturgical 'Depositio' Drama* (New York: Garland, 1978); J. Tripps, *Das handelnde Bildwerk in der Gotik* (Berlin: Mann, 1998), pp. 122–41; C. Bernardi, 'La funzione della deposizione di Cristo il venerdi santo nella chiesa francescana di S. Angelo a Milano (secolo XVII)', *Medioevo e Rinascimento* 6:3 n.s. (1992), pp. 235–49; and John Paoletti, 'Wooden sculpture in Italy as sacral presence', *Artibus et historiae* 13:26 (1992), pp. 85–100, esp. 93–4. The classic study of liturgical plays is Karl Young's *The Drama of the Medieval Church*, 2 vols (Oxford: The Clarendon Press, 1933). See also N.C. Brooks, *The Sepulchre of Christ in Art and Liturgy*, University of Illinois Studies in Language and Literature vol. 7, 2 (Urbana: University of Illinois, 1921).

29 Gesine and Johannes Taubert, 'Mittelalterliche Kruzifixe mit schwenkbaren Armen: Ein Beitrag zur Verwendung von Bildwerken in der Liturgie', *Zeitschrift des Deutschen Vereins für Kunstwissenschaft* 23 (1969), pp. 79–121; Johannes Taubert, *Farbige Skulpturen: Bedeutung, Fassung, Restaurierung* (Munich: Callwey, 1978); Ulla Haastrup, 'Medieval props in the liturgical drama', *Hafnia: Copenhagen Papers in the History of Art* 11 (1987), pp. 133–70; Rhinehard Rampold, 'Gotische Kruzifixe mit schwenkbaren Armen: Neuentdeckung in Tirol', *Schler* 73 (1999), pp. 425–36; A. Pacia, *Restauri a Caravaggio: Dipinti e sculture delle chiese di San Giovanni Battista e di San Bernardino* (Bergamo: Lubrina, 2001); M. Burresi (ed.), *Sacre Passioni: Scultura lignea a Pisa dal XII al XV secolo* (Milan: F. Motta, 2000); Giuseppe Capriotti, 'Simulacri dell'invisibile: "Cultura lignea" ed esigenze devozionali nella Camerino del Rinascimento', in Raffaele Casciaro (ed.), *Rinascimento scolpito: Maestri del legno tra Marche e Umbria*, exh. cat., Convento San Domenico, Camerino,

5 May–5 November 2006 (Cinisello Balsamo, Milan: Silvana, 2006), pp. 72–83 esp. 78 and 83, n. 34 and 65.

30 Evelyn Welch, 'The moaning crucifixion: An automata for Francesco Sforza, 1462', in Arnaldo Ganda et al. (eds), *Arte e storia di Lombardia: Scritti in memoria di Grazioso Sironi* (Rome: Società editrice Dante Alighieri, 2006), pp. 55–62, esp. 55–6.

31 Bernardi, 'Deposizioni', p. 82. See M. Senesi, 'Fraternite disciplinate e sacre rappresentazioni a Foligno nel secolo XV', *Bollettino della Deputazione di Storia Patria per l'Umbria* 71 (1974), pp. 193–4.

32 Bernardi, 'Deposizioni', p. 79. See Young, *Drama of the Medieval Church*, vol. 1, p. 164.

33 Cristina Galassi, 'Arte e serialità nella bottega di Nero Alberti a Sansepolcro', in Cristina Galassi (ed.), *Sculture 'da vestire': Nero Alberti da Sansepolcro e la produzione di manichini lignei in una bottega del Cinquecento*, exh. cat., Museo di Santa Croce, Umbertide, 11 June–6 November 2005 (Perugia: Mondadori Electa, 2005), pp. 15–104, esp. 31.

34 Albertus Magnus wrote 'in ligno jacet animalis natura', an attitude inherited from Aristotle. H. Balss, *Albertus Magnus als Biologe* (Stuttgart: Wissenschaftliche Verlagsgesellschaft, 1947), p. 106; and Albertus Magnus, *De vegetabilibus*, ed. E. Meyer and C. Jessen (Berlin: Typis et impensis Georgii Reimeri, 1867), book VII, noted by Pastoureau, 'Introduction à la symbolique médiévale du bois', p. 26.

35 Theophrastus, *Enquiry into Plants*, trans. Arthur Hort, 2 vols (Cambridge, MA: Harvard University Press, 1999), vol. 1, pp. 16–23.

36 Theophrastus, *Enquiry into Plants*, pp. 434–5.

37 'Et sucus pomiferum arborum . . . comparator sanguine hominis.' Hildegard von Bingen, *Physica: Liber subtilitatum diversarum naturarum creaturarum. Textkritische Ausgabe*, ed. Reiner Hildebrandt and Thomas Gloning (Berlin and New York: De Gruyter, 2010), vol. 1, p. 49.

38 Pastoureau, *Une histoire symbolique*, p. 82. See Albertus Magnus, *De animalibus*, ed. H. Stadler (Munster: Aschendorff, 1913), vol. 22: pp. 65–6; and vol. 36: p. 2.

39 Crescenzi, *Trattato*, vol. 1, p. 66.

40 Crescenzi, *Trattato*, vol. 1, p. 92.

41 Leonardo da Vinci, *The Manuscripts of Leonardo da Vinci in the Institut de France*, trans. John Venerella, Manuscript G (Milan: Ente Raccolta Vinciana, 2002), fol. 17r, [I], p. 27; Leonardo da Vinci, Royal Library, Windsor 19074 v; Leonardo da Vinci, *Treatise on Painting* [*Codex Urbinas Latinus 1270*], trans. A. Philip McMahon (Princeton, NJ: Princeton University Press, 1956), 2:6, fol. 250r, 883, noted by William A. Emboden, *Leonardo da Vinci on Plants and Gardens* (Portland, OR: Dioscorides Press, 1987), pp. 110, 169, and 171.

42 See, for instance, Crescenzi, *Trattato*, vol. 1, p. 72; and Vincent de Beauvais, *Speculum naturale* (Douai: 1624), book VII, chapters 50–1, col. 456–7, the latter cited by Pastoureau, *Une histoire symbolique*, p. 82.

43 See, for instance, Claudia D'Alberto, 'Il crocifisso parlante di Santa Brigida di Svezia nella Basilica di San Paolo fuori le mura e i crocifissi replicati, copiati e riprodotti a Roma al tempo del Papato avignonese', *Studi Medievali e Moderni* 1–2 (2011), pp. 229–55; Katherine Allen Smith, 'Bodies of unsurpassed beauty: "living" images of the Virgin in the high Middle Ages', *Viator* 37 (2006), pp. 167–87, esp. 168 and note 6; and Jacqueline E. Jung, 'The tactile and the visionary: Notes on the place of sculpture in the medieval religious imagination', in Colum Hourihane (ed.), *Looking Beyond: Visions, Dreams, and Insights in Medieval Art and History* (Princeton, NJ: Index of Christian Art, Princeton University; University Park, PA: Penn State University Press, 2010), pp. 203–40, esp. 233.

44 One might object that in this chapter I am collapsing together distinct discourses in which the term 'living' participates: specifically the physiological understanding of wood as humoral and living, which is different from the way in which sculptures were believed to have the capacity to come alive. This deserves further investigation. However, as evidence

of the potential connection between these different realms there are the many examples of sculptures with animated physiologies, whose sweat and blood were an attempt to make them impressively lifelike. My thanks to one of the volume's anonymous reviewers for highlighting this problem for me.

45 Alberti, *On the Art of Building*, pp. 40–1.

46 Alberti, *On the Art of Building*, pp. 39–40.

47 Zahira Véliz, 'Wooden panels and their preparation for painting from the Middle Ages to the seventeenth century in Spain', in K. Dardes and A. Rothe (eds), *The Structural Conservation of Panel Paintings* (Proceedings of a symposium at the J. Paul Getty Museum, 24–28 April 1995; Los Angeles: The Getty Conservation Institute, 1998), pp. 136–48, esp. 137. See Esteban García Chico, *Documentos para el studio del arte en Castilla*, 3 vols (Valladolid: Universidad de Valladolid, 1946), vol. 3, p. 160.

48 Michael Baxandall, 'The perception of Riemenschneider', in *Tilman Riemenschneider: Master Sculptor of the Late Middle Ages*, exh. cat., National Gallery of Art, Washington, DC, 3 October 1999–9 January 2000; and The Metropolitan Museum of Art, New York, 7 February–14 May 2000 (New Haven, CT, and London: Yale University Press, 1999), pp. 83–98, esp. 95ff. (including note 5). For an unusual case, see Dieter Eckstein, 'Wood science and art history: Interdisciplinary research illustrated from a dendrochronological point of view', in Carl Van de Velde, Hans Beeckman, Joris Van Acker, and Frans Verhaeghe (eds), *Constructing Wooden Images: Proceedings of the Symposium on the Organization of Labour and Working Practices of Late Gothic Carved Altarpieces in the Low Countries, Brussels* (Brussels: VUB, 2005), pp. 19–26.

49 F.W. Jane, *The Structure of Wood* (London: Adam & Charles Black, 1956; rev. ed. 1970); and R. Bruce Hoadley, *Understanding Wood: A Craftsman's Guide to Wood Technology* (Newtown, CT: The Taunton Press, 2000).

50 Baxandall, *Limewood Sculptors*, pp. 36–8.

51 Exceptions are Donatello's *Crucifix* (Basilica del Santo, Padua) and Niccolò Baroncelli's *Crucifix with Virgin, Sts John, George and Maurelius* (1456) for Ferrara Cathedral, both in bronze. Paoletti, 'Wooden sculpture', pp. 88 and 100, note 56.

52 Moshé Lazar, 'Le Légende de "l'arbre de paradis" ou "bois de la croix"', *Zeitschrift für romanische Philologie* 76 (1960), pp. 34–63. On the wood of the cross see Mirella Levi d'Ancona, *The Garden of the Renaissance: botanical symbolism in Italian Painting* (Florence: Leo S. Olschki, 1977), pp. 85, 135–6, 142, 184, 197, 233, 250, 263, 282, 304, 371, 373, 387.

53 *Martin Luther und die Reformation: Ausstellung zum 500. Geburtstag Martin Luthers*, exh. cat., Nuremberg, 1983 (Frankfurt am Main: Insel Verlag, 1983), no. 470, cited by Christopher Wood, *Albrecht Altdorfer and the Origins of Landscape* (Chicago: University of Chicago Press, 1993), p. 186.

54 R. Hatfield, 'The tree of life and the holy cross: Franciscan spirituality in the Trecento and the Quattrocento', in T. Verdon and J. Henderson (eds), *Christianity and the Renaissance: Image and Religious Imagination in the Quattrocento* (Syracuse, NY: Syracuse University Press, 1990), pp. 132–60, esp. 141–2.

55 Corine Schleif, 'Nicodemus and sculptors: Self-reflexivity in works by Adam Kraft and Tilman Riemenschneider', *The Art Bulletin* 75:4 (December 1993), pp. 599–626, esp. 607–9.

56 Antonio Palomino, *Museo pictórico y escala óptica*, 3 vols (Madrid: 1724); Antonio Palomino, *Lives of the Eminent Spanish Painters and Sculptors*, trans. Nina Ayala Mallory, 3 vols (Cambridge and New York: Cambridge University Press, 1987), vol. 3, p. 70, cited by Gridley McKim-Smith, 'Spanish polychrome sculpture and its critical misfortunes', in Suzanne L. Stratton (ed.), *Spanish Polychrome Sculpture, 1500–1800, in United States Collections*, exh. cat., The Spanish Institute, New York, NY, 4 November 1993–4 January 1994; Meadows

Museum, Southern Methodist University, Dallas, TX, 28 January–26 June 1994; Los Angeles County Museum of Art, Los Angeles, CA, 21 April–26 June 1994 (New York: Spanish Institute, 1993), pp. 13–32, esp. 23.

57 Alessandro Bagnoli, 'Lando di Pietro, *Crocifisso*', in *Scultura dipinta: Maestri di legname e pittori a Siena 1250–1450*, exh. cat., Pinacoteca Nazionale, Siena, 16 July–31 December 1987 (Florence: Centro Di, 1987), pp. 66–7, cat. 12; and Catherine King, 'Effigies: Human and divine', in Diana Norman (ed.), *Siena, Florence and Padua: Art, Society and Religion 1280–1400*, 2 vols (New Haven, CT: Yale University Press in association with the Open University, 1995), vol. 2, pp. 105–27, esp. 126–7.

58 See, for instance: Luca Uzielli, Marco Fioravanti, Ottaviano Allegretti, Riccardo Ballerini, Marino Piva and Renzo Ricci, 'Il nuovo ancoraggio per il crocifisso ligneo di Andrea Orcagna nella chiesa di San Carlo a Firenze', in Laura Sperenza (ed.), *La scultura lignea policroma: Ricerche e modelli operative di restauro* (Florence: Centro Di, 2007), pp. 71–88, esp. 71; Giancarlo Gentilini (ed.), *Proposta per Michelangelo giovane: Un Crocifisso in legno di tiglio*, exh. cat., Museo Horne, Florence, 8 May–4 September 2004 (Turin: U. Allemandi, 2004); Maria Donata Mazzoni, Rosanna Caterina Proto Pisani, and Laura Speranza, 'Il Crocifisso di Badia a Passignano: Considerazioni e problematiche conservative', in Sperenza (ed.), *La scultura lignea policroma*, pp. 115–22; Rita Bernini and Milena Dean, 'Il Maestro dei crocifisso bellunesi: Considerazioni in margine a due recuperi', in Spiazza and Majoli (eds), *La scultura lignea*, pp. 187–206, esp. 193; Barbara Schleicher, 'The Restoration', in Michele Maccherini (ed.), *Benedetto da Maiano a San Gimignano: La riscoperta di un crocifisso dimenticato*, exh. cat., Galleria d'arte moderna e contemporanea, San Gimignano, 21 March–21 June 2009 (San Gimignano: Comune di San Gimignano, 2009), pp. 61–75, esp. 62–3; Cristina Galassi, 'Arte e serialità', pp. 81–4; Achille Pellerano, Fabrizio Vona, Francesca Dentamaro, and Maria Marmontelli (eds), *Sculture lignee e dipinti su tavola in Puglia: Cinque casi di studio dalla diagonistica al restauro* (Foggia: C. Grenzi, 2008), p. 137; Raffaele Casciaro (ed.), *La scultura lignea lombarda del Rinascimento* (Milan: Skira, 2000), cat. 113, p. 323. According to Tanya Ann Jung ('The phenomenal lives of movable Christ sculptures' (PhD dissertation, University of Maryland, 2006), p. 21), most sculptures of Christ with movable limbs from southern Germany were made from limewood.

59 See, for example: Gianluigi Canocchi, Marco Ciatti, and Antonello Pandolfo, 'La scultura dipinta: Nota su alcuni restauri', in Sperenza (ed.), *La scultura lignea policroma*, pp. 17–34, esp. 20; Massimo Vezzosi (ed.), *Quattro crocifissi lignei restaurati*, exh. cat., Greve in Chianti, Chiesa Propositurale di Santa Croce, 12 September 1998 (Florence: Edizioni Polistampa, 1998); and Casciaro (ed.), *La scultura lignea lombarda*, cat. 114, p. 324.

60 Ovid, *Metamorphoses*, trans. F.J. Miller (Cambridge, MA: Harvard University Press, 1951), vol. 2, pp. 340–66, noted by Levi d'Ancona, *Garden of the Renaissance*, p. 319.

61 See, for instance: Barbara Schleicher, 'Relazione di restauro', in *Il Crocifisso di Camaggiore ritrovato*, exh. cat. ex-church of San Francesco, Imola (Imola: La Mandragora, 2000), pp. 57–63, esp. 57; Luca Bonetti, 'Relazione sul restauro del Crocifisso ligneo di Sant'Andrea in Pistoia', in Max Seidel, *La Scultura Lignea di Giovanni Pisano* (Florence: Edam, 1971): pp. 23–6, esp. 23; Giuseppe Capriotti, 'Scultore tedeschizante, *Crocifisso della beata Battista*', and 'Bottega di Domenico Indivini (Sebastiano d'Appennino?), *Crocifisso*'; Francesca Coltrinari, 'Sebastiano di Giovanni d'Appennino, *Crocifisso*', and 'Sebastiano di Giovanni d'Appennino, *Crocifisso*', in Casciaro (ed.), *Rinascimento scolpito*, pp. 162–53 and 166–7, esp. 162 and 166; and pp. 220–1 and 222–3, esp. 220 and 222; Galassi, 'Arte e serialità', p. 85; Peter Stiberc, '45. Crocifisso', in Clara Baracchini (ed.), *Scultura lignea: Lucca 1200–1425*, 2 vols, exh. cat. Museo nazionale di Palazzo Mansi and the Museo nazionale di Villa Guinigi, 16 December 1995–30 June 1996 (Florence: SPES, 1995), vol. 2, p. 106; Veronica Hartam, '49. Crocifisso', in Baracchini, *Scultura lignea* p. 117; and Alessandro Bagnoli, 'Marco Romano e collaborator, "8. Crocifisso"', in Alessandro Bagnoli (ed.), *Marco Romano e il contesto artistico Senese fra la fine del Duecento e gli inizi del Trecento*, exh. cat.,

Museo civico archeologico e della Collegiata, Casole d'Elsa, 27 March–3 October, 2010 (Cinisello Balsalmo: Silvana, 2010), pp. 182–5, esp. 182.

62 See Peter Stiberc, 'La scultura lignea policroma del Rinascimento fiorentino: Osservazioni sulla tecnica scultorea', in Sperenza (ed.), *La scultura lignea policroma*, pp. 195–212, esp. 205–6; Fidanza, 'Caratteristiche tecnologie e formali delle specie legnose', p. 45; M.G. Ciardi Dupré Dal Poggetto (ed.), *La bottega di Giuliano e Benedetto da Maiano nel Rinascimento fiorentino* (Florence: Octavo, 1994); and Deborah Strom, 'Studies in Quattrocento Tuscan wooden sculpture' (PhD dissertation, Princeton University, 1979), pp. 128 and 131.

63 Augustine's theological writings, for instance, were frequently copied and published during the early modern period and his ideas were accessible to a wide audience, including artists. Meredith Gill, *Augustine in the Italian Renaissance: Art and Philosophy from Petrarch to Michelangelo* (Cambridge: Cambridge University Press, 2005), pp. 16–26.

64 *Analecta Hymnica Medii Aevi*, 55 vols (Leipzig, 1886–1922), vol. 54, p. 154, no. 100, strophe 19, noted by d'Ancona, *Garden of the Renaissance*, pp. 245–8.

65 Saint Ambrose, *Hexaemeron*, in J.P. Migne (ed.), *Patrologiae cursus completus: Series Latina* (Paris: Migne, 1844–64), vol. 14, p. 179, noted by d'Ancona, *Garden of the Renaissance*, pp. 93–5.

66 Augustine in *Patrologia Latina*, 211, p. 707; Pliny, *Naturalis historia* vol. 15, p. 92; vol. 17, p. 147; and Andrea Alciati, *Emblemata*, noted by Lucia Impelluso, *Nature and Its Symbols*, trans. Stephen Sartarelli (Los Angeles: J. Paul Getty Museum, 2004), pp. 172 and 187.

67 Alciati, *Emblemata*, p. 154.

68 Donatello's *Mary Magdalen* (1457, Museo dell'Opera del Duomo, Florence) was carved from poplar. (Stiberc, 'La scultura lignea policroma del Rinascimento fiorentino', pp. 205–6). Unfortunately the wood for the other Tuscan examples (Santa Maria Maddalena, Pescia; Collegiata Museum, Empoli; Casa di Vasari, Arezzo; and a statue by Brunelleschi originally in Santo Spirito, destroyed by fire in 1471) have not been identified. (Strom, 'Studies in Quattrocento Tuscan wooden sculpture', pp. 26 and 111–13). Another example, not mentioned by Strom, attributed to Francesco da Sangallo, is at Santo Stefano al Ponte, Florence (Alan Phipps Darr and Rona Roisman, 'Francesco da Sangallo: A rediscovered early Donatellesque "Magdalen" and two Wills from 1574 and 1576', *The Burlington Magazine* 129: 1017 (December 1987), pp. 784–93).

69 Sirio Lupi, Mario Venturi and Silvano Vestri, 'Maddalena', *OPD Restauro* 2 (1990), pp. 155–60, pp. 155–6.

70 Petrus Berchorius, *Prima pars dictionarii (repertorium morale)*, 3 vols (Nuremberg: Anton Koberger, 1499), vol. 1, p. 102, noted by d'Ancona, *Garden of the Renaissance*, p. 408.

71 Hrabanus Maurus, *De universo*, in *Patrologia Latina*, 111, p. 519, noted by d'Ancona, *Garden of the Renaissance*, p. 408.

72 Richard of Saint Laurent compared the willow to the Virgin's chastity (Anthony S. Mercatante, *The Magic Garden: The Myth and Folklore of Flowers, Plants, Trees, and Herbs* (New York: Harper and Row, 1976), p. 69).

73 Psalm 137:1–2, noted by d'Ancona, *Garden of the Renaissance*, pp. 407–8.

74 Saint Melito, *Clavis*, in Jean-Baptiste Pitra, *Spicilegium solesmense*, 4 vols (Paris: F. Didot fratres, 1852), vol. 2, p. 365, noted by d'Ancona, *Garden of the Renaissance*, pp. 407–8.

75 Pliny the Elder, *Naturalis historia*, vol. 15, pp. 53–6, noted by Impelluso, *Nature and Its Symbols*, p. 154.

76 Matteo Mazzalupi, 'Lucantonio di Giovanni Barberetti, *San Rocco*', in Casciaro (ed.), *Rinascimento scolpito*, pp. 196–9, esp. 196; Tommaso Mozzati, '*San Rocco*', Cristina Galassi, '*San Rocco*, 1528', Fabio Marcelli, '*San Rocco*, 1550 circa', and Giovan Battista Fidanza, 'Intaglio e plastica: Considerazioni formali e tecniche su alcune statue della bottega in Nero Alberti',

in Galassi (ed.), *Sculture 'da vestire'*, pp. 149–50, 157–8, 159, and 109–14; and Casciaro, *La scultura lignea lombarda*, cat. 98, p. 313.

77 Benedetta Montevecchi, 'Il restauro di alcune sculture lignee cinquecentesche', in Giovan Battista Fidanza (ed.), *Scultura e arredo in legno fra Marche e Umbria: Atti del primo Convegno, Pergola 24/25 October, 1997* (Perugia: Quattroemme, 1999), pp. 235–40, esp. 236; and Baxandall, *Limewood Sculptors*, p. 273.

78 Ovid *Metamorphoses*, vol. 2, pp. 340–66; Pliny the Elder, *Naturalis historia*, vol. 14, p. 10; and vol. 35, p. 13. This has been noted by Impelluso, *Nature and Its Symbols*, p. 59.

79 Thomas the Cistercian, *In Cantica Canticorum . . . Elucidatio*, in *Patrologia Latina*, 206, 205, noted by d'Ancona, *The Garden of the Renaissance*, p. 136.

80 'Fuit lignum quod plantatur locis in humentibus, Rochus sacer, dum ornatur plurimis virtutibus' and 'hic quae stulto placet mundo, vanitatem respuit et se fructu perfecundo servum cunctis obtulit.' Bollandisti, *Acta Sanctorum* (1737), vol. 3, pp. 389–90, noted by B. Bertoli, *Arte e teologia nel culto di San Rocco*, Quaderni della Scuola Grande Arciconfraternita di San Rocco, 3 (Venice: Grafiche Veneziane, 1996), pp. 32–3, quoted by Galassi, 'Arte e serialità', p. 35. Thanks to Alex Jones for the translation.

81 Bertoli, *Arte e teologia nel culto di San Rocco*, p. 31; and Tommaso Mozzati, '4. San Rocco, 1527–1528', in Galassi (ed.), *Sculture 'da vestire'*, p. 155.

82 Fabio Marcelli, '6. San Rocco, 1550 circa' in Galassi (ed.), *Sculture 'da vestire'*, p. 159; and Galassi, 'Arte e serialità', pp. 31–4.

83 Cited in Louise Marshall, 'Manipulating the sacred: Image and plague in Renaissance Italy', *Renaissance Quarterly* 47:3 (Autumn, 1994), pp. 485–532, p. 496.

84 Marshall, 'Manipulating the sacred'.

85 A. da Cipressa, *Discorso storico intorno alla prodigiosa effigie di Gesù Bambino che si venera nella chiesa di S. Maria in Aracoeli* (Rome: Tipografia Monaldi, 1861).

86 Michele Bacci, 'Le sculture lignee nel folklore religioso: Alcune considerazioni', in Baracchini (ed.), *Scultura lignea*, vol. 1, pp. 31–42, esp. 34; and Michele Bacci, 'San Cristoforo', in Baracchini (ed.), *Scultura lignea*, vol. 1, p. 47.

87 Ilaria Bischi Ruspoli and Michele Maccherini, 'Giuliano o Benedetto da Maiano: Crocifisso (1474 circa)', in Maccherini (ed.), *Benedetto da Maiano*, pp. 105–9, esp. 106–7. See Enrico Castaldi, 'Artefici che lavorarono nella insigne collegiate ai tempi dell'operario Onofrio di Pietro', in Castaldi and Guido Traversari, *Ricordi da vecchie carte sangimignanesi* (Poggibonsi: Cappelli, 1909), pp. 39–50.

88 Guillame de Deguileville, *Le Pèlegrinage de l'âme* . . . , ed. J.J. Stürzinger (London: The Roxburgh Club, 1895), lines 5674–84, 5809–24. The same idea had been expressed earlier by Saint Ambrose (*Expositio Evangelii Secundum Lucam*, in *Patrologia Latina*, 15, p. 1614), noted by d'Ancona, *The Garden of the Renaissance*, p. 386.

89 This is one of the *Miracles de Nostre Dame* compiled by thirteenth-century Benedictine abbot Gautier de Coincy, cited by Smith, 'Bodies of unsurpassed beauty', p. 168.

90 Smith, 'Bodies of unsurpassed beauty', pp. 176–8.

91 Biblioteca Nacional de España, Madrid (Mss 1713, fols. 283 and 290), trans. Xavier Bray, *The Sacred Made Real: Spanish Painting and Sculpture 1600–1700*, exh. cat. National Gallery, London, 21 October 2009–24 January 2010; and National Gallery of Art, Washington, DC, 28 February–31 May 2010 (London: National Gallery Company Limited, 2009), p. 194.

92 See, for instance, Antonio P. Torresi (ed.), *Il ricettario Bardi: cosmesi e tecnica artistica nella Firenze medicea* (Ferrara: Liberty House, c. 1994). Thanks to Montserrat Cabré for this reference.

93 Xavier Bray, 'The sacred made real: Spanish painting and sculpture 1600–1700', in Bray, *Sacred Made Real*, pp. 15–43, esp. p. 19.

11 ✧ *Arti povere*, 1300–1650

Michael Cole

IN HIS BOOK *Tintoretto: Tradition and Identity*, Tom Nichols drew out connections between the Venetian artist's pictorial manner and the economics of his practice. As contemporary writers regularly noted, Tintoretto worked unusually quickly. His paintings, to quote Pietro Aretino, 'were finished in less time than normally might have been devoted to the mere consideration of the subject'.[1] And by his late career, Tintoretto's employers at San Rocco were taking advantage of that, contractually requiring the artist to produce large amounts of work in short order. This commitment, in turn, encouraged Tintoretto to break from traditional techniques. He rejected, for example, the time-consuming gesso preparations other artists used and began to paint directly on a dark ground.[2] In a painting like the *Baptism of Christ* (Figure 11.1), from the Sala Superiore, the gloom has the same motivation as the quick handling.

By delivering more painted canvas in less time, Tintoretto could charge less for individual works than his contemporaries did. Using inexpensive pigments – Nichols speculates that Tintoretto procured his red lakes from the local dying industry, in which his family worked – cheapened his production still further.[3] Such cost-cutting might have helped any artist anywhere win commissions, but the look that resulted from Tintoretto's approach also lent itself particularly well to the nature of his assignments at San Rocco, where he was painting for a confraternity dedicated to the care of the poor, and where many of the scenes he depicted take place in a dilapidated world. As Nichols sees it, however, Tintoretto's manner was not just an index of a competitive market or pictorial function but also a distinctive, personal response to a broader tradition. When Tintoretto nodded to Michelangelo's *Day* in his depictions of the miracles of Saints Augustine and Roch, this humbled a Roman (we might rather say 'Medicean') sort of magnificence.[4] When Tintoretto rejected colour in favour of light–dark drama, he cast himself

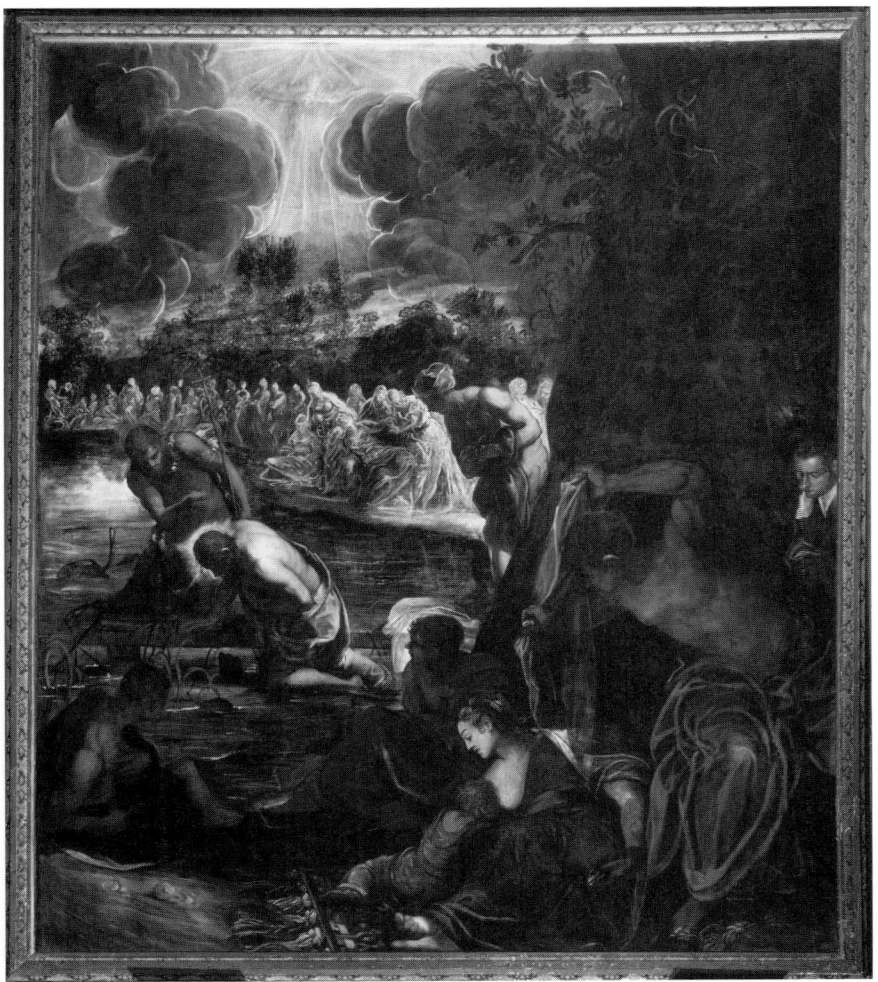

11.1. Tintoretto, *Baptism of Christ*, 1579–81, oil on canvas, Sala Superiore, Scuola Grande di San Rocco, Venice

as a strong local alternative to the greatest living Venetian painter, Titian. Titian's painting, Nichols suggests, foregrounded his medium, while 'Tintoretto's technique . . . [acted] at once to dematerialize and to spiritualize the painted surface'.[5]

Nichols's book represents not only an original reading of Tintoretto but also one of the most perceptive recent reflections on the materiality of Renaissance painting. At the same time, casting the topic as a study of Tintoretto's 'identity' and approaching the question of tradition as a matter of 'self-fashioning' or individual pictorial style might lead us to miss one larger historical frame.

Consider, for comparison, this excerpt from a 2008 *New Yorker* interview with the video artist Paul Chan. Chan has just been talking about his decision to animate Caravaggio's *Basket of Fruit:* he was attracted, he explains, to the 'gravity' of the original, and he wanted to invert that, causing individual pieces of fruit to float upwards. But then Chan remarks on how his revision of Caravaggio generated dissatisfaction with the direction his work was going:

> It still has the lines and shapes and colours of 'My birds' [an earlier video] and you're still looking at it through the camera obscura of the past. I realized that what I had to do was impoverish the image. I had to give up all the things that I thought were my strengths – the vibrant colour, the brutal clarity of line that comes from digital animations, the sort of depth I got by almost putting the foreground and the background together. If you're willing to impoverish, you can go on to something else.[6]

What Chan is describing here is a change in style – a new avoidance of bright colour and linear clarity – which he casts as a kind of progress. More strikingly, he presents both the change and the forward movement in terms of an 'impoverishment'. Chan shares something with Tintoretto, but it is not a conception of self or even a style so much as a *strategy*: 'If you're willing to impoverish, you can go on to something else.'

It is useful to evaluate Nichols's take on Tintoretto with Chan in mind not only because the comparison shows the extent to which Tintoretto's four-hundred-year-old concerns are still with us but also because Chan himself demonstrates a historical sensibility, having arrived at his interest in 'impoverishing' his video work in the course of studying Caravaggio. These artists' respective conjunctions of progressive art and impoverishment do not seem to point to a peculiarly modern idea, or even quite to an enduring Renaissance legacy. Rather, they represent iterations of or variations on a more broadly shared intuition.

Impoverishment themes are bound up with the very idea of the Renaissance. The letter from Giovambattista Adriani with which Vasari prefaced his 1568 edition of the *Lives* imagined a time 'when our citizens were rough and our commonwealth poor, where they had many images of those gods that they adored, made of terra cotta, and the vases used in the sacrifices made at those images were of clay. And we believe that the poverty and simplicity of those centuries pleased the Gods much more than the gold and silver that followed.'[7]

The association between antiquity and poverty here is twofold. To remodel the present on an ancient past was to abandon a more recent decadence. Yet it was also to return to an ancient idea, a classical trope.

Here is the ancient Roman historian Pliny, writing on the Greeks who preceded his own people:

> It was with four colours only that Apelles, Echion, Melanthius, and Nicomachus, those most illustrious painters, executed their immortal works; melinum for the white, Attic sil for the yellow, Pontic sinopis for the red, and atramentum for the black; and yet a single picture of theirs has sold before now for the treasures of whole cities. But at the present day, when purple is employed even for colouring walls, and when India sends to us the slime of her rivers and the corrupt blood of her dragons and her elephants, there is no such thing as a picture of high quality produced. Everything, in fact, was superior at a time when the resources of art were so much fewer than they now are.[8]

If Adriani's evocation of an earlier moment of impoverishment underwrote a new modern aesthetic, it did so by repeating a Plinian scheme.

Jan Białostocki identified numerous examples of the medieval afterlife of this idea in his classic essay 'Ars auro prior'. He took his title phrase from a twelfth-century reformulation of what he considered to be an Ovidian *topos* – an important early text for Białostocki was Ovid's description of the Palace of the Sun at the beginning of Book 2 of the *Metamorphoses* – and he focused especially on the conviction numerous later theologians articulated that one could acknowledge and even expect material preciousness in a sacred object while also admiring a facture that was at odds with this. Thus he pointed to the rapture medieval viewers described experiencing when they stood in the presence of mosaics like those in Santa Maria dell'Ammiraglio in Palermo, while also citing Abbot Suger to the effect that, before church decorations, 'the onlooker should wonder not at the expense and not at the gold, but at the workmanship, the "art"'.[9] By no later than the twelfth century, Białostocki believed, viewers had arrived at a twofold way of seeing, one that provided the basis for later outright rejections of material splendour.

For the post-medieval Italian tradition, the monument that served as the real touchstone for tensions of this sort was the Franciscan mother church at Assisi. Early modern artists would regularly look back to the thirteenth- and fourteenth-century frescoes there, or at least the idea they embodied: Nichols, for example, characterizes Tintoretto's San Rocco paintings at one point as an instance of 'Franciscan naturalism', and a painting of Saint Francis counts among Caravaggio's first religious works. As Donal Cooper and Janet Robson have recently underscored, here, too, we have documented responses to artistic patronage that make the question of luxury and poverty a central theme. Especially telling are the writings of Ubertino da Casale, an early fourteenth-century spokesman

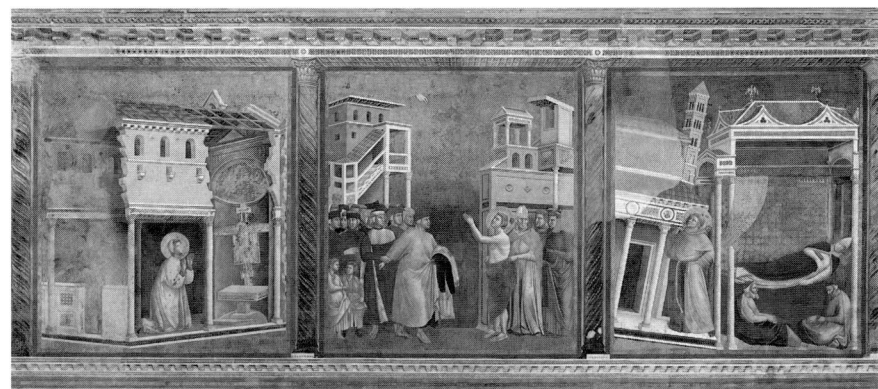

11.2. Giotto, *Miracle of the Crucifix*, fresco, Upper Church, San Francesco, Assisi

for a breakaway faction that condemned the laxity of conventual Franciscans and regarded their architecture and its decoration as a tell-tale sign of this. Members of the order, Ubertino reminded his readers, were supposed to live by a vow of poverty, yet the friars at Assisi not only accepted offerings from the laity but also used these to construct 'sumptuous, superfluous and richly decorated' buildings.[10]

Ubertino's target included the Upper Church, but do the murals there make or undermine his point? One (Figure 11.2) shows Francis praying in the decrepit church of San Damiano before a crucifix that spoke to him, saying 'Francis, go and restore my house, which is in danger of collapsing'.[11] Francis would subsequently set out to restore San Damiano itself, only then to realize that God in fact meant for him to repair the institution of the Church, not one of its buildings. Accenting the deteriorating fabric of a physical structure, the fresco foreshadows Francis's misconstruing of God's own instructions, and other paintings in the same cycle underscore the saint's ultimate, exemplary self-abnegation. Adjacent to the San Damiano scene is the episode in which Francis's father hauls him before the bishop and accuses him of giving away the family possessions; Francis, in response, hands his father the clothes off his back. In another image (Figure 11.3), Francis preaches before Honorius III, and the painter emphasizes the difference between Francis's simple habit and the fine textiles that cover every surface of the Pope's chamber. Are these frescoes to be taken as virtual tapestries, comparable in kind to those that cover the depicted room's walls, or does the fact that they in fact consist of nothing more than cheap paint make them more like Francis himself, clothed in coarse fabric as he delivers his message?[12]

In 1309, Pope Clement V had Bonagrazia of Bergamo and Raymond of Fronsac draft a reply to Ubertino's criticisms. Their tract took as its

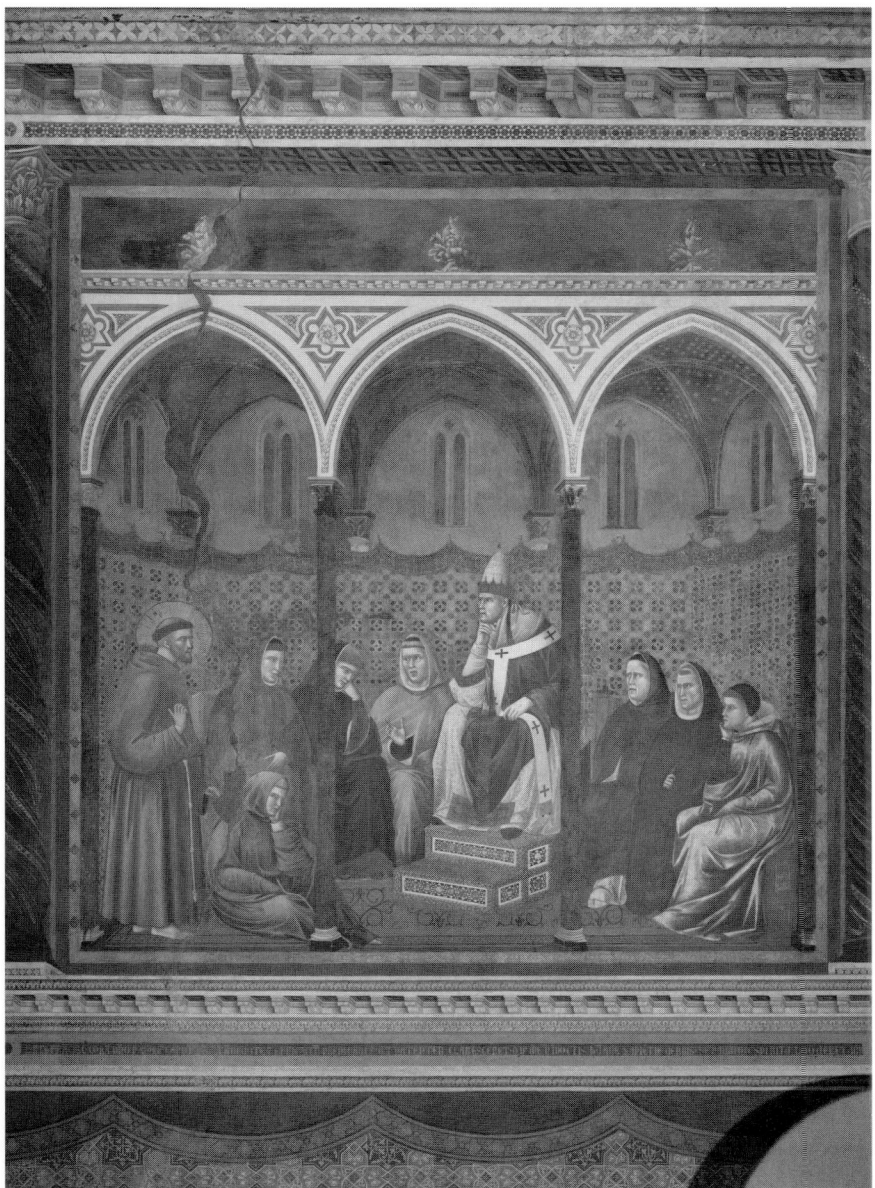

11.3. Giotto, *Christ Preaching before Honorius III*, Upper Church, San Francesco, Assisi

point of departure an earlier bull by the Franciscan Pope Nicholas IV, one that explicitly directed the use of alms to 'conserve, repair, build, modify, enlarge, furnish and decorate' the Assisi basilica.[13] This reply, in turn, must form part of the background for the paintings added to the crossing of San Francesco a few years later. In one spandrel (Figure 11.4),

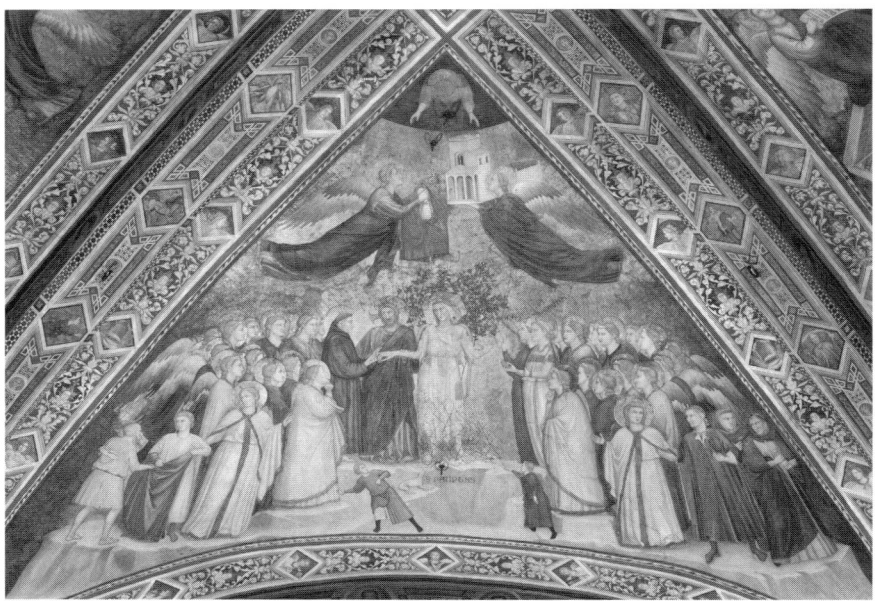

11.4. *Allegory of Poverty*, c. 1330, Lower Church, San Francesco, Assisi

Christ officiates at a wedding between Saint Francis and a personification of Poverty, whose bridal gown is sewn from rags, and at whom children derisively throw rocks rather than rice. The fresco reasserts the fundamental commitments that Ubertino's Spiritualist followers had accused the order of forgetting, even while it flouts the central point these opponents made: by the standards of anything in the basilica dating to before 1310, this is a 'rich' thing, arraying its protagonists against a sky of gold. The painting, with its promotion of Franciscan poverty, would seem self-contradictory, even hypocritical, were it not for the acts that take place at its margins. At bottom left, a young man imitates one of Francis's own most celebrated deeds and gives his cloak to a beggar. Above, God receives a similar, perhaps identical, cloak in offering. Gestures to the poor, the painting suggests, are gestures to God. Yet more remarkable is the motif with which the angelic cloak-bearer is paired – the elevation of a complete church. The reference, in this case, must be to the basilica itself, or rather to its decoration; the painting, like others in the church, implies a connection between human dress and the art that covers church walls. But it also equates the prospect of impoverishing oneself to help the poor – giving away enough that one ends up in a Franciscan habit or in Poverty's rags – with that of *art patronage*, the sponsorship of churches and their decoration. Suddenly, the painting's expense looks like evidence of an especially generous donation, the patron's possibility of imitating Francis in a way befitting his own station.

The early Franciscan paradigm provides terms that help make sense of a longer tradition. There is, to begin, the putative author of the hagiographic cycle in Assisi's Upper Church: Giotto. Lorenzo Ghiberti's *Commentaries* introduced an episode that would appear repeatedly in the later biographies when he wrote that Cimabue discovered the boy 'seated on the ground, drawing on the slab of rock'. He asked Giotto's father, 'who was very poor', to place the boy in his care, and Giotto then proceeded to lead a revolution against the 'Greek style' that Cimabue represented. What facilitated Giotto and his disciples as they 'brought about natural art' in Assisi and elsewhere was the fact that Giotto himself came from the humblest of origins, and learned to draw by using simple materials.[14] Vasari's later Giotto biography goes so far as to locate the painter's most ground-breaking displays of artfulness in his renderings of the poor: 'The foreshortenings, next, that are seen in another picture among a quantity of beggars that he portrayed, are very worthy of praise and should be held in great price among craftsmen, because from them there came the first beginning and method of making them, not to mention that it cannot be said that they are not passing good for early work.'[15]

Yet it was not just the condition of the painter that mattered for the heirs of the Assisi models but also the patronage debate. William Hood has noted that when Fra Angelico painted the *Annunciation* in one of the cloister cells at San Marco in Florence, he rendered the Virgin with the grey contour line and red wash modelling that artists typically used when preparing to apply lapis lazuli, then left the figure in this unclothed state. Hood goes on to note the absence of blue throughout the cells, 'a concession to the [Order's] rule of poverty'.[16] In this case, the site was an Observant Dominican rather than a Franciscan house, but the self-consciousness about avoiding luxuries in a mendicant context responds to scepticism in the vein of Ubertino da Casale's critiques. Or consider another Franciscan painting, Michele Giambono's c. 1430 *Man of Sorrows* in the Metropolitan Museum (Figure 11.5). Behind the head of Christ is a large gold halo with punchwork and etched ornaments; both are positioned before a cross which stands against a backdrop decorated with gilding in a manner that evokes a costly tapestry, and the artist has used additional gold to render the embroidered cloth that appears to have fallen from Christ's body. The entire work has a splendour that contrasts pointedly with the diminutive figure of Saint Francis to the left: the hierarchy of scale corresponds to a hierarchy of materials. And yet the painting departs in subtle ways from the conventions of gold-ground panels. Artists conventionally used *pastiglia* (gesso relief)

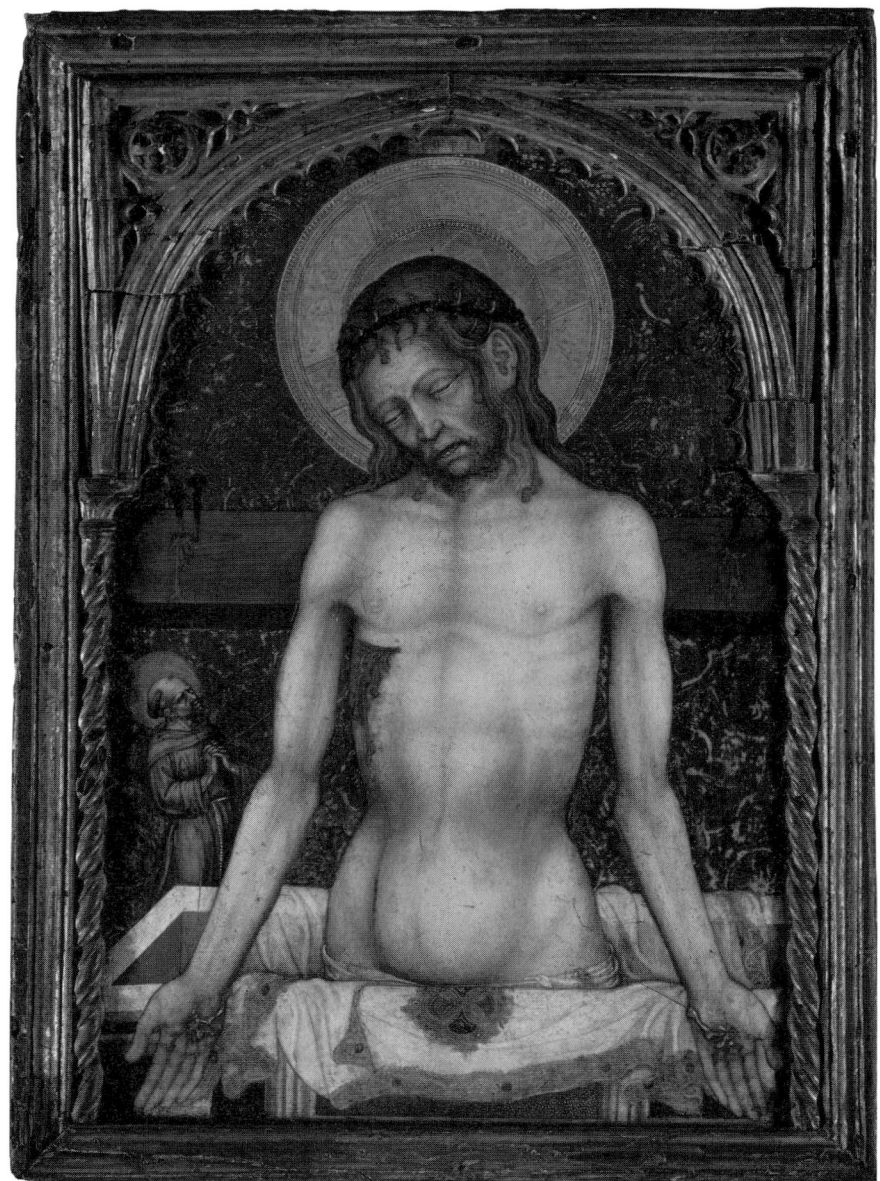

11.5. Michele Giambono, *Man of Sorrows*, c. 1430, tempera and gold on panel, Metropolitan Museum of Art, New York

to produce virtual goldsmithery: Gentile da Fabriano's c. 1420 *Coronation* in the Getty Museum (Figure 11.6), for example, employs the technique for rendering the Virgin's crown, the brooch that closes her drapery, and Christ's gold belt. The *pastiglia* in Giambono's painting, by contrast, realizes

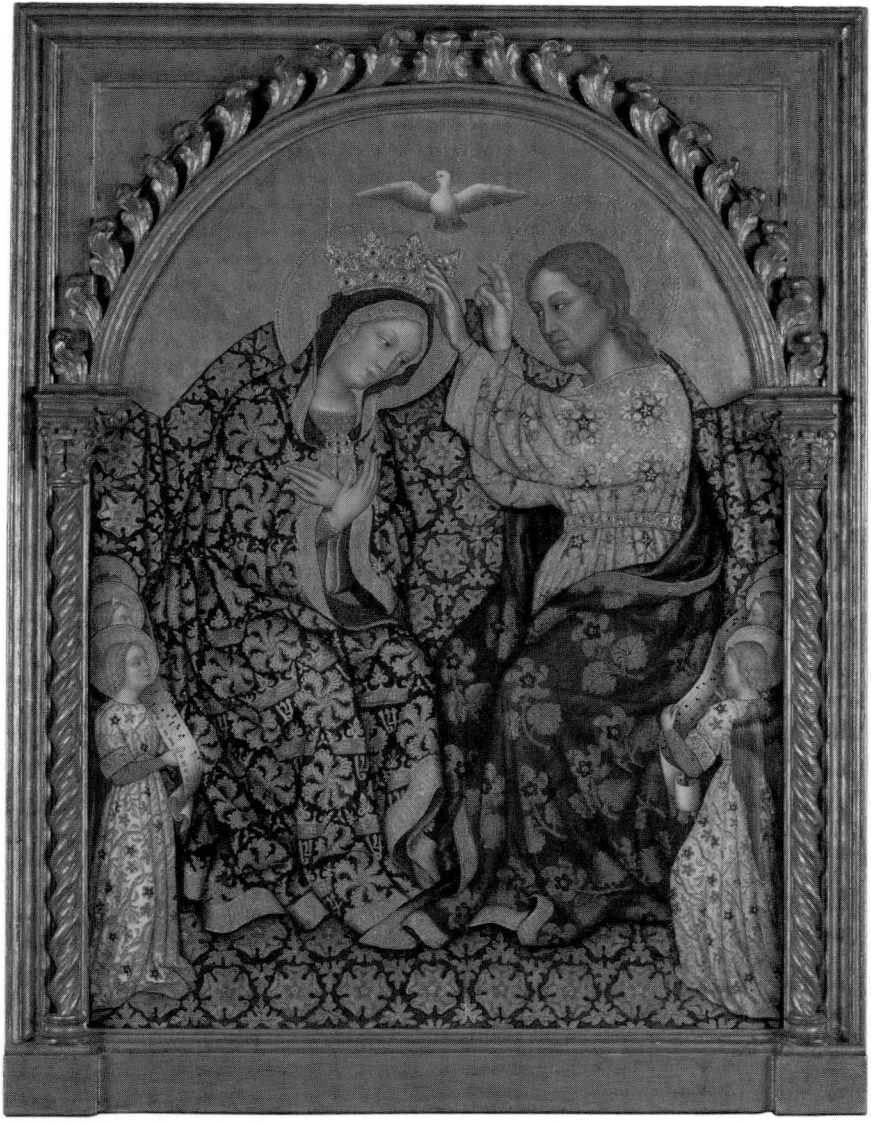

11.6. Gentile da Fabriano, *Coronation of the Virgin*, c. 1420, tempera and gold on panel, J. Paul Getty Museum

the blood that flows from Christ's wounds. This amplifies the Franciscan dimension of the *Pietà* form, since it is from the same wounds that the rays effecting Francis's stigmatization emerge. Yet historically considered, the picture exhibits a replacement, blood taking over for gold.

Paintings like this point to a fundamental question that the makers and patrons of Renaissance art confronted: should paintings of the

Virgin and Christ elevate them with regal splendour or humble them with saintly poverty? Surely such a dilemma was felt at the court of the single Franciscan Pope of the Quattrocento, Sixtus IV, who in summoning a group of Florentine masters to paint the Sistine Chapel brought something like the Assisi cycle to Rome itself. Its type–antitype pairs include, for example, one between the followers of Moses, who worship an idol cast from golden earrings, and the good Christians who listen to Christ's Sermon on the Mount, which begins, 'blessed are the poor'. It also included a ceiling of ultramarine and gold.

Perhaps the most pointed confrontation with the Franciscan ideal in those years, however, is the bronze tomb Giovanni de' Medici commissioned from Antonio Pollaiuolo to honour Sixtus after his death (Figure 11.7). The inscription at the foot of this announces Sixtus's membership in the Franciscan order and also nods to the fact that Sixtus had asked to be buried in the floor rather than in a wall tomb, as a sign of humility.[17] Such a gesture was, by this point, a familiar one: Andrew Butterfield, picking up on an earlier argument by Julian Gardner, has noted that when early Renaissance cardinals rejected the option of a wall tomb in order to be buried in the floor, their wills typically specified that that tomb was to be *humile*, and more recently Ingo Herklotz has given us a history of the medieval tomb that turns on the opposition between the 'sepulchre' and the 'monument'.[18] Yet the gesture to humility in this case must have seemed ironic, since the bronze tomb Giovanni ordered was more costly than many a wall monument. Surely he would have been familiar with conflicting sentiments like those of Maffeo Vegio, who asserted that the expense of Eugenius IV's tomb greatly displeased the pope. The tension provides context for the remarkable additional inscription on Sixtus's own monument, which insists that Cardinal Giovanni erected that moment 'with more piety than expense'. As Alison Wright has observed, this formula 'neatly draws attention to, rather than veils, the cardinal's munificence in paying for it'.[19]

Do we take the phrase 'MAIORE PIETATE QVAM IMPENSA F[ECIT]' to mean that the patron's piety exceeded even the tomb's mammoth price, or does it deny that the work cost as much as it appears to? Giovanni must have known that such denials had a good Medici tradition. To follow Vasari, Cosimo I de' Medici – Giovanni's great grandfather – had mitigated the risky ostentation involved with building the grandest private palace in Florence by circulating the story that the patron had rejected a still more lavish proposal from Brunelleschi on grounds that it 'was too sumptuous and magnificent, and more likely to stir up envy among his fellow citizens than to confer grandeur or adornment on the city'.[20] More relevant still is another work of bronze, Donatello's *Judith and Holofernes*, which Giovanni's grandfather Piero had outfitted with the

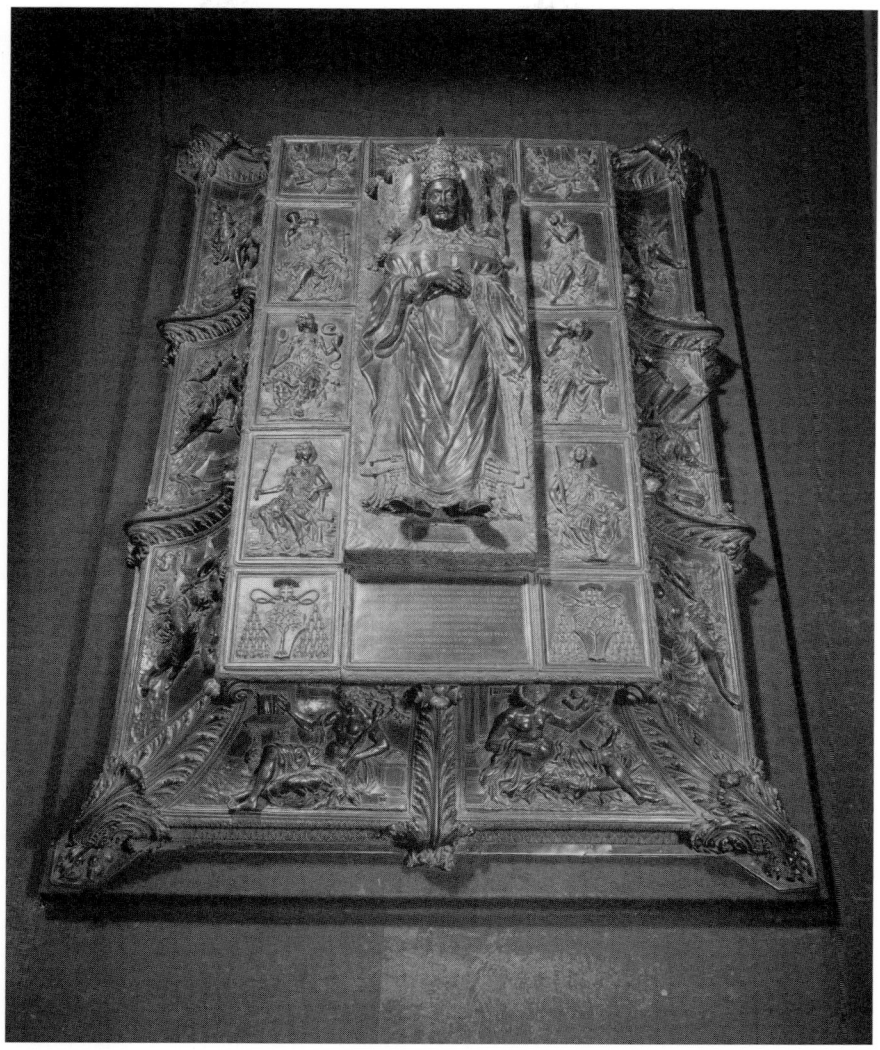

11.7. Antonio del Pollaiuolo, *Tomb of Sixtus IV*, 1484–93, bronze, St Peter's, Vatican

inscription, 'Kingdoms fall through luxury, cities rise through virtues; behold the neck of pride severed by the hand of humility.' However we read the words on the tomb, it demonstrates the cardinal's awareness that spending vast sums of money on art violated at least some viewers' sense of propriety, not all of them Franciscan.

An extensively gilded fresco in a Franciscan basilica could affirm the order's commitment to poverty; a large bronze tomb monument could insist that it was not, primarily, a display of wealth: in view of examples like these, how can we know 'arte povera' when we see it? Expenditure was always relative; objects could be placed under competing labels. Repeatedly, an expectation of sumptuary restraint found itself with competition with the virtue of magnificence, such that patrons needed to identify paths towards impressive display that did not work in terms of cost alone. In his classic book *Painting and Experience in Fifteenth Century Italy*, Michael Baxandall found in the contracts that Quattrocento patrons drew up with artists 'a lessening preoccupation with precious pigments'. '[A]s the conspicuous consumption of gold and ultramarine became less important in the contracts, its place was filled by references to an equally conspicuous consumption of something else – skill.'[21] Baxandall took this change in painting to be part of a 'general shift away from gilt splendour'; he associated it both with neo-Ciceronian humanism (returning us to the latter-day Roman appreciation of the Greek four-colour system), and with 'accessible sorts of Christian asceticism', of which the Franciscan example would certainly be one. Indeed, Hood writes of Fra Angelico that it was 'characteristic of him to have pushed his technique as a painter to the point at which his hand could compensate for the material wealth that would have been inappropriate for dormitory decoration, however sacred both the subject and its function.'[22] Yet Baxandall's own chief example was no longer a mendicant image: it was a Pinturicchio fresco in which landscape had become a newly prominent feature.

The disappearance of gold and ultramarine from the painter's palette, to follow Baxandall, did not mean that painting over the course of the century became any less costly. Rather, it meant that craftsmen became artists when patrons started paying them to. Looking forward rather than back, in fact, we might invert Baxandall's formulation and say that the emergence of the artist depended upon – that it first became visible through – a conspicuous cheapening of paint. It is not just Tintoretto's style but Renaissance artfulness as such that amounts to a sort of anti-materialism. What Baxandall observed happening with gold and ultramarine repeated itself across other media: in the same period, canvas replaced panel, and from the beginning artists like Mantegna would save costs by using size as a medium, eliminating the time-consuming step of preparing a gesso ground. Paper would replace parchment as the preferred drawing support, and the printing press would make the individual image less expensive still. The example of Michelangelo would help marble overtake the equally established but far more expensive material of bronze in prestige; stucco would soon thereafter begin taking the place of marble.[23]

Yet even this requires qualification. In a December 1523 letter, Michelangelo recorded a now famous response to the suggestion of Pope Julius II that the painter compose the Sistine Chapel ceiling frescoes around a series of apostles: 'I said to the Pope that if I were to make the Apostles alone there, it would turn out to be a poor thing... for they, too, were poor.'[24] Reading the first part of the remark, it would be tempting to take its notion of the 'poor' as nothing more than a manner of speaking: Michelangelo essentially rejects the Pope's proposal for being insufficiently ambitious. But then the conclusion puts weight on the expression, elevating it to the level of a more serious metaphor. What is most remarkable, especially in the context of an amplification of the chapel built and named for a Franciscan pontiff, is the assertion that a decorative programme celebrating apostolic poverty was unworthy of the modern papacy.

Complicating things still further is the conversation between Michelangelo and the pope that Vasari reports (or imagines), one that seems to reverse this very sentiment. When Michelangelo had broken off work and had the scaffolding removed, Vasari writes, the painter:

> desired to retouch some portions of the work *a secco*, as had been done by the older masters who had painted the stories on the walls; he would also gladly have added a little ultramarine to some of the draperies, and gilded other parts, to the end that the whole might have a richer and more striking effect. The Pope, too, hearing that these things were still wanting, and finding that all who beheld the Chapel praised it highly, would now fain have had the additions made, but as Michelangelo thought reconstructing the scaffold too long an affair, the pictures remained as they were, although the Pope, who often saw Michelangelo, would sometimes say, 'Let the Chapel be enriched with bright colours and gold; it looks poor.' When Michelangelo would reply familiarly, 'Holy Father, the men of those days did not adorn themselves with gold; those who are painted here less than any, for they were none too rich; besides which, they were holy men, and must have despised riches and ornaments.[25]

It is an odd, contradictory, passage: can it really be that Michelangelo wished to add ultramarine to his work, then later simply found a way to justify the state in which it had been left? Just which 'none too rich' 'men of those days' did Vasari have in mind, when after all Michelangelo had rejected the proposal of painting humble apostles in favour of a Genesis sequence, surrounded by prophets, sibyls, and an elaborate genealogy? How is the celebration we hear from Vasari's Michelangelo of characters who 'despise riches' to be reconciled with the disdain his letter expresses toward poor pictures of poor people? In the end, it is tempting to conclude that Vasari himself did not know what to make of the ceiling, how to describe its richness in terms of the aesthetic of poverty that readers by 1568 expected.

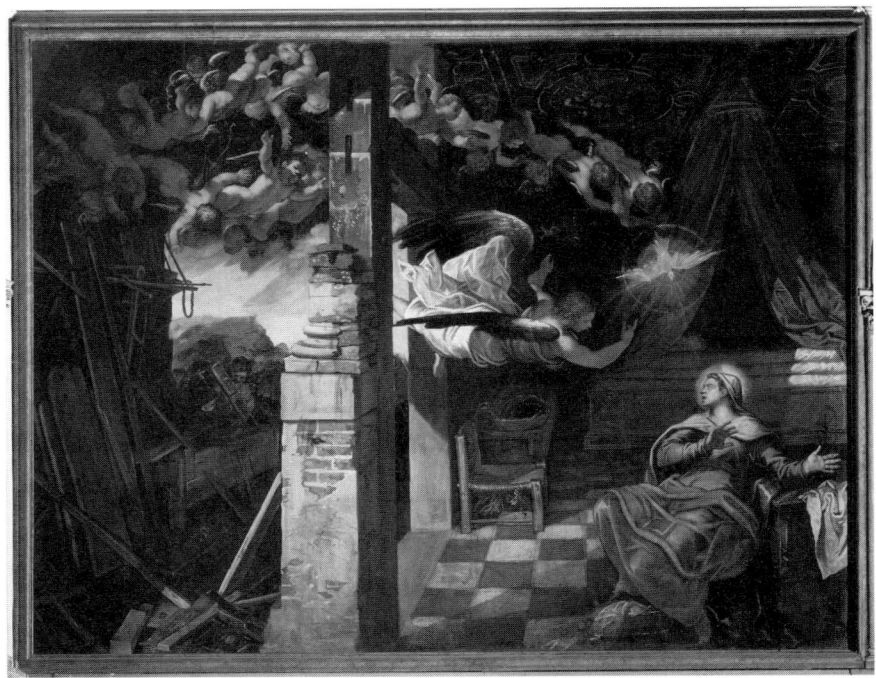

11.8. Tintoretto, *Annunciation*, 1583–87, oil on canvas, Sala Inferiore, Scuola Grande di San Rocco, Venice

Or perhaps it is art itself that could not quite resolve such conflicting demands. Vasari's Michelangelo conveys a double sense of art's potential: its depictions of poverty can signify holiness, but glorious art can just as well give a holy aura to magnificence. Tintoretto's patrons may have accepted his way of painting and appreciated his low prices, but they also placed his paintings in gilded frames. Nor are the paintings of the Scuola di San Rocco themselves always straightforward. Among the most derelict of Tintoretto's depicted spaces is the chamber in which the *Annunciation* takes place (Figure 11.8): everything is dingy, the chair at the edge of the room is broken, and the whole exterior of the building seems to have collapsed. Yet the depicted interior is also an obvious extension of the architecture of the Scuola itself, picking up both the marble floor and gilded, coffered ceiling. How is it that the Virgin could occupy such a house unless she was of the same privileged social class as Tintoretto's patrons? Perhaps the point is related to that in Giotto's depiction of San Damiano: the confraternity's reform mission includes the rebuilding of the Church. But it is also possible to read Tintoretto's setting as an intentional impoverishment, even a 'soiling', of the space it was meant to decorate. The painting might work against the architecture here, much as Nichols proposed that the ideological orientation of Tintoretto's painting in general stood at odds with the classical ornamentation on the building's exterior. That would suggest that where there was a question of the painting's place between luxury and poverty, the interests of painter and patron might not stand in complete harmony.

Compare this to the situation of Tintoretto's contemporary Giambologna in Florence. While Tintoretto was painting in San Rocco, Giambologna was overseeing the execution of a chapel in San Marco – the same mendicant church for which Fra Angelico had worked – that broke all local codes of sumptuary restraint. At the ceremony inaugurating the space, in fact, Bishop Ugolino Martelli felt compelled to give a sermon justifying the expenditure, and the chapel's imagery itself takes up related arguments. The right-hand wall centres on a painting of the banker Saint Matthew relinquishing his worldly possessions so as to join Christ. The Latin inscription 'relictis omnibus secutus est eum' ('and leaving all things, he rose up and followed', Luke 5:27–28) equates the Apostolic mission with the abandonment of money and provides a point of identification for the chapel's banker-patrons. On the opposite wall, one patron's namesake, Edward, holds a church, echoing the Assisi mural by presenting the sponsorship of ecclesiastical settings as a saintly act.

What is most striking in this case, though, is not the chapel's representation of patronage but rather the difference between its excess and persona of the architect in charge. The Urbinate ambassador Simone Fortuna reported on visiting Giambologna while he was at work on San Marco, and finding that the Fleming was 'the best person you could ever meet, not greedy in the least, as his absolute pennilessness shows. Everything he does is in the pursuit of glory, and he has ambition in the extreme to match Michelangelo.'[26]

Here we have an artist who seems to associate the task of living up to Michelangelo – what he calls *ambizione* – with pennilessness. The idea that the pursuit of art might be at odds with the pursuit of money dates at least to Ghiberti, who began the autobiographical section of his *Commentaries* with the line: 'I, O most excellent reader, not having to obey money, dedicated myself to the study of art.'[27] Vasari opened his life of Perino del Vaga with the generalization that art is a gift, one that 'with no regard to abundance of riches, to high estate, or to nobility of blood, embraces, protects, and uplifts from the ground a child of poverty much more often than one wrapped in the ease of wealth.'[28] And Michelangelo himself – 'a rich man who lived like a pauper', to quote Wittkower – might have seemed to reinforce that very idea.[29] Leone Leoni's medal of around 1560 – made of lead rather than a precious metal – showed the artist as a simple pilgrim, virtually a beggar.[30]

Giambologna's example differs from these precedents in the explicit dis-identification of the artist with the costly things he made. What we seem to have by the 1580s, in fact, is an artist who recognized the attraction of *arte povera* – he saw that the path to being Michelangelo involved the rejection of wealth – but who found himself in circumstances (employ as a court artist) that made such a path impossible. Could it even be the case that the patronage system in Italy, the expectation that the best artists would attach themselves to wealthy households, worked against a set of pictorial values that both the Franciscan tradition and the classical example of Apelles might otherwise have encouraged? Tintoretto notwithstanding, it is difficult to find close Italian parallels for the numerous northern European artists who both claimed to be impoverished and made pictures that in one way or another adhered to that image of self.

That situation, in fact, adds to the interest of an etching like Salvator Rosa's *The Genius of Salvator Rosa* from about 1662 (Figure 11.9). A variation on an earlier print by Giovanni Benedetto Castiglione (Figure 11.10) that itself responded to a series of etchings by Pietro Testa, Rosa's invention included an inscription that clarified his more distinctive point: 'sincere, free, equable painter and igniter, despiser of wealth and of death: this is my genius.' At the heart of the conceit is the by now familiar image of the poor artist. What is not conventional, though, is Rosa's sense that living up to this image meant rejecting the court system, and indeed commissioned works generally.[31] What his inscription replaced, in fact, was the dedication to the patron that earlier artists, Castiglione among them, had added to their own prints. Rosa wrote in a 1666 letter that he painted not to enrich himself, but for his own satisfaction.[32] As a matter of practice, Rosa put his economic fate in the hands of the print-buying public. And the image in this case – of a genius at odds with wealth, literally turning away from money – conformed to the medium, a cheap paper multiple that Rosa could undertake on his own initiative. *Arte povera* here has become more than just a style or a way of living; now it is a means of artistic freedom.

Rosa's etching, relative to Castiglione's, is also considerably less calligraphic. In rhetorical terms, it exemplifies a 'plain style', reminding us that the pursuit of an impoverished art could go beyond the question of materiality altogether.[33] In this respect, Rosa belongs not in the tradition of other printmakers, but of Caravaggio, who provided a model from his own day right up to that of Paul Chan for how to impoverish one's art. Caravaggio's early paintings rejected the landscapes and other displays of manual virtuosity that Baxandall found to have taken the

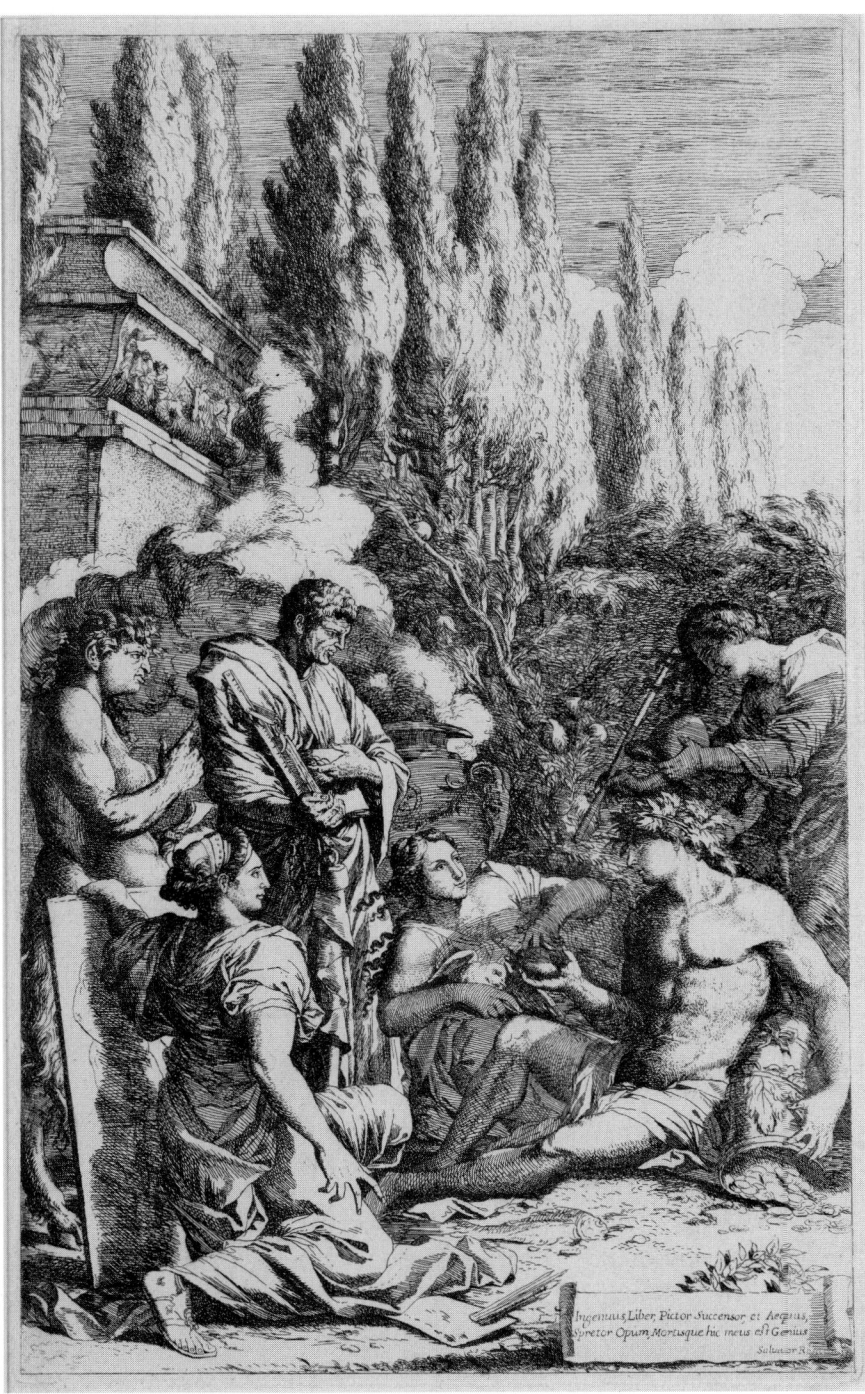

11.9. Salvator Rosa, *The Genius of Salvator Rosa*, c. 1662, engraving

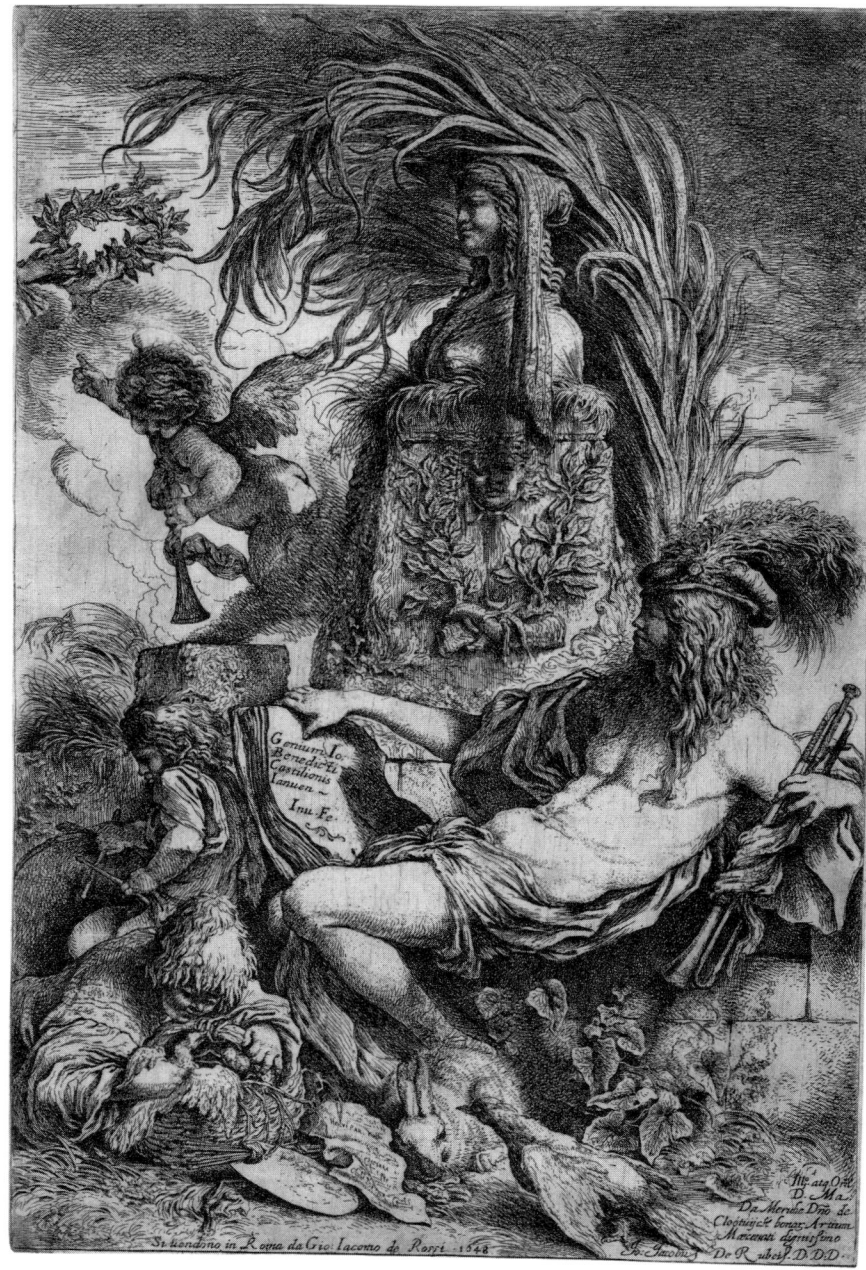

11.10. Giovanni Benedetto Castiglione, *The Genius of Castiglione*, c. 1645–47, engraving

place of precious materials, yet they also gave up on the rendering of nude bodies in complex postures that artists from Michelangelo to Tintoretto identified with 'art'. Over time, moreover, Caravaggio reduced his paintings in other ways as well, eliminating colour, restricting himself to a palette that consisted of little more than browns and a bit of red – as though he, like the child Giotto, were painting with dirt. To moderns, these decisions have sometimes made Caravaggio look like the first 'Realist' painter: if we find in 'neo-Realists' like Rossellini or De Sica a recycling of Caravaggio's subject matter, which contemporaries of all three took to consist of characters pulled in from the street, so might we see in Caravaggio the origins of the chiaroscuro effect that became so central to later cinema.[34] To become a Caravaggist, indeed, has often been to *amplify* Caravaggio's own poverty: when a French painter like Valentin 'corrected' Caravaggio's model by adding more characters, he darkened it, exaggerated its low-life elements. Yet, ironically, this gesture has only lent to Caravaggio's original simplicity. When Fréart de Chantelou first saw the *Fortune Teller* that arrived in Paris in 1662 (Figure 11.11), he reacted with a dismissal that has come to look like a compliment: this, he wrote, is 'a poor painting'.[35]

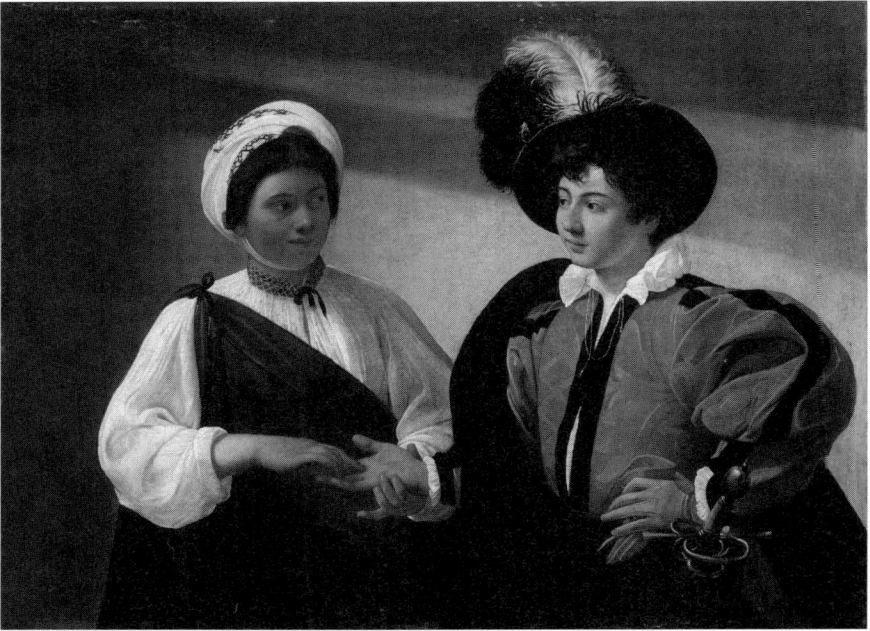

11.11. Michelangelo Merisi, called 'Caravaggio', *The Fortune Teller*, 1595, oil on canvas, Louvre, Paris

Notes

My initial thinking on this topic owed much to my collaboration with Stephen Campbell on our book *Italian Renaissance Art* (London: Thames & Hudson, 2011). Readers will find my discussions of Fra Angelico, Pollaiuolo, and Tintoretto take up themes we addressed there. Diane Bodart drew my attention to Giambono's use of *pastiglia*. I presented an earlier version of this chapter in 2010 at the University of St Andrews. I thank Fabio Barry and Alistair Rider for the invitation and for helpful comments.

1. Tom Nichols, *Tintoretto: Tradition and Identity* (London: Reaktion Books, 1999), p. 38.
2. Nichols, *Tintoretto*, p. 200.
3. Nichols, *Tintoretto*, p. 202.
4. Nichols, *Tintoretto*, p. 210.
5. Nichols, *Tintoretto*, p. 214.
6. Calvin Tomkins, 'Shadow player: The provocations of Paul Chan', *The New Yorker*, 26 May 2008.
7. Georgio Vasari, *Le opera di Giorgio Vasari*, ed. Gaetano Milanesi (Florence, G.C. Sansone, 1906), vol. 1, p. 54: quando i cittadini vi erano rozzi ed il commune povero, dove ebbero molte imagini di quelli Dei, che essi adoravano, di terra cotta; e ne' sacrificj appresso di loro furono in uso i vasi di terra. E molto piu si crede che piacesse alli Dei la semplicita e povera di quei secoli, che l'oro e l'argento e la pompa di coloro li quali poi vennero.'
8. Pliny the Elder, *Natural History*, trans. H. Rackham (Cambridge, MA: Harvard University Press, 1938), p. 299.
9. Jan Białostocki, 'Ars auro prior', in *Aesthetics in 20th-Century Poland: Selected Essays* (Cranbury, NJ: Associated University Presses, 1973), pp. 270–85, here p. 276.
10. Donal Cooper and Janet Robson, '"A great sumptuousness of paintings": Frescoes and Franciscan poverty at Assisi in 1288 and 1312', *The Burlington Magazine* 151 (2009), pp. 656–62, here p. 659.
11. Thomas of Celano, *St Francis of Assisi: First and Second Life of St Francis with Selections from The Treatise on the Miracles of Blessed Francis*, trans. Placid Hermann (Chicago, IL: Franciscan Herald Press, 1988), p. 144.
12. For the importance of clothing as a metaphor in this period, see the excellent article by Philine Helas, 'The clothing of poverty and sanctity in legends, and their representations in Trecento and Quattrocento Italy', in Kathryn M. Rudy and Barbara Baert (eds), *Weaving, Veiling, and Dressing: Textiles and their Metaphors in the Late Middle Ages* (Turnhout: Brepols, 2007), pp. 245–87.
13. Cooper and Robson, 'A great sumptuousness of paintings', p. 659.
14. Lorenzo Ghiberti, *I commentarii*, ed. Lorenzo Bartoli (Florence: Giunti, 1998), pp. 83–4. (English trans.: Christie Knapp Fengler, 'Lorenzo Ghiberti's *Second Commentary*: The translation and interpretation of a fundamental Renaissance treatise on art' (unpublished PhD dissertation, University of Wisconsin, 1974), pp. 17–18.)
15. Giorgio Vasari, *Lives of the Painters, Sculptors and Architects*, trans. Gaston du C. de Vere (New York: Everyman's Library, 1996), vol. 1, p. 108; cf. Vasari, *Le opera*, vol. 1, p. 393.
16. William Hood, *Fra Angelico at San Marco* (New Haven, CT, and London: Yale University Press, 1993), p. 236. When, in the following decade, Paolo Uccello began painting frescoes in terra verde, he enacted a different kind of 'disrobing' of the painting, first in the Olivetan San Miniato al Monte, then in the Dominican S. Maria Novella. Later viewers regularly identified Uccello's reduction of pictorial means with his modernism.
17. Alison Wright, *The Pollaiuolo Brothers: The Arts of Florence and Rome* (New Haven, CT, and London: Yale University Press, 2005), p. 377.

18. Andrew Butterfield, 'Social structure and the typology of funerary monuments in early Renaissance Florence', *RES: Anthropology and Aesthetics* 26 (1994), pp. 47–67, esp. p. 58; Ingo Herklotz, *'Sepulchra' e 'monumenta' del medioevo: Studi sull'arte sepolcrale in Italia* (Naples: Liguori, 2001), p. 337.
19. Wright, *The Pollaiuolo Brothers*, p. 373.
20. Vasari, *Lives*, vol. 1, p. 379.
21. Michael Baxandall, *Painting and Experience in Fifteenth-Century Italy: A Primer in the Social History of Pictorial Style* (Oxford: Oxford University Press, 1988), p. 15.
22. Hood, *Fra Angelico*, p. 236.
23. For a relevant example of this as a theme in Renaissance printmaking, see Madeleine Viljoen, 'Paper value: Marcantonio Raimondi's "Medaglie Contraffatte"', *Memoirs of the American Academy in Rome* 48 (2003), pp. 203–26. Cristina Acidini Luchinat has observed that the blue Andrea della Robbia began to achieve in his terracotta glazes would previously only have been obtainable 'solo con stesure pittoriche costose', the use of the rare pigments like lapis lazuli. The art that aligns with impoverishment is in this case an alchemical one. See 'Del blu in città', in Giancarlo Gentilini (ed.), *I Della Robbia e l'arte nuova della scultura invetriata* (Florence: Giunti, 1998), pp. 9–16.
24. Paula Barocchi and Giovanni Poggi (eds) *Il carteggio di Michelangelo* (Florence: Sansoni, 1973), vol. 3, pp. 8, 11: 'dissi al papa come facendovi gli Apostoli soli, mi pareva che riuscissi cosa povera ... perché furon poveri anche loro.'
25. Vasari, *Lives*, vol. 2, p. 668.
26. Paola Barocchi and Giovanna Gaeta Bertelà (eds), *Collezionismo mediceo Cosimo I, Francesco I e il Cardinale Ferdinando* (Modena: Franco Cosimo Panini, 1993), p. 181: 'Egli è poi la migliore personcina che si possa trovar mai, non punto avaro, come dimostra l'esser egli poverissimo e in tutto e per tutto volto alla gloria, avendo una ambizione estrema d'arrivare Michelangelo et a molti giudiziosi par già che l'abbi arrivato e vivendo sii per avanzarlo e tale opinione ha il Gran Duca ancora.'
27. Ghiberti, *Commentarii*, p. 92: 'Et io, o excellentissimo, non ò a ubbidire la pecunia, diedi lo studio per l'arte.'
28. Vasari, *Lives*, vol. 2, p. 152; cf. Vasari, *Le opere*, vol. 5, p. 587.
29. Rudolf and Margaret Wittkower, *Born Under Saturn* (New York: Random House, 1963), p. 263.
30. For the Leoni medal, see the discussion in Andreas Schumacher, 'Leone Leonis Michelangelo-Medaille: Porträt und Glaubensbekenntnis des alten Buonarroti', in Georg Satzinger (ed.), *Die Renaissance-Medaille in Italien und Deutschland* (Münster: Rhema, 2004), pp. 169–94; also Tom Nichols, *The Art of Poverty: Irony and Ideal in Sixteenth-Century Beggar Imagery* (Manchester: Manchester University Press, 2007), p. 242.
31. This aspect of Rosa's career – though not its relevance to the *Genius* etching – had already been noted by Francis Haskell, *Painters and Patrons: A Study in the Relations between Italian Art and Society in the Age of the Baroque* (New Haven, CT, and London: Yale University Press, 1980), p. 15.
32. Haskell, *Painters and Patrons*, p. 22, note 1: 'io non dipingo per arrichire mà solamente per propria sodisfazione.'
33. See the still fundamental discussion in Marc Fumaroli, *L'Âge d'éloquence* (Geneva: Droz, 1980).
34. One provocative take on the themes of this essay as it bears on Rossellini and De Sica is André Bazin's. See, for example, 'An aesthetic of reality: Cinematic realism and the Italian school of the liberation', in *What is Cinema?* Vol. 2, trans. Hugh Gray (Berkeley and London: University of California Press, 1971), esp. p. 29 (on the realism that resulted

from the technical limitations Italian directors faced) and p. 31 (on what he terms 'modal poverty').

35 Paul Fréart de Chantelou, *Diary of the Cavaliere Bernini's Visit to France*, ed. Anthony Blunt, trans. Margery Corbett (Princeton, NJ: Princeton University Press, 1985), p. 239: 'I afterwards discussed with him the pictures that Prince Pamphili had sent to the King. I said that they were all mediocre, the one by Albani being among his least successful pictures; the landscapes by Carracci are remarkable only for the freedom with which they are painted; they lack nobility; the *Gypsy* by Caravaggio is a poor work, lacking originality or spirit.' Cf. Chantelou, *Journal de voyage du cavalier Bernin en France*, ed. Milovan Stanic (Paris: Macula, 2001), p. 212: 'J'ai parlé, après, de ces tableaux que le prince Pamphili a envoyé au roi . . . la *Cingara* du Caravage un pauvre tableau, sans esprit ni invention.'

12 ✧ Polish stone, Venetian glass, and red Hungarian marble: the materials of a Renaissance chapel in Jagiellonian Poland

Katie Jakobiec

THE SIGISMUND CHAPEL epitomizes the material richness of Polish Renaissance architecture (Figure 12.1). Constructed from local sandstone and imported precious materials, including Hungarian red marble and Venetian glass, the chapel articulated the tastes and ambitions of its patron, King Sigismund I of the Jagiellonian dynasty. Annexed to the south choir aisle of the red-brick Gothic Wawel Cathedral in Krakow, Sigismund's mausoleum was erected on the site of an earlier chapel. Thus the building commission stressed dynastic succession, while its novelty was a statement of triumph. Like a new and shining jewel, the Renaissance chapel introduced new forms, materials, and surface textures into an established building tradition (Figure 12.2). By

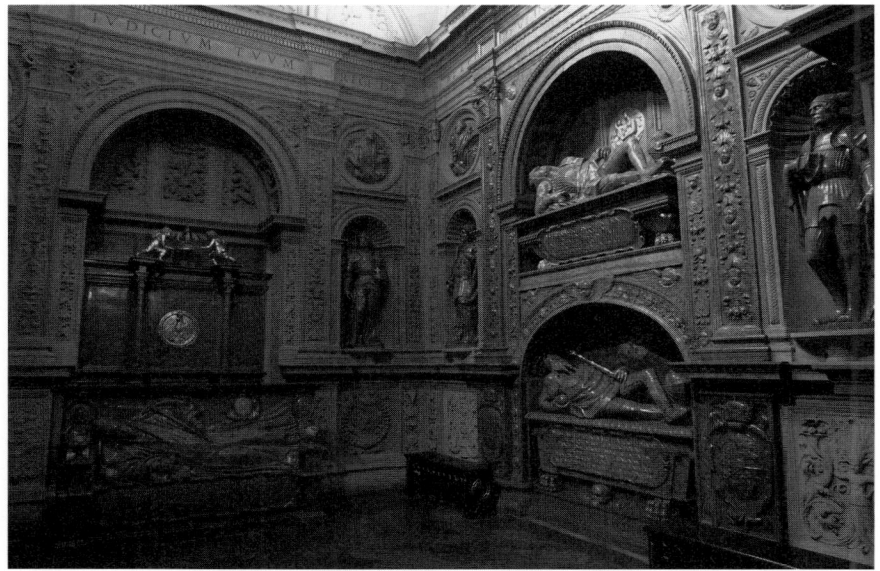

12.1. Bartolommeo Berrecci, Sigismund Chapel (interior), 1519–33, Krakow

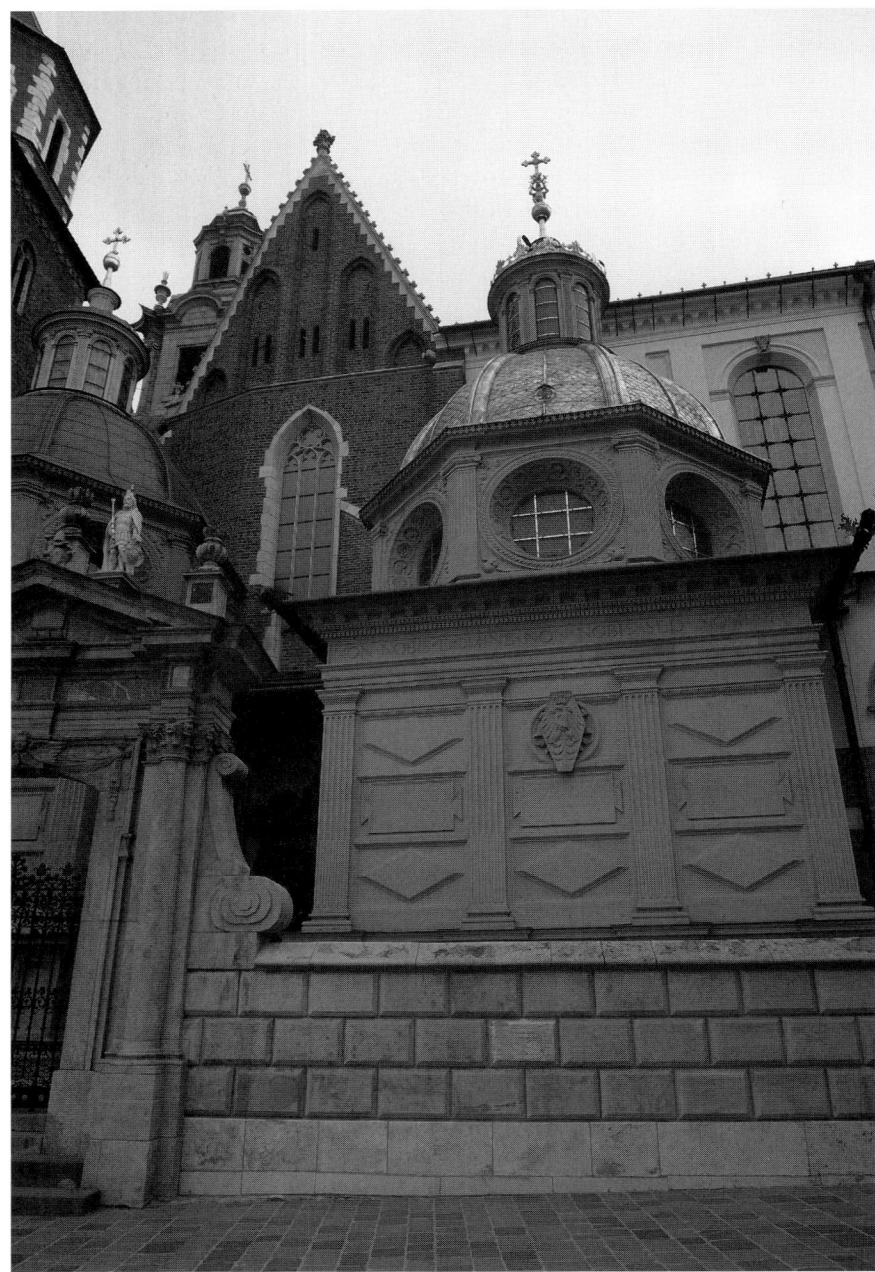

12.2. Bartolommeo Berrecci, Sigismund Chapel (exterior), 1519–33, Krakow

fusing classical forms and material splendour, the Sigismund Chapel heralded a change in Polish architecture. However, despite the innovative architectural language, the act of building itself expressed lineage and a respect for tradition. By portraying himself as King Solomon, Sigismund's building project was imbued with the discourse of power and magnificence that was centuries old (Figure 12.3). Erecting buildings meant finding highly skilled architects and craftsmen; selecting, acquiring, and importing desired building materials; and, finally, arranging the logistics of their timely delivery. Materials used in the Sigismund Chapel articulated the wealth, power, and wisdom of the ruler-patron, while strengthening the imperial ambitions of the Jagiellonian dynasty, helping to demarcate their vast territory, and showcasing its reaches and international connections.

Commissioned and closely supervised by King Sigismund I the Old (r. 1506–48), the chapel was built by the Italian architect Bartolommeo Berrecci (c. 1480–1537) and his workshop between 1519 and 1533.[1] The centrally planned cubical structure was surmounted by an octagonal drum with lunettes and pendentives supporting a dome, which was covered by metallic sheets. Finally, the entire structure was crowned by a lantern. On the four interior walls of the chapel, the architect incorporated triumphal arch elements which functioned as framing devices for the entrance, altar, throne, and Sigismund's effigy. Symmetry and clarity were achieved by the careful measurement of proportions and the repetition of *all' antica* parts for which the chapel has been hailed

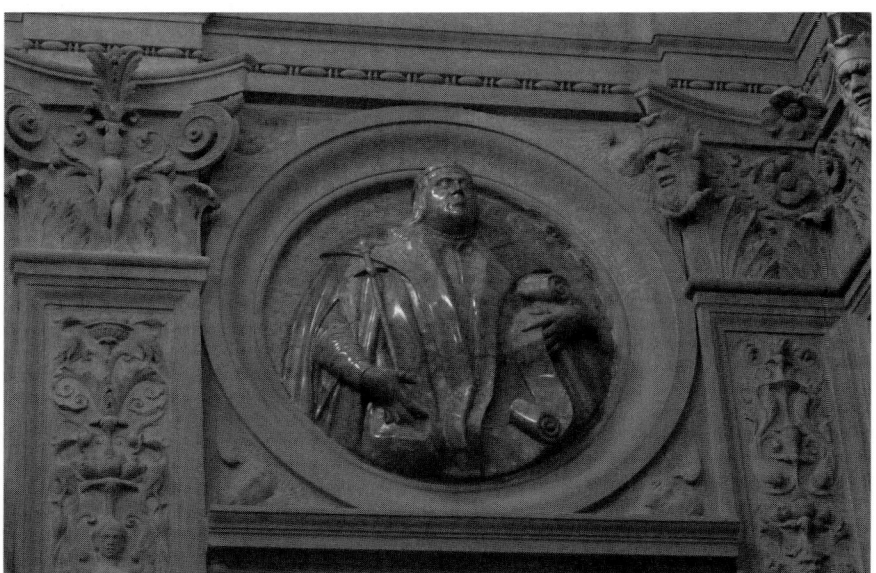

12.3. Bartolommeo Berrecci, Sigismund Chapel (detail), 1519–33, Krakow

as the 'pearl' of Renaissance architecture north of the Alps.[2] The importance of this monument is reflected in the extensive attention it has received in Polish art and architectural historiography, a vast body of literature that established the Sigismund Chapel as a significant exemplum for a new classical idiom in the early modern Polish architecture that followed.[3]

As the product of the collaboration between the Polish ruler-founder and an Italian architect, the Sigismund Chapel can therefore be studied as one of the many instances of the influence, reception, and adaptation of Italian Renaissance style outside of Italy. While this chapter does, to a certain extent, discuss the routes by which Italian architects and artisans made their way to this region, I am more interested in the complex and multi-faceted issues of architecture, such as the materials out of which it is constructed, and the meanings that are achieved by the combination of form and material. Form (or style) in architecture is only one consideration of building, which is often secondary to other considerations, such as the technical requirements (both in the sense of engineering and/or workmanship or skill) and the materials of building, including their physical properties and expressive potential to convey meaning. By shedding light on the actual *fabrication* of buildings, it becomes clear how closely the process of making is tied to the material. Existing archival documentation concerning the project of the Sigismund Chapel includes correspondence, excerpts from chronicles, and invoices kept by Jan Boner and later by Seweryn Boner, the treasurers of the crown.[4] These archival sources show the concerns and motives of the patron, and materials are at the forefront of the discussion. This essay explores these references to materials in light of the process of building and examines the ways in which materials contribute to the meaning of the finished architectural monument. Examining the material qualities of architecture not only offers insights into early modern Poland as an important centre of production, it is also a rich approach to understanding the diversity of European architecture in general.

In 1517, two years before construction of the Sigismund Chapel began, Sigismund addressed a letter to Jan Boner outlining the plans for his mausoleum:[5]

> The Italian was here with the model of the chapel [*exemplo sacelli*] which he will build for us and we liked it well, but we ordered him to change a few things in accordance with the views which he expressed. We have indicated to him also how much we want in the tomb to be made of marble, which you will learn better from him and from the papers. You should, therefore, arrange for as much marble to be brought from Hungary as will be needed, since he says that the marble there is more suitable for such a

work than elsewhere and the transportation from there is more convenient. [*Itaque cures, ut ex Hungaria tantum marmoris, quantum sat erit, illi adaucatur, nam ibi potius esse dicit pro tali labore, quam alibi et commodius est illinc ducere.*] He told us also that he would need eight collaborators to carve the statues and once having them he would like to complete the chapel in three years and a half, which is certainly later than we would desire, but if we care so much about temporary buildings, why should we stint the means we use for those in which we have to dwell forever [*in quibus est perpetuo habitandum*]?[6]

The *Italus* mentioned in the letter was most probably Bartolommeo Berrecci, a native of Florence, who was called to the court in Krakow via Hungary around 1515.[7] To discuss the plans of the mausoleum with the king, the architect travelled to Vilnius and presented a model (*exemplum sacelli*), which does not survive. It could have been a wooden construction or a set of architectural drawings.[8] The architect's recommendation of the red Hungarian marble and his knowledge of shipment routes suggest that he worked in Hungary before arriving in Krakow. After consulting with the architect, Sigismund proceeded to make practical arrangements, delegating orders to Jan Boner for the acquisition of materials and workmen, showing erudition and experience in the practices of managing building projects. Jan Boner was a member of the German family of merchants who became bankers to the king and the Polish nobility, like the Fuggers did in Germany. The Boners acted as important players in architectural and artistic commissions in Krakow.[9] Their international contacts with merchant networks allowed for the acquisition of commodities that were desired by the court. Boner kept account books for the king, where the scrupulous documentation provides information on the progress of the building stages of the Sigismund Chapel.[10] Yet despite Boner's important role in overseeing the project, in one of the letters from 1517, while still in Vilnius, Sigismund demanded that work be suspended until his return to Krakow.[11] This was also the case in 1513 and 1514, while building his residence in the city of Sandomierz, when Sigismund ordered that materials be prepared, but work should not proceed until he approved the plans (*nec volumus ut aedificatur prius quam conspexerimus quo modo et quid aedificandum sit*).[12] Sigismund's insistence that he be present during the early stages of building highlights how seriously he took his role as the patron and the tasks that were his to execute. The planning stages of architecture were of great importance and were the domain of a wise, knowledgeable, and erudite patron-builder.

King Sigismund's active role in the planning stages of his building commissions fundamentally involved selecting craftsmen and materials. The accounts disclose the complex and diverse origins of the materials used in the Sigismund Chapel, which became a bold statement of the ways in which materials communicate political power, wealth, wisdom, and privilege. On the exterior of the chapel, four hundred and sixteen sheets of copper were used for the dome. The copper came from a mine in Hungary owned by the Fuggers. Berrecci selected the material himself and devised the distinctive patterning of overlapping scales, which were then covered with silver.[13] At the very top of the stone lantern, copper was again used to create the cross, crown, and a kneeling putto.[14] The architect also used sandstone, which was described in 1526 as quarried from *de monte Myslimicensi*, a region of the town Dobczyce, not far from Krakow.[15] This local material and its variants included a greenish-grey sandstone, with a fine-grain consistency, a dark-green sandstone, and a yellowish-grey sandstone, and all had a slightly different tint and technical properties due to the grain.[16] Berrecci's inexperience with Polish stone is evident in the receipts and accounts of the Boners, who recorded that the sculpture often broke during execution due to the structural flaws of the material, which was perhaps incorrectly matched or selected to meet the demands of the architect's design.[17] Berrecci used two types of marble. One type was used to lay the floor of the chapel (since replaced), which was shipped via the Vistula River from Gdansk in February 1527.[18] The second type was a crimson limestone, the so-called 'red Hungarian marble', imported from quarries located at the foot of the Gerecse Mountain, near Esztergom and Szekesfeherwar and shipped via the Danube River and its tributaries.[19] Again, a careful process took place in the selection of marble, wherein the block that was used for the king's effigy was of the highest quality, chosen over the initially selected block, which failed to meet the high standards and was rejected and demoted to another work.[20] In 1525, five crates of Venetian glass were purchased, an amount that exceeded the need for the chapel; however, precautions were taken in case of damage and imperfections.[21] The forethought that went into the material acquisition and selection is extraordinary, as it demonstrates the wide qualification of the architect, whose job was to oversee quality standards. Berrecci was not only expected to manage the workshop and the realization of his design, but was also responsible for the selection of quality materials, which required knowledge of local geology and natural history that would allow him to discern between appropriate materials. The architect was expected to react accordingly to unexpected outcomes, and adapt to situations where materials caused challenges to the building schedule. One such challenge involved the Hungarian marble, which was so important to the king. When the Turkish invasion made it difficult to obtain the material from Hungarian quarries, Sigismund urged Berrecci to study Polish geology to see whether suitable marble could be obtained within the country.[22]

Polish stone, Venetian glass, and red Hungarian marble 269

At the beginning of 1525, work on the chapel stopped as Berrecci left Krakow in order to find suitable marble to execute the sculpture planned for the chapel.[23] He sent his workers to Nysa, Kazimierz Dolny, Olkusz, and Tenczyna (all cities in Poland) to search for appropriate marble, all without success.[24]

The commitment to acquiring the best materials meant that Sigismund and Berrecci had to muster all the resources at their disposal to obtain the desired supplies. Sandstone, red marble, gold and silver, and glass indicted the opulence of this commission and demonstrated that no effort and cost was spared to acquire the best from different parts of Europe, including Hungary, Venice, and Nuremberg. The richness and variety of materials used in the Sigismund Chapel translates into an array of colours, textures, and reflective surfaces, all of which help to order the individual parts of the chapel into a unified whole. In the Sigismund Chapel, materials were selected and used in order to articulate a hierarchy of value and direct the visitor's attention on the places of prominence. While the architectonic parts within the chapel, like the niches, were rendered from a pale local grey sandstone, red marble was used to articulate the areas of greatest importance. The figures of St Peter, St Paul, St Wenceslaus, St Florian, St Wacław, St John the Baptist, and St Sigismund, as well as the medallion busts of the Evangelists, King David, and King Solomon, and finally the effigy of King Sigismund, were sculpted from red marble.[25] In contrast to the matte surface of the sandstone, which absorbs sunlight and recedes into the background, the marble's polished surface reflects light and becomes animated (Figure 12.4). Marble's special reflective quality to engage light makes

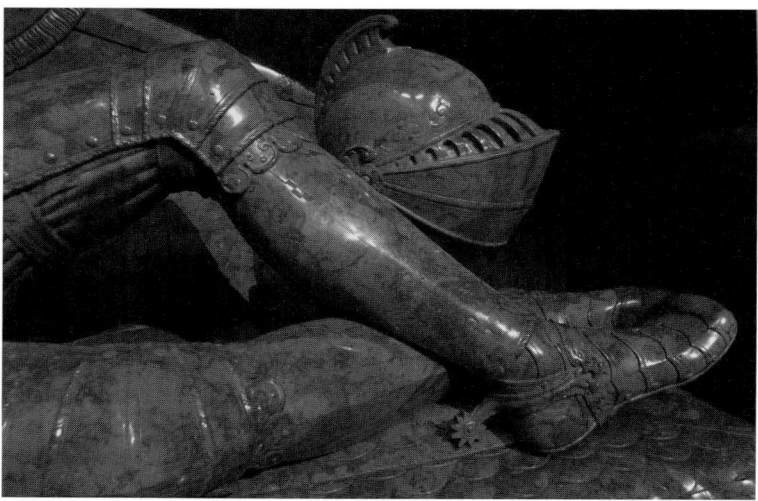

12.4. Bartolommeo Berrecci, Sigismund Chapel (detail), 1519–33, Krakow

it the most suitable material to render the king's reclining body, dressed in armour and crown. The deep crimson hue and the perfectly polished surface, transformed from the rough state of the marble, rendered the king's political body immortal; light brings the material to life, animating the figure shown seemingly asleep. Not only was red Hungarian marble costly and imported; its deep red colour as well as the texture and patterning of the marble's veins, and the highly polished reflective surface, were employed by Berrecci to convey a quality appropriate to the status of the subject. As expressed in his letter, Sigismund believed marble carried within it an inherent quality of permanence, thus it was most appropriate for a building that was to withstand the 'forever'.

Sigismund and Berrecci fully understood the power of architecture as an element of its material essence. In his chapel, Sigismund was portrayed not only in his effigy, but also in one of the tondos, sculpted from red marble, as the supreme ruler-builder King Solomon.[26] The selection of materials, the discernment of their quality, and finally their deliberate use in the chapel expressed the qualities of the wise patron-builder, who used the biblical archetype King Solomon, the magnificent ruler-architect, as a prototype.[27] In the Book of Kings, Solomon proceeds to organize the construction of the Temple of Jerusalem (1 Kings 5:6–18). He prepares and delegates beforehand, importing cedars from Lebanon, transporting the logs, removing large blocks of quality stone from the quarry. The passage explains the details and specifications of the temple's furnishings and most importantly emphasizes the preoccupation with materials, their quality, their worth, and their transformation from their natural state into something finished and perfect. Moreover, King Solomon's dedication to finding and approving men with skills was made possible by his knowledge and wisdom, which he had gained from God. King Solomon, as the builder of the Temple of Jerusalem, served as a paradigm for Christian princely patrons, who fashioned themselves within this lineage, as the New Solomons.

By choosing King Solomon as a model, Sigismund emphasized royal lineage in order to claim the attributes of the biblical figure. While using his own features in the portrait bust, he borrowed qualities such as wisdom, justice, and divine right. By doing this, he justified and validated his commission in its splendour, opulence, and magnificence. An inscription on the western wall of the interior of his mausoleum reads: DOMINE DILEXISTI DECORVM DOMVS TV[A]E (You have loved, O Lord, the beauty of thy house),[28] an inscription that boldly declares God's approval of the beauty of the chapel. The concept of *decorum*, or appropriateness of architecture, reflects the idea that building fuses natural wonders in the choice of materials, virtuosity of architects and craftsmen, and the patron's wisdom, which are all God-given gifts. Building is thus an exchange or a dialogue between the natural and the divine. As a wise ruler-builder Sigismund enacted a Solomonic reciprocal exchange by orchestrating the union of material and man's skill in the building of God's house. Given the great attention Sigismund placed in selecting materials, God's admiration of the decorum of his house was first and foremost an admiration of the shaping of *matter*.

The attention placed on building materials and their multi-national origin should be seen therefore as a framework for the genesis of the Sigismund Chapel itself. The process of building relied on considerations of materials based on their value and reputation for quality, and appropriateness for the work intended. This discernment by the patron also applied to the selection of craftsmen and architects, based on their knowledge and skill. In his letter from 1517, when devising his mausoleum, Sigismund did not voice his concern about style or the formal qualities of his chapel, which perhaps hiring an Italian would guarantee, but rather, about the materials of construction. The process of importing a new architecture was more complex than having craftsmen shift their repertoire of forms naively. The king requested Italian designers and craftsmen because they were trained in Italy (Berrecci's workshop included men from Florence and Fiesole), where they acquired the skills that the king valued.[29] Architects and craftsmen were selected based on their knowledge and skill in working with materials, quarrying and transforming them into wonderful monuments pregnant with meaning. Especially in its material substance, the Sigismund Chapel raises challenging questions about the notion of Renaissance architecture in Poland as simply an Italian import. The chapel did not solely arise out of the dissemination of designs from Italy; it was shaped by a complex process of selection that took into account a variety of architectural concerns. The employment of Italian, German, and Polish artisans was determined by their strengths and talents, not their nationality. In a poem praising Sigismund for his virtue and glory, Berrecci is also admired for making mute marble speak: 'Ut cunctorum hominum Sigismundum fama loquatur/ Virtute et meritis, praestitit ipse suis./ Illius ut laudes ne marmora muta silerent/ Effecit tua nunc Bartholomaee manus.'[30] The architect's virtuosity turns silent stone into a work of wonder, which becomes a statement of Sigismund's magnificence and virtues.

Poland around 1500 was a territory in constant flux. The sons of King Casimir IV (Kazimierz Jagiellończyk; r. 1447–92) dispersed the Jagiellonian dynasty to far regions of Europe. The eldest, Vladislav II (Władysław Jagiellończyk), was elected to the Bohemian throne in 1471 and the Hungarian throne after the death of Matthias Corvinus (r. 1458–90) in 1490.[31] The early death of Jan Olbracht (r. 1492–1501) in 1501 passed the Polish crown to Aleksander (r. 1501–06), who had been the Grand Duke of Lithuania since 1492, and who spent a fair share of his reign in Vilnius.[32] Eventually, the youngest prince, Sigismund, became the King of Poland in 1506. The Jagiellonians manifested a strong presence in the cultural sphere of their vast multi-cultural empire, and their imperial pretensions spurred the building of architectural monuments. Although the complex political context of the Jagiellonian dynasty is beyond the scope of this essay, the issues of lineage, dynasty, genealogy, and continuity were important tools used in buttressing their political legitimacy, which was challenged from every angle. Building was an effective way to presence and permanence in the political landscape. The Jagiellonian realm was not only an imagined territory: Sigismund and his brothers actually travelled to Prague, Buda, and Vilnius. Their experience of this vast and multi-cultural boundary indicates the ways in which they understood the space of their empire and its physical conditions. Considering the architectural projects of the Jagiellonians, they wished to forge an identity that was articulated by materials and building processes. It was precisely this common cultural network, mercantile connections, and material sources, such as quarries and markets, which forged a world in which influential patrons and artists commingled.

The Jagiellonian imperial pretensions, while threatened and challenged, produced a political realm that was linked by cultural interests and made manifest in a shared architectural patronage. The dynasty's period in Hungary (1490–1526) was decisive for Sigismund when he spent years at the court of his brother Vladislav II, between 1490 and 1493, and again between 1498 and 1501.[33] In Hungary, he came into contact with a new method of building initiated by Matthias Corvinus and continued by his successor, Vladislav Jagiellon, an architecture executed in the classical style and ideology. The cultural and intellectual climate developing in Krakow during the fifteenth century provided the foundation for Sigismund's interests in classicism and humanism,[34] while his marriage to the Italian Bona Sforza in 1518 further justified his preference for the Italian workshops.[35] At Vladislav's court he had access to Corvinus's famous library containing architectural treatises by Vitruvius, Alberti, and Filarete (Antonio Averlino).[36] In Buda he increased his vocabulary of forms and witnessed the power of materials, especially red marble. Sigismund imported red Hungarian marble, while Florentine/Italian craftsmen like Francisco della Lora (known as Franciscus Florentinus in Poland) made their way north to Krakow to carry out new commissions.[37] Sigismund may also have purchased architectural drawings from an Italian in Buda, as the invoice from 19 November 1502 records the purchase of *picturas edificiorum* for which he paid half a florin.[38] Sigismund's immersion in this fertile architectural environment suggests that he read Alberti and explored Corvinus's library, but, more importantly, that he was a witness to a significant architectural building site in Buda of the Corvinian past, projects that were being continued by Vladislav. Sigismund's interest in the physicality of architecture and the process of building is evident by his possession of architectural sketches, and through the mechanics of architectural production in the selection of skilled masons and arranging the logistics of acquiring materials. The use of the red marble in royal commissions was a distinctive quality of Jagiellonian building, and the material triggered associations with another Jagiellonian court in Buda and thus carried with it an association of imperial power and triumphal supremacy.

At the Jagiellonian court in Hungary, Sigismund was introduced to an entire system of Renaissance building practices, treatises, drawings, *all'antica* architectural monuments, and great patron builders: Corvinus, Vladislav, and Bakócz. Although Sigismund himself never saw the Bakócz Chapel (1507–17) at Esztergom Cathedral, built for his good friend Cardinal Tamás Bakócz, it served as a model for Sigismund's mausoleum.[39] The Hungarian chronicler Evlia Tchélébi described the chapel in 1663 'like a bowl of copper with a golden net inside'.[40] The colours and materials, such as copper, bronze, and red Hungarian marble, and the ways in which light reflected the surfaces, amazed visitors to the chapel.[41] Sigismund's confidence in Bakócz's taste, but also perhaps the spreading word of the chapel's splendour, spurred Sigismund to send a draughtsman to bring back drawings for the design of the bronze grille.[42] For the Sigismund Chapel the final bronze grille was poured in 1525 by a master from Brussels; however, it was lost in a fire that destroyed his workshop.[43] The king requested a master from Nuremberg to complete the project.[44] The Boners arranged the commission with Hans Vischer in a contract that specified that the iron grille would be poured in Nuremberg and personally delivered to Krakow by the master.[45] The similarities between the two chapels are present in both the classical style and use of materials. As a political statement, red marble was a powerful reference to dynastic power and magnificence, functioning as a visual cue, connecting dispersed political realms.

The Jagiellonians shifted between Gothic and Renaissance styles for their architectural commissions. However, while both styles were used interchangeably (and often in the same building), the admiration for architecture originated in its materiality and the ways in which materials metamorphose into a demonstration of skill and virtuosity. Vladislav's architectural patronage and the importance of building materials are evident in the imposing Vladislav Hall at Hradčany, executed by Benedikt Ried in 1500 and vaulted in 1502 (Figure 12.5). The spacious hall was vaulted with double-curved ribs that form repeating six-petalled flowers.

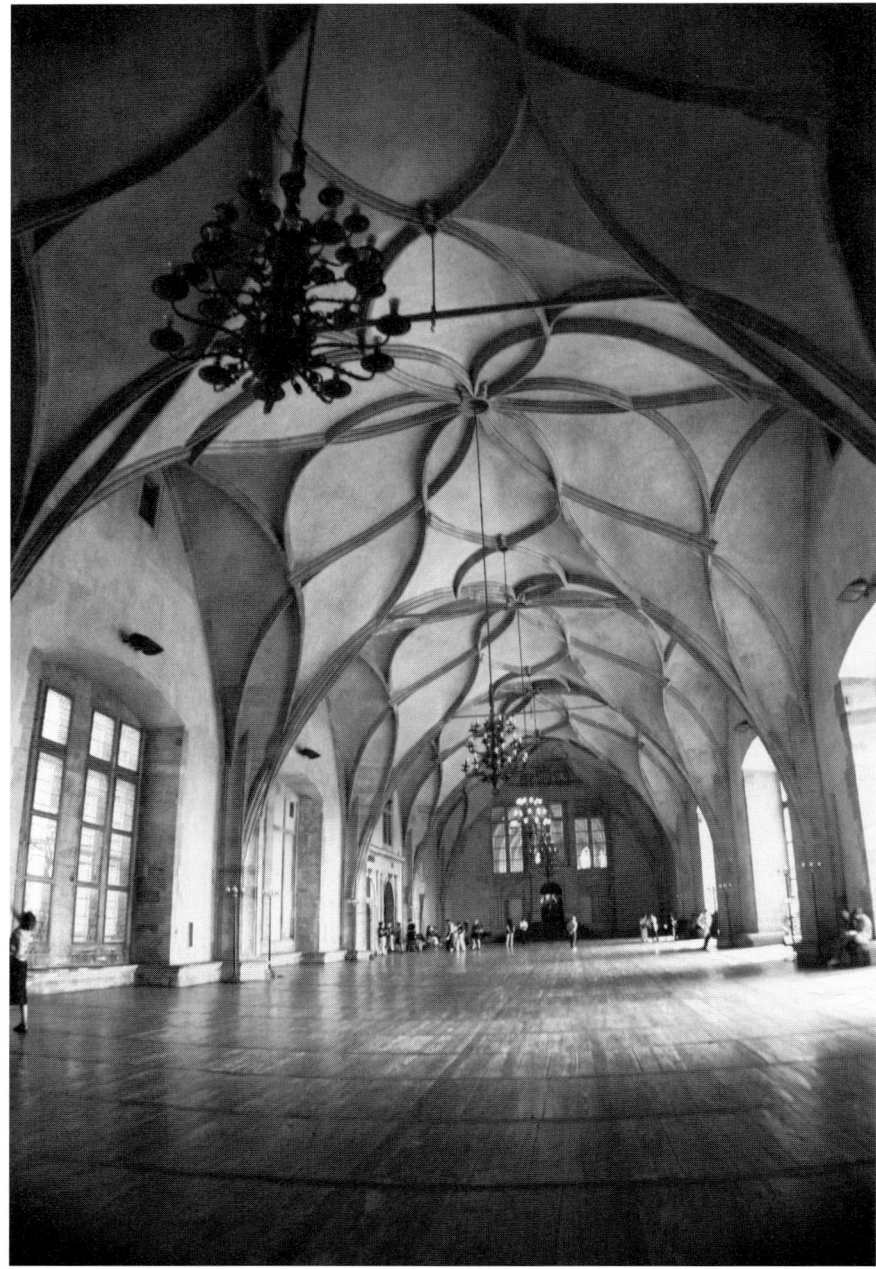

12.5. Benedikt Ried, Vladislav Hall, c. 1500, Prague

Ried's mixture and fusion of styles are evident in the juxtaposition of the vault and the Renaissance portal and exterior façade. The Louis Wing in Hradčany (1500–10) recalls the façades of the Buda palace.[46] Ried's more dynamic work is the Riders' Staircase, which led riders into the great hall. Exuberant vaults display the architect's skill and desire to push traditional architectural elements to new limits and amaze the viewer with the craftsmen's technical mastery (Figure 12.6). The Renaissance Gothic of this region was not only a melange of forms that

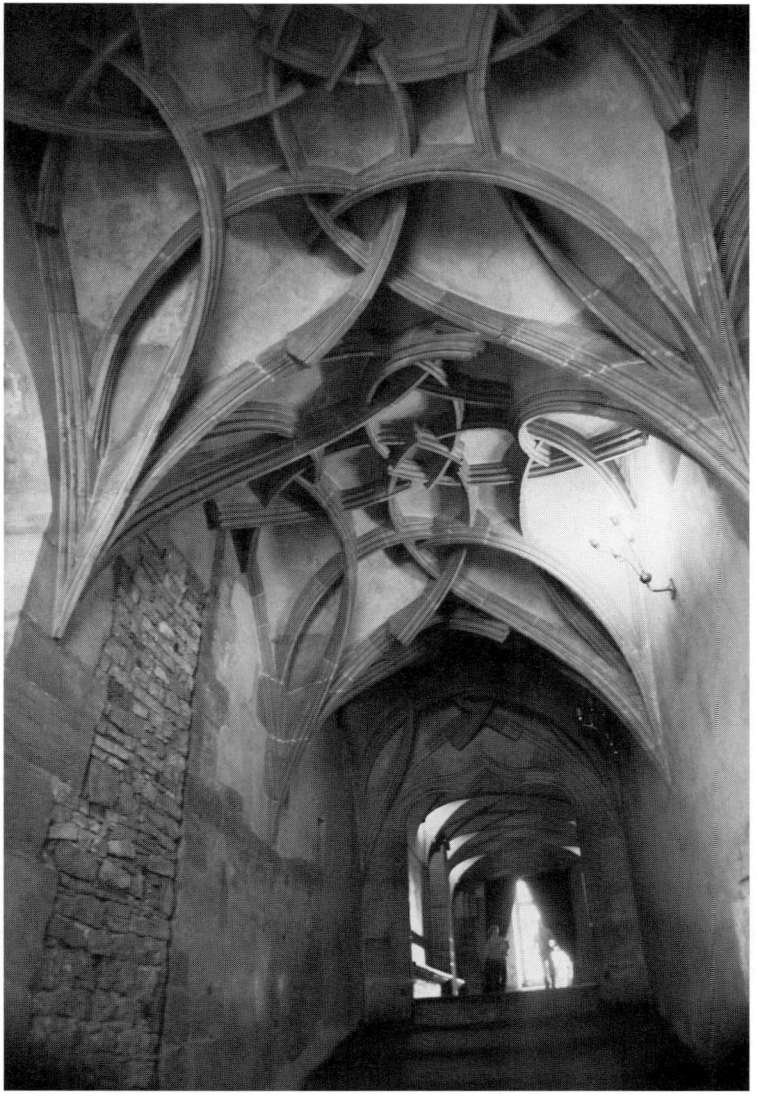

12.6. Benedikt Ried, Riders' Staircase, Prague

created a new visual language that triggered association and meaning; the technical knowledge that was required to push materials to new limits and exploit their full potential was the quality that was most admired.[47] Architecture expressed a delight in exploring the expressive potential of materials, while animating and activating a space. As the transformative qualities of materials were explored, they were understood to have metamorphosed from their raw state into something that appears technically impossible, crossing over into the realm of wonder. Furthermore, architects and craftsmen showcased the playful visual tricks of building materials, which imitate other materials, such as the Vladislav Oratory at St Vitus Cathedral executed by Hans Spiess in 1490–93 (Figures 12.7 and 12.8).[48] Here, tree branches are loosely tied by rope (*Astwerk*); the stone vault ribs have been transformed into botanical matter.[49] This material conceit not only visually undermines the human-made architectural structure (held up by tree branches); the architect reminds the beholder that surfaces are deceiving. One witnesses a tug of war between the rather primal forces of nature, which have been ordered and controlled by the architect, who has shown his dexterity and a certain *sprezzatura*, as a master of physical matter.

Perhaps there is no other building within the Jagiellonian territory that better displays the preoccupation with materials, animation, and craftsmanship than the façade of St Anne's Church in Vilnius (Figure 12.9), which was commissioned by Aleksander Jagiellon around 1501. The unidentified builder, with the skill of a goldsmith, pushed his technical

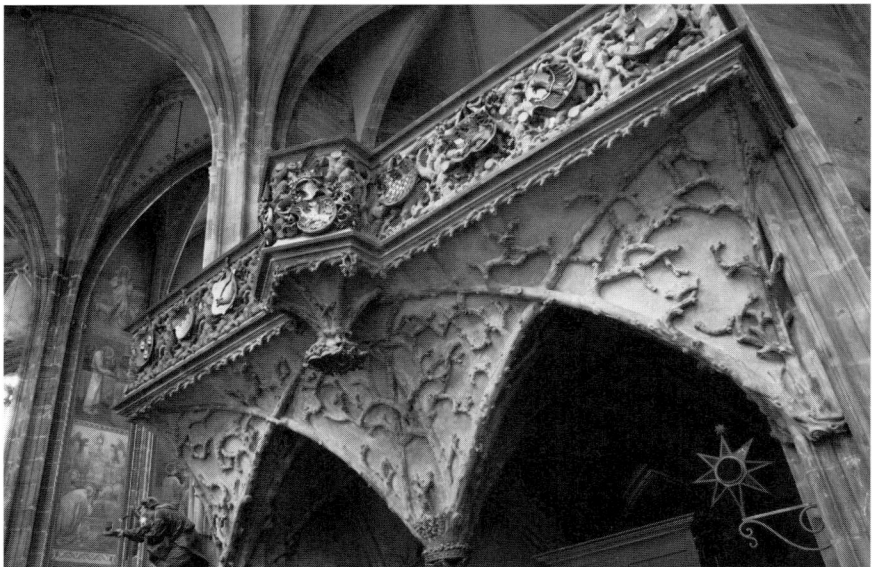

12.7. Hans Spiess, Vladislav Oratory, St Vitus Cathedral, 1490–93, Prague

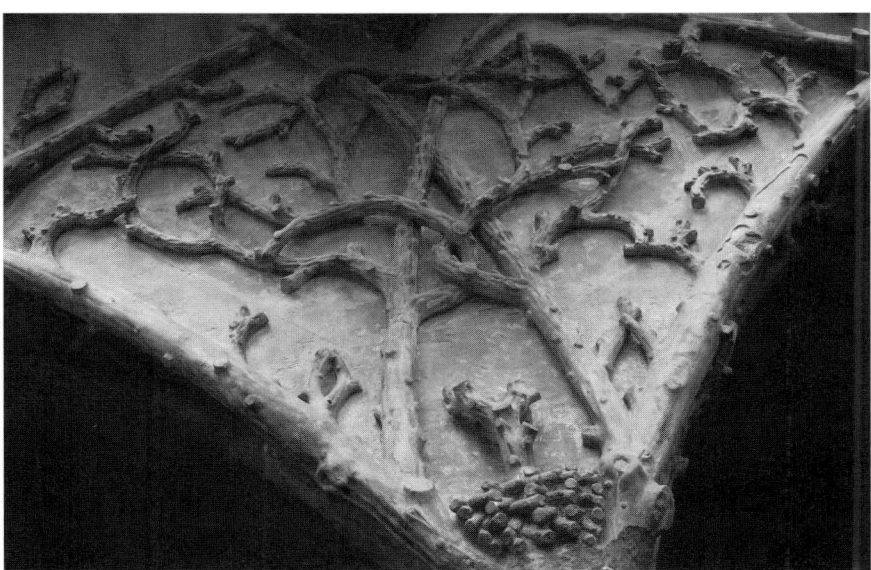

12.8. Hans Spiess, Vladislav Oratory (detail), St Vitus Cathedral, 1490–93, Prague

abilities to the limit.[50] St Anne's is a display of decorative extravagance, where the architect had shown off his extraordinary control over the brick material – the *brickness* becomes the chief characteristic of the church. It was constructed of thirty-three differently shaped bricks, ingeniously laid to create the elaborate profile of the façade (Figure 12.10).[51] The monumental colour of the red brick and the virtuosity of the brick building set the façade of the church in motion. The master of this church is unidentified; however, it is very likely that German craftsmen were called to Vilnius from Gdansk, where they were building magnificent church gables with extraordinary attention to the brick material.[52] Sigismund, who knew the church in Vilnius as he was devising his plans for his mausoleum in Krakow, would have admired the façade of St Anne's as a manifesto of material, with its wondrous tactile quality, texture, colour, and expressive abilities.

The concern with buttressing their political legitimacy led the Jagiellonians to shape the architectural landscape of their empire by carefully crafting how tradition and dynastic continuity, as well as novel models of building, might express magnificence and power. Style in architecture was one way to accomplish these aspirations; however, given the employment of Gothic and Renaissance forms, it is clear that style was an option and not a set formula.[53] In Sigismund's material acquisition and the employment of specially selected craftsmen and architects, building required knowledge and skills that were technical and highly specialized, including the knowledge of geology and natural science:

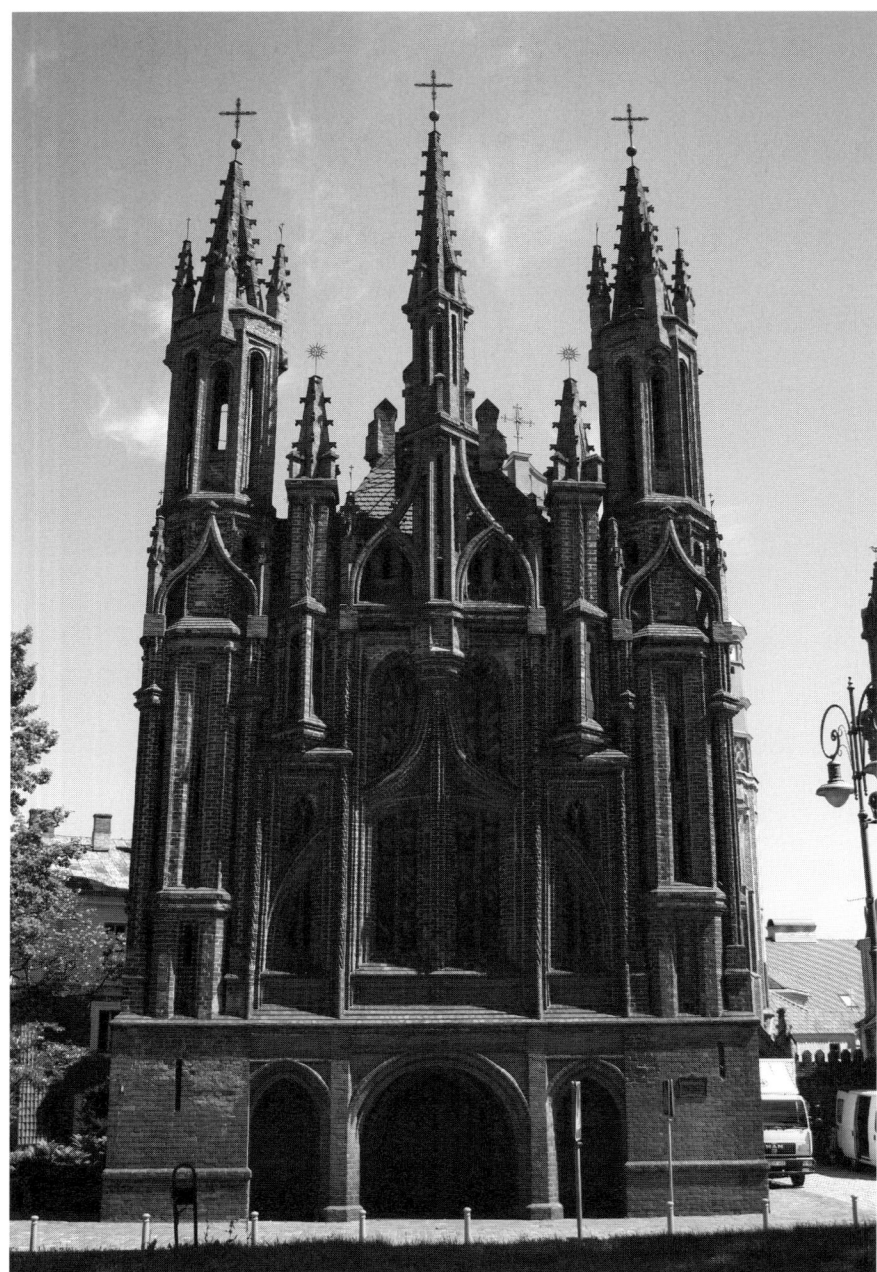

12.9. St Anne's Church, c. 1501, Vilnius

Polish stone, Venetian glass, and red Hungarian marble

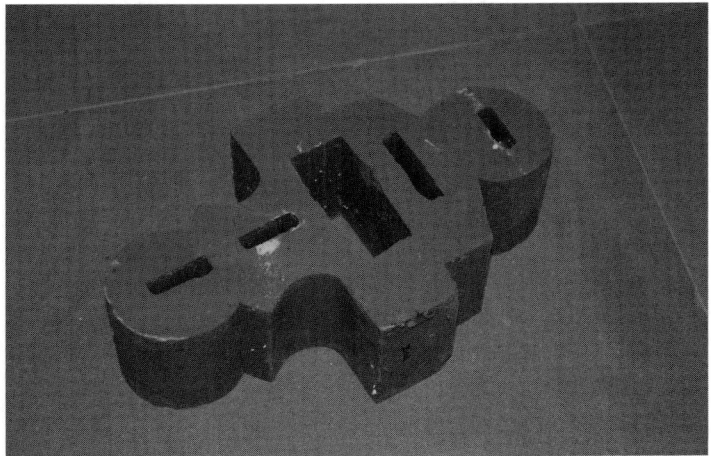

12.10. St Anne's Church (detail of brick), c. 1501, Vilnius

understanding the intrinsic qualities of materials in a microscopic sense, and being adept at understanding a material down to the level of its grain particles. Understanding materials meant having the technical skill and the power to animate and allow architecture to perform. Such were the values and expectations of Sigismund I in the building of his chapel-mausoleum. In a poem, published in Krakow in 1524, entitled *Encomium Sigismundi regis Poloniae post partam de Tartaris victoriam*, the author declared that the Sigismund Chapel triumphed the seven wonders of the world, and thus it was a home worthy of the almighty God: 'Quodque strutis cineri septem miracula mundi/ Vincit opus, summo Numine digna domus.'[54] Seeing the Sigismund Chapel as a wonder speaks about the highest admiration for the collaboration of a great patron-builder and the architect in transforming the natural world into a masterpiece or a marvel inspiring the senses. It is also a statement recognizing the chapel as permanent, withstanding the tests of time, a building worthy of God in which Sigismund intended to dwell forever.

Notes

1. Stefan S. Komornicki, 'Kaplica Zygmuntowska w katedrze na Wawelu 1517–1533', *Rocznik Krakowski* 23 (1932), p. 64. Komornicki provides 17 May 1519 as the day in which foundations were laid.
2. Komornicki, 'Kaplica Zygmuntowska', pp. 47, 49. Komornicki states that the Sigismund Chapel 'is the most outstanding work of art on Polish soil' and is considered a 'Polish cultural treasure'. Komornicki makes reference to the art historian August Essenwein, who declared the Sigismund Chapel a 'pearl of the Renaissance on this side of the Alps'. See also Jan Białostocki, *The Art of the Renaissance in Eastern Europe: Hungary, Bohemia, Poland* (Ithaca, NY: Cornell University Press, 1976), pp. 2, 37, 40, 43–4. Jan Białostocki states:

'In Hungary, Slovakia or Poland, we can meet the Renaissance – at least in the early stages of its development – in a more original, pure form', while the Sigismund Chapel 'was the first splendid Renaissance building erected in Poland from the ground and it remained unique in its stylistic purity and beauty'. The Sigismund Chapel is perhaps the most influential architectural monument in terms of its dissemination via 'copies' throughout the region, imitated by the Polish gentry, and the extent of historical attention it has received.

3 Stanisław Mossakowski, *Kaplica Zygmuntowska (1515–1533): Problematyka Artystyczna i Ideowa Mauzoleum Króla Zygmunta I* (Warsaw: Liber Pro Arte, 2007), p. 9.

4 Komornicki, 'Kaplica Zygmuntowska', pp. 50, 57. See also Kenneth F. Lewalski. 'Sigismund I of Poland: Renaissance king and patron', *Studies in the Renaissance* 14 (1967), p. 60. See also Mieczysław Morka, *Sztuka dworu Zygmunta I Starego: Treści polityczne i propagandowe* (Warsaw: Argraf, 2006), p. 38, note 87.

5 Komornicki, 'Kaplica Zygmuntowska', p. 52. See also Mossakowski, *Kaplica Zygmuntowska*, p. 44.

6 Białostocki, *The Art of the Renaissance in Eastern Europe*, p. 35. The Latin text is provided by Komornicki, 'Kaplica Zygmuntowska', p. 53.

7 It is uncertain if the Italian in Vilnius was indeed Berrecci. It is likely and thus an accepted hypothesis by scholars. Komornicki, 'Kaplica Zygmuntowska', p. 54. See also Rózsa Feuer-Tóth, *Renaissance Architecture in Hungary* (Budapest: Magyar Helikon, 1977), p. 20; Mossakowski, *Kaplica Zygmuntowska*, p. 23.

8 Komornicki, 'Kaplica Zygmuntowska', p. 53; Mossakowski, *Kaplica Zygmuntowska*, p. 35.

9 Norman Davies, *God's Playground: A History of Poland, Vol. 1: The Origins to 1795* (Oxford: Oxford University Press, 2005), pp. 102–3.

10 Komornicki, 'Kaplica Zygmuntowska', pp. 50, 57–8. The Boners even recorded funds spent on nails, p. 77.

11 Tadeusz Zadrożny, 'Starotestamentowa geneza relacji między twórcami Kaplicy Zygmuntowskiej, królem i Berreccim', *Biuletyn Historii Sztuki*, 67/2 (2005), p. 14, note 14.

12 Tomasz Ratajczak, *Mistrz Benedykt: Królewski Architekt Zygmunta I* (Krakow: Universitas, 2011), p. 59.

13 Komornicki, 'Kaplica Zygmuntowska', pp. 70, 73.

14 Komornicki, 'Kaplica Zygmuntowska', p. 72.

15 Ireniusz Płuska, M. Rembiś, and A. Smoleńska, 'Kamień w architekturze i dekoracji Kaplicy Zygmuntowskiej', *Biuletyn Historii Sztuki*, 67/1–2 (2003), pp. 147, 153.

16 Płuska et al., 'Kamień w architekturze i dekoracji', p. 148.

17 Płuska et al., 'Kamień w architekturze i dekoracji', p. 154.

18 Płuska et al., 'Kamień w architekturze i dekoracji', p. 149.

19 Płuska et al., 'Kamień w architekturze i dekoracji', p. 149. See also Feuer-Tóth, *Renaissance Architecture in Hungary*, p. 13, who states that the material was quarried on the estate of the archbishops of Esztergom, at Süttő and Tardos (approximately 50 kilometres from Buda). See also Płuska et al., 'Kamień w architekturze i dekoracji', p. 161. See also Pál Lővei, 'Routes and meaning: The use of red marble in medieval central Europe', in Jaynie Anderson (ed.), *Crossing Cultures: Conflict, Migration and Convergence. The Proceedings of the 32nd International Congress in the History of Art* (Carlton, Victoria: The Miegunyah Press, 2009), pp. 477, 480.

20 Komornicki, 'Kaplica Zygmuntowska', p. 75. The costs of the marble including its quarrying and shipment, from 24 November 1525 until 13 June 1526, totalled 558 florins; see pp. 74, 76.

21 Komornicki, 'Kaplica Zygmuntowska', p. 70; see also Morka, *Sztuka dworu Zygmunta I Starego*, p. 209.

22 Lewalski, 'Sigismund I of Poland', p. 63; see also Feuer-Tóth, *Renaissance Architecture in Hungary*, p. 23.

23 Płuska et al., 'Kamień w architekturze i dekoracji', p. 147; see also Stanisław Mossakowski, 'Kiedy, jak i przez kogo wznoszona była i dekorowana Kaplica Zygmuntowska', *Kwartalnik Architektury i Urbanistyki*, 39/2 (1994), 103, p. 107. Mossakowski states that from April to November in 1524 and from February to November in 1525 intensive work was carried out in stone quarries.

24 Komornicki, 'Kaplica Zygmuntowska', p. 69. See also Płuska et al., 'Kamień w architekturze i dekoracji', p. 147.

25 Mossakowski, Kaplica Zygmuntowska, pp. 264–76; Morka, *Sztuka dworu Zygmunta I Starego*, p. 261.

26 Białostocki, *The Art of the Renaissance in Eastern Europe*, p. 39.

27 Zadrożny, 'Starotestamentowa geneza', pp. 9–57. For a discussion of the 'reactivation' of the Temple of Jerusalem see Alexander Nagel and Christopher S. Wood, *Anachronic Renaissance* (New York: Zone Books, 2010), p. 65.

28 Mieczysław Morka, 'Kaplica Zygmuntowska: Król Salomon – princeps fundator', *Biuletyn Historii Szuki* 1–2 (2005), pp. 60, 94. See also Zadrożny, 'Starotestamentowa geneza', p. 15, note 22. Or Mossakowski, *Kaplica Zygmuntowska*, pp. 54, 260.

29 Komornicki, 'Kaplica Zygmuntowska', p. 61. Komornicki states that at least four of the workers came from Florence or Fiesole. See also Mossakowski, *Kaplica Zygmuntowska*, pp. 20, 46.

30 Mossakowski, 'Kiedy, jak i przez kogo', p. 126.

31 Davies, *God's Playground*, pp. 110–13. See also Białostocki, *The Art of the Renaissance in Eastern Europe*, p. 4, and Feuer-Tóth, *Renaissance Architecture in Hungary*, p. 7.

32 Robert M. Kunkel, 'Fundacje Aleksandra Jagiellończyka w Wilnie i Krakowie', *Sztuka około 1500. Materiały Sesji Stowarzyszenia Historyków Sztuki Gdańsk, listopad 1996* (Warsaw: Arx Regia, 1997), p. 141.

33 Feuer-Tóth, *Renaissance Architecture in Hungary*, p. 20.

34 Mossakowski, *Kaplica Zygmuntowska*, p. 18. Sigismund was educated by Jan Długosz and Filip Kallimach. See also Lewalski, 'Sigismund I of Poland', pp. 51–3, 57.

35 For more on Bona Sforza's journey to Poland published in English see: Lewalski, 'Sigismund I of Poland', p. 49. Bona's role in commissioning works in the Italian style is a large topic that can't be treated in this essay.

36 Feuer-Tóth, *Renaissance Architecture in Hungary*, p. 9; Białostocki, *The Art of the Renaissance in Eastern Europe*, pp. 7, 9. See also Thomas DaCosta Kaufmann, *Court, Cloister, and City: The Art and Culture of Central Europe, 1450–1800* (Chicago, IL: University of Chicago Press, 1995), p. 53; Mossakowski, *Kaplica Zygmuntowska*, p. 33.

37 Białostocki, *The Art of the Renaissance in Eastern Europe*, pp. 29, 35. See also Lewalski, 'Sigismund I of Poland', pp. 55–6. Francisco della Lora stayed in Poland from around 1501 until his death in 1516.

38 Morka, *Sztuka dworu Zygmunta I Starego*, p. 170. See also Białostocki, *The Art of the Renaissance in Eastern Europe*, p. 19; Mossakowski, *Kaplica Zygmuntowska*, p. 32.

39 Mossakowski, *Kaplica Zygmuntowska*, p. 22. Mossakowski states that Cardinal Tamás Bakócz might have had recommended Berrecci to Sigismund.

40 Białostocki, *The Art of the Renaissance in Eastern Europe*, p. 32. Białostocki footnotes the following: Evlia Tchélébi's text in Balogh, 1956, p. 176.

41 Białostocki, *The Art of the Renaissance in Eastern Europe*, p. 32.

42 Komornicki, 'Kaplica Zygmuntowska', p. 69. See also Lewalski, 'Sigismund I of Poland', p. 65. Also, Morka, *Sztuka dworu Zygmunta I Starego*, p. 207. Morka states that, in 1524,

the painter Sebald Singer was asked to design the bronze grille, which was not approved by Seweryn Boner, who sent a copier to Esztergom Cathedral.

43 Komornicki, 'Kaplica Zygmuntowska', pp. 80–1; Morka, *Sztuka dworu Zygmunta I Starego*, p. 207.
44 Komornicki, 'Kaplica Zygmuntowska', p. 81.
45 Komornicki, 'Kaplica Zygmuntowska', pp. 81–2.
46 Feuer-Tóth, *Renaissance Architecture in Hungary*, p. 20.
47 I thank Professor Ethan Matt Kavaler for introducing me to the topic of Renaissance Gothic. My work on St Anne's Church in Vilnius, as a Renaissance Gothic monument within the Jagiellonian realm, is a future project. See Ethan Matt Kavaler, *Renaissance Gothic: Architecture and the Arts in Northern Europe, 1470–1540* (New Haven, CT: Yale University Press, 2012).
48 Jiřína Hořejši, 'Podstawy ideowe architektury dworskiej za panowania Władysława Jagiellończyka', *Sztuka i ideologia XV wieku: Materiały sympozjum komitetu nauk o sztuce polskiej akademii nauk Warszawa, 1–4 grudnia 1976*, ed. Piotr Skubiszewski (Warsaw: Wydawnictwo PWN, 1978), p. 481.
49 Norbert Nussbaum, *German Gothic Church Architecture*, trans. Scott Kleager (New Haven, CT: Yale University Press, 2000), p. 191.
50 Fryderyk Papée, *Aleksander Jagiellończyk* (Krakow: PAU, 1949), pp. 23–4.
51 Władysław Zahorski, *Kościół Św Anny w Wilnie* (Vilnius: Druk. J. Zawadzki, 1905), p. 14.
52 Kunkel, 'Fundacje Aleksandra Jagiellończyka', p. 131. Aleksander would have seen these building practices during his stay in Gdansk from 25 May until 7 June in 1504.
53 Kaufmann, *Court, Cloister, and City*, p. 57. See also Lewalski, 'Sigismund I of Poland', p. 50.
54 Mossakowski, 'Kiedy, jak i przez kogo', p. 94.

13 ✧ Reveal or conceal: chopines and the display of material wealth in early modern Valencia and Venice

Elizabeth Semmelhack

THE DRESS of upper-class women in early modern Europe was marked by an ostentatious use of rare and exotic materials as well as the responsibility of consuming and displaying materials of local manufacture. Footwear was integral to this sartorial splendour and none more so than the towering platform shoe known as the chopine,[1] one of the most extraordinary forms of footwear ever worn in Western dress. The wide variety of imported and domestic luxury materials used in early modern European women's dress has long been the subject of study, but the role of the chopine in both the consumption and display of these materials as well as the materials used in the making of chopines themselves has been neglected.[2]

Women throughout Europe wore chopines, but this form of footwear never represented a pan-European fashion; rather, chopines were expressly linked to Spain, Portugal, and Italy, where the fashion flourished. However, even within southern Europe chopines do not represent a single monolithic style; the materials with which they were made and the materials that they were designed to display varied by region. A comparison of the distinctive styles of chopines in Valencia and Venice will illuminate some of these differences.

Both Valencia and Venice were renowned during the fifteenth, sixteenth, and early seventeenth centuries for the high chopines worn by the women of the wealthiest families. Each city, however, produced distinctly different forms of chopines and they were worn in strikingly different ways. This essay will show the ways in which these fashion developments were constrained and fostered by locally available – often remarkably humble – materials, as well by local social and economic factors, such as familial prestige, civic identity, and the promotion of the industries that drove local economies.

Luxury chopines from Valencia were made with cork platforms completely covered in gilt leather, frequently embellished with precious stones and festooned with silk ribbons. They were the pride of the city and were worn as prominent accessories of dress for 'important women',[3] whose skirts grazed the tops of these ostentatious forms of footwear. In contrast, chopines made for upper-class women in Venice had wooden bases that soared much higher than Valencian models. These wooden platforms were also completely covered in leather, but only minimally ornamented, reflecting the fact that Venetian chopines were not worn as visible accessories of dress but instead functioned as foundation garments completely concealed under women's skirts. The primary function of Venetian chopines was to aid in the display of dress fabric, thereby increasing the amount of textile required to make the wearers' skirts.[4]

Origin of the chopine

Since antiquity, high platform footwear has been a gendered article of dress in the West. Evidence can be found as far back as the sixth century, when Greek statues, such as the Phrasikleia Kore and the Berlin Kore, were sculpted as wearing thick-soled footwear as part of their elaborate attire.[5] Greek-art historian Katherine Morrow, discussing the fifth-century sculptures from the east frieze of the Parthenon, notes that thick-soled footwear was a feature of feminine dress in Greek fashion.[6] The materials used in the creation of this footwear appear to have been varied. Some extant sculptures suggest layered leather soles such as the high platform footwear comprised of five distinct layers, seen on the foot of the figure of *Tragoidia* from Pergamon. Others appear to depict platform footwear featuring leather-covered bases perhaps of cork, such as the exceptionally high sandals depicted on the numerous terracotta figurines of Aphrodite from Myrina, Corinth, and Tangara (Figure 13.1). The ivory and gold sculpture of Athena created by Pheidias in 438 BCE for the Parthenon featured thick, wood-soled platform sandals which the poet Kratinus described as Tyrrhenian sandals from Etruria decorated with a narrative scene in relief.[7]

The women of ancient Rome wore platform footwear similar to, and often in emulation of, Greek and Etruscan examples.[8] As in ancient Greece, artistic depictions and textual references exist but archaeological evidence has also survived. The boggy conditions found in the northern provinces of the Roman Empire have preserved examples of Roman footwear with layered leather or cork soles, but these soles only rise a centimetre or so in height.[9]

If the platform footwear of ancient Greek women inspired the fashion among Roman women, the expansion of the Roman Empire disseminated it to a much wider populace. As the work of Carol van Driel-Murray has demonstrated, the arrival of Romans into newly conquered territories brought a radical transformation of local dress.[10] Her careful study of

Reveal or conceal 285

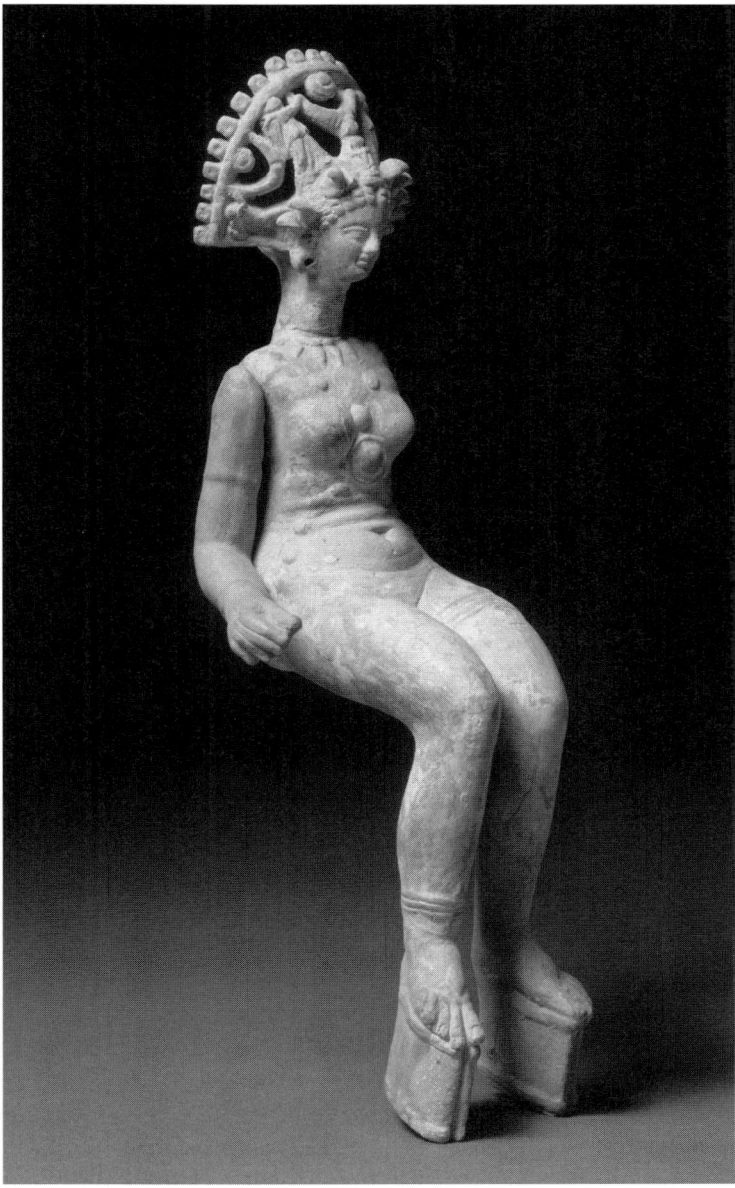

13.1. Small terracotta statues of Aphrodite wearing high platform footwear were made in great quantity in Myrina, Tangara and Corinth. This first-century example depicts the goddess wearing an ornate *stephane*, jewellery, and exceptionally high platform sandals. Greek, first century BCE, Louvre, Paris

archaeological evidence suggests that local women in civilian settlements were the first to take up the full range of Roman footwear styles; examples of fashionable footwear have been found even in isolated frontier communities.[11] At Vindolanda in Northumbria, Driel-Murray has noted that cork-soled slippers account for 5 per cent of the excavated footwear.[12] Although no extant Roman period footwear has survived on the Iberian Peninsula, Roman artworks reveal the presence of platform footwear and it is to this region with its abundance of cork that we must turn our attention.

All the cork in Spain: chopines in Valencia
Scholars have long acknowledged the importance of Iberian agricultural and metallurgic resources to Rome. One of the peninsula's most notable assets was its forests of *Quercus suber*, or cork oak, which was used by the Romans in the production of footwear. Although remains of Roman-period cork-soled footwear have been found in places as remote as Northumbria in the UK, archaeological evidence of cork-soled footwear production and wear in Iberia has not survived, due to environmental conditions. Artworks, however, provide good reason to believe that this type of footwear was a part of Iberian dress in Roman times.

Clearer evidence that cork-soled footwear was produced and worn on the Iberian Peninsula dates to the period of Moorish dominance of Iberia (718–1492). Costume historian Yedida Kalfon Stilman suggests that cork-soled footwear was one of the few aspects of Iberian culture embraced by the conquering Arabs.[13] Historian Thomas Glick has established that the Andalusi Muslims were heir to a number of oak-based industries developed by the Romans including the making of cork-soled shoes, and that, under Moorish rule, cork-soled shoes became a staple of the export trade.[14] An eleventh-century document records an order for 'twenty corkwood shoes of which ten should be made plain, of the type you have previously imported'.[15] The primacy of the material aspects of these shoes is reflected in the Arab word for this Iberian cork-soled footwear which was *aqraq* (singular *qurq*), coming from the Latin word *quercus* or cork. The term subsequently returned to Castilian as the cognate *alcorque* meaning cork or cork-soled shoes.[16] Evidence for the manufacturing of *aqraq* in Muslim Spain can be found in the *darb*, or small urban quarters established during Moorish rule, where members of particular guilds lived and worked. Granada, for instance, had a *darb* called *al-Qarraqin*, where *aqraq* were made.[17]

Information concerning the wearing of platform footwear by women in Moorish Spain and across the Maghreb is exceptionally difficult to find because mentions of women's clothing in Arab chronicles are almost non-existent.[18] The scant evidence that does exist suggests that high platform shoes were associated exclusively with female dress. Early evidence of thick platform footwear worn by upper-class Christian women in Spain comes from the grave of Doña Teresa Petri, founder of the Cistercian monastery of Santa Maria la Real de Gradefes in León, who died in 1187.[19] The Spanish used the term *chapín* for chopines. The 1611 dictionary by Covarrubias suggests that the word *chapín* came from the Arabic term *chipin*, which itself was related to the word *sapin*, meaning fir tree.[20] This muddle of terms reflects the continued use of platform footwear across the Iberian Peninsula as well as the centrality of the materiality of the chopine. The suggestion that Spanish chopines may have been linked in some way to fir trees also suggests the fluidity of fashion across cultural borders as Italian chopines were almost exclusively made of soft pine wood such as fir.

The style of these chopines also provides evidence of the influence of Moorish taste on upper-class Christian dress. One of the hallmarks of extant sixteenth-century Spanish chopines is the use of finely tooled leather in keeping with the ornate embellishment of leather found on other luxury goods such as leather-bound books and wall hangings. Doña Teresa Petri's chopines indicate that this tradition of covering cork platforms with tooled leather dates at least to the twelfth century. The upturned and closed toes of Doña Teresa Petri's chopines are unique among extant Spanish chopines and may reflect Moorish fashion.

The Catholic *reconquista* of Spain in 1492 brought the impact of Moorish material culture on Iberian dress into greater focus. As Christian Spaniards struggled to create a distinctive identity, nearly every aspect of culture, especially dress, came under scrutiny to determine if it was Muslim or Christian in origin.[21] Despite its potentially confusing cross-cultural use, the chopine escaped censure because it signified luxury more than it signified cultural identity and thereby remained a central accessory of upper-class dress.[22]

The wearing of cork-soled footwear in early modern Christian Spain spanned cultural affiliation, gender, and socioeconomic status. Mentions of low cork-soled shoes called *alcorque* and *pantofle* can also be found in inventories of men's wardrobes.[23] The late fifteenth-century sculpture of Juan II of Castile by Gil de Siloé at the Monastery of Miraflores shows the king in shoes with leather or fabric covered soles 'two corks' high; that is to say, soles made using two layers of cork and measuring around 4 centimetres in height.

Women also wore *alcorque* and *pantofle*, but the *chapín* was explicitly feminine. It was the height of the sole that identified chopines as exclusively female forms of footwear. The use of three layers of cork seemed to be enough to confirm the gender of the wearer. Yet elevation alone was not enough to establish socioeconomic status. Rather, it was the materials used to cover the cork platforms of Spanish chopines that signified privilege.

On the Iberian Peninsula the waterproof qualities and insulating properties of cork were exploited to make simple unembellished overshoes worn by the women of the lower classes. In contrast, the tall cork chopines covered in luxury leather or textiles were the prerogative of upper-class women, who wore them for the purpose of display rather than protection. The luxury materials used to make them were specifically related to the cladding of chopines. It was the silk brocade fabric and gilded leather covering the cork bases that transformed Spanish chopines from practical forms of footwear into accessories of upper-class dress whose function lay in the consumption and display of the rare and expensive materials that decorated them rather than as a means of navigating muddy byways.

Extant footwear, works of art and social commentaries from the sixteenth century reveal the fashion for highly embellished chopines encrusted with jewels and precious metals in the wardrobes of women from the elite Christian families of Spain.[24] Surviving inventories and other records include mentions of chopines, but only those from Valencia receive special notice. *Tapines*, as they were called in Valencia, account for thirty-seven of the seventy pairs of chopines in the wardrobe of Juana, Queen of Castile and Aragon.[25] The *guardaroba* inventory of Lucrezia Borgia, daughter of the Valencian pope Alexander VI, further distinguished between the *tapines* of gilded and painted leather from Valencia and the other *tapines* in her wardrobe.[26] Others outside of Spain also coveted *tapines*; a youthful Lorenzo Strozzi of the powerful Florentine banking family wrote home to Florence while in exile in 1450 about a pair of golden chopines he had seen in Valencia, regretful that he couldn't buy them because they were too expensive.[27]

The precise cost of these elegant chopines is difficult to ascertain, but comments such as Lorenzo Strozzi's indicate that they were costly. Although not identified as Valencian, the two pairs of chopines embroidered with gold thread ordered for the wedding of the Infanta Isabel, daughter of Ferdinand and Isabel I, in 1490 cost more than three-quarters the price of a team of mules.[28] The term *chapín de la reina* or the 'Queen's chopine' was used when the people were pressed into service and/or forced to contribute revenue to cover the expense of royal weddings.[29] These anecdotal references suggest that luxury chopines were highly priced and designed to be worn as extravagant items of dress.

The use of elaborately decorated leather and the multiple rows of eyelets to accommodate silk or velvet ribbons suggest that chopines such as these were designed to be seen. Indeed, there is ample evidence to suggest that Spanish women in many places allowed the hems of their dresses to skim the tops of their chopines. Cesare Vecellio's book *Habiti antichi et moderni di tutto il mondo* (*Ancient and Modern Clothes from Various Places of the World*), published in 1590, although not always reliable as a source, describes the manner in which Spanish chopines were worn: 'Underneath they wear a floor-length gown of gold brocade or of silk or *damasco* and on their feet certain high *pianelle*, which are tied as are those of the Clogging Friars; these ties are of velvet, and they are visible because the gown does not reach down to the *pianelle* themselves.'[30] Numerous works of art also show that many Spanish women wore their chopines fully visible (Figure 13.2).

The fact that many Spanish women's dresses skimmed the tops of their chopines may have given rise to the common misconception that

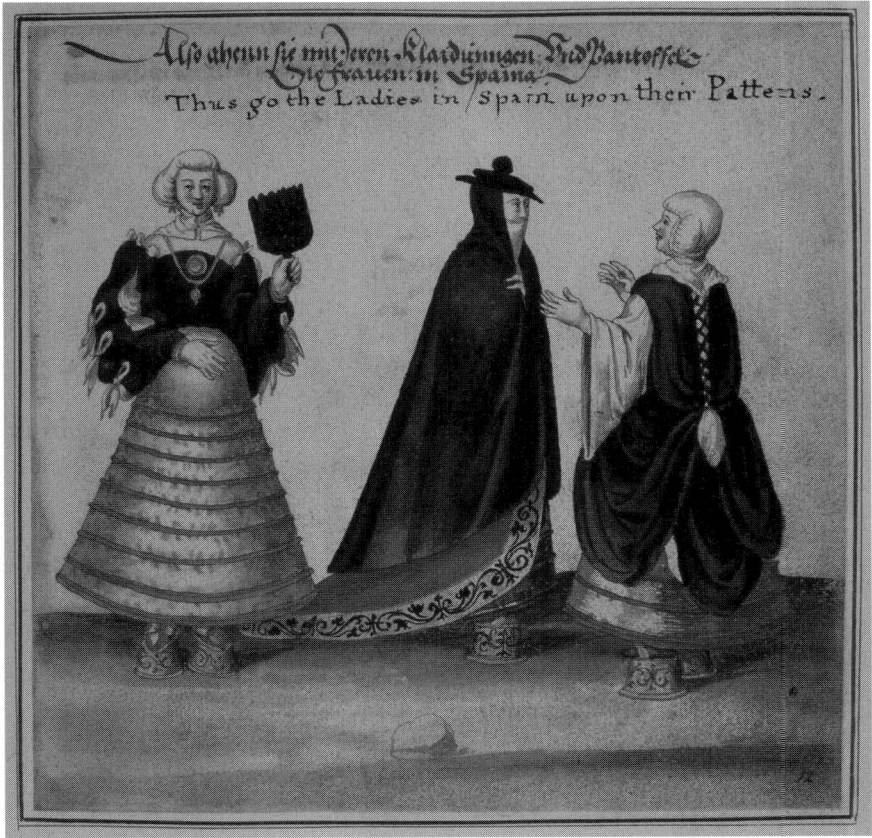

13.2. This watercolour shows Spanish women wearing their distinctive farthingales and high chopines. The hems of their farthingales do not conceal the footwear; instead they skim the tops of the chopines allowing the brightly coloured and ornately ornamented footwear to catch the viewer's eye. The chopines lift the women and their dresses above the ground but the highly embellished nature of their chopines brings their use as practical overshoes into question. Spanish Ladies, c. 1540, Museo Stibbert

all chopines, regardless of region, were worn to raise women's dresses above the ground. Although upper-class Spanish chopines were worn in the manner of overshoes, meaning that they were slipped on over footwear and worn out-of-doors, their elaborate decoration and their use of fine materials such as gilded kid, brocaded silk, or sumptuous velvet provide evidence of their real function, which was the proclamation of the wearer's status rather than protection from the dirt of daily life.

In Valencia, *saboteurs* (shoemakers) and *tapiners* (chopine makers) established separate guilds in the fourteenth century. This division of labour stipulated that *tapiners* were not allowed to make shoes, while the shoemakers could only make chopines for their own wives.[31] The *Libre del mustaçaf* (*Book of the Inspector of Weights and Measures*) from 1563 held in the Valencia Municipal Archives devotes five folios to *tapin* makers, suggesting the importance of this luxury commodity to the city.[32] Revisions to the *Libre del mustaçaf* in Valencia in 1583 indicate that the making of gilded chopines had become a matter of civic pride in Valencia and assert the demand for quality control.[33] Many cities in Spain were associated with exceptionally fine leather, but no other city had the reputation for making such fine chopines. The revisions include the stipulation that no chopine maker be permitted to use anything other than metal-leafed goatskin in the fabrication of *tapines* and that the use of gilded sheepskin was 'a deceit and a fraud'.[34] The soles were required to be of the best ox leather, and the use of new cork was made mandatory, revealing support of the local suppliers of the component materials from which chopines were made.[35]

Close examination of a pair of early sixteenth-century chopines currently held in Museu Diocesà in Solsona, Spain, offers insight into Spanish and probably Valencian chopines (Figure 13.3).[36] The size of the chopines is quite small. They measure a mere 17.5 centimetres in length and may have been made for a young girl. The platforms measure 7.45 centimetres at the front and because of a slight incline of the platform measure 9.1 centimetres at the back. X-rays of these chopines taken on behalf of the author reveal that they were made using four layers of cork. These layers of cork served as a common way of describing the height of Spanish chopines. Thus this pair is 'four corks high'. It has been assumed that cork-soled chopines were made by stacking layers of cork that are fixed in place; a fragmentary example found at the Alhambra reveals that its cork layers were secured with reed pegging.[37] X-rays of the Solsona chopines, however, do not show pegging.[38] Instead the X-rays reveal distinct hollows in the interior suggesting that the middle two layers are doughnut-shaped, with a hollow core.

The removal of the interior cork was not required to make the cork lighter. Yet it would have taken effort and had to have been done to

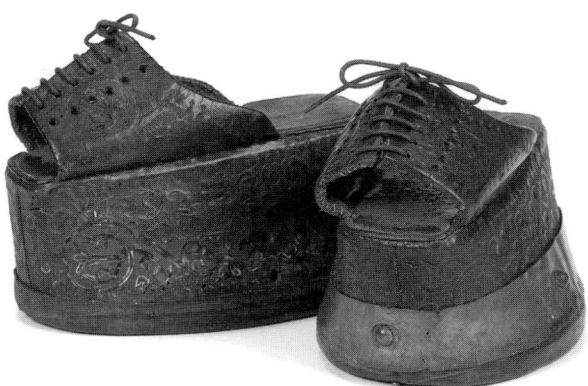

13.3. Although Spanish chopines were made using lightweight cork, their blocky design makes them appear ponderous and heavy. This pair was covered in expensive leather that was elaborately tooled and gilded. Remnants of the gilding can be seen along the lower edge of the chopine, which is missing its protective metal guard. Probably Valencian, sixteenth century, Museu Diocesà i Comarcal de Solsona, Spain

some end. Since the cork was completely hidden from view beneath the chopine's leather 'envelope' perhaps the Solsona chopines provide evidence of, or can shed light on, some kind of 'deceit'. Perhaps the excised cork was repurposed for something else – the making of cork stoppers for glass bottles appears to have only begun in the sixteenth century. Or perhaps this effort was undertaken to increase the chopines' stability. Although the void created by the missing cork may seem to have introduced structural weakness, the hollow may also have made allowances for the natural elasticity of cork and allowed the layers to be laminated without the need for pegging, thus introducing greater stability. In addition, the terms 'old' and 'new corks' mentioned in the *Libre del mustaçaf* might refer to when cork was harvested rather than to the reuse of cork or to the hollow revealed by the X-rays. All of this simply highlights the challenges faced when attempting to unravel the history of the chopine.

Without pegging, it appears that the layers of cork used to make the Solsona chopines were glued together. Valencian chopine makers are known to have used rice starch as an adhesive. The exterior of each layered cork platform is wrapped in a single piece of leather, which is assumed to be vegetable-tanned goat skin. The leather is secured with a single lapped centre seam that runs vertically up the front of the platform; glue was also probably used to adhere the skin to the cork base. Ruth Matilda Anderson's examination of the damaged chopines recovered from a pile of refuse under a stair at the Alhambra reveals that the leather used to cover the bases was sometimes lined with coarse linen and interlined with paper most likely to add rigidity to the thin and delicate goat skin.[39] The upper is what today would be called an open-toed split vamp, but in sixteenth-century Valencia this style was termed a 'closed vamp' (*capellada*). A *capellada* featured two leather side pieces each pierced with two rows of six eyelets through which ribbons were laced. Currently the *capelladas* are secured with a single leather lace, but artworks such as Jan Cornelisz Vermeyen's *Seated Oriental Woman* of 1545 suggest that textile ribbons were laced through all of the holes to decorative effect.

The footbed and the vamp are lined with brown leather. The footbed leather is stamped with a regular pattern of circles in varying sizes. The sole is probably ox hide glued to the base of the cork. X-rays reveal that a single nail enters the platform at a forty-degree angle at the site of the vertical centre seam, piercing the sole leather, platform leather, and interior cork base. The leather that covers the cork platform and the leather of the vamp are elaborately stamped and tooled with foliate and geometric designs evidencing Moorish influence. One of the chopines retains a ring of lead that encircles the base of its platform. The other chopine is missing this metal band, revealing the original gilding of the leather. Here the extravagance of this pair of chopines is revealed.

Fine leather and luxury leather goods made up some of Spain's most famous export products. The English term *cordwainer*, meaning shoemaker, comes from the word *cordovan* used for the fine leather from Cordoba. Valencia was also renowned for its expensive leather. Much of the finest leather was decorated with stamping, embossment, and gilding. Silver-foil and tin were commonly used to 'gild' sixteenth-century Spanish leather, including the leather used to make Valencian chopines. According to J.W. Waterer, before cutting, skins were entirely silver or tin-leafed. After being leafed, they were then covered in a yellow glaze to impart a gold colour and then were stamped and worked with the intended design.[40] The Solsona pair seems to have been gilded in such a manner. Where the gilding is still extant on this pair it retains a very bright sheen and in the areas where the gilding has worn away one can see the original layers of white gesso and red bole used to enhance the brilliance of the gold varnish that would have been applied over the top. The areas where the gold colour has escaped damage still gleam because of the application of *glair*, a glaze of egg white that was commonly applied to gilded leather to keep the silver from tarnishing.[41] Although it might seem wasteful that entire hides were gilded, Waterer maintains that it would have been considerably more labour intensive to accurately gild small surface areas after they were cut. The design on the Solsona chopines includes the typical stippled *gullioché* pattern in the background to add a glittering quality to the leather while the larger foliate designs and their unbroken surfaces allowed the gilt to shine.

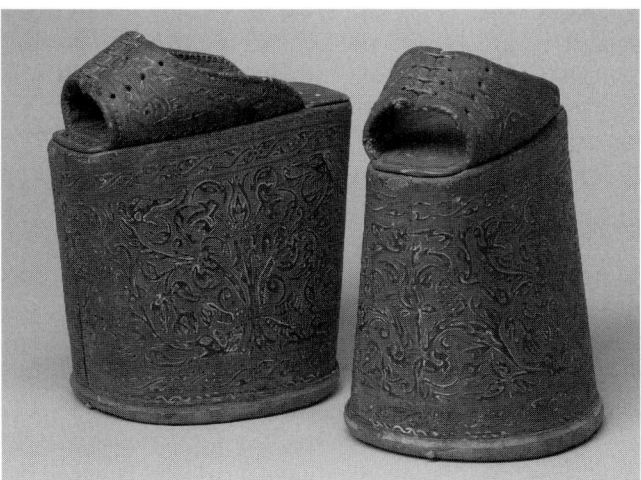

13.4. This pair of high Spanish chopines is evidence of the 'elbow high' chopines worn by women in Spain. Like the pair from Solsona, these chopines feature tooled leather and four sets of eyelets through which expensive ribbon would have been laced. Probably Valencian, before 1540. Kunsthistorisches Museum Wien, Sammlung Schloss Ambras

Examination of another extant pair of Spanish chopines held in the collection of the Kunsthistorisches Museum Wien, Sammulung Schloss Ambras, also shows traces of gilding, but reveals no evidence of gesso or bole (Figure 13.4). X-rays instead suggest that the white painted details may be lead-based and were intended to be seen. Certainly the black painted details on the surface are decorative. The little bit of metallic finish that can still be seen may be silver or tin glazed to appear gold; the quality and effect are quite different from the 'gilding' on the pair from Solosona. The chopines held in the Ambras Castle collection are substantially taller than the Solsona chopines, and X-rays reveal that they comprised ten layers of cork. The late fifteenth-century *arcipreste* Alfonso Martínez de Toledo lamented that there was hardly enough cork in Spain to satisfy the demands of women for chopines and that by his estimation chopines had risen as high as the 'length of an elbow'.[42] Toledo's comments about the heights of fashionable chopines may seem an exaggeration, but extant chopines such as the pair from Ambras Castle as well as period artworks corroborate his observation As with the Solsona pair, the layers of cork are not held together by any central pegging and there is a void in the centre. Only the top and bottommost layers of cork seem to be solid layers. These chopines were also made for a small foot and, like the Solsona pair, may have been intended for wear by a relatively young girl.

In Spain, social standing was proclaimed through dress, and women's dress, in particular, offered opportunities to flaunt familial wealth as well as the wealth of the empire. As a Spanish writer of the period commented, the whole world was reflected in the dress of a Spanish woman; her pearls were from the West Indies, her gold trimmings from Milan and her chopines were from Valencia.[43] Feast days and other holidays offered opportunities for upper-class women and their clothing to be viewed, but on daily outings, such as attending church, respectable women were expected to be completely veiled, hiding themselves as well as their garments, leaving only their chopines visible. Perhaps the visibility of the chopine beneath the hems of their dresses was designed to offer hints of the sumptuous dress that lay beneath the veil. Certainly chopines such as the gilded ones made in Valencia would have caught the eye and promoted the fame of Valencian leather and the wealth of the individual wearer.

Both of the chopines examined here were made for individuals with small feet and may have been worn by young brides; one of the most important moments for the display of wealth through feminine attire was weddings. In the late fifteenth century, the phrase *ponerse en chopines* or 'to put into chopines' came to mean to marry off a daughter, as girls received their first pair of chopines upon betrothal.[44] Evidence that this tradition was still being practised over one hundred years later is seen in a comment by the Tuscan ambassador to Spain, Averardo de' Medici di Castellina, in correspondence with the Medici Court, telling of the Infanta Doña Maria wearing *ciappini* (chopines) for the first time in connection with her betrothal. Perhaps the two pairs of chopines above were preserved because of their association with this rite of passage as well as being prized as Valencian.

In sixteenth-century Spain some people lauded chopines and saw them as expressions of status and as a means of enhancing female dignity by causing women to walk at a slow and stately pace.[45] One writer, however, cheekily stated that although chopines had been invented to keep women at home, women had overcome this impediment by instructing their chopine makers to use cork, rather than heavy wood, when making their chopines.[46] Although this statement may have been only an attempt at humour, the suggestion that Spanish women's chopines may have been originally made from wood is interesting because most Italian chopines were made with wood rather than cork platforms.

Half-woman, half-wood: chopines in Venice

There is ample evidence for the wearing of chopines on the Italian Peninsula from as early as the thirteenth century. What is not clear is whether there was an unbroken continuity of wearing platform footwear from Roman times onward or if the chopine was re-introduced through trade with the Spanish or Moors. The thirteenth-century Franciscan friar

Jacopone da Todi used the term *suvarati* for footwear that he described as transforming short women into giants.[47] The word *suvarati* is linked to the Latin term for cork tree, *quercus suber*, and suggests a tantalizing connection to Iberian models. In Sicily, the term for chopine was *tappini*, a term directly linked to the Valencian word *tapin*.[48] Although Sicily was ruled at different times by both the Moors and the Spanish, the use of the Spanish term suggests a possible link to the footwear worn in Valencia.

An image of a high platform shoe, drawn by the secretary of the Venetian Major Council in 1430 to illustrate the legal limit for the height for women's platforms, depicts a blocky chopine that shares formal similarities to Spanish examples.[49] Yet, within the body of the document, the shoe is identified by the Italian term *zoccoli*, suggesting that the platform of the illustrated Italian chopine was made of wood. Perhaps this illustration depicts a type of shoe that was Spanish in form but made using local materials. By the sixteenth century, however, there were striking formal differences between the cork-soled *chapines* of Valencia and the wooden *calcagnetti* of Venice.

In Italy, as in Spain, a number of different words were used to describe the chopine. *Zoccoli, pianelle*, and *pantofole* all appear to have been in common use throughout Italy. Andrea Vianello notes that in one Venetian family account book from 1460 a pair of chopines is described as 'very tall *zoccoli*, that is very tall *pianelle*',[50] and he also quotes a 1522 law that describes platform shoes as '*zoccoli* otherwise known as *pantofole*'.[51] Of all these terms, *zoccoli* is the most confusing because it could mean a humble wooden overshoe or a luxurious chopine. There were regional words for platforms as well. In Milan, chopines were referred to as *zibre, zibroni*, and *solee*.[52] In Palermo and Sicily the term was *tappini*[53] and in Venice they were called *calcagnini* and *calcagnetti*.[54]

One of the earliest references to chopines in Venice dates to 1283, when the Doge is recorded as extending his thanks to the shoemakers' guild in Venice, the Scuola dei Calegheri, for making his wife a beautiful pair of chopines.[55] By 1308 the guild had divided into two distinct branches: the *calegheri* who were responsible for shoemaking, and the *zuravati*, also called the *zoccoleri*, who were dedicated to making *zoccoli*.[56] Given that *zoccoli* was also a term for chopines, it is tempting to imagine that this was the primary form of footwear made by the *zoccoleri*, but it appears that the *zoccoleri* were in fact responsible for making inexpensive wooden overshoes. The question therefore arises if there is any connection between the simple wooden *zoccoli*, worn by Zoccolanti monks as a sign of poverty, and by the lower classes because of actual poverty, and the finely made wooden-soled chopines worn by upper-class women in Venice.

The history of stilted wooden footwear, like the history of the platform shoe, goes back to antiquity and deserves consideration. The stilted wooden *sculponea* of ancient Rome spread across the Maghreb and Near East only to be reintroduced into Western dress in the twelfth century as a signifier of the 'Orient'.[57] Although this tangled history goes beyond the scope of this chapter, the heirs to this tradition were the embellished and elevating wooden *qabâqib*, as they were known in Arabic, or *nalin*, as they were called in Turkish, worn across the Near and Middle East. The wooden structure of *qabâqib* was never concealed and the deep colour of the wood was often set off with inlays of mother-of-pearl. Depictions of women wearing *qabâqib* show them being worn fully visible and when worn in bathhouses *qabâqib* were often the only item of dress.

There is evidence that highly embellished *qabâqib* were available in Venice in the sixteenth century and there is also some suggestion that imitation *qabâqib* were made domestically.[58] Images of Turkish women with *nalin* also circulated in sixteenth-century Venice and were included in books on costume.[59] It is important to consider *qabâqib* because they are often cited as the primary model for the Venetian chopine. However, the formal differences between the Near Eastern *qabâqib* and the Venetian chopine are notable. The heights attained by many *qabâqib* may have provided inspiration for the height achieved by the chopines of Venice but the majority of Venetian chopines share little of the *qabâqib* architecture. Rather than having two stilts, Venetian chopines featured solid columnar pedestals and their wooden bases were completely covered in either leather or textile rather than being embellished with bone, ivory, and mother-of-pearl.

A challenge to the research of Venetian chopines is that very few examples have survived. Extant chopines of established Venetian origin feature carved wooden platforms covered in white or dark brown leather. They also typically feature closed-toed vamps in the style of mules decorated with slashing and cutwork over textile. There are a number of extant wooden-soled chopines that are covered in textile, typically unfigured velvet rather than leather; however, these cannot yet be confirmed as Venetian. The majority of these textile-covered, wooden-soled chopines feature open-toed split vamps with four rows of eyelets very much in keeping with Spanish examples. They are also lower in height than the leather-covered chopines. This particular set of chopines displays a hybridity of Italian and Spanish elements that could suggest regional difference among Italian chopines. There is also the possibility that lower, textile-covered, wooden-soled chopines were worn at home in Venice. This may explain the presence of a pair of red textile-covered chopines in the famous sixteenth-century Venetian painting, *Two Venetian Ladies* by Vittore Carpaccio held at the Museo Correr. Identification of

Reveal or conceal

the top half of this same painting in the Getty collection allows its original appearance to be appreciated and the women in the foreground to be understood in their intended context. The claim by John Ruskin in the nineteenth century that the two women depicted in the painting were courtesans has been refuted. Instead, the painting most probably depicts a young bride and her mother-in-law. The new wife is identified by her pearl necklace. Her red chopines also probably signified her new social status; in Venice as in Valencia it seems that a girl received her first pair of chopines upon betrothal.

Lower chopines may have been worn at home, but the infamously high Venetian chopines were designed to be worn in public. Tall Venetian chopines are held in a number of museum collections, the most famous being two pairs in the Museo Correr. The tallest extant chopine is held at the Museo Stefano Bardini in Florence and measures 54 centimetres in height (Figure 13.5). The Bardini also has a chopine that is

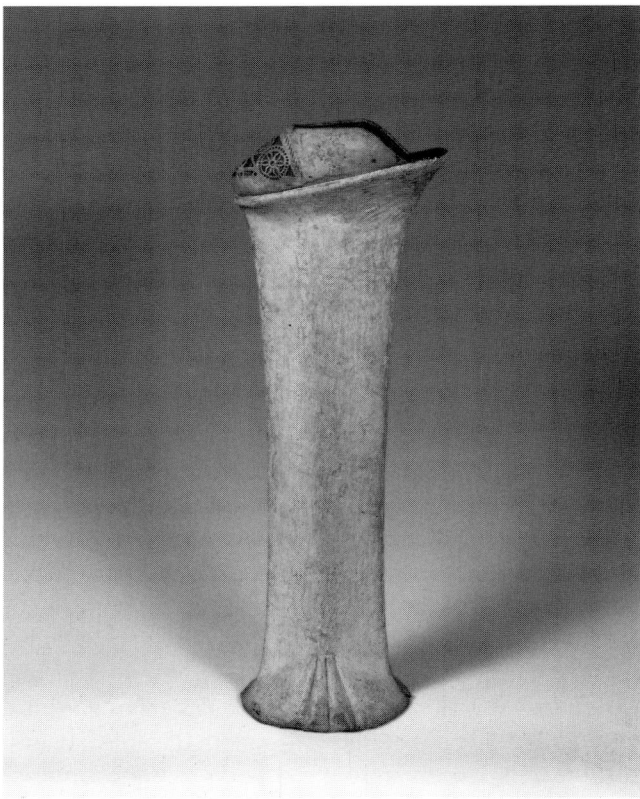

13.5. Venetian chopines, in contrast to Spanish examples, were made of wood and reached much greater heights. This chopine measures 54 cm in height but would have been unseen when worn. Chopines were hidden underneath Venetian women's skirts and were worn as a means of displaying greater amounts of dress material. Venetian, late sixteenth century, Museo Stefano Bardini

slightly lower, measuring 36 centimetres. Both have carved wooden bases covered in white kid. The leather used to make these chopines could have been of local manufacture or was perhaps imported alum-tanned Spanish cordovan leather. It is also possible that fine Hungarian leather was used. Both examples are missing their sole leather, revealing that a soft wood, most probably pine, was used to create the platforms. X-rays of other Italian chopines reveal the use of soft wood in the creation of platforms. Each sole has a shallow hollow carved out of the base with nails embedded in the middle of each hollow. This is consistent with other Italian chopines, where X-rays show that the nails were used to secure the sole leather to the wooden platform. Many Italian chopines are missing their sole leather, suggesting that Italian chopine makers did not copy the Spanish method of gluing the sole leather to the platform base. The hollow seems to be related to the placement of the nails so that they don't protrude, rather than being an attempt to reduce the weight of the wooden platforms.

Concern for weight does seem to explain the typical fluted shape of Venetian chopines. Despite the reduction of the amount of wood used to create the pedestals, Venetian chopines are substantially heavier than Spanish examples. The Bardini chopines weigh 1,281 grams and 754 grams respectively, compared to the 431 grams of the Ambras Castle example, 294 grams for the chopine from Solsona with the metal band and 243 grams for the one without the metal band. Venetian examples have markedly lower pedestals, such as an example held in the Victoria and Albert Museum that has a pedestal height of 21.5 centimetres and weighs 563 grams.

If the narrow pedestals were designed to make the chopines less heavy, the flared bases so typical of Venetian chopines were designed to offer some stability to the wearer. Both Bardini chopines have fluted bases carved in flower-like shapes. The scalloping that creates the flower-like base continues in sculptural form up the side of each pedestal. The taller of the two chopines features three fluted shapes on either side of its base while the other example has four. The leather that covers the base of the shorter chopine was painstakingly stitched along the recesses of the fluting to emphasize the sculptural nature of this detail. The effect is suggestive of the ripple of material. Some Venetian chopines feature even more of these 'ripples' at the base while others have simpler shapes with only a single notch in the base and a single notch running up the sides of the base. Silk tassels decorate the lower Bardini chopine where the pedestal leather meets the sole leather. Other Venetian examples also feature silk braid decoration and silk tassels on the platform base.

The base of each Bardini chopine is covered in two pieces of white leather that are seamed vertically at the front and back. The leather would have been applied wet and stretched taut over the wooden base so that when it dried the leather would conform to all of the sculpted subtleties of the wood base. Inspection of these chopines also reveals that the wooden base was covered in a paste to adhere the leather to the wood. The result is a very fine and smooth leather surface covering the wooden bases. However, the leather bases were not completely featureless; both half pairs were embellished with stamped or tooled details on their pedestals. The taller chopine features a large and ornate circular design stamped directly above the 'ripple' detail and two smaller circular designs on either side of the front centre seam. Two rows of stamped circular motifs encircle the base of the platform just above the sole and continue up the fluted 'ripples' as well. Damage to the taller of the chopines reveals a white gesso-like substance painted on to the wood but it is unclear if this is an underlay that is being revealed by the loss of leather or if it was an earlier conservation attempt since the leather appears to be painted in places as well. The uppers of the chopines are mules made from fine white leather lined with coarser brown leather; the sock or footbed is also made of leather. The vamps feature cut-out designs reminiscent of Venetian lace, and both chopines have fabric underlining. The taller chopine has faded silk cloth with blue pinstripes; the shorter chopine has remnants of red silk.

In contrast to Spanish examples, Venetian chopines are plain. However, despite being relatively unadorned the use of fine white leather and the addition of details such as silk tassels along the edge of the sole suggest that they were not worn as practical overshoes as is so commonly asserted. Venetian chopines were worn under women's skirts and their skirts were required to graze the ground. Therefore, Venetian chopines were not worn to raise women and their expensive clothing above the outdoor debris. Chopines are conspicuously absent from portraiture and are only seen in artworks that depict women in states of undress. Women were also instructed about how to always keep their chopines concealed. The dance master Fabritio Caroso da Sermoneta writing in 1581 on the subject of dance and comportment provided explicit instructions on how to avoid showing one's chopines. In discussing taking one's seat, Caroso writes: 'seated in the middle of the seat, the gown shall come to remain even with the ground, nor will it show yet moreover in this manner the *pianelle*'.[60]

The reason for the chopine's invisibility is explained by the display of textile wealth through women's dress. The wearing of tall chopines required a significant increase in the length of women's skirts and therefore a substantial increase in the amount of expensive cloth required to make those skirts. Indeed, one of the most common criticisms concerning chopines was directly related to the extravagant use of cloth resulting from the increased length of women's skirts. When addressed in sumptuary laws chopines are likewise criticized for their role in increasing textile consumption. This connection between textile consumption and chopines is fundamental to understanding the role of the Venetian chopine in the sixteenth century. It is also essential to factoring the true expenditure represented by chopines.

While chopines are mentioned in bridal trousseaus, wills, and inventories, they are frequently left unvalued like other forms of women's footwear and were counted among the more private and personal aspects of what a woman wore.[61] The few documents that list values suggest that chopines were quite expensive relative to other forms of footwear.[62] However, the actual cost represented by a pair of chopines had to include the sum for the additional dress material that was required to ensure that the chopines remained hidden beneath the wearer's skirts. When this is taken into consideration, the real expense suggested by chopines was much greater than the simple price of the shoes themselves.

The value of cloth to the economy of early modern Venice should not be underestimated. The demand for luxury textiles across Europe was so universal that textiles served as a form of common currency; wages and debts were frequently paid in cloth.[63] Venice derived its immense wealth and influence from its role in the trade of both imported fabrics from the Near East and locally manufactured luxury textiles, promoted in part by the extravagant dress of upper-class women. The importance of the textile trade to the city's economy invested female attire with the responsibility of displaying civic wealth. The role of women's dress in the expression of familial wealth was related to the fact that Venice was a republic whose ruling men expressed their confraternity through the uniformity of their dress. Cesare Vecellio, in discussing the notable homogeny of dress among Venetian noblemen, wrote in 1590 that 'its uniformity is perhaps no small reason for the harmony and concord with which this immense Republic has always been governed. Actually, this simplicity of dress can be seen more in men than in women, who through their natural inclination are always attracted to new fashions.'[64] Thus the wealth of both the city of Venice as well as the specific wealth of each individual family was proclaimed through the dress of its women.

By the end of the sixteenth century and into the seventeenth century new stresses to the Venetian economy ranging from dowry inflation to New World exploration challenged Venice's position as lynchpin between East and West, and amplified the responsibility placed on upper-class women's dress to signify wealth. Upper-class women's attire was also clearly a matter of civic pride in Venice and the appearances of highly ornamented women were orchestrated events anticipated by visitors who flooded the city. This was further heightened by the fact that Venetians famously kept their women sequestered, making their rare public appearances important occasions for the proclamation of the wealth of their families and their city. The relationship between female dress and civic pride was made especially clear at major public events such as the Ascension Day Fair. This annual festival demanded the proud display of everything that Venice had to offer, and visitors flocked to the city to enjoy the spectacle. The trades and goods associated with Venice filled Piazza San Marco, and the placement of the craftsmen's stalls was determined according to the prestige of their wares. Silk merchants held pride of place but the stalls of shoemakers were also given prominence.[65] The occasion of the fair was the Feast of the Ascension but the focus of the celebration was the ceremonial marriage between Venice and the sea. This annual ritual of symbolic marriage connected the fair to the provisioning of brides.

Nothing rivalled weddings in the advertisement of family wealth through dress. Bridal clothing and its attendant trousseau declared the prosperity of the two uniting families. Dowry inflation ballooned between the fifteenth and seventeenth centuries, and the importance of bridal display took on an ever greater and more public economic significance leading to fewer but more lavish displays in which higher chopines played a role. In many works of art, brides are as easily identifiable by their height as they are by the other aspects of bridal clothing. Mounted on high chopines and supported by two servants, brides slowly walked from their natal house to their nuptial home, adorned from head to toe in the vestments of family honour and prestige (Figure 13.6).

As Jutta Gisela Sperling has suggested, inflated dowries and the resulting reduction in the number of marriages at the end of the sixteenth century, as well as the cloistering of excess daughters in nunneries or at home, were part of the 'patriciate's most conspicuous form of consumption: the competitive exchange of women'.[66] The dramatic reduction in the number of marriageable females also invested the display of those girls selected for marriage alliances with greater importance. It is in relation to these pressures that the Venetian chopine reached its greatest height. The surge in chopine heights was noted by Vecellio in 1590 in the section of his book which looked at the clothing of Venetian women from fifty years earlier.[67]

The drastic reduction in marriage prospects throughout the second half of the sixteenth century also gave rise to a new form of Venetian sex worker, the state sanctioned 'honest courtesan'. Like her counterpart, the bride, the highly ornamented 'honest courtesan' proclaimed what money could buy. The dress of these elite courtesans was meant to mimic the dress of respectable women, including the wearing of high

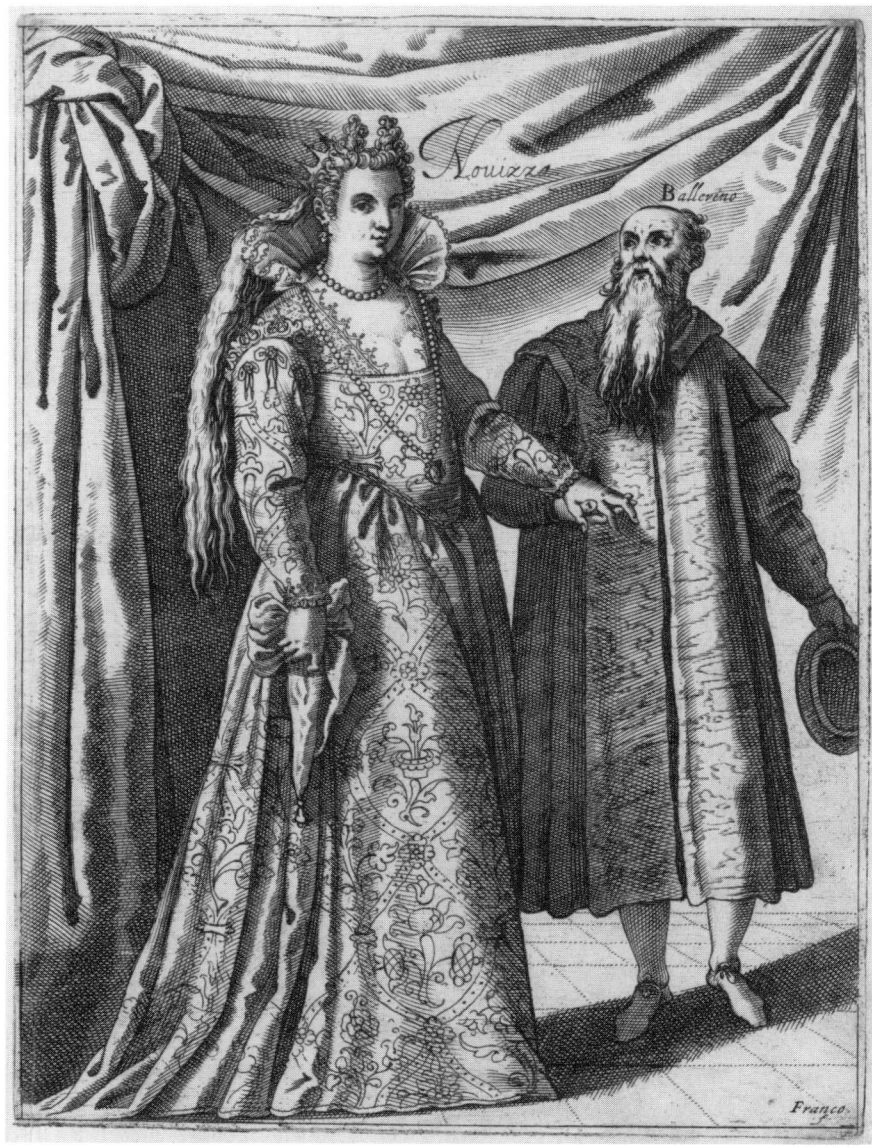

13.6. A bride and her dancemaster train in this print by Giacomo Franco. Dancemasters taught brides how to walk in high chopines with grace and dignity. Although the bride's chopines are hidden under her dress, her towering height provides evidence of their wear. Venetian, Giacomo Franco, c. 1591–1609, The Metropolitan Museum of Art, Harris Brisbane Dick Fund, 1938 38.38.7

Reveal or conceal

chopines.⁶⁸ Vecellio writes that 'prostitutes who want to win respect by means of feigned modesty wear widow's and married women's styles of dress, especially in the colours worn by brides.'⁶⁹ And again he comments in regard to an illustration in his book that courtesans wore the dress depicted 'just as virtuous women of good reputation do'.⁷⁰ In a city of sequestered women, the dress of Venetian courtesans was both exciting and confusing, making them one of the city's notable tourist attractions. Numerous prints illustrating courtesans and their dress were made as souvenirs. One extant print from the end of the sixteenth century was designed so that the skirt of the courtesan could be lifted to reveal her undergarments, including her chopines (Figures 13.7 and 13.8). The erotic value of chopines seems to be related to their function as undergarments.

Comments such as Vecellio's suggesting that women were naturally inclined towards fashion as an explanation for the extravagances of women's attire might make it easy to assume that women were responsible for how they were presented in public. However, the financial investment represented by clothing and the function of female attire in

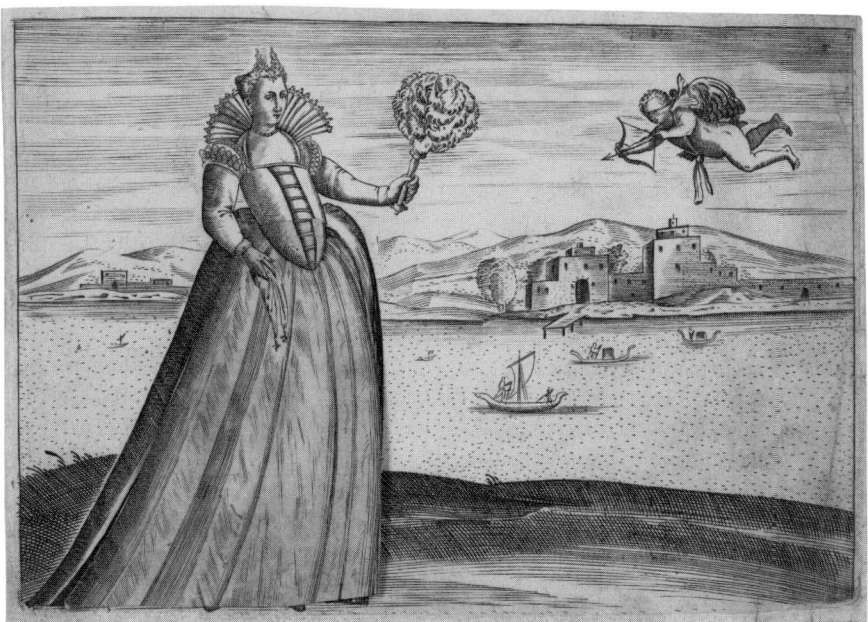

13.7. The extravagant dress of Venetian courtesans was one of the city's tourist attractions. Numerous prints, such as this one, were made as souvenirs. This print was designed so that the skirt of the courtesan can be lifted to reveal her undergarments, including her chopines. Venetian, *Courtesan and Blind Cupid*, publisher Pietro Bertelli, c. 1563, Metropolitan Museum of Art, 55.503.30

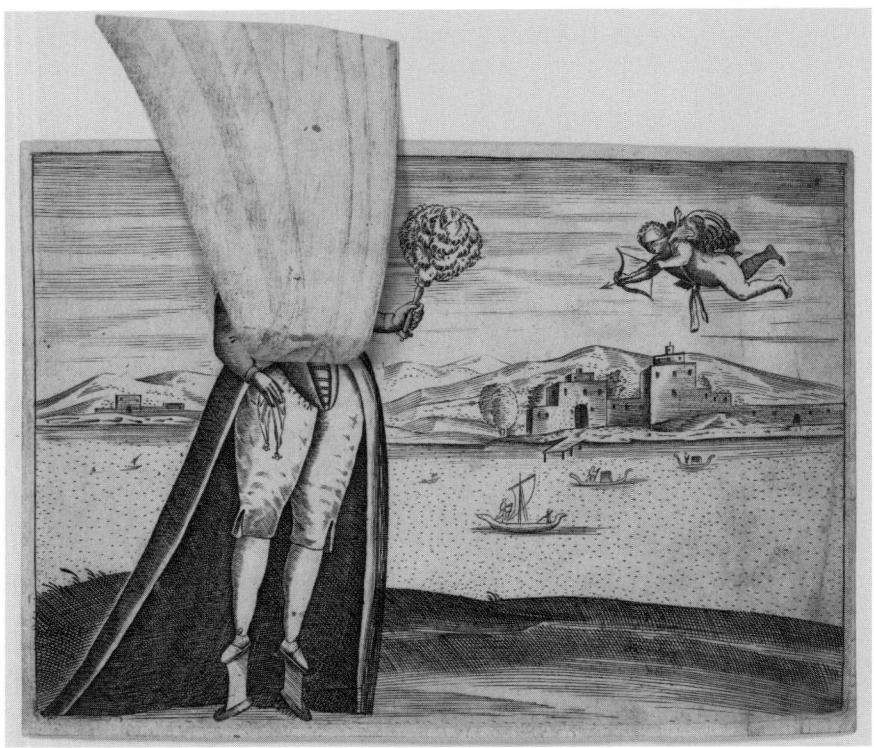

13.8. Lifting the courtesan's skirt reveals substantially high chopines in keeping with the dress of wealthy Venetian matrons. Venetian, *Courtesan and Blind Cupid*, publisher Pietro Bertelli, c. 1563, Metropolitan Museum of Art 55.503.30

the proclamation of familial and civic wealth meant that in reality heads of households exerted control over women's dress. Evelyn Welch has pointed out that the dressing and provisioning of a household was a distinctly male privilege in Venice.[71] Even women's underwear and stockings were acquired by the heads of their households, suggesting that women had very little agency concerning dress.[72]

Women's clothing was also subject to legal regulation. Sumptuary laws offer particular insight into how women's attire was assessed and controlled at a civic level. Chopines were the focus of many sumptuary laws, and the focus of the efforts to limit their height was almost always linked to attempts to manage the consumption of dress material. The general tone towards women's finery set by these laws is one of disapproval, consternation, and concern about women's unrelenting vanity. Although laws concerning women's dress were directed by men of means toward men of lesser station, they are typically cast as paternalistic moralizing directed at women. Sumptuary laws were not devised to actually curb spending and display, but rather to control it and to establish discernible distinctions between social classes and genders. With female dress as a prime signifier of male status, the regulation of female 'vanity' can be understood as a means of regulating homosocial competition between men just as the wearing of high chopines in Venice can be understood as a means of displaying familial textile wealth rather than an expression of female agency in dress.

Conclusion

In Valencia and Venice humble cork and wood were transformed by chopine makers into platforms for the display of luxury materials. Valencia gilt leather chopines were luxury products in their own right as well as a means for displaying the famous Valencian leather. In Venice, chopines were foundation garments that allowed for increased lengths of textile, the material of Venetian wealth, to be advantageously displayed. By the beginning of the seventeenth century, however, the fashion for chopines in both Valencia and Venice was coming to an end. In Valencia, the Golden Age of Spain was on the wane. World exploration had established greater access to Eastern goods to the detriment of the local silk and leather manufacturing centres in Spain, and cities such as Valencia suffered. Chopines accompanied Iberian women to the New World, where they served as a means of establishing ethnic as well as socioeconomic difference,[73] but in Spain the time of the chopine was reaching its end. In Venice the chopine reached its zenith just as the fortunes of the republic were diminishing. The capitals of fashion were shifting to France and northern Europe. Venice's luxury textiles were beginning to lose their lustre – both Venetian chopines and the textiles they were meant to display had reached their height. A new era with new priorities was dawning and a new form of elevating footwear, the high heel, was stepping in to replace the chopine.

Notes

1 Although I will identify regional terms for platform shoes, for ease of reading I will use the English term chopine whenever possible.
2 This chapter is greatly indebted to the work that I did in 2009 related to the exhibition *On a Pedestal: From Renaissance Chopines to Baroque Heels* at the Bata Shoe Museum, 19 November 2009 to 20 September 2010 and the attendant book *On a Pedestal: From Renaissance Chopines to Baroque Heels* (Toronto, ON: Bata Shoe Museum, 2009). However, research concerning the fabrication of chopines was only conducted at the close of the exhibition when many of the exhibition lenders generously allowed their chopines to be measured and weighed. Many also allowed their chopines to be X-rayed. The cooperation of these institutions was essential to this chapter and is greatly appreciated. Lenders to the exhibition included Bayerisches Nationalmuseum, Munich; Civiche Raccolte d'Arte Applicata: Castello Sforzesco, Milano; Fondazione Musei Civici di Venezia: The Collections

of Museo Palazzo Mocenigo and Museo Correr; Kunsthistorisches Museum Wien, Sammlung Schloss Ambras; Musei Civici Fiorentini; Museo Stefano Bardini, Firenze; Museu Diocesà i Comarcal de Solsona, Spain; Museum of Fine Arts, Boston; Royal Ontario Museum, Toronto, Canada; Skokloster Castle, Sweden; Victoria and Albert Museum, London; and The Royal Armoury, Stockholm, and all are greatly thanked.

3 'Important women's shoes' was a common descriptor used for chopines in Spain.
4 Semmelhack, *On a Pedestal*, p. 48.
5 Katherine Dohan Morrow, *Greek Footwear and the Dating of Sculpture* (Madison: University of Wisconsin Press, 1985), p. 24.
6 A fragment of a foot identified as Zeus' wears a thick-soled sandal, and Apollo Patroos also sports a pair of platforms. However, he is also dressed in a *peplos*, which is typically female attire. Morrow, *Greek Footwear*, pp. 55, 75.
7 Morrow, *Greek Footwear*, p. 62.
8 Norma Goldman, 'Roman footwear', in Judith Sebesta and Larissa Bonfante (eds), *The World of Roman Costume* (Madison: University of Wisconsin Press, 1994), pp. 101–29.
9 Goldman, 'Roman footwear', p. 109.
10 Carol van Driel-Murray, 'Vindolanda and the dating of Roman footwear', *Britannia* 32 (2001), p. 91.
11 Van Driel-Murray, 'Vindolanda', pp. 192–4.
12 Van Driel-Murray, 'Vindolanda', p. 191.
13 Yedida Kalfon Stillman, *Arab Dress: Short History From the Dawn of Islam to Modern Times* (Leiden: Brill, 2000), p. 90.
14 Thomas F. Glick, *Islamic and Christian Spain in the Early Middle Ages* (Princeton, NJ: Princeton University Press, 1979), p. 229.
15 S.D. Goitein, *A Mediterranean Society: Jewish Communities of the World as Portrayed in the Documents of the Cairo Geniza* (Berkeley: University of California Press, 1999), pp. 6, 163.
16 Glick, *Islamic and Christian Spain in the Early Middle Ages*, p. 229.
17 James Dickie, 'Granada: A case study of Arab urbanism in Muslim Spain', in Salma Khadra Jayyusi (ed.), *The Legacy of Muslim Spain* (Leiden: Brill, 1992), p. 92.
18 Stillman, *Arab Dress*, p. 77.
19 I wish to thank Hilary Davidson, Curator of Fashion and Decorative Arts at the Tower of London, for bringing this to my attention.
20 Sebastián de Covarrubias, *Tesoro de la lengua castellana o española* (Madrid, 1611). http://books.google.ca/books?id=qKm8nzelynUC&printsec=frontcover&dq=Sebastián de Covarrubias&hl=en&sa=X&ei=Pkv3UOKME-ar2AXeoICoAg&ved=0CD8Q6AEwAw (accessed on 14 February 2014).
21 Barbara Fuchs, *Exotic Nation: Maurophilia and the Construction of Early Modern Spain* (Philadelphia: University of Pennsylvania Press, 2009), pp. 60–87.
22 Fuchs, *Exotic Nation*, p. 71.
23 Ruth Matilda Anderson, *Hispanic Costume, 1480–1530* (New York: The Hispanic Society of America, 1979), p. 81.
24 Ruth Matilda Anderson, 'El chapín y otros Zapatos Afines', *Cuadernos de la Alhambra* 5 (1969), p. 35–6.
25 Anderson, 'El chapín y otros Zapatos Afines', p. 37.
26 Michelle O'Malley points this out in 'A pair of little gilded shoes: Commission, cost and meaning in Renaissance footwear', *Renaissance Quarterly* 63:1 (2010), pp. 47–8.

27 Andrea Vianello, '"Courtly lady or courtesan?"': The Venetian chopine in the Renaissance', in Giorgio Riello and Peter McNeil (eds), *Shoes: A History from Sandals to Sneakers* (Oxford: Berg, 2006), p. 81.

28 Anderson, 'El chapín y Otros Zapatos Afines', p. 36.

29 S.D. Juan Eugenio Hartzenbusch, *La Saviduría de las Naciones ó los Evangelios Abreviados: Probable Origen Etimologiay Razon Historicade Muchos Proverbios, Refranes y Modismos Uusados en España* (Barcelona: Imp. de El Porvenier, de Buenaventura Bassas, Tallers, n. 51 y 53, 1862), p. 186.

30 Cesare Vecellio, *Habiti antichi et moderni di tutto il mondo* (*Ancient and Modern Clothes from Various Places of the World*) (1590), trans. Margaret F. Rosenthal and Ann Rosalind Jones, *Cesare Vecellio's Habiti Antichi et Moderni, The Clothing of the Renaissance World: Europe, Asia, Africa, the Americas* (London: Thames & Hudson, 2008), p. 337.

31 Anderson, 'El chapín y Otros Zapatos Afines', p. 37.

32 Anderson, 'El chapín y Otros Zapatos Afines', p. 37.

33 Anderson, 'El chapín y Otros Zapatos Afines', p. 37.

34 Anderson, 'El chapín y Otros Zapatos Afines', p. 37.

35 Anderson, 'El chapín y Otros Zapatos Afines', p. 38.

36 Anderson, *Hispanic Costume*, p. 234.

37 Anderson, *Hispanic Costume*, p. 35.

38 X-rays were taken with the generous cooperation of the Royal Ontario Museum.

39 Anderson, *Hispanic Costume*, p. 229.

40 John William Waterer, *Spanish Leather: A History of Its Use from 800 to 1800 for Mural Hangings, Screens, Upholstery, Altar Frontals, Ecclesiastical Vestments, Footwear, Gloves, Pouches and Casket* (London: Faber & Faber, 1971), p. 30.

41 Waterer does specify that glair was used to keep silver from tarnishing. Waterer, *Spanish Leather*, p. 30.

42 Anderson, 'El chapín y Otros Zapatos Afines', p. 38.

43 Anderson, *Hispanic Costume*, p. 234.

44 Anderson, *Hispanic Costume*, p. 263.

45 Anderson, 'El chapín y Otros Zapatos Afines', p. 39.

46 Anderson, 'El chapín y Otros Zapatos Afines', p. 39.

47 Vianello, 'Courtly lady or courtesan?', p. 81.

48 Maria Giuseppina Muzzareli. *Guardaroba medievale: Vesti e società dal XIII al XVI secolo* (Bologna: Società editrice il Mulino, 1999), p. 296.

49 Vianello, 'Courtly lady or courtesan?', p. 82.

50 Vianello, 'Courtly lady or courtesan?', p. 79.

51 Vianello, 'Courtly lady or courtesan?', p. 79.

52 Grazietta Butazzi, 'Tipologie delle calzature rinascimentali', in *Raccolta delle Stampe A. Bertarelli Raccolte di arte Applicata Museo degli Strumenti Musical:. Rassegna di Studi e di Notizie*, Vol. 11: *Anno X Castello Sforzesco* (Milan: Ripartizione Cultura e Spettacolo, 1983), pp. 122–3.

53 Butazzi, 'Tipologie delle calzature rinascimentali', p. 123.

54 Vianello, 'Courtly lady or courtesan?', p. 79.

55 Gabriella Giurato Faoto, *L'arte dei Calegheri e dei Zavareti di Venezia dal medievo ad oggi* (Venice: Il Gassettino, 1999), p. 6.

56 Vianello, 'Courtly lady or courtesan?', p. 81.

57 For a more detailed discussion on the history of the of wooden stilted footwear in Roman times, the Near East and Europe see Semmelhack, *On a Pedestal*, pp. 39–45.

58 The Museo Correr has a pair of *nalin* identified as made in Venice.

59 Nicolas Nicolay's *Navigations et pérégrinations orientales, avec les figures et les habillements au naturel, tant des hommes que des femmes* (*Navigations and Pilgrimages in the Orient with Natural Figures and Costumes, Both of Men and Women*), printed in Lyon in 1567–8, has one of the earliest and most widely copied European images featuring *nalin*.

60 Fabritio Caroso da Sermoneta, *Il Ballarino* (1581), full text www.pbm.com/~lindahl/caroso/ transcription (accessed on 14 February 2014).

61 Carole Collier Frick, *Dressing Renaissance Florence: Families, Fortunes, and Fine Clothing* (Baltimore, MD: Johns Hopkins University Press, 2002), p. 140. Also see O'Malley, 'A pair of little gilded shoes'.

62 Determining the cost of Venetian chopines is extremely difficult. There is some extant information concerning the price of chopines across Italy but it is extremely limited, geographically scattered and covers a large expanse of time. The chopines listed for sale in an early fifteenth-century Perugian tanners shop cost twenty-five soldi a pair, pricey compared to fourteen to seventeen soldi for the other kinds of shoes on offer. The inventory of the estate of the shoemaker Francesco Magri from 1592 includes a list of the footwear in his shop. Of the wide variety of shoes and *zoccoli* listed, *the zoccoli da donna de legno incanadi*, the wooden *zoccoli* for women, are also the most expensive footwear valued at just over fifty-four *soldi* a pair. In 1600, there were roughly one hundred and twenty-four soldi to the florin, suggesting that chopines could represent a significant purchase.

63 Rosamond E. Mack, *Bazaar to Piazza: Islamic Trade and Italian Art, 1300–1600* (Berkeley: University of California Press, 2002), p. 27. An elegant discussion of this can also be found in Ulinka Rublack, *Dressing Up: Cultural Identity in Renaissance Europe* (Oxford: Oxford University Press, 2010).

64 Rosenthal and Jones, *Cesare Vecellio's Habiti Antichi et Moderni*, p. 158.

65 Evelyn Welch, *Shopping in the Renaissance: Consumer Cultures in Italy, 1400–1600* (New Haven, CT: Yale University Press, 2005), p. 179.

66 Jutta Gisela Sperling, *Convents and the Body Politic in the late Renaissance Venice* (Chicago, IL: University of Chicago Press, 1999), p. 59.

67 'Their *pianelle* did not have soles as high as they do today.' Rosenthal and Jones, *Cesare Vecellio's Habiti Antichi et Moderni*, pp. 152–3.

68 It should also be noted that chopines were a legally mandated aspect of dress for prostitutes in many parts of Italy. A typical example of this is the 1384 order by the Florentine Office of Decency stipulating that prostitutes wear platform footwear. Sicilian law required that prostitutes wear *tappini*. There is also a recorded dispute between a nun and a priest where the priest, in his effort to besmirch the nun's character, accuses her of wearing 'zoccoli da cortesana' – that is, *zoccoli* worn by courtesans. The reasons for these associations, what *zoccoli da cortesana* looked like, and whether or not they were the same as upper-class women's chopines are unclear and remain to be researched.

69 Rosenthal and Jones, *Cesare Vecellio's Habiti Antichi et Moderni*, p. 190.

70 Rosenthal and Jones, *Cesare Vecellio's Habiti Antichi et Moderni*, p. 196.

71 Welch, *Shopping in the Renaissance*, p. 219.

72 Welch, *Shopping in the Renaissance*, pp. 219–20.

73 Sara Vicuña Guengerich, 'Unfitting shoes: Footwear fashions and social mobility in colonial Peru', *Journal of Spanish Cultural Studies* 14:2 (June 2013), pp. 159–85.

14 ✧ Entanglements of body, text, and stone: the crafting and connoisseurship of inkstones in eighteenth-century China

Dorothy Ko

AN INKSTONE (or inkslab), a piece of stone no bigger than an outstretched palm, carries hefty meanings that exceed its materiality (Figure 14.1). As an instrument for grinding ink, a collectable object, a token of exchange among friends, and an inscriptional surface, an inkstone is entangled with the production of texts and the culture of *wen* (culture, civility) in multiple ways. This chapter adopts a 'geography of skills' approach to illuminate the skills, knowledge, and bodily investments involved in the making and connoisseurship of inkstones in the mid-Qing dynasty (1644–1911) in general, and in the case of the female

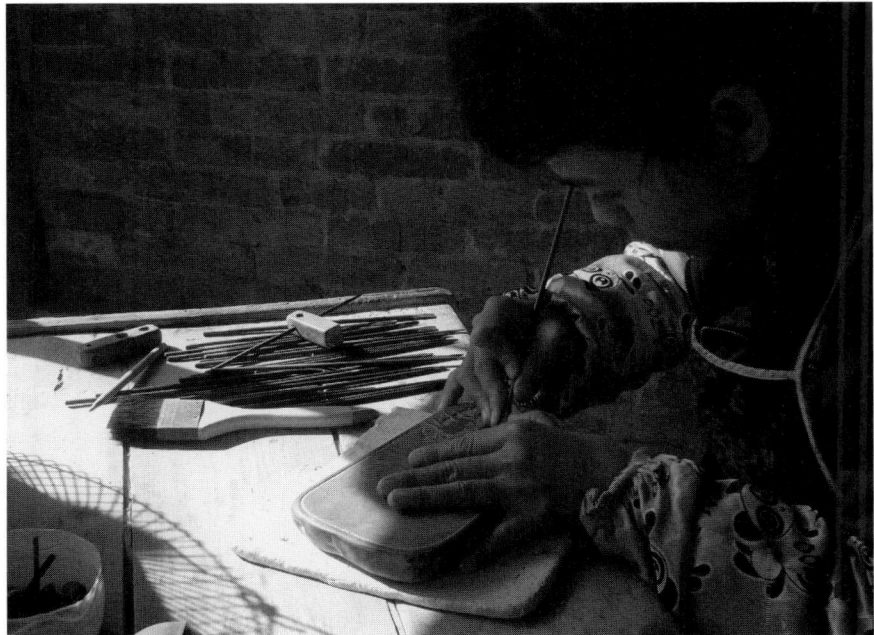

14.1. Carving an inkstone, Huanggang village, Zhaoqing, Guangdong province, China

inkstone carver Gu Erniang (fl. 1700–24) and her patron Huang Ren (1683–1768) in particular.

Appadurai's seminal *Social Life of Things* has changed the way many historians understand the identity and value of objects – not as something intrinsic to the object but as constituted in social discourse.[1] Building on this notion, 'geography of skills' tracks the skills 'embodied in the construction, display, use, representation, and interpretation of one artefact, or a genre of artefacts'. Without an a priori assignment of the relative value of skills, the historian can map 'crisscrossing trajectories of manual, mental, sentient, and social skills' that went into the social life of that artefact – inkslabs made of Duan river stones in this case.[2] In juxtaposing three kinds of skill sets and the knowledge associated with them – that of the quarrier, connoisseur/patron, and artisan – this chapter seeks to map the unevenness in social and discursive power that attended the social life of inkstones in the eighteenth century. The power of texts – handwritten, carved, and imprinted – in shaping the culture of craft and in altering the physical appearances of inkstones emerges in clear relief.

The body of the quarrier: harvesting Duan stones

Today, the making of an inkstone involves five steps: mining the stone, assessing the raw material (*weiliao* 維料), carving, box-making, and polishing.[3] Some master carvers also assess and select the stones, but mining is a separate operation handled by specialist workers. The first two steps take place at the quarry whereas the other three are executed in workshops or artisan studios that can be far removed. Although the first three steps all involve tactile handling of the stone, the tools and skills required in each are different.

To understand the challenge of mining the stones one needs to visit the site and to ponder the technology of writing – or the mechanics of grinding ink, to be specific. From the Southern Song dynasty (1127–1279) at the latest to the present day, the most desirable material for inkslabs has come from two mountain ranges on the banks of the Xijiang river and its tributary Duan 端溪 in the western part of Guangdong province on the southern edge of the empire. The area, near present-day Zhaoqing 肇慶, was known by its Sui dynasty (581–618) name of Duanzhou 端州.[4] Geologically, Duan stone is a shale whose main contents include mica, clay, and silica with traces of mineral salts – mostly iron, potassium, and magnesium – the source of its characteristic deep purple colour. The foliated rock, formed by metamorphic compression over 600 million years ago, is fine-grained and of medium hardness (about 3.5 on the Mohr scale, or on a par with a copper penny; by comparison, a lead pencil is 1, and a knife blade, 5.5).[5]

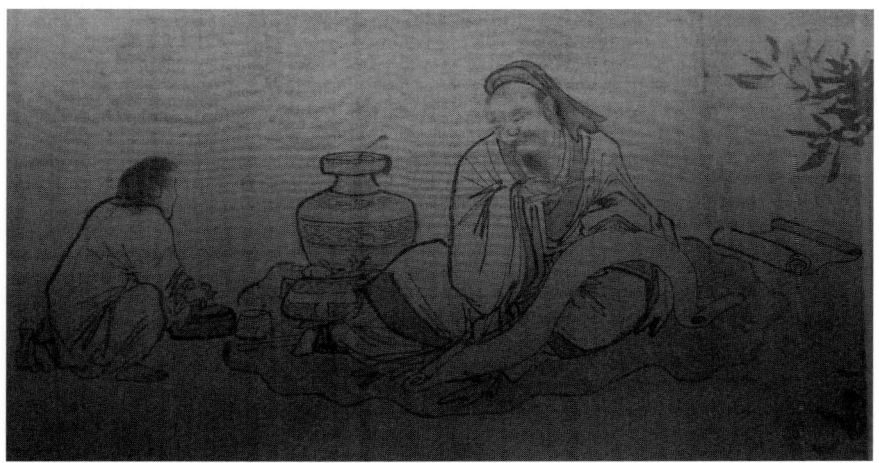

14.2. A scholar sitting on an outdoor mat, holding a writing brush and a blank scroll; his butler grinding ink on an inkstone. Detail from Zhang Lu 張路 (1464–1538), Handscroll of the Lord of Huainan Seeking Immortality, Collection of the Tianjin Museum, Tianjin. China

Before the modern advent of fountain pens, inkstones were first and foremost functional objects for the writer and painter. To produce ink, the artist rubbed a moistened inkstick, a finger-length stick made of soot and glue, on the face of the inkstone in a deliberate circular motion (Figure 14.2). The technical requirement for the ideal inkstone, encapsulated in the expression 'producing ink without hurting the brush' (*famo er busunhao* 發墨而不損毫) involves a fine balancing of opposites: the stone should be coarser and harder than the inkstick (2.2–2.4 on the Mohr scale) but softer than the bristle of the brush. Furthermore, the stone should have just the right absorbency – if too porous, the ink would disappear into the stone; if too impervious the ink would be too thin.[6] Duan stones, especially those from the three most desirable mines in Fuke Mountain 斧柯山 on the southern bank of the Xijiang river, fit the bill perfectly.

Of the three, the oldest and most prestigious was the Old Pit (*laokeng* 老坑, also called Underwater Lode, *shuiyan* 水岩), which was first mined during the mid-Tang (618–907). The second in history and prestige. the Small Pit (*kengzai* 坑仔), was a drift mine first opened in the Northern Song Zhiping reign (1064–67). The third, the Poker-Mark Pit (*mazi keng* 麻子坑), was first opened in the Qianlong reign (1736–95) and included both an underwater and a dry pit. To harvest the lode from the dry pits, workers dug a tunnel into the steep hillside as they would any mine. The submerged pits, where the lode lay at a level below the bed of the Xijiang River, had to be pumped dry before mining could ensue. Before the modern convenience of electric pumps, teams of workers were assembled with the onset of the dry winter months in November to December. Descending into the diagonal shaft, they formed an assembly line conveying jugs of water in clay pots. Manual removal of water required a team of over 200 workers alternating in day and night shifts for over a month, leaving a mining season of three to five months. By May, rain would swell the river and the pit would again be submerged.[7]

The scholar-official Li Zhaoluo 李兆洛 (1769–1841), a geographer who visited Zhaoqing in 1820, described the commingling of stone and water common in the pits as well as the corporeal nature of the operation:

> All inkstone pits, be they on top of the mountain or at its foot, have water in them. To harvest the stone one has to first remove the water. Also, inside the shaft the air is warm even in the winter months, hence all must strip bare their bodies before entering. The tunnels are without fail pitch black, so the miners have to carry lamps. The lamps have no space to ventilate, so the soot from the burning coal all settles on the human bodies. Those who emerge from the tunnel are caked with yellow mud on their lower bodies and fumigated by coal on their upper bodies. Naked and squalid, they all look like ghosts.[8]

That quarrying Duan stones is filthy and backbreaking labour does not detract from the necessity of expert knowledge accumulated by way of the mindful eye and hand. Embedded in layers of waste rock, the raw material for inkstones is a snake-like vein (*shimai* 石脈) which measures about 10–30 centimetres at its thinnest and 40–60 centimetres at its widest. The lode, although hard and resistant to compression, is so brittle that the use of explosives would reduce it to rubble. Its delicacy mandates that even in modern times the vein is harvested manually with hammer and chisels (with round and flat cutting edges). With each hammering, the miner intuits the trajectory of the hidden vein and moves with it: a little to the left; a little further up. The waste rock, called 'the bones' (*shigu* 石骨), has to be left undisturbed.[9] The miner is thus in possession of a 'tacit knowledge', or a skill that is embodied and transmitted by sensory facilities (such as an apprentice watching his teacher) instead of textually.[10]

According to Li Zhaoluo, when blocks of usable stones (called *liao* 料 in today's parlance) are carried from the tunnels, workers mark the harvest date in vermilion and the lot is closely guarded. As the mining season comes to an end and the tunnels are sealed, the investors and workers draw lots to split the bounty: seven parts for the former group and three for the latter.[11] Eventually the boulders pass into the hands of an 'assessor' who has an uncanny ability to intuit what lies underneath the coarse shell of each boulder. Stone-workers envision each block in terms of four layers: a coarse top layer to be discarded, the layer underneath it and a base layer that are dry but often usable, and finally a core layer that would eventually be fashioned into inkstones (called 'the flesh', *shirou* 石肉, today). What we have just differentiated as four layers in analytic and conceptual terms is, however, inchoate visually.

It is the assessor who sizes up the surface of the boulder, visualizing the trajectory of the layers underneath as well as the type and location of the valued mineral features each piece may contain, which are to be showcased on the front of the finished inkstone. He has to emplot the size and shape of the inkstones to be cut from the block by conjuring a three-dimensional map in his head. He then picks up the hammer and chisel to divide up the stone into individual raw pieces (*pu* 璞), which will be sold to a collector or handed to an inkstone carver, who in turn makes the design and executes it. The cunning knowledge of the assessor, or the ability of his eyes to 'penetrate the stone' (*kanchuan shi* 看穿石), is rooted in his intimate knowledge of the geology of the pits often gained from early experience as a miner.[12] A faint green spot on the surface may well mean that a cherished 'eye' which derives its yellow or green colour from ferrous oxide is buried inside, and so on.

Connoisseurs have praised this local, tacit knowledge of the miner and assessor in terms of a familiarity with 'the patterned principles of the lode' (*shi shanshi zhi wenli* 識山石之文理).[13] The terminology of moral philosophy seems alien to the local way of knowing, which as we have seen envisions the mountain as a human body with the structural integrity of 'skeletons'; the lode is called a 'vein' and the most lustrous part of the vein 'flesh'. Indeed, as Mircea Eliade observed, mining and metallurgy in many civilizations were sexualized and understood in terms of gynaecology and obstetrics – the ores are embryos of the Earth Mother.[14] Inkstone connoisseurs, too, spoke of the rare occurrence of 'child stones' (*zishi* 子石) in Zhaoqing, which some writers construed as one stone giving birth to another, whereas others took it to mean as the embedding of one round stone within another.[15]

The body figures in the mining of Duan stones not merely as metaphor but at the centre of the physical extraction of the stone: the tacit knowledge of the miner and stoneworker can only be embodied; mining and assessing require manipulation of the stone using eyes, head, and hand. Since tacit and cunning knowledge, along with the corporeal exertion it implied, were denigrated by the literati who wrote, it was not textualized and hence was resistant to generalization. The image of the miner emerging from the underground tunnel captured by Li Zhaoluo's documentary mode of narration is symptomatic of the lowly status of the stoneworker: caked in mud and soot, the miner's naked body is ghost-like in that it is at once visible and invisible.

Although striking in its visceral corporeality, the body is masked from sight by defilement, which renders it illegible in history.

The body of the connoisseur

The connoisseurship of inkstones engages the sensory faculty of the literati, albeit this bodily investment is of a different kind from the miner's due to the mediating work of texts. Connoisseurship became possible when the stone acquired aesthetic traction that exceeded its functionality. Textual production of male scholars – poetry in the Tang and treatises in the Song – was key to this aestheticization. The purple Duan stone and the dexterity of the stoneworkers, for example, were eulogized in a poem by the maverick mid-Tang poet Li He (791–817). About a century later, the inkstone garnered separate treatment in its own chapter in the connoisseurship treatise *Four Articles from the Scholar's Studio* (*Wenfang sipu* 文房四譜) by Su Yijian 蘇易簡 (958–996). With a profusion of treatises that ensued during the Song from such major intellectual and artistic figures as Ouyang Xiu, Mi Fu, and Su Dongpo, the status of Duan inkstones as a premier object of desire and subject of specialized knowledge of the elite men of letters was ensured.[16]

These seminal treatises established the tradition of calling the collecting of inkstones by the verb *xu* 蓄, which refers to the keeping of animals, boy actors, or concubines as pets.[17] Since the stone is believed to be animated or alive, prolonged contact with the human skin serves to enhance its luminosity and efficacy. Mi Fu (1051–1107), the calligrapher and inkstone connoisseur par excellence, once acquired a prized inkstone with protruding peaks from a monk and 'hugged it in bed for three days'.[18] Improving on an ancient Yuefu poet's love of his sword, the seventeenth-century connoisseur Zhang Chao thus described the joy of cuddling up with inkstones: 'Having gathered ten thousand stones in one room, you [and the stones] can spend time in each other's company. In a day you can cradle and caress them repeatedly; it gives more pleasure than being with a fifteen-year-old female. What joy can surpass this?'[19] The 'keeping' of a stone acquired a downright erotic charge as the action shifted from the studio to the bedroom in a legend about the Qing connoisseur Huang Ren 黃任 (1683–1768), who was said to have ordered each of his ten teenage maids to carry an inkstone against her body in the daytime and to cradle it at night. The super-yin *qi* of the young girls was supposed to enhance the inkstone's jade-like lustre. The modern connoisseur Zhang Genji 張耕汲 (d. 1919) was famed for bedding down with the crown jewel of his inkstone collection himself.[20]

Legends aside, the tactility of their sensuous surface is key to the appreciation of Duan stones, which are prized for their fine texture and

Entanglements of body, text, and stone

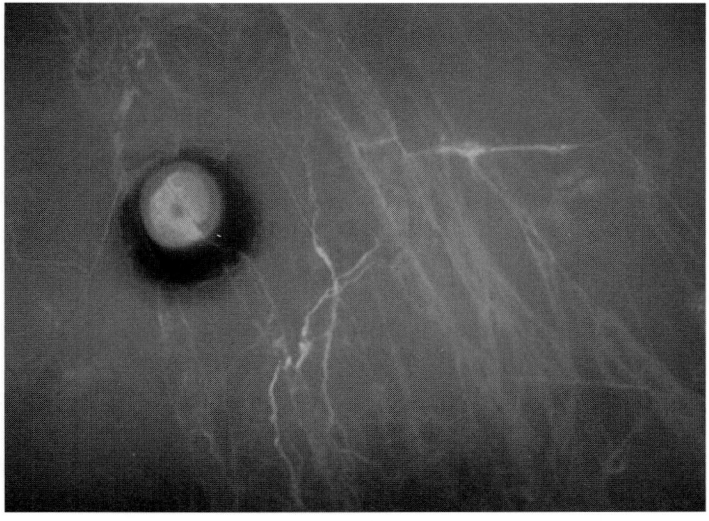

14.3. Fetishized imperfections (*shipin* 石品) on the surface of Duan stone. Showing stone's eyes (round button), banana leaf white (greenish white patch), fish brain freeze (white patch), ice crackle (white streaks in ice crackle pattern), gold streaks, silver streaks. Duan Inkstone Factory, Zhaoqing, Guangdong province, China

warm, lustrous touch – the simile favoured by modern connoisseurs is baby's skin. Also notable are patterns of mineral deposits that show up on the surface of the polished stone as yellow-greenish dots, metallic veins gold or silver in colour, or faint red highlights (Figure 14.3). These imperfections were isolated and given such lyrical names as 'blackbird eye', 'gold streaks', 'yellow dragon', and 'charred by fire' in the connoisseurship literature of the southern Song. Their numbers proliferated in the Qing, when such new features as 'banana leaf white' (a white patch of clouds), 'fish brain' (a whiter patch of clouds), 'sky blue' (a faint bluish hue), 'oil glow' (a pearly reflection), and 'five-coloured nail' (a multi-coloured blot) were identified and named.[21] Reification of the mineral imperfections on the surface of the stones enhanced their monetary value, part of the craze in Duan inkslabs in the Qing that surpasses the previous dynasties in intensity as well as material and textual productions.

Belying the analytically distinct nomenclature, some of these marks can be inchoate and difficult to discern to the untrained eye. Increasingly the ranking of stones became esoteric knowledge. The 'blue spot' (*qinghua* 青花), for example, considered the most reified feature of all, is imperceptible to the naked eye. The tiny dots can barely be made out when the stone is placed in water or under strong artificial light. The same can be said about the legendary 'wood sound' (*musheng* 木聲):

when tapped with fingers the stones are said to give a crisp and distant echo but emit no sound with the grinding of the inkstick. But the exact tone of the 'wood sound' is as varied as the metal content in the stone and the judgement of the expert.

Be that as it may, the connoisseurship of Duan stone involves the eye, hand, and ear and their pedagogy – it requires not only arcane knowledge about the geology and location of the quarries but also the active employment of the sensory faculties of the scholar. Increasingly by the eighteenth century, both the arcane and sensory knowledge were textualized; mastery of texts became the prerequisite and ultimate purpose of connoisseurship.

Inscribing elite male subjectivities

The thing-ness of Duan inkstones was actualized in their social life, as they changed hands in the form of tribute, gift, commodity, and other ways. These exchanges, which altered the physical appearance of the stones, were always entangled with the written word.[22] As early as the Tang, the poems of several scholars attest to a burgeoning traffic between words and things among the emergent scholar-official group: a purple-stone inkslab which an exam candidate gave to Liu Yuxi (772–842) was 'answered' with a poem; a certain gift from Lu Guimeng (d. 881) to his friend Pi Rixiu (c. 834–83) elicited counter-gifts in the form of a purple-stone inkslab and a poem; Lu himself responded to the gift of a purple-stone inkslab from another friend using an active verb that connotes the bodily gesture of embracing – he composed a poem to 'greet' it (*yingzhi* 迎之).[23]

As the connoisseurship of inkstones reached its height in the eighteenth century, these slabs of stones became the lynchpins in the making of elite male subjectivities and sociabilities. The Qing connoisseur Huang Ren, who was said to have his maids cradle his prized collection, offers an instructive case study. In Huang's two extant poetry collections (numbering over 960 poems) no mention of maids cradling stones can be found, but the centrality of inkstones in his psyche and everyday activities, as well as the extent to which inkstones structured his emotional, social, and artistic lives, is palpable. Huang Ren, a poet from Yongfu, Fujian province, was initiated into the connoisseurship of inkstones by his father.[24] He had the good fortune of serving as magistrate of Sihui in Guangdong in 1725, where his duties included supervising the quarries in neighbouring Gaoyao, home of the famous Duan stones. In 1646, the Shunzhi emperor ordered the reopening of the dry mines as soon as peace was barely secured in the area. Five more operations were ordered between 1646 and 1687. In 1725, Huang oversaw another mining, this time from the beds buried deep under water. As can be imagined, it was a lucrative post. Huang ruffled powerful feathers, however, and was impeached several years later. Proclaiming his innocence, Huang maintained that he returned home carting nothing but a bundle of poems and several small slabs of Duan stones.[25]

There is no doubt that Huang Ren was a historical figure, but certain facets of his biography conform to age-old tropes of an iconic inkstone-lover-cum-upright-official. The trope of his leaving Duanzhou impoverished harks back to that of the incorruptible Northern Song magistrate Bao Gong (999–1062), who was said to have left his post in Duanzhou without taking even one slab of stone.[26] If Huang Ren's persona as a public official is thus mediated by inkstones, the same is even truer for his persona as a retired gentleman at home. In life and in legend, Huang Ren fits the bill of Judith Zeitlin's obsessive collector whose love of inkstones was an expression of a radical subjectivity in vogue in the seventeenth century.[27] What renders his life unmistakably 'real' and singular is the emotional poignancy and visceral corporeality with which he cared for his stones.

The verb 'mosuo 摩挲' (to caress) recurs in his poems on inkstones. For example, in a eulogy to one particular slab simply entitled 'Inkstone 硯', he addressed the slab using the personal pronoun '*jun* 君' for close (human) friends:

Blue spots, leaf-white patch on a ground of clear sky-blue,	青花白葉蔚藍天
An old encomium, newly carved, etched in a small seal script.	古款新銘小篆鐫
Every day I caress you three or two times,	每日摩挲三兩遍
With you, we pass the time for hundreds and thousands of years.	與君上下百千年

The scholar's identification with his anthropomorphized inkstone is a form of self-loving-the-self. Hence Huang began his colophon for his life-long friend and fellow connoisseur Lin Fuyun's 林涪雲 painting, 'Washing Inkstones',[28] with these lines:

A scholar's inkstone is like a beauty's mirror,	美人之鏡名士硯
In the course of a day you caress it over and over.	入手摩挲日幾遍
Relying on you to magnify and make us glow,	托君照耀生光華
How can we let our implement be covered in grime?	詎忍文房受垢面

One day when he was fondling an inkstone that was smooth, lustrous and lovely (*huani keai* 滑膩可愛), it slipped and fell to the ground. It was cracked but did not shatter. Huang wrote a poem to record his shock and recovery:

The beauty has such fine skin and muscles,	美人好肌膚
Born and brought up in the garrison of hibiscus,	生長芙蓉邏
Stroke her and she does not stick to your fingers.	拊之不留手
One slip, by accident –	偶然失一蹉
My soul scattered – A hairline crack!	驚魂裂微痕
. . .	
This old dejected thing in the connoisseur's studio,	蕭齋老棄物
Keeping our three-some company	與汝成三個
Decrepit, but still useful	坐廢仍有用
In writing this song for you.	短歌為汝賀[29]

In assigning the female gender to his inkstone, Huang highlighted his own masculinity in his identification with her.

In the eighteenth century, the entanglement between text and stone reached new heights. Conforming to a range of basic designs, Song inkstones were relatively simple in shape and sparse in surface decoration. Not only did these shapes become increasingly fanciful, by Huang Ren's time it was common for collectors to tamper with the surface of the stones. Treating the surfaces of an inkstone as an open canvas, they would inscribe a poem, a seal, or an encomium on the back, sides, or even the front of the slab in the same way that admirers embellished a painting with their own calligraphy and seals.[30] Furthermore, rubbings were often made of the carved surfaces and given to friends or included in published catalogues. Thus inkstones enjoyed increasingly complicated social lives and in different modalities – as objects, texts, and images.

Huang Ren, for example, presented a Duan inkstone to a friend Li Lincun with a poem to him carved on the stone.[31] In the opposite direction of give-and-take, Huang once sent a poem to his close friend Yu Dian 余甸 (Tiansheng 田生, *jinshi* degree 1706) requesting an inscription for an ancient drum-shaped inkstone in Huang's collection. Yu, a well-known calligrapher and inkstone collector, entertained similar requests from all kinds of people who 'kept' inkstones. Having met his social obligations, he copied these gifts of words and mounted them on to a scroll for himself.[32] A gift of inkstones was a particularly effective way of initiating or maintaining contact with superiors. Hence in 1741 Huang reluctantly gifted the crown jewel of his collection, an inkstone with a cloud and moon design, to a powerful official, Zhao Guolin (1673–1751). The latter composed an inscription, had it carved on the stone, and sent a rubbing of it to Huang, who responded with four new poems.[33] The stone-to-text-to-stone chain reaction could go on for some rounds, cementing elite male social networks across temporal and geographic distances around the scholars' shared dedication to the practice of *wen*.

Huang Ren's remembrance of his intimate friends (inkstone lovers all) was mediated by inkstones and the encomiums they inspired. One day, Huang chanced upon an old inkstone inscription composed over twenty years before during a visit with his calligrapher teacher Lin Ji 林佶 (Jiren 吉人, Luyuan 鹿原, *jinshi* degree 1712) in Beijing. The two made an excursion to the periodic fair on the grounds of Ciren Temple and netted several slabs of inkstones. The joy of the discovery climaxed in the composing of inscriptions. The events of the day, so commonplace and yet so special, unfolded as if it were in front of his eyes, and Huang Ren wrote a poem to express his longing for his teacher.[34]

For Huang Ren, composing inkstone inscriptions was by nature a social activity. Xu Xuecun, a maternal cousin, was Huang's roommate when they sojourned in Suzhou as aspirant students, where they developed the habit of inscribing each other's inkstones. Decades later, when Huang Ren was magistrate in Guangdong he sent Xu an inkstone but did not inscribe it. In his acknowledgement letter, Xu expressed his regret, hence the two made a date to get together upon retirement and to while away the time by composing encomiums for each other's inkstone collections. But it was not meant to be. In 1730, Xu, still in his prime, died suddenly in his office while investigating an embezzlement case. Huang's heart-wrenching lament took the form of a poem carved on an inkstone.[35]

In sum, as one of the 'four treasures' on a scholar's desk (along with paper, writing brush, and inkstick), the inkstone became a quintessential elite male object in the eighteenth century; it embodied the identity of the scholar who collected, inscribed, used, and bequeathed it. The appreciation of the inkstone – as both a utilitarian and aesthetic object – required the engagement and investment of the male connoisseur's body, in the process of which the stone was animated and sometimes feminized or eroticized.

Gu Erniang the inkstone carver: kinship and status

One of the artisans who carved inkstones for Huang Ren and his friends was a most unusual woman, Gu Erniang (fl. 1700–24), who excelled in a profession normally gendered male. Although the village of Huang-gang 黃岡 in Guangdong, an inkstone-carving centre near Zhaoqing, was said to produce the 'majority of its output from female hands', which numbered in the thousands in the mid-Qing,[36] they made functional objects to supply the needs of numerous students and functionaries in the empire. At the elite end of the practice, all of the inkstone carvers mentioned in the connoisseurship literature – surprisingly only a handful – were male with the exception of Gu Erniang.

Gu, a daughter of the Zou 鄒 family in Suzhou, was known by her marital name of Gu Erniang 顧二娘 or Gu Qinniang 顧親娘. Her father-in-law, Gu Delin 德麟, gave up studying to become a inkstone carver of some repute. Erniang's husband Qiming 啟明 was the sole inheritor of the family craft, but he died young without an heir. Gu Erniang learned the craft from her father-in-law and adopted Qiming's nephew Gongwang 公望 as the heir. Gongwang, who was in turn taught by Erniang, became so skilled that he was summoned to serve in the imperial household agency of emperor Kangxi's court. In the absence of Gongwang, Erniang sustained the family business at home in Suzhou. Her reputation surpassed that of her male relatives, and according to the Suzhou gazetteer it was Erniang who emerged as 'the sole transmitter of Gu Delin's artisanship (*dushan qiyi* 獨擅其藝) for twenty-some years'.[37]

As daughter-in-law and widow, Erniang became the lynchpin in the survival of a family craft normally passed on through the male line. Although nominally patrilineal, the Chinese family was flexible and pragmatic in practice; widows and sometimes daughters could inherit and transmit the family learning, craft, or business as substitute males. Yet even the expedient recruitment of females was no guarantee for success. When Gongwang died without an heir, the Gu family craft went into oblivion. Abiding by the formal genealogical reckoning, some local historians made it clear that, however accomplished, Erniang was merely a placeholder in a male line of descent.

In a rare account originally carved on the back of an inkstone, a Suzhou connoisseur called Huang Zhongjian 黃中堅 recounted his decades-long patronage of the family, which began with his encounter with an inkstone Delin made for one of his cousins. Delin was already renowned as one of the premier carvers in Suzhou. Although 'others tried to appropriate and imitate his work, eventually they all fell short'. Huang was so enamoured by this inkstone with a knotted design that he handed over (*shouzhi* 授之) two slabs of Duan stone and asked Delin to make the same. But the results were somehow less than satisfactory. Thinking that the problem lay with the inferior quality of the slabs, Huang was attempting to locate a better one and to 'order' (*mingzhi* 命之) Delin to re-carve it, when the latter passed away. Finding a superior stone also proved to be elusive.[38]

Over ten years had passed before Huang finally procured a slab for three pieces of gold. By then Delin's heir Qiming had also died, and Delin's grandson Gongwang had been summoned into the inner palace. Huang wrote:

> There were no other skilled hands in Suzhou. I have heard that Qiming's wife had in fact inherited the family mantle [*shiwei jiachuan* 實為家傳], but had not realized that her fame was rising day by day. In mid-autumn of

the year *renchen* [1712], I ordered her to execute it in a spontaneous, whimsical style [*ling suiyi zhizhi* 令隨意製之] in whatever design she pleased. She opted for the knot. When I inspected the inkstone closely, the knot appeared a bit too contrived and crafted [*guoyu gongqiao* 過於工巧] and not as archaistic and unkempt [*gupu* 古樸; literally, antique simplicity] as Delin's work. But otherwise it is warm, pure, archaistic, and elegant [*wenchun guya* 溫純古雅], which befits the [Gu] legacy.

Huang was satisfied: 'Hence my desire of twenty years was realized in one day. In my delight, I composed two eulogies [to inscribe on the stone].'[39]

This anecdote yields valuable information about the social status of an inkstone carver as well as the roles played by kinship and gender in his or her success. Huang's choice of imperative verbs – to hand over, to order (both Delin and Erniang) – leaves no ambiguity about the status differential between patron and artisan. Delin was said to have studied the classics but failed to ascend the examination ladder. His biographer in the Suzhou gazetteer emphasized that, although he left no publications, 'there are stashes of poetry drafts at home', implying that he partook in the literati pastime of drinking with friends and matching each other's compositions. Indeed, in the affluent and consumerist cultures of seventeenth-century Jiangnan, such Suzhou artisans as the bamboo carver Pu Zhongqian 濮仲謙 (b. 1582) mingled with his learned patrons at dinner parties, but Delin does not seem to have circulated in such a fashion to promote his business.[40] His reputation derived from his father, and potential clients came to him by word-of-mouth. His carvings and the Gu name spoke for him.

Similarly, Huang Zhongjian identified Erniang as 'the Gu wife', highlighting the family name as her biggest asset, a fact confirmed by his earlier disclosure that he decided to entrust her with his rare stone upon hearing that she had inherited the family mantle. Huang never wavered in his confidence that *he* was the arbiter who assessed the artisan's work and defined the essence of the Gu family style.

The branding of Gu Erniang

The social status of artisans, the spatial arrangement in the workshop, the process of commissioning objects of art, and the economics involved in the transaction are important topics that deserve further research. Anecdotal evidence in Huang Ren's poetry confirms the impression given by Huang Zhongjian that, even among artisans, there was a hierarchy of artistry and the status of inkstone carver was rather low. Apparently, although seal-carving became an esteemed pursuit for the literati in the sixteenth century, a trend facilitated by the use of such soft stones as soapstone, scholars did not normally pick up the knife to carve inkstones.⁴¹ Huang Ren's friend Lin Fuyun was such a dedicated lover of inkstones that his practice of carving inscriptions in a minute seal script with his own hand was singled out for comment.⁴² When Huang Ren was magistrate in Sihui, he hosted two inkstone carvers skilled in the seal script, Dong Cangmen 董滄門 and Yang Dongyi 楊洞一, in his official compound for three years. Although Huang referred to them as 'my friends' (*yuyou* 余友), suggesting a certain social parity, it is more accurate to construe them as literate and highly experienced artisans who supplied the magistrate with carved Duan slabs for his incessant gift-giving.⁴³

Not only was the inkstone carver relatively low in status, the value of his or her labour was also subservient to that of the stone and the name of the owner. When collectors refer to a particular piece of inkstone, most often they refer to the design or pattern (inkstone with twin swallows, for example); when the stone has a distinguished feature they refer to the stone itself (inkstone with blue spots). When the inkstone is identified with an illustrious person, it is seldom the carver but almost always the owner, user, or collector associated with the stone. In this the inkstone is different from a work of calligraphy or a painting, whereby the artist's hand matters the most. Huang Ren, who mentioned his friend Yu Dian's popularity as a supplier of inkstone inscriptions, put it succinctly:

A mere piece of stone, vying to be ranked and commented on,	片石爭求月旦知
Unless it is being inscribed on [by a famous person] it is nothing extraordinary.	不經題品不稱奇⁴⁴

It is a tribute to Huang Ren's passion and expertise that collectors and curators today refer to many inkstones associated with him – that he commissioned, inscribed on or once owned – by *his* name instead of by the design, shape, or features of the stone.

These observations about the status of the stone and its (erased) authorship, conjectural as they may be, shed light on the peculiar nature of the reception of Gu Erniang's work. By all accounts a well-known and sought-after artisan in her lifetime, Erniang was said to be the first of the Gu family carvers to have left signature marks on her work. A brief survey of seven extant inkstones bearing such marks shows that they appear in a variety of scripts – regular, clerical, small seal, and others – a standard repertoire of a calligrapher or seal carver. All are variants of 'Made by Gu Erniang of the city of Suzhou' (吳門顧二娘製、造; Figure 14.4) or 'Made by Gu Erniang' (顧二娘製、造).⁴⁵ There must

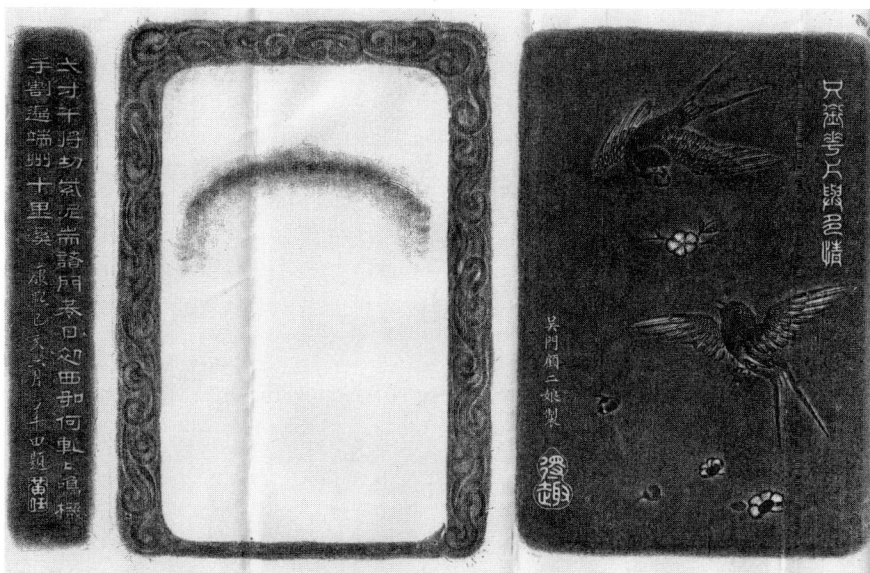

14.4. Rubbing of 'Twin swallows' inkstone bearing Gu Erniang's mark, from left: side, front, and back of the inkstone, Gu's trademark: 'Made by Gu Erniang of Suzhou (*Wumen Gu Erniang zhi*) is on the lower left corner of the back, Qing dynasty (1644–1911), Collection of Tianjin Museum, Tianjin, China

have been a large number of inkstones bearing such marks; even today, occasionally an inkstone bearing some version of the designation will surface at auctions in Beijing or Shanghai. Qing observers remarked that Gu became so popular that forgeries appeared in the market within her lifetime, and that Qing antique-dealers would take a Ming stone that *pre*-dated Gu – normally more valuable than a Qing stone – to pass off as hers. We may thus conclude that many of the stones bearing Gu's signature were forgeries. Since none of Gu's inkstones with unequivocal textual references, such as those mentioned by Huang Ren and Huang Zhongjian, can be identified today, and, conversely, none of the extant stones bearing her signature mark enjoys solid provenance, the authenticity of her works remains a matter of subjective judgement and hence considerable dispute.[46]

The very attempt to use signature marks – be they inscribed by Gu, her workshop, her patrons, or her forgers – to identify an inkstone by its carver is unprecedented and a significant fact for the social historian. Gu Erniang achieved a feat that none of her male counterparts could match: to become not merely a commodity but a brand. Her name and the cult of her persona trumped the value of the patinated veins on the stone and rivalled the fame of her patrons and their learned inscriptions.

This was because Gu was exceptional by dint not of her skills, which were no doubt outstanding, but of her female gender.

The body of the female artisan

Gu Erniang's gender was marked by an excessive attention to her body in legends that developed around her person and work. The first of two that concerns us read in part:

> During the Shunzhi (1644–1661)–Kangxi (1662–1722) reigns, Gu Erniang became renowned as a maker of inkstones. Refusing to apply her carving knife unless it was a fine stone from the old caves of River Duan, she had made no more than a hundred inkstones in her lifetime. As legends have it, she could discern the [interior] flaws of an uncut stone merely by touching it with the tip of her shoes. This is indeed an extraordinary skill. In her own words: 'An inkstone is *carved* from a piece of stone. It would have to appear round, lively, fatty, and lustrous in order to show off the magic of the meticulous carving. If it appears to be dull, static, skinny and stiff, then it is in fact the original state of the piece of stone. What good did the carving do?' The inkstones she made evoke both an antiquarian elegance and a rich splendour. They were peerless among her contemporaries.[47]

This story highlights two equally miraculous aspects of Gu Erniang's artistry: the omniscient power and uncanny accuracy of her 'eyes' and the alchemical transformation effected by her hands. The latter was presented in Gu's own words, an eloquent statement of the artist's craft as an improvement upon nature. The goal of artisanal creation was to bestow life on an inanimate object. Both the process of crafting and its results were described in corporeal terms: 'round, lively, fatty, and lustrous' (*yuanhuo er feirun* 圓活而肥潤) is commonly used to describe people or jade, a stone which is believed to have the ability to take on the aura of its owner.

Indeed, Gu Erniang's body was present at the front and centre of her legend. The displacement of her discerning eyes to her feet (or the tip of her shoes to be exact) is curious. To a reader familiar with the profusion of poetic and pictorial images depicting the tip of lotus slippers peeking out from underneath a woman's long skirt, the description conjures up the image of a desirable female with dainty feet. Although it is not known if Gu Erniang had bound feet (most likely not), her persona thus acquired an unmistakable gendered identity. In a later variation on the same theme, Erniang was moved closer to the field of action while the allusion to her feet became explicit: she was said to have diagnosed the quality of the uncut stone at the quarry by 'feeling the rope of the pulley with her slender feet'. To go even further, some authors referred to her by the moniker of 'Gu-the-Tiny-Feet' (Gu Xiaojiao 顧小腳). It is extremely unlikely that Gu Erniang was involved in the process of assessing and selecting stones at the quarry, legends notwithstanding.

In another legend, after his impeachment Huang Ren was said to have carried an exquisite piece of Duan stone in his sleeves, looking for a worthy carver. After ten years, he landed on Gu Erniang's doorstep in Suzhou. She 'saw and took a liking to it', and agreed to carve the stone for him.[48] Huang commemorated the collaboration in a poem:

A one-inch blade gliding into purple clay,	一寸干將切紫泥，
Twilight begins to descend on Zhuanzhu Lane.	專諸門巷日初西。
How come the hands that make a loom sing ya-ya,	如何軋軋鳴機手，
Have cut through the ten-mile river in Duanzhou.	割遍端州十里溪。[49]

The second line pays tribute to Gu Erniang's skills, which eclipsed others in her marital home on Zhuanzhu Lane, situated in a neighbourhood in Suzhou famous for its jade carvers and other artisans. The last two lines laud Gu by highlighting the *un*naturalness of her achievements: a woman's hand should be wielding a shuttle, not a carving knife. This contrast between weaving, the intended female occupation, and Gu's *actual* occupation accentuated the feminine identity of the artisan. The last line comes close to declaring outright that inkstone-making is a masculine undertaking. The verb to 'cut through' is unnecessarily violent; coming at the heels of the 'sharp blade' in the first line it depicts stone-carving as an act of aggression.

Appearing on many inkstones attributed to her, this poem had become as commonplace as Gu's signature marks. The story of Huang's encounter with the female artisan was widely transmitted because it mirrors the structure of romance fiction. Gu Erniang's craft was construed as a love match between Gu and Huang that was destined to happen: she chanced upon a stone worthy of her craft while he finally discovered an artisan worthy of his stone (and exquisite taste). The stone was animated in its role of matchmaker. By way of stories like this, Gu Erniang's inkstones were feminized at the same time as the profession of inkstone-making was being masculinized.

In sum, although Gu Erniang learned her craft from a man and managed to sustain and transmit a nominally male family tradition, her inkstones were feminized in multiple ways. They were feminized in the very act of commission by the gendered expectations of the patron, who preferred such eroticized motifs as banana leaf, paired swallows, and phoenix. The stones were feminized yet again when they were being collected, forged, and eulogized. Ironically, the high regard that the patrons and collectors accorded Gu's work reflected her socially inferior status as artisan; the fame she enjoyed was predicated on her culturally inferior position as woman.

Concluding remarks: on making and corporeal investments

The quarrying of stones and the making of inkstones are corporeal processes; the connoisseurship of things also requires embodied knowledge and sensory engagement. Yet these are two vastly different kinds of corporeal investments in things, each governed by a different economy. Co-extensive with textual production, the investment of the scholar-connoisseur is grounded in the pre-modern or non-modern economy of cosmogenesis: bodies are not containers of individual selves but sites of cosmological transformation; the boundaries between self and others are fluid and mutable.

In this economy, the more one gives of his body-self, the more he may have or become. Witness the corporeal investment of such inkstone connoisseurs as Huang Zhongjian and Huang Ren. Their sentimental, financial, and corporeal investments in the stone and the attendant texts served to enlarge their social networks and to extend their existence through time. Their love of inkstone was an expression of their textualist faith in the power of writing as a vehicle of communication across temporal and spatial boundaries, indeed as a vehicle of immortality. Their mode of investment was one of incorporation, of encompassing if not appropriating the bodily investments and labours of others.[50]

In contrast, the body of the artisan belongs to a modern economy of a zero-sum game that is grounded in the modern notion of the body as a personal, bounded, and finite entity – as the container of the individuated self. The corporeal investment of the nameless quarriers as well as such artisans as Gu Erniang and her male relatives belonged to this economy of expiration and exhaustion. Their bodies were simply used up, like the corroded hands of Guan Honghui 關紅惠, a female inkstone carver who has mastered her craft in the apprenticeship system in the socialist Duan Inkstone Factory and today, after the dissolution of the government monopoly enterprise, is successful enough to operate a workshop under her own name in Zhaoqing. Her shop is located at a site on Duanzhou No. 2 Road not far from the historic village of Huanggang, where hundreds of young women who can barely write sit by small tables carving inkstones day after day. Still in her early 40s, over two decades' grappling with the piece of stone and exposure to the dust of the stones has eaten into and toughened Guan's skin; she smiled an embarrassed smile while remarking that she has 'the hands of an eighty-year-old granny'. Her pair of hands serves to remind us that not only was there a status differential between the male patron and the female artisan, there also existed a hierarchy among crafts that no amount of romanticization of the 'female hand' could conceal or wish away.

As an artefact, the inkstone was made – acquired a material form and presence – by the cunning knowledge and embodied skills of the quarrier and the carver. Yet the contributions of both were effaced if not erased in the connoisseurship discourse; the surface of the carved stones bore witness to the brilliance of the scholars who owned and inscribed on it, who possessed expert knowledge on geology and nomenclature, and who lodged feelings of nostalgia and mourning in the stone. The emotional comforts afforded by the inkstone, the pleasures of caressing it, not to mention the facility of grinding ink with it, all served to refer the materiality of the inkstone – its thing-ness – back to the male author of texts. So what does it matter that Gu Erniang was female? The maker of things was always already feminized in subject position, regardless of his or her identity in terms of social gender.

From this perspective, the connoisseurship discourse that reached its height during the Qianlong reign in the eighteenth century had the same cultural effect as the Enlightenment discourse in eighteenth-century Europe in one regard: the bifurcation of 'head' and 'hand' and denigration of tacit craft knowledge that resists textualization.[51] Surely, the denigration had existed as long as the history of writing, and I do not intend to suggest that it occurred only in the high Qing. Yet the specific form that the triumph of textual over embodied knowledge took – as the colonization by literati painting of such other art forms as embroidery and inkstone carving – deserves further analysis from art historians, specialists of literature, and cultural historians.

The codification of 'literati painting' as a cultural system in the late thirteenth and early fourteenth centuries, the very same time when 'literati values' and identities were threatened by the Mongol conquest, changed literati culture and the status of writing in common culture in indelible ways. As literati painting became a distinct art form it also became exclusive, accessible only to those educated viewers with the cultural skills to decipher the colophons and decode the image. Both the distinctiveness and exclusivity are rooted in a metaphoric continuum between calligraphic texts and pictorial images on the conceptual space of the painting surface. In this new 'ecology of painting', the ink traces on the tactile surface of the paper provide visual unity to the calligraphic texts and images.[52] The calligraphy, poetic inscriptions, encomiums, and colophons – texts all – thus enjoyed robust social lives and augmented cultural prestige beyond the printing press and the culture of books with which texts were previously associated. The supremacy of literati painting as the highest artistic achievement of the male scholar, established by the seventeenth century, thus represents a triumph of the (hand)written word and the mode of textuality associated with it.

The paradigm of a metaphoric continuum between text and image was so powerful that it found its way into other mediums beyond painting. The self-conscious modelling of Gu family embroidery after literati painting in the early seventeenth century was a salient example: the female embroiderers executed the underdrawing by wielding a painting brush; colophons were added and stitched with black silk floss; the faces of embroidered figures were embellished with a brush to enhance their pictorial effect. None of this was common practice in the centuries before. The embroidered works of the Gu workshop, mounted as album leafs or scrolls, were being sold and collected *as paintings*. The impoverished family secured the endorsement of Dong Qichang, *the* literati painter of his generation, to establish the brand name.[53]

The transformation of the material format of the inkstone is another example of the power of the paradigm of literati painting to penetrate if not 'colonize' the culture of craft. Whereas the inkstone made in the Tang and Song dynasties is impressive in its *object*hood, with hefty and simple form and convoluted surfaces, the inkstone of the late Ming and Qing calls attention to its surface as a coherent conceptual space. Late imperial inkstones increasingly resemble a tablet, a veritable piece of stone-paper that produces flat surfaces for inscription on the four sides, front, and back. The growing fad for naming and cherishing mineral imperfections encourages the collector to fixate on the surface of the stone. The popularity of the inscription of poems and encomiums, rare in previous centuries, echoes the increasing emphasis on mimetic representation in the design motif: flower, bamboo, swallow, phoenix, banana leaf, moon, rocks (!), and landscape all found their way to the front and back of inkstones.

The inkstones commissioned by Huang Ren and his friends appear as veritable literati paintings on the back. One favourite subject is that of Chan meditation, which recurs in inkstones in Huang's collection. Framed by the edges of the stone, a portrait of the Bodhi-dharma is carved in the centre; a poem by Huang appears on top; on the lower left corner are artist and collector seals. The metaphoric continuum between calligraphic text and image directs the viewer's attention and imagination in the same way as in a literati painting. In another example, this time of playful self-referentiality, Huang presents the portrait of himself as a farmer holding a hoe in his right hand and an inkstone in his left (Figure 14.5). To the left is a self-encomium followed by his signature and seal. As poet, calligrapher, farmer, and lover of elegant things, the connoisseur incorporated into himself all cultural and economic values before externalizing them on to the back of an inkstone,

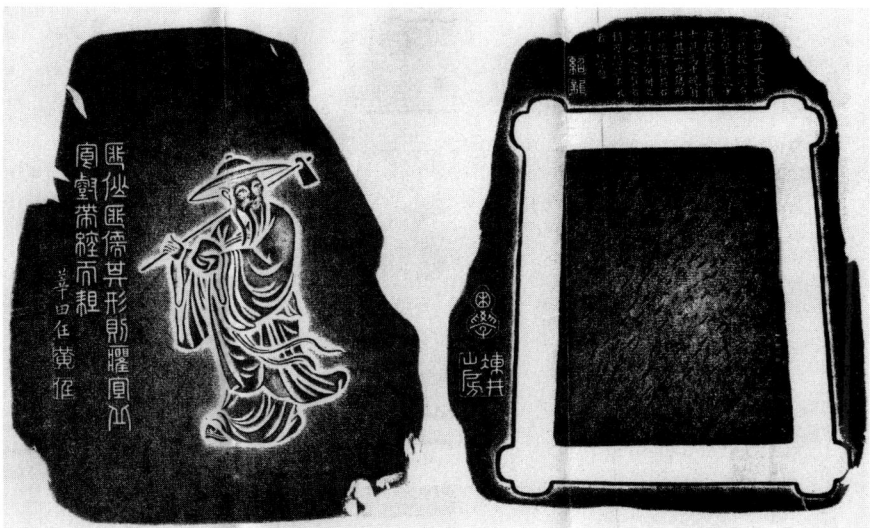

14.5. Rubbing of 'Ink drops' inkstone showing Huang Ren's portrait, From left: back, front of the inkstone, Qing dynasty (1644–1911), Collection of Tianjin Museum, Tianjin, China

hence allowing us glimpses into a time when the supreme value of *wen* was manifest in all visual and material cultures.

Notes

1. Arjun Appadurai (ed.), *The Social Life of Things: Commodities in Cultural Perspective* (Cambridge: Cambridge University Press, 1988).
2. The term is Lissa Roberts's, in Lissa Roberts, Simon Schaffer, and Peter Dear (eds), *The Mindful Hand: Inquiry and Invention from the Late Renaissance to Early Industrialisation* (Chicago: University of Chicago Press, 2008), pp. 216–7. Because skills are contextual, it is useful methodologically to focus on one genre of artefact at a time. This approach also has the advantage of avoiding a bifurcation of production and consumption, theory and practice, applied and pure knowledge and so on.
3. Liu Yanliang, *Duanyan de jianbie he xinshang* (Wuhan: Hubei meishu chubanshe, 2002), pp. 42–4. In today's Zhaoqing, the boxes are made by carpenters and polishing is relegated to less experienced workers.
4. Duan stones were mined as early as the Tang, but the discourse of their superiority (especially over She stones from Anhui) did not emerge until the Song. According to Qing writer Ji Nan 計楠, ink slabs made of Duan stones first appeared during the reign of emperor Gaozu of the Tang (r. 618–26). Cited in Liu Yanliang, *Duanyan de jianbie he xinshang*, p. 3. For an introduction to the history of Duan stones, see Liu Yanliang, *Duanxi mingyan* (Guangzhou: Guangdong renmin, 1979). The name Duanzhou was changed to Zhaoqing in 1118 during the reign of Song emperor Huizong.
5. Green and white Duan stones also exist, albeit quite rare. White Duan stones, rich in mica, were formed 70 million years later than the purple and green ones. For geological formation and qualitative analysis, see Liu Yanliang, *Duanyan*, pp. 17–19, 24–6; Duanyan daguan bianxiezu, *Duanyan daguan* (Beijing: Hongqi, 2005), pp. 1–32.

6 The expression is used by, for example, Qing connoisseur Chen Gongyun (1631–1700), in Duanyan daguan bianxiezu, *Duanyan daguan*, p. 5. When the inkstick is being rubbed against the moistened slab, a fine amount of the stone is ground into the ink, which is a mixture of ink, water, and stone dust. R.H. van Gulik, *Mi Fu on Ink-stones* (Peking: Henri Vetch, 1938), p. 22.

7 The expenses involved in labour outlay and logistical support meant that mining was sporadic, often spurred by an entrepreneurial magistrate who assembled a team of investors to finance the operation. Li Zhaoluo suggested that the mining of the Old Pit had to be approved by the prefectural magistrate and the mining of the Poker Mark Pit, by the county magistrate. The lesser pits were open to the exploits of private investors (*Duanyan daguan*, pp. 233–4). For a list of the years when Old Pit was mined during the Ming and Qing dynasties, see Liu, *yanjiu*.

8 Li Zhaoluo, 'Duanxi yankeng ji', in *Duanyan daguan*, p. 233. For a biography of Li, see Ye Yanlan and Ye Gongzhuo, *Qingdai xuezhe xiangzhuan heji* (Shanghai Guji, 1989), pp. 321–2.

9 The term 'skeleton' is from Li Zhaoluo, 'Duanxi yankeng ji', p. 232. The implication is that if the skeleton is weakened, the shaft may collapse.

10 Pamela H. Smith thus said of craft knowledge: 'Craft involved a way of knowing nature that was largely tacit and transmitted by social practices and institutions not generally recognized today as producing theoretical knowledge. This knowledge has an unfamiliar appearance to scholars because it is produced by bodily labour, rather than by words, and is often embodied in objects (and in artisan's practices), rather than in texts.' (*Mindful Hand*, p. 34)

11 The 'parts' are called 'days', (*ri* 日) in the Qing. Li Zhaoluo, 'Duanxi yankeng ji', p. 234.

12 The term is in Liu Yanliang, *Duanyan de jianbei*, p. 42.

13 Su Yijian, 'Wenfang sipu', juan 3, *Duanyan daguan*, p. 4. Cf. Tang Xun, 'Yanlu', in *Duanyan daguan*, p. 101.

14 Eliade, *The Forge and the Crucible*, trans. Stephen Corrin (London: Rider & Company, 1962), pp. 26–33. In this world of creation-as-procreation, the metalsmith's tools are sexualized and endowed with magical powers. Body metaphors also structure theories of calligraphy, as expounded by John Hay, 'The human body as a microcosmic source of macrocosmic values in calligraphy', in Susan Bush and Christian Murck (eds), *Theories of the Arts in China* (Princeton: Princeton University Press, 1983), pp. 74–102.

15 On child-stones, see Van Gulik, *Mi Fu on Inkstones*, pp. 32–6; *Duanyan daguan*, pp. 152–3.

16 Ironically, Mi Fu's seminal treatise on inkstone, *Yanshi*, cemented its status as an aesthetic object by inaugurating a discourse of function.

17 The Tang calligrapher Liu Gongquan might have been the first to use the term 'xu yan' (keeping an inkstone) in his 'Lunyan'. Liu, *Duanxi mingyan*, p. 12.

18 The monk Mouzhou 懋周 had a Duan stone that had protrusions like a peak. Mi Fu got it, hugged it in bed for three days, and asked Su Dongpo to compose an encomium (Yu Huai, *Yanlin*, 4b).

19 Yu Huai, 'Yanlin xiaoyin', *Yanlin*, 1b.

20 Lin Wanli, *Shengchunhong shi jinshi shuji*, pp. 39, 2–3.

21 Summarizing the connoisseurship literature from the successive dynasties, local authorities in Guangdong promulgated a list of nomenclature and definitions of these features in an effort to install accountable industry standards as inkstones became highly prized collectibles in post-Reform China. See *Guangdong sheng difang biaozun: Duanyan* (n.p., Guangdong sheng jiliang jishu jianduju, 2006). For their history in the Qing, see *Duanyan daguan*, pp. 27–32.

22 Some scholars have argued that locals of Zhaoqing sent Duan inkstones to the court as tribute as early as the Tang. Liu, *Duanyan de jianbie*, pp. 13–4.

23 Inkslabs excavated from Tang tombs also suggest an increasing emphasis on surface decoration since the mid-Tang, serving as supporting evidence for their emergent status as aesthetic objects. Liu, *Duanyan de jianbie*, p. 3.

24 Also known as Yuxin 于莘; Xintian 莘田; Elder with Ten Inkstones (Shiyan weng 十硯翁). He received his *juren* degree in 1702.

25 These biographical details are compiled from several biographies, with varying degrees of veracity. The biographies by Yu Wenyi, Zheng Fangqun, and preface by Chen Zhaolun in *Xiangcaozhai shizhu* give useful personal information. Information on the opening of the quarries is from Xu Kang, *Qianchen mengying lu*, shang, pp. 171–2, in *Meishu congshu*. Huang Ren's life and inkstones was a subject of mythologizing and forgery in the late Qing.

26 Bao Gong was said to have thrown the stones that locals gave him as departure gifts into the Xijiang river, which became an islet. Today there still stands a shrine on the islet (Liu Yanliang, *Duanxi mingyan*, 20–1). See a similar story about a Magistrate Zhao (Yu Huai, *Yanlin*, 13b).

27 Judith Zeitlin, 'The petrified heart: obsessions in Chinese literature, art and medicine', *Late Imperial China* 12:1 (June 1991), pp. 1–26. The radical subjectivity was expressed as an act of the self-loving the self.

28 The washing of inkstones is a routine but delicate operation. If washed too often or too much the inkslab would dry up; if ink was allowed to cake the surface the stone would lose its porosity.

29 'Garrison of hibiscus' refers to Zhaoqing. 'Xiaozhai', literally 'cold studio', is the name of the studio of seminal art critic Zhang Yanyuan.

30 This practice of inscribing words on inkstones was extremely rare in the Song. An exhibition of the inkstones listed in emperor Qianlong's catalogue of his inkstone collection, the *Xiqing yanpu*, at the Taipei Gugong shows a lot of early stones being inscribed retroactively with Qianlong's intrusive poems and seals. Only one Song inkstone bears the signature of its original owner, Su Dongpo, and his poem (*Xiqing*, pp. 174–5).

31 Huang Ren, *Xiangcaozhai shizhu* (n.p., 1814), 5.20b.

32 Huang Ren, *Qiujiang ji* (n.p., 1756), 4.7b; *Xiangcaozhai shizhu*, 4.10b; 4.11b.

33 Huang, *Xiangcaozhai shizhu*, 5.20b; *Qiujiang ji*, 5.12a-b. Huang Ren addressed Zhao by his honorific name, Taian Gong. Zhao served as the provincial governor (the highest civilian official) of Fujian in 1730–34. Zhao subsequently named his studio the Cloud Moon Inkstone Studio. Huang and other local Fujian scholars cultivated Zhao with the hope that Zhao would promote them and their sons in court (which he often did).

34 The Ciren temple was inside the Guangning Gate; temple fairs were held three times a month, on the first, fifteenth, and twenty-fifth days. Huang Ren, *Qiujiang jizhu* (n.p., 1843), 4.10b.

35 Huang, *Qiujiang ji*, 4.5a-b. Huang's Ren's remembrance of his wife, Madam Zhuang, was expressed by way of her love of inkstones over jewellery (*Qiujiang jizhu*, 5.32a; *Xiangcaozhai shizhu*, 5.35a).

36 Huang Ren, *Xiangcaozhai shizhu*, 4.12b; *Qiujiangji zhu*, 4.15b.

37 Li Mingwan et al. (eds), *Suzhou fuzhi* (1883; reprinted 1970), 110.20b. The entry, under Gu Shengzhi, appeared in the 'Yishu' (artistry) section. Erniang was not mentioned by name, only as 'daughter-in-law' (*xi*). The late-Qing writer Xu Ke suggested that Gu Erniang adopted two sons and taught both stone-carving but one died and the other was Gongwang

According to Xu, Gongwang was not a nephew of Qiming but was a Zou, a nephew of Erniang herself. *Qingbai leichao* 5, in *Guangdong gongyi meishu shiliao*, p. 262. Xu's source about the Zou nephew is probably Zhu Xiangxian, *Wenjian oulu*, *Congshu jicheng xubian*, v. 96 (Shanghai: Shanghai shudian, 1994), pp. 628–9.

38 Huang Zhongjian, 'Shiyan ming bingxu', *Shuzhai erji*, in *Siku weishoushu jikan*, 8:27 (Beijing: Beijing chubanshe, 1997), p. 458.

39 Huang Zhongjian, 'Shiyan ming bingxu', p. 431.

40 Li, *Suzhou fuzhi*, 110.20b. Pu Zhongqian's year of birth is from Wang Shixiang, *Jinhuidui*, 1 (Beijing: Sanlian shudian, 1999), p. 282. Other famous bamboo carvers include Zhang Xihuang and the Zhu's in Jiading, founders of the Jiading school of bamboo carving. The second generation Zhu Xiaosong (1520–87) befriended such literati as Xu Xuemo who wrote his funerary epitaph. Of his three sons, one became a student and the other two inherited his artistry (Wang, *Jinhuidui*, p. 286). The Jiading literatus Li Liufang carved bamboo himself. On the status anxieties associated with the social ascent of craftsmen in the late Ming, see Chu-Tsing Li and James C.Y. Watt (eds), *The Chinese Scholar's Studio: Artistic Life in the Late Ming Period* (New York: Asia Society Galleries, 1987), p. 9; Craig Clunas, *Superfluous Things: Material Culture and Social Status in Early Modern China* (Honolulu: University of Hawaii Press, 2004), pp. 60–7, 140–7.

41 For the popularity of seal-carving as literati self-expression, see Li and Watt, *Chinese Scholar's Studio*, pp. 11–3.

42 Huang Ren, *Qiujiang ji*, 4.5b.

43 Huang, *Qiujiang ji*, 4.6b. Both Yang and Dong studied calligraphy with Lin Ji. In sub-tropical Guangdong the two old men worked outdoors, under sugar palm trees. In present-day Zhaoqing, there is a division of labour between inkstone carvers who specialize in pictorial elements and in texts. The latter tend to be male and better educated. I do not know if this was the case in the mid-Qing.

44 Huang, *Qiujiang ji*, 4.5a.

45 The one departure from this formula is 'Wumen Gu Dagu' (Gu Dagu of Wumen [Suzhou]) on an inkstone with phoenix and cloud design. Zhu Jiajin, *Gugong tuishilu* (Beijing: Beijing chubanshe, 1999), pp. 236–8. I am dubious about the authenticity of this attribution. 'Dagu' (general address for a respectable woman) may signify Gu's status as a master of her craft in the eyes of her patrons (or forgers), or it may be a specific reference to the honorary name of Han scholar and poet Ban Zhao (45–120), Cao Dagu.

46 Complicating the issue further, inkstones without Gu's signature marks could have been carved by her. If Huang Zhongjian's descriptions were typical, the making of an inkstone was, even in Gu's time and in her case, a collaboration between the patron and the artisan, with the former dictating the format and motifs. The unequivocal notions of authorship or authenticity demanded by the market or connoisseurship are thus misguided. I have studied the 'inkstone with paired swallows' at the National Palace Museum in Taipei, another one with the same name at the Tianjin Museum, both bearing Gu's signature marks, and the 'Dongtian yipin' attributed to her at the Palace Museum in Beijing. An analysis of these stones and their attributions is the subject of another paper.

47 Yi Zongkui, *Xinshishuo* (Taipei: Mingwen shuju, 1985), 18.562. See a similar rendition in Xu Ke, *Qingbai leichao* 5. Gu's remarks about her own artistry were first transmitted by Zhu Xiangxian in his *Wenjian oulu*, p. 628. Zhu (1663–1733) was a rough contemporary of Gu Erniang.

48 Although the poem is verifiable, the dating of the encounter in the legend is spurious. Huang's commissions were likely made before his departure for Guangdong in 1725, which is reasonable in light of the fact that Erniang was active in the 1700s to 1720s and Huang Ren had sojourned in Suzhou as a young scholar.

49 The poem is included in two of Huang Ren's poetry collections, *Xiangcaozhai shizhu*, 2.23b and *Qiujiangji zhu*, 2.33b-34a. Yuan Mei, however, disputed the attribution and ascribed it to a Liu Ci in his *Suiyuan shihua*. See the discussion in Cai Hongru, *Zhonghua guyan yibai jiang* (Tianjin: Baihua wenyi, 2007), pp. 43–47.

50 We are reminded of what Charlotte Furth has said about the gender inequality in the Taoist practice of inner alchemy – male practitioners worked to regenerate their vital energies in an economy of regeneration whereas female practitioners battled their bodies of depletion. Furth, *A Flourishing Yin: Gender in China's Medical History, 960–1665* (Berkeley: University of California Press, 1999).

51 Roberts et al., *Mindful Hand*, p. 310.

52 The same can be said about the inscriptional surfaces of inkstones after the latter increasingly took on the format of a literati painting. The term 'ecology of painting' is John Hay's. See his 'Surface and the Chinese painter: the discovery of surface', *Archives of Asian Art* 38 (1985), pp. 95–123. The surface of literati paintings also becomes a site of the active production of pleasures according to Hay, 'Boundaries and surfaces of self and desire in Yuan painting', in John Hay (ed.), *Boundaries in China* (London: Reaktion Books, 1997), pp. 124–70.

53 For Guxiu, see the pioneering research of Huang I-Fen, 'Gender, technical innovation, and Gu family embroidery in late-Ming Shanghai', *EASTM* 36 (2012), pp. 77–129.

Index

Page numbers in *italic* refer to illustrations

Abu-Lughod, Janet Lippman 79
Acosta, José de 190
actor–network theory 3, 26, 32, 34, 63n.4
Adimari, Alemanno 88n.1
Adriani, Giovambattista 242–3
affordances 8, 31–4, 36
agency 3, 26, 30, 32–3, 35
Agricola, Georgius 8, 51–62 *passim*, 66n.65, 67n.91
Alberti, Leon Battista 86, 224, 225, 272–3
Alberti, Nero *230*
Albertus Magnus 49–52, 67n.91, 83–5, 143, 146–50, 155, 225
alchemy 10, 49–50, 52, 84, 170, 179n.63, 333n.50
Alcuin 122
Al-Faziri 77
al Hamdani 77
Allegory of Poverty 245–7, *246*
Ambrose 227
Anaxagoras 148, 155
Anderson, Ruth Matilda 291
Angelico, Fra 247, 252, 255
Apelles 243, 256
Appadurai, Arjun 310
Aquinas, Thomas 123–4, 125
architecture 12, 164, 190–2, 201n.57, 273, 275, 277
    materials 266–79
    Polish 14, 263–79, 279n.2
Aretino, Pietro 160–1, 170, 240
Aristotle 22, 49, 50, 52, 65n.28, 83, 147, 155
    on memory 166, 172
    Pseudo-Aristotle 57

Arnheim, Rudolf 26–27
ars nova 28, 39n.37
artisans 9–10, 13, 23, 321, 326–7
Arts and Crafts movement 5–6
Augustine 82, 124, 132, 227, 238n.63, 240
Avery, Charles 174n.7
Avicenna 83
azurite 76, 93n.60, 219
Azymite Controversy 121–2

Bachelard, Gaston 4–5, 211
Bakócz, Tamás 273
Baldinucci, Filippo 161
Bandinelli, Baccio *165*, 175n.21
Bao Gong 317, 331n.26
Barba, Alvaro Alonso 55
Bartholomeus Anglicus 219n.1
Baxandall, Michael 5, 13, 226, 252, 256
Becon, Thomas 120
Bellini, Giovanni 166
Belting, Hans 22
Benedetto da Mariano 231, *232*
Benintendi, Orsino 168
Berchorius, Petrus 228
Berrecci, Bartolommeo 263–5, 265–71, *269*, 280n.7
Berry, Jean de 213
Bewer, Francesca G. 45
Białostocki, Jan 243, 279n.2
Biringuccio, Vannoccio 8, 53–4, 56, 58, 60–1, 179n.63
blood 44–5, 100, 122, 140, 225, 249
Boccaccio, Giovanni 86, 96n.83
Boehm, Gottfried 22
Boerhaave, Herman 63, 64n.11

Index

bole 56, 74, 107–8, 114n.39, 176n.29, 292–3
Bonagrazia of Bergamo 244
Bona Sforza 272, 281n.35
Bonaventure 231
Boner Jan 266–7, 273
Borghini, Raffaello 161
Boucher, Bruce 170
bronze 8, 11, 17n.26, 45, 61, 160, 161, 223, 228, 252, 273
Brunelleschi, Filippo 250
Burgh, John de 124
Butterfield, Andrew 250
Bynum, Caroline 135n.7

candles 166–8
Caravaggio, Michelangelo Merisi da 242, 243, 256, 259, *259*
Caroso da Sermoneta, Fabritio 299
Carpaccio, Vittore 296–7
carving 5, 224, 324–5
Castiglione, Giovanni Benedetto 256, *258*
Catalan Atlas 81, *82*
Cellini, Benvenuto 62, 161, 164
Cennini, Cennino 74, 75, 76, 80, 85–7, 108, 110n.15, 149–50
  on gilding 103–5, 112n.26, 113n.28–9, 114.n39, 176n.29
  on lead white, 144–5, 146, 148–9
Chan, Paul 242, 256
Charles the Bold 210, 214–15
Chastellain, Georges 209–10, 212
Chaucer, Geoffrey 145–6, 148, 150, 155
Chevalier, Étienne 205–6, 209
Chinggis Khan and sons 78–9
chopines, *see* shoes
Cieza de León, Pedro de 198n.5
Cimabue 247
clay 11, 35, 50, 60–2, 160–2, 164–5, 168–73, 178n.55
Cobo, Bernabé 181–2, 184, 187, 190
Cole, Michael W. 45
Commynes, Philippe de 214
connoisseurship 13, 310, 313–19, 327, 330n.21
Cooper, Donal, and Janet Robson 243
copper 45, 51, 54, 61, 147, 268, 273
Corvinus, Matthias 272–3
courtesans 209, 297, 300–3, *303–4*, 308n.68
Crescenzi, Piero de' 224, *225*
Cresques, Abraham 81

Ctesias 81
Cummins, Thomas 187

De Landa, Manuel 4
de Lorris, Guillaume, and Jean de Meun 145, 153–4
Desiderio da Settignano 228, *229*
Detti di filosofia in versi provenzali 84, *85*
Dewey, John 35
Didi-Huberman, Georges 172
Diego de la Cruz *129*
Domenico di Fazino 223
Donatello 238n.68, 250
Dong Cangmen 322, 332n.43
Dong Qichang 328
Driel-Murray, Carol van 284, *285*
Duccio 80
Dürer, Albrecht 25, 218
Dym, Walter 56–7

Egbert 125
Eliade, Mircea 313
Elkins, James 25
Encomium Sigismundi 279
Ercker, Lazarus 53
Erhart, Michel 224
Eucharist 10, 119–33
Eurasian trade 6, 8, 76–80, 91n.43
ex voti 168, *169*, 173

Fernández, Gregorio 226
Filarete 272
Fortuna, Simone 255
Foscolo, Jacobello 224
fossils 48, 53, 55
Foucault, Michel 209
Fouquet, Jean 12, 205–7, *206*, 209, 210, 212, 217–18, 220nn.7–8
Fra Angelico, *see* Angelico, Fra
Francesco di Giorgio Martini 224
Francesco di Valdambrino 223
Francisco della Lora 272, 281n.37
Francis of Assisi 244–5, 247
Franco, Giacomo *302*
Fraser, Valerie 188–9, 191–3
Fréart de Chantelou, Paul 259, 262n.35
Freedberg, David 200n.30
Friedländer, Max 28
Fugger family 267, 268
Furth, Charlotte 333n.50

Garcilaso de la Vega 192–3, 198n.14
Gardner, Julian 250

Geber, *see* Jabir Hayyan, Abu Ibn Musa
Gell, Alfred 3, 30–31
gems 7, 12–13, 48, 68, 82, 205–19, 219n.1
  exotic origins 215–16
  See also painting: gemstone backings; pearls; shoes
genealogie de Jean le Blanc, La 119, 119–21, 130
Gentile da Fabriano 8, 68, *69–70*, 74, 82, 86–7, 88nn.1–2, 106, 248, *249*
Gentilini, Gian Carlo 168, 170
gesso 74, 107–8, 161, 179, 224, 240, 292–3
  See also plaster
Ghent Altarpiece, *see* van Eyck, Jan
Ghiberti, Lorenzo 247, 255
Giambologna 161–2, *163*, 255–6
Giambono, Michele 247, 248, *248*
Gibson, James J. 8, 31–2
Gilbert, John 141
Gil de Siloé 287
Giotto 115n.44, *244*, 244–5, *245*, 247, 254, 259
Giuliano 231, *232*
glass-making 146, 148
Glauber, Rudolf 63
Glick, Thomas 286
Godefroy, Denis 209
gold 9, 45, 77–8, 82–3, 97–109, 109n.8, 109n.12
  coins 9, 74, 77–8, 97–103, 111n.21, 113n.29
  dust 75
  gold leaf 9, 74, 84, 97–8, 102–9, 109n.1, 112n.23, 112–13nn.26–28, 176n.29
  painting uses 74–5, 77, 87, 89n.11, 98, 102–6, 247–9, 252–3
  properties 55
  sources 9, 50, 77, 81–2, 97–101
  supernatural properties 84, 95n.77
Goldthwaite, Richard 163
Gongwang 320, 331n.37
Guaman Poma de Ayala, Felipe 198n.8
Guan Hongshi 326
Guarico, Pomponio 166, 170–2
Gu Delin 320–1
Gu Erniang 310, 319–28, *323*, 331n.37, 332nn.45–6
Guglielmo 98, *99*, 106–7
guilds 74, 97, 102–6 *passim*, 110–11nn.15–16, 112n.25, 223, 290, 295
Guillaume de Deguileville 231

gypsum 74, 163–4, 166, 172, 175n.21, 175n.22

Hegel, Georg Wilhelm Friedrich 1, 23, 24
Hemming, John, and Edward Ranney 187
Herklotz, Ingo 250
Hermens, Erma 38n.27
Hermes Trismegistus 148
Herodotus 81, 82
Hildegard of Bingen 225
Hood, William 247, 252
Host mill retable 132–3, *133*, 139–40nn.45–6
host press *126–7*
Huang Ren 314, 316–19, 322–8 *passim*, 329, 331n.25, 331n.35, 332–3n.48–9
Huang Zhongjian 320–1, 323, 326
human body and materiality 42–8, 52, 63, 146–7, 223, 225, 235n.44, 319, 326–9
hylomorphic paradigm 22, 26, 34–5

Ibn Battuta 92n.47
Illich, Ivan 14
Ingold, Tim 1, 3, 7, 9, 42
Inka culture 11, 16n.23, 180–97, 199n.26
inkstones 13, 309–29, *309*, *311*, *323*, *329*, 331.nn22–3, 331n.28, 331n.30, 333n.52
Isidore of Seville 80–1

Jabir Hayyan, Abu Ibn Musa 80
Jacopone da Todi 295
Jean Le Begue 84
Jean le Blanc 10, 120
Joan of Arc 209
John of Plano Carpinis 79
Jonston, Joannes 46

kamay 187–8, 194–5
Killick, David 155
Kilwardby, Robert 146
Klein, Ursula 30
Komornicki, Stefan S. 279n.2
Kratinus 284
Kubilai Khan 82
Kunstwerden 8, 24, 26, 27, 34, 37n.20
Kunstwollen 8, 23–4, 37n.17, 37n.20

Lando di Pietro 226, *227*
lapis lazuli 6, 12, 68, 76, 78, 80, 81, 90n.24, 92n.51, 219, 247, 261n.23
  supernatural properties 83–4
Latini, Brunetto 81

Index

Latour, Bruno 3–4, 21, 26, 27, 28, 30, 33–4, 38n.32
Law, John 26
lead 11, 51, 55, 59, 75, *143*, 143–4, 147, 152, 159n.84
lead white 10–11, 75, 86–7, 141–56, 156n.9
Lechtman, Heather 184
Leinberger, Hans 47
Leonardo da Vinci 225
Leoni, Leone 255
Leo of Rozmital 212–3
Lessing, Gotthold Ephraim 29
Liber claritas 80
Libre del mustaçaf 291
Li He 314
Li Lincun 318
Lin Fuyun 317, 322
Lin Ji 319, 332n.43
Liu Gongquan 330n.17
Liu Yuxi 316
Livre des simples médecines, see Platearius, Matthaeus
Li Zhaoluo 312, 313, 330n.7
Lomazzo, Gian Paolo 155
Lorenzetti, Pietro 69, *71–3*
Lucretius 4
Lu Guimeng 316
Lup, Lio 224

Macclesfield Psalter 151–4, *151–4*
Malafouris, Lambros 35
Malsystem 30
Mandeville, Sir John 80
Mannying, Robert 129–30, 131–2
Mantegna, Andrea 252
Mappae clavicula 145, 148
maps 21, 80–2
Marbode 83–5
marble 14, 48, 51, 55, 160, 166, 223, 228, 252, 266–70, 273
'Märe vom Feldbauer' 53
Margaret of York 210, *211*
Martínez de Toledo, Alfonso 293
Martínez Montañés, Juan 231
Marx, Karl 1, 6
masonry, *see under* stones
Master of Rosano 98, 106–7
material culture, defined 2–3, 12
materialism vs idealism 21–5, 35, 131–3
materials, theory of 7–8, 21–36
Mathesius, Johannes 66n.65
Medici, Cosimo I de' 250
Medici, Giovanni de' 250

Medici, Piero de' 250
medicine 52, 60, 63, 84, 95n.77, 150
medieval European cosmology 146–52, 155–6
medieval European worldview 76–7, 80–7
Memmi, Lippo 69
mercury 54, 83, 147
Merrifield, Mary 6
metalworking 8, 45, 48–9, 60, 63 330n.14
metric system 1–2, 4
Metz, Christian 199n.25
Michelangelo 160–1, *162*, 175n.25, 240, 252–4, 256, 259
Mi Fu 314, 330n.16, 330n.18
minerals and ores 44–5, 48, 50–63, 65n.34, 67n.91, 215
   fat and lean paradigm 59–63, 66n.65, 66n.68, 67n.96
   See also stones
mining 8, 45–59, 62–3, 158n.56, 313
   Chinese 13, 51, 311–13, 330n.7
   See also gems; metalworking prospecting
Mitchell, William T.J. 22
Mondrian, Piet 68
Moronzone, Jacopo 224
Morrow, Katherine 284
Mouzhou 330n.18
Murúa, Martín de 193

Nair, Stella 198n.10, 201n.52
neo-Realist cinema 259
Newton, Isaac 67n.97
Nicholas of Cusa 150
Nichols, Tom 240–3
Nicodemus 226
Niles, Susan 182

Ogburn, Dennis 199n.26
oil medium 8, 27–33, 35, 75, 76, 141
Orosius 80
Ortiz Rescaniere, Alejandro 196–7
Österreichische Museum für Kunst und Industrie 23
Ouyang Xiu 314
Ovid 149, 226–7, 243

Pacheco, Francisco 231
painting 5, 6, 8–9, 12–13, 27–36, 86, 102, 141, 218–19
   gemstone backings 68–73, 87
   'literati' 327–8, 333n.52
   Netherlandish 27–9, 31–2, 35
   tempera materials and techniques 72, 74–7, 86, 163
   See also lead white; oil medium; pigments

Palissy, Bernard 66n.65
Palmieri, Matteo 167
Panofsky, Erwin 24–5, 28, 33, 218
Paracelsus 42, 47–8, 57–8
paragone debate 160, 168
pearls 205, 207, *208*, 215, 294
Pegolotti, Francesco 82
Peto, John Frederik 31
Petri, Teresa 287
Pheidias 284
Philip the Good 212–13
Physiologus 207
Piccolpasso, Cipriano 170
pigments 5, 9–10, 27, 28, 31, 45, 75–6, 80, 84, 141–2, 149, 155, 240, 252
Pinturicchio 252
Pi Rixiu 316
plaster 11, 160–1, 163–6, 172–3
Platearius, Matthaeus *208*, 215
Pliny 13, 49, 52, 59, 81, 84, 105, 166, 178n.53, 243
Pollaiuolo, Antonio del *171*, 171–2, 250, *251*
polychromy 165–6, 170, 173, 231
Polo, Marco 80, 81–2, 216
Polo de Ondegardo, Juan 190
poverty and art 242–59
Prester John 81, 97
prospecting 48–9, 52–8, 62
　dowsing 56–7
　practices and beliefs 57–8
prostitutes, *see* courtesans
Protzen, Jean-Pierre 182, 198n.10
puruawqa 181, 182
Pu Zhongjian 321

Rashid al Din 80
Raymond of Frosac 244
recipes 45, 59, 84, 102, 110n.14, 231
Richard of Saint Laurent 227
Richardus Anglicus 148
Ried, Benedikt 273–5, *274*
Riegl, Alois 8, 23–4, 37n.20, 38nn.22–3
Rembrandt 25
Robbia, Andrea della 261n.23
Roch 228, 230–1, *230*, 240
Romance of the Rose, see de Lorris, Guillaume, and Jean de Meun
Rosa, Salvator 256, *257*
Rowe, John 184–5
Ruissel, Hermann 213
Rülein von Calw, Ulrich 51–2, 53
Ruskin, John 6, 297
Ryman, James 131

San Cristoforo 231
Santo Bambino 231
Savonarola, Michele 95n.77
Schlosser, Julius von 5
Scully, Vincent 201n.57
sculpture 5, 21, 11, 160–73
　materials 160–73
　wood 13, 223–31
Segala, Francesco 176n.32
Semper, Gottfried 8, 23–4, 26, 27, 35, 37n.20, 38n.22
Sennert, Daniel 46
shoes 14, 283–305, *285*, *289*, *291*, *293*, *297*, 308n.62, 324
　cork-soled 283, 284, 286–7, 290–5, 305
　gem embellishments 283–4, 288
　wooden-soled 284, 294–9, 305
Sigismund I 263–7, 269–73, 277, 279
Sigismund Chapel, *see* Berrecci, Bartolommeo
silver 45, *46*, 51, 77–8, 110n.12, 147
　coins 61, 77, 100–1
　prospecting 54, 55
Sirigatti, Ridolfo 161
Sistine Chapel 250, 252–3
Sixtus IV 250, *251*
Skylax 81
smelting, *see* mining
Smith, Pamela H. 23, 330n.10
Solomon 265, 269–71
Sorel, Agnes 209–12, 220n.7, 220n.9
Sperling, Jutta Gisela 301
Spies, Hans 276–7
Squarcione, Francesco 164, 166
St Anne's Church 276–7, *277–9*
Steinberg, Leo 230
Stillman, Yedida Kalfon 286
Stokes, Adrian 5
stones 11–12, 31, 50–1, 82–4
　classifications 83–6
　Duan 310–16, *315*, 320, 325, 329nn.4–5
　Inka stonework 180–97, *183*, *185–6*, *194–5*
　precious stones, *see* gems
　sacred 180–2, 188, 196, 200n.30
　stonemasonry 11–12, 50, 182, 184–90, 193, 198n.15, 199n.20, 199n.24
　supernatural properties 82–4, 86, 95n.73, 215, 313, 314
　transportation of 12, 181–2, 192
Stoss, Veit 223
Strozzi, Lorenzo 288
Su Dongpo 314, 330n.18
Suger 82–3, 243

Index

sulphur 52, 54–5, 83, 147
Su Yijian 314

terracotta 12, 161, 170–2, 242, 284
Tchélébi, Evlia 273
Testa, Pietro 256
textiles 6–7
Theodulf of Orléans 125–6
Theophilus 29, 99, 103–5, 106, 108, 113n.28, 142–4, 146, 148, 150
Theophrastus 52, 60, 142–3, 225
Thomas the Cistercian 228
Three Brothers' Brooch 213, *214*
tin 55–6, 61, 74
Tintoretto 240–3, *241*, 252, 254–5, *254*, 256, 259
Titian 241
Tribolo, Il 175n.25

Ubertino da Casale 243–5, 247
Uccello, Paolo 260n.16
urban planning 14, 188, 191

Valentin de Boulogne 259
van Eyck, Jan 27–9, 216–19, *217*
Vasari, Giorgio 160, 166, 168, 175n.25, 178n.53, 255
  on Cosimo I de' Medici 250
  on Giotto 247
  on Michelangelo 253
  on oil painting 28
  on sculpture 161, 168
  on wood 224
Vecellio, Cesare 289, 300, 301, 303
Vegio, Maffeo 250
Venetian glass 263, 268
Vermeyen, Jan Cornelisz 292
Vernatti, Philiberto 144
Verrocchio, Andrea del 166, 168
Vianello, Andrea 295

Victoria and Albert Museum 15n.10
Vischer, Hans 273
Visconti, Valentina 210
Vitruvius 142–3, 272
Vladislav II Jagiellon 272, 273
Voltaire 220n.7

Wallace, William F. 175n.19
Waterer, J.W. 292
wax 5, 11, 160, 166–8, 172–3, 177n.43
Welch, Evelyn 304
Werkbund 32
Westminster Retable 141
wheat 119–31 *passim*
White, Raymond, and Ashok Roy 29
Wittkower, Rudolf and Margaret 255
wood
  cultivation 43
  footwear and, *see under* shoes
  glass-making and 157n.29
  painting use 74, 88n.8
  sculpture use, *see under* sculpture
workshop practices 6, 43, 97, 102, 166
Wright, Alison 172, 250

Xu Ke 331n.37
Xu Xuecun 319

Yang Dongyi 322, 332.n43
Yasser, Chalid *ii*
Yu Dian 318, 322

Zeitlin, Judith 317
Zhang Chao 314
Zhang Genji 314
Zhang Lu *311*
Zhang Yanyuan 331n.29
Zhao Guolin 318, 331n.33
Zibaldone da Canal 78, 91n.35
Zoppo, Marco 164, 175n.22